Charles I
A Political Life

Charles I

A POLITICAL LIFE

Richard Cust

PEARSON
Longman

Harlow, England • London • New York • Boston • San Francisco • Toronto
Sydney • Tokyo • Singapore • Hong Kong • Seoul • Taipei • New Delhi
Cape Town • Madrid • Mexico City • Amsterdam • Munich • Paris • Milan

PEARSON EDUCATION LIMITED

Edinburgh Gate
Harlow CM20 2JE
United Kingdom
Tel: +44 (0)1279 623623
Fax: +44 (0)1279 431059
Website: www.pearsoned.co.uk

Hardback edition published in Great Britain in 2005
This paperback edition published 2007

© Pearson Education Limited 2007

ISBN 978 1 4058 5903 5

British Library Cataloguing in Publication Data
A CIP catalogue record for this book can be obtained from the British Library

10 9 8 7 6 5 4 3 2
15 14 13 12

Set by 35 in 9/13.5pt Stone serif
Printed and bound in China
EPC/02

For Alice and David

Contents

CONTENTS

Preface

So much has been written about Charles I in the last 30 years that any biography must, to a considerable extent, be a work of synthesis. This is particularly true of this book. My footnotes demonstrate how heavily I have drawn on the work of others and benefited from their insights. I am particularly grateful to Tom Cogswell, Ken Fincham, Ann Hughes, Sean Kelsey, Peter Lake, Anthony Milton, Brian Quintrell, Ian Roy, David Scott, Kevin Sharpe, Malcolm Smuts, Christopher Thompson, Nicholas Tyacke and Malcolm Wanklyn. Their generosity in commenting on drafts and discussing ideas has been invaluable. My greatest intellectual debt, however, is to Conrad Russell. This book is the product of a dialogue about Charles which has been going on for nearly 30 years. I was going to say there are still lots of things on which we disagree, and I know that he will continue to enjoy arguing about them; however, just as I was completing this typescript I learnt of his death. I hope this book can stand as a tribute to his love of scholarship and his inspirational qualities as a teacher.

On a personal level I could not have completed this book without the support and encouragement of my friends. I am particularly grateful to John Bourne, Jacqueline Eales, Jeff Goodman, Eric Ives, Bob Knecht, George Lukowski, Brendan Mannion, Angela Trikic, Ian Williams, Diana and Nigel Wood and my friends at Lichfield Cricket Club and in the history department at Birmingham University. I also want to thank Heather McCallum and Keith Robbins for their patience and support as this book got longer and longer. Generations of Birmingham students have had Charles inflicted on them without showing too many signs of boredom. I am grateful for their enthusiasm and interest, in particular that of Peter Holland. Finally I want to thank Ann, Alice and David for their help, encouragement and much else besides. Alice and David have still to be convinced that history is 'cool', but they have listened politely while I have droned on about it.

Lichfield   RICHARD CUST
October 2004

Abbreviations

APC	*Acts of the Privy Council*
Basilicon Doron	*Basilicon Doron* in *King James* VI *and* I. *Political Writings*, ed. J.P. Sommerville, Cambridge, 1994
BIHR	*Bulletin of the Institute of Historical Research*
BL	British Library
Bod. Lib.	Bodleian Library
Chamberlain	*The Letters of John Chamberlain*, 2 vols., ed. N.E. McLure, Philadelphia, 1939
CJ	*Commons Journals*
Clarendon, *History*	Edward, earl of Clarendon, *The History of the Rebellion*, ed. W.D. MacRay, 6 vols., Oxford, 1888
Clarendon, *Life*	Edward, earl of Clarendon, *The Life of Edward, Earl of Clarendon*, 3 vols., Oxford, 1828
Clarendon State Papers	*State Papers Collected by Edward Earl of Clarendon*, 2 vols., Oxford, 1767
Commons Debates 1621	*Commons Debates in 1621*, 7 vols., eds. W. Notestein, F.H. Relf and H. Simpson, New Haven, 1935
Commons Debates 1629	*Commons Debates for 1629*, eds W. Notestein and F.H. Relf, Minneapolis, 1921
Constitutional Documents	*Constitutional Documents of the Puritan Revolution 1625–1660*, ed. S.R. Gardiner, 3rd edn, 1906
Court and Times	*Court and Times of Charles* I, 2 vols., ed. T. Birch, 1848
CSP Dom.	*Calendar of State Papers Domestic*
CSP Ven.	*Calendar of State Papers Venetian*

DNB	*Dictionary of National Biography* (all references are to the original *DNB*; the 2004 version appeared too late for me to take account of it)
EHR	*English Historical Review*
Eikon Basilike	*Eikon Basilike*, ed. P.A. Knachel, Ithaca, NY, 1966
Evelyn	*The Diary and Correspondence of John Evelyn*, ed. W. Bray, 1890
Hist.	*History*
HJ	*Historical Journal*
HLQ	*Huntington Library Quarterly*
HMC	Historical Manuscripts Commission
HR	*Historical Research*
JBS	*Journal of British Studies*
JEH	*Journal of Ecclesiastical History*
Laud, *Works*	W. Laud, *The Works*, 6 vols., Oxford, 1853
Letters of Charles I	*The Letters of King Charles I*, ed. C. Petrie, 1935
Letters of Henrietta Maria	*Letters of Queen Henrietta Maria*, ed. M.A.E. Green, 1857
LJ	*Lords Journals*
NA	National Archive
NAS	National Archive of Scotland
Nicholas	*Nicholas Papers, i. 1641–1652*, ed. G.F. Warner, Camden Society, New Series, vol. 40, 1886
NLW	National Library of Wales
P & P	*Past & Present*
Proceedings in Parliament 1625	*Proceedings in Parliament 1625*, eds M. Jansson and W.B. Bidwell, New Haven, 1987
Proceedings in Parliament 1626	*Proceedings in Parliament 1626*, 4 vols., eds W.B. Bidwell and M. Jansson, New Haven, 1991–6
Proceedings in Parliament 1628	*Proceedings in Parliament 1628*, 6 vols., eds R.C. Johnson, M.F. Keeler, M.J. Cole and W.B. Bidwell, New Haven, 1977–83
Proclamations of Charles I	*Stuart Royal Proclamations, vol. II. Royal Proclamations of King Charles I*, ed. J.F. Larkin, Oxford, 1983
Rupert and the Cavaliers	*Memoirs of Prince Rupert and the Cavaliers*, 3 vols., ed. E. Warburton, 1849

Rushworth	J. Rushworth, *Historical Collections*, 7 vols., 1659–1701
Strafforde Letters	*The Earl of Strafforde's Letters and Dispatches*, 2 vols., ed. W. Knowler, 1729
TRHS	*Transactions of the Royal Historical Society*
Warwick Memoirs	Sir Philip Warwick, *Memoirs of the Reign of Charles I*, Edinburgh, 1813

Place of publication is London unless otherwise stated.

Chapter 1

A political apprenticeship, 1600–1622

Prince of Wales

Early one morning in 1623, Matthew Wren was summoned to Whitehall to meet his patron, Lancelot Andrewes. He had recently returned from Spain where he had been acting as Prince Charles's chaplain during the farcical bid to marry the Infanta. In an atmosphere heavy with conspiracy, he was ushered into the presence of Andrewes and his fellow anti-Calvinists, Richard Neile and William Laud, and charged to tell them 'how the Prince's heart stands to the Church of England that when God brings him to the crown we may know what to hope for'. Wren's reply is one of the most interesting early assessments that we have of Charles. He was careful to cover himself, emphasising that he attended on the prince for only two months of the year, then only in his closet and at meal times. But he delivered the opinion that while

my master's learning is not equal to his father's, yet I know his judgement to be very right; and as for his affections for upholding the doctrine and discipline of the church, I have more confidence of him than of his father, in whom they say is so much inconstancy in some particular cases.

Neile and Laud then proceeded to argue over this verdict until Wren was dismissed, still not quite sure whether he had told them what they wanted to hear.[1]

---

[1] *Parentalia, or Memoirs of the Family of Wren*, ed. S. Wren, 1760, pp. 45–7.

Wren's assessment proved remarkably astute. He was certainly right about Charles's loyalty to the Church of England, or at least to the hierarchical, non-puritan church that the anti-Calvinists wanted. Right up to his death this was probably his most consistent priority. He was also right about Charles being less learned than his father. Charles was intelligent and well educated, and probably had a more refined aesthetic taste than any other English monarch, but he could not match his father's native wit or assured grasp of ideas. Perhaps the most interesting aspect of the whole episode, however, was the uncertainty it revealed about the young prince's religious and political inclinations. He was 22 when Wren delivered his verdict and few heirs to the throne in this period could have remained quite so inscrutable to those whose futures depended on them. But Charles was very much a late developer, largely as a consequence of a difficult and precarious childhood.

He was born at Dunfermline Castle on 19 November 1600 and throughout his early years suffered from a combination of poor health and lack of parental attention. When his family moved south in March 1603, on James's accession to the throne of England, Charles remained behind in Scotland because he was considered too sickly to cope with the journey. When he did finally come to England, in July 1604, it was difficult to find a noble family to look after him because of fears that he might die on their hands. He was eventually placed with Sir Robert Carey and his wife Lady Elizabeth who provided him with a stable home until 1613 when he was considered old enough to set up his own household. During these early years, Charles saw little of his parents or his elder brother and sister, Henry and Elizabeth, and such contact as he had was often discouraging. There is a story of Prince Henry teasing him when he was nine by snatching off Bishop Abbot's hat, placing it on his head and telling him that he was such a swot that when he was king he would make him archbishop of Canterbury. He was also largely ignored by the general public who devoted most of their attention to the glamorous Henry. This hardly changed even when he became heir to the throne after Henry's death from typhoid fever in November 1612. There was surprisingly little of the romantic gossip which normally attaches to a future king; and after a flurry of dedications of literary works to him in the year after Henry's death, aspiring authors looked elsewhere. It was, perhaps, indicative of his lack of impact that when he was installed as Prince of

Wales in 1616, the bishop of Ely made the Freudian slip of praying for Prince Henry.[2]

Charles's public profile remained remarkably low until about 1619. This was partly a consequence of personal difficulties. There were still doubts about his health and physical development which led the Venetian ambassador to report as late as 1616 that he would not be ready to marry for another two or three years. He was also notably shy and diffident, completely lacking in the self-confidence which enabled Henry to project himself as the focus of a popular cult dedicated to the revival of chivalry. Above all, however, it was due to James's determination to keep him under his thumb. Towards the end of his life Henry, like a Hanoverian Prince of Wales, had threatened to establish a reversionary interest which would offer an alternative to the king's court as a focus for politics and policy making. The prince became identified with an Elizabethan policy of war and alliance with Protestant powers on the continent. This was something James went out of his way to prevent in the case of his second son, not least because he planned to marry him to a Catholic. He announced 'that the young prince [would] be kept within a stricter compass than the former' and allowed only five of Henry's household of over a hundred to be continued in office.[3] He also kept him on a tight rein in terms of exercising the responsibilities appropriate for a future monarch. Charles attended with his father on state occasions, such as the opening of the 1614 Parliament, but he was not allowed to accompany him on his progress to Scotland in 1617, in spite of his express desire to learn the customs of the kingdom he would one day rule. In addition, he appears to have been largely excluded from influence over patronage. In 1616, one of the few occasions when there is evidence of him intervening in a suit, his petition for the bishopric of Carlisle on behalf of his chaplain, George Carleton, was brushed aside in favour of a much more obscure candidate backed by George Villiers.[4] James made life

---

[2] C. Carlton, *Charles I. The Personal Monarch*, 1983, pp. 1–18; B.W. Quintrell, *Charles I*, Harlow, 1993, pp. 8–9.

[3] K. Sharpe, *Politics and Ideas in Early Stuart England*, 1989, pp. 288–91; M.D. Shepherd, 'Charles I and the distribution of political patronage', University of Liverpool, Ph.D., 1999, pp. 328–9.

[4] Quintrell, *Charles I*, p. 9; K. Fincham, *Prelate as Pastor. The Episcopate of James I*, Oxford, 1990, pp. 26, 30.

difficult for his son during his adolescence, and Charles lacked the assertiveness to stand up to him, instead showing himself almost pathetically eager to please. However, the young prince was able to form one relationship which gave him a measure of confidence and support, with George Villiers.

Villiers became firmly established as James's favourite and homosexual lover during 1615. Much of the time their relationship was akin to that of doting father and surrogate son, with Villiers spending much more time in James's company than Charles and referring to him as his 'Dear Dad'. The young prince found this extremely hurtful, and an incident in 1616 when, in the presence of the court, he turned a water fountain on Villiers and soaked him to the skin, was perhaps indicative of his frustration. At first Villiers (from 1617 earl, then later marquis and duke, of Buckingham) made little effort to soothe Charles's feelings, but he was sufficiently astute to recognise the dangers in alienating the future king and eventually set about cultivating his friendship. The breakthrough came in the summer of 1618 when the favourite provided an elaborate banquet for the king at his house at Wanstead, without inviting the prince who was staying nearby. Charles was reported to be very upset, and Buckingham, realising that he had gone too far, immediately rode over to apologise. A week later he held an even more splendid banquet for Charles, as well as his father, which came to be known at court as 'the friends' feast'. From this point onwards the relationship between the two blossomed. Charles began to address Buckingham using James's nickname of 'Steenie' and signing his letters 'your constant, loving friend'. Before the end of year he had given him his reversion of the office of lord admiral, and was said to be allowing him to handle 'all his business of importance'. By the beginning of 1620 Buckingham was reported by the Venetian ambassador to be 'as great a favourite with the prince as with his father'. This was to be the most secure and fulfilling relationship of Charles's early years. He seems to have found in Buckingham a replacement for the elder brother he had never really known; and increasingly he turned to him for guidance and help, particularly in dealings with his father.[5]

Between 1619 and 1621 a series of incidents showed Charles beginning to emerge from his shell and take a more prominent role in politics. The first of these was in March 1619 when both his parents fell seriously

---

[5] R. Lockyer, *Buckingham*, Harlow, 1981, pp. 33–4; *CSP Ven. 1619–21*, p. 138.

ill. Ann eventually died, with Charles attending at her bedside and then taking on the responsibility for managing her funeral. James recovered, but at one point he briefed Charles on how to take over, telling him to trust in the wisdom of his councillors, especially Buckingham, and protect the Church of England and its bishops. This episode showed Charles being thrust into a more adult role than any he had experienced before and finding that he was able to cope.[6]

The second incident was the crisis in the Palatinate that allowed Charles for the first time to develop a distinctive political identity. The Palatinate was to be the issue that dominated English foreign policy for the next 20 years. The crisis began in September 1619 when Frederick of the Palatinate in Rhineland Germany accepted an invitation to become ruler of Bohemia. This escalated the religious conflict in Europe, which had begun the previous year when Protestant nobles in Bohemia had rebelled against the Holy Roman Emperor, and also ensured that England became involved because Frederick had married Charles's sister Elizabeth in 1613. To punish Frederick, Spain, the Emperor's Hapsburg ally, invaded the Palatinate in August 1620. Frederick and Elizabeth were driven first of all out of Bohemia and then out of the Palatinate, where resistance to the Spanish finally collapsed in 1622. James was determined to keep England out of a continental religious war, but dynastic loyalty demanded that he do something to rescue his son-in-law. He therefore set about reviving negotiations begun in 1614–17 for a marriage between Charles and the Spanish Infanta, hoping that the Palatinate could be restored to Frederick and Elizabeth by diplomatic means. However, there was also a strong lobby in England that welcomed the prospect of armed intervention in support of the Protestant cause, and for a time in 1620 it looked as if Charles might be offering himself as its leader.[7]

Charles's sympathy for his sister and brother-in-law probably dated back to the period when they were in England for their wedding. He had spent a good deal of time in their company and developed a warm, if fleeting, friendship with Frederick. Unlike his father, he welcomed the fateful decision to accept the crown of Bohemia, openly declaring how glad he was

---

[6] Quintrell, *Charles I*, pp. 10–11.

[7] S. Adams, 'Spain or the Netherlands? The dilemmas of English foreign policy', in H. Tomlinson ed., *Before the English Civil War*, Basingstoke, 1983, pp. 79–101.

that 'my brother is so ripe of judgement and so forward in inclination for the good of Christendom'. During the following months he took a particular interest in the Bohemians' struggle, and was said to have declared that their 'claims' were 'well founded'. Then, when news came that the Spanish had invaded the Palatinate, he was influential in persuading James to issue a declaration supporting the Union of Protestant Princes in Germany. It was said that 'he spoke strongly in council and this encouraged many of the councillors while it dismayed the opponents'. The defeat of Frederick and the Bohemian army at the Battle of the White Mountain in November 1620 was said to have caused him such grief that he spent two days locked up in his room.[8] All of this happened at a time when it also looked as if Charles was about to take up the chivalric mantle laid down by Prince Henry. During his youth he had aroused considerable admiration for his skill in horseman-ship and the knightly exercise of 'running at the ring'. Now, in March 1620, he made his first entry at an accession day tilt, leading the procession dressed in full armour and then jousting with various offspring of the aristocracy. This made a considerable impression on contemporaries since the accession day tilt was the central event in the revival of English chivalric culture.[9] At last Charles was beginning to assume an identity in the eyes of the public; and there was speculation that he might also be about to develop a reversion-ary interest of his own, based on revived chivalric values and a Protestant war policy. But this was premature. It was some time before Charles was to become sufficently self-assured to risk contradicting his father. Although he was reported to be unenthusiastic about the negotiations for a Spanish marriage, he continued to cooperate with the project; and when he made an offer to fight for the Palatinate in person he qualified it with the proviso that he would go only 'if the king my father will give me leave'.[10]

The third episode that brought Charles into the open was involvement in the 1621 Parliament. He was too young to make any impression on the previous parliament of 1614; but now he sat in the House of Lords, attend-ing 63 of the 89 sessions and serving on several committees including the

---

[8] Carlton, *Charles I*, pp. 14–15; NA, SP 81/16/127; *CSP Ven. 1619–21*, pp. 151, 431.

[9] A. Young, *Tudor and Jacobean Tournaments*, 1982, p. 40; J.S.A. Adamson, 'Chivalry and political culture in Caroline England', in K. Sharpe and P.G. Lake eds, *Culture and Politics in Early Stuart England*, 1994, p. 165.

[10] *CSP Ven. 1619–21*, p. 238; Carlton, *Charles I*, p. 29.

one dealing with the patentee, Sir Giles Mompesson. During the first session (30 January–4 June) some of his interventions were rather naive and ill-judged, notably in February when he got into a muddle after promising to present a petition from the Lords against excessive creations of new peers and then finding that James disapproved of it. However, he did reassure the Commons with his opposition to Mompesson and was also able to make it clear that he would stand firm if anyone slighted the king's honour. In late April, when Sir Henry Yelverton attacked Buckingham in the Lords by comparing him with Hugh Despencer, one of Edward II's favourites, Charles immediately interrupted him. He declared that he would not permit his father's government to be 'paralleled and scandalised' in this way and led the calls to imprison Yelverton in the Tower. During this first session, however, his most significant impact was probably a less obvious one. His mere presence in the Lords appears to have done much to extinguish early stirrings of opposition to Buckingham.[11]

During the second session of the parliament (20 November–19 December) when foreign policy became the main concern, Charles himself took centre stage. James was absent from London throughout the session, convalescing at Newmarket with Buckingham. Charles was given the task of staying behind and liaising with 'those of the council that the king trusts most', then passing on their collective advice to his father and the duke. He took his responsibilities seriously, delivering his advice with great earnestness and working hard to bring the session to a successful conclusion. But, at the same time, he harboured considerable suspicions about the intentions of the House of Commons and was very alert to any signs of it infringing on royal authority.[12] On 23 November, when a group of MPs in the lower house caused a row over the issue of freedom of speech and the king's right to exclude troublesome MPs, he took the relatively indulgent view that the king should be patient and avoid taking drastic action until it could 'be seen whether they mean to do good, or persist in their follies.' However, in a covering letter to Buckingham, he also urged that a commission be sent down to him with authority 'to set seditious fellows

---

[11] R. Zaller, *The Parliament of 1621*, Berkeley, 1971, pp. 60–1, 74, 116–24; C.S.R. Russell, *Parliaments and English Politics 1621–1629*, Oxford, 1979, pp. 85, 108.

[12] On Charles's conduct during this second session, see my forthcoming article on 'Prince Charles and the second session of the 1621 Parliament'.

fast' in order that they 'might be made an example to others'.[13] Five days later, after the Commons' foreign policy debate, he was again taking a moderate line, urging that since the Commons had agreed to grant a subsidy, its request to complete the session before Christmas should be granted; however, at the same time, he advised that the king should 'command them not to speak any more of Spain, whether it be of that war, or my marriage'.[14] When the Commons proceeded to do just this – drawing up a petition which urged James to go to war with Spain and ensure that his son was 'timely and happily married to one of our religion' – the prince's earlier tolerance vanished. He complained that his marriage 'was continually prostituted in the lower house' and sent his father a copy of the offending document.[15]

Charles's protest set in motion the train of events which was to lead to the premature dissolution of the parliament. James responded on 3 December by writing an angry letter declaring that he would not permit further discussion about Spain or the marriage, nor would he 'deign the hearing' of any petition concerning these matters. He blamed the whole episode on 'some fiery and popular spirits' in the Commons who, emboldened by his absence, had begun to debate 'matters far beyond their reach or capacity and so tending to our high dishonour and to trenching upon our prerogative royal'. The Commons was at first stunned, since it had been invited to draw up the petition by Buckingham's client, Sir George Goring, and had therefore assumed that the king would welcome it. However, it rallied behind it, preparing a declaration to explain its proceedings and assert its 'ancient and undoubted right' to freedom of speech in such matters. Once this issue was out into the open it became very hard for either side to draw back.

---

[13] Bod.Lib., Tanner MS 73, fos. 79–80. The dating of this letter presents a problem. Charles dates the letter at the bottom in his own hand 'Fryday, 3 No. 1621', but this is plainly impossible because parliament was not sitting at this time and the Friday in 1621 fell on the 2nd not the 3rd of November. S.R. Gardiner, *The History of England 1603–1642*, 10 vols., 188–4, vol. 4, p. 250n, has 'Monday, 3 December' which also seems unlikely. The date which best fits the contents of the letter, with its references to Charles's discussions with councillors and his hope that although ' the lower house has been a little unruly . . . it will turn to the best, for before they arose they began to be ashamed of it', is Friday, 23 November, as suggested by R.E. Ruigh, *The Parliament of 1624*, Cambridge, Mass., 1971, p. 12n. For a fuller discussion of this letter, see my forthcoming article.

[14] BL, Harl. MS 6987, fos. 205–6. For the dating again see my article and Ruigh, *Parliament of 1624*, p. 13n.

[15] *Commons Debates 1621*, vol. 5, pp. 237–8; Russell, *Parliaments and English Politics*, p. 137; Zaller, *Parliament of 1621*, p. 165.

Charles, who by this stage had recovered some of his equanimity, joined with the privy councillors in doing his best to calm things down and James made various conciliatory gestures.[16] However, it was to no avail. The row intensified when a majority in the Commons backed a Protestation of their privileges and this led James to adjourn and, eventually, dissolve the parliament.[17] Charles made an effort to be statesmanlike in the second session of 1621; but his wounded sense of honour and his sensitivity to encroachments on the prerogative had done more than anything to provoke the confrontation which wrecked the parliament.

This episode is notable because it marked the first occasion on which the young prince's interventions can be shown to have had a significant impact on national politics. However, it is perhaps even more interesting as a sign of what was to come. Indignation at the Commons' infringement of the royal prerogative and recourse to a rhetoric that blamed this on 'seditious fellows' were to be recurring themes in Charles's dealings with parliaments in the later 1620s. Conrad Russell and Kevin Sharpe have argued that such concerns developed largely as a consequence of the Commons' failure to fulfil 'engagements' given in 1624 to finance his wars.[18] But Charles's reactions in 1621 suggest that they were already part of his mindset, feeding off anxieties which, as we shall see, his father had been voicing for some time.

Charles's intervention in the second session of 1621 marked his emergence as a significant figure in the politics of the court. Although not formally sworn in as a privy councillor until March 1622, he had been attending meetings since 1620 and was now playing an important part in its deliberations. He was also becoming a power in the king's bedchamber where, increasingly, crucial policy decisions were made before being presented to the council as a *fait accompli*. Much of Buckingham's dominance as favourite was built on his command of this inner sanctum which gave him unrivalled access to the king and control of the sign manual, used for authorising grants. But by 1622 Charles was working alongside him as joint

---

[16] Zaller, *Parliament of 1621*, pp. 151–63; *Commons Debates 1621*, vol. 7, pp. 624–5.

[17] Zaller, *Parliament of 1621*, pp. 165–87; 'The examination of Mr Mallory after the Parliament of 1621', in C.S.R. Russell, *Unrevolutionary England*, 1990, pp. 81–8.

[18] The nature of a parliament in early Stuart England', in Russell, *Unrevolutionary England*, p. 21; Russell, *Parliaments and English Politics*, pp. 397–9; K. Sharpe, 'The Personal Rule of Charles I', in Tomlinson ed., *Before the English Civil War*, pp. 54–6.

head of the bedchamber, and was able to take a full part in the discussions there which initiated policy. He had also come to enjoy a significant role in the distribution of patronage, with much of the day-to-day business now being handled by two of the grooms of his own bedchamber, Endymion Porter and the duke's brother, Viscount Purbeck.[19] The area where Charles's higher profile was most apparent, however, was foreign policy where he continued to take a much more bellicose line than his father. He put himself forward as principal champion of the cause of his sister and brother-in-law, and after the fall of Heidelberg in September 1622 there were plans for him to lead a relief army of 20 000 infantry and 3 000 cavalry to operate in conjunction with the Dutch. The prince had taken his place alongside James and Buckingham in the triumvirate which determined royal policy; but any prospect of the reversionary interest emerging was still forestalled by his eagerness to please his father. He remained very much the junior partner, 'Baby Charles' as both king and favourite persisted in nicknaming him.[20]

In spite of the attention which was now being given to him by commentators, Charles also remained something of an unknown quantity. Andrewes, Laud and Neile were not alone in finding that he was hard to predict or get to know. As late as 1624, John Chamberlain, one of the best informed of contemporary newsletter writers, expressed surprise at the quality of his contributions in the parliament, commenting that it was the 'received opinion he concealed himself before'.[21] Inscrutability was to remain a feature of Charles's make-up for the rest of his life; but, in other respects, he showed every indication of emerging from his political apprenticeship to take on the role of king-in-waiting.

Attitudes and influences

Recent scholarship has tended to draw sharp distinctions between James I and Charles I. Whereas James is seen as a peacemaker who was content

---

[19] N. Cuddy, 'The revival of the entourage: the bedchamber of James I, 1603–1625', in D. Starkey ed., *The English Court*, Harlow, 1987, pp. 214–25.

[20] T.E. Cogswell, *The Blessed Revolution*, Cambridge, 1989, pp. 58–9, 61–2.

[21] *Chamberlain*, vol. 2, p. 550.

to leave well alone, Charles 'suffered from energy' and disliked his father's willingness to swallow his pride in the interests of a quiet life. James is depicted as a ruler who liked to operate by debate, argument and negotiation, while his son preferred visual symbolism and display, and sought to persuade his subjects to conform to ideal patterns of behaviour. James was willing to step down from his throne and engage in the hurly-burly of politics while Charles tended to remain reserved and aloof; and where James was patient, subtle and flexible, his son was rigid and insensitive.[22] There is a good deal in these contrasts. They point up considerable differences of style and approach, and also help to explain why Charles was generally a less successful ruler than his father. But just to emphasise the differences is misleading. There were also similarities and continuities. They were agreed on the meaning and implications of divine right monarchy and, after trying his hand at war during the 1620s, Charles reverted to his father's peaceful foreign policy. Moreover, the young prince revered his father as a model of what a good king should be and did his best to emulate him.

Perhaps the most striking testimony to this reverence is the painted ceiling of the Banqueting House at Whitehall which was built in the 1620s as the setting for great occasions of state. Charles commissioned the ceiling from the Flemish artist, Peter Paul Rubens, in 1629, and it was completed around 1635. It showed James at his most majestic and heroic. The first of the main panels depicted him as Solomon presiding over the unification of England and Scotland, with the approval of Minerva, the goddess of wisdom. In the second he was again Solomon, ushering in an age of peace and plenty and subduing the evils of conspiracy and popular rebellion. And a third panel showed his apotheosis, as he was transported up to heaven to take his place alongside God.[23] The ceiling was both a celebration of James's achievements and a representation of the qualities divinely-ordained monarchs were supposed to aspire to. It was a constant reminder to Charles of what it meant to be a good king.

---

[22] For these contrasts, see K. Sharpe, *The Personal Rule of Charles I*, 1992, p. 197; Russell, *Parliaments and English Politics*, p. 422; Cogswell, *The Blessed Revolution*, p. 62; Sharpe, *Politics and Ideas*, pp. 47–8; J. Wormald, 'James VI and I: two kings or one?', *Hist.*, vol. 68, 1983, pp. 193–209; C.S.R. Russell, *The Fall of the British Monarchies 1637–1642*, Oxford, 1991, pp. 31–6.

[23] R. Strong, *Britannia Triumphans. Inigo Jones, Rubens and Whitehall Palace*, 1980, pp. 7–64.

The qualities summed up in the Whitehall ceiling were described at length by James himself, in his advice book, the *Basilicon Doron*. This was written in 1598 for Prince Henry; but what it had to say was just as relevant for Charles, and it is likely that the young prince read the book closely. In the original preface, James had urged his son to keep the book 'ever with you as Alexander did the Iliads of Homer', to treat it as 'a just and impartial counsellor', and 'to follow and put in practice, as far as in you lieth, the precepts'. Charles was reminded of this in the 1616 reissue where he was urged to imitate 'the good precedents of a good father' and let 'the advice lie before you as a pattern'.[24] He appears to have taken this to heart and, as he sensed his own death was approaching, he would prepare something similar for his son.[25]

Basilicon Doron was not a particularly original work. It belonged to the Renaissance genre of advice books and 'mirrors for princes' in which the reader was offered guidance through a distillation of received wisdom and moral precepts. The advice it contained was extremely conventional and, because of this, most historians have tended not to look very closely at its content. But, as Kevin Sharpe has pointed out, this is a mistake.[26] Charles was considerably influenced by conventional ideas about kingship, and *Basilicon Doron* tells us a good deal about the sort of king that he aspired to be.

---

[24] K. Sharpe, 'Private conscience and public duty in the writings of Charles I', *HJ*, vol. 40, 1997, p. 643; *Basilicon Doron*, pp. 2–3; *The Workes of James, King of Great Britaine, France and Ireland, published by James Bishop of Winton*, 1616, 'the epistle dedicatorie'.

[25] This was published as chapter 27 of *Eikon Basilike*, pp. 158–71. At the beginning of the chapter Charles summed up his intention in the advice:

Son, if these papers, with some others wherein I have set down the private reflections of my conscience and my most impartial thoughts touching the chief passages which have been most remarkable or disputed in my late troubles, come to your hands, to whom they are chiefly designed, they may be so far useful to you as to state your judgement aright in what hath passed . . . and . . . also give you some directions how to remedy the present distempers and prevent, if God will, the like for time to come.

The advice was written in late 1648 or early 1649, perhaps in November 1648 when he was preparing other pieces of advice for his son and had doubts about whether he would ever be allowed to communicate with him again: see below pp. 445–7; for other sets of advice from this period, see *Clarendon State Papers*, vol. 2, pp. 448–9 and *Letters of Charles I*, pp. 239–41. According to the royalist historian, Sir William Sanderson, the advice was entrusted to Bishop Juxon before Charles died: W. Sanderson, *A Compleat History of the Raigne of King Charles*, 1658, p. 1140.

[26] Sharpe, 'Private conscience and public duty', pp. 645–7.

The book begins with 'A King's Christian Duty towards God' in which James outlined his son's religious obligations. Foremost among these, and the key to all the rest, was obeying his conscience. 'Above all, my son,' said James, 'labour to keep sound this conscience'. Conscience was the 'right knowledge and fear of God' and provided an understanding of 'all the things necessary for the discharge of your duty both as a Christian and as a king'. It would remind him, according to James, that he had been placed on his throne by God and therefore owed God his principal duty of service; that he must be diligent in prayer and reading the Scriptures and count even the smallest sin a breach of God's laws; and that he must take responsibility for promoting godliness in the church, which meant advancing 'godly, learned and modest men' and banishing the arrogance and 'conceited parity' of the puritans.[27] All of this Charles accepted and did his best to pass on to his own son. 'My . . . conscience', he wrote towards the end of his life, 'is dearer to me than a thousand kingdoms.' He explained how he had endeavoured to put conscience before all considerations of worldly success or political gain, and urged the young Charles to do likewise. This meant cultivating his personal piety, ensuring that 'the sceptre of his word and spirit . . . rule in your heart' and 'advancing God's glory in the maintenance of true religion and the church's good'.[28]

The most specific advice on religious policy that James delivered in the *Basilicon Doron* was to steer a middle course between the pride and error of popery and the arrogance and extremism of the puritans.[29] Beyond this he did not go into detail; however, this did not preclude him from having a profound impact on the development of his son's religious ideas. Charles described his own version of the ideal church in very similar terms to his father. 'After much search and many disputes', he told his son, he had concluded that the Church of England was 'the best in the world . . . keeping the middle way between the pomp of superstitious tyranny and the meanness of fantastic anarchy'.[30] The terms in which Charles understood this 'middle way' – as filling the space between Rome and Geneva – owed much to James's influence.

---

[27] *Basilicon Doron*, pp. 13, 17–19, 27, 39.

[28] *Eikon Basilike*, pp. 170, 159–60.

[29] *Basilicon Doron*, pp. 5–8, 25–7.

[30] *Eikon Basilike*, p. 167.

Charles's early religious development has long been shrouded in mystery; but now, thanks to the researches of Peter McCullough, it is apparent that his anti-Calvinist convictions did not come to be formed until he was in his early twenties. Initially his religious upbringing was directed by staunch Calvinists. The Careys, his first guardians, had a reputation for puritanism and his Scottish tutor from the age of six, Thomas Murray, was a Presbyterian. It was predictable, therefore, that when Charles established a household at court in 1613, it was dominated by evangelical Calvinists. His first chaplains, George Hakewill and Richard Milborne, were appointed with express instructions to act as what McCullough calls 'anti-Catholic bodyguards'; and they were joined by others with similar credentials, such as George Carleton, John Preston and his puritan clerk of the closet, Henry Burton. All the indications are that during his teens Charles was brought up in the same way as his elder brother and sister had been, as a zealous Calvinist. Hakewill who prepared him for confirmation in 1613 later claimed that the prince's exemplary responses had inspired him to write a Calvinist defence of the rite as practised in England. The court sermons surviving from the period suggest that Charles was treated to a rich diet of Protestant moralising, warning him of the dire consequences of sinfulness and reminding him of the godly example that a prince should set his people. On occasion, the warnings were very explicit. In 1621 Hakewill preached 12 sermons in his presence in which he castigated the immorality of James's court, and explicitly condemned the policy of appeasement towards Spain and the intended marriage with the Infanta.[31] The influence of these Calvinist chaplains may well be discernible in the reports from this period of Charles's support for a Protestant war policy and unhappiness at the prospect of a Spanish marriage. In the longer term, it is probably apparent in the moral earnestness with which he approached his religion and his profound belief in providence. Charles always took his faith very seriously, reading the Bible every day for guidance, seeking out chaplains and bishops to discuss matters that afflicted his conscience, and striving to set an example to others.[32] He also fully internalised the view set forth in detail by Calvinists such as Hakewill, that it was God's sovereign will and

---

[31] P.E. McCullough, *Sermons at Court. Politics and Religion in Elizabethan and Jacobean Preaching*, Cambridge, 1998, pp. 194–204.

[32] Sharpe, *The Personal Rule*, pp. 280–1.

providential judgements that determined what happened in the world.[33] Had it not been for the intervention of Lancelot Andrewes, the young prince might well have progressed from this early indoctrination to the full-blown Calvinism of his sister Elizabeth.

According to Peter Heylyn, the Laudian polemicist, when James lay in the grip of his near-fatal illness at Royston in 1619, Andrewes approached his bedside and expressed his concern about the church's future in the hands of a prince who was 'not well principled by those which had the tutelage of him, either in the government or liturgy of the Church of England'. James acknowledged this and promised that, if he recovered, he would make amends.[34] He was apparently as good as his word. Years later Charles remarked with some pride that the chief 'instructor', 'who laid in me the grounds of Christianity', had been his own father. Precisely what these 'grounds' consisted of he did not spell out; but his comments imply that they included a strong belief in the necessity for bishops and a conviction that the liturgy of the Church of England had been 'perfected' under Elizabeth.[35] James also introduced anti-Calvinists into the prince's entourage, partly, it would seem, in response to Calvinist opposition to the Spanish Match. In January 1622, Matthew Wren, Andrewes's protégé and domestic chaplain, was brought into the prince's household and, at the same time, Murray was replaced as Charles's secretary by the pro-Spanish Sir Francis Cottington. Andrewes's initiative finally bore fruit in 1623 when crucial decisions were taken about the religious establishment that was to accompany Charles on his trip to Spain. Hakewill and Burton claimed the right to go by dint of their seniority; but James blocked this and ordered that Wren and another anti-Calvinist, Leonard Maw, be sent instead. The content of the prince's services was also carefully supervised. James issued instructions that, in order to reassure the Spanish, all ceremonies were to be 'as near the Roman form as can lawfully be done'; and the prince's portable chapel may have

---

[33] For George Hakewill's *Apologie of the power and providence of God*, 1627, see A. Walsham, *Providence in Early Modern England*, Oxford, 1999, pp. 23–4. For references by Charles to God's 'justice' and 'providence' and his role as 'sovereign disposer of the kingdoms of the world', see his advice to the Prince of Wales in *Eikon Basilike*, pp. 158–71. For fuller discussion of Charles's belief in providence, see below pp. 398, 409–10, 419, 428, 460, 467–8.

[34] P. Heylyn, *A Short View of the Life and Reign of Charles I*, 1658, pp. 17–18.

[35] *The Papers which passed at Newcastle betwixt his Sacred Majestie and Mr Al. Henderson concerning the Change of Church Government in 1646*, 1649, pp. 1–4, 15–21.

included altar rails and other items of furnishing modelled on Andrewes's own.[36] Nicholas Tyacke has suggested that it was on the trip to Spain – when he had to make up his mind about which version of Protestantism he could subscribe to in the face of his hosts' efforts to convert him to Catholicism – that Charles became a convinced anti-Calvinist.[37] This would make sense in terms of the assessment of the prince's beliefs that Wren was able to pass on after his return home. The hopes of the Calvinist contingent in Charles's household revived in 1624, when he appeared wholeheartedly to embrace anti-popery. But once he ascended the throne it became clear that he was determined to stand by the anti-Calvinists' vison of the church as a 'middle way' between Rome and Geneva.

Book 2 of the *Basilicon Doron* covered 'A Kings Duty in his Office'. Here James ranged widely over the responsibilities attendant on his son's 'calling' as a monarch. These could be divided into two categories: one involved 'establishing and executing good laws among your people', the other setting a personal example that would 'glister and shine before the people' and provide 'a pattern of godliness and all honest virtues'. The key to fulfilling these objectives was, of course, first and foremost 'the right knowledge and fear of God', but beyond this to strive to conquer and order one's passions. 'He cannot be thought worthy to rule and command others', James insisted, 'that cannot rule . . . his own proper affections and unreasonable appetites.' This meant adopting the approach of the neo-Stoics and cultivating the four cardinal virtues of wisdom, justice, temperance and fortitude. Of these, temperance was the most critical because 'wise moderation . . . first commanding yourself shall as a queen command all the affections and passions of your mind'. The good prince must show restraint in language, dress and manners, and avoid the 'beastly vice of drunkenness'; he must practise 'clemency, magnanimity, liberality, constancy, humility and all other princely virtue'; and he must establish his family and household as a model of harmony and decorum.[38]

Charles's whole education and upbringing inclined him in the direction prescribed by his father. We know relatively little about the course of study

---

[36] McCullough, *Sermons at Court*, pp. 204–9; J. Davies, *The Caroline Captivity of the Church*, Oxford, 1992, p. 20.

[37] N.R.N. Tyacke, *Anti-Calvinists. The Rise of English Arminianism, c. 1590–1640*, Oxford, 1987, p. 114.

[38] *Basilicon Doron*, pp. 12–13, 19–20, 42–3, 49–54.

he pursued under Murray, although it appears to have followed the conventional grounding in the classics, languages, mathematics and theology, supplemented by training in specific skills such as riding, fencing and dancing. However, we do know that he was a bookish and attentive student whom James was inclined to compare favourably with his less diligent brother. He read widely and carefully, adopting the contemporary practice of commonplacing, which involved noting and classifying memorable aphorisms so that they could be studied as guides to conduct. Several collections of Charles's aphorisms survive, and as an adult he displayed a considerable fondness for quoting them whenever he was conducting a debate or giving advice.[39] The content of much of this reading and notetaking centred on the principles of neo-Stoic moral philosophy. The young prince grew up during the 1610s and 1620s when the influence of neo-Stoicism on English culture was at its height. The Senecan ideal of cultivating a detachment from the chaotic swirl of everyday events in order to achieve constancy in the pursuit of virtuous principles was held up as a model by contemporaries such as Shakespeare, Jonson and Bacon.[40] It was an ideal Charles sought to fulfil in his own life. He was renowned for his displays of patience and self-control, and for the chastity and decorum he sought to infuse into his family and household. He also urged the same standards on his son. 'We have learnt to own ourself by retiring into ourself', he told him, and urged him to 'let no passion betray you to any study of revenge'.[41]

One aspect of Charles's neo-Stoicism that is of particular interest when it comes to assessing his kingship is his understanding of political 'prudence'. This was a concept that became fashionable in England during the 1590s, with the revival of interest in Tacitus. Tacitus's penetrating analysis of the motivation of politicians and the dissimulation of rulers was seen as having a particular relevance when it came to understanding how to cultivate the Stoical qualities of constancy and detachment. He encouraged contemporaries to delve into the mysteries of state and to treat the study

---

[39] M.B. Pickel, *Charles I as Patron of Poetry and Drama*, Columbia, 1936, pp. 17–21; *CSP Dom. 1611–18*, p. 273; *CSP Ven. 1603–7*, p. 513; Sharpe, *The Personal Rule*, p. 193. For one of the collections of Charles's adages, see *Witty Apophthegms delivered at several times by King James, King Charles*, 1658.

[40] For the importance of neo-Stoicism for contemporary culture, see R. Tuck, *Philosophy and Government 1572–1651*, Cambridge, 1993, ch. 2.

[41] *Letters of Charles I*, p. 240; *Eikon Basilike*, pp. 158–9, 166.

of politics as a branch of knowledge and wisdom. James also invited such an approach with his advice that his son should 'study to know well your own craft', and that the best means to do this was by reading 'authentic histories' and 'applying bypast things to the present state'.[42] Charles appears to have absorbed many of the implications of this advice. He read and noted the works of Guicciardini and Francis Bacon, two of the leading authorities on the subject.[43] He adopted the vocabulary of their style of analysis, talking about 'policy' – by which he meant the legitimate means for a ruler to bolster his power and secure political advantage – and 'prudence' – which he used to refer to the understanding of the causes and effects of political action.[44] He also, as we shall see, took a certain pride in his ability to dissect political tactics and motivation.

This, however, presents a conundrum which has been highlighted by Kevin Sharpe. If Charles was drawn to the prudential approach to politics, how could he reconcile this with his insistence on the primacy of conscience? The former was generally associated with the Machiavellian view that politics occupied a sphere apart from religion and morality, while the latter belonged to a world in which providence and God's judgements loomed large. In fact, the problem is more apparent to later historians than it was to Charles. For him, there appeared to be no conflict. 'The prudential part of any consideration', he told his counsellors in 1646, 'will never be found opposite to the conscientious.'[45] Charles was using this view to justify the specific argument that abandoning episcopacy would not only go against his conscience, but would also be bad politics, since the bishops were an essential bulwark of royal authority. However, as he well recognised, in practice it was not as simple as this. On this occasion,

---

[42] *Basilicon Doron*, pp. 44, 46. For the impact of Tacitism, see R.M. Smuts, *Culture and Power in England 1585–1685*, Basingstoke, 1999, pp. 32–40 and M.B. Peltonen, *Classical Humanism and Republicanism in English Political Thought 1570–1640*, Cambridge, 1995, pp. 124–36.

[43] For Charles's reading of Guicciardini, see R. Dallington, *Aphorisms, civill and militarie, amplified with authorities*, 1613, 'preface' addressed to Charles; for Bacon, see his annotations on the copy of Francis Bacon, *The Advancement of Learning*, 1640, pp. 302–23 in the British Library (C.46.vi.l).

[44] For these usages, see Sharpe, 'Conscience and public duty', pp. 648–9 and *The Princely Pellican*, 1649, p. 5.

[45] *Clarendon State Papers*, vol. 2, p. 260; C.S.R. Russell, *The Causes of the Civil War*, Oxford, 1990, p. 198.

having apparently refused any compromise, he promptly worked out a scheme that would involve sacrificing the bishops for the time being so as to be able to strengthen his position and restore them in the future.[46] In other words, he recognised that conscience did allow space for flexibility and manoeuvre. He had a strongly developed sense of what it ultimately required of him; but the boundaries of what was permissible could vary, and up to the point at which conscience kicked in he saw it as entirely legitimate to apply principles of 'policy' and 'prudence'. Charles's understanding of these principles is something that needs to be borne in mind before dismissing him as somehow 'unpolitical' or unwilling to engage in political calculation. Whether he made the right political judgements is a separate issue. In terms of his understanding of the 'craft' of kingship, he was very conscious that a ruler needed to be attuned to a world of tactics and manipulation.

The core of James's advice about 'establishing and executing good laws' was to strive at all times to serve the public good. This picked up on one of the central concepts of Renaissance political thought, the distinction between the 'public' and the 'private'.[47] The main difference between a good ruler and a tyrant, according to Aristotle, was that the tyrant put his own, selfish, 'private' interests first, whereas the good ruler served the public good and the 'common weal'. This was the view endorsed in the *Basilicon Doron*. The 'good king', according to James, was like 'a natural father' to his people, 'subjecting his own private affections and appetites to the weal and standing of his subjects, ever thinking the common interest his chiefest particular'. The tyrant, on the other hand, followed only his 'unruly private affections . . . building his surety on his people's misery'. A monarch belonged to his people. He had been set on his throne by God, and endowed with his royal prerogative and kingly wisdom, not for his own glory, but to govern in the interests of those set under him. He was 'rather born to *onus* than *honos*'. His 'daily care' must consist of 'hazardous painstaking for the dutiful administration of that great office', which should mean governing in partnership with parliament, executing justice impartially, abiding by existing laws, refraining from excessive taxation and ruling with mildness and generosity. His reward would come when 'good and loving subjects may not only live

---

[46] For a fuller discussion of these manoeuvres, see below pp. 424–6.

[47] For 'public' and 'private', see Q. Skinner, *The Foundations of Modern Political Thought*, 2 vols., Cambridge, 1978, vol. 1, pp. 221–8 and Peltonen, *Classical Humanism and Republicanism*, pp. 62–5, 147–8.

in security and wealth but be stirred up . . . to open their mouths in the just praise of you and your so well moderated regiment'.[48]

Charles urged similar priorities on his own son. He would have him, he said, rather 'be Charles *le Bon* than *le Grand*, good rather than great'. 'Princes should always remember they are born and by providence designed' to serve 'the public good'. Their 'true glory' lay in 'the public interest and good of the community'. This meant pursuing the policies advocated by his father. He should aim to uphold 'the settled laws of the kingdom' which offered an ideal balance between the 'liberty and happiness' of the subject and the 'majesty and prerogative' of a king. He should exercise his prerogative with restraint, 'there being nothing worse than legal tyranny'. And he should recognise that mildness and tolerance were often the best way to defuse 'passions, humours, or private opinions'.[49] Most strikingly, he delivered a ringing endorsement of the benefits of parliament. He would not have his son

entertain any aversion or dislike of parliaments, which in their right
constitution . . . will never injure or diminish your greatness, but will rather
be as interchangings of love, loyalty and confidence between a prince and
his people . . . Nothing can be more happy for all than in fair, grave and
honourable ways to contribute their counsels in common, enacting all things
by public consent without tyranny or tumults.[50]

Charles wrote this advice at a time when he was working especially hard to project an image of himself as a constitutional monarch. But there is no reason to doubt that it genuinely represented his aspirations. His coronation oath bound him 'to hold and keep the laws and rightful customs which the commonalty of this your kingdom have', and he often referred back to this as imposing a particularly powerful sense of obligation.[51] At moments of crisis he could display an instinctive constitutionalism which was not necessarily in his own best interest.[52] Charles was very aware of

---

[48] *Basilicon Doron*, pp. 20–1, 2, 31.

[49] *Eikon Basilike*, pp. 159, 162–4.

[50] Ibid., p. 168.

[51] Rushworth, vol. 1, pp. 200–1. For the importance of his coronation oath, see below pp. 103, 424–5.

[52] A good example of Charles's 'constitutionalism' is his handling of the attempt on the Five Members in early 1642: see below p. 321.

the judgements and punishments that awaited tyrants. He was not about to let himself in for the 'infamous memory . . . and the endless pain' that James anticipated as their fate.[53]

Both James and Charles were very conscious of the dangers of monarchical government degenerating into tyranny. Their advisers warned repeatedly against the flattery and evil counsel which were the bane of princely courts, and the 'private' interests which inevitably lurked in any form of government.[54] However, when it came to diagnosing the ills of the common weal, they were much more concerned with the shortcomings of another of the classical forms of government, democracy – or what contemporaries often referred to as 'popularity'. This was a central preoccupation of sixteenth and early seventeenth-century political theorists, and during Elizabeth's reign became a major concern for active politicians as well.[55] Peter Lake has demonstrated that 'popularity' was virtually invented, as a term of current political usage, by John Whitgift during his confrontations with the Presbyterian Thomas Cartwright in the 1570s. He took Cartwright's vision of a church based on democratic principles and 'active godly citizenship' to be the clerical equivalent of the quasi-republican forms of secular politics that were being widely espoused at the time. He then proceeded to attack both of these approaches as dangerously 'popular' since they threatened to pull down existing hierarchies and undermine authority by stirring up a fickle and novelty-addicted populace. His assault was developed and intensified from the 1590s onwards, notably in Richard Bancroft's attacks on Presbyterians, and Robert Cecil's diatribes against oppositionist MPs in the House of Commons.[56] In the process, contemporaries were given a language and

---

[53] *Basilicon Doron*, p. 21.

[54] Ibid., pp. 20–1, 34–7; *Eikon Basilike*, pp. 164–5; *Clarendon State Papers*, vol. 2, p. 448.

[55] 'Introduction. The 1590s: the second reign of Elizabeth I' in J.A. Guy ed., *The Reign of Elizabeth I. Court and Culture in the Last Decade*, Cambridge, 1995, pp. 1, 11. For a fuller discussion of the contemporary concern with 'popularity', see R.P. Cust, 'Charles I and popularity', in T.E. Cogswell, R.P. Cust and P.G. Lake eds, *Politics, Religion and Popularity*, Cambridge, 2002, pp. 237–41.

[56] P.G. Lake, 'Popularity, puritanism and anti-puritanism, or John Whitgift, Martin Marprelate and Richard Bancroft discover the limits of "the Elizabethan public sphere"'; R.P. Cust, '"Patriots" and "popular spirits": narratives of conflict in early Stuart politics', in N.R.N. Tyacke ed., *The English Revolution and its Legacies* (forthcoming, Manchester).

set of assumptions that provided a template for analysing the effects of 'popularity'. James adopted this in book 2 of the *Basilicon Doron*.

Here he dissected the causes of the sedition he had faced in Scotland. He argued that these could be traced back to the character of the Scottish Reformation, 'wherein many things were inordinately done by a popular tumult and rebellion . . .' At an early stage,

some fiery spirited men in the ministry got such a guiding of the people . . .
as finding the gust of government sweet they began to fantasy to themselves
a democratic form of government . . . [and] fed themselves with the hope to
become tribuni plebis *and so in a popular government by leading the people*
by the nose to bear the sway of all rule.

Their efforts had helped to destroy the rule of his grandmother and his mother, and during his own minority had succeeded in overwhelming the loyal majority in the church and interposing 'parity, the mother of confusion and enemy of unity'. Even more alarmingly, there was the danger that 'once established in the ecclesiastical government, the politic and civil estate should be drawn to the like'. 'Take heed therefore', he urged his son, of

such puritans, very pests in the church and common-weal . . . breathing nothing
but sedition and calumnies, aspiring without measure, railing without reason
and making their own imaginations . . . the square of their conscience . . . suffer
not the principals of them to brook your land if you like to sit at rest.[57]

James's sensitivity to the dangers of popularity was not confined to religion. Once in England, he also developed the habit of assimilating opposition to his secular policies to a broad popular challenge to monarchy. Common lawyers who contested his use of the prerogative he saw as being led on by 'a vain popular humour' to dispute 'the mystical reverence that belongs unto those that sit in the throne of God'. More divisively, he also applied this rhetoric to the House of Commons. In 1610, after the attacks on impositions, he accused it of having 'wounded our reputation, emboldened an ill-natured people, encroached on many of our privileges'. Its aim, he said, was to leave him with no more power than a doge of Venice. After challenges in the 1614 Parliament, he was even fiercer in his condemnation. Those who criticised him, 'cannot be content with the present form

---

[57] *Basilicon Doron*, pp. 25–7.

of government, but must have a kind of liberty in the people'. 'In every cause that concerns prerogative [they] give a snatch against monarchy through their puritanical itching after popularity.'[58] Taken in such a context, his denunciation of 'fiery and popular spirits' in 1621 was clearly no mere irrational outburst. It represented the logical response of a king who had grown used to the idea of a popular plot to undermine monarchy.

Popularity had become the basis for a conspiracy theory that could be used to label the actions of almost anyone who appeared to be challenging royal authority as inherently subversive; and, increasingly, this was used to legitimate authoritarian readings of the power of monarchy. From the 1590s onwards, as Lake, John Guy and others have demonstrated, it was a key ingredient in the reaction that took place against the quasi-democratic politics of Elizabeth's 'monarchical republic'. The openness, participation and involvement of the public which, in many respects were the hallmarks of the early Elizabethan regime, were retyped as dangerous, subversive and potentially destructive of order. This led to the emergence of a much more limited vision of the state in which the involvement of aristocratic and democratic elements was reduced, and the power of the divinely ordained monarch and his natural allies, the *iure divino* bishops, were presented as the principal guarantors of hierarchy and stability. The roles of parliament and 'active citizens' were played down, and there was a renewed emphasis on keeping the *arcana imperii* hidden from public view and making clear that the giving of counsel and redressing of grievances was to be regulated by the monarch. The tension between these conflicting visions of politics did much to feed the political conflicts of the late Tudor and early Stuart period, and also did much to shape Charles's understanding of the threats and challenges he faced.[59]

When he turned to the topic of disorder and rebellion in his advice to the young Prince Charles, he identified the prime mover in the civil war as an explosive mixture of religion and popularity. 'Rebellion', he warned

---

[58] Ibid., pp. 213, 222; R.P. Cust, *The Forced Loan and English Politics 1626–1628*, Oxford, 1987, p. 19; J.P. Sommerville, 'James I and the divine right of kings: English politics and continental theory', in L.L. Peck ed., *The Mental World of the Jacobean Court*, Cambridge, 1991, p. 66.

[59] Lake, 'Popularity, puritanism and anti-puritanism'; J.A. Guy, 'The Elizabethan establishment and the ecclesiastical polity', in Guy ed., *The Reign of Elizabeth I*, pp. 126–49; Cust, 'Patriots and popular spirits'.

his son, would always tend to take on 'this mask of religion' because 'under the colours of piety, ambitious policies march not only with greatest security, but applause as to the populacy'. The obvious manifestation of this was Presbyterianism. During the early part of his reign it had remained largely quiescent in England, but at the first sign of trouble in 1640 it had re-emerged, preaching its doctrines of 'parity' and 'sedition'. It was the Presbyterians who had inflamed 'ill humours' and drawn together 'all the lesser factions', and their determination to root out episcopacy that had provided the one irreconcilable obstacle to a settlement in 1642. But the 'popular' challenge had not confined itself to the church. It had also wrecked the healing and reforming potential of parliament. Charles explained how the loyalty and goodwill of the Long Parliament had been destroyed by 'distempers' that he had hoped had been laid to rest by the Personal Rule. The warning signs were there in the parliamentary elections of 1640, many of which had been 'carried' with 'partiality and popular heat'. Demagogues, driven on by 'private men's covetous and ambitious designs', had then whipped up the 'vulgar', and the resulting 'tumults' had destroyed whatever hopes there might have been of implementing a programme of measured reform. They had intimidated the 'wiser statesmen' in both Lords and Commons and forced him to withdraw from his capital. What Charles called 'this black parliament' had been turned against him, through the 'insolencies of popular dictates and tumultuary impressions'.[60]

Charles approached most of the political crises of his reign with a similar mindset, and fear of popular conspiracy coloured his thinking in some very significant ways. Once he had identified 'the multitude' and popular demagogues with elements among his own people, this made many of their activities profoundly suspect. Legitimate calls for reform could come to be seen as threats to his authority; appeals to the rule of law could seem like challenges to the prerogative; and the activities of parliament could appear as part of a plot to undermine kingly power. Popularity, then, provides one of the keys to understanding how Charles's apparently benign aspirations could be transformed into policies that seemed to many to be authoritarian and unconstitutional.

If the king's anxieties and prejudices drew much of their force from a fear of 'popularity', however, his more 'positive' impulses remained rooted

---

[60] *Eikon Basilike*, pp. 160–2, 168; see also pp. 4, 15–16, 40–1.

in the standards set in the *Basilicon Doron*. It should be emphasised that measured against this benchmark he matched up rather well. Like his contemporary, Philip IV of Spain, he had a very strong sense of what was expected of him and made a determined effort to fashion himself into the ideal of the virtuous and godly prince.[61] He took personal charge of government in the way monarchs were supposed to do and set a rather better example in his personal and family life than his father had done. However, this could only take him so far. Contrary to the assumptions of contemporary moralists, virtue, conscience and self-control did not make an effective ruler. In the hard world of princely politics – as Machiavelli had recognised – a huge amount depended on personal skills. To succeed, a ruler needed to be shrewd and ruthless in the art of man-management, sensitive to threats and challenges, a good judge of when to intimidate and when to compromise, and sufficently forceful to stamp his authority on those around him. Before concluding this discussion of Charles's early life and influences, then, it is worth looking more closely at his personality.

One does not need to be a psychoanalyst to recognise that the combination of ill-health, lack of parental affection and his father's determination to keep him on the sidelines had a profound effect on Charles' character. In the shrewdest analysis we have of this, Conrad Russell has drawn attention to his 'constant nagging doubt about his status and capacity'.[62] He seems to have felt this doubt particularly strongly whenever he measured himself against his father. In February 1626, for example, he complained to Scottish privy councillors who were reluctant to agree to proposals to reform the Court of Session that they had disobeyed him and 'you durst not have done so to my father'. As Russell points out, it was odd to be talking in this way as early as the first year of his reign unless Charles expected to be slighted.[63]

This basic lack of confidence showed in the crucial art of man-management where he displayed little of James's perceptiveness. In his dealings with courtiers and counsellors he often found it hard to take a

---

[61] For Philip, see J.H. Elliott, *Richelieu and Olivares*, Cambridge, 1984, pp. 40–8.

[62] For this analysis, see 'The Man Charles Stuart', chp. 8 of Russell, *Causes of the Civil War*; the quotation is on p. 204.

[63] HMC, *Supplementary Report on the MSS of the Earl of Mar and Kellie*, 1930, pp. 145–6; Russell, *Causes of the Civil War*, p. 204.

detached view, and tended either to go to extremes in his affection for those he felt were serving him loyally, or to form strong dislikes that were almost impossible to shake. Buckingham and Weston were two of the principal beneficiaries of this. Having decided that they were serving him loyally, Charles stuck by them when it would have been politically advantageous to let them go. The corollary of this was that two of James's more capable ministers, Archbishop Abbot and Lord Keeper Williams, found it almost impossible to function under Charles, because of his personal animosity.[64]

Charles also had what Russell calls 'a somewhat two-dimensional view of people' and an inability to comprehend 'ordinary human reactions which did not happen to be within the limits of his current concerns'. As an example, he cites his obliviousness to the plight of Sir Francis Cottington in 1633 after the death of his wife in childbirth. Cottington, who had been Charles's servant for many years, wrote a very hurt letter to Viscount Wentworth describing how 'in a whole week' the king 'never sent to take notice of my loss', but instead summoned him to court in the midst of mourning to attend to his service. One can contrast this with the empathy displayed by his father during a progress in Northamptonshire in 1616. In conversation with Sir Edward Montague, he recalled how he had been told about Montague's mother who, although completely blind, was remarkably skilled at needlework. The next day Montague presented him with one of her embroidered handkerchiefs, which James showed to the courtiers in attendance and promised to treasure thereafter. It is not hard to see why the old king generated considerable affection among those who got to know him, whereas close contact with Charles often produced frustration and bewilderment.[65] However, it is important not to draw the contrast too strongly. Charles was quite capable of displaying considerable warmth and graciousness. On a visit to the Isle of Wight in 1628, Sir John Oglander recorded how 'he took me by the hand and held me a long time riding together' as the king persuaded him to go on with the unwelcome task of billeting Scottish troops. Charles was also good at conveying a sense of trust and obligation which Edward Hyde seems to have found irresistible

---

[64] Sharpe, *The Personal Rule*, p. 192; Cust, *The Forced Loan*, p. 26.

[65] Russell, *Causes of the Civil War*, pp. 206–8; HMC, *Report on the MSS of the Duke of Buccleuch and Queensberry*, 1899, vol. 1, p. 249.

when they first met in April or May 1641.[66] Nonetheless, the personal insensitivity that he displayed on occasion does seem to have been symptomatic of an inability to see things from the perspective of others. This extended to his understanding of views about politics.

There is no doubt that, compared with his father, Charles's political antennae were severely underdeveloped, and he often found it very hard to foresee reactions to his decisions or gauge their impact on others. A particular blind spot was in comprehending the religious sentiments of English puritans or Scottish Presbyterians; but this also extended to a repeated misunderstanding of the aims of parliament. Again, it is important not to exaggerate his failings. He was not stupid, and could sometimes produce quite a shrewd reading of the political situation. But, again and again, this was revealed as one of his main weaknesses as a politician.

Another facet of Charles's character that seems to have owed a good deal to his upbringing was the lack of confidence he displayed in his ability to secure loyalty and obedience, particularly during his early years. The habit of command was not something that came easily to him. This showed in dealings with courtiers and ministers. Much of the time Charles was able to rely on a routine deference to get his way, but when he had to resort to argument or coercion he was much less comfortable. The encounter with the Scottish privy councillors in February 1626 revealed a king who found face-to-face confrontations very difficult to handle. He delivered a series of prepared arguments, but then seemed at a loss over how to justify them, and finally lapsed into a reproachful silence. English councillors in this situation would probably have conceded the point, but the Scots were accustomed to a less deferential political culture and persisted with their case. Eventually Charles had no choice but to foreclose further discussion by falling back on his authority as king.[67]

This lack of assurance extended to political negotiations more generally. Charles was much less at home than his father had been when it came to

---

[66] *A Royalist's Notebook. The Commonplace Book of Sir John Oglander of Nunwell*, ed. F. Bamford, 1936, pp. 43–4; Clarendon, *Life*, vol. 1, pp. 92–4; see also the instances described in K. Sharpe, 'The image of virtue: the court and household of Charles I, 1625–1642', in Starkey ed., *The English Court*, pp. 246–7.

[67] HMC, *Supplementary Mar and Kellie MSS*, pp. 133–46. For a fuller discussion of this encounter, see below pp. 214–16.

bargaining and deal making. There were several reasons for this. Partly, it seems to have been due to a limited faith in his own powers of persuasion. He sometimes felt a basic want of fluency when it came to using words and argument, not helped by his famous stutter, which once prompted him to admit 'I know I am not good to speak much'.[68] It also had to do with his inability to see the other side's point of view, which he himself implicitly acknowledged when he confided to Laud that he would never have made a lawyer because 'I cannot defend a bad nor yield a good cause'.[69] Perhaps more than anything, it reflected the inherent inflexibility that came out in his fondness for rules and aphorisms. His ministers were forever reciting 'that rule which the king hath set himself' or 'the rule [he] gave me' as justifications for their actions, and these rules – or 'grounds' as he often called them – considerably limited his scope for reaching an accommodation with opponents.[70] The overall result was a style of government with much less room for discussion and compromise than under his father. With Charles, it was generally a case of laying down the law and expecting those he was dealing with to accept it.

Once again it is important not to draw the contrast too starkly. Charles could be an eloquent and effective public speaker who often impressed observers with his command of argument. It should also be emphasised that he gained considerably in self-confidence as his reign went on. The young prince who was at a loss when facing his Scottish councillors in 1626 had transformed himself into an articulate and confident debater by June 1640 when he reportedly ran rings round the Covenanter leadership in discussions at Berwick.[71] Nonetheless, it is apparent that Charles's instinct was to allow a much less open-ended approach than his father; and this often meant, as Russell puts it, that he had 'to stake his authority where a more prudent king might have held it in reserve'.[72]

A third area where Charles's upbringing influenced his character as a politician was in his sensitivity about personal honour. During his

---

[68] *Proceedings in Parliament 1626*, vol. 1, p. 20.

[69] Laud, *Works*, vol. 3, p. 147.

[70] Sharpe, *The Personal Rule*, pp. 183, 188–91; Laud, *Works*, vol. 7, p. 102; *CSP Dom. 1634–5*, p. viii.

[71] For a fuller account of the Berwick negotiations, see below pp. 247–8.

[72] Russell, *Causes of the Civil War*, p. 205.

adolescence and early manhood, he was bombarded with challenges to his masculine self-esteem. His father's overt homosexuality, his embarrassing failure when it came to wooing the Spanish Infanta in 1623 and his problems with asserting his authority over Henrietta Maria in 1626 all struck at his sense of personal potency. The latter episode must have been particularly wounding. It culminated in June 1626 in an argument conducted in the royal bed when the queen refused point-blank to accede to his requests to veto her choice of servants. He tried to persuade her by pointing out that, as his wife, she was duty-bound to respect his views and 'ought not to use me so'; but still she defied him.[73] This had especial significance for his sense of himself as a ruler because contemporaries so often equated a man's capacity to govern with his ability to control his wife and household.[74] Matters improved enormously once he had developed a close relationship with the queen in 1628 and she began to bear his children; but these early experiences left their scars. He remained acutely sensitive to anything that might be construed as a personal slight or humiliation, and this invariably brought out the vengeful side of his character.[75]

At the same time, his sense of honour was closely tied up with broader values and ideals. Through his reading and education, he absorbed the humanist-inspired notion that honour derived from virtue, wisdom and self-control. He was also influenced by traditional notions that equated it with ancient blood and lineage, or the chivalric values of courage and assertiveness.[76] In particular, he internalised the aristocratic principle that his word was his bond. Once he had pledged himself, whether to an individual or a cause, he saw it as a matter of supreme importance to abide by what he had undertaken. This explains his intense feelings of guilt after abandoning Strafford in 1641, and also his powerful sense of obligation to the French Huguenots in the late 1620s.[77]

---

[73] Charles's account of this episode to Buckingham still makes painful reading: *Letters of Charles I*, pp. 42–5.

[74] E. Foyster, *Manhood in early Modern England*, Harlow, 1999, pp. 3–5.

[75] One of the signals he tended to give when he felt he was being treated in this way – at any rate in the context of domestic politics – was to talk about his royal authority being reduced to that of a duke of Venice. For more on this, and Charles's sense that he was being subjected to a process akin to emasculation, see below pp. 230–1.

[76] For contemporary honour codes, see Smuts, *Culture and Power*, pp. 8–17.

[77] For further discussion of these episodes, see below pp. 50–1, 73, 77, 281–2, 287–8.

Charles's touchiness on matters of honour was not helpful when it came to trying to defuse political conflicts. He tended to resort to the language of honour where a more neutral rhetoric might have sufficed, often serving to personalise confrontations, and making it harder for either side to back down. As we shall see, this was to be another powerful obstacle to political settlement.

Recent judgements of Charles have tended to be very critical. One historian has described him as 'woefully inadequate', another as 'unfit to be king' and a third as 'the most inept monarch to occupy the English throne since Henry vi'.[78] He has been widely blamed for causing the English Civil War, bringing about the defeat of the Royalists and sabotaging the chances of a post-war settlement. Without wishing to anticipate the argument of this book, it has to be said that several of these verdicts appear unduly harsh. Investigation of Charles's early life and influences suggests that he was neither 'unfit' nor 'inadequate'. He was far from stupid; he thought long and hard about the 'craft' of kingship; and, in terms of his aspirations, he matched up well to what contemporaries expected. The reasons why he came unstuck have to do with much more than failings of character or aptitude. They relate to the difficulties of applying particular attitudes and convictions to the solution of complex political problems, as well as specific mistakes and misjudgements made in the handling of crises. Beyond certain limited achievements, one would be hard put to argue that Charles was a successful king. But the spectacular nature of his downfall should not obscure the qualities that he brought to the role.

---

[78] L.J. Reeve, *Charles i and the Road to Personal Rule*, Cambridge, 1989, p. 3; Russell, *Causes of the Civil War*, p. 208; B. Coward, *The Stuart Age*, 2nd edn, Harlow, 1994, p. 158. The main exception to this is the work by Kevin Sharpe who has approached Charles on his own terms and presented a much more sympathetic portrait: see Sharpe, *The Personal Rule*, pp. 179–208 and Sharpe, 'Conscience and public duty', pp. 643–65.

Chapter 2

Charles and Buckingham, 1623–1628

The Blessed Revolution

The clearest indication that Charles was becoming a force to be reckoned with in politics came when he and Buckingham returned from Madrid and quite unexpectedly launched the so-called 'Blessed Revolution'. This over-turned the policy of peace with Spain that James had maintained since 1604 and determined that from now on the struggle to recover the Palatinate was to be built around a continental war. Suddenly it appeared that the reversionary interest had taken over. In fact, behind the scenes, James con-tinued to cling to power and remained the key decision maker in foreign affairs; but this episode did witness the prince's transformation from 'Baby Charles' into a politician of real substance.

The celebration that greeted the prince's return in October 1623 was one of the most memorable displays of popular emotion in the entire seventeenth century. Thomas Cogswell has described how bonfires were lit and bells were rung throughout the kingdom: one observer noted 335 fires between Whitehall and Temple Bar in London alone. 'The salutations of joy' convinced Sir Edward Conway, secretary of state, that 'there was not a sober head between Southampton and . . .': at first he wrote Royston, then Cambridge, but finally settled on 'God knows where . . .' When Charles rested at York House the crowd who gathered to greet him was so dense that his coach could not get out and had to be carried through the mass. Charles 'leaned his body out of the coach, with his hat in his hand and gave thanks to them all for their loves'; in response they shouted, 'we have him . . . we have our prince again'.[1] This was the first time Charles had experienced the full warmth of popular acclaim. It did much to bolster his confidence and self-esteem; and – since the crowds were cheering because he had returned home having *not* married the Infanta – it reinforced his growing conviction that the best way to deal with the Spanish was by force.

The Spanish Match was deeply unpopular in England, raising fears of a toleration for Catholics and a return to the horrors of the last time an English monarch had married a Spaniard. However, for much of 1622 and 1623 it seemed that nothing could prevent it from going ahead. The dissolution of the 1621 Parliament removed the possibility of rallying the nation behind a war and left James with little option but to draw closer to Spain. At the same time, Charles's personal feelings had become part of the equation. He was now a spirited young man of 21 who had overcome much of the awkwardness of his adolescence and taken on the chivalric mantle bequeathed by his elder brother. His thoughts were turning to romance and he became increasingly besotted with the Infanta Maria. He lapped up reports of her dancing, pestered James's special envoy to Spain, the earl of Bristol, for a portrait of her and began taking Spanish lessons. He even told the Spanish envoy, Gondomar, that he was prepared to go to Madrid to woo her in person. What James, in a characteristically piquant phrase, called 'the cod-piece point', gave added impetus to negotiations.[2]

Historians have long debated the reasoning behind Charles and Buckingham's dramatic trip to Spain in February 1623. Some have suggested that it was the reckless venture of a young prince whose head was full of notions of romance and chivalry. Others see it as part of a machiavellian scheme by Buckingham to detach Charles from his father and secure his future as royal favourite.[3] Both verdicts have some validity, but they overlook the serious diplomatic calculation that was also an element in the decision. Since the dissolution of the 1621 Parliament, the Spanish had slowed

---

[1] Quotations are from T. Cogswell, 'England and the Spanish Match', in R.P. Cust and A.L. Hughes eds, *Conflict in Early Stuart England*, Harlow, 1989, pp. 107–9.

[2] Ibid., pp. 111–26; G. Redworth, 'Of Pimps and Princes: three unpublished letters from James I and the Prince of Wales relating to the Spanish Match', *HJ*, vol. 37, 1994, pp. 401–9; Lockyer, *Buckingham*, pp. 134–5.

[3] Lockyer, *Buckingham*, p. 137.

the pace of negotiation over the marriage, confident that they could string England along and thus achieve their main objective, which was to prevent England from joining forces with Spain's enemies. James tried to speed things up by sending Endymion Porter on a special mission to Madrid; but his interview with the Count of Olivares, Philip's leading minister, simply raised suspicions that even if the marriage went ahead Spain had no intention of pressuring the Emperor into restoring the Palatinate. James was prepared to continue on the basis of earlier Spanish assurances; however, Charles and Buckingham were becoming frustrated by the delays and increasingly sceptical about whether the Spanish would actually deliver. The Madrid trip offered a means of cutting through the diplomatic evasions and securing a decision.[4]

Charles was certainly greatly attracted by the prospect of marrying Dona Maria and wanted to speed things up as much as possible; but equally he seems to have been determined to secure a breakthrough over the Palatinate. He grew particularly close to his sister Elizabeth during 1622 and 1623 and there was much talk in court circles of the need to rescue her honour. If this could be achieved by a Spanish marriage then all well and good; but if not, then both Charles and Buckingham showed that they were still interested in the military option. The young prince put himself forward to lead the proposed Anglo-Dutch relief force in September 1622, and the favourite was taking lessons in the drillyard and going out of his way to cultivate veterans of the Elizabethan wars, like Sir Edward Conway. However, they needed to know what Spain's intentions were one way or the other. The Madrid trip was an effective means of discovering these. Even James, who was initially opposed, was forced to concede it would bring matters to a head: 'if my baby Charles's credit in Spain mend not these things I will bid farewell to peace in christendom'.[5]

The main impetus behind the decision to go to Spain appears to have come from Charles himself. James later recalled that it was 'upon your earnest entreaty' that he had agreed to 'so hazardous a journey'. Charles had begged the king, on his knees, that he be allowed to go to Madrid to fetch his bride in person. When James hesitated, Charles persuaded Buckingham to blackmail him by warning that if he refused a request so important

---

[4] Ibid., pp. 129–34.

[5] Cogswell, *The Blessed Revolution*, pp. 58–61.

for Charles's future happiness it would jeopardise his love for him. Significantly, this was the first time Charles pushed through an important political initiative against his father's wishes, although he still depended on Buckingham to act as intermediary.[6]

The trip itself was a mixture of farce and frustration; again, however, it showed Charles growing into a more independent and commanding role. The would-be suitors tried to slip out of England disguised as 'Tom' and 'John Smith', complete with false beards. At Canterbury the two suspicious strangers were arrested by an over-enthusiastic mayor and Buckingham had to pull down his beard and reveal his identity as the lord admiral on the way to a surprise inspection of the fleet. They travelled through France and Spain on horseback and at one point nearly fought a duel with two Spanish soldiers over the virtue of the ladies of their respective nations. Once in Madrid, Charles was given only tantalising glimpses of his prospective bride, but this was enough for him to become thoroughly infatuated. Buckingham reported to the king that 'Baby Charles is so touched by the heart that he confessed that all he ever saw is nothing to her'; and at one stage, desperate for closer contact, he scaled the wall of her privy garden and advanced towards her, whereupon she fled in the opposite direction, shrieking for her chaperone.[7]

By the time Charles and Buckingham arrived in Madrid in March 1623 Spanish attitudes towards the marriage had shifted. Philip IV and his council of state had decided that the benefits of peace with England, and the possibility of England's future return to the Catholic fold, outweighed any disadvantages from restoring the Palatinate. Olivares disagreed, but for the time being he had to go along with the majority view. Charles was given a reception befitting a future brother-in-law of the king of Spain and was both impressed and flattered. During the spring and early summer, negotiations proceeded apace. The Spanish were somewhat put out when it became clear that Charles was not going to convert to Catholicism; however, they were reassured by his willingness to allow his children to be brought up in the faith until the age of 12 and his offer of an immediate suspension of the recusancy laws in England. Buckingham upset his hosts and

---

[6] Carlton, *Charles I*, pp. 36–7.

[7] Ibid., pp. 38–42.

quarrelled openly with Olivares; but Charles stepped in to smooth the differences and keep negotiations on track. By July most of the obstacles appeared to have been removed and it was agreed that the couple should marry in September. At this point, however, two unexpected developments upset the whole process.[8]

The death of the pope necessitated a fresh dispensation for the marriage, which caused unavoidable delay. But much more significantly, doubt was now cast on whether the Spanish would actually deliver over the Palatinate. Charles had all along been working on the assumption that marriage and restoration were inextricably linked. During August, however, it emerged that the Spanish council of state had agreed to a proposal by Olivares that restoration should be conditional on Frederick and Elizabeth marrying their eldest son to the daughter of the Emperor and sending him to Vienna to be brought up as a Catholic. Charles knew that his sister and brother-in-law would never consent to such a humiliation. When he pressed Olivares for assurances that their original understanding would be honoured, the count was evasive and eventually conceded that it had never been agreed with the Emperor. Charles was deeply upset. He had engaged himself to do all in his power to assist Frederick and Elizabeth and had been receiving reminders from England about just how desperate their plight had become after the surrender of their final toehold in the Palatinate in April. Their cause took precedence even over his own feelings for the Infanta. He refused to be mollified when Philip promised to do all in his power to return the Palatinate as a wedding present and on 28 August took his leave. He had undertaken to abide by the marriage articles already agreed and signed documents allowing the union to take place by proxy once the new papal dispensation arrived; but his misgivings were clear. He left behind instructions that Sir Walter Aston, the resident ambassador, was not to deliver the proxy except with his express approval. At the same time, he wrote to his sister, assuring her that he 'would not be engaged till he might g[a]uge what would become of your business'.[9]

The Madrid trip had three important political consequences. First of all it firmly cemented the relationship between Buckingham and Charles. In spite of their differences in the latter stages of negotiations, the whole

---

[8] B.C. Pursell, 'The end of the Spanish Match', *HJ*, vol. 45, 2002, pp. 699–715.

[9] Ibid., pp. 715–26; Cogswell, *The Blessed Revolution*, pp. 60–1.

venture served, in the words of one historian, as 'an intense bonding experience'. After their return, it was reported that the two men 'never go asunder but arm in arm' and throughout the following months they remained politically inseparable. Second, it made Charles into a more mature politician. He had taken responsibility during some difficult negotiations and shown that he could act forcefully and independently. As if to emphasise this, he returned from Spain with a newly grown beard.[10] Third, it opened the way for the about-turn in English foreign policy.

Several historians have ascribed this largely to personal pique. Once Charles left Spain, the Infanta's spell over him was quickly broken and feelings of love were replaced by resentment. Both he and Buckingham felt insulted by the apparent duplicity of the Spanish, so the argument goes, and were determined to exact revenge. This may explain the vehemence with which they took up the cudgels on their return home, but it does not do justice to the motivation behind their policy. If it achieved nothing else, the trip to Madrid clearly revealed that the Spanish were not to be trusted over the restoration of the Palatinate. As Buckingham put it to the French ambassador, they were shown to have been leading James 'par le nez'. In these circumstances, it was logical to turn to the military option. This now seemed to offer the likeliest means of putting effective pressure on the Spanish, while at the same time offering a means to satisfy the clamour to rescue the 'Protestant cause' in Germany, which had taken a fearful battering during the run of Hapsburg military successes. It was out of a mixture of realism, idealism and their sense of slighted honour, then, that the prince and favourite began putting together the anti-Spanish coalition needed to support a war.[11]

The new policy was a joint effort, so much so that it is impossible to say with any certainty who was the dominant partner. S.R. Gardiner saw the favourite as very much in charge and, in a celebrated judgement, described the opening of the 1624 Parliament as the beginning of the reign of 'King' Buckingham.[12] But such a verdict seems misconceived. If anything, as we have seen, it was Charles who had shown the greater commitment

---

[10] M.B. Young, *Charles I*, Basingstoke, 1997, p. 20; Cogswell, *The Blessed Revolution*, pp. 64, 98–9.

[11] Young, *Charles I*, pp. 19–21; Cogswell, *The Blessed Revolution*, pp. 61–2, 67–9.

[12] Gardiner, *History of England*, vol. 5, p. 184.

to war since 1620. With his strong sense of right and wrong, it appears that he was the one who provided much of the conviction and clarity of purpose needed to get the policy launched. Buckingham, on the other hand, ever sensitive to the demands of royal favour, seems to have tried to anticipate his views and move to meet them. However, the prince was not yet up to acting on his own and it was the duke who supplied the gumption needed to hold the policy together, offering advice and support, and stiffening Charles's resolve when he looked like wavering. The two men came to form a supremely effective double act. Buckingham took responsibility for the day-to-day detail of power broking and negotiation, and acted as public spokesman. Charles remained more aloof, but was always ready to step in and use his growing prestige to overawe opposition.[13]

The first problem facing the 'patriot coalition', as it became known, was how to handle James. After the return from Madrid, the king had been pushed to the sidelines, partly due to illness and partly because his own foreign policy had effectively collapsed. However, he remained the final arbiter in such matters and all his instincts were against going to war. The coalition did its best to present him with a strategy he could live with – stressing the need to counter Hapsburg imperialism rather than engage in any sort of confessional crusade – but he was still tempted by Spanish offers of a peaceful restitution of the Palatinate and was supported by a powerful lobby in council. The key to dealing with James was the power that Buckingham and Charles wielded at court. The favourite used his control of the bedchamber to supervise access to him and prevent the pro-Spanish lobby from putting their case. The prince took over the chairing of the privy council's foreign policy committee and also secured control of the correspondence with Bristol and Aston in Madrid, using this to insist that his proxy could only be delivered after specific undertakings on the Palatinate. The crunch came in January 1624 when Philip offered to restore the Lower Palatinate by the summer if the marriage went ahead. The foreign policy committee voted by five to three to accept these terms and James was undoubtedly attracted by them; however, Charles played his trump card by refusing, under any circumstances, to accept the Infanta and this effectively put an end to marriage speculation. Throughout these difficult negotiations, the prince had played a crucial role, displaying for the first time an awareness of the

---

[13] Cogswell, *The Blessed Revolution*, pp. 64, 114, 171.

power that he wielded as heir to the throne. He was also beginning to impress contemporaries, with Sir Edward Zouch, a seasoned courtier, describing in November 1623 how he was now 'entering into command of affairs . . . and all men addressed themselves to him'.[14]

Charles's new-found authority, together with a growing fund of popular goodwill, became important as the coalition worked to build up support. They needed to outflank the powerful pro-Spanish lobby at court, led by Lord Treasurer Cranfield, and also make preparations to carry the forthcoming parliament. Charles's presence offered crucial reassurance to those who still did not entirely trust Buckingham. He helped to recruit 'undertakers' to act as the coalition's parliamentary spokesmen from among those who had opposed the crown in 1621. Of these, Sir Edward Coke in particular seems to have been drawn in by the prospect of serving the future king. He also did much to win over some of the more difficult senior figures at court. Foremost among these was the earl of Pembroke who profoundly resented Buckingham and, for a time, seemed prepared to put personal animosity before his long-standing hatred of Spain. To the dismay of court commentators it looked as if he might support the proposal to go ahead with the match; however, Charles stepped in – with a threat 'to remember' all those who advocated the marriage – and by January 1624 Pembroke and other anti-Spanish 'grandees' had fallen into line.[15]

The 1624 Parliament (19 February–29 May) was the most successful of the decade, due in no small part to Charles's involvement. Most politicians were looking to the future and were eager to make the right impression on their prospective monarch. Charles reciprocated with a performance that was both confident and constructive. As in 1621, he attended assiduously in the House of Lords, made regular contributions to debate and mediated between parliament and the king. But there was none of the sourness in his relations with the Commons that had marred the latter stages of 1621. Throughout he remained positive and encouraging, offering repeated assurances that the future of parliament would be safe in his hands. At one point, his father predicted that 'he would live to have his belly full of parliaments'; but there was no sign of this in 1624. As far as he was concerned,

---

[14] Ibid., pp. 69–76, 87–9, 128–31; NA, SP 14/154/10.

[15] Cogswell, *The Blessed Revolution*, pp. 164–5; Russell, *Parliaments and English Politics*, pp. 147–8.

parliament was behaving just as it was supposed to. It listened to the case put by the coalition, then demonstrated its loyalty by dissolving the Spanish treaties and making a large grant of supply. When he declared, in 1628, that 'at the first I liked parliaments', it was 1624 that he had in mind.[16]

The parliament was the key to the coalition's strategy. They had to persuade MPs to break off the treaties with Spain and vote a generous supply, while avoiding specific discussion of the war, which might upset James or jeopardise treaty negotiations with the French and Dutch. Rejection of the Anglo-Spanish treaties was by no means a foregone conclusion. Some MPs shared James's reservations and wanted to continue the policy of peaceful diplomacy. However, coalition spokesmen were able to stoke up a mood of hostility, greatly helped by the drama of Buckingham's Relation on 24 February, which exposed in minute detail the duplicity of the Spanish during the marriage negotiations. By early March, the Commons was recommending that the treaties be terminated. Charles's main contribution at this stage was to deliver part of the Relation, which helped dispel any suggestion that the favourite might have misrepresented what had happened.[17]

Obtaining the grant of subsidies without tying James to a particular war policy was more problematic, since many MPs felt cheated by the lack of action following the grants made in 1621. The coalition's first attempt to move a grant on 5 March ran into opposition from MPs who wanted specific undertakings about redress of grievances. A better coordinated bid on 11–12 March did produce agreement in principle; but James then threatened to disrupt things by insisting on a totally unrealistic grant of six subsidies, part of which must be used to discharge his debts. At this point Charles and Buckingham had to step in and engage in frantic lobbying to scale down the demand and earmark the money for the war. On 19–20 March the Commons was finally persuaded to offer three subsidies and three fifteenths, with specific discussion of the nature of the war being carefully avoided.[18]

---

[16] Cogswell, *The Blessed Revolution*, p. 148; Ruigh, *The Parliament of 1624*, p. 336; *Proceedings in Parliament 1628*, vol. 2, pp. 324–5.

[17] Cogswell, *The Blessed Revolution*, pp. 147, 166–7, 171–83; Ruigh, *The Parliament of 1624*, pp. 163–7.

[18] Cogswell, *The Blessed Revolution*, pp. 182–218.

This phase of the parliament ended in a mood of great optimism. James graciously accepted the offer of subsidies and promised to do everything possible to restore Frederick and Elizabeth to the Palatinate, while Charles dropped broad hints about the war and promised that a speedy grant would lead to more frequent parliaments. 'If you go on with courage and show alacrity and readiness in this business', he told the committee for supply, 'you shall so oblige me unto you now that I will never forget it hereafter.' This was widely reported and, according to the student diarist, Simonds D'Ewes, 'did much comfort all their hearts and made every man's mouth almost full with the discourse of it'.[19]

During the latter stages of the parliament, Buckingham fell seriously ill and the prince took charge of the coalition, displaying considerable drive and determination. In the first place, he brought negotiations for a military alliance with the Dutch to a successful conclusion, after they had looked like foundering on James's lack of enthusiasm for war. Second, he took over management of the parliamentary impeachment of Cranfield who had become a serious threat to the coalition, not only because he continued to press a pro-Spanish foreign policy, but also because he was trying to entice James with a new homosexual favourite, Arthur Brett. Charles organised the group of Buckingham clients who had been hounding the lord treasurer in the Commons and himself led the attack in the Lords. James was dismayed by this partisanship and warned prophetically that his son would live to regret his part in reviving the impeachment of royal ministers; but Charles achieved his objective. Cranfield was dismissed from office and, briefly, imprisoned in the Tower. Then, third, he demonstrated that he could get his way in the rough and tumble of court faction. He headed off Cranfield's continuing efforts to unseat Buckingham by becoming 'a bedchamber man', which meant keeping a constant watch on the king to deny Brett and his mentor access. He also dealt with a more serious plot against the duke, hatched by the Spanish ambassadors and pro-Spanish elements at court. In late April, the earl of Kellie, who had been worsted by Buckingham in a battle for bedchamber influence in 1622, used his position as groom of the stool to admit the ambassadors to a private audience with James. They accused Buckingham of the cardinal sin of 'affecting popularity' and claimed that he was planning to retire the king

---

[19] Ibid., pp. 193–4; *The Diary of Sir Simonds D'Ewes*, ed. E. Bourcier, Paris, 1974, p. 185.

to a country house so that his son could rule in his place. James took the charges seriously enough to interrogate his councillors on oath and bar the favourite from his presence; however, the prince saved the day by making it clear to all and sundry that he remained Buckingham's 'true friend', which effectively prevented any of the councillors from testifying against him. When the duke finally recovered his health in June, the king welcomed him back to court as warmly as ever.[20]

Over the summer months of 1624, the 'patriot coalition' carried all before it and the political reputations of Charles and Buckingham reached their apogee. Anti-Spanish and anti-Catholic pamphlets were published in huge numbers, typified by the writings of Thomas Scott, the puritan propagandist, who portrayed the duo as heroes of the hour for exposing the treachery of Spain. This was also the theme of Thomas Middleton's *Game at Chesse* which, during its brief run in August, was probably the most heavily attended stage play of the period. The breach of treaties and the alliance with the Dutch produced something approaching a war fever and there was even optimism about a league with the French who seemed prepared to drop any demands for concessions to Catholics.[21] Within less than a year, however, the mood had altered dramatically. The Spanish war had failed to develop; there were loud complaints about costs and the way strategy was being conducted; the French alliance was condemned as a sell-out; and Charles's honeymoon with the English people was over. The change of mood was decisive and set the tone for the politics of the later 1620s. But what brought it about?

This question has aroused considerable debate. Conrad Russell and other 'revisionist' historians have argued that it happened largely because Charles and Buckingham misjudged the mood of the nation. Few people really wanted a war and when the full costs became apparent there was a widespread reluctance to pay for it. Russell points to the lack of specific discussion of war in the House of Commons in 1624 as evidence that MPs and their constituents were far more interested in local matters. 'The impression', he argues, 'is not of a House of Commons eager to seize the

---

[20] Cogswell, *The Blessed Revolution*, pp. 234–8, 255–6, 268–70; Ruigh, *The Parliament of 1624*, pp. 336–40, 272–87; Cuddy, 'Bedchamber of James I', pp. 223–4.

[21] Cogswell, *The Blessed Revolution*, pp. 274–8, 281–307.

initiative in foreign affairs, but rather of one deferring the involvement which was asked of it until the last possible moment.'[22]

This conclusion has been answered very persuasively in Thomas Cogswell's book, *The Blessed Revolution*. He shows that the absence of detailed discussion in the Commons can be attributed not to a lack of interest in a war, but to the coalition's efforts to steer MPs away from controversy. He also stresses the positive evidence of an enthusiasm for war, in the sermons and pamphlets published after Charles's return from Madrid, the excitement and anticipation in the summer of 1624 and, above all, the size of the Commons' grant of supply. The Commons could simply have rejected the crown's request, but instead – in full expectation that the money would be used to pay for a war – they agreed to pay an unprecedented £300 000. What was unpopular, Cogswell concludes, was not the war itself, but the type of war that was fought and the lack of success which attended it.[23]

The source of these problems can be traced to the last months of James's reign, when the old king effectively crippled the war effort. This is a reminder not to exaggerate the dominance of the reversionary interest in this period. Some historians have consigned James to a premature grave and, in the process, seriously underestimated his continued capacity to shape events. Once he had recovered from the coalition's initial onslaught, he showed he could still take charge at court. Buckingham was so shocked by the investigation into the Spanish ambassadors' allegations that he spent the rest of the reign trying to mend his relationship with James. The old king also retained control of the prerogative and, through this, the ultimate direction of war strategy and diplomacy. Charles and Buckingham had hoped to pursue a 'blue water' policy based on a naval war against Spanish colonies and shipping lanes. This was a roundabout way of recovering the Palatinate, and it was unlikely to produce results quickly; but it had the advantage of being popular in parliament and playing to England's military strengths. James, however, had different ideas. He was convinced that England's best chance was a land war aimed directly at relief of the Palatinate. In the end it was the king's approach that prevailed. While the

---

[22] Russell, *Parliaments and English Politics*, pp. 161–2.

[23] Cogswell, *The Blessed Revolution*, pp. 309–12, 317–18.

English navy lay in harbour, Count Mansfeldt's force of mercenaries and conscripts set out for Germany in May 1625; but it got no further than the Netherlands before starting to disintegrate. This cast a blight over the early stages of the war, and James made matters worse by forcing through a disastrous treaty with the French. He believed, with some justification, that Spain could only be defeated if England became part of a non-denominational alliance aimed at curbing Hapsburg imperialism. However, this made him so desperate for a league with the French that they were able to manoeuvre him into conceding much more than was prudent. He agreed to suspend the recusancy laws, which directly contravened assurances he had given to the 1624 Parliament, and also promised to lend ships to Louis xiii, which were later used to suppress an uprising by French Huguenots. In return, all England received was some financial support for Mansfeldt. James's pursuit of the French treaty was to cause enormous damage; but by the time he died in March 1625 it was too late to undo it.[24]

The period between Charles's return from Madrid and his accession showed him emerging decisively from his father's shadow. James was no longer able to dominate him and found that it was now he who was being pressed into following the initiatives launched by his son. This period also provides a fleeting opportunity to observe Charles's performance as a politician having to compete with other politicians rather than being raised above the fray as king. The impression he created was very favourable. He showed considerable abilities in his role as a party leader – abilities which, as Russell observes, he was to reveal again in the 1640s. These were based on his obvious commitment to causes he believed to be just and honourable and his considerable drive and energy. He also revealed a surprising talent for public relations, projecting himself as the ideal of the parliamentary prince who was about to lead his nation to war. When Sir Edward Coke thanked him for his speech to the committee for supply, he evoked images of the Black Prince and the young Henry v.[25] It seemed to Englishmen that under the leadership of their vigorous young prince they were about to embark on a new age of martial glory. But the strengths that made Charles such an impressive Prince of Wales could become liabilities when he was king.

---

[24] Ibid., pp. 313–17.

[25] Ibid., p. 194.

His sense of conviction, which was invaluable when particular goals were being pursued, might be a source of weakness when he needed to be able to see the bigger picture and adopt a more flexible approach. There was also some justice in the earl of Kellie's charge that he had become 'a little too popular'. The partisanship and tendency to play to the gallery that he displayed in the Cranfield impeachment would, as James had warned, make a rod for his back in future parliaments.[26] The 'Blessed Revolution' was a triumph for Charles and Buckingham. But it created the problems that overshadowed the first three years of the new reign.

The parliaments of 1625 and 1626

Charles's honeymoon with the English people lasted three months into the new reign. It was brought to an abrupt end by the divisions of the 1625 Parliament. Writing six years later, Sir John Eliot vividly recalled the nation's hopes at Charles's accession.

King James being dead and with him the fearful security and degenerate vices of a long corrupted peace in hope and expectation laid aside, with the new king a new spirit of life and comfort possessed all men.[27]

Nostalgia for this fleeting moment no doubt led Eliot to exaggerate the mood of optimism; but there was a good deal of truth in his description. Charles was still enormously popular, with commentators vying to outdo each other in the praise of his piety and virtue; and the death of the old king did herald a new vigour in the preparations for war. Mansfeldt's forces were finally put to good use in assisting the Dutch to relieve the siege of Breda; Charles's uncle, Christian of Denmark, was promised £30 000 a month to mount an offensive in Germany; and preparations were at last under way to unleash the English navy. Warrants were issued to prepare the fleet and levy 10 000 men for an expedition against either Dunkirk or Cadiz, while the long-awaited 'blue water' policy seemed about to be launched with plans

---

[26] HMC, *Mar and Kellie*, pp. 202–3. For the double-edged nature of popularity, as experienced by Buckingham, see T.E. Cogswell, 'The people's love: the duke of Buckingham and popularity', in Cogswell, Cust and Lake eds, *Politics, Religion and Popularity*, pp. 235–58.

[27] *Proceedings in Parliament 1625*, p. 491.

to establish a joint-stock privateering company. The cloud on the horizon was the terms of the French alliance. Charles issued an order to suspend the recusancy laws on 1 May, thus allowing the marriage with Henrietta Maria to go ahead and also securing the first half of her dowry. But, with the nation gearing itself up for war against the greatest Catholic power in Europe, this was not a time to appear soft on popery.[28]

The first parliament of the new reign was critical if the war effort was to be credible. A substantial grant of supply was needed to help cover costs, estimated at around £1 000 000 a year, and it was also important to obtain a display of national unity. However, in contrast to 1624, the preparations made by Charles and Buckingham were wholly inadequate. There was little they could do about the plague that broke out in London in May and created an anxious and restive mood throughout the session. They were also unfortunate that the French were determined to celebrate Henrietta Maria's marriage in style. The new queen arrived in London with a train of 1 000 attendants two days before the parliament opened and most of the court's energies during June and July were absorbed by an exhausting round of balls and receptions.[29] However, the main problem was that there was no organised lobby of crown supporters in the parliament. Lord Keeper Williams reminded Charles before the meeting that in the past 'the king's servants and trustiest friends' had used their influence in elections to recruit a block of sympathetic MPs. But no such effort was made in 1625 and even the 'undertakers', who had played such an important role in 1624, were largely ignored, with the result that their interventions during the session were either unhelpful or positively obstructive.[30] Charles seems to have thought the Commons could be relied on simply to carry on where it had left off the previous summer and this proved disastrous.

The 1625 Parliament met on 18 June and lasted, with a break to adjourn to Oxford, until 12 August. The crown's basic aim was to secure a quick grant of supply and postpone discussion of grievances for a later

---

[28] T.E. Cogswell, 'Crown, Parliament and War, 1623–25', Washington University, St Louis, Miss., Ph.D., 1983, pp. 508–9; Russell, *Parliaments and English Politics*, pp. 206–9.

[29] Russell, *Parliaments and English Politics*, pp. 205–6, 212–14, 218–19; Cogswell, 'Crown, Parliament and War', pp. 512–19.

[30] J. Hacket, *Scrinia Reserata. A Memorial of John Williams D.D.*, 2 parts in 1 vol. (1693), pt. 2, p. 3; Cogswell, *The Blessed Revolution*, pp. 300, 314.

session. Charles was convinced that the Commons was under an 'engagement' to support the war because of its promise in 1624 to 'assist . . . in a parliamentary course' if James broke off the Spanish treaties. This was the theme of his characteristically terse opening speech. He reminded the house that it was 'engaged' by its earlier actions and stressed that 'it would be a dishonour to him and to us not to perfect it'. The lord keeper followed this up by promising discussion of grievances at a later session and underlining its responsibility to fulfil the 'engagement'. He also made it clear that any decisions about the treatment of Catholics would be reserved to the king alone. According to Eliot, most MPs 'liked' Charles's speech, comparing it favourably with James's long-winded orations.[31] But, lacking the support of an organised lobby, it was never likely to be enough to secure an adequate grant.

Within three days some MPs were proposing an immediate adjournment of the parliament because of the plague. When this was headed off, they latched on to the sensitive issue of the recusancy laws and began to discuss a petition on religion. A motion for supply was finally made on 30 June; however, it came not from one of the crown spokesmen, but from Sir Francis Seymour, a backbencher who was notably unsympathetic to the war effort. He proposed a grant of one subsidy and one fifteenth, worth just £100 000. Pembroke's client, Sir Benjamin Rudyerd, tried to explain that the costs of the fleet alone amounted to more than £300 000 a year; but to little effect. The decisive contribution came from one of the 1624 'undertakers', Sir Robert Phelips, who answered Charles's point about an 'engagement' by arguing that this was in respect of a war and no war had been formally declared. He also voiced a general concern about the crown's determination to consider grievances only after supply had been granted. In the end a decision was taken to offer just two subsidies, worth £140 000.[32]

Charles and Buckingham clearly mismanaged the early stages of the parliament. It did not help that, as king, Charles no longer attended debates. Had he done so he might have been more sensitive to MPs' worries about the plague and the relaxation of the recusancy laws. But the main problem

[31] *Proceedings in Parliament 1625*, pp. 492–3; Russell, *Parliaments and English Politics*, p. 219.

[32] Russell, *Parliaments and English Politics*, pp. 220–46; C. Thompson, 'Court politics and parliamentary conflict in 1625', in Cust and Hughes eds, *Conflict in Early Stuart England*, pp. 172–5.

continued to be complacency. The young king appears to have assumed that the notification of his wishes and a reminder about the 'engagement' would be enough to secure compliance. He showed no readiness to engage in the traditional processes of bargaining with the Commons and he had no strategy for dealing with opposition.

Once the size of the grant had been decided, Charles and Buckingham's best course would probably have been to accept the offer graciously and hope for additional supply from a later session. At first this was what they seem to have resolved to do. On 4 July, Lord Keeper Williams delivered a message expressing satisfaction with the grant and leaving MPs to conclude their business and go home. However, on 8 July the policy was suddenly reversed. This decision revealed a split at the centre of government which was to be one of the themes of court politics for the remainder of the decade. Charles and Buckingham argued that they must have additional supply to equip the fleet, otherwise the expeditionary force would be a disaster. The subsidies already granted should simply be regarded as a goodwill offering, traditional at the start of a new reign, in which case the crown was entitled to further support for its military ventures. This line was resisted by a lobby of courtiers and councillors – among whom the lord keeper and Sir Humphrey May were the most conspicuous – who feared such action would destroy good relations with parliament. The request for additional supply, at a time when many MPs had absented themselves from the Commons because of the plague, would be seen as a betrayal of trust. Moreover, it would be dishonourable to ask for more when the subsidies had already been accepted. Such arguments were brushed aside, however, and on the 8th Buckingham's client, Sir John Coke, put the motion for extra subsidies. The Commons' response was almost entirely negative. MPs either failed to comprehend what was being asked of them or opposed the request outright. Nonetheless, Charles and Buckingham pressed on and staggered MPs by announcing that, instead of bringing the session to an end, they would adjourn it to meet in Oxford at the start of August.[33]

The few days spent at the Oxford meeting of the 1625 Parliament (1–12 August) were among the most turbulent and dramatic of the decade. The spread of the plague to Oxford helped to create a frenetic atmosphere

---

[33] Thompson, 'Court politics and parliamentary conflict', pp. 175–9; Russell, *Parliaments and English Politics*, pp. 236–7.

in which the crown tried three times to secure further supply and MPs responded by launching an attack on Buckingham. Charles eventually dissolved the parliament amid murmurings about the dangers of 'popularity' and the need for 'new counsels'. Most of the tensions that damaged good relations between crown and subject for the rest of the decade came to the surface during this meeting.

Charles and Buckingham's priority continued to be to secure adequate supply while making as few concessions as possible. Initially they intended to explain their military strategy and the extent of their needs, and then rely on the goodwill of the Commons. But this was soon abandoned in favour of a harder-nosed approach. On 4 August, Charles staked his personal credit by addressing the Commons in person. He reminded it again of its 'joint and mutual engagements'; then urged MPs to consider whether the danger to 'the reputation of the kingdom' was not rather greater than any immediate danger from the plague; and finally dramatised the whole situation with a characteristic appeal to honour.

Better far it were, both for your honours and mine, that with hazard of half the fleet it were set forth than with assured loss of so much provision stayed at home.[34]

In spite of the fact that he was now supported by a well-organised lobby of royal officials, the appeal fell on deaf ears. MPs were much more concerned to discuss the lenient treatment of Catholics or the even more explosive issue of what happened if too much power was concentrated in the hands of one man. Alarmed by the drift of the debate, Buckingham and his clients worked behind the scenes to arrange a deal, the essence of which was that the Commons grant £40 000 to allow the fleet to set out in return for immediate concessions on religion and the direction of the war. In line with this, on 8 August Charles promised full enforcement of the recusancy laws and sought to exonerate himself by describing how he had stuck to the priorities set out in 1624. He then invited the Commons to name its prospective enemy. Had the king stuck with this approach he might still have won over a majority in the Commons; but he was undone by a lack of patience. On 10 August he sent a message announcing that

---

[34] *Proceedings in Parliament 1625*, p. 133.

if the Commons made an immediate offer of supply he would allow it another meeting to complete discussion of its grievances; otherwise he would bring the session to an end. Once again he was ably seconded by crown spokesmen; but the hint of blackmail in his message, and the prospect of grievances going unredressed until later, were too much for the lower house. They stepped up the attacks on Buckingham and began to pursue Phelips's complaint that if the king was unable to borrow as small a sum as £40 000 then the fault must lie with his advisers. The next day Charles sent a further message, offering to allow time at Oxford for the discussion of grievances; however, by now the Commons appeared to be out of control and criticism of the favourite simply increased. That evening, after meeting with the privy council, he decided to dissolve the parliament.[35]

At the council *post-mortem*, it was generally agreed that parliament's problems had been caused by a group of 'stirring men' who had followed 'the popular way' in initiating attacks on Buckingham. Charles himself complained that the Commons had sought 'to touch his . . . sovereignty' by seeking to interfere with his choice of ministers and there were hints that he was beginning to contemplate alternatives to parliamentary supply.[36] For the time being, however, he decided to take a relatively relaxed view of the Commons' behaviour. In September, it was being reported in court circles that he was 'not . . . much troubled' by the attacks on Buckingham and that 'for the distemper of 5 or 6 men he would not be angry with his people but still endeavour to preserve their love to him'.[37] He and Buckingham therefore set about trying to rebuild the coalition that had been so effective in 1624. The promise of sterner measures towards Catholics, which had been made on 8 August, was followed by a proclamation to banish Jesuits and seminary priests and an order to disarm recusants. A new offensive treaty was concluded with the Dutch, which envisaged joint fleets operating against Spain and the Indies. And the war effort against Spain was launched in earnest when the fleet set out to attack Cadiz in October.

---

[35] Thompson, 'Court politics and parliamentary conflict', pp. 179–84; Russell, *Parliaments and English Politics*, pp. 238, 241–52.

[36] Hacket, *Scrinia Reserata*, pt. 2, pp. 10, 17; *CSP Ven. 1625–6*, p. 147.

[37] NA, SP 84/129/fo. 28.

But perhaps the most significant element in the new policy was an about-turn in attitudes towards France.[38]

Charles and Buckingham gave up their efforts to draw the French crown into a union against Spain and instead took sides with the French Calvinist Huguenots. The main reason for this was the loss of face they suffered over the loan ships promised by James. These had finally been released to the French crown in July 1625 when it appeared that its differences with the Huguenots were about to be settled; but the conflict suddenly revived, and in September the ships were used to defeat the Huguenot fleet at Oleron and then help in the blockade of their stronghold at La Rochelle. Buckingham was severely embarrassed since he had assured the 1625 Parliament that the loan ships would never be used against fellow Protestants. It was also humiliating for Charles, who saw himself as having inherited Elizabeth's mantle of protector of the French Calvinists. During the following months relations between the two countries deteriorated rapidly. When Charles demanded the return of the ships, the French evaded the issue and complained about the enforcement of the recusancy laws and interference with the queen's household. Eventually, on 12 December, after negotiations with Huguenot exiles in England, the privy council approved plans to fit out a fleet to relieve La Rochelle. Four days later it also agreed to send out the writs for a new parliament.[39]

The shift in foreign policy was an enormous gamble, running counter to all the diplomatic wisdom of the period. The assumption behind Charles and Buckingham's strategy hitherto had been that to fight Spain effectively they needed to be allied with France. Taking on both powers at the same time was never in their original plan; but it was not entirely nonsensical. They had at first hoped that they could meet their next parliament with a military success behind them. That possibility vanished with the disaster at Cadiz in October, when the expeditionary force failed to capture the Spanish treasure fleet and suffered heavy losses. With the new policy, they could still offer the next best thing: a popular war. It allowed king and favourite to present themselves, unambiguously, as supporters of 'the

---

[38] T.E. Cogswell, 'Foreign policy and parliament: the case of La Rochelle, 1625–1626', *EHR*, vol. 99, 1984, pp. 246–9.

[39] Ibid., pp. 249–56.

Protestant Cause'. There was no longer a need for the compromises towards Catholics that had bedevilled the 1625 Parliament. Instead, they could hope to rally the nation behind the religious war that it apparently yearned for, and thereby secure both unity and financial assistance. The policy also had the appeal of satisfying Charles's sense of honour. He felt bound by both justice and tradition to defend the Huguenots, particularly after the mistake with the loan ships. This was a way of discharging his obligation and at the same time freeing himself from the tangle of deceit and compromise that had characterised negotiations with the 'inconstant false Monsieurs'. Finally, it offered a lifeline to Buckingham. His reputation had been severely damaged by the mishap over the loan ships and the failure at Cadiz; but now he could present himself once again as a Protestant champion and hope to salvage some of his political credit. The problem was that the whole scheme depended on the conflict continuing in France and this did not happen. On 26 January 1626 Louis and the Huguenots signed a treaty at Fontainebleau that left the crown without a clear foreign policy when parliament opened on 8 February.[40]

Their initial response was to put everything on hold until the diplomatic dust had settled. The opening of the session was deliberately low key. Charles excused himself from making any statement about policy and the lord keeper delivered a discourse on parliament's role in uniting king and people. There was no reference to foreign policy or supply. The Commons was then allowed to spend the next three weeks catching up with its backlog of minor legislation. This made sense in that the treaty at Fontainebleau had not been finally ratified by the Huguenot communities and there were also disputes to be sorted out concerning English goods impounded in retaliation for seizures of French shipping. A war with France was still possible. However, the absence of any major issues for MPs to focus on allowed Buckingham's critics freedom for manoeuvre and time to develop their case.[41]

Charles thought that he had dealt with this problem by 'pricking' the ringleaders of the attack at Oxford as sheriffs, so that they could not sit in

---

[40] Ibid., pp. 249–62; T.E. Cogswell, 'Prelude to Re; the Anglo-French struggle over La Rochelle, 1624–1627', *Hist.*, vol. 71, 1986, pp. 8–9; Adams, 'Spain or the Netherlands', p. 88. The description of the French was Buckingham's, but Charles held the same opinion, only more.

[41] *Proceedings in Parliament 1626*, vol. 1, pp. 20–1; Cogswell, 'Foreign policy and parliament', pp. 262–3.

the present parliament. Coke, Seymour and Phelips were excluded in this way, along with others who were only suspected of opposition to the duke, like Sir Thomas Wentworth. However, other MPs were ready to step into their shoes and they were supported by powerful figures in the House of Lords, notably the earl of Pembroke who now saw an opportunity to condemn Buckingham for undermining the 'common cause' against Spain. An even greater danger to the favourite came from the groundswell of hostile public opinion. He was universally blamed for the disaster at Cadiz, while the sudden shifts in policy towards France had cast doubt on his ability to handle foreign affairs. There seemed little point in giving support to the war effort as long as he remained in charge. His position, therefore, became the main grievance of the parliament, and the Commons pursued it singlemindedly from late February, when Sir John Eliot questioned his trustworthiness as lord admiral by launching an enquiry into the arrest of the French merchant ship, the *St Peter*.[42]

The drift in proceedings came to an end in the second week of March. On the 7th, the crown's spokesmen at last put forward a request for supply – to pay the subsidies promised to the Danes and also prepare defences against a possible Spanish invasion. Then on the 11th, Dr Turner, a client of Pembroke, broadened the attack on Buckingham by suggesting that most of the evils in the kingdom, including the spread of recusancy, could be traced back to the monopoly of power enjoyed by himself and his relatives. The two central issues of the parliament were now out in the open. Over the next few weeks the Commons investigated Turner's queries, which eventually became the basis for their articles of impeachment. The Commons also agreed in principle to grant the crown three subsidies and three fifteenths, worth £300 000; however, mindful of their experience of 1625, MPs made it clear that the grant would only be translated into a formal bill when the king redressed their grievances.[43]

Charles's reaction to all this was one of increasing exasperation. Since the 1625 Parliament, he had made substantial concessions to the Commons

---

[42] Cogswell, 'Foreign policy and parliament', pp. 263–5; T.E. Cogswell, 'War and the liberties of the subject', in J.H. Hexter ed., *Parliament and Liberty from the Reign of Elizabeth to the English Civil War*, Stanford, Calif., 1992, pp. 239–40; Russell, *Parliaments and English Politics*, pp. 262, 266–7, 278–82.

[43] Russell, *Parliaments and English Politics*, pp. 287–91; Gardiner, *History of England*, vol. 6, pp. 76–7, 80–1.

and apparently dealt with the small core of troublemakers; yet MPs persisted in making life difficult for him. Not only were they mounting an attack on the man who above all others supported and sustained him, but they had the effrontery to try to blackmail him over a grant of supply to which he was entitled anyway. Perhaps not surprisingly, he began to suspect them of darker and more sinister designs. On several occasions he tried to deflect criticism from Buckingham by making it clear that he had been acting on his orders, as his servant.[44] When this failed, he drew the dangerous conclusion that he himself was the real object of the Commons' attack. His choice of language during a private interview with the earl of Totnes shows that even at this early stage in his reign he could view his relationship with them in starkly polarised terms. Urging the earl to stand firm against the lower house's attempts to interrogate members of the council of war, he assured him that

Let them do what they list, you shall not go to the Tower. It is not you they aim at, but it is me upon whom they make inquisition; and for subsidies, that will not hinder it. Gold may be bought too dear . . .[45]

Charles's disenchantment with the Commons was the main theme of an address to the two houses at Whitehall on 29 March. Because of his lack of confidence in his powers of oratory, it was his habit on such occasions to allow the lord keeper or another senior councillor to do most of his talking for him. This tended to mean his views were watered down before they reached the ears of MPs. However, on this occasion, with the king sitting next to him, the new lord keeper, Sir Thomas Coventry, did not mince his words.

Charles himself began by thanking the Lords for their efforts to meet the crown's needs and reprimanding the Commons for 'some errors' and 'unparliamentary proceedings'. Coventry then picked up the theme. He started by insisting that 'there was never king more truly loving of his people nor better affected to the right use of parliament', as was illustrated by Charles's readiness 'to hear and answer . . . just grievances' and accept that 'parliament is his council and therefore it ought to have the liberty

---

[44] *Proceedings in Parliament 1626*, vol. 2, pp. 285, 294.

[45] NA, SP 16/22/51. He also famously remarked of the Commons' attack on Buckingham: 'If the duke is Sejanus, I must be Tiberius.': Gardiner, *History of England*, vol. 6, pp. 107–8.

and freedom of a council'. However, there were limits to this freedom, and it was the responsibility of the king to maintain the 'difference between counselling and controlling, between liberty and abuse of liberty'. He then warned the Commons that while Charles regarded most of the members as 'wise and well tempered men, well affected to the public good and his Majesty's service', he also believed it was being led astray by 'the corrupt humours of some particular persons'. This had become apparent in its determination to pursue Turner's complaints. Even after the king had explained that Buckingham was simply doing his bidding, it had continued to hound him and question his actions. How could it expect 'a great king or a good master' to abandon his servant in such circumstances? Its persistence could only be taken to indicate that, although 'pretended against the duke of Buckingham', its real aim was 'to wound the honour and government of his Majesty and his late blessed father'. Its proceedings also betrayed a damaging lack of trust. Charles had offered every indication over recent months that he would reform abuses, but, instead of trusting him to deal with these himself, it was attempting to coerce him by holding back the supply essential to maintaining a war for which it was responsible. This was not only unjust, it was also 'dishonourable and full of distrust':

for though you have avoided the literal words of a condition . . . yet has it the effect of a condition . . . This is not a parliamentary way nor a way to deal with kings.

He ended with an ultimatum. The Commons must show its 'cheerful obedience' by making an unconditional grant of supply and abandoning its attack on Buckingham, or else face dissolution. Charles then added an even more menacing postscript:

Remember that parliaments are altogether in my power for the calling, sitting and continuance of them. Therefore as I find the fruits either good or evil they are to continue or not to be.[46]

This was not only the fullest address from the throne delivered to parliament during the late 1620s, it was also the most revealing. It encapsulated Charles's basic view of parliament, a view that appears to have changed

---

[46] *Proceedings in Parliament 1626*, vol. 2, pp. 391–5.

little during the course of the decade, or indeed the reign as a whole. He accepted that a good king should meet parliaments regularly and do his best to cooperate with them, which meant hearing and remedying their grievances and allowing them some leeway in offering advice. But in return, he required parliaments to trust and obey him, and refrain from challenging his honour by engaging in the sort of coercive bargaining envisaged in 1626. When this happened he tended to assume that it was a result of 'popularity', working through a few MPs to destroy the loyalty of the Commons as a whole. In such circumstances, he was quite prepared to contemplate doing without parliament altogether. His final statement on 29 March was certainly no idle threat. It was to provide the rationale for dispensing with parliament during 'the Personal Rule' and, indeed, during the 18-month period that followed the dissolution in 1626.[47]

In spite of the lord keeper's ultimatum, however, the Commons pressed on, drawing up a Remonstrance in reply to the charge that its proceedings were 'unparliamentary' and naming Buckingham as chief cause of its grievances. At this point one might have expected Charles to dissolve the parliament; however, he kept it together until 15 June, even allowing MPs to deliver their charges against the duke. Why did this happen? The short answer appears to be that the crown needed money. Conrad Russell has suggested that this was an unlikely reason because the amount offered by the Commons fell well short of its needs, which Sir John Coke on 21 March estimated at £1 067 211. However, Thomas Cogswell has pointed out that Coke's figure was grossly inflated for the purposes of bargaining. The crown's immediate requirement was for about half that sum, which the £300 000 on offer (£350 000 after the Commons pledged an additional subsidy on 26 April) would have gone a considerable way towards meeting. Not only this, but subsidies were also the surest means of actually raising fresh revenue. Recent attempts to pawn the crown jewels had failed and most other potential sources of income were either pledged in advance or unpredictable in their yield. A grant from parliament provided what one leading creditor described as 'a perfect security' for raising the big money market loans needed to equip military expeditions – and in both 1625 and 1628 it was used in just this way almost as soon as it had been approved.

---

[47] R.P. Cust, 'Charles I and a draft declaration for the 1628 Parliament', *HR*, vol. 63, 1990, pp. 143–57.

So, if the crown could hang on and secure a deal, it would obtain most of what it needed to carry on with the war.[48]

But if Charles kept parliament together to raise supply, how was he to deal with the threat to Buckingham? Here it is important to recognise that the process of parliamentary impeachment was much less formalised than it later became. It was by no means clear what direction the Commons assault would take. It might lead to an inquiry rather than a trial, and if charges were drawn up they were just as likely to be adjudged by the king as by the House of Lords. So Charles could feel he still had plenty of room for manoeuvre.[49]

It was also likely that any trial would be pre-empted by a deal struck between the duke and his enemies at court. Speeches by Buckingham's clients on 2 May make it clear that negotiations were going on behind the scenes to secure a 'reformation of the duke', rather than his judicial punishment. The details of these have remained secret, but Russell has pieced together their probable content. The main objective would have been to appease Pembroke and other enthusiasts for the war against Spain, who included the duke's main antagonists in the Commons, Eliot and Sir Dudley Digges. This could have been done by Buckingham giving up the post of lord admiral – which might then have been entrusted to an advocate of the 'blue water' policy, such as the earl of Warwick – and Charles showing a readiness to consult more closely with the privy council. Turner's other queries about damage to the king's revenues and the spread of recusancy could have been answered by appointing a new lord treasurer and dismissing the notoriously Catholic Lord Scrope from the presidency of the Council of the North. And, since there appears to have been no attempt to remove Buckingham from his court offices, he could have held on to his position as the king's favourite and confidant. Hopes of a compromise, however, were thwarted, largely because of the intransigence of the Commons.[50]

During April, Charles allowed them to go ahead with preparing its charges while keeping up the pressure for a bill to confirm the grant of supply. This

---

[48] Russell, *Parliaments and English Politics*, pp. 270, 292; T.E. Cogswell, 'A Low Road to Extinction? Supply and redress of grievances', vol. 33, 1990, pp. 294–5; Cust, *The Forced Loan*, p. 15.

[49] Russell, *Parliaments and English Politics*, pp. 272–3, 294, 303–4.

[50] Ibid., pp. 293–9.

produced the extra subsidy agreed on the 26th, but no relaxation of conditions. The critical point for the policy of negotiation was reached on 2 May when the Commons debated whether to have its charges heard by the king or the House of Lords. Buckingham's followers and, significantly, Pembroke's clients, such as William Coryton, argued strongly for adjudication by the king; but the house as a whole decided to go to the Lords. At this point the prospect of a compromise settlement collapsed. Nonetheless Charles persisted with the parliament through May and early June.[51]

The principal reason remained the need for money; but coupled with this there was now an urgent concern on the part of some councillors to maintain a dialogue with the people. The alternative was outlined in a speech in the Commons by Sir Dudley Carleton, recently returned from the embassy in France. He painted a grim picture of life in a country where parliaments had ceased to exist; then issued a warning that echoed Charles's remarks on 29 March.

Move not his Majesty with trenching upon his prerogatives, lest you bring
him out of love with parliaments . . . he hath told you that if there were
not correspondency between him and you, he should be enforced to use new
counsels.[52]

'New counsels' were not something most privy councillors wished to contemplate. When the possibility of a dissolution had been discussed in March, the Venetian ambassador reported that the lord president, the earl of Manchester, and Sir Humphrey May had talked Charles out of it, emphasising the 'impossibility of subsisting unless they were at one with the people'.[53] Again and again, through April and May, council spokesmen tried to get the Commons to see sense and recognise that national unity, as well as the war effort, depended on them confirming their grant. By early June, however, even they were giving up hope, as was vividly expressed in a letter from Secretary Conway to his old friend, the earl of Carlisle. Conway had, he said

---

[51] Ibid., pp. 299–305.

[52] Gardiner, *History of England*, vol. 6, p. 110.

[53] *CSP Ven. 1625–6*, p. 380.

*spoken with three or four of the parliament, the wisest of my acquaintance,
and find so little to build any hope upon as if I did not defy despair it would
take up every corner of me . . . I cannot see any help than that which they used
to say in the plague time, every man for himself, Lord have mercy upon us.*[54]

This from a former leading member of the 'patriot coalition' registered an
important shift in the views of those at the heart of government. The
Commons' intransigence had made it appear that appeals to its sense
of responsibility, even when coupled with substantial concessions, were
unlikely to succeed. With this the policy of fighting a war in partnership
with the Commons was effectively at an end and 'new counsels' became
the obvious alternative.

On 9 June the king followed the logic of Conway's analysis and
delivered a final ultimatum demanding that the Commons finalise the bill
for supply or take responsibility for the consequences.[55] The indications are
that he had already given up on them; however, he and Buckingham now
had another reason for keeping the parliament going just a little bit longer
– to secure the conviction of the earl of Bristol.

The former ambassador to Spain had been a thorn in their sides ever
since the return from Madrid. He persisted with efforts to try to arrange
the marriage long after they had turned against it and then tried to cause
trouble for Buckingham by alleging that he had taken Charles to Spain
in order to convert him to Catholicism. Since the 1624 Parliament he had
been under house arrest at Sherborne Castle, but he successfully petitioned
the Lords to be allowed to take his place in 1626 and then made the even
more sensational claim that Buckingham had administered a fatal dose of
medicine to James to prevent him from hearing Bristol's complaints. This
was too much for Charles, who had been present at his father's deathbed
and, by implication, stood accused of being an accessory to murder. He was
determined that Bristol should be tried by his peers and punished. The Lords,
not surprisingly, proceeded with great caution. During early June it still looked
as if Charles might obtain the condemnation that he sought. However, on
the 13th, when the peers acceded to Bristol's request that his witnesses be
examined by impartial judges, it became clear that the most likely outcome

---

[54] NA, SP 78/79, fo. 64. I am grateful to Tom Cogswell for this reference.

[55] *Proceedings in Parliament 1626*, vol. 3, p. 406.

was deadlock. Then, the following day, the Commons prepared a further Remonstrance against Buckingham. At this point Charles decided enough was enough. On 15 June he instructed Coventry to announce a dissolution. A delegation of senior councillors sitting in the Lords petitioned him to think again, but he was adamant, declaring that the 'wound is not from your lordships, but the house of commons'.[56]

The 1625 and 1626 parliaments were pivotal for the politics of Charles's reign. They marked the point at which his honeymoon with the English people and his hopes of partnership with the House of Commons came unstuck. But what brought this about? Why had the 'patriot coalition', in which he and Buckingham invested so much of their political credit, proved unworkable? Conrad Russell and other 'revisionist' historians have laid most of the blame on the House of Commons, arguing that having encouraged the crown to enter the war it was now refusing to support it. This is in accord with Charles's view that they were reneging on the 'engagements' of 1624. The main reason for this, in Russell's analysis, was MPs' determination to protect the interests of their constituents. The mood in the house, particularly in 1625, was 'overwhelmingly local'. The main issue was not redress of grievances, the running of the war, or even hostility to Buckingham, but 'reluctance to give away the country's money'. 'It was Charles and Buckingham's failure to face this central fact which produced most of the troubles of the next three years.'[57]

However, this interpretation has again been contested by Thomas Cogswell. He attributes the Commons' restiveness to the crown's failure to offer prompt redress of grievances and deliver the type of war that it expected. There was a well-established convention that grants of supply in parliament should go hand in hand with redress of grievances. The Commons allowed exceptions to this in 1621 and in the Westminster meeting of 1625, but had gained little in return. It was therefore understandably wary when Charles requested additional supply without offering concessions. There was a danger of establishing an unfortunate precedent that could upset the balance between crown and subject. 'We cannot give without wrong to our successors', as one speaker explained it. This anxiety

---

[56] Russell, *Parliaments and English Politics*, pp. 309–21.

[57] Ibid., pp. 252–9; see also Young, *Charles I*, pp. 37–8 and Lockyer, *Buckingham*, pp. 471–2.

was compounded by unease over the way the war was being run. In 1624 the 'patriot coalition' had offered the prospect of a war on the Elizabethan model, with stern measures against Catholics at home and a 'blue water' policy abroad. But this had failed to materialise. Instead there were the costly failures of the Mansfeldt and Cadiz expeditions, an agreement with the French that allowed Catholics greater toleration and the fiasco of the loan ships. The Commons vented its frustration first of all by petitioning about religion and complaining that 'We know not our enemy', then, more dangerously, by attacking Buckingham. During the latter half of 1625 he became identified with everything that was going wrong and there was a growing clamour for his dismissal.[58] MPs recognised that it was asking a lot of Charles to give up his favourite, but until he did so there seemed little point in granting further supply for the war. 'Any money that we shall or can give will through his misemployment be turned rather to the prejudice and hurt of this kingdom than otherwise', they explained in their final Remonstrance of 1626 and, in these circumstances, they became more and more intransigent.[59] For Cogswell, then, it was the type of war and its lack of success, rather than war itself, which caused the difficulties in parliament.

His analysis directs attention back to the role of Charles and Buckingham. They must bear a considerable share of responsibility for the failure of the two parliaments. It is possible to feel some sympathy for their problems over the direction of the war. They did try to give the nation the war it wanted, but their efforts were hamstrung by James's interference and the duplicity of the French. Their handling of the House of Commons, however, undoubtedly left a good deal to be desired. In both 1625 and 1626 there was a lack of organisation in the early stages that allowed proceedings to drift out of control. This was remedied later on, but in each case the damage had already been done. Even more significant was their unwillingness to play the traditional game of exchanging redress for supply. The conventions governing grants of subsidies did require the crown to make meaningful concessions; however, as he made clear in 1626, Charles regarded any pressure in this direction as 'dishonourable' and tantamount

---

[58] Cogswell, 'War and the liberties of the subject', pp. 235–41; Cogswell, 'Supply and redress of grievances', pp. 291–5.

[59] *Proceedings in Parliament 1626*, vol. 3, p. 441.

to blackmail. What he offered was too grudging and too late. In 1625 the first signs of compromise came only after the failure of his appeal on 4 August, and these were mainly from Buckingham. The king continued to press for an immediate grant of supply, seemingly oblivious to any priority except the vindication of his honour. In 1626 the scheme for a 'reformation of the duke' was only proposed after the opposition had built up a formidable head of steam. On both occasions, the crown lost the initiative basically because of Charles's inflexibility and lack of judgement. This was to be a recurring problem throughout the reign.

The king's conduct also brings into question the strength of his commitment to parliaments. Crown spokesmen referred to this repeatedly, praising the enthusiasm he had shown in 1624 and describing him as a prince 'bred in parliaments'.[60] Russell has concluded that 'only a principled belief in parliamentary institutions can explain the efforts Charles made to work them between 1625 and 1628'.[61] However, this is not entirely borne out by his actions in 1625 or 1626. He may have shown himself prepared to work with parliament, but only on his own terms. As Christopher Thompson has pointed out, in 1625 Charles gives the impression of having viewed parliament 'essentially as a subservient instrument for funding his war policies . . . useful to him only insofar as it complied with his will'.[62] Much the same comment could also be made about 1626. It seems that the king was seeking what the French ambassador in 1640 described as a 'Parlement à sa mode'.[63] However, this was not the sort of parliament that contemporaries had in mind when they enthused about its role as 'a point of contact', bringing together crown and subject. If anyone was concerned about achieving this it would seem to have been the moderate councillors who urged the king to back off and not push the Commons too hard.

There were also alarming signs that Charles had reverted to the view he held of the Commons in the final session of 1621. The tendency to blame any problems on a small group of troublemakers, playing to the popular gallery, had resurfaced in 1625. During 1626 it became a constant

---

[60] *Proceedings in Parliament 1625*, p. 29; *Proceedings in Parliament 1626*, vol. 1, pp. 20–1.

[61] Russell, *Parliaments and English Politics*, p. 237.

[62] Thompson, 'Court politics and parliamentary conflict', p. 187.

[63] Russell, *The Fall of the British Monarchies*, p. 93.

refrain in court circles and there was also talk of a broader popular conspiracy working through the Commons 'to pull the feathers of royalty' and debase 'this free monarchy . . . through the duke's sides'.[64] By the end of the session both king and favourite appear to have believed that the Commons was completely out of control and this provided the basic rationale for 'new counsels'. The emergence of such views so early in the new reign was ominous. It suggested that Charles's enthusiasm for parliaments was strictly conditional, dependent on their displaying a degree of submissiveness and docility that was at odds with many of the political conventions of the period.

The forced loan and the 1628 parliament

Charles's decision to dissolve the 1626 Parliament precipitated a period of political turmoil as the crown sought other ways of raising revenue. The king himself emerged as the dominant decision maker and domestic policy was shaped by distrust of the House of Commons. He took the lead in voicing this. During the summer months there were several references to his continuing displeasure with parliament, including a report of a conversation with the queen's almoner, the bishop of Mende, about 'the means used by the kings of France to rid themselves of parliament'.[65] But there was also no shortage of courtiers and advisers to encourage him in this course. Buckingham's role was ambiguous. He had a good deal to fear from another parliament, and behind the scenes almost certainly opposed it; but in public he sought to repair his image by giving the impression that he favoured a resummons.[66] His closest supporters, however, were less squeamish, particularly the earl of Dorset and Bishop Laud. They played up the threat of popularity, harped on a highly divisive distinction between the loyal and the disloyal – who were defined largely in terms of their attitudes to Buckingham – and offered the king a variety of schemes to

---

[64] 'To his sacred Majesty, Ab Ignoto', printed in *Cabala Sive Scrinia Sacra*, 3rd edn, 1691, pp. 255–7. The implications of this important document are discussed more fully in Cust, 'Charles I and popularity', pp. 237–8 and idem., *The Forced Loan*, pp. 17–23, 27–9.

[65] *CSP Ven. 1625–6*, p. 508.

[66] Cust, *The Forced Loan*, p. 43.

raise money through 'new counsels'. In conversation with the Venetian ambassador, Dorset provided an analysis of the political situation that verged on the apocalyptic, but nonetheless reflected the new mood at court.

The king's distress is at its height more from the necessity of having recourse to some violent remedy against his subjects than from any other reason . . . war must be maintained with the property of the subject, all being bound to contribute where it is just, and if in the last parliament the people had agreed to the promised contribution they would have paid much less than the king will eventually compel them to disburse . . . at any rate there was no fear of insurrection in this kingdom as it contained no fortresses . . .[67]

Charles's more authoritarian instincts, together with recent experience, pushed the crown towards an acceptance of the approach outlined by Dorset; but, nonetheless, it remained abhorrent to a solid core of senior privy councillors. They continued to take the view that it was important to maintain good relations with the subject and wanted Charles to summon a fresh parliament as soon as possible. Their philosophy had been summed up in the peers' petition of 15 June. Only by using legal and parliamentary means could 'these great and apparent dangers, both at home and abroad . . . be prevented, and your Majesty made happy in the duty and love of your people, which we hold to be the greatest strength and security of a king'.[68] For the time being such pleas had little impact; but the moderate councillors did manage to mount a successful rearguard action against the worst excesses of 'new counsels' and eventually win the struggle for another parliament.

Over the summer months of 1626 the government faced a series of foreign policy emergencies. First of all there was an invasion scare which the privy council took very seriously after reports that the Spanish were preparing 200 boats and 40 000 men in Flanders. No sooner had this passed than there was a new crisis in relations with France. At the end of July, Charles expelled the French attendants in his wife's household, thereby antagonising Louis XIII who regarded it as a monumental slight on himself and his

---

[67] *CSP Ven. 1625–6*, p. 528; see also Cust, *The Forced Loan*, pp. 27–30.

[68] *Proceedings in Parliament 1626*, vol. 1, p. 633.

sister. Meanwhile the French crown appeared about to make another move against the Huguenots. Since the spring Richelieu had been building up a fleet in Brittany and it was widely believed that he would use this to relaunch the attack on La Rochelle. Charles responded in August by meeting with the Huguenot leader, Soubise, and drafting a plan to send 6 000 English veterans from the Low Countries to garrison the town against assault. However, this had to be shelved in early September when news arrived that Christian IV of Denmark had been defeated by the Emperor's forces at the Battle of Lutter. This was a disaster for English hopes of recovering the Palatinate and also a personal humiliation for Charles, because Christian was his uncle and had depended on English subsidies that had rarely been paid. He responded immediately, cutting short his summer progress and returning to London to assure the Danish ambassador that 'he would render his uncle every assistance, even at the risk of his own life'. Within a week, the council had decided to divert the Low Country veterans to Denmark and finance further assistance with what became known as the forced loan.[69]

Charles firmly stamped his authority on the council during these discussions. He began to attend meetings on a more regular basis and took the chair for important policy discussions, leaving councillors in no doubt about his opinions. When some of them tried to discuss a proposal to resummon parliament, he was reported to have 'disliked it utterly' and declared that 'they might pledge his word and crown, but there was to be no question of a parliament'.[70] The king's unequivocal attitude – usually voiced in the bluntest language – came to supply much of the drive behind 'new counsels' and ensured that for the time being the more moderate councillors kept their heads down. However, he was not simply an autocrat. His style may have been domineering, but he remained very respectful of the tradition whereby English monarchs consulted their councillors and, as we shall see, was still open to being persuaded to follow a policy which ran counter to his initial instincts.[71]

---

[69] Gardiner, *History of England*, vol. 6, pp. 131–2, 134–8; Cogswell, 'Prelude to Re', pp. 10–13; Cust, *The Forced Loan*, pp. 39–41.

[70] *Court and Times*, vol. 1, p. 149.

[71] Cust, *The Forced Loan*, pp. 41–3; Russell, *Causes of the Civil War*, pp. 189–90.

The most important domestic initiative of the period was the forced loan, which was collected between October 1626 and the end of 1627. In fact it was a tax rather than a loan, assessed at the same rate as the £300 000 that parliament had agreed to grant in 1626. It earned the epithet 'forced' because non-payers were summoned before the privy council and imprisoned or even pressed to serve in the king's armies. In financial terms, the levy was a considerable success, producing over £243 000; but it caused enormous political damage, raising, in the starkest possible terms, difficult issues about the scope of the royal prerogative and the future role of parliaments. Over a hundred leading gentry were imprisoned for refusing to pay and the Five Knights Case provoked a national outcry because the crown appeared to be violating the subject's right to habeas corpus.

Taxation had always been a very sensitive area for English political theorists. It was often argued, particularly in the House of Commons, that there was a fundamental principle, enshrined in law, that the king could only tax with the consent of parliament. This principle had, however, long been disputed by the crown and it was not accepted by James. The issue had come to a head in 1610 when the Commons challenged his right to collect the customs levies known as impositions. James responded with a classic exposition of his responsibilities as a divinely-ordained monarch. He accepted that he had a moral obligation to rule within the customary law and that he 'leaves off to be a king and degenerates into a tyrant as soon as he leaves off to rule according to his laws'. But he also insisted that he had an absolute discretionary power, in the form of the royal prerogative, to take whatever measures he deemed necessary to promote the public good. In exercising this he was accountable to God alone. If his people disliked what he was doing, their only recourse was to 'prayers and tears'. They had no right to resist him, but must simply await God's providential judgements. This meant that the right to levy impositions must be regarded as one of 'the points of his regality', which he could not give up even if he wanted to.[72] Charles took a similar view of the forced loan. With his approval, anti-Calvinist apologists, such as Robert Sibthorpe and Roger Mainwaring, hammered home the message that he was simply carrying out his godly

---

[72] J.P. Sommerville, 'Ideology, property and the constitution', in Cust and Hughes eds, *Conflict in Early Stuart England*, pp. 50–9; idem., 'James I and divine right of kings', p. 64; G. Burgess, 'The divine right of kings reconsidered', *EHR*, no. 425, 1992, pp. 837–61.

duty to provide for the welfare of his people, and that any withholding of payment was tantamount to resistance.[73]

The king became the driving force behind the most coercive aspects of the loan and directly responsible for much of the damage that it caused. Because he had engaged his honour to help his uncle, he treated payment in very personal terms. He took an unusually active role in keeping councillors up to the mark, demanding that they supply him with regular reports of proceedings and even ordering them to forgo their summer holidays to keep up the pressure. He also wrote individually to each member of the peerage, asking them to set an example and letting it be known that they could not expect to find favour unless they cooperated. His sense that his personal honour was involved led to damaging doubts about the loyalty of his subjects and equally damaging displays of vindictiveness. Prior to the loan, Charles had requested a benevolence from taxpayers that was presented in part as a test of personal loyalty. If the money was paid, he had declared, this would 'give us an ample testimony of the dutiful and good affections of our people' and 'just encouragement the more speedily to meet a parliament'. Unfortunately it was not, and this was taken to indicate that the forces that had disrupted the parliament were at large in the nation. From the start the council expected opposition to the loan and was determined that it should be severely punished. Their instructions to commissioners included an unprecedented provision to examine refusers on oath 'whether any publicly or underhand be workers or persuaders of others to dissent'. They also considered some remarkably draconian measures, including a proposal to hang Essex defaulters 'in the next tree to their dwellings for an example and terror unto others'. The king himself was very much to the fore in pushing the hard line. When the judges refused to subscribe to the legality of the loan in November 1626, he accused them of 'great insolency' and vowed that he would 'sweep their benches'. He had a signet letter drafted ordering that 150 Gloucestershire refusers be pressed for service abroad, on account of having 'obstinately refused to assist us in this extremity, thereby discovering their disaffection to their prince and country'. And he humiliated his own archbishop of Canterbury, George Abbot, by placing him under house arrest when he refused to license Sibthorpe's

---

[73] Cust, *The Forced Loan*, pp. 62–7.

sermon. He was also determined to ram home lessons about royal authority. Mainwaring's controversial sermon on the loan was printed with the
rubric 'by his majesty's special command', in spite of a warning from the
normally hawkish Laud that it contained 'many things which will be very
distasteful to the people'.[74]

The more moderate members of the council did their best to limit the
damage and had some success. Manchester and Conway, for example,
managed to prevent the signet letter about the Gloucestershire refusers being
sent out. But there were limits to what they could achieve. Where the king's
attention was engaged by an issue they had little choice but to concede
and respect his wishes. This was demonstrated in the Five Knights Case.
For much of 1627, senior councillors had carefully avoided allowing any of
the gentry refusers to come to trial, recognising that a public test of the
loan's legality could only add to the outcry against it. Charles, however,
saw things differently. At the end of October, he overturned the council's
strategy and ordered the judges to hear the petition of the five knights, apparently believing that a verdict against them would strengthen his hand
for the future. He also took the precaution of interviewing the judges
and letting them know that he expected a favourable decision. The case,
however, brought none of the dividends he had hoped for. The judges did
rule against the loan refusers, but only on the technical grounds that since
the plaintiffs had been imprisoned 'by his Majesty's special commandment'
they were not eligible for bail. There was no confirmation of the loan's legality and when the attorney-general, acting on the king's instructions, tried
to tamper with the official record he was unsuccessful. This was a classic
example of the dangers inherent in Charles's lack of judgement and tendency to get over-involved in the political process. He failed to achieve
his ends and the revelations about his interference only strengthened the
resolve of the 1628 Parliament to curb his power of imprisonment.[75]

By the end of 1627 events abroad were prompting a reconsideration
of the policies associated with 'new counsels'. The war against Spain began

---

[74] Ibid., pp. 46–51, 54–5, 57, 62–3, 105–6, 137; *The Diary of Sir Richard Hutton 1614–1639*,
W.R. Prest ed., Seldon Soc., suppl. ser. vol. 9, 1991, pp. 64–6; NA, SP 16/89/4; Rushworth,
vol. 1, pp. 434–58, 'Archbishop Abbot his narrative'.

[75] Cust, *The Forced Loan*, pp. 57–62; *Diary of Hutton*, p. 72; J.A. Guy, 'The origins of the
Petition of Right reconsidered', *HJ*, vol. 25, 1982, pp. 289–312.

to wind down following the opening of peace negotiations in early 1627; and Christian of Denmark's war effort collapsed in the summer, with the subsidies promised by Charles still unpaid. The main focus of English attention once again became France. Relations with the crown had taken another turn for the worse in late 1626 when Richelieu seized the English wine fleet at Bordeaux and Louis repudiated a settlement of the differences over Henrietta Maria's household. At the same time, another attack on La Rochelle appeared imminent and the Huguenot leaders pleaded with the king to intervene. The reasons that had led him to pledge himself to their defence in December 1625 still applied. It would satisfy his sense of honour by enabling him to discharge his obligations, as well as avenging Richelieu's duplicity over the loan ships and, perhaps, restoring the political credit of Buckingham. Once again Charles threatened the French with war, but this time, despite continuing diplomatic efforts, they refused to back down and he had little choice but to fight.[76]

The English fleet, with 6 000 troops on board, set sail under Buckingham's command in June 1627. The aim was to capture the Isle de Rhé, just outside La Rochelle, which would force Richelieu to lift his blockade. From July to September the English besieged the fort at St Martin, which was the key French stronghold; but, just as it was about to capitulate, help arrived and at the end of October Buckingham was forced to retreat, having lost 4 000 of the troops. This was a political disaster for the crown. It undermined the credibility of its foreign policy and exposed the full depth of its financial problems. For the first time, splits emerged in the council, with some advocating concentration on the struggle against Spain and others abandonment of war altogether. Charles was determined to soldier on and mount another expedition to Rhé in 1628; but the cost of this was enormous, with one estimate showing that £600 000 was urgently needed to re-equip the fleet and also stave off another threat of invasion from Flanders. A sum of this size could only be raised through taxation which, inevitably, opened the way for renewed discussion of a parliament.[77]

---

[76] Cogswell, 'Prelude to Re', pp. 13–18. For the importance of Charles's honour, see the royal 'Manifest' drawn up to explain the reasons for launching the Rhé expedition which stated forthrightly that 'that which hath enforced us to this resolution . . . is chiefly our honour pledged to the [French] protestants'.: T.E. Cogswell, 'The politics of propaganda: Charles I and the people in the 1620s', *JBS*, vol. 29, 1990, p. 206.

[77] Gardiner, *History of England*, vol. 6, pp. 171–200; Cust, *The Forced Loan*, pp. 73–6.

The council debate that followed was one of the bitterest and most divisive of the decade, exposing differences in political philosophy at the heart of government. Charles chaired the main sessions and at the start attempted to rule out a resummons by declaring that 'the occasion will not let me tarry so long'. He was supported by Buckingham's clients, although once again the duke himself sat on the fence, still trying hard to give the impression that he was in favour of a parliament, while apparently relying on Charles to prevent it. This involved some tortuous manoeuvring, including one rather unlikely audience at court, during which the favourite prostrated himself before the king – declaring that if he 'was found worthy of death [by parliament] let them not spare him' – until Charles made it clear that a resummons was out of the question.[78]

The king's main concern continued to be the loyalty of his people. He was said to be determined to impose another unparliamentary tax lest an immediate resummons be seen as countenancing the defiance met with from the loan refusers. Council hardliners reinforced this by resurrecting fears about the attitude of the Commons. In an important memorandum – which highlighted some of the more avant-garde thinking behind 'new counsels' – Laud argued that 'factious spirits . . . will study revenge, at least unquiet' and

will take hart if they see the king yield to them without any submission of theirs, as some were seen to laugh outright in the last parliament when they got their ends upon the king.

They must therefore be denied opportunities to organise, which meant avoiding another parliament. Laud also sought to demonstrate how important it was to maintain the crown's right to tax without consent. Using arguments put forward by Sibthorpe and Mainwaring, he claimed that royal authority was something that derived from above, owing little to the consent of the people. In times of need, taxes were due to the king as of right, and parliament's role was to decide on the manner of a grant, not whether it should be made. This ruled out any necessity for the sort of bargaining that the Commons had envisaged in 1626. Indeed, such bargaining was positively dangerous since by this means 'the flowers of the crown are parted with,

---

[78] Cust, *The Forced Loan*, pp. 77–8; *Court and Times*, vol. 1, p. 305.

and the prerogative so decreased as I dare not speak of the consequence'. Viewed in such terms the king had little to gain from a parliament and everything to lose.[79]

This approach, however, was anathema to a majority of councillors. Led by senior figures such as Lord President Manchester, Lord Keeper Coventry and the earl of Pembroke, they looked to a parliament not only for money, but also to heal the wounds opened up by the forced loan. Their hope was that 'king and people may [have] peace again and the kingdom not bee endangered by this division'. During the weeks of the debate they did their best to allay the king's fears by promising to prevent another attack on Buckingham and offering assurances about the conduct of loan refusers. They also persuaded him that a ship money levy proposed in February 1628 together with another scheme to collect privy seal loans were impracticable. In the end, Charles was faced with either summoning a parliament or abandoning his foreign policy. So, on 20 February, he reluctantly gave way.[80]

The 1628 Parliament appeared to many contemporaries to be a critical moment in the history of the institution. Charles had ruled without it for the past 18 months – in the midst of a war, when tradition suggested he should be meeting his people regularly – and this showed that there was a real danger of English parliaments following their continental counterparts and ceasing to exist. Sir Benjamin Rudyerd, the earl of Pembroke's spokesman, was not exaggerating when he solemnly declared 'this is the crisis of parliaments. We shall know by this if parliaments live or die'.[81] Moderates in both the council and parliament were, therefore, more keenly aware than ever of the need to produce a workable settlement.

The immediate problem was that neither the king nor the more militant MPs appeared in any mood to compromise. For Charles, parliament was very much on probation. In his opening speech on 13 March, he offered some comforting assurances of his intention to rule with parliament, but then proceeded to warn that this was no time for 'long consultation' and that 'if you do neglect your duties herein I must then be forced, for the preservation of the public and that which by the folly of particular men

---

[79] NA, SP 16/94/88.

[80] Ibid.; Cust, *The Forced Loan*, pp. 80–5.

[81] *Proceedings in Parliament 1628*, vol. 2, p. 58.

may be destroyed, to take some other course'. He then added, rather gratuitously, 'I would not have you take this as a threatening for I scorn to threaten any but my equals.'[82] This was not just the king showing his usual lack of tact in hammering out the implication of statements better left vague; it also indicated that he had barely shifted his ground since the preliminary discussions in council. The approach of many MPs was similarly unyielding. After three years of wartime expedients from the council they were determined to re-establish the rule of law, which meant putting an end to forced loans and imprisonment without showing cause, and also curbing the prerogative powers of the lieutenancy and banning the compulsory billeting of soldiers. Moreover, they had unfinished business with Buckingham.[83] In the event, it was left to moderate councillors to try to build bridges between the two sides.

During the early weeks of the parliament – with Sir John Coke, Sir Thomas Edmondes, Sir Humphrey May and Rudyerd as their spokesmen – they were remarkably successful. At the first major debate in the Commons, on 22 March, they headed off an attack on the duke and persuaded the house to concentrate on their other grievances. They then chivvied MPs along with promises that the king would remedy their grievances until, on 4 April, they were able to secure agreement to grant an unprecedented five subsidies, worth £300 000. Just as important, they were successful in managing Charles. The flow of information to him about what was happening in the Commons was carefully controlled and he was prevented from making any more personal appearances. Instead, his views were relayed through messages, usually drafted and delivered by Secretary Coke who was far more emollient than the king in his choice of language.[84] The culmination of the moderates' efforts came on the evening of 4 April, when Coke delivered news of the Commons' grant to the privy council. For once, Charles responded warmly and graciously. 'This contents me', he declared

that it is not done by any man's labour, but it is the work of the whole house.
Another thing that gives me content is that although 5 subsidies be inferior to

---

[82] Ibid., pp. 8–9.

[83] Russell, *Parliaments and English Politics*, pp. 331–40.

[84] R.P. Cust, 'Charles I, the privy council and the Parliament of 1628', *TRHS*, 6th ser., vol. 2, 1992, pp. 30–4.

*my wants, yet it is the greatest that ever was; and now I see with this I shall
have the affections of my people and this will be greater to me than all value.
At the first I liked parliaments, but since (I know not how) I was grown to
distaste of them. But I am now where I was. I love parliaments. I shall rejoice
to meet with my people often.*[85]

Buckingham also seized the moment to declare himself a reformed character. He no longer wished to be thought of as 'a man of separation', he said,
but rather a 'good spirit', dedicated to promoting unity. The euphoria was
not to last, but for the time being the moderates had the upper hand. Those
who doubted the success of the parliament were silenced and there was the
prospect that if the king could just hang on and settle with the Commons,
his immediate financial worries would be over.[86]

Unfortunately, during the next phase, prospects of a general settlement
receded as Charles grew increasingly distrustful of the Commons. This
happened largely because, as in 1626, the house held back the passage of
the subsidy bill until grievances had been redressed. On most issues the crown
was prepared to concede. The forced loan, compulsory billeting and the
use of martial law against civilians were all, in Secretary Coke's words, 'confessed to be unlegal'. However, Charles insisted on maintaining the right
to imprison without showing cause which he regarded as an essential part
of the prerogative. The result was deadlock. The Commons would not confirm
its grant and Charles would not back down. The Lords tried to find a
way out of the impasse by proposing that the king be allowed to imprison
without showing cause only when reason of state required. Charles himself
offered a personal assurance that he would do nothing to infringe the
traditional liberties enshrined in Magna Carta. But the Commons refused
to compromise, and when the path to legislation was blocked in early May
they decided to proceed by Petition of Right. Charles's response to all this
became less and less tolerant. He cast off the restraining influence of
his councillors and demanded that the Commons confirm their grant of
subsidies and give up on imprisonment. On 5 May, Lord Keeper Coventry
warned on his behalf that 'if you seek to bind the king by new and indeed
impossible bonds, you must be accountable to God and the country for

---

[85] *Proceedings in Parliament 1628*, vol. 2, pp. 324–5.

[86] Cust, 'Charles I, the privy council and the Parliament of 1628', pp. 34–5.

the ill success of this meeting'. This sounded ominously like a rerun of the final stages of 1626 and it was accompanied by discussion about a return to 'new counsels'.[87]

An important insight into Charles's attitude at this stage is provided by a declaration of his reasons for dissolving parliament, drafted by the attorney-general, Sir Robert Heath. It showed that prerogative taxation was still very much on the agenda. The original version of the document contained a promise not to reimpose the forced loan, which was in line with assurances given by councillors in the Commons; however, there is a note alongside this, suggesting that it be omitted and elsewhere a warning that the king must now make whatever provision was necessary for the security of the realm. Even more significantly, the draft made it clear that Charles continued to be alarmed about the scope of the Commons' actions. It described how 'some of the members of the house, blinded with a popular applause, have, under the specious show of redeeming the liberty of the subject, endeavoured to destroy our just power of sovereignty'. The popular conspiracy theory that had caused such damage in 1625 and 1626 clearly remained an important influence on the king's thinking.[88]

In spite of this, on 12 May Coventry announced that the parliament would continue. The reason for this was, once again, money. A new fleet, under the command of the earl of Denbigh, had set sail for La Rochelle late in April. Early reports suggested that it had succeeded in breaching the harbour defences, which created an urgent demand for cash so that reinforcements could be sent to exploit the opportunity. In the event it failed and retreated back to England in mid-May; but this did not remove the need for supply. Charles interpreted the failure as a personal disgrace and on 18 May decided that the fleet must return to France as soon as possible. This was going to be impossible unless new sources of revenue could be found. It therefore remained imperative to keep the parliament going until the subsidies had been confirmed.[89]

The crown's strategy now was to rely on the House of Lords. Charles wrote personally to the peers, appealing to them to safeguard the prerogative,

---

[87] Ibid., pp. 36–8.

[88] Cust, 'Charles I and a draft declaration for the 1628 Parliament', pp. 143–61.

[89] Cust, 'Charles I, the privy council and the Parliament of 1628', pp. 40–3; Gardiner, *History of England*, vol. 6, pp. 291–3.

while councillors of all shades of opinion rallied to its defence. The problem with this, as Conrad Russell has shown, was that too many peers had been alienated by Charles and Buckingham's recent actions. So in late May, when the Commons rejected the Lords' attempt to attach a saving clause to the Petition of Right, a majority of the peers opted to support the document in its original form.[90] Charles, however, was still reluctant to concede. He consulted the judges and drafted a series of possible answers to the Petition; then, on 2 June, delivered what the Commons considered to be the least satisfactory of these, a simple declaration that 'right be done according to the laws of the realm'. As was so often the case with Charles, this clumsy attempt at subterfuge proved counter-productive. If he had simply given way with a good grace that would have been an end of the matter. Instead, the Commons was so outraged that it immediately began drawing up a Remonstrance which condemned Buckingham as 'the cause of all our miseries'. The king was once again faced with either dissolving parliament and losing his money, or giving way. After a six-hour discussion in council on 5 June he decided to give way, and on the 7th he consented to the Petition of Right in terms that gave it the effect of law. The subsidy bill was finally passed on 16 June, although even before this the council had begun to spend the money.[91]

During the final weeks of the session, which ended on 26 June, some of the earlier tension eased as it appeared that both sides were getting more or less what they wanted. The king received his subsidies, the Commons secured the Petition of Right and was allowed to present its Remonstrance, and Buckingham was given protection. The new spirit of reconciliation was reflected in the duke's assurances to the Lords that the crown had no intention of raising taxes outside parliament. Even Laud caught the mood, declaring on Charles's behalf, in a draft reply to the Remonstrance, that 'we would be glad to see such moderate parliaments that we may love them and make them more frequent'.[92] The one person who threatened to spoil everything was Charles himself. Having obtained his grant, he reverted to a style of dealing with the Commons that was as grating as anything that had gone before. When the Commons presented the Remonstrance against

---

[90] Russell, *Parliaments and English Politics*, pp. 371–4.

[91] Cust, 'Charles I, the privy council and the Parliament of 1628', pp. 41–3.

[92] NA, SP 16/108/67.

Buckingham he told it not to interfere with matters that did not concern it, and then gave the favourite his hand to kiss in public. He also resorted to forestalling criticism of his servants by taking responsibility for their actions on to himself. When the Commons tried to investigate Sir Edward Sawyer's role in raising customs rates he stopped it by declaring that this had been done at his behest. Even more alarmingly, he began to backtrack on the Petition of Right. It had initially been printed with only his second answer attached; however, three days after the end of the parliament, apparently without consulting the council, he ordered the attorney-general to call in all the existing copies, 'to be made waste paper', and then commissioned a second printing. This contained his first, unsatisfactory, answer, a series of qualifications to his second answer and a copy of his closing speech to the parliament. In this he had warned categorically that 'my meaning was not to grant any new privileges but to reedify your old' and also asserted his right to collect tonnage and poundage, even though this had never formally been agreed to. The effect, as Russell has commented, was to undercut the agreements reached during the parliament and leave the liberties of the subject resting on the king's goodwill and readiness to execute the law.[93]

In the final analysis the 1628 Parliament failed to provide the decisive shift in one direction or another that many had anticipated. Moderate councillors achieved a good deal in showing Charles that parliament could be made to work and in managing him during the crucial first phase. However, their influence was limited. During the second phase, when the Commons took their stand on imprisonment, they could do little to prevent the king taking offence and undoing much of their earlier good work. In the latter stages it is less easy to discern what was going on behind the scenes, but such evidence as there is suggests the moderates had considerable success in persuading Charles to make concessions. There remained, however, the difficulty emphasised by Russell, that although he was willing to be counselled over the means by which he pursued his policies, he could rarely be persuaded to alter his ends. It appears doubtful whether he ever really intended to abide by the terms of the Petition of Right, and in the

---

[93] Cust, 'Charles I, the privy council and the Parliament of 1628', pp. 43–5; E.R. Foster, 'The printing of the Petition of Right', *HLQ*, vol. 28, 1974, pp. 81–3; Russell, *Parliaments and English Politics*, pp. 81–3.

end it was his backtracking that undid the moderates' efforts to build a lasting settlement.[94]

Charles's attitude to the House of Commons continued to be dominated by his perception of the popular threat. Sir Robert Phelips noted shrewdly that 'nothing so endangers us with his Majesty as that opinion that we are antimonarchically affected'.[95] It was not that Charles was opposed to parliaments in principle. His 4 April speech showed that he continued to believe in the tradition of meeting his people and engaging in acts of mutual cooperation. The problem was that he expected cooperation on his own terms. When this did not happen, he began to suspect the Commons of all sorts of disloyal and subversive intentions, and, as Heath's draft demonstrated, these were taken to include the aim of destroying monarchy itself. His stance, however, was not fixed or permanent. The Commons could still redeem itself if it behaved the right way and in 1628 he decided to give it another chance. So, instead of dissolving the parliament, he prorogued it until 20 October 1628. Meanwhile, Buckingham set about building bridges for the coming session by wooing former enemies, such as the earl of Arundel and Sir Thomas Wentworth.[96]

Once the parliament had finished, the attention of king and favourite shifted back to foreign affairs. The war of the Mantuan succession which had broken out early in 1628 gave them a fresh opportunity. France and Spain were now so preoccupied with fighting each other that they were more willing to settle their differences with the English. An embassy was dispatched in July to seek peace with Spain and the nation's military effort became focused on rescuing the Huguenots. Sir John Coke, the council's most effective organiser, was sent down to Portsmouth to prepare the fleet, and elaborate plans were made to use fireships to break through the floating palisade that had defeated Denbigh. In late July, Buckingham arrived to take command. The fleet was almost ready to sail when, on 23 August, he was stabbed to death by John Felton.[97]

This dramatic event brought to an end the first phase of Charles's reign. After a brief period of mourning there was a scrabble for places at court,

---

[94] Russell, *Causes of the Civil War*, pp. 189–90.

[95] *Proceedings in Parliament 1628*, vol. 2, p. 432.

[96] Russell, *Parliaments and English Politics*, p. 390; Lockyer, *Buckingham*, p. 448.

[97] Lockyer, *Buckingham*, pp. 444–54.

out of which the new lord treasurer, Sir Richard Weston, emerged as the most powerful minister. The expected parliament was postponed until the following January amid renewed mutterings about the dangers of popular unrest and the irresponsibility of MPs. And the war policy, which was the main reason for persevering with parliament, was gradually wound down. The fleet did finally set sail in September, with the king insisting that its main task was to rescue his honour and the honour of the nation. But it failed to breach the harbour defences and this led the Rochellese to surrender. Charles's struggle to rescue the Huguenots was now effectively at an end and peace was concluded with France in April 1629. Negotiations with the Spanish took rather longer but here, too, an agreement was reached in November 1630.[98]

The assassination was also an important turning point for Charles personally. He was deeply traumatised. Clarendon describes how on first receiving the news he exercised enormous self-control, continuing 'unmoved, and without the least change in his countenance' until the end of his morning prayers; but then he suddenly broke down, shut himself up in his chamber 'and threw himself upon his bed, lamenting with much passion and with abundance of tears'.[99] This was understandable. For ten years Buckingham had been both his mentor and his closest friend. He had filled the role of elder brother far more sympathetically than Henry had ever done and he was the one person with whom Charles felt able to share his anxieties and frustrations. He desperately needed a replacement and found it in Henrietta Maria. She comforted him through the period of mourning and then became a constant companion. By October it was reported that the couple were doting on each other and the king's new habit of lying 'with the queen every night' seemed set to become 'the fashion at court'.[100] The clearest sign of their changed relationship was that around this time, after three and a half years of marriage, they conceived their first child. The queen was to be an important influence in shaping Charles's political opinions and the royal love affair one of the central motifs of his kingship.

---

[98] Gardiner, *History of England*, vol. 6, pp. 361–70; Cust, 'Charles I, the privy council and the Parliament of 1628', pp. 48–9; NA, SP 16/118/66; *CSP Ven. 1628–9*, pp. 373, 376.

[99] Clarendon, *History*, vol. 1, p. 37.

[100] Sharpe, *The Personal Rule*, pp. 46–7; Shepherd, 'Charles I and the distribution of political patronage', p. 66.

Charles also emerged from the period of mourning determined to show that he was in sole charge of the government. According to his new secretary of state, Viscount Dorchester, he resolved to take the 'total directory' of affairs into his own hands. He announced an intention to preside continuously at the council and threw himself into a round of frantic activity, dispatching more business in a fortnight, according to one report, than the duke had managed in the previous three months. This was not to last; but Charles had at least created a strong impression of a king acting as contemporaries expected him to. On the strength of this, several historians have seen Buckingham's death as marking the real beginning of his 'personal rule'.[101] Such a verdict, however, seems misconceived because, in most respects, Charles was already in command.

The stages by which the relationship between Charles and Buckingham developed are by no means easy to plot. But it does appear that around the time of his accession, he became much less willing to defer to his more experienced companion. There are some intriguing hints that he deliberately set out to put Buckingham in his place, or at least establish clear limits to his influence. Although it was obvious that he was to continue as royal favourite, he was not allowed to achieve the dominance at court that many observers expected. Charles made an effort to reconcile the factions that had emerged at the end of his father's reign, pardoning Cranfield and appointing the earl of Pembroke to the junta on foreign affairs. He also denied the duke the degree of control over the royal bedchamber that he had enjoyed under James. His appointment as a gentleman of the bedchamber was confirmed and he was issued with a golden key that symbolised his right of access at any time of the day or night. But the crucial position of groom of the stool went to Sir James Fullerton, who had served Charles in this capacity when he was Prince of Wales.[102] In some of his personal exchanges, too, Charles was prepared to make it clear that he now considered

---

[101] Gardiner, *History of England*, vol. 6, pp. 359–61; Sharpe, *The Personal Rule*, p. 50; Carlton, *Charles I*, pp. 60–1. For an astute assessment of the limits of Buckingham's power, see Quintrell, *Charles I*, pp. 45–6.

[102] Sharpe, 'The image of virtue', pp. 252–4; Lockyer, *Buckingham*, p. 235. Sir Roger Mostyn's report of the changes at court at Charles's accession makes it clear that he was determined to keep on as many of his former servants as possible; and also that Buckingham came under considerable pressure to surrender his position of master of the horse: NLW, Wynn MSS 1336 (I am grateful to Brian Quintrell for this reference).

his relationship with Buckingham to be that of master and servant. In October 1625, for example, he insisted that the duke go and sort out the defence of Essex before departing on a long embassy to the Netherlands, in spite of his desire to spend time with his young family. 'My service', Charles insisted, must take precedence; and his only concession was to 'give you leave to make your return to Kate without coming to give me an account'.[103]

Buckingham's response to all this appears to have been one of more or less willing acquiescence. He was always acutely conscious that his political survival depended on bending to Charles's wishes – and a less exposed role in policy making may not have been unwelcome, particularly after the attacks in 1625. From this point onwards his approach most of the time was to operate in the king's slipstream, adopting views and taking up positions that reflected those of his master. He continued to exercise a good deal of control over patronage – although even here Mark Shepherd has detected a weakening of the influence he enjoyed under James[104] – but it was Charles who was making the running in dealings with parliament, in religious policy, in the collection and enforcement of the loan and in most other areas where important executive decisions had to be made. The one area where Buckingham was still able to shape policy was in foreign affairs. His position as chief negotiator and spokesman for the crown, particularly in dealings with the French, continued to give him considerable power and it may be that he was able to rein in some of the king's aggression and stave off open war until 1627. But, even here, the king prevailed in the end and policy was driven forward largely by his affronted sense of honour.[105] So there would seem to be considerable justification in the claim made by Charles soon after Buckingham's death that, in spite of what most people thought, he had always accepted the role of 'faithful and obedient subject'.[106]

It might have been better if Buckingham had been able to assert himself more effectively. Ever the pragmatist, his political instincts were more accommodating than Charles's and he had a much clearer sense of how a

---

[103] Quintrell, *Charles I*, pp. 95–6.

[104] Shepherd, 'Charles I and the distribution of political patronage', p. 69.

[105] Cust, *The Forced Loan*, pp. 43–4; Cogswell, 'Foreign policy and parliament', pp. 255–6; Cogswell, 'Prelude to Re', pp. 8–9.

[106] Sharpe, *The Personal Rule*, p. 48.

particular policy would play before a public audience.[107] The compromises he offered, to parliament in particular, could well have avoided some of the more fraught political clashes of the period. These often arose not, as contemporaries believed, because Charles had too little control over government, but because he had too much. One can see emerging several of the traits that were to cause conflict later in the reign. His lack of political antennae led to him staking far too much of his political credit on the vexed issue of unparliamentary taxation, where he was almost bound to arouse opposition. His tendency to want to hammer out issues that were better left vague made life difficult for moderate councillors who wanted to put a reassuring gloss on his actions. His curtness and inflexibility when it came to negotiating made it much harder to operate the bargaining processes that were crucial to sustaining a good relationship with parliament. And already, in his backtracking over the Petition of Right, one can see evidence of the transparent deviousness that made him so hard to trust.

Two aspects of his conduct, in particular, were serious causes for concern. One was his apparent distrust of his people. During the forced loan, in particular, he seems to have been in the grip of something approaching paranoia whenever he considered whether they were loyal and obedient. He repeatedly sought to turn the whole issue of taxation into a test of allegiance. His letters over the benevolence and the loan, his use of oaths, his warnings that those who failed to respond would be remembered and the vindictiveness with which he pursued refusers, all suggest that he expected to be disobeyed – and, almost inevitably, he was. His anxiety created a spiral of mistrust which incidents like the assassination of Buckingham only added to. When the smooth functioning of the political system depended so much on goodwill and a willingness to cooperate this could not but be extremely damaging.[108]

Just as harmful was his refusal to lay the blame for disruptive policies on 'evil counsellors'. This was crucial to sustaining the subject's belief in the essential soundness of their monarch, and both Elizabeth and James had managed it when it became necessary. But Charles, out of a mixture of stubbornness and conscientious scruple, refused to play the game. He

---

[107] On Buckingham and the public audience, see Cogswell, 'Buckingham and popularity', pp. 211–34.

[108] Cust, *The Forced Loan*, p. 88; Russell, *Causes of the Civil War*, pp. 201–5.

was fully aware of what was expected, on one occasion announcing to the House of Lords that it was 'a general maxim of kings to leave harsh commands to their ministers, themselves only executing pleasing things'; however, he seems to have felt it was both more virtuous and more honourable to take responsibility onto his own shoulders and make it clear that policy emanated directly from him.[109] The damaging effects of this can be seen in his widely reported hostility to parliament between late 1626 and early 1627. Instead of allowing Buckingham to shoulder the blame for this, he deliberately contrived that everyone should know that it was he who stood in the way of a resummons. Hardly anything could have been more calculated to alarm the sensibilities of ordinary Englishmen and upset the delicate balance of faith and trust on which political stability rested. Charles's approach meant that critics of crown policy very quickly found themselves running up against the king himself. Much of the neutral ground in politics – where a certain amount of pushing and shoving could be tolerated in the interests of accommodating a wide spectrum of opinion – was cut away. And, because of this, challenging royal policy came to involve much higher stakes than under his father.

Conrad Russell and other revisionist historians have argued that the political conflicts of the late 1620s were caused mainly by parliament's failure adequately to fund the war. There is much to support this verdict. Charles's resentment at what he saw as the Commons' unwillingness to fulfil its 'engagements' certainly helped to poison good relations; and the lack of subsidies in 1626 was the immediate cause of the forced loan. But it was not the whole story. Charles had a choice over how he dealt with his financial difficulties. He could have decided to continue working with parliament as his moderate councillors wanted. When he did this, and was prepared to make realistic concessions, as in 1628, he could obtain much of the money that he needed. Instead, he chose to adopt 'new counsels' and all that these entailed, because of worries about his people's loyalty, fears of a popular conspiracy to undermine monarchy and a determination to uphold the prerogative and royal authority. All this suggests, then, that when it comes to explaining the political conflicts of the period, a crucial role must be assigned to Charles himself, to his decisions and his interventions.

---

[109] *LJ*, vol. 4, p. 43.

The effects of these were damaging, but not disastrous. The forced loan raised tension and conflict to levels not previously experienced in the early seventeenth century, but most of the harm could be repaired. Contemporaries were very aware – to an extent that has not always been appreciated by later historians – that Charles was still relatively young and inexperienced. They recognised that his style of kingship had yet to be shaped and moulded and this encouraged them to make some important allowances. At the height of the forced loan, for example, a correspondent of Sir Robert Phelips could comment that Charles was still widely regarded as 'a most virtuous young prince, only thought misguided by his affections, which time, experience, good counsel and sundry accidents may rectify'. The writer's main concern was that the opposition to the loan should not cause him to become 'so exasperated and embittered as that there should settle in him any disaffection to his people'.[110] A similarly indulgent view can be seen in some of the letters of Sir Thomas Barrington, the son of one of the leading organisers of opposition to the loan. He insisted that 'Princes should in policey have some time and way left to evade when point of honour is in competition.' This meant that 'if they acknowledge their acts past illegal and their ministers confess it and plead ignorance' then there was no reason why the people should not accept this as a 'reasonable satisfaction'.[111] Barrington was referring to tonnage and poundage when he made these remarks, but his comments could be applied more widely, particularly in the aftermath of the Petition of Right. There was a desire to draw a line under the grievances and abuses, and move on. One area where this looked like being difficult, however, especially for a puritan like Barrington, was over the king's religious policy.

The Caroline religious settlement

The nearest thing Charles had to a religious mentor – apart from his own father – was Lancelot Andrewes. It was Andrewes who, in 1619, persuaded James to entrust his future religious education to anti-Calvinists like Matthew

---

[110] Somerset Record Office, Phelips MSS 219/35.

[111] *Barrington Family Letters 1628–1632*, ed. A. Searle, Camden Soc., 4th ser., vol. 28, 1983, p. 59.

Wren; Andrewes to whom Charles turned within a few days of his accession for advice on the vexed issue of predestination; and Andrewes whose works, alongside those of Richard Hooker and William Laud, he recommended to his children the night before his execution. He may even have contemplated making Andrewes archbishop of Canterbury in succession to George Abbot, although he was over 70. It was not until a few days after Andrewes's death that Laud received the famous promise from the king that he would be given the reversion of the office.[112] Charles's admiration for Andrewes was highly significant because it played a critical role in moulding the religious settlement that took shape in the opening months of his reign.

Under the later Tudors and James, the accession of the new monarch had become an important moment for redefining the religious direction of the nation. Charles's entry to the throne was no exception. The Caroline religious settlement, which unfolded between April 1625 and June 1626, although not enshrined in any notable decrees or enactments, nonetheless produced a dramatic shift in the balance of the church. At Charles's accession it was still dominated by Calvinist bishops and Calvinist doctrine. Within less than 18 months, however, it was set on a very different trajectory that favoured anti-Calvinists such as Andrewes. The struggle between the two sides had been gathering momentum during the early 1620s, but it was the young king's arrival on the throne that finally resolved it.

James's approach to the church in England was heavily influenced by his Calvinist upbringing in Scotland. He remained sympathetic to the doctrines of reformed Protestantism and tended to entrust power and responsibility in the upper levels of the church to those who shared his perspective. His archbishop of Canterbury after 1611, Abbot, two of his archbishops of York, Matthew Hutton and Toby Matthew, and the majority of his bishops – including James Montague, Bishop of Winchester, who has been described as the equivalent of his personal confessor – all belonged to this tradition. His Calvinist instincts also encouraged him to accommodate the puritans who had caused so much trouble under Elizabeth. He made clear at the start of his reign that he shared their theological beliefs and recognised the need to promote a vigorous preaching ministry; but, at the same time, he insisted that he would not tolerate those who supported the

---

[112] McCullough, *Sermons at Court*, pp. 204–9; Laud, *Works*, vol. 3, p. 160; N.R.N. Tyacke, 'Archbishop Laud', in K. Fincham ed., *The Early Stuart Church*, Basingstoke, 1993, pp. 62–4.

Presbyterian programme of abolishing bishops or who openly refused to conform to the church's discipline and ceremonies. This had the effect of driving a wedge between the radical and moderate wings of the movement, encouraging the latter to compromise and work within the Church of England. Up until the early 1620s, this approach was very successful. Presbyterianism was effectively removed from the reforming agenda; reluctant conformists were won round and devoted their energies to preaching and the parish ministry; and the dominant style of churchmanship became an evangelical, sermon-centred, piety that accorded with the preferences of the majority of the clergy and godly laity.[113]

Much of the cement holding together this accommodation was supplied by the Calvinist doctrine of predestination, which stated that God had predestined some to salvation, but most to damnation. The world was sharply divided between elect saints and the reprobate or damned, although only God knew for certain who these were. This was the basis for the theology taught in the universities, published in the presses and approved by James when he sent a British delegation to the Synod of Dort (1618–19) to help sort out doctrinal controversies in the Netherlands. It supplied what Nicholas Tyacke has called 'a common and ameliorating bond', uniting different strands of Protestant opinion and persuading the majority that, for all its imperfections, the Church of England was a true church, in contrast to the debased version offered by the papists. Not everyone, however, subscribed to this doctrine. There was a small, but significant, group of bishops, and Oxford and Cambridge theologians, who challenged the certainties of Calvinist predestinarianism by suggesting that God's saving grace was available to all and that human beings had the free will to play a role in their own salvation. They were known to their opponents as Arminians, because their views were similar to those of the Dutch anti-Calvinist, Jacobus Arminius. Andrewes was their most articulate and influential spokesman.[114]

For most of James's reign, these anti-Calvinists faced an uphill struggle. James was quite prepared to promote some of their number to the episcopal

---

[113] K. Fincham and P.G. Lake, 'The ecclesiastical policy of James I', *JBS*, vol. 24, 1985, pp. 169–97.

[114] N.R.N. Tyacke, 'Puritanism, Arminianism and counter-revolution', in idem, *Aspects of English Protestantism, c. 1530–1700*, Manchester, 2001, pp. 132–55.

bench and to senior positions at court. This fitted with his policy of trying to maintain a balance between different religious viewpoints and his personal readiness to accept that the whole doctrine of predestination was sufficiently complicated to allow a diversity of opinion. But he was not prepared to countenance them speaking out openly on the issue, lest England be sucked into the doctrinal controversies that divided the Dutch. Even Andrewes, who was able to use his privileged position as James's favourite preacher to argue against the Calvinist stress on sermons, had to keep quiet about predestination. However, until this central doctrine could be publicly challenged the anti-Calvinists were condemned to remain an embattled minority. Their opportunity came in the early 1620s with the furore over the Spanish Match.[115]

Zealous Calvinists regarded the Match as a threat to the very survival of Protestantism in England and there was a concerted campaign to alert the public to the dangers of marrying an idolator. The king was furious at what he saw as a blatantly popular attempt to stir up public opinion and encroach on the *arcana imperii*. In the summer of 1622 he ordered Archbishop Abbot to issue directions that banned preaching on matters of state. But the protests continued, and, to James's dismay, were supported by senior churchmen, including his son's chaplain, George Hakewill, and Abbot himself. In these circumstances, much of the rhetorical initiative at court passed to anti-Calvinist divines, like Andrewes, who defended the Match and at the same time warned about the dangers of puritan sedition. This reawakened James's long-standing fears of populist puritanism and made him increasingly receptive to the message that his policy of accommodation had created a dangerous fifth column inside the church.[116]

It was against this background that Richard Montagu, with the blessing of Richard Neile, leader of the anti-Calvinist lobby at court, published *A New Gagg for an Old Goose*. Ostensibly a reply to Roman Catholic criticism of the Church of England, this was, in fact, a carefully calculated challenge to the Calvinists. It argued that predestination was no part of the teachings of the church as enshrined in the Thirty-Nine Articles, but was really the doctrine of the puritans, and therefore schismatic. This provocative message

---

[115] Tyacke, *Anti-Calvinists*, pp. 87–105; P.G. Lake, 'Calvinism and the English church', *P & P*, no. 114, 1987, pp. 47–54.

[116] Fincham and Lake, 'Ecclesiastical policy of James I', pp. 198–202.

met with a hostile response in the 1624 Parliament, where the Commons referred the whole matter to Abbot. The archbishop wanted to send a clear message that such views would not be tolerated within the English church, but he was frustrated by James who simply urged Montagu to clarify his position. Montagu responded with the *Appello Caesarem* which was published in 1625 after being read and approved by the king. This was an even more aggressive assault on the Calvinists, employing throughout an anti-puritan and anti-Calvinist language which, in the past, the Arminians had only dared to use selectively. It accused the puritans of being a dangerous religious faction who were trying to pass off their 'private opinions' and 'some classical resolutions of the bretheren' as the settled teaching of the church. Predestination was again presented as the distinctive doctrine of puritanism. The king's earlier efforts to define puritans in terms of nonconformity or Presbyterianism were overridden and Montagu proposed that all doctrinal Calvinists belonged to this category, and were therefore part of a subversive threat to the established religion. James's sudden death means that it is impossible to tell how far he had been converted to Montagu's line. But it is clear that as soon as he ascended the throne Charles decided to embrace it wholeheartedly and immediately set in motion the changes that brought the anti-Calvinists to power.[117]

The young king's role in this process has recently been the subject of considerable debate. Tyacke, in his classic account of the rise of Arminianism, and Ken Fincham and Peter Lake in their work on James and Charles's ecclesiastical policies, have seen his personal impact as crucial. They depict Charles as a monarch who was willing to cast aside the ambiguity and restraint of his father and wholeheartedly embrace the anti-Calvinist agenda to which he had recently been converted.[118] This view has, however, been challenged by Julian Davies and Kevin Sharpe. Both argue that Charles had little interest in Arminian doctrine. His main concern was to silence controversy over the whole issue of predestination and concentrate on what he saw as the far more important issues of ritual, conformity and personal

---

[117] Tyacke, *Anti-Calvinists*, pp. 125–8, 147–50; Fincham and Lake, 'Ecclesiastical policy of James I', pp. 202–6.

[118] Tyacke, 'Puritanism, Arminianism and counter-revolution', pp. 144–6; K. Fincham and P. Lake, 'The ecclesiastical policies of James I and Charles I', in Fincham ed., *The Early Stuart Church*, pp. 36–40.

devotion. Davies has also argued that in the early months of the reign it was Buckingham, rather than the king, who was supplying much of the impetus behind religious policy.[119] The work of these two scholars is a useful reminder that doctrinal divisions were not always clear-cut and were not the only source of religious conflict during Charles's reign. Nonetheless, a close examination of these early months does suggest that Montagu's challenge to predestinarian doctrine was widely regarded as the litmus test of the new regime. For those in the know, it appeared to be the critical issue which would define the future direction of the church. Both sides threw themselves into the struggle to secure a favourable ruling and, at the same time, Charles emerged as the main champion of the anti-Calvinist ascendancy.

The most revealing account we have of these events is the diary of William Laud, who suddenly found himself thrust into the limelight as principal intermediary between Charles and the anti-Calvinists.[120] Laud had been Buckingham's chaplain and religious confidant since 1622 and it was this which gave him his key role. The duke's own approach to religion was relatively flexible and he was just as ready to seek guidance from an ardent Calvinist, like John Preston, as from Laud. But he also recognised the strength of the young king's convictions and was aware that his own future might depend on giving him the sort of church that he wanted. He therefore used Laud to channel advice and information to Charles, and keep himself in touch with the various options.[121] During these early months, king and favourite were working together closely in the making of religious policy. But it was Charles who provided most of the conviction and leadership.

Events moved rapidly in the weeks after James's death. The first significant step recorded by Laud came on 5 April 1625, when he drew up a list of leading churchmen marked 'O' for Orthodox or 'P' for Puritan. The original list has not survived, but it appears to have provided information

---

[119] Davies, *The Caroline Captivity*, pp. 12, 25, 108, 111; Sharpe, *The Personal Rule*, pp. 279–84.

[120] Laud, *Works*, vol. 3, pp. 158–208. When using Laud's diary, account must be taken of his concern to protect himself against future Calvinist retribution by presenting Charles as the main author of ecclesiastical policy. But, even allowing for this, the diary reveals a king who was very positive about the direction in which he wanted the church to go.

[121] Lockyer, *Buckingham*, pp. 114–15; Davies, *The Caroline Captivity*, pp. 106–7.

that ensured the virtual exclusion of Calvinists from a number of important episcopal committees over the following months and, in the longer term, helped secure anti-Calvinist dominance of appointments to bishoprics. A few days later, Laud received direction from the king to consult Andrewes over 'what he would have done in the case of the church', especially with regard to the five decrees supporting predestination issued at Dort. This was very significant. Whereas James's objective had been to secure silence over this critical doctrine, Charles's initial inclination appears to have been to open it up for discussion. Experience was to teach him the perils of such a course, and from June 1626 he reverted to his father's policy. But his readiness to consult Andrewes – who he must have known was far from neutral on this issue – clearly indicated where his sympathies lay.[122] A couple of weeks later Charles also secured the anti-Calvinists' base at court with a decision to keep Richard Neile in the important post of clerk of the closet, with Laud as his deputy. His determination to brook no dissent in this matter was revealed when Henry Burton, whose claims to the office had been ignored, tried to protest that both Neile and Laud were 'popishly affected'. On Burton's account, Charles started to read his letter sitting in front of him, 'but perceiving the scope of it he gave it me again and bade me forbear any more attendance in my office until he should send for me'.[123] His dismissal was the start of a process by which the three key religious offices at court – clerk of the closet, dean of the chapel and royal almoner – all passed into the hands of anti-Calvinists and the Calvinists found their opportunities to preach before the king severely curtailed.[124]

These developments demonstrated to insiders where Charles's religious sympathies lay. This started to become apparent to a wider public in July 1625, during the parliament. Having failed to secure Montagu's condemnation by means of Archbishop Abbot in 1624, the Commons decided to indict him for contempt in publishing the *Appello* while his case was still under consideration. Montagu himself had considerable doubts about whether he could rely on Charles to support him, as James had done; but he need not have worried. Within two days of the Commons ordering his

---

[122] Laud, *Works*, vol. 3, pp. 159–61; Tyacke, *Anti-Calvinists*, p. 167.

[123] Henry Burton, *A narrative of the Life of Mr Henry Burton*, 1643, p. 3.

[124] Fincham and Lake, 'Ecclesiastical policy of James and Charles', p. 38.

arrest, Charles declared that he was a royal chaplain and therefore exempt from its jurisdiction. At a time when the Commons was worried about religion, this was clearly not the best way to appease it; but it was a big boost to the confidence of the anti-Calvinists.[125] A few days later, three of their supporters among the bishops, including Laud, wrote to Buckingham commending the king's readiness to take the whole business 'into his own care' and openly declaring their opposition to the decrees passed at Dort.[126]

Over the following months Charles continued to give his wholehearted support to the anti-Calvinist agenda. In January 1626 he invited Andrewes and other like-minded bishops to advise him on how to proceed in the Montagu case and received the predictable advice that, since his doctrine was the doctrine of the Church of England, he must stand by him. At his coronation on 2 February, Laud and Neile were given pride of place as his chief 'supporters'; while John Cosin, the Arminian spokesman at the York House Conference a few days later, took a prominent role as master of ecclesiastical ceremonies. Then on 6 February, at the opening of the parliament, Laud delivered a blistering attack on the puritans that was evidently approved by the king.[127] By this stage, however, the Calvinists were beginning to organise a counter-attack.

This involved two different strategies. Abbot and other leading members of the Calvinist church establishment, supported by the two most zealous Calvinists among the court peerage, Warwick and Lord Saye, several senior officeholders, such as Secretary Coke and Attorney-General Heath, and various assorted MPs, favoured a direct assault. They sought to take advantage of the king's new-found desire to present himself as a champion of 'the Protestant cause' to secure two important concessions: first, a condemnation of Montagu's writings as heretical and, second, a restatement of the orthodoxy of the Church of England that incorporated the decrees of Dort or the Lambeth Articles issued after a similar confrontation with anti-Calvinists in 1595. Heavyweight Calvinist authors, such as Bishop Carleton of

---

[125] Tyacke, *Anti-Calvinists*, pp. 151–2; Russell, *Parliaments and English Politics*, pp. 231–6.

[126] Laud, *Works*, vol. 6, pp. 244–6.

[127] Ibid., vol. 3, pp. 178–9; Bod. Lib., Ashmole MS 857, pp. 154–6; Rushworth, vol. 1, pp. 200–1; Laud, *Works*, vol. 1, pp. 82–3. Charles attended the sermon and it was immediately published by 'his Majesty's command'.

Chichester, one of the delegates at Dort, and Abbot's chaplain, Daniel Featley, swung into action with books denouncing Montagu and the Arminians as latter day Pelagians, while Warwick and Saye used their influence with Buckingham to summon a conference on doctrine.[128]

Meanwhile, the earls of Pembroke and Carlisle tried a subtler approach. Mindful of the need to preserve a united front behind the war effort and, perhaps, also of the strength of Charles's attachment to the anti-Calvinists, they sought to defuse the whole issue. The key to their strategy was a work written by their client Joseph Hall early in 1626 entitled the *Via Media*. Hall was another member of the Calvinist delegation to Dort, but with the reputation of being a professional moderate, which made him ideally suited to the purposes of the two earls. His book provided a definition of the middle ground of the Church of England which was in line with the doctrines approved at Dort, but then offered a reading of Montagu's works that allowed them to be incorporated within this middle ground. It also endorsed James's view that there were certain doctrinal truths that should not be openly discussed and urged Charles to restrict debate on such matters. The effect of all this, as Peter Lake has argued, was to offer both Montagu and the king an end to the witch-hunt over doctrine in return for subscribing to a view of orthodoxy compatible with the moderate Calvinism of Hall and his patrons. If accepted, it would have produced something like a return to the *status quo* under James.[129]

Charles and Buckingham's response to these initiatives was deliberately ambiguous. While the 1626 Parliament was in session, they were willing to give ground to the Calvinists, partly in the hope of concluding a deal over supply and partly to try to prevent the Montagu case becoming entangled with impeachment proceedings. At the same time they continued to send signals to the anti-Calvinists which confirmed their support. The conference on doctrine took place at York House on 11 and 17 February 1626 in the presence of senior privy councillors, including Pembroke, Carlisle, Manchester, Dorset and Coke. As an attempt to solve the religious problem, it was inconclusive. The anti-Calvinist spokesmen, Francis White and John Cosin,

---

[128] Tyacke, *Anti-Calvinists*, pp. 152–5.

[129] P.G. Lake, 'The moderate and irenic case for religious war: Joseph Hall's *Via Media* in context', in S.D. Amussen and M. Kishlansky eds, *Political Culture and Cultural Politics in Early Modern England*, Manchester, 1995, pp. 67–79; Davies, *The Caroline Captivity*, p. 110n.

were able to cloud the issues sufficiently to prevent any clear condemnation of Montagu, even though most of the delegates were Calvinists; and when Warwick and Saye proposed to end the controversy by establishing the decrees of Dort as authoritative in England, only Coke supported them. Politically, however, the conference yielded important benefits for the king and favourite. The Montagu case surfaced only briefly during the parliament and never came before the Lords where it might have caused real problems. Just as crucially, the Calvinist peers remained divided, with Pembroke and Carlisle refusing to follow Warwick and Saye down the path to confrontation.[130] The anti-Calvinists' escape from censure bolstered their confidence considerably and in the aftermath of the conference Cosin jubilantly declared that 'the king swears his perpetual patronage of our cause'.[131] However, while there remained a possibility of parliamentary supply, they were not out of the wood.

On 17 April the Montagu case again came before the Commons. Charles responded to its complaints that he had denied the doctrine of perseverance contained in the Thirty-Nine Articles with a message declaring 'his dislike of Mr Montagu his writings'. He also indicated his readiness to refer the whole matter to Convocation as proposed by one of Pembroke's clients during the negotiations for 'reformation of the duke'.[132] These were hopeful signs for the Calvinists and they were followed by Charles instructing Attorney-General Heath to draw up a proclamation banning further discussion of disputed points of doctrine. Heath's first draft of this specifically blamed 'some questions and opinions broached by Richard Montagu and others' for destroying the peace of the church, and called for a moratorium on the discussion of doctrine.[133] Meanwhile Montagu himself was becoming concerned about losing the king's support and was apparently willing to subscribe to Hall's gloss on his writings. It seemed that the sort of settlement Pembroke hoped for was about to take shape.[134] The appearance of a proclamation for the peace of the church in tandem with

---

[130] Tyacke, *Anti-Calvinists*, pp. 164–80; B. Donagan, 'The York House Conference revisited: laymen, Calvinism and Arminianism', *HR*, vol. 64, 1991, pp. 312–30.

[131] Tyacke, 'Puritanism, Arminianism and counter-revolution', p. 144.

[132] *Proceedings in Parliament 1626*, vol. 3, p. 30.

[133] NA, SP 16/29/78. On Heath's loathing for Arminians, see Cust, 'Charles I and a draft declaration', pp. 145–6.

[134] Russell, *Parliaments and English Politics*, pp. 298–9.

Hall's *Via Media*, perhaps supported by a statement from Montagu, could have silenced further discussion of predestination, but with a presumption in favour of the Calvinists. What in fact happened was very different, and it decisively shaped the religious history of Charles's reign.

In the final days of the parliament, Laud and Charles took control of drafting the proclamation and revised it to remove any reference to Montagu or the Arminians. Now it simply stated the king's 'utter dislike' of those who 'stir up or move any new opinions differing from the sound and orthodoxall grounds of the true religion . . . established in the Church of England'. Crucially, there was no attempt to define what these 'new opinions' were.[135] The consequences of this became apparent two days after the proclamation was issued on 14 June when Neile, acting, he claimed, on Charles's instructions, warned the authorities at Cambridge University not to go ahead with a commencement disputation in support of predestination. Two weeks later, the Court of High Commission in London cited the proclamation as justification for banning the writings against Montagu prepared earlier in the year, and Hall's *Via Media*, although already licensed, was withdrawn from the press.[136] Those on the inside quickly saw what was happening. Bishop Davenant, another former member of the Dort delegation, worried about 'how far those of Durham House' (i.e. Neile and the anti-Calvinists) might 'stretch the meaning' of the proclamation. His ally James Ussher, archbishop of Armagh, went further and preached a sermon in front of Charles deploring the new fashion for branding Calvinists with the 'odious name' of puritans and predicting disastrous doctrinal conflicts.[137]

Ussher was not overstating the case. The June 1626 proclamation was a critical turning point for the Calvinists' fortunes. Prior to this their views on predestination had been largely accepted as the official doctrine of the Church of England; but now, with no guidelines for interpreting

---

[135] NA, SP 16/540/404; 29/79; *Proclamations of Charles I*, pp. 90–3. The proclamation referred specifically to having been drafted with the advice of the bishops which was very unusual and probably refers to Laud drawing on a conclave of anti-Calvinist bishops, as on other occasions during this period: Russell, *Causes of the English Civil War*, p. 201.

[136] Tyacke, *Anti-Calvinists*, pp. 48–9; Davies, *The Caroline Captivity*, p. 112; Lake, 'Joseph Hall's *Via Media*', pp. 78–9.

[137] M. Fuller, *The Life, Letters and Writings of John Davenant D.D. 1572–1641, Lord Bishop of Salisbury*, 1897, p. 167; Tyacke, *Anti-Calvinists*, pp. 56–7.

the proclamation, they were at the mercy of Laud, Neile and other anti-Calvinists with the ear of the king. This shift had been engineered by Charles himself, as a matter of deliberate choice.

In retrospect, it seems all too clear that the basic character of the Caroline church was established during the first 15 months of the reign; however, for those involved there still appeared to be much to play for. The anti-Calvinists had certainly gained an advantage; but Calvinists remained in the majority on the privy council and meetings of parliament continued to offer opportunities to claw back lost ground. For the next three years, then, the struggles over doctrine continued.

Following the dissolution of the 1626 Parliament, the anti-Calvinists steadily strengthened their grip on the upper levels of the church. Buckingham became chancellor of Cambridge University at the beginning of June 1626 and, with the king's encouragement, used his position to suppress predestinarian teaching at what had previously been a bastion of Calvinist orthodoxy. In October, a few days after the death of Lancelot Andrewes, Laud was made dean of the Chapel Royal and then told that Charles intended him to succeed Abbot as archbishop of Canterbury. The following April both he and Neile were promoted to the privy council. Then, in July 1627, Abbot was sequestered from his archbishopric and replaced by a committee of anti-Calvinist bishops for refusing to license Sibthorpe's sermon.[138] Royal policy clearly favoured the anti-Calvinists; however, the flow was not all in one direction. During 1627, mainly after Buckingham's departure for the Isle de Rhé, the Calvinists staged a partial recovery. In August, Henry Leslie, a royal chaplain, was able to preach a sermon before Charles that contained an uncompromising assertion of Calvinist doctrine. This was immediately published at the behest of Pembroke's brother, the earl of Montgomery. Then, in November 1627, Hall was able to breach the apparent ban on Calvinists being promoted to bishoprics by securing the see of Exeter, again probably with backing from Pembroke and Carlisle.[139] As parliament reconvened in March 1628 there were further possibilities for progress.

Again the different wings of the Calvinist movement pursued different strategies. The more zealous continued to promote a head-on confrontation.

---

[138] Tyacke, *Anti-Calvinists*, pp. 48–9, 167–8.

[139] Cust, *The Forced Loan*, pp. 74–5.

The Commons revived its case against Montagu, spurred on by tracts from Henry Burton and Jeremiah Dyke that equated Arminianism with popery and warned of God's judgements against the nation unless it was eradicated. They also attempted to give statutory authority to the Thirty-Nine Articles and the Irish Articles of 1615 (which incorporated the Lambeth Articles). In both cases their efforts were abortive, mainly because the attention given to the Petition of Right meant there was little time to discuss religion.[140] Meanwhile, Pembroke and his allies persisted in their efforts to get Charles to distance himself from the anti-Calvinists. Hall and Davenant were recruited to preach before the House of Lords – to offer a public reminder that moderate Calvinism was both responsible and respectable – while Sir Humphrey May dropped hints in the Commons that the king was about to disown the Arminians. This policy appeared to be bearing fruit during the final stages of the meeting when Charles declared in council that he 'did utterly dislike these novelties' whereupon Laud and Neile fell to their knees to 'disavow and protest that they did renounce the opinions of Arminius'.[141] However, as usual, once the parliament had ended Charles's basic inclinations came to the fore. In June he ordered pardons to be prepared to protect Montagu and Roger Mainwaring, and in July Montagu was made bishop of Chichester.[142]

As we shall see, the Calvinists were to have a final opportunity to reverse the situation in the winter of 1628–9, as part of the policy of a 'new deal' with parliament. But this was to prove abortive. By mid-1630, with the issuing of new Instructions to the Clergy and other measures to restrict Calvinist preaching, the world had been made safe for the anti-Calvinists and the direction of the church had been fixed for the following decade.[143] There is little doubt that Charles supplied much of the drive and conviction that enabled all this to happen; but his reasons for doing so still require explanation. What was it that drew him to the style of churchmanship espoused by Andrewes, Laud and other anti-Calvinists? And why was he so determined to support their efforts to displace Calvinism as the doctrinal orthodoxy of the church?

---

[140] Tyacke, *Anti-Calvinists*, pp. 154–60.

[141] Cust, 'Charles I, the privy council and the Parliament of 1628', pp. 35–6, 43–4.

[142] Davies, *The Caroline Captivity*, pp. 113–14.

[143] See below, pp. 110–12, 116, 123–4.

The first and foremost reason appears to have been his deep loathing for puritanism. Conrad Russell has described Charles as 'a man with a real allergy to puritanism in all its forms'.[144] He was rarely capable of distinguishing the moderate and extreme manifestations of the creed in the way his father had done. As far as he was concerned, all puritans were tarred with the same brush and they stood for everything he detested, both in church and state. His view of them was basically that set out by James in the *Basilicon Doron*. He saw them as a populist sect bent on spreading sedition and undermining order. On one of the few occasions when he reflected in writing on the nature of the Church of England – in exchanges with the Scots Presbyterian Alexander Henderson in 1646 – the puritans emerged as the opposite of everything he valued. One of the principal guarantees of the purity and integrity of the church, as he saw it, was the fact that reform in England had been carried out 'neither with multitude nor with tumult, but legally and orderly and by those whom I conceive to have the reforming power'. The puritan approach of 'popular reformation' was 'little better than rebellion'.[145]

A more detailed impression of how he regarded them emerges in the sermons of anti-Calvinist court preachers who knew Charles and were eager to preach what they thought he wanted to hear. Again and again the puritans were depicted as the chief agents of a popular conspiracy to destroy order, obedience and unity. In his sermon at the opening of the 1626 Parliament, Laud assimilated this to the threat from Presbyterianism:

A parity they would have: no bishop, no governor . . . and they, whoever they be, that would overthrow sedes ecclesiae *. . . will not spare if they get the power to have a pluck at the throne of David. And there is not a man that is for parity – all fellows in the church – but he is not for monarchy in the state.*

Isaac Bargrave, in the context of the forced loan, accused them of fomenting resistance. They were those whose 'purity consists in parity, whose conscience in disobedience'. Matthew Wren went even further and branded them as potential regicides. In a sermon preached in the aftermath of

---

[144] Russell, *Unrevolutionary England*, p. 246.

[145] *The Papers which passed at Newcastle*, pp. 3, 38. For a similar view of the 'popular'/ puritan threat to the church see Charles's preface to the Canons of 1640: Laud, *Works*, vol. 5, pp. 610–11.

Buckingham's assassination, he described them as that 'most pernicious sect and dangerous to a monarch', who 'held the same tenet that their head fellow Felton doth, viz. that it is lawful to kill any man that is opposite to their party, and that all their whole doctrine and practice tends to anarchy'.[146] These were images that spoke to Charles's worst nightmares.

What is more difficult to discern is how far he also accepted Richard Montagu's line: that all predestinarian Calvinists could be assimilated to the subversive image of the puritan. One can find examples of doctrinal Calvinists whom he revered and respected. Perhaps the outstanding instance was his chaplain Robert Sanderson, of whom he is reputed to have said 'I carry my ears to hear other preachers, but I carry my conscience to hear Dr Sanderson.'[147] On the other hand, any suspicion of Calvinist zeal could be fatal to one's chances of winning royal favour. When the earl of Leicester found himself accused of puritanism by one of his enemies at court in the late 1630s, he compiled a long, self-justificatory memorandum for Charles. This basically argued that he could not be a puritan because he subscribed to 'the Christian faith established in the Church of England'. On precisely what this 'faith' consisted of he remained silent, and he carefully avoided any reference to his predestinarian beliefs. The implication would seem to be that this would not have helped his case with the king.[148]

Charles's attitude appears to have stemmed from an ambiguous approach to the doctrine of election. The view he generally expressed was that of his father: that this was something ordinary mortals should not attempt to delve into. It was part of God's mystery, beyond human comprehension and therefore best treated with an awed silence and respect.[149] He was also

---

[146] Laud, *Works*, vol. 1, pp. 82–3; Cust, *The Forced Loan*, p. 66; *Court and Times*, vol. 1, p. 410. Bargrave had been Charles's chaplain since 1622: *DNB*, 'Isaac Bargrave'.

[147] *DNB*, 'Robert Sanderson'; P.G. Lake, 'Serving God and the Times: the Calvinist conformity of Robert Sanderson', *JBS*, vol. 27, 1988, pp. 103–8. For the influence of Sanderson's *De Juramento* on his conscience, see below pp. 424–5.

[148] HMC, *Report on the De L'Isle and Dudley MSS*, vol. 6, 1955, pp. 355–8.

[149] See for example the views he expressed to Bishop Davenant in 1630: cited below pp. 123–4. This view was faithfully echoed by Laud in writing to Samuel Brooke in 1630 to discourage him from publishing a tract on predestination: 'I am yet where I was that somewhat about these controversies is unmasterable in this life', adding 'I do much doubt whether the king will take any man's judgement so far as to have these controversies any further stirred . . . ': Laud, *Works*, vol. 7, p. 275.

very conscious that allowing people to discuss such matters could only lead to division and turmoil. This was the justification for the ban on doctrinal debate in the June 1626 proclamation and a Declaration prohibiting further debate about predestination with which he prefaced a reissue of the Thirty-Nine Articles in late 1628. It also appears to have been the rationale behind his occasional and – on the face of it – somewhat surprising public condemnations of the 'Arminians'. Several times between 1628 and 1631 he went out of his way to make it clear that he would have no truck with either Arminians or Calvinists who tried to preach openly on the doctrine of predestination – and indeed that he regarded 'Arminians' as almost as disruptive an influence within the church as the puritans. It was this that produced the spectacle of Laud and Neile on their knees in council in May 1628 disavowing the opinions of Arminius, and which, as we shall see, opened up an opportunity for Calvinist councillors to secure a condemnation of Montagu in the winter of 1628–9.[150] What Charles meant by 'Arminians' is not clearly stated, but a reading of the June 1626 proclamation and the one issued in January 1629 to suppress Montagu's *Appello* suggests that he saw them as crypto-Catholic, aggressively polemical and expressing views that were incapable of being glossed in accord with the Thirty-Nine Articles.[151] It was the style and language that was being attributed to Montagu and others that Charles appears to have objected to, rather than the views themselves. He had no quarrel with the anti-predestinarian theology of grace, but he did not like it being expressed in ways that stirred up controversy and division.

Some of the implications of this position emerged at an important meeting at Woodstock in August 1631 when three Calvinist fellows from Oxford University were convented before Charles for preaching against Arminian views on predestination in defiance of his ban. During the hearing it became evident that rumours were circulating that while Calvinists at Oxford were being harassed, 'Arminians' were allowed to preach their views openly. Charles stepped in and ostentatiously insisted that equal 'diligence' be shown in bringing 'Arminians' to book, 'he having ever desired that those points should be forborne on both sides

---

[150] See below pp. 110–12.

[151] *Proclamation of Charles I*, pp. 90–3, 218–20.

and indifferently'.[152] This episode has persuaded Julian Davies that in doctrinal matters Charles was basically neutral, while Kevin Sharpe has gone further and argued that he was 'genuinely and impartially committed to unity'.[153] This may well have been what the king, in all sincerity, intended; but the end result was somewhat different. Like Andrewes and Laud – who expressed similar views on the need for silence[154] – he approached the whole issue of doctrine with a strong presumption in favour of the anti-Calvinist position. At the Woodstock hearing, the three Calvinist fellows were banished from the university and Dr Prideaux, the Calvinist Regius Professor of Divinity, was rapped over the knuckles for appearing to countenance their actions. This must have been just what Laud was hoping for when he had brought the matter to the king's attention. It sent an important message that while the king was ostensibly in favour of an even-handed approach, in practice some opinions were more unacceptable than others.[155] Another indication of where his sympathies lay was his indulgent attitude towards the court sermons of Robert Skinner during the 1630s. As Peter Lake has shown, these presented a clear statement of the Arminian position on predestination, denouncing Calvinist doctrine over issues such as perseverance and the limited nature of atonement, and asserting that Arminian teaching on the conditionality of God's will was doctrinal orthodoxy. Although Skinner dressed this up in a rhetoric of restraint and moderation, it still constituted a breach of the royal ban. However, in contrast to Bishop Davenant – who was slapped down when he preached a predestinarian sermon at court in 1630[156] – Skinner escaped royal censure and was rewarded with promotion to the bishopric of Bristol.[157] It seems that Charles was in fact guilty of applying a double standard in matters of doctrine. While making clear his disapproval of Calvinist preaching, he was prepared to allow Arminians a

---

[152] Bod. Lib., Jones MS 17, fo. 303.

[153] Davies, *The Caroline Captivity*, pp. 120–2; Sharpe, *The Personal Rule*, p. 283.

[154] Lake, 'Calvinism and the English church', pp. 73–4.

[155] Bod. Lib., Jones MS 17, fos. 307–9. For a very perceptive reading of this episode as a subtle exercise in public relations designed to counter accusations that the king's Declaration was being enforced in a biased fashion, see D. Como. 'Predestination and political conflict in London', *HJ*, vol. 46, 2003, pp. 264–5, 291–2.

[156] See below pp. 123–4.

[157] Fincham and Lake, 'Ecclesiastical policy of James and Charles', p. 40.

good deal of latitude.[158] This did not quite amount to a presumption that predestinarian Calvinists were potential puritans, but it came close.

On the positive side, Charles's approach to religion was shaped by a strong sense of the responsibilities inherent in his role as Defender of the Faith. For most of his subjects, this meant defending Protestant doctrine and resisting popery; for Charles it was mainly about restoring the Church of England to its former glories. His view was that the English Reformation had been 'perfected' in Elizabeth's time, when the church had 'come nearest to the purity of the primitive doctrine and discipline'; since then 'rites and ceremonies' had 'begun to fall into disuse' and through the influence of the puritans 'foreign and unfitting usages by little and little to creep in'. The task he set himself, as he explained in the preface to the Canons of 1640, was to ensure a 'return unto the true, former splendour of uniformity, devotion and holy order.'[159] His understanding of how this could be achieved – and indeed his vision of what the Elizabethan church had been like – appears to have been heavily influenced by his reading of Hooker and Andrewes and the tutelage he had received from Laud, Wren and others. Three aspects appear to have been of paramount concern: first, restoring 'rites and ceremonies' as the basis for religious practice in the church; second, upholding 'uniformity' and 'holy order' as a means of reforming society as a whole; and third, strengthening the position of the clergy and, in particular, the bishops.

When Laud became dean of the Chapel Royal in October 1626, he made a significant change to the nature of court services. The Jacobean practice of cutting off set prayers to proceed straight to a sermon on the entry of the king was abandoned and the liturgy was kept going through to the end. This was warmly approved by Charles. He liked sermons and listened to them regularly and attentively; but he appears to have shared Andrewes's view that they were less important than prayers or the eucharist in nurturing a saving faith. This was because listening to sermons was essentially

---

[158] As David Como points out, in the diocese of London no Arminian was ever questioned for preaching in breach of the ban: 'Predestination and political conflict', p. 289.

[159] *The Papers which passed at Newcastle*, pp. 17, 43; Laud, *Works*, vol. 5, pp. 610–11. See also his comments on the church in his 1629 Declaration of the reasons for dissolving parliament (*Constitutional Documents*, p. 89) and Tyacke, *Anti-Calvinists*, p. 239. Charles's determination to model himself on Elizabethan 'best practice' also came through in the household reforms he introduced soon after his accession: see below pp. 150–1.

passive, whereas prayer allowed the ordinary Christian to participate actively in worship, and the eucharist brought him into direct contact with the mystical body of Christ.[160] Charles took a deep personal interest in liturgical practice, writing his own prayers and making extensive corrections to one of the drafts of the Scottish prayerbook. He also set a much-praised example through the personal piety he displayed at services, Peter Heylyn declaring that 'his Majesty's religious observance in the house of God' was an 'excellent sermon' on 'decency and comeliness'.[161]

Another area of especial concern to the king was the architectural setting for worship. He shared the anti-Calvinists' respect for the church as the place where God was most obviously present and where everything was suffused with an aura of sanctity which could communicate itself to the worshipper. Hence his enthusiasm for the programme for 'beautifying' St Paul's, and his habit of inspecting cathedrals and parish churches while on progress and ordering changes in their layout and furnishings.[162] He was also supportive of the practice of moving communion tables to the east end, turning them 'altarwise' and railing them off, which constituted the most dramatic alteration to church interiors since the Reformation. Julian Davies has argued that Charles was, in effect, the author of this policy, setting an example with railed-off communion tables in the chapels royal from early in his reign and steering the anti-Calvinists towards the adoption of this policy more generally. Ken Fincham has demonstrated, however, that this is overstating the case. Charles wanted a placement of the communion table that would reflect the 'primitive' practice of the Elizabethan era, but he was initially somewhat confused over what this practice involved. As we shall see, at the hearing of the St Gregory's case in 1633 he appears to have believed that it meant upholding the 1559 Injunction to move the communion table into the chancel during the time of communion. He had to have it explained to him that, on the contrary, in 'the primitive church' the table was set in the position of the altar, which meant at the east end. Charles still appeared uncertain on this issue during the following year; however,

---

[160] McCullough, *Sermons at Court*, pp. 155–67; P.G. Lake, 'The Laudian style', in Fincham ed., *The Early Stuart Church*, pp. 164–80.

[161] Sharpe, 'Private conscience and public duty', pp. 654–5; Fincham and Lake, 'Ecclesiastical policies of James and Charles', pp. 42–3.

[162] Lake, 'The Laudian style', in Fincham ed., *The Early Stuart Church*, pp. 164–5; Fincham and Lake, 'Ecclesiastical policies of James and Charles', pp. 42–3.

by 1636 he had grasped the point of the railed-off, east end, altar and, having done so he embraced the new policy enthusiastically, not only on grounds of decency and order, but also as an expression of the centrality of the eucharist in the church's liturgy. By the late 1630s he was leading the way in the custom of going up to the rails and kneeling to receive communion.[163]

In promoting ceremonial, the king's concerns were not solely theological. He recognised that it could also help to instil order and deference into his people. Like most of his contemporaries, he took the view that church and commonwealth were inseparable. Order in one depended on order in the other, and without religious discipline and a formal liturgy it would be hard to maintain royal authority.[164] It was one of his principal objections to Presbyterian services in Scotland that they contained no set prayers. 'Preachers and readers and ignorant schoolmasters', he observed, were simply allowed to pray extempore, and 'sometimes so ignorantly as it was a shame to all religion to have the Majesty of God so barbarously spoken unto, sometimes so seditiously that their prayers were plain libels, girding at sovereignty and authority'.[165] Much of the appeal of anti-Calvinism was that it encouraged just the opposite. As Tyacke puts it, 'against the incipient egalitarianism of Calvinism, Arminians stressed the hierarchical nature of both church and state in which the office not the holder was what counted'.[166] This was not just a feature of their preaching; it was also inherent in their services, which were believed to inculcate positive principles through the repetition of rituals of order, hierarchy and worship. Anti-Calvinist preachers regularly drew parallels between the effect of their liturgical practice and ceremonial at court. Richard Steward, clerk of the closet during the 1630s, observed that 'good carriage is as well a part of religion as civility . . . no less in the Temple than the court', while Fulke Roberts, compared bowing to the altar to paying respect to the chair of state.[167] These were comparisons that Charles

---

[163] Davies, *The Caroline Captivity*, pp. 20–1, 209–12; K. Fincham, 'The restoration of altars in the 1630s', *HJ*, vol. 44, 2001, pp. 926–7.

[164] For this view, see Sharpe's discussion of one of Charles's favourite works, Laud's conference with Fisher: *The Personal Rule*, pp. 288–9.

[165] *The Large Declaration*, p. 16; Russell, *Fall of the British Monarchies*, pp. 44–5.

[166] Tyacke, *Anti-Calvinists*, p. 246.

[167] Davies, *The Caroline Captivity*, pp. 18–19.

himself recognised and understood. Just as his reforms at court were intended to provide a model for ideal patterns of behaviour, so he envisaged the restored 'rites and ceremonies' of the church, particularly those relating to the eucharist, as helping to instil order and reverence into his people.[168]

Charles looked on the clergy as natural allies in this process. Partly this was for religious reasons. He appears to have accepted the anti-Calvinist line that they were entitled to more status and respect than ordinary mortals because they led the laity in worship.[169] But it was also because he recognised their broader role in guiding the people into the ways of order and sustaining the authority of the crown. This led him to make strenuous efforts to strengthen and regulate their position. In April 1626 he commissioned Laud, Harsnett and Morton to undertake a wide-ranging review of the state of the church, including the vexed question of impropriations, and at the same time rebuked the bishops as a whole for not speaking out more forcefully on such matters.[170] He followed this up by giving his backing to the clergy's efforts to increase their tithe revenue and supporting them in struggles with town corporations over jurisdictional rights.[171]

Charles was especially concerned with the bishops. Like his father, he believed in the doctrine of *iure divino* episcopacy. This was the idea that bishops had been established by Christ as the best possible form of church government and that their authority came directly from God. Although such a role might appear to challenge the royal supremacy, in practice bishops were always seen as subject to the power of the king because he alone could determine whether they had the right to exercise their authority. James clearly regarded the two offices as complementary and interdependent. When he thought he was dying in 1619 one of the main pieces of advice he gave to Charles was to respect the bishops as 'grave and wise men and the best companions to princes'.[172] Charles took this to heart. He

---

[168] For Charles's reforms at court, see below, pp. 149–52.

[169] Lake, 'Laudian style', pp. 174–80.

[170] Laud, *Works*, vol. 3, pp. 186–9.

[171] Fincham and Lake, 'Ecclesiastical policies of James and Charles', p. 41, 48; A. Foster, 'Church policies of the 1630s', in Cust and Hughes eds, *Conflict in Early Stuart England*, p. 208; C. Pattinson, 'Corporations, cathedrals and the crown: local dispute and royal interest in early Stuart England', *Hist.*, vol. 85, 2000, pp. 546–71.

[172] J.P. Sommerville, *Politics and Ideology in England 1603–40*, Harlow, 1986, pp. 208–11; Fincham, *Prelate as Pastor*, pp. 34–41.

displayed a close personal interest in the membership of the episcopal bench, promoting only those whom he knew personally; and he used the bishops to spearhead the ecclesiastical reforms of the 1630s, monitoring them closely by requiring annual reports on the state of their dioceses.[173] He also took extremely seriously the oath made at the time of his coronation to 'protect and defend' them to the uttermost of his power.[174] In the face of the later rebellions in Scotland and England, this was the one issue on which he steadfastly refused to compromise.

The full impact of what Nicholas Tyacke has described as the 'Arminian revolution' was not to be felt until the 1630s. But the die was cast with the displacement of Calvinism as the doctrinal orthodoxy in the opening months of the new reign. Charles's role in this was critical and it demonstrated one of the most striking features of his style of kingship – his refusal to compromise where he believed his conscience was engaged or his God-given royal authority was at stake. Whereas his father would probably have met the Calvinists halfway and accepted the relatively painless climbdown offered by Pembroke and Hall, Charles was determined not to concede. Each time he felt he was freed from the necessity to appease parliament, he would revert to his basic convictions and back the anti-Calvinists to the hilt. Over the course of his reign there was, perhaps, nothing he did that caused more damage to the peace and stability of his kingdoms.

---

[173] See below, pp. 135–6.

[174] Rushworth, vol. 1, pp. 200–1.

Chapter 3

The Personal Rule, 1629–1640

The Road to Personal Rule

The policy of rule without parliament was not dreamt up in 1629. Charles had been talking about 'new counsels' since 1626; and these had first become a serious possibility after the watershed assembly of 1614 when the Commons' intransigence over supply led James to dissolve parliament as a punishment. This had a profound effect on the political landscape. The whole future existence of parliaments was suddenly thrown into question – especially as 1614 was followed by James's own 'seven years' personal rule'. The king's councillors became divided between those who wanted him to go on ruling with parliaments and those who urged him to find money elsewhere; and the issue of popularity – and how far 'factious spirits' in the Commons constituted a threat to royal authority – was pushed up the political agenda.[1] However, if the Personal Rule was a possibility from the middle of James's reign, it still required several other things to happen before it became an established fact. The wartime conditions that made the crown so dependent on parliamentary subsidies had to change. The pro-parliament majority in council that continued to support a resummons, even in the difficult days of the forced loan, had to be reduced or, somehow, silenced.

---

[1] C.S.R. Russell, *The Addled Parliament of 1614: the Limits of Revision*, Reading, 1992, pp. 13, 25–6; A. Thrush, 'The personal rule of James I, 1611–20', in Cogswell, Cust and Lake eds, *Politics, Religion and Popularity*, pp. 84–102; Cust, 'Charles I, the privy council and the Parliament of 1628', pp. 27–8.

Above all, Charles himself had to be finally persuaded that meeting his people in parliament – as good kings were supposed to do – was no longer worth the risk. The 'Road to Personal Rule' is basically the story of how these preconditions fitted into place. This was not something that happened suddenly or as the result of any clearly defined decision. Rather, it came about by default, as the climate of opinion made it harder and harder to justify a parliament and opportunities for a successful meeting steadily slipped by.

To start with, the death of the duke looked like an opportunity for a fresh start with parliament. Writing in late September 1628, Viscount Dorchester reported a division of opinion among councillors about the prospects for the next session in January 1629. Some saw the assassination as increasing the chances of a successful meeting on the grounds of 'a presumed desire the parliament will have to make it appear by their fair and moderate proceeding their former distempers were rather personal than real, & that the cause . . . being taken away the effect should cease'. This would appear to have been the line being pushed by those councillors who from the beginning of the year had been so anxious to re-establish good relations with the subject. Certainly one of the earl of Pembroke's first thoughts when he heard of the assassination was that this raised hopes that the next session would 'see a happy agreement between [his Majesty] and his people'. On the other side, however, Dorchester detected a view that the assassination had unleashed dangerous popular forces. The people were being compared to 'a sea moved by tempest which though the wind be still doth not immediately calm'. On this account, the best remedy was 'a settled and constant form of government' that would allow the '*aegritudo* which is in men's minds' to disperse.[2] This was the tone of much of the comment in the pro-Spanish circles around Lord Treasurer Weston, and also among the anti-Calvinist leadership at court. Both had good reason to fear a parliament, since it was likely to revisit the changes in the church and direct its fire towards 'evil counsellors'.[3] For the time being, however, the political initiative lay with the moderates.

Across the broader political landscape in late 1628 there were a number of factors that encouraged optimism about the prospects for parliament. The

---

[2] NA, SP 16/117/83; 529/9.

[3] HMC, *Report on the MSS of H.D. Skrine*, 1887, p. 74; NA, SP 16/123/8.

first was the new power structure at court. Weston was firmly installed as first minister, backed by a solid phalanx of pro-Spanish courtiers, including Arundel and Bristol who had recently been restored to favour.[4] But it was clear that he enjoyed a much less dominant position than the duke. The king had decided, according to Dorchester, 'not to discharge himself so much of affairs upon any one man, but to take the main direction to himself, & leave others, every man, to the duty of his charge'.[5] This was apparent in September when, after busying himself with arrangements for the dispatch of the fleet, he hurried back to Whitehall and, unaided, took the important decision to postpone parliament. It was now the conventional wisdom that he was 'holding in his hands the total directory . . .'[6] This opened up what, for many, was the enticing prospect of a return to an Elizabethan style of court politics. The days of the single favourite would be over and there would be opportunities for different interest groups to push alternative policies with Charles as supreme arbiter. This new 'Elizabethanism' was described in Sir Robert Naunton's *Fragmenta Regalia*, which was written around this time, as the monarch ruling 'by faction and parties which [he]she both made, upheld and weakened as [his] her own great judgement advised'.[7]

---

[4] NA, 16/529/15, 17, 20; *CSP Ven. 1628–9*, pp. 394, 398.

[5] NA, SP 16/114/17.

[6] NA, SP 16/117/83.

[7] *Fragmenta Regalia*, ed. J. Cerovski, Washington, 1985, p. 41. Naunton's study of Elizabethan politics was put together in its final form c. 1633: ibid., pp. 25–6. Charles's own 'Elizabethanism' is a topic that would repay further investigation. It appears that he was strongly drawn to the myths and images of Elizabeth that were current in the 1620s. The two best documented examples of this are the appeal of Elizabeth's supposedly chaste and virtuous court and the attraction of the Hookerian image of Elizabeth's church, supposedly embodying the best of 'primitive doctrine and discipline' (see pp. 99, 150). But there was another version of Elizabeth that also exerted a strong appeal. This was the image of the 'politic' princess and heroic Protestant warrior that was presented in the 1625 English translation of William Camden's *Annals* and a treatise addressed to the privy council in January 1628 by Camden's friend and collaborator, Sir Robert Cotton. These works harked back to the triumphs of the Spanish Armada and the war against Spain when the queen, guided by sage and public-spirited councillors like Burghley, had won the hearts of her people through observing the rule of law and meeting regular parliaments: 'Introduction' and P. Collinson, 'William Camden and the anti-myth of Elizabeth: setting the mould?', in S. Doran and T. Freeman eds, *The Myth of Elizabeth*, Basingstoke, 2003, pp. 5–9, 81–5; Cogswell, *The Blessed Revolution*, pp. 96–7; Rushworth, vol. 1, pp. 467–72. This was the role that Charles and Buckingham had espoused as leaders of the patriot coalition in 1624–5, and it was the role the patriots were seeking to revive in 1628–9.

In this changed political world if anyone seemed likely to exert a personal influence over Charles it was the queen. The closeness of their relationship impressed all around and it was widely reported that she was his only 'favourite'. But court commentators were still not sure what to make of her. She was accessible and intelligent, and well equipped to build a following; however, she was still only 19 and some believed she was too frivolous and easily distracted to have a consistent impact.[8] No one was discounting her at this stage, but the main beneficiary of speculation about her influence was the earl of Carlisle. His wife, the redoubtable Lucy, was her closest English friend, and he himself was the obvious candidate to lead a queen's party at court. Throughout the autumn his friends were urging him to return home from his embassy to Savoy as quickly as possible. The hope was that he would come back to provide the sort of mature, pro-Protestant, counsel needed to counterbalance the suspect influence of Weston. But by the end of the year this had evaporated as the news leaked that he, himself, had turned Spanish.[9] The net result, however, was to direct attention to a more consistent and determined supporter of 'the Protestant cause', Pembroke.

The earl had been given a new lease of life by Buckingham's death. While the favourite still dominated at court, Pembroke often seemed diffident and hesitant, and there were reports during July that he was about to retire to the country and surrender his office of lord steward.[10] The assassination came not a moment too soon from his point of view and it was little wonder that he saw it as a providential deliverance, for himself as much as the country.[11] He was attending the king in Hampshire at the time and immediately threw himself into managing the preparations for Rochelle. He gratified Charles by working closely with Weston and it was soon being reported that 'he wins exceedingly upon the king's favour and was never out of his sight'. There were even rumours that he was about to be made

---

[8] *CSP Ven. 1628–9*, pp. 310–11; R.M. Smuts, 'The puritan followers of Henrietta Maria in the 1630s', *EHR*, vol. 93, 1978, pp. 27–8; HMC, *Skrine*, p. 165.

[9] R.E. Schreiber, *The First Carlisle*, Philadelphia, 1984, pp. 117–18; NA, SP 16/529/15,20; 118/14; 121/34,38; 122/58.

[10] HMC, *Cowper*, vol. 1, p. 359; *Letters of John Holles 1587–1637*, ed. P.R. Seddon, 3 vols., Thoroton Soc. Record Ser., xxxi, xxxv, xxxvi, 1975–83, vol. 3, p. 386.

[11] NA, SP 16/529/9.

the new lord admiral, which would have effectively put him in the position of commander-in-chief of the nation's forces.[12] A revitalised Pembroke, drawing on the high personal regard that Charles had for him, was an entirely credible candidate for the leadership of a new patriot coalition.

However, if this was to get off the ground there needed to be a reorientation of English foreign policy. Here the rapidly shifting situation offered hope for those who wanted England once again to concentrate its efforts on the war against Spain. Buckingham had died with two peace initiatives on the table. Of these, the negotiations with the Spanish at first looked the more likely to bear fruit. Endymion Porter had been dispatched to Madrid in August 1628 to push them along and at the beginning of October Charles wrote personally to the Abbé Scaglia thanking him for his role in the discussions and expressing his own desire to end the Spanish war.[13] However, progress was agonisingly slow and by December doubt was being cast on the whole scheme by the Spaniards' usual reluctance to link peace to the restoration of the Palatinate, and also by news that their treasure fleet had been seized by the Dutch.[14] This last event caused great excitement in London, with predictions that the Spanish war effort in northern Europe was about to collapse and fresh speculation about the benefits of the blue water policy which had long been favoured in patriot circles.[15]

At the same time as prospects for a Spanish treaty were on the wane, an agreement with the French appeared imminent. The main stumbling block had always been Charles himself who had repeatedly declared that he was honour bound to relieve the Huguenots at La Rochelle.[16] He stuck to this line through September and October, long after it became clear that it was virtually impossible for his fleet to clear a channel into the town. However, the Huguenots' surrender removed the main reason for him to

---

[12] *Court and Times*, vol. 1, p. 406; NA, 16/116/58; 121/38,52; *CSP Dom. 1628–9*, pp. 322, 333; HMC, *Skrine*, p. 165.

[13] Gardiner, *History of England*, vol. 6, pp. 333–4; Reeve, *Road to Personal Rule*, pp. 43–4, 52–3.

[14] Reeve, *Road to Personal Rule*, pp. 54–6; HMC, *Skrine*, pp. 163–4, 171–2; HMC, *Cowper*, vol. 1, p. 378; *CSP Ven. 1628–9*, p. 503.

[15] BL, Harl. MS 383, fos. 74–6; NAS, GD 406/1/11,134.

[16] On Charles's sense of the obligations of honour, see his instructions to Lindsey before the final attempt to relieve La Rochelle: NA, SP 16/118/6.

go on fighting. He continued to complain of French duplicity, and refused to offer any undertaking on the vexed question of the queen's household, but the way to a settlement now lay open. By 10 January 1629 the Venetian ambassador believed that a treaty had been secured and, with the encouragement of Dorchester the ambassador's thoughts were turning to rebuilding the 'common cause' against the Hapsburgs.[17]

If this was to happen, then the obvious contribution England could make would be to assist Christian of Denmark. The expeditionary force sent out under Sir Charles Morgan in 1627 had surrendered in April 1628 and further defeats left Denmark itself open to attack. Charles, who was always very conscious of his obligation to help his uncle, responded by dispatching an embassy in November with promises of aid and early in 1629 the privy council began making military preparations. If England did re-enter the war in Germany then this would create a fresh demand for subsidies and strengthen the hand of those seeking to work with parliament.[18]

The third reason for optimism about parliament's prospects was Charles himself. The indications are that during the autumn of 1628 he was taking very seriously the possibility of a 'new deal' with his people. One of those who picked up on this was the earl of Dorset. Dorset had previously been a robust opponent of a summons, but he had changed his mind to such an extent that he was now predicting the next parliament would be a great success. He based this on the demeanour of the king who was showing himself 'so capable of good counsel, so patient to hear truth, so loving justice, so discerning right and so zealously affecting the good of his people' that the coming session was set to be 'a day of jubilee . . . striking a covenant between sovereign and subject of continual peace and happiness'.[19] This could all have looked wildly optimistic were it not for the fact that on 27 November – three days after the earl wrote his letter – Charles summoned his councillors to an after-dinner meeting and told them of his desire to clear the way for 'a good proceeding in

---

[17] Gardiner, *History of England*, vol. 6, pp. 363–71; *CSP Ven. 1628–9*, pp. 397, 404, 430, 465, 488–91, 505; HMC, *Skrine*, p. 169.

[18] Gardiner, *History of England*, vol. 6, p. 346–7, 372; Reeve, *Road to Personal Rule*, pp. 41, 59; *CSP Ven. 1628–9*, p. 432.

[19] NA, SP 16/529/40. For Dorset's previous attitude to parliaments, see Cust, *The Forced Loan*, pp. 29, 77.

parliament'. 'He knew', he said, that 'the Commons would first begin with religion' and that there were two particular issues that 'they would stumble at, the papists and Arminians'. In the case of the papists, 'he would have them all turned out of office and out of commission unless they would conform'; as for the Arminians, 'he would have the bishops about the town compare them with the book of articles and to condemn all such tenets as were not agreeable thereunto'. He then entrusted the whole matter to a council committee, consisting of four members of the House of Lords and four from the Commons.[20]

This was a highly significant initiative. On no previous occasion had Charles invited his councillors to engage in organised discussion of the concessions needed to appease a forthcoming parliament. Yet here he was giving them a specific mandate to meet in committee and come up with ways to remedy the subjects' grievances. Perhaps most strikingly, he was encouraging them to come forward with initiatives on religion, an area of policy making that he had previously kept to himself, Buckingham and a few select bishops.[21] Charles's willingness to allow the moderates to act freely may have had something to do with the persuasive powers of Pembroke. The earl had written to Carlisle the previous day in a state of high optimism about the prospects for the session; and as soon as Charles had finished speaking on the 27th he rose to declare that this was 'a princely resolution' and 'he was no good subject that durst oppose it'.[22] But it also seems likely that he had been caught up in the buoyant mood of Dorset's letter. He was still young and impressionable, and anxious to prove himself a good king which, according to conventional wisdom, meant being seen to promote the welfare of his people. The idea of what Dorset called 'new courses & new resolutions' was very appealing.

Over the following weeks, councillors devoted considerable time and energy to their preparations.[23] The main focus of activity was religion.

---

[20] BL, Harl. MS 383, fos. 72–3; *Barrington Letters*, p. 38.

[21] Privy councillors had, of course, been involved in discussions about religion at the York House Conference, but in a much more passive role.

[22] NA, SP 16/121/66; BL, Harl. MS 383, fos. 72–3.

[23] For more detail on these preparations and the politics of this period, see R.P. Cust, 'Was there an alternative to the Personal Rule? Charles I, the Privy Council and the 1629 Parliament', *Hist.*, vol. 90, 2005, pp. 330–44.

Working in tandem with Archbishop Abbot, who was restored to favour in early December, they set out to overturn the Caroline church settlement by producing a statement of doctrine that could be glossed as a condemnation of Arminianism. The key to this lay in exploiting Charles's willingness to make concessions in the run-up to the parliament and his desire to silence controversy. In a half-hidden, but highly significant struggle with the anti-Calvinist bishops, they achieved considerable success.

The first round went to the anti-Calvinists. After extensive discussion in council committee, followed by a meeting of the bishops at Lambeth, it was decided to reissue the Thirty-Nine Articles accompanied by a lengthy Declaration in the king's name. This said that everyone should accept the articles as the standard statement of the church's doctrine and that henceforth all 'curious search' or 'dispute' as to their meaning should be abandoned and they should be understood in their 'literal and grammatical sense'.[24] The aim of the Declaration was to silence controversy on the doctrine of predestination in the same way as had been attempted in the June 1626 proclamation. The problem was that the 'literal and grammatical sense' of the articles was left undefined, which, on the basis of past experience, suggested they would be interpreted in a way that suited the anti-Calvinists. The Calvinist councillors, however, were not deterred and turned things round at the second attempt. Following up on an initiative taken by Attorney-General Heath, at the start of October, they put considerable pressure on Richard Montagu to withdraw the views he had expressed in his *Appello Caesarem*. The matter was being discussed during November when an aggrieved Montagu was informed by Laud that 'his great friends at court would take no blows for him'.[25] At the start of December he caved in and wrote a letter to Abbot in which he was reported to have disowned the *Appello*, subscribed to the Synod of Dort and rejected 'the five tenets of Arminianism touching predestination, general grace, freewill etc.'. The whole climbdown appears to have been arranged without Charles being consulted, but it had the desired result in that on 17 January 1629, just three days before the parliament, a proclamation appeared in which the *Appello* was identified as 'the first cause of these disputes and differences',

---

[24] For the text of this Declaration, see Gardiner, *History of England*, vol. 6, pp. 21–2.

[25] G. Ornsby ed., *The Correspondence of John Cosin*, Surtees Soc., vol. 53, 1868–72.

and the order was given for it to be suppressed.[26] Appearing so close to the reissue of the Thirty-Nine Articles, this ensured that the immediate gloss put on these would be in favour of the Calvinists, which was precisely what Abbot and his allies had been working for.

The moderate councillors' platform, however, was not confined to religion. There is evidence in an undated set of propositions, drawn up by Heath, of an intention to establish a wide-ranging partnership with the subject.[27] It suggested a series of legal initiatives designed to offer reassurance about the king's willingness to abide by the rule of law. Care was to be taken 'that the king's gracious and royal answer to the Petition of Right, in the true and right understanding thereof, be not broken'; and an attempt was made to defuse the explosive issue of tonnage and poundage.

This had become a problem initially because Charles's first parliament tried to use confirmation of the grant – which in previous reigns had been automatic – to secure parliamentary control over impositions. There was insufficient time to complete the negotiations and, as a result, the king was left with having to collect customs duties without the support of parliamentary statute. This worked until 1627 when London merchants started to use non-renewal of the grant as an excuse for evading payment of duties. The whole issue was discussed again in the 1628 Parliament, but this simply increased the divisions. The Commons renewed its complaints about impositions, investigated the recent Book of Rates and eventually condemned tonnage

---

[26] BL, Harl. MS 383, fos. 77–8, 80–1; *Court and Times*, vol. 1, p. 449; vol. 2, pp. 2–3. 'A Proclamation for the suppressing of a Booke intituled *Appello Caesarem, or An Appeale to Caesar', Proclamations of Charles I*, pp. 218–20. A letter from Sir John Coke to Abbot at this time implies that Montagu's recantation was the result of an arrangement between him and the privy council: BL, Add. MS 64, 898, fo. 38.

[27] L.J. Reeve, 'Sir Robert Heath's advice for Charles I in 1629', *BIHR*, vol. 59, 1986, pp. 215–24. John Reeve has ascribed this memorandum to the period after the dissolution of the parliament; but it makes more sense as a contribution to the debates that preceded it. It appears to have been drawn up between 27 November 1628 when Charles gave the go-ahead for the council to prepare for the parliament and 10 January 1629 when the council drew up detailed proposals for guarding the seas as suggested in the memorandum. Dorchester may have been referring to these proposals when he told Carlisle on 19 December 1628 that 'all things by his Majesty's personal order in council, as well in church and commonwealth, are provisionally so disposed that he may hope for a fair and loving meeting with his people': *Court and Times*, vol. 2, p. 2; see also Sir Robert Aiton's description of these discussions: NA, SP 16/122/58.

and poundage as a breach of the Petition of Right. Charles then raised the stakes by declaring that it was 'a flower of my crown, without which I neither may nor can subsist'. Following the parliament, merchants of the East India and Levant companies mounted a tax strike and, after one of their number had been imprisoned for complaining that merchants 'are in no part of the world so screwed and wrung as in England', smuggling and refusal to pay duties became widespread. In November 1628 the Barons of the Exchequer sought to calm the situation down by giving assurances that the whole issue would be settled in the coming parliament where they had 'no doubt but that there would be a perfect agreement between king and subject'.[28] Heath's proposals sought to build on this by ordering customs officials 'not to provoke any by harsh or indiscreet words or acts'. But neither intervention appears to have had much impact, and settling the whole issue had become a matter of the utmost urgency, not least because the crown's income was being seriously eroded.

A further section of Heath's proposals related to foreign policy. There was a suggestion that steps be taken to guard the narrow seas, protect trade and establish the king's sovereignty, which bore fruit in council proposals of 12 January 1629 to assign five naval squadrons for this purpose.[29] More intriguingly, there was also a proposal that 'such as would adventure to the sea by letters of marque' be allowed a reduction in the duties paid on any goods seized in order to encourage them 'by the hope of gain'. This appears to have been a response to the excited talk in November of huge profits to be made out of privateering and the seizure of Spanish treasure. If adopted, it could have provided a shot in the arm for the blue water policy and helped to relaunch war against Spain. Pembroke may have had something like this in mind when he wrote to Carlisle in late November of his hopes for 'the beginning of raising again our lost honour'.[30]

What Heath's memorandum offered, then, was the agenda for a new patriot coalition in which, in return for supply, councillors would deliver assurances about the liberties of the subject and the defence of Calvinist

---

[28] L.S. Popofsky, 'The crisis over Tonnage and Poundage in parliament in 1629', *P & P*, vol. 126, 1990, pp. 51–61; Gardiner, *History of England*, vol. 7, pp. 2–6; BL, Harl. MS 383, fos. 72–3.

[29] HMC, *Cowper*, vol. 1, pp. 378–9.

[30] NA, SP 16/121/66.

orthodoxy, and also begin the process of relaunching the war in support of the Protestant cause. The king had already given tacit approval to parts of this. The patriots' hope was that the momentum provided by a successful parliament would persuade him to go along with the rest. The problem was that the political mood of the moment was against them.

Since the late summer, public opinion, particularly in London, had become increasingly restive. This was partly a consequence of the merchants' resistance over tonnage and poundage, but more particularly of the continuing agitation caused by the assassination of the duke. Felton was not tried and executed until late November and in the meantime he was hailed as a Protestant hero and there was much talk of taking revenge on the enemies of the people. In such a frenetically polarised atmosphere, there was little chance of appeals to the middle ground making much headway.[31] On top of this, the 'parliament men' had become extremely frustrated at the apparent ineffectiveness of the measures they had taken in 1628. Their thoughts were directed not towards the council's carefully leaked proposals for accommodation, but the evidence that Charles was flouting the provisions of the Petition of Right and sabotaging their efforts to punish leading Arminians. This was to produce a degree of hostility during the parliament that royal servants had rarely experienced before and provide fertile ground for Sir John Eliot's calls to safeguard privileges and strike down evil counsellors.[32]

The difficulties faced by councillors became apparent almost as soon as the session started on 20 January 1629. Their first priority was to make headway over tonnage and poundage and, in keeping with the mood at court, Charles tried to settle the matter in as inoffensive a manner as possible. Four days into the parliament, he summoned the Lords and Commons to the Banqueting House at Whitehall and told them that he wished 'to remove all obstacles that may hinder the good correspondency betwixt me and this parliament'. He assured them that his intention at the last meeting had not

---

[31] On the mood in London around the time of the trial, see A. Bellany, ' "The Brytnes of the Noble Lieutenant's Action": an intellectual ponders Buckingham's assassination', *EHR*, vol. 118, 2003, pp. 1242–63 and his unpublished paper on ' "The Enigma of the World": mourning and memorializing the duke'. I am grateful to Alistair Bellany for alerting me to the consequences of this mood for the parliament. On the agitation over tonnage and poundage, see *Court and Times*, vol. 2, pp. 5–6.

[32] Russell, *Parliaments and English Politics*, pp. 396–7, 412–13.

been to claim customs duty as his 'hereditary prerogative', but merely to demonstrate 'the necessity . . . by which I was to take it until you had granted it to me'. He then asked them to pass the bill for tonnage and poundage 'as my ancestors have had it' – which would 'put an end to all the questions arising from this subject' by giving retrospective authorisation for his actions – and, at the same time, confirm the principle that customs were paid by the consent of parliament. The tone was very different from Charles's pronouncements at the end of the 1628 Parliament. He was doing his best to offer a way out of the whole impasse and was explicitly setting aside any claim that the levy was his by right. But the Commons refused to follow his lead. Its overriding concern was to hold the crown accountable for the undertakings given in the last parliament and pursue what it took to be a series of breaches of good faith. On the second day of the meeting, it had uncovered the disturbing story of the second printing of the Petition of Right and promptly set up a committee to investigate. The next day it began to explore the seizure of merchants' goods by customs officials, which quickly turned into an issue of parliamentary privilege. As a result, when Secretary Coke proposed that they read the bill for tonnage and poundage he got short shrift and the house voted instead to concentrate on Arminianism.[33]

Conrad Russell has written as if this doomed the parliament to failure because it diverted attention from the issue that mattered most for Charles.[34] However, this fails to recognise that such a move was playing to the patriots' strength since they had already taken steps to deal with the problem. It was possible to visualise a situation in which having helped to put in place a statute that bolstered Calvinism the council lobby would be able to return to tonnage and poundage with enhanced credibility. The biggest difficulty was likely to be persuading Charles to accept this. But in late January he still appeared to be more or less on board. The message delivered to the Commons on the 28th, after he had heard that they would not be proceeding with tonnage and poundage was, by his standards, remarkably restrained. He told the house that as long as they handled religion 'with moderation

---

[33] *Commons Debates 1629*, pp. 10–11; C. Thompson, 'The divided leadership of the House of Commons in 1629', in K. Sharpe ed., *Faction and Parliament*, Oxford, 1978, pp. 251–2; Russell, *Parliaments and English Politics*, p. 403.

[34] Russell, *Parliaments and English Politics*, p. 408.

and meddle not with what belongs to his Majesty', he would be 'ready to receive any notice therein from us of anything whereof consideration hath not been already taken'.[35] This was as much of a green light as the patriots could reasonably hope for.

The initiative in pushing for a religious settlement came from John Pym and Sir Nathaniel Rich who throughout this session appear to have been acting in concert with the main council spokesmen, Coke, Sir Humphrey May and Sir Benjamin Rudyerd.[36] Their aim was to set up the Thirty-Nine Articles as an unimpeachable standard of doctrinal orthodoxy, fit to stand alongside the Petition of Right. The problem with this – as councillors had recognised – was that it was hard to guarantee that the articles would always be understood in a Calvinist sense since interpretation was ultimately in the hands of the bishops. One intriguing way round the problem – suggested by the Commons committee on religion – was for all bishops to be appointed with the advice of the privy council. But the solution finally arrived at was to establish an unambiguous link between the formularies of faith contained in the Thirty-Nine Articles, the Lambeth Articles of 1595, the Irish Articles of 1615 and the resolutions at Dort by giving them all statutory confirmation. This would have reinstated Calvinism as the orthodoxy of the Church of England.[37] However, the scheme failed when MPs became embroiled in trying to decide what should or should not be given statutory authority and then became diverted into an investigation of Arminian evil counsellors. This was an easier issue for the house to tackle, but it undercut the whole strategy of the councillors, which was to avoid witch-hunts – something that could only upset Charles – and concentrate on the doctrinal settlement.[38]

After a couple of weeks the religious debate lost impetus and the lower house returned to the issue of tonnage and poundage. This was another

---

[35] *Commons Debates 1629*, p. 113.

[36] The evidence for this is discussed more fully in Cust, 'Was there an alternative to the Personal Rule?' and Thompson, 'Divided leadership', pp. 249–50, 254–60, 263–70.

[37] Thompson, 'Divided leadership', pp. 255–62; Russell, *Parliaments and English Politics*, pp. 406–12. For the proposal on bishops, see *Commons Debates 1629*, p. 100.

[38] Just how counter-productive the Commons' pursuit of evil counsellors was is illustrated by the fact that their enquiries led them into hounding Heath and Dorchester, two of their main council allies against the Arminians: *Commons Debates 1629*, pp. 39–40.

chance for the patriots to make a success of the assembly. Pym and Rich, supported by the council lobby, urged the house to look again at the king's bill and accept it as a way of resolving the whole complicated issue by giving retrospective statutory authorisation for his actions. However, they came up against Eliot's determination to punish those responsible for the illegal collection of duties, and the anxieties MPs had about defending their privileges. The discussion eventually resolved itself into the question of how to deal with those customs officials who had collected duties illegally and impounded merchants' goods. The Commons was determined to punish them in order to vindicate its privileges, but this quickly ran into the difficulty that the officials claimed to be acting under royal warrant, which meant further proceedings would lead to a confrontation with the crown. An ingenious way round this was found by declaring that the officers had in fact seized goods for their own profit and thereby exceeded their warrant. Had Charles been prepared to accede to this – and thus demonstrate the sincerity of his earlier assurances – this might have paved the way for a successful vote on the tonnage and poundage bill. However, any hopes were dashed by his tendency to see attacks on his servants as challenges to his own honour. In a message on 23 February that was read out twice by Secretary Coke, he insisted that

what these men did they did it by his express command or by the council board, he being by in person or directing; that this can not be divided from his own act and that there be no proceeding against them as highly concerning his honour.[39]

The house was stunned by the bluntness of the response. A decision was taken to adjourn proceedings until 25 February; then another adjournment was ordered by the king until 2 March.

In the meantime, there were covert negotiations for a compromise which, according to the Venetian ambassador, broke down on the intransigence of the two sides. The Commons' leaders insisted that the customs officials be punished for breaching parliamentary privilege, while Charles was adamant that if he set a precedent by abandoning his servants 'none

---

[39] *Commons Debates 1629*, pp. 236–7; Popofsky, 'Tonnage and poundage', pp. 64–8; Thompson, 'Divided leadership', pp. 262–70, 275, 280–1.

would ever obey him again'.[40] This led to the ugliest parliamentary scenes of the decade when the house reassembled on 2 March. The speaker, Sir John Finch, announced a further adjournment at the king's command until 10 March and then tried to rise to end the sitting. As he did so, Denzil Holles and Benjamin Valentine forced him back into his chair so that Eliot could read out a declaration condemning Weston for wishing to 'break parliaments' and Bishop Neile for promoting Arminianism. It then proposed that anyone who supported 'innovation in religion', or who advised the collection of tonnage and poundage, or who even so much as paid the levy, 'shall be reputed a capital enemy to the kingdom and commonwealth'.[41] Although Eliot requested that his resolutions be communicated to the king, they were really directed to the people. Like the Grand Remonstrance of 1641, they had what Russell describes as the 'potentially revolutionary' aim of 'appealing over the king's head to the country at large'. The most remarkable thing about this act of defiance was that it had the support of most of the MPs present. The Commons had apparently moved beyond the point where it could cooperate with even the most moderate of councillors. There was a real sense – previously only apparent at the Oxford session of 1625 and the worst moments of 1626 – that they were divided between two sides and could no longer serve both king and country.[42]

Even after Eliot's act of defiance on 2 March there were councillors who continued to urge 'gentleness', but the debate was won by Weston and Laud. They had been keeping their heads down for much of the parliament, but now seized the opportunity to revive talk of 'popularity' and threats to royal authority. On 4 March Charles issued a proclamation announcing parliament's dissolution and at the same time nine of the ringleaders of the demonstration were arrested. Sir Thomas Roe, one of the patriot councillors' principal allies, wrote of the sense of disappointment over the Commons' intransigence and gloomily predicted that the 'parliament doors [would be] sealed for many years'.[43] No less frustrated, probably, was Charles himself.

---

[40] *CSP Ven. 1628–9*, pp. 579–80.

[41] *Commons Debates 1629*, pp. 258–61; *Constitutional Documents*, pp. 82–3; Thompson, 'Divided leadership', pp. 270–3.

[42] Russell, *Parliaments and English Politics*, pp. 415–16, 397, 412–13.

[43] *CSP Ven. 1628–9*, p. 580; Reeve, *Road to Personal Rule*, pp. 81–2; L.J. Reeve, 'Sir Thomas Roe's prophecy of 1629', *BIHR*, vol. 56, 1983, pp. 120–1.

He had made a real effort to get the parliament to work, and right up to the final stages was offering to trade further concessions on religion for passage of the tonnage and poundage bill. His sense of being let down was all the greater, because he had been trying so hard to promote a 'new deal'. In these circumstances, he quickly reverted to a familiar explanation of the causes of breakdown. The fault, he told the House of Lords at the formal dissolution on 10 March, lay not with a majority of MPs who were 'as dutiful subjects as any in the world', but with 'some few vipers that did cast the mist of undutifulness over most of their eyes'.[44] This analysis was extended and developed in a declaration published a few days later.

His majesties declaration of the causes which moved him to dissolve the last parliament is one of the most revealing political statements to survive from this period. Charles probably did not write it himself. His normal method was to delegate the drafting of declarations, proclamations, signet letters and other royal statements to trusted servants, often his secretaries of state; but he would then carefully read and vet them as his interlinings on numerous documents testify. On one occasion he confided to his clerk of the signet, Sir Philip Warwick, that 'he would willingly make his own dispatches but that he found it better to be a cobbler than a shoemaker'. He also told Warwick that of all his secretaries, Dorchester was the most in tune with his thinking: he 'ever brought me my own sense in my own words'. Dorchester may well have penned the 1629 *Declaration*, but it also very clearly reflected Charles's own views; and it can tell us much about his thinking at a critical turning point in the reign.[45]

Throughout the *Declaration*, emphasis was given to the king's moderation and willingness to abide by tradition and precedent. There were reminders that he had allowed the Commons considerable latitude in debating its grievances in 1628, and since then had made numerous concessions over religion and offered an eminently reasonable settlement of tonnage and poundage. With some justification, he expected that 'according to the candour and sincerity of our own thoughts . . . men would have framed themselves for the effecting of a right understanding between us and our

---

[44] *LJ*, vol. 4, p. 43.

[45] *Warwick Memoirs*, pp. 70, 72; Sharpe, *The Personal Rule*, pp. 201–2. We know that Dorchester drafted the proclamation about parliament on 27 March which was amended and corrected by Charles: Reeve, *Road to Personal Rule*, pp. 106–12.

people'. Instead, he had been confronted by 'turbulent and ill affected spirits' who rejected the bill for tonnage and poundage, turned legitimate concern about religion into 'a plausible theme to deprave our government' and intimidated 'the sincerer and better part of the house' with the demonstration on 2 March. Just as disturbingly, their 'spirit' had become 'infused' into the political nation as a whole. The people were being stirred up by 'rumours and jealous fears', the merchants were encouraged to increase their resistance to the payment of duties and even local subsidy commissioners were reluctant to make proper assessments. Their behaviour had transgressed the bounds of what any reasonable ruler could tolerate, particularly in their questioning of judges and royal officials. 'Their drift was to break, by this means, through all respects and ligaments of government and to erect an universal over-swaying power to themselves, which belongs only to us and not to them.' Any suggestion that this was simply a result of having been provoked by the duke of Buckingham was nonsense.

Now it is manifest the duke was not alone the mark these men shot but was only as a near minister of ours taken up on the by and in their passage to their more secret designs which were only to cast our affairs into a desperate condition, to abate the powers of our crown and to bring our government into obloquy that in the end all things may be overwhelmed with anarchy and confusion.[46]

The only sensible response to all this was a period of calm reflection in which royal authority could be re-established and the effects of the turmoil allowed to subside. Meanwhile, as Charles announced in a proclamation of 27 March, 'we shall account it presumption for any to prescribe any time unto us for parliaments'.[47]

The *Declaration* demonstrated the full extent of Charles's disillusionment after the events of 2 March. It appeared that once and for all his eyes had been opened to the scope of the Commons' challenge to royal authority and his faith in the assembly had been definitively undermined. It also did much to shape the direction of future policy. This was one of the most effective exercises in royal propaganda of the entire reign, seizing on a moment

---

[46] *Constitutional Documents*, pp. 83–99.

[47] *Proclamations of Charles I*, pp. 226–8.

when most political observers felt that the Commons had overreached itself and presenting an analysis that was both coherent and compelling. It relied for its impact on feeding anxieties about 'turbulent spirits' and 'false rumours' which were part of the increasingly familiar discourse about the evils of 'popularity'; and it drew readers to the obvious conclusion that if 'anarchy and confusion' were to be averted it would be better if, for the time being, parliament did not meet.[48] This helped to create a climate of opinion in which even the instinctively moderate Viscount Dorchester was drawn into adopting the rhetoric of conspiracy and disobedience and became, in John Reeve's words, 'a fellow traveller for new counsels'.[49] For the time being, the prospects for a new parliament were very bleak.

During the latter part of 1629 and early 1630 government decision-making took place in an atmosphere of perpetual crisis. Dearth, unemployment in the cloth trade and rioting in London, Essex and the West Country led to fears of a collapse of social order; the discovery of an absolutist tract in the library of Sir Robert Cotton resulted in the trial of several leading peers for supposedly defaming Charles's government; the circulation of a series of inflammatory sermons and libels asserting that the suppression of predestinarian doctrine heralded a descent into tyranny brought limitations on Calvinist preaching; and even such a mundane matter as quarrels within the corporation of Great Yarmouth provoked alarm about 'popular' challenges to hierarchy. Above all there was the problem of how to deal with the imprisoned MPs whose defiance was thought to be encouraging all sorts of opposition, especially from the merchants who were persisting with their tax strike.[50] In these circumstances, royal policy became markedly

---

[48] For reactions to the dissolution and the *Declaration*, see Sharpe, *The Personal Rule*, pp. 55–6; *The Diary of John Rous*, ed. M.A. Everett Green, Camden Soc., 1st ser., lxvi, 1856, pp. 36, 39–40. The evils of popularity were a prominent theme in two important political treatises written around this time by gentlemen closely connected to the court: Sir Robert Filmer's *Patriarcha* (on which see Robert Filmer, *Patriarcha and Other Writings*, ed. J.P. Sommerville, Cambridge, 1991, pp. viii, x, xxxii–iv, 24–33) and Francis Kynaston's 'A True Presentation of Forepast Parliaments' (on which see E.S. Cope, *Politics Without Parliaments 1629–1640*, 1987, pp. 27–8).

[49] Reeve, *Road to Personal Rule*, p. 163.

[50] B. Sharp, *In Contempt of All Authority*, Berkeley, chps. 2–4; Reeve, *Road to Personal Rule*, pp. 115–16, 158–64; R.P. Cust, 'Anti-puritanism and urban politics: Charles I and Great Yarmouth', *HJ*, vol. 35, 1992, pp. 1–26.

harsher and more arbitrary. Charles's priority was to make an example of the prisoners by dealing with them as severely as possible. This was supported by Weston, and probably other councillors opposed to a parliament, such as Laud; however, there remained a majority, led by Pembroke and Dorchester, who were committed to upholding good relations with the people. The principal difficulty for the moderates remained how to strike the right balance. They had to go along with stern measures in order to convince Charles that the prerogative was secure, in spite of all the talk of 'popular' conspiracy. At the same time they had to try to reassure the public that they were willing to act within the law, even when denying prisoners the bail to which they were entitled under the terms of the Petition of Right.[51]

In the event, this proved largely beyond them. Ingenious efforts to persuade the detainees to accept bail under royal letters patent – so that this could be made to appear an act of prerogative, without invoking the Petition of Right – failed because they recognised what was going on and refused to make the necessary submission. The trial itself proved difficult to manage because of uncertainty about how best to defeat the prisoners' defence of parliamentary privilege. Eventually judgement was passed in King's Bench in February 1630 and Eliot, Holles and Valentine were incarcerated at the royal pleasure with no prospect of release until they had submitted and paid hefty fines. By this stage, too, the merchants' resistance to tonnage and poundage had largely fizzled out and the customs revenues were starting to pick up. However, in the interim, the public spotlight had been focused more or less continuously on the MPs' plight, which aroused concern that the crown was disregarding the spirit if not the letter of the Petition of Right. Just as damagingly, Charles himself proved very difficult to restrain and began to act as arbitrarily as he had done during the forced loan. He bullied the judges, dismissing Chief Justice Walter when he delivered the opinion that prosecution of the MPs could be blocked by the plea of parliamentary privilege; he quite cynically subverted efforts to hear the prisoners' bail application in King's Bench by moving them overnight to the Tower of London; and he hounded Eliot with a vindictiveness that suggested deep personal spite. His relatives were even refused permission to take his body back to Port Eliot after he died in 1632.

---

[51] Reeve, *Road to Personal Rule*, pp. 117, 132–4.

The sourness and distrust so apparent in the 1629 Parliament had, if anything, become more pronounced.[52]

This was not helped by developments in the church. The hounding
of Arminian supporters during the second and third weeks of the 1629
Parliament had reminded Charles why he so disliked Calvinists and once
the session had ended he ran true to form and turned against them. In April
1629, his irritation over the sermons on predestination and the activities
of puritan ministers who 'seditiously divulge that religion doth totter' led
to an order to punish any preacher who tried to suggest that there had been
'innovation or alteration in religion'. This was the ecclesiastical equivalent
of the measures taken to deal with 'popular' MPs, and the two threats were
seen as closely linked.[53] Then in December new royal instructions were issued
to the clergy, the main effect of which was to restrict Calvinist preaching.
Stipendiary lectureships, financed by town corporations, were to be suppressed;
ordinary lecturers were required to read the liturgy before preaching and to
substitute catechising for their afternoon sermons; and the ban on discussing
controversial doctrine was reiterated.[54]

This last point was made even more forcibly in March 1630 when Bishop
Davenant sought to test the water at court by preaching a predestinarian
sermon. He was immediately told that 'his Majesty was much displeased
that [he] had stirred this question' and treated to a dressing down in front
of the council by Samuel Harsnett, the anti-Calvinist archbishop of York.
The following day, when he went to seek the king's pardon, Charles told
him in no uncertain terms that

*he would not have this high point meddled withal or debated either one way
or the other, because it was too high for the people's understanding; and other
points which concern reformation and newness of life were more needful and
profitable.*[55]

---

[52] Ibid., pp. 115–56; Gardiner, *History of England*, vol. 7, pp. 109–119; Quintrell, *Charles I*,
p. 44.

[53] NA, SP 16/140/37. On the association with parliament, see the king's comments to
Chateauneuf in August 1629: cited below, p. 132.

[54] Davies, *The Caroline Captivity*, pp. 27–31; Fincham and Lake, 'Ecclesiastical policies of
James and Charles', pp. 40–1.

[55] Fuller, *Life, Letters and Writings of John Davenant*, pp. 311–13.

Davenant and his friends interpreted this as a clear indication that a Calvinist reading of the 1628 Declaration would no longer be acceptable. From this point onwards they became very wary of speaking out about doctrine in public.[56] The final blow was the death of Pembroke in April 1630. Not only did this remove arguably the most effective coordinator of resistance to the anti-Calvinists, it also opened the way for Laud to become chancellor of Oxford University where he quickly imposed the same restrictions on predestinarian preaching as had long since applied at Cambridge.[57] By the summer of 1630 the direction of the church had been fixed for the remainder of the decade and the anti-Calvinist takeover was assured.

In spite of the attention given to domestic matters, however, the crucial question of whether or not to resummon parliament hinged on developments in foreign policy. Here the main priority remained recovery of the Palatinate. There was a division of opinion as to how this could best be achieved. Supporters of the Protestant cause argued that the best course of action was to draw closer to the Dutch and French, and negotiate while threatening the Hapsburgs with war. Within such a strategy, parliament had a crucial role, because a successful meeting would lend credibility to the war effort and increase diplomatic pressure. However, this approach was resisted by the peace lobby who placed all their faith in closer ties with Spain. As usual, the final arbiter was Charles himself and he opted decisively for peace and Spanish friendship, thereby inaugurating a shift in policy that was in many ways as dramatic as the original 'Blessed Revolution' of 1623–4.[58]

Charles's approach was shaped in part by personal sentiment. He shared his father's dislike of the Calvinist, republican Dutch, while past dealings with the 'false inconstant Monsieurs' made him disinclined to enter any new alliance with the French. By contrast, he had enormous respect for the Spanish, with their *gravitas* and instinctive sense of honour and hierarchy.[59] He was also influenced by the increasing power of the peace lobby at court.

---

[56] Lake, 'Calvinism and the English church', pp. 64–6.

[57] Tyacke, *Anti-Calvinists*, pp. 78–82.

[58] Reeve, *Road to Personal Rule*, pp. 52–7, 229–38.

[59] S. Adams, 'Foreign policy and the Parliaments of 1621 and 1624', in Sharpe ed., *Faction and Parliament*, pp. 141, 149; Adams, 'Spain or the Netherlands', pp. 88–90. For Charles's respect for the Spanish, see also below p. 150.

Weston and the chancellor of the exchequer, Sir Francis Cottington, were able to control much of the advice he received on foreign affairs; and they were consistently supported by Laud, Wentworth, the earl of Arundel and more minor figures with close personal ties to Charles, such as Endymion Porter. The patriots found themselves increasingly outgunned, particularly after the deaths of Pembroke and Dorchester (in February 1632). Their eclipse was confirmed by the appointment of Laud's client, Sir Francis Windebank, to the vacant secretaryship in the summer of 1632, ahead of the 'Protestant causer' Sir Thomas Roe. One of the most powerful arguments Weston was able to offer in favour of peace was the buoyant state of the customs revenues. Once the merchants' opposition to tonnage and poundage had been broken, and the trade slump of 1629–31 was over, these began to increase rapidly. By 1635 they were worth £358 000 a year – well over half the crown's annual income – and for the first time under the early Stuarts the exchequer was in surplus on its ordinary revenues. Since most of the trade on which this revenue depended was with the Mediterranean and the Iberian peninsula, and Charles was also being offered lucrative profits on minting Spanish silver, there was clearly a strong financial incentive for him to maintain peace with Spain. Finally, in a less tangible way, he may have been encouraged in this direction by the birth of Prince Charles in May 1630. There is some evidence that during the later 1620s he was nervous about the much greater public approval enjoyed by his sister Elizabeth and felt under pressure to be seen to be doing something positive to rescue her position in the Palatinate. This reinforced his sense of the need for aggressive military action. Once his line was secured, however, his sister no longer represented the reversionary interest and he became more relaxed about the whole issue. A by-product of this appears to have been a greater willingness to accept vague Spanish assurances where before he had insisted on substantive concessions.[60]

The king's directing role in foreign policy emerges very clearly from the diplomatic correspondence of this period. He made most of the key decisions in person, after consulting whichever of his advisers he trusted most over a particular initiative – usually Weston and Cottington if it involved negotiations with Spain, more occasionally Dorchester if he was considering

---

[60] Reeve, *Road to Personal Rule*, pp. 179–94, 204–7, 222–4; Sharpe, *The Personal Rule*, pp. 126–30.

alliance with the northern Protestant powers. The council as a whole was barely involved, except to rubber-stamp decisions already made. Thus when the Hapsburg envoy, Peter Paul Rubens, came to England in the summer of 1629 he spent long periods closeted with Charles and Weston and barely saw other councillors. The decision to follow up these talks by sending Cottington to Madrid was forced through council by the king and lord treasurer with no opportunity for discussion.[61]

Charles began the negotiations with Spain apparently determined to obtain the guarantee of full restoration of the Palatinate that he had promised to Frederick and Elizabeth. But this was gradually watered down as it became clear that no such guarantee would be forthcoming, and the alternative would be a continuation of the war in alliance with the Dutch and another meeting of parliament. The turning point in the negotiations came early in 1630, after Cottington had dispatched a series of gloomy reports to Charles, expressing doubts about whether the Spanish could deliver on the Palatinate and questioning the legitimacy of negotiating independently of the Dutch. Dorchester stepped in to remind Charles of Spain's duplicity in the past and to advocate renewal of the war; however, this backfired. Charles's mind was set on securing a peace and he responded to Cottington by making it clear that he had no qualms about abandoning the Dutch and was now prepared to trust a vague assurance from Philip that he would do his best over the Palatinate. The ambassador was able to soften his demands and negotiate the Treaty of Madrid, which largely reaffirmed the Anglo-Spanish peace of 1604. The Palatinate was dealt with separately in the draft of a remarkable agreement known as 'the Cottington treaty'. In this, as the *quid pro quo* for restoring Frederick and Elizabeth, the king committed England to joining the Spanish in invading the Netherlands. It was a staggering turnaround. Charles was apparently prepared to wage war on his Protestant neighbour in alliance with the foremost Catholic power in Europe, thus completely reversing the alignments of the past 70 years. How far he really intended to do this, and how far the agreement was simply another negotiating ploy, is uncertain; but he recognised that the whole deal was sufficiently sensitive to be kept secret from some of his senior councillors.[62]

---

[61] Reeve, *Road to Personal Rule*, pp. 198–9, 234–8, 244–7, 275–6.

[62] Ibid., pp. 242, 247–60.

Having apparently thrown in his lot with Spain, Charles then spent most of 1631 backtracking. There were two reasons for this: first of all the Spanish failed to deliver on their assurances over the Palatinate; and second Gustavus Adolphus's military successes – particularly his defeat of the Hapsburgs at Breitenfeld in September 1631 – offered a golden opportunity to restore Frederick and Elizabeth by force. As the Swedish king advanced on the Palatinate in November, his sister implored him to seize the moment, 'for by treaty it will never be done'. Charles had already established contact with Gustavus through the volunteer force led by the marquis of Hamilton which set out to assist them in July. Now the Swedish king appeared quite willing to restore Frederick and Elizabeth for the price of a £200 000 subsidy. This sort of money could only be raised quickly through a parliament and there was immediately feverish speculation that it was about to be resummoned. Even an obvious opponent like Weston attempted to take out insurance by making overtures to Eliot and Selden. However, Charles himself remained adamantly opposed.[63] The decisive moment came at a council debate on 21 December 1631. Adopting the line he had taken in the early stages of the forced loan, he firmly ruled out a summons without allowing any opportunity for discussion. According to reports of the meeting, his attitude had been decisively coloured by the continuing defiance of Sir John Eliot. He began by complaining that Eliot was 'more frequented with visits and used more feasting and jollity than became a prisoner in the Tower' and ordering that he be moved to 'a meaner lodging'. Then he warned that

by the discourses of many concerning a parliament he was now offended and his proclamation violated, and therefore wished all men to be wary how they displeased him in that kind, adding farther that he would never be urged by necessity or against his will to summon one.[64]

This harking back to the terms of his March 1629 proclamation was a chilling reminder to the moderate councillors of just what they were up against. The king apparently now saw parliament as having taken on the character of a personal enemy and, in this frame of mind, was not prepared to give it another chance.

---

[63] Ibid., pp. 266–82.

[64] NA, C 115/M35/8387.

Dorchester used his personal credit with Charles to keep discussions with the Swedes going during the winter months of 1631–2; and there remained a slim possibility that Gustavus's demands could be scaled down to £10 000 which might be met from extra-parliamentary sources. However, the secretary of state's death in February 1632 allowed Weston to take control of the negotiation and quickly wind it down. Gustavus continued to carry all before him and during the summer actually occupied the Lower Palatinate. But the peace party dominated at court and Charles remained immune from any temptation to intervene. In November 1632 Gustavus was killed at Lutzen and 12 days later Frederick himself died. The opportunity for intervention had passed.[65]

From mid-1632 to mid-1635 England was locked firmly into the Spanish alliance. Efforts to secure the restoration of the Palatinate rested entirely on diplomacy. The problem was that the English had little to offer as an incentive to positive action. The Spanish were mainly concerned to stop them assisting the French and the Dutch with their fleet and had long since discovered that the best way to achieve this was to dangle the prospect of restoration but never actually deliver, because to do so would be to sacrifice their main bargaining counter. This led to a lot of dipomatic activity, but little solid achievement. Then, in the summer of 1635, everything was suddenly thrown back into the melting pot. France formally declared war on Spain, thus raising the value of English friendship; Lord Treasurer Weston died, weakening the Spanish lobby's grip at court; Charles launched his first ship money fleet, giving England renewed credibility as a military force; and the Peace of Prague confirmed Hapsburg recognition of Maximilian of Bavaria as Elector Palatine, thus clearly demonstrating that the Spanish had been deceiving Charles and merely humouring him. The French ambassador, supported by Henrietta Maria, Elizabeth and 'the Protestant causers' began to lobby hard for a French alliance, while the arrival in England of the young elector Charles Louis in November 1635 prompted renewed enthusiasm for entry into the Thirty Years War. Charles decided to keep his options open and early in 1636 dispatched embassies to Vienna and Paris. The earl of Arundel, who had gone to Vienna, spent the summer in fruitless negotiation until it became clear that the Emperor had no intention of cooperating with a restoration, even after Maximilian's death.

---

[65] Reeve, *Road to Personal Rule*, pp. 279–91.

Meanwhile in Paris the earl of Leicester laid the foundations for a treaty by which the English would offer France the assistance of their ship money fleet in return for French agreement to offer Lorraine as an exchange for the Palatinate. Charles hesitated, reluctant to commit himself to an alliance that would almost certainly mean war; however, Arundel's return to court in early 1637, complaining that the nation's honour had been impugned by the Emperor, immediately made him much more aggressive. The young elector was instructed to protest about the recent election of the King of the Romans without his consent and promised the backing of a small fleet. By February 1637 there was a widespread expectation, even among pro-Spanish councillors, that the country was about to go to war. However, in March the French started to quibble over the terms of the agreement; then in July the prayerbook rebellion broke out in Scotland, forcing Charles to direct much of his attention elsewhere. By the end of the year England was firmly back in the Spanish camp and was to stay there for the remainder of the Personal Rule.[66]

The biggest puzzle in all this is how seriously Charles intended to go to war. Kevin Sharpe has argued that when Charles threatened war he meant it, pointing out that, unlike his father, he was willing to fight when the situation seemed to demand it, and particularly when he felt the need to vindicate his honour. However, this analysis has been questioned by Ian Atherton who argues that all along the king's intention was simply to put extra diplomatic pressure on the Hapsburgs, in line with a maxim that he himself enunciated that 'the best treaty is with a drawn sword'. Atherton points to the crucial ambiguities in some of Charles's actions; for example, his insistence that the ships given to Charles Louis sail under the Palatine flag so that he could disown them if they became embroiled in a conflict with the Spanish. He also highlights some important exchanges with the Irish lord deputy, Wentworth, at the height of speculation about the war early in 1637. In response to Wentworth's anxious arguments against entering the conflict, the king assured him that he still regarded it very much as a last resort, to be used only if the diplomatic pressure failed. 'By your

---

[66] Sharpe, *The Personal Rule*, pp. 73–5, 83–6, 88, 94–6, 509–36; Quintrell, *Charles i*, pp. 68–72; Smuts, 'Puritan followers of Henrietta Maria', pp. 36–40; J.H. Elliott, 'The year of the three ambassadors', in H. Lloyd-Jones, V. Pearl and B. Worden eds, *History and Imagination*, 1981, pp. 166–81.

favour', he told the lord deputy, 'you mistake the question. For it is not whether I should declare a war on the House of Austria or not, but whether I shall join with France and the rest of my friends to demand of the House of Austria my nephew's restitution and so hazard (upon refusal) a declaration of war.'[67] In the final analysis, it is impossible to tell how far Charles was prepared to go. He was engaged in an elaborate game of poker and, perhaps, even he himself was uncertain whether he would carry out his threats.

What does seem clear, however, is that if he had gone to war it would have been without summoning a parliament. In February 1637 the 12 common law judges delivered their opinion in favour of the collection of ship money, thus apparently securing for Charles a source of revenue worth the equivalent of four subsidies a year. He could now contemplate fighting a naval war without recourse to parliamentary supply; and if there was to be a showdown with the Spanish this was the type of conflict he envisaged, assuring Wentworth that 'what great inconvenience this war can bring (now that my sea contribution is settled . . .) I cannot imagine . . .'[68] This helps to explain why, even in the midst of the feverish speculation of early 1637, the council does not appear to have been given the opportunity to discuss a summons. Rule without parliament had become an established fact.

This account has identified two decisive moments on 'the Road to Personal Rule'. The first was the failure of the 1629 Parliament, in spite of all the talk of a 'new deal' and the king's apparent willingness to return to policies associated with Queen Elizabeth. For a few weeks in late 1628 and early 1629 it looked as if the patriots might persuade him to re-commit to war against Spain and pro-Calvinist/pro-parliament policies at home. However, the whole scheme fell apart in the face of the Commons' intransigence. The second decisive moment was the decision *not* to summon a parliament in December 1631. At just the point when it seemed that the principal objective of English foreign policy since 1620 was within the king's grasp, he turned away and refused to act. As John Reeve has stressed, the decision to rule without parliament was never 'a decision neatly made'.

---

[67] Sharpe, *The Personal Rule*, pp. 535–6; I. Atherton, 'John, 1st Viscount Scudamore (1601–71). A career at court and country, 1601–43', University of Cambridge, Ph.D. thesis, 1993, pp. 198–215, 241–5; *Strafforde Letters*, vol. 2, p. 78.

[68] *Strafforde Letters*, vol. 2, p. 53.

Rather it was a result of a conjunction of circumstances that diminished the support within government for another meeting, at the same time as making it both less necessary and less attractive.[69]

The first of these circumstances was the ending of the war and the adherence to a peaceful foreign policy. This immediately removed much of the need for extra money, or indeed the display of national unity, which a successful parliament could provide. Moreover, peace had allowed the crown to improve its finances to the point where for the first time in the seventeenth century it was solvent. A summons of parliament would jeopardise this since it would in all probability reopen discussion of impositions and tonnage and poundage which were the main sources of royal income.[70] If the king wanted to fight he could now do so without parliamentary assistance, as was demonstrated when the army against the Scots was funded from extra-parliamentary sources in 1639. Providing Charles could limit the scale of any conflict – and preferably concentrate his effort into the navy – it must have seemed to him that there was no reason why he should need to summon parliament again.

The king also found that he was under much less pressure from within his own council. In the late 1620s the patriot lobby had played a crucial role in keeping parliament on the agenda and twice talked the king into resummoning it. However, from 1629 onwards they were largely in eclipse. This was partly due to shifts in the balance of power at court. After the deaths of Pembroke and Dorchester there were no court heavyweights left in the moderate camp. Councillors like Coke, Coventry and Manchester had been very effective advocates for a parliament while their patron Buckingham was alive, but no longer exerted much influence. Instead, the king tended to listen to Weston and Laud who, for different reasons, were strongly opposed to it. It was also becoming much harder to argue the case for a resummons, with all the talk of 'popular' conspiracy and disobedience. The Venetian ambassador noted that senior councillors dared not even raise the issue 'because they are afraid of irritating the king'.[71] These difficulties persisted even after things had settled down. When Coventry tried to

---

[69] Reeve, *Road to Personal Rule*, p. 279.

[70] This point is made in Quintrell, *Charles I*, p. 60.

[71] *CSP Ven. 1629–32*, pp. 204–5.

discuss a summons in 1633 Cottington noted sardonically that 'the king . . . so rattled my lord keeper that he is now the most pliable man in England and all thoughts of parliament are quite out of his pate'.[72] Even amid the speculation about war in 1635–7 the only senior politicians who appear to have been prepared to raise the matter with Charles directly were non-councillors like the earl of Warwick.[73] The king had asserted himself very effectively and for much of the decade, within the inner circles of government, the case for a parliament largely passed by default.

But what of Charles's own views? These were the most important ingredients in the situation, but also, in many ways the most elusive. Much of the time he simply did not talk about parliament, but when he did his comments tended to be extremely hostile. In August 1629 he told Châteauneuf, the French ambassador, that the Commons leadership was in the hands of puritans and proto-republicans who were bent on reducing his powers to nothing.[74] Writing to Wentworth in 1634 he famously described the assembly as 'that Hidra', and urged him to 'take good heed, for you know that I have found it as well cunning as malicious'.[75] There was no longer any mention of the 'wise and well tempered men' who in the 1620s he had presumed to be a majority in the lower house. The impression given is that when he thought of parliament now it was in terms of Eliot and his accomplices.

One of the clearest insights into Charles's thinking on parliaments, as Anthony Milton has suggested, comes from his further exchanges with Wentworth over whether to hold a meeting in Ireland in 1634–5.[76] Wentworth was a shrewd and knowledgeable observer of the king; so his comments can be taken as a good indication of what he wanted to hear. The lord deputy put forward the case for a summons premised on the view that parliament should be allowed no opportunity to bargain with the monarch or challenge the royal prerogative, and that if it tried to do so it

---

[72] *Strafforde Letters*, vol. 1, p. 141.

[73] Smuts, 'Puritan followers of Henrietta Maria', pp. 36–40; for the very different atmosphere behind the scenes, see the newsletter cited in Quintrell, *Charles I*, p. 108.

[74] Reeve, *Road to Personal Rule*, p. 132.

[75] *Strafforde Letters*, vol. 1, p. 233.

[76] A. Milton, 'Thomas Wentworth and the political thought of the Personal Rule', in J.F. Merritt, *The Political World of Thomas Wentworth, Earl of Stafford 1621–1641*, Cambridge, 1996, pp. 142–9.

should be dissolved at once. He therefore devised a scheme for dividing the parliament into two sessions. The first was to focus on providing Charles with an unconditional grant of supply. Only after this was forthcoming would MPs be allowed – in a second session – to discuss grievances, and then any concessions made would be entirely at the king's discretion. The trade-offs that were a normal part of parliamentary politics in England were to be entirely dispensed with. As Wentworth explained to Secretary Coke, the parliament must

put an absolute trust in the king without offering any condition or restraint upon his will . . . he would be provided for as the head and care for his people as the members, through all the expressions of a gracious king, but still according to the order of reason, nature and conscience, himself first and his people afterwards.[77]

This appears to have chimed in perfectly with Charles's thinking and probably did much to persuade him to allow the parliament in Ireland to go ahead. However, even after it had delivered a grant with no strings attached the king remained suspicious. In January 1635 he insisted that Wentworth discontinue it at the earliest opportunity, offering some gratuitous comments about parliaments being 'of the nature of cats: they ever grow curst with age'.[78] In the final analysis, it is this guardedness and hostility, the bleakness of this vision of what a parliament had to offer, which explains why for 11 years Charles ruled without it.

Laudianism and the Personal Rule

In August 1633 Laud at last succeeded Abbot as archbishop of Canterbury. This coincided with a rapid acceleration in the anti-Calvinist programme of church reform. The republication of James I's *Declaration of Sports* in October 1633 led to a challenge to puritan sabbatarianism; the decision in the St Gregory's case in November marked the start of the policy of moving communion tables to the east end of churches and railing them off; and

---

[77] *Strafforde Letters*, vol. 1, p. 237.

[78] Ibid., vol. 1, p. 365.

the commissions for collecting money for the refurbishing of St Paul's, which went out in December, were intended to establish the cathedral as a showpiece for the beautifying of churches. Traditionally these events have been regarded as closely connected. Laud's arrival at Canterbury is seen as supplying an energy and clarity of vision that had previously been lacking, enabling Charles to turn his anti-Calvinist inclinations into practical policies. The archbishop was the driving force behind a new emphasis on order and the beauty of holiness in the church that matched the Rule of Thorough in the state.[79] From a Calvinist perspective he was, in Patrick Collinson's words, 'the greatest calamity ever visited upon the English church'.[80]

Recently, however, this view has been challenged in the work of Julian Davies and Kevin Sharpe. They see Charles as the real initiator of change, with Laud largely content to act as his master's servant. The archbishop's reputation as the domineering 'evil counsellor' was, they argue, largely a consequence of the case made against him at his trial in the early 1640s, when the aim was to lay the blame on him for unpopular policies so that Charles could be given room to reach a settlement. In fact, he was a moderate, essentially conservative figure, intent on achieving uniformity within the church, but through persuasion rather than compulsion. It was Charles who gave anti-Calvinist policies their cutting edge.[81]

This interpretation, in turn, has been criticised by Kenneth Fincham and Peter Lake. They point out that the Davies/Sharpe reading of Laud is based on the defence he made of his actions at his trial and therefore deserves to be treated with a certain amount of scepticism. They also emphasise that there are real difficulties over attributing final responsibility for any of the religious policies to either king or minister. Charles, for a variety of reasons, was anxious to be seen as the one in charge; while Laud was adept at covering his tracks and concealing the extent of his role because he was always conscious of the danger of being called to account before parliament. The best way to view their relationship, they suggest, is as a

---

[79] Gardiner, *History of England*, vol. 7, pp. 254–9, 299–322; vol. 8, pp. 8, 106–29.

[80] P. Collinson, *The Religion of Protestants*, Oxford, 1982, p. 90.

[81] Davies, *The Caroline Captivity*, pp. 300–4; Sharpe, *The Personal Rule*, pp. 284–92; Sharpe, *Politics and Ideas*, pp. 123–8.

partnership, 'a practised double act', in which each needed the other. Laud depended on the king's prestige and authority to overcome opposition to anti-Calvinist policies, both inside and outside the church, while Charles looked to his archbishop to translate his concerns and preferences into practical policy. The relationship worked mainly because the two men shared the same basic aims and assumptions.[82]

The circumstances in which Charles and Laud were operating during the 1630s were subtly different from those in the 1620s. It was no longer a matter of issuing directives and taking control of what passed for religious orthodoxy. If anti-Calvinism were to have a lasting impact, the emphasis now needed to be on effecting change at a parish level. This placed a premium on the administrative and managerial skills that the archbishop possessed in abundance. A good indication of the dynamics of his relationship with the king over this period is provided in the annual reports on the state of the dioceses sent in by the bishops, then summarised by himself and Neile, archbishop of York from 1632. Several of these survive with extensive marginal annotation by Charles, which Sharpe has taken as evidence for his detailed oversight of church affairs.[83] In fact, the impression they give is of a more complex set-up in which the king, while appearing to take control, was actually being prompted and led towards particular responses. Laud carefully selected the material in the summaries to reassure him on some matters and draw his attention to others. He was also very adept at throwing in rhetorical formulae and catchphrases to which Charles was almost certain to react. References to 'a seditious lecture' and 'nurseries of inconformity' almost invariably elicited approving feedback.[84] On one occasion, Laud passed on a report from Bishop Williams of a scheme by the Mercers company to establish a stipendiary lectureship in Huntingdon with the warning that this would give them the power to 'put in or put out any lecturer'. The king responded with predictable indignation, declaring,

---

[82] Fincham and Lake, 'Ecclesiastical policies of James and Charles', pp. 44–7.

[83] Sharpe, 'The Personal Rule of Charles I', pp. 62–3.

[84] Laud, *Works*, vol. 5, pp. 320, 323. Another example was when Laud complained of the difficulties of suppressing separatists in his diocese without the help of the secular judges. Charles wrote in the margin 'Demand their help and if they refuse I shall make them assist you': Ibid., vol. 5, p. 355.

certainly I cannot hold fit that any lay person or corporation should have the power these men would take to themselves. For I will have no priest have any necessity of a lay dependency. Wherefore I command you to show me the way to over throw this and to hinder the performance in time to all such intentions.

Laud was then able to refer this back to Williams, citing the king's words, and insisting that he take steps to suppress the scheme.[85] The king evidently trusted his archbishop to see things the same way as he did. This allowed Laud considerable freedom of action and at the same time created opportunities for him to invoke Charles's authority to reinforce his own. But there were limits to what he could do. He had always to recognise that this trust would only last as long as he was seen to be addressing the king's preferences and priorities.

Another aspect of the relationship about which we know a good deal is the operation of ecclesiastical patronage. Fincham has described how Laud was able to use his position as Charles's 'trusted lieutenant' to establish 'a partnership between prince and prelate unparalleled since the Reformation'.[86] Charles set the ground rules – for example, in insisting that senior posts in the church be filled by his own chaplains – but within the prescribed framework Laud enjoyed considerable discretion. His influence was based on careful attention to the machinery of ecclesiastical patronage. He knew how the system worked inside out, which made him indispensable when Charles needed advice on how an appointment was to be made or who was best qualified to fill it. He was also very industrious when it came to sorting out the administrative formalities of signifying the king's wish that a grant be made and ordering the bill to be drawn up. This gave him the dominant voice in determining who received what, especially when it came to the all-important appointments to bishoprics. The king himself was undoubtedly active in ecclesiastical patronage. He chose some of those who became royal chaplains because he was impressed with their ability as preachers; and on occasion he overrode Laud, for example in refusing to

---

[85] Ibid., vol. 5, p. 321; vol. 6, pp. 349–50; see also Fincham and Lake, 'Ecclesiastical policies of James and Charles', p. 46.

[86] K. Fincham, 'William Laud and the exercise of Caroline ecclesiastical patronage', *JEH*, vol. 51, 2000, p. 93.

approve his taking the see of Winchester in 1632. But he was too busy or too limited in his knowledge of what was going on to exercise consistent oversight. It was Laud whose influence normally prevailed, as other suitors recognised. When the marquis of Hamilton wanted to secure the deanery of Durham for his client Walter Balcanquall, it was to Laud that he wrote, urging that 'if your grace will move the king in it, I do believe he will not deny me this favour . . .' Laud was able to oblige, even though Charles had previously advised Balcanquall to seek another living.[87]

As this example suggests, Laud became adept at nudging and steering the king in a particular direction. Charles generally had an idea of what he wanted, but did not always know how to achieve it. Laud did, and in providing the king with practical solutions, he often exercised his greatest influence. The significance of his interventions was perhaps best demonstrated in the St Gregory's case. As we have seen, Charles wanted a placement of communion tables that reflected the practice of 'the primitive church'; but he was initially uncertain what this involved. As a result, a coherent altar policy emerged by fits and starts, and then largely through the efforts of Laud and Neile. Both men had shown themselves supporters of east end altars as early as 1617, and during the early 1630s were using their episcopal powers to enforce this arrangement at a local level. However, without explicit royal sanction they were cautious about extending the policy to the church as a whole. This was what they were seeking in the St Gregory's case.[88] The matter was brought before the king and privy council in November 1633 after Laud had intervened to prevent the Court of Arches making a decision in the case. What was at issue was whether or not the parishioners of St Gregory's should be allowed to obstruct an order by the dean and chapter of St Paul's for moving the communion table to the east end. The fullest account we have of the hearing suggests that Laud opened the case by citing the 1559 Injunction, to the effect that the communion table should normally be 'set in the place where the altar stood'. The parishioners responded by quoting the gloss on this in the 1604 Canons that allowed the table to be moved into the 'church or chancel' during a service. Charles, who seems to have been a little confused by the

---

[87] Ibid., pp. 69–93.

[88] Davies, *The Caroline Captivity*, pp. 207–8; Fincham, 'Restoration of altars', pp. 924–7.

conflicting precedents, consulted the book of canons and then declared that it was his view that the table should stand not in the body of the church but in the middle of the chancel during communion time. This was not what Laud was looking for and he came back with a robust affirmation that the communion table was always called the altar in 'the primitive church' and should therefore be set in the position of the altar. Charles, still anxious to follow what he took to be precedent, then expressed a willingness to allow the churchwardens to take the table down into the church at communion time, whereupon Laud retorted

they would have it down to vex their minister, that they would not kneel and they were but a few puritans who when the example of the cathedral churches and your Majesty's chapel royal was urged said that though your Majesty suffer idolatry in your chapel they will not do so in their church.

This carried the day. Charles pronounced his dislike of 'innovation' and his determination to see parish churches guided by the practice of their 'cathedral mother church', then declared that the 'altarwise' position be maintained in this case and that in future the judgement of the 'ordinary' (here the dean and chapter) should be final.[89] This was not quite the directive that Laud and Neile had been seeking, but it was a start, and over the following three years, they were able to extend the policy country-wide.[90]

This account of the St Gregory's case comes from a biased source, one of the witnesses against Laud at his trial, but the evidence it presents does ring true. The scenario of a slightly baffled king, struggling to reconcile his anti-Calvinist instincts with his desire to uphold precedent, and an archbishop who was able to clinch his case by invoking the threat from puritanism was repeated on other occasions.[91] It suggests that ultimately it was often a case of Laud giving the lead for his less astute royal master to

---

[89] NA, SP 16/499/42.

[90] Fincham, 'Restoration of altars', pp. 927–40.

[91] For other examples, see Fincham and Lake, 'Ecclesiastical policies of James and Charles', pp. 45–7. The reissue of the *Book of Sports* may be yet another instance. At first Charles was reluctant to go ahead with this, but was persuaded by Laud who was probably able to exploit the argument being put to the king that 'the Humorists [i.e. puritans] increase much in those parts and unite themselves by banding against those feasts': Laud, *Works*, vol. 6, p. 319; K. Parker, *The English Sabbath*, Cambridge, 1988, pp. 189–91; Sharpe, *The Personal Rule*, pp. 353–5.

follow. However, there is more to it than this. The manipulation was not all one way and Charles's own views could never be discounted. He always retained the capacity to surprise and discomfort his archbishop, perhaps most notably, as we shall see, over the appointment to the lord treasurership in March 1636. This ensured that Laud was always conscious of a need to demonstrate loyal service, which meant sticking closely to the priorities which Charles had done so much to establish in the 1620s. It may be appropriate, as Fincham argues, to describe the religious reforms of the Personal Rule as 'Laudianism' rather than 'Carolinism' – since this highlights the archbishop's crucial guiding role – but the term should not be allowed to obscure the king's continuing active contribution to religious change.[92]

King and archbishop worked closely together over a long period, but their approach to ecclesiastical matters was often very different. Charles, with his strong sense of conviction and moral righteousness, was generally direct and forceful. He had little time for opposition, and little understanding of its strength or resolve. Laud was equally clear about where he wanted to go, but tended to be more cautious and tactical. The differences can be seen if we look at the efforts made during the 1630s to restrict puritan lecturing. Concern about the subversive effects of this first became widespread during the period of the Spanish Match in the early 1620s and then re-emerged amid the general alarm about 'popularity' following the 1629 Parliament. Charles commissioned Samuel Harsnett, archbishop of York, who had led the earlier campaign against lecturers, to draft proposals for 'the better settling of church government'. These became the basis of the Royal Instructions of December 1629 which, as we have seen, imposed extensive restrictions on puritan lecturers.[93] The policy was enforced rather unevenly in the dioceses. Some bishops, notably Wren at Norwich and Piers at Bath and Wells, interpreted the instructions as a green light for shutting down lectureships and bringing to an end afternoon sermons. Laud's approach, however, was more flexible. Conscious of just how sensitive an issue this was for Calvinists, he enforced the instructions selectively. He insisted, for instance, that the liturgy be read as an accompaniment to preaching; he

---

[92] Fincham, 'Restoration of altars', p. 940. For other resonances of the term 'Laudianism', see Lake, 'Laudian style', pp. 61–2 and A. Milton, 'The creation of Laudianism: a new approach', in Cogswell, Cust and Lake eds, *Politics, Religion and Popularity*, pp. 162–84.

[93] Davies, *The Caroline Captivity*, pp. 27–31, 130–2.

also made an example of a few notable puritans such as Thomas Hooker, the lecturer at Chelmsford, or John Workman, lecturer at Gloucester. Otherwise he was willing to allow a fair amount of latitude, giving ministers time to become accustomed to the policy and conform of their own volition rather than suspending them in large numbers.[94] David Como has demonstrated how, as Bishop of London in the early 1630s, Laud adopted a similarly tactical approach to suppressing Calvinist preaching on predestination. Recognising the dangers of antagonising moderate opinion, he used private audiences and behind the scenes pressure to intimidate the Calvinists, while maintaining the public fiction that Charles's ban was being enforced impartially.[95] It was an approach that was politically sensitive and recognised the limitations of the machinery of enforcement; but it had little appeal for Charles who did not see his role as being to appease or reconcile opposing interests, but to lay down clear principles and ensure that these were adhered to. Over lectureships, he shared his father's view that they represented the spearhead of a populist puritan conspiracy to subvert royal authority and, given the opportunity to intervene, he favoured as restrictive a reading of the 1629 Instructions as was feasible. Hence he supported the view that all ministers, and not just lecturers, should provide catechising instead of afternoon sermons; while his comments on the Huntingdon lectureship, cited earlier, suggest that he was opposed to all stipendiary lecturers, regardless of whether they held a parish living.[96] Great Yarmouth, in particular, felt the force of his dislike. During 1629 he received information from Harsnett and Attorney-General Heath that the town was a hotbed of sectarianism. He therefore authorised Heath to draw up a new charter for the corporation in order to limit the influence of the puritan aldermen; and when the local stipendiary lecturer, John Brinsley, was cited before the privy council for nonconformity, he chaired the hearing, and ordered that he be barred from preaching and four of the aldermen arrested. At stake in Yarmouth, he declared, was not just 'ecclesiastical authority and discipline', but the very basis of 'civil order and government'. There was a need to put a stop to 'popular elections' and curb

---

[94] Ibid., pp. 132–61; Tyacke, *Anti-Calvinists*, pp. 188–92.

[95] Como, 'Predestination and political conflict', pp. 278–84.

[96] Davies, *The Caroline Captivity*, p. 136.

'the busy humours of those whose ears itch after novelty'.[97] This readiness to view the challenge of a few local puritans in such fundamental terms does much to explain why Charles was so rigid in his approach to the enforcement of ecclesiastical policy. Where puritans were concerned it was hazardous to compromise.

The Great Yarmouth case also offers an insight into the impact of Charles's interventions. Much of the time he was too busy and too pre-occupied elsewhere to follow up his directives. This was inevitable in an administrative system where in theory the final decision always lay with the king, but in practice the bureaucracy was too primitive and under-resourced to enable him to keep track of what was going on. It meant that on the ground royal orders were often bypassed, or even contradicted. Thus, in Yarmouth the puritan aldermen were able to deflect the efforts to alter the charter by working through their high steward, Dorset, and were even able to install a new puritan lecturer with the assistance of Secretary Coke.[98] However, these obstacles did not preclude a process of 'working towards the king' which in many respects – in this and other areas of policy – provided the most effective means of implementing the royal will. It was a process that ran parallel to, and often in tandem with, the 'work-ing towards the archbishop' that Anthony Milton has identified during the 1630s. As Milton explains it, Laud encouraged those who sought his favour to come forward with policy initiatives and the intellectual rationales to support them, simply through letting it be known that he wanted to promote greater ceremonial conformity and the suppression of puritans. This enabled him to push forward an increasingly radical version of 'Laudianism', without having to take direct responsibility for doing so, which, given his nervousness about being called to account, was always an important consideration.[99] Much the same can be said for the influence of

---

[97] R.P. Cust, 'Anti-Puritanism and urban politics', pp. 1–26.

[98] Ibid., pp. 15–17, 20–22.

[99] Milton, 'Creation of Laudianism', pp. 177–80. This concept was originally developed by Ian Kershaw in his biography of Hitler. He demonstrates that within the flimsy and over-lapping bureaucracies of the Nazi state the most effective means of implementing the Führer's wishes was to encourage a cut-throat competition for favour among subordinates who came up with all sorts of creative and imaginative programmes designed to meet with his approval: I. Kershaw, *Hitler 1889–1936: Hubris*, 1998, p. 530.

Charles – although in his case the main concern was to find a way of infusing into his servants his own ideological imperatives. Awareness of the king's loathing for puritans and desire to restore the church to its 'primitive' purity permeated the administrative and ecclesiastical hierarchies. Subordinates were very conscious that the way to promote both themselves and their interests was to adopt the rhetoric of anti-Calvinism and be seen to be working towards these ends. This paid dividends on both sides. In Yarmouth, the anti-puritan minority, who were outgunned at a local level, were nonetheless able to gain central backing for the revision of the charter, while the king was able to uncover and – in some respects, at least – curb the activities of local puritans. It was this process – of subordinates fitting their language and actions around the king's anti-Calvinist prejudices – that gave the religious policies of the Personal Rule so much of their hard-edged dynamic.

But what of the effects of Laudianism? What impact did it have on the religious landscape of Caroline England? Its greatest success was in controlling what happened at the upper levels of the church. Appointments to bishoprics and senior positions in the universities were dominated by anti-Calvinists, to such an extent that between 1625 and 1641 there were only three obvious examples of Calvinists being promoted on the episcopal bench (Hall at Exeter in 1627, Potter at Carlisle in 1629 and Morton at Durham in 1632). By the mid-1630s Laud and Charles had created a new anti-Calvinist ecclesiastical establishment.[100] They also achieved some success in revising what passed for religious orthodoxy in the Church of England. Preaching at court and at public showpieces, such as the Paul's Cross sermons, was carefully regulated under the term's of Charles's 1628 Declaration to exclude predestinarian doctrine. The change in the content of the Paul's Cross sermons was especially striking. Prior to 1628, all those published sermons back to 1570 which dealt with the issue of predestination took a Calvinist line. But these came to an abrupt end to be replaced by a cluster of overtly anti-Calvinist sermons from 1632 onwards.[101] The output of the presses reflected a similar shift. Anthony Milton has shown that in spite of all the loopholes and inconsistencies in the licensing system, anti-Calvinists were

---

[100] Fincham and Lake, 'Ecclesiastical policies of James and Charles', p. 37.

[101] Tyacke, *Anti-Calvinists*, pp. 248–65.

able to exert a broadly effective control over what was presented in print as mainstream orthodoxy. Predestinarian works by moderate Calvinists such as Bishop Davenant and Bishop Downham of Derry were suppressed and anti-Calvinists and ceremonialists were encouraged to offer their work for publication for the first time. There were also instances of Calvinists having their work co-opted to legitimate Laudian policies. For example, John Prideaux, the fiercely anti-Arminian Regius Professor at Oxford, had a treatise on the sabbath republished in 1634 with a preface by Heylyn that made it appear that he was supporting the new *Book of Sports*.[102]

Success in enforcing Laudian policy at a local level was much more variable. A good deal depended on the lead given by individual bishops and here there was a wide range of responses. Hardliners, like Wren, were prepared to enforce the policies to the letter and suspend ministers in large numbers for non-compliance; but, at the opposite end of the spectrum, there were Calvinists, like Hall, who were willing to go through the motions when under pressure, but put little energy into enforcement.[103] Perhaps the most impressive achievement was the administration of the altar policy. During the mid-1630s all the bishops, with the exception of Williams at Lincoln, issued visitation articles supporting the policy. These often had a considerable impact. In the diocese of Peterborough, for example, where Bishop Dee had been one of the first to impose the new requirements, a 1637 survey revealed that only 13 had failed to place the table at the east end and altarwise.[104] This was, perhaps, exceptional, but it showed what could be achieved with vigorous action by local court officials; and there is no doubt that the policy produced highly visible changes in the layout of large numbers of parish churches.[105] Elsewhere, the success of Laudian policies is less easy to measure. The instructions over preaching and lecturing probably had a mixed impact, although in the judgement of Patrick Collinson the new emphasis on 'orthodoxy' and 'conformability' drained much of the

---

[102] A. Milton, 'Licensing, censorship and religious orthodoxy in early Stuart England', *HJ*, vol. 41, 1998, pp. 625–51.

[103] Davies, *The Caroline Captivity*, p. 218; Tyacke, *Anti-Calvinists*, p. 213.

[104] Fincham, 'Restoration of the altars', p. 931.

[105] On the success of the altar policy, see ibid., pp. 928–40; Davies, *The Caroline Captivity*, pp. 220–1; Foster, 'Church policies', pp. 202–5.

evangelical energy out of 'combination' lectures, which from the king's point of view was the principal objective.[106] The reissuing of the *Book of Sports* challenged puritan sabbatarianism and gave a boost to festive culture as part of Charles's campaign to bolster the traditional social hierarchy, but the requirement that it be read out by ministers in all parish churches appears to have been enforced only sporadically.[107] To be really effective, Laudian policy needed a broad base of support among the clergy and, even more importantly, among the laity. This was still developing during the 1630s. John Evelyn could later look back on the period as a golden age in which the Church of England enjoyed 'her greatest splendour';[108] but he was in a small minority. The attacks on altar rails and the petitions to the Commons against abuses in the early 1640s showed the rooted hostility of the majority.

Where Laudian policies did have a very considerable impact was in sweeping away the religious middle ground that had developed out of James's support for moderate evangelical Calvinism. Practices that had been taken for granted in the earlier period were proscribed and prohibited, and the radical tendencies inherent in puritanism became much more pronounced. Some Calvinists who were willing to conform during the 1620s were driven into nonconformity or even separation. John Davenport, an influential London conformist, was so appalled by the upsurge of Arminian doctrine that in 1633 he fled to Amsterdam; while John Ley, another conformable minister from Cheshire, warned his local bishop that as a consequence of the 'schismatical' altar policy moderate puritans like himself would become 'stiff in standing out against conformity'. One of the chief casualties of this process were the bishops themselves. In James's reign most Calvinists had regarded them as natural allies in the cause of godly reform, but by the mid-1630s their complicity in the programme of Laudian reform had laid them open to William Prynne's charge that they were no better than 'pontifical lordly prelates'. Out of this developed calls for their abolition in the early 1640s, often supported by relatively moderate figures, like Ley.[109]

---

[106] P. Collinson, *Godly People*, 1983, pp. 488–92.

[107] Foster, 'Church policies', pp. 206–8; Davies, *The Caroline Captivity*, pp. 180–95.

[108] *Evelyn*, p. 7.

[109] Tyacke, *Anti-Calvinists*, pp. 186–7, 223–6.

In political terms, however, there is no doubt that the most dangerous reaction of all was the upsurge in anti-popery.

Fear of popery was rooted in the Calvinist view of Roman Catholicism as the antithesis of true religion, based on ignorance, superstition and adherence to a pope who was the Antichrist. It gained a wider currency from the association of popery with threats to national security and challenges to traditional liberties. The Spanish Armada, the Gunpowder Plot and Catholic aggression abroad were all connected in the minds of ordinary Englishmen with the menace of Rome. At the same time, popery was equated with tyranny and authoritarianism, and was seen as threatening parliament and the rule of law through the influence of popish counsellors at the royal court. Linking these concerns was a consciousness that if England did not oppose popery and stand up for true religion this would bring down God's providential judgements. During the 1620s – with the Spanish Match, the forced loan and the disasters of the wars – belief in a popish plot to destroy Protestantism and traditional liberties was widespread. It became even stronger during the 1630s. Laudian ritual and ceremonial aroused fears that Catholic worship was being reintroduced by the back door; the high-profile activities of Henrietta Maria and other Catholics at court fuelled alarm over the activities of 'evil counsellors'; and the king's failure to play the role of Protestant champion in the Thirty Years War – when the very survival of the faith appeared to be at stake – added to the sense of crisis.[110]

Charles did little to dispel these fears. He was quite clear in his own mind that he was not a Catholic and got particularly upset when he was accused of this in the parliamentarian propaganda of the 1640s. In response to one of the petitions from the Oxford Parliament of 1644 he went out of his way to stress that 'it had pleased God to enlighten our understanding to discern the clear truth of the Protestant Religion, in which we have been born and bred, from the mists and clouds of popery' and that 'if it shall not please God to enable us by force to defend it, we shall show our affection and love to it by dying for it'.[111] This was a statement intended for public

---

[110] P.G. Lake, 'Anti-popery: the structure of a prejudice', in Cust and Hughes eds, *Conflict in Early Stuart England*, pp. 72–106.

[111] Rushworth, vol. 5, p. 599. See also his defence against charges of popery in the preface to the 1640 Canons: below, pp. 261–2.

consumption; but there is no reason to doubt that Charles meant what he said, at least insofar as it applied to his understanding of Protestantism. He respected his wife's Catholicism, but it seems to have been accepted by both of them that faith was something on which they must agree to differ.[112] Contrary to her wishes, and the terms of the French marriage treaty, he insisted that his sons be baptised as Protestants. He was also just as hostile to Catholic zealots as he was to puritans, expressing fury over the well-publicised conversions of courtiers such as Wat Montagu and the countess of Newport during the 1630s.[113] However, this was not the impression he gave to many of his subjects. His oft-voiced conviction that his Catholic subjects had a greater sense of loyalty to him than puritans or Presbyterians,[114] his cosmopolitanism and admiration for all things Spanish, his obvious affection for his Catholic wife, his favouritism towards the papal envoy George Con and his desire to distance himself from Calvinist anti-popery, all encouraged the suspicion that at the very least he was a Catholic sympathiser. Further evidence for this was provided in the mid-1630s by his willingness to encourage talk of a reunion with Rome. What seems to have been envisaged – according to discussions that took place in 1635–6 between Richard Montagu and the papal agent who preceded Con, Gregorio Panzani – was a scheme whereby the English church would acknowledge the pope's position as head of Christendom, but would continue with distinctively Protestant practices, such as communion in both kinds, and retain its independence in a similar fashion to the Gallican church in France. How serious Charles was about the whole project is unclear. He had much to gain from drawing closer to the papacy at this juncture, both in terms of securing diplomatic support for a solution to the Palatine problem and persuading his own Catholic subjects to take the Oath of Allegiance. However, in conversations with Con, he was certainly prepared to banter about the advantages and disadvantages of ecumenicism and advocate the reunification of Christendom previously proposed by his

---

[112] See, for example, *Charles I in 1646*, Camden Soc., 1861, pp. 21, 24.

[113] C.M. Hibbard, *Charles I and the Popish Plot*, Chapel Hill, N.C., 1983, pp. 39, 22–3, 62.

[114] For a particularly clear statement of this view, see *Eikon Basilike*, p. 89.

father.[115] Negotiations for reunion largely petered out by the end of 1637. But Charles's goodwill towards Catholic powers did bear fruit in the closer relationship with Spain between 1638 and 1640.

Awareness of the reunion scheme does not appear to have reached beyond the court; but the sense that royal policy was dangerously biased towards Catholics was growing, with sinister consequences. Londoners were dismayed in the late 1630s when the earl of Arundel, at the time commander-in-chief of the English army, was seen travelling to a council meeting in George Con's coach, emblazoned with the papal coat of arms.[116] Belief in a popish plot was becoming even more widespread than before. One of the most articulate expressions of this was provided by Henry Burton, whose warnings to the young king had been ignored in 1625. He claimed, in his Gunpowder Plot anniversary sermon in 1636, that the encouragement given to Arminian doctrine, the silencing of preaching ministers and the moving of communion tables were all elements in a 'plot or practice . . . for the suppressing of the true religion here established [and] for the bringing in of popery'.[117] What was particularly dangerous about this version of the plot was that the king no longer appeared immune to the blandishments of the papists. In his diary for September 1637, Robert Woodford, the puritan town steward of Northampton, recorded a prayer 'for the king's majesty for his conversion, to enlighten his eyes, to stir him up to drive away the wicked from the throne and to make choice of such as will be faithful'. On this and other occasions there seems to have been some question in Woodford's mind as to how far the 'evil counsellors' had actually succeeded in converting him to their point of view.[118] Like most of his fellow puritans, he was probably still prepared to give Charles the benefit of the doubt. But the seeds of mistrust had been sown, and in the minds of many, over the following four to five years, these were to mature into a conviction that the king was at the centre of the Catholic plot. Once this happened, civil war became a distinct possibility.

---

[115] A. Milton, *Catholic and Reformed*, Cambridge, 1995, pp. 353–73; Hibbard, *Charles i and the Popish Plot*, p. 49.

[116] Hibbard, *Charles i and the Popish Plot*, pp. 99–100.

[117] Tyacke, *Anti-Calvinists*, pp. 227–8.

[118] J. Fielding, 'Opposition to the Personal Rule of Charles i: the Diary of Robert Woodford, 1637–1641', *HJ*, vol. 31, 1988, pp. 782–3.

The image of virtue

It has been argued in some of the recent writing on Charles that he was too lazy and too uninterested in politics to make an effective ruler. He is seen as having preferred a life that was essentially 'private and apolitical', taking every opportunity to withdraw from public affairs into his family and the art and ceremonial of the court.[119] There is some truth in this verdict, but as an assessment of the nature of Charles's engagement with politics it is well wide of the mark. He may have lacked the relaxed skills of his father, but he took his kingly duties extremely seriously and was far more diligent in attending to the day-to-day business of government. It also fails to appreciate that in this period the 'private' very often was 'political'. Charles was devoted to his family and his artistic interests, but he did not regard these as in any sense alternatives to the world of politics. Rather, they were an extension of it. Like most contemporaries, he viewed his family and household as a commonwealth in miniature. *A looking Glass for Prince and People* explained in 1632 that

the court of kings is an abridgement of their kingdom . . . it is a proof of the government of their persons and an image of the ruling of their states . . . as is the prince, so is his court . . . as the court is so the country will be.[120]

In other words, the king's court should be seen as an expression of his personality and capacity as a ruler and, at the same time, as a means of shaping the attitudes of his subjects. Everything that happened there – from the elaborate ceremonial to receive ambassadors to the most intimate domestic arrangements – provided an example to guide the nation. Charles was acutely conscious of this and devoted considerable effort to making his family and court an image of the virtue he wished to instil into his people.

The king's relationship with his family was at the core of this personal and political identity. He was the first English monarch for well over a hundred years to enjoy anything approaching a happy and fulfilled family life and it did much to define his kingship. The warmth and closeness of his relationship with the queen was the source of frequent comment by his

---

[119] Reeve, *Road to Personal Rule*, p. 196.

[120] Cited in Sharpe, *The Personal Rule*, p. 210.

courtiers and emerges clearly from his own correspondence. The royal couple found it very hard to be apart, even for short periods. The devotion that was so evident in 1628 was still apparent in 1637 when the king was said to dine and sup with the queen and sit by her 'the greatest part of the day' while she was expecting their fifth child. His affection for his offspring was just as evident. The birth of Prince Charles on 29 May 1630, followed by James (in 1633) and Henry (in 1639), and Mary (in 1631), Elizabeth (in 1635), Anne (in 1637) and Henrietta (in 1644) were events that he celebrated and cherished. He had one of Van Dyck's delightful group portraits of his children hanging over his breakfast table and kept a silver staff on which he recorded their growth. There are some charming descriptions of the time he spent with them, such as the occasion when the whole family went 'a maying into St James's Park', or when the infant princes 'welcomed him home with the prettiest innocent mirth that can be imagined' after his progress to Scotland in 1633.[121] Charles's family provided him with a sense of happiness and fulfilment that he had rarely felt in his earlier life. They also enabled him to feel, perhaps for the first time, that he was making a success of being a king. He had, after all, discharged the first responsibility of any monarch, which was to secure his succession. Beyond this they provided a model for the way in which he visualised the relationship with this subjects. Images of the love and harmony of the royal couple, and of the king as father of his people, were central motifs in the style of kingship that he promoted during the 1630s.

A similar connection between the personal and the political was envisaged in measures taken to promote reform at court. There were two established models of court etiquette that Charles could follow: the French, where the monarch lived out his life in the public gaze, constantly surrounded by his leading subjects; and the Spanish, where he was shut away in private and surrounded by ceremonial to enhance the mystical status of kingship.[122] James favoured the French model, cultivating a sprawling, densely populated, inclusive court in which, as he often protested, he was accessible to suitors day and night. This allowed him to supervise the factions among his leading nobles and demonstrate to the world the reality of the union between

---

[121] Ibid., pp. 170–1, 183–8, Carlton, *Charles I*, pp. 133–4.

[122] On the character of European courts in this period, see J.H. Elliott, 'The court of the Spanish Hapsburgs', in idem, *Spain and its World 1500–1700*, 1989, pp. 142–61.

England and Scotland. But there were frequent complaints of corruption and immorality that Charles found distasteful. Within a a few weeks of his accession he had issued a proclamation describing how 'in the late reign of our dear father . . . we saw much disorder in and about his household' and, 'finding [this] to bring much dishonour to our house have resolved the reformation thereof'.[123]

The gloss put on this 'reformation' at the time was that it was an attempt 'to bring [the court] to the ancient form' and reinstate 'the rules and maxims of the late Queen Elizabeth'.[124] As in the church, Charles apparently saw himself as working to restore 'primitive' standards of purity and decorum. In fact, the reforms he made probably owed rather more to the features of the Spanish court that he had observed at first hand on his trip to Madrid. Contemporaries associated the Spanish style with honour and *gravitas*, with the ideals of the old nobility, and with a high moral tone and sense of order and permanence. All of these were values with which Charles strongly identified. The formality of the Spanish also doubtless appealed to his reserve and love of privacy. He adopted their more restrained dress code, following the example set by the earl of Arundel in the 1610s and attiring himself all in black.[125] He also established the Spanish fashion of decorating royal palaces with collections of paintings, to enhance the impression of majesty. Most conspicuously, he incorporated their sense of distance and aloofness into his court ceremonial. The Venetian ambassador noticed a difference within a few weeks of his accession.

The king observes a rule of great decorum. The nobles do not enter his apartments in confusion as heretofore, but each rank has its appointed place . . . The king has also drawn up rules for himself, dividing the day from his

---

[123] *Proclamations of Charles I*, pp. 37–9.

[124] Cited in Shepherd, 'Charles I and political patronage', p. 62.

[125] Sharpe has suggested that Charles identified so strongly with the values of the Spanish court in part because of the dislocation of his early years: *The Personal Rule*, p. 183. To judge by his portraits his dress was at its most austere in the mid-1620s when he was, perhaps, trying hardest to impress those around him with his *gravitas*: see particularly the Mytens portrait of c. 1623 reproduced in J. Peacock, 'The visual image of Charles I', in T. Corns ed., *The Royal Image. Representations of Charles I*, Cambridge, 1999, p. 223 and the Van Doort portrait of c. 1624–5, reproduced in *Dynasties*, ed. K. Hearn, 1995, p. 225 and featured on the cover of this book.

very early rising, for prayers, exercises, audiences, business, eating and sleeping.[126]

Once the war was ended, Charles took this process further, setting up a commission of peers with the task of restoring the court to its 'ancient splendour'. Their proposals formed the basis for a book of orders establishing new codes of behaviour and regulations for access within the royal household.[127]

Although the standards achieved by Charles never matched the awe-inspiring formality of the Spanish, they were much closer to this than anything that had gone before. Three sets of principles can be discerned in the new regulations. First, they were meant to ensure that 'our house may be a place of civility and honour', with scrupulously high moral standards. Any royal servant found to be 'so vicious and unmannerly that he is unfit to live in virtuous company' was to be banished from the household, as was anyone 'noised to be a profane person . . . a notorious drunkard, swearer, railer or quarreler'. Charles was quite prepared to show that he meant business. When Henry Jermyn, the queen's favourite, made her maid, Elizabeth Villiers, pregnant, he told him that he must either marry her or leave the court.[128] Second, the new regulations were intended to reinforce hierarchy and order. This was achieved by making access within the court more exclusive the closer one approached to the royal presence. The privy chamber was now barred to all except noblemen, councillors and gentlemen of the privy chamber, while the bedchamber, where Charles slept and took most of his meals, became accessible only to princes of the blood and the gentlemen and grooms who attended there.[129] In the third place, the reforms stressed the reverence due to the king's semi-divine person. The preservation of a proper distance between king and ordinary mortals was insisted on at all times and objects that came into contact with his body were treated with a quasi-religious reverence. Ushers were deputed to ensure that in his absence no one stood under the canopy of state or leaned on his bed; and after he had been washed in the

---

[126] *CSP Ven. 1625–6*, p. 21.

[127] This was probably finalised around 1630: see Sharpe, *The Personal Rule*, p. 211.

[128] Ibid., pp. 190, 211–12.

[129] Sharpe, 'The image of virtue', pp. 233–5, 244–5.

morning the royal towel was raised above the gentleman usher's head
as he left the presence chamber. Services in the Chapel Royal were especially carefully choreographed. The king's offertory was brought in by a
gentleman usher and passed to the senior nobleman present who then
handed it to the kneeling king, who finally presented it to the officiating
cleric.[130] The aim of these regulations was partly to impress foreign ambassadors and visiting dignitaries, but more especially to provide a model
for his people. The new household orders stated quite explicitly that the
intention was 'to establish government and order in our court which from
thence may spread with more order through all parts of our kingdoms'.[131]
This was to become the centrepiece of an extensive programme of social
and political reform.

The impulse to order the kingdom through reform of the court also played
an important role in Charles's patronage of court culture. He attached great
importance to images and patterns when it came to communicating with
his people or seeking to instil unity and obedience. This accorded with the
belief that was widespread among Renaissance writers and artists, that
the purpose of their work was as much political as aesthetic. Literature and
the visual arts should not only be pleasing to the eye or ear, but also instruct
their audience in the virtuous principles that would produce a more
civilised society. Ben Jonson, the playwright and poet laureate to James I,
declared on one occasion that poetry was an art that disposed men 'to all
the civil offices of society . . . and guides us by the hand to action, with a
ravishing sweetness'.[132] Similarly Inigo Jones, who was Charles's chief
architect and artistic adviser, believed that classical buildings, through their
ordered and harmonious proportions, could instil reason and moral virtue
and teach people how to live ordered lives. He wrote a book about
Stonehenge premised on the assumption that it had been built by the Romans
to civilise the barbarous ancient Britons.[133] The application of these ideas
can be seen very clearly in the court masques of the period.

---

[130] Ibid., pp. 242–3; Sharpe, *The Personal Rule*, pp. 218–19.

[131] Cited in Sharpe, *The Personal Rule*, p. 210.

[132] Cited in R.M. Smuts, 'The political failure of Stuart cultural patronage', in G.F. Lytle
and S. Orgel eds, *Patronage in the Renaissance*, Princeton, 1981, pp. 167–9.

[133] R.M. Smuts, *Court Culture and the Origins of a Royalist Tradition in Early Stuart England*,
Philadelphia, 1987, pp. 165–6.

These masques are a curious phenomenon. There is nothing quite like them in modern drama and attempts to restage them have been unsuccessful because modern audiences are unfamiliar with their conventions. Yet they were vehicles for the talents of many of the outstanding dramatists of the period – including Jonson, William Davenant and James Shirley – and they were seen as an indispensable part of the exercise of divine-right monarchy. Charles himself took a leading role in the productions, discussing designs with Jones, who was the chief producer, and dancing with the queen in each of the annual performances between 1631 and 1640. The masques were also conceived in such a way as to enhance the sense of awe at the king's majesty. They were the only stage plays of the period that employed perspective scenery – and Jones's sets were full of visual pyrotechnics and spectacular illusions that were regarded as part of the mystery of divinely ordained kingship. Moreover they took place inside a specially constructed theatre in which the only 'true' perspective for events on stage was that enjoyed by the king and queen. They sat at the centre of the auditorium with the court arranged around them in order of seniority. This ensured that the audience watched the royal couple as much as the masque, and emphasised again that monarchy was the ethical and symbolic centre of the whole performance.[134]

The basic aim of the masque was to proclaim the authority of the king and celebrate his achievements through a representation of his role in the ongoing struggle between virtue and vice. Performances generally began with what was known as the antimasque, in which a world of order and harmony was plunged into chaos by vices and evil influences. The forms taken by these vices are instructive because they illustrate the court's perception of its enemies during the Personal Rule. Often they were fairly abstract, representing forces like greed and selfishness which led people to put their own private interests before the public good. But on occasion they were more immediate and concrete. In *The Temple of Love* the main threat to the rule of true love was identified as the puritan, who is described as 'a sworn enemy of poetry, music and all ingenious arts, but a great friend of murmuring, libelling and all sorts of discord, attended by his factious

---

[134] S. Orgel, *The Illusion of Power*, Berkeley, 1975; R. Strong, *Splendour at Court*, 1973, pp. 153–70.

followers'; while in *Britannia Triumphans* London was reduced to 'a horrid hell' by, among others, the leaders of popular rebellions against the crown, Jack Straw, John Cade and Robert Kett.[135] The antimasque was followed by a middle section in which the evils were banished by the appearance of all sorts of virtues. This was usually the point at which the king and queen arrived on stage, accompanied by various of their nobles and ladies in waiting. Charles generally appeared, according to Jones's description in *Tempe Restored*, as 'the prototype to all the kingdoms under his monarchy of religion, justice and all the virtues joined together'.[136] Henrietta Maria was invariably presented as a manifestation of pure, uncorrupted love and beauty.[137] This was often the longest section of the masque, as a chorus discoursed on the two monarchs' capacities for bringing harmony and understanding, while they and their attendants danced in front of Jones's backdrops of classical architecture and ordered landscapes. Finally, the masquers on stage descended into the auditorium to join with other members of the court in a crowning expression of unity.

The masques were full of messages that illustrated the belief in the civilising power of images and patterns. This can be demonstrated by looking in more detail at *Salmacida Spolia*, the last of Charles's masques, performed in January 1640. The spoils of Salmacis were the fruits of victory won by persuasion rather than force, and the masque can be read as an allegory of Charles's efforts to deal with the rebellious Scots. In the opening scene, 'Discord, a malicious fury', envious of the peace that prevails in Britain, sought to stir up conflict by introducing the vices of falsehood, avarice, pride and ambition. The people, lulled into complacency by their good fortune, succumbed to these 'evil spirits' and a storm ensued. However, it was suddenly stopped by the appearance of 'a secret power whose wisdom . . . will change all their malicious hopes . . . into a sudden calm'. This was the first reference to Charles who took the role of 'Philogenes, a lover of his people'. The scenes that followed proclaimed his virtues. 'Concord' and 'the Good Genius of Great Britain' applauded his patience and forbearance in

---

[135] M. Butler, 'Reform or reverence? The politics of the Caroline masque', in J.R. Mulryne and M. Shewring eds, *Theatre and Government Under the Early Stuarts*, Cambridge, 1993, pp. 144–51; the quotation is cited on p. 144.

[136] Cited in R. Strong, *Charles I on Horseback*, 1972, pp. 89–94.

[137] Strong, *Splendour at Court*, p. 161.

the face of 'the people's folly'; a chorus praised his reliance on 'inward helps, not outward force', against the backdrop of 'craggy rocks and inaccessible mountains which represented the difficult way which heroes are to pass'; and the proscenium arch, which framed the stage, depicted the qualities of 'the good prince': 'Reason', 'Counsel', 'Resolution', 'Prudence', 'Doctrine' and 'Discipline'. Eventually Charles himself was glimpsed with his nobles, seated on 'the Throne of Honour', whereupon the queen and her ladies in waiting were sent down from heaven to join them. The finale involved the king and queen and their attendants dancing together in front of Jones's stage set of magnificent classical buildings linked together by a bridge, while the chorus sang of the harmonising influence of the royal couple.

All that are harsh, all that are rude,
Are by your harmony subdued;
Yet so into obedience wrought,
As if not forc'd to it but taught.[138]

Salmacida Spolia took place when Charles was preparing to meet the Short Parliament and deal once again with the rebellious Scots. These circumstances gave it a very specific political meaning. The stress on Charles's patience and self-restraint can be read, as Martin Butler has shown, as a declaration of his commitment to reconciliation, directed both at the Covenanters and the parliament.[139] There are also images of the king as conqueror, which may refer to his preferred option of subduing the Scots by force. But, beyond these there were the more general messages that could be found in the other masques of the period. The tributes to the royal marriage, as an example of the pure and virtuous love that could teach the people how to control their corrupting passions, were common to most of them. So, too, was the contrast between a Europe riven by war and Britain enjoying the benefits and happiness of the Caroline peace. Less common, but still an important theme of masques like *Coelum Brittanicum*, was the celebration of the ancient glories of Great Britain and, by implication, the feat of James and Charles

---

[138] The text of the masque is in S. Orgel and R. Strong, *Inigo Jones. The Theatre of the Stuart Court*, 2 vols., 1973, vol. 2, pp. 730–34. For commentaries on it see Smuts, *Court Culture*, pp. 255–7 and M. Butler, 'Politics and the masque: *Salmacida Spolia*', in T. Healey and J. Sawday eds, *Literature and the English Civil War*, Cambridge, 1990, pp. 59–74.

[139] Butler, '*Salmacida Spolia*', pp. 64–71.

in uniting the three kingdoms. Finally, like most of the masques, *Salmacida Spolia* addressed the central issue of how virtue in its various forms could dispel the disordered passions and unruly vices of the antimasque.[140]

It is important to emphasise this last point because some historians have depicted the masques as a form of escapism by which Charles sought to isolate himself from unpalatable realities and enjoy the 'illusion of control' over his political difficulties.[141] This is to misunderstand their purpose. If one interprets them within the context of ideas about the civilising power of images, they can be seen, as Malcolm Smuts has argued, 'not as substitutes for political reality, but as guides to statesmanship'. They were not intended to achieve political realism, or confront detailed policy issues, because they were in essence allegorical. However, they did represent the world of politics in the terms in which Charles himself often appears to have understood it: as 'a great drama of conflicting passions' in which an enlightened, virtuous, noble elite, with the king at its apex, sought to regulate the disordered impulses of a plebeian multitude.[142]

Similar themes emerge in the court painting of the period. Painting was Charles's great enthusiasm. Most of his personal friendships with courtiers were based on this shared passion. Endymion Porter and Sir Kenelm Digby, two of the grooms of the bedchamber closest to him, were fellow connoisseurs, as were Arundel, Hamilton and the third and fourth earls of Pembroke.[143] Painting also provided some of the few occasions when he threw off his normal reserve and really warmed up. The Venetian ambassador recorded a delightful episode in 1636 when a new consignment of pictures arrived from the Vatican.

As soon as the king was told by the queen that she had received the pictures he rushed to see them, calling to him Jones, the earl of Holland and the earl of Pembroke. The very moment Jones saw the pictures he greatly approved of them and in order to be able to study them better threw off his coat, put on his

---

[140] Smuts, *Court Culture*, pp. 245–53; Strong, *Splendour at Court*, pp. 161–4; Strong, *Charles I on Horseback*, pp. 83–8; M. Butler, 'The invention of Britain and the early Stuart masque', in R.M. Smuts ed., *The Stuart Court and Europe*, Cambridge, 1996, pp. 65–85.

[141] Orgel, *Illusion of Power*, pp. 88–9; Strong, *Splendour at Court*, pp. 157, 169–70.

[142] Smuts, *Court Culture*, pp. 169, 255–7.

[143] Ibid., pp. 120–3; Reeve, *Road to Personal Rule*, pp. 196–7.

eyeglasses and together with the king began to examine them very closely, admiring them very much.[144]

The next day, Charles put Jones's expertise to the test by removing the labels from the paintings to see how many he could recognise by the artist's hand. Jones was still boasting of his success a week later.

Charles was extremely knowledgeable about painting. He developed the expertise in his youth when art collecting was becoming fashionable among the European nobility. During the trip to Madrid he had the opportunity to view some of Europe's finest masterpieces at first hand and on his return quickly established himself as an outstanding patron. He used the crown's resources to buy up important collections, such as the duke of Mantua's, which cost him £15 939 when the crown's bankruptcy was at its height in 1627.[145] He also attracted leading painters to England, the most important of whom was the Flemish artist, Sir Anthony Van Dyck. Charles set him up with a house and studio in Blackfriars and provided a pension, a knighthood and enough commissions to keep him in England from 1632 until his death in 1640. He visited the studio regularly to watch the master at work and legend has it that, on occasion, he took up the brush himself to supply the finishing touches.[146]

Charles believed that paintings, like court masques, should enlighten and civilise as well as being aesthetically pleasing. Most of the major commissions of his reign were representations of kingship, designed to be displayed in the royal palaces where they could provide images to both inspire and instruct. The first of these was the ceiling of the Whitehall Banqueting House which was planned when Rubens visited England on an embassy in 1629, and finally installed between 1635 and 1637. It has been plausibly suggested that Inigo Jones, the original architect of the Banqueting House, provided the allegorical programme on which the paintings were based, but Charles, with his highly developed understanding of the medium, must also have been involved. The themes closely matched those of the court masques. In the main panels, James was represented in the familiar guises of peacemaker,

---

[144] Cited in Smuts, *Court Culture*, p. 122.

[145] R.M. Smuts, 'Art and the material culture of majesty in early Stuart England', in Smuts ed., *The Stuart Court and Europe*, pp. 96–7, 102–3.

[146] C. Brown, *Van Dyck*, 1982, pp. 137–40.

unifier of England and Scotland, the personification of wisdom and justice and defender of the faith. There were also images from the antimasque – of envy, ignorance, avarice and intemperance, together with a many-headed monster, a snaky-haired fury and an armed man brandishing a torch, which represented war, discord and popular rebellion.[147] Once again the central messages were about the harmonising and civilising power of the king's virtue.

This theme was also central to the iconography of Van Dyck's paintings of Charles, but presented in a much more original way. Van Dyck was arguably the greatest visual image maker that any English ruler has ever had the good fortune to employ and he completely transformed the representation of Charles. Lack of height, heavy features, a long face and a rather tense demeanour made him an unpromising subject for the portrait painter. Sir Anthony's predecessor, Daniel Mytens, struggled to convey much in the way of dignity or substance. Yet, within a few months of his arrival in England, Van Dyck was producing portraits that depicted the king as the epitome of baroque notions of majesty and kingship. He overcame his physical defects by posing him on horseback, elongating his hands and fingers, ageing him by about five years and giving his face a distant, melancholy expression suggestive of wisdom and maturity.[148] As his subject matter, he adopted the various roles expected of 'the good prince'.

One of his earliest portraits, known as 'the great peece', represented Charles as the father of his people (see Plate 3). It showed him seated in the middle of a family group, gazing calmly at the viewer. Henrietta Maria and the baby Princess Elizabeth were turned slightly towards him, to emphasise his command of the scene, and the infant Prince Charles rested his hand on his knee, to suggest informality and tenderness. At the side of the group is the crown, orb and sceptre of state and in the background the parliament house. The painting, which was hung in the Long Gallery at Whitehall Palace, captured brilliantly the link between the 'public' and 'private' roles of the king. Here was Charles as head of his family and head of his people, commanding both spheres with an air of relaxed confidence.[149]

---

[147] Strong, *Britannia Triumphans*, pp. 7–64.

[148] Strong, *Charles I on Horseback*, pp. 27–43; Brown, *Van Dyck*, pp. 142, 164; Smuts, *Court Culture*, p. 204.

[149] O. Millar, *Van Dyck in England*, 1982, pp. 46–7; Sharpe, *The Personal Rule*, p. 185.

Van Dyck's two great equestrian portraits, 'Charles with Monsieur de St Antoine, his riding master' (c.1633 – see Plate 4), hung at the end of the gallery at St James's palace, and 'Charles on horseback' (c.1637 – see Plate 5), a smaller version of which was hung in the throne room at Whitehall, conveyed a different side of kingship. Here Charles was represented as the conquering hero, clad in jousting armour, wielding the baton of command and – in the portrait with M. de St Antoine – riding through a triumphal arch. The depiction of the king on horseback deliberately echoed the Roman tradition, in which this form of representation was reserved for Emperors, and at the same time conveyed the impression of his command over nature, by showing his skill in horsemanship. The later portrait also included a cartouche with the inscription *'Carolus Rex Magnae Britanniae'*, a reminder of his status as king of Great Britain just when this was being contested by the rebellious Scots. This was an image of the king as commander and leader of his people, a figure of awesome power and majesty.[150]

A third aspect of kingship was captured in the portrait of 'Charles à la chasse' (c.1635 – see Plate 6), which showed him resting after the hunt. This was Charles as the ultimate courtier, elegant, well-dressed, poised and relaxed, but at the same time clearly in command of his surroundings. He gazed out at the viewer with an air of serene self-possession, suggesting the inner strength and control over unruly passions which was regarded as the essence of true nobility. Like the central figures in many of Van Dyck's other portraits, Charles radiated a quality that Malcolm Smuts has described as 'psychic balance'. He was the image of a king who 'could rule the kingdom because he had first learned to subdue his own lusts'. Again this was Charles as Philogenes, the Stoical philosopher king, but depicted in a way that was both novel and arresting.[151]

These portraits had a particular resonance for contemporaries and later generations, and probably also for Charles himself. Because of his closeness to Van Dyck, and his highly developed knowledge of painting, it can be assumed that he exercised more control than most patrons over the images that finally emerged. Perhaps more than any of the texts produced in the

---

[150] Strong, *Charles I on Horseback*, pp. 45–57; Millar, *Van Dyck in England*, pp. 50–2.

[151] Smuts, *Court Culture*, pp. 172–7; Brown, *Van Dyck*, p. 169. On the notion of 'psychic balance', see Smuts, *Court Culture*, pp. 203–9; Sharpe, *The Personal Rule*, pp. 223–7.

1630s, they capture the essence of how he liked to imagine himself and wanted others to imagine him.

Court art and court ceremonial were fused together in Charles's reform of the Order of the Garter. This was part of an important reorientation of chivalric culture in England, marked by a shift away from the martial values of the accession day tilts, which Charles had embraced so enthusiastically in his youth. After 1622 the annual tilts were discontinued and by the 1630s Charles was taking other steps to distance himself from the Elizabethan military tradition that had become something of an embarrassment with the pursuit of peace. The tapestries which James commissioned to celebrate the victory over the Spanish Armada were transferred from his main palace at Whitehall to the relative obscurity of Oatlands and court masques poked fun at the Don Quixote figure of the knight-errant. This reorientation was not total. Charles himself, after all, was still being painted in jousting armour.[152] But there was a definite shift of emphasis that accommodated the king's pursuit of peace and also his desire to stress the civilising and sacred aspects of kingship.

The reinvention of the Order of the Garter was at the centre of this process. Charles took his role as Garter Sovereign extremely seriously. His first action on rising each morning was to put on the medal of St George which he is shown wearing in the majority of his portraits. According to Sir Thomas Roe, appointed chancellor of the Order in 1637, his priority was 'to restore' it 'to the primitive institution', although, as with the Church of England, this became a justification for far-reaching changes.[153] Under Elizabeth and James, the Order had retained its associations with martial valour, and its main ceremony was a parade through Whitehall by the knights of the garter and their retinues. Charles changed this by reviving the practice of holding parades in the more private surroundings of Windsor Castle and stressing their civil and spiritual aspects. He himself processed under a golden canopy, accompanied by choristers and clergymen from the chapel of St George chanting the litany, with the knights walking two by two, without their retinues. The knights were also required to wear newly designed cloaks bearing the cross of St George surrounded by an aureole

---

[152] Adamson, 'Chivalry and political culture', pp. 161–82.

[153] HMC, *Report on the MSS of the Marquess of Salisbury, XXII*, 1971, p. 294.

of silver rays in emulation of the French Order of the Holy Spirit.[154] This shift of emphasis received, perhaps, its clearest expression in Rubens's 'A landscape with St George and the dragon' (see Plate 7), painted on his 1629 visit to England. It depicted Charles as St George, having slain the dragon, presenting himself to a princess who is Henrietta Maria. According to Malcolm Smuts's reading, the landscape can be understood as an image of England, freed by the saint from the devouring monster of war and disorder, while the presence of the queen can be taken as inferring the way in which love has tempered his valour and helped to establish a reign of peace and harmony. The religious dimension is very prominent. St George was both a soldier and a martyr for Christ. The slaying of the dragon can be seen as symbolic of the Christian's victory over Satan, and the inclusion of the holy lamb, and Lambeth Palace in the background, as underlining the king's role as Defender of the Faith.[155] This was an image of Charles as priest/king, highlighting the sacerdotal elements of his kingship in contrast to the more secular qualities emphasised by Van Dyck.

One of the effects of Charles's reforms and artistic patronage was to introduce a new cosmopolitanism into English court culture. For much of Elizabeth and James's reigns the country had been cut off from European fashions for baroque painting, and classicising poetry and architecture. Charles brought it back into the international mainstream and in the process gained a great deal of prestige among art connoisseurs and visiting dignitaries.[156] Rubens, as early as 1625, described him as 'the greatest amateur of painting of all the princes of the world'.[157] However, this made a much less favourable impression on his own people. Most Englishmen, even the most educated, were conditioned to understand an artistic culture rooted in medieval and north European ideas about liberality, magnificence and spectacle. They were impressed by displays of lavish materials and flamboyant decoration of the type seen in the Jacobean 'prodigy houses'. The discipline, restraint and austere classicism of Jones's architecture or Van Dyck's paintings was largely alien to their experience.

---

[154] Sharpe, *The Personal Rule*, pp. 219–22; Adamson, 'Chivalry and political culture', pp. 174–5; Strong, *Charles I on Horseback*, pp. 62–3.

[155] Smuts, *Court Culture*, pp. 247–9.

[156] Smuts, 'Art and material culture', pp. 86–112; idem, *Court Culture*, pp. 185–9.

[157] Brown, *Van Dyck*, p. 138.

This led to a cultural divide that some historians have seen as opening up a split between 'Court' and 'Country'. To the English people, they argue, the court came to appear superficial, wasteful, corrupt and imbued with the ideas of popery and continental absolutism, all of which helped to distance it from the English people and exacerbate political tensions.[158] This view has been justifiably criticised for presenting an overly straightforward account of the impact of court culture. It overlooks the court's own diversity and also its capacity for self-criticism. In ideological terms, it embraced a huge range of cultural, political and religious opinions, many of which accorded with those of the 'country', while many of the most trenchant criticisms of its failings came from within its own ranks, from writers like Ben Jonson who saw themselves as fulfilling a philosophical duty to expose the vice and corruption that existed in all court-based societies.[159] Charles's reforms had a less clear-cut impact than these historians have suggested. Nonetheless, they did contribute in significant ways to the political differences of the period.

One of their most obvious consequences was to reinforce the court's sense of itself as a beleaguered minority, assailed on all sides by enemies. Many of the masques and paintings of the period were structured around a narrative in which order and hierarchy were threatened by seditious puritans, ambitious demagogues, the many-headed monster of popular insurrection or some other challenge to royal authority. This helped to confirm political assumptions that were already prevalent among Charles and his advisers. A vivid illustration of the process is provided by the newsletter account of a comedy performed before the king and queen when they visited Oxford in August 1636.[160] Entitled *Passions Calm'd or the Floating Island*, it described the struggles of 'Prudentius' (Charles) to bring good government to his people, aided by 'Intellectus Agens', a 'wise and active' counsellor

---

[158] L. Stone, *The Causes of the English Revolution 1529–1642*, 1972, pp. 105–6; P.W. Thomas, 'Two Cultures? Court and country under Charles I', in C.S.R. Russell ed., *The Origins of the English Civil War*, Basingstoke, 1973, pp. 168–93.

[159] R.M. Smuts, 'Cultural diversity and cultural change at the court of James I', in Peck ed., *The Mental World of the Jacobean Court*, pp. 102–6; idem, *Court Culture*, pp. 79–82.

[160] George Leyburn to Edward Bennett, 3 September 1636. This was discovered by Michael Questier and is included in his forthcoming edition of *Newsletters from the Caroline Court, 1631–1638: Catholicism and the Politics of the Personal Rule*, Camden Soc. I am most grateful to him for sharing it with me.

who was taken to represent Laud, chancellor of the university and sponsor of the performance. The main obstacle to Prudentius's efforts was the 'unrulye and disobedient passions' which, according to the letter writer, the queen's Catholic chaplain, George Leybourne, represented 'the puritans and all such as are opposite to the courses which our king doth run in his government'. The main comic turn was Malancholio, 'a puritan minister who made very good sport', at which 'their majesties laughed heartily'. The 'Passions' forced 'Prudentius' to give up his crown and in his place elected 'Lady Fancy', 'under whose government they fell into bitter discord and dissensions'. But the situation was rescued when 'Intellectus Agens' persuaded the 'Passions' to reinstate their former king and make 'acknowledgement of their foul errors'. Prudentius forgave them in a speech 'full of mercies, signifying that the courses which he ran in his government was for their good, and as for the navy it was to defend them and the kingdom'. The only sour note was sounded by Malancholio who when he came to tender his submission said 'O king, I kneel not to thee but to power; neither do I adore thee.'

This was an occasion which, in many ways, captured the *zeitgeist* of the 1630s. It showed Charles confronting the forces of puritanism and popularity and, for the most part, subduing them, not through force, but by the power of wit and reason. Sharing in the royal couple's laughter at the mockery of the puritans were a collection of courtiers, Catholics members of the queen's household and the two papal envoys Gregorio Panzani and George Con. The message of the occasion was similar to that of the court masques, that those who shared in Charles's mission to bring order, stability and good government were not the 'patriots' and 'commonwealthmen' lionised by the political nation, but a small elite of courtiers and noblemen, as likely to be Catholics as Protestants. It is significant that in none of the masques performed at court in the 1630s is there any suggestion that those outside it have any positive role to play in establishing order and harmony. Parliament never appears and the people are cast either as the potentially rebellious characters of the antimasque or as loving, but essentially passive, subjects who look on while their king performs all sorts of heroic and creative acts.[161] The only assistance he received was

---

[161] I am grateful to Martin Butler for advice on this point.

from subordinate virtues striving to imitate his perfection, which were the roles taken by members of the nobility present at court. This reinforced the assumption that those who mattered in the distribution of political power were the king and the court-based peerage, a belief also apparent in the attention Charles lavished on the Order of the Garter and the decision to summon a gathering of nobles rather than a parliament before going to war with the Scots in 1639. It was a vision of the political order that matched the seating plan of one of Jones's perspective theatres: Charles at the centre, selected peers, councillors and courtiers arranged in hierarchical order around him, and the rest of the political nation shut outside.

Almost as damaging was the way in which the culture of the court tended to close down opportunities for the discussion of policy options. The strongest and most persistent theme running through the poetry and paintings, as well as the masques, of the 1630s was the benefits of the Caroline peace. The dominant motifs were the cult of pure love associated with the royal couple, Jones's images of peaceful landscapes and depictions of holy knights turning their back on martial values. Only one of the court masques of the decade made an approving reference to the glories of war. This was *The Triumph of the Princes d'Amour* which, significantly, was written not for Charles but the Prince Palatine, and was performed in 1636 during the brief period when continental involvement was being actively considered.[162] For most of the rest of the decade the images and arguments associated with peace were so overpowering as to stifle the expression of any alternative. The broader climate of ideas at court also made it hard to get the king to recognise a need to consult his people in parliament. As *Salmacida Spolia* demonstrated, masques were potentially a means of counselling the king through reminding him of the desirability of ruling in a tolerant and conciliatory manner – and the point could be underlined by involving courtiers who had misgivings about the direction of policy in the performance. However, as Martin Butler has shown, where such an approach might come into conflict with the masques' basic aim of praising the monarch and affirming his supremacy, it was the latter that took precedence. More authoritarian images tended to overpower the conciliatory, and the causes of disharmony were almost invariably traced back not to

---

[162] Smuts, *Court Culture*, p. 250; M. Butler, 'Entertaining the Palatine Princes: plays on foreign affairs, 1635–1637', *English Literary Renaissance*, vol. 3, 1983, pp. 319–44.

any failing on the part of Charles, but to the stubbornness and subversiveness of disruptive elements among the people.[163]

Good relations with the subject were further damaged by the way in which the culture of the court, in its broadest sense, tended to distance the king from his people. The English expected their monarchs to be visible and accessible. They associated royal majesty with public pageants in which the king or queen paraded before them amidst richly dressed courtiers, displaying the trappings of wealth, rank and status. The earl of Newcastle explained the power of such displays in a letter of advice to his tutee, the young Prince Charles, in the late 1630s. 'What protects you kings', he said, was, above all, ceremonial and spectacle:

the distance people are with you, great officers, heralds, drums, trumpeters, rich coaches . . . marshal's men making room . . . I know these master the people sufficiently. Aye even the wisest . . . shall shake off his wisdom and shake for fear of it, for this is the mist is cast before us and masters the commonwealth.[164]

Both Elizabeth and James understood this very well. Elizabeth displayed a genius for playing to the audience on her progresses and ceremonial entries into London and succeeded in emphasising both the majesty that raised her above her people and the emotional bonds that united her to them. James was less enamoured of large crowds, but still catered for popular taste by making elaborate entries in 1604 and 1606 and sponsoring lavish pageants for Henry's inauguration as Prince of Wales and Elizabeth's marriage to Frederick of the Palatinate. Charles was much more reluctant. It was widely anticipated that he would hold a coronation pageant in 1625–6, and the city even set up ceremonial arches; but this was first postponed because of the plague and then cancelled altogether. Thereafter he abandoned the practice of ceremonial entries, until November 1641 when he was trying to rally political support in the city. The main pageant in the court's calendar became the highly ritualised St George's day procession that took place

---

[163] Butler, 'Reform or reverence?, pp. 118–56; idem, '*Salmacida Spolia*', pp. 64–71.

[164] R.M. Smuts, 'Public ceremony and royal charisma: the English royal entry into London, 1485–1642', in A.L. Beier, D. Cannadine and J.M. Rosenheim eds, *The First Modern Society*, Cambridge, 1989, pp. 65–80; the quotation is on p. 67.

in the semi-private surroundings of Windsor Castle.[165] It was much the same story with royal progresses. His summer journey to Scotland in 1633 involved the customary civic receptions and entertainments at country houses, but this was very much the exception. Most of the time he stayed in royal palaces and hunting lodges, and often went out of his way to discourage direct contact with crowds, for example by imposing strict limitations on access to him by Oxford students when he visited Woodstock in 1631.[166]

There appear to have been two main reasons for Charles's reluctance to parade himself before his people. Partly it was a matter of money. Civic ceremonial cost tens of thousands of pounds and in the late 1620s, when the exchequer was seriously depleted, he evidently felt there were more pressing calls on his resources.[167] However, money was less of a problem in the 1630s and Charles's avoidance of pageants at this time seems to have had more to do with a dread of close contact with his subjects. As Prince of Wales, on the return from Madrid, he showed that he could work a crowd with the best of them and gave every impression of having enjoyed the experience. But once he became king he was much more guarded. The Spanish emphasis on distance and formality, the political rebuffs of his early months, the unseemly behaviour of some of the London crowds – particularly their open rejoicing at Buckingham's assassination – and his lack of confidence in his people's approval, all appear to have encouraged a tendency to withdrawal.[168] He understood that showing himself to his subjects was a necessary part of kingship, but he still found it hard to do.[169]

Judith Richards has suggested that Charles's reluctance to meet his people – together with an apparent neglect of the traditional kingly duties of touching for 'the king's evil' and receiving his subjects' petitions – meant that he was more withdrawn than any other English monarch had been for generations.[170] This is surely overstating the case. The evidence of the

---

[165] Ibid., pp. 82, 90–2; J. Richards, ' "His nowe majestie" and the English monarchy: the kingship of Charles I before 1640', *P & P*, vol. 113, 1986, pp. 82–3.

[166] Sharpe, *The Personal Rule*, p. 779; Richards, 'The kingship of Charles I', pp. 83–6.

[167] Smuts, 'The political failure of early-Stuart cultural patronage', pp. 172–4.

[168] Smuts, 'Public ceremony and royal charisma', pp. 84–7.

[169] See his willingness to go along with Nicholas's preparations for his entry into London in November 1641: *Evelyn*, pp. 771, 783, 791, 793–4.

[170] Richards, 'The kingship of Charles I', pp. 79–93.

books of petitions among the state papers, and the quantities of gold 'angels' minted to be given to those whom the king touched, suggests that he was at least as attentive to these duties as his father had been.[171] However, her argument does highlight an important issue – the extent to which Charles was damaged politically by a failure to be as open or as accessible as his people expected. This applies not just to access to his person, but also to his willingness to engage with a new style politics of public relations and news management.

Peter Heylyn, writing in the 1650s, insisted that he would have been much better able to rally popular loyalist sentiment in the civil war if he had displayed 'a little popularity' and done more to sell himself to his people.[172] His judgement reflects an awareness that politics had become something that took place in the full glare of public scrutiny. By the 1620s, and, indeed, well before, developments in the circulation of news and the dissemination of opinion had opened up the political arena. Ideas, rumours and reports were now being communicated with unprecedented speed and reaching a far wider audience than previously; and a variety of different 'publics' were encouraged to debate issues on which they would not previously have been supposed to have an opinion. Politics had become 'popular', and appealing to, and manipulating, the opinions of the people was now an essential part of the process. Most leading politicians recognised this fact, however much they might deplore it.[173] The problem for the crown was that neither James nor Charles felt particularly comfortable with this situation.

In 1621 James had a golden opportunity to take control of the processes of news management by publishing 'a gazette of weekly occurants'. According to the promoter of the scheme, John Pory, it would

---

[171] Sharpe, *The Personal Rule*, pp. 199–200; H. Farquhar, 'Royal charities, part 1 – Angels as healing pieces for the king's evil', *British Numismatics Jnl.*, vol. 12, 1915, pp. 111–14, 132; Fincham and Lake, 'Ecclesiastical policies of James and Charles', p. 44.

[172] Smuts, 'Public ceremony and royal charisma', p. 90.

[173] For discussions of this new style politics, see R.P. Cust, 'News and politics in early seventeenth-century England', *P & P*, vol. 112, 1986, pp. 60–90; A. Bellany, ' "Rayling rhymes and vaunting verse": libellous politics in early Stuart England, 1603–1628', in Sharpe and Lake eds, *Culture and Politics in Early Stuart England*, pp. 285–310; P.G. Lake and M. Questier, 'Puritans, papists and the "public sphere" in early modern England: the Edmund Campion affair in context', *Journal of Modern History*, vol. 72, 2000, pp. 587–627.

establish a speedy way whereby to dispense into the veins of the whole body of the state such matter as may best temper it to the disposition of the head and principal members.[174]

The success that Richelieu enjoyed with a similar scheme in France suggests that Pory's claim was not exaggerated.[175] But James turned down the proposal, perhaps because of his oft-expressed dislike of encouraging any sort of public discussion of the *arcana imperii*.

Charles's accession offered a fresh opportunity. His own experiences at the time of the 'Blessed Revolution' made him aware of the effectiveness of appeals to public opinion; and in Buckingham he had an adviser who was a relatively skilled, if not always successful, practitioner of the new techniques.[176] Again, however, the crown failed to make the most of its opportunities. One of the moments of decision came in the summer of 1627 when Secretary Coke drew up a lengthy 'Manifest' containing a well-argued explanation of the reasons for the Isle de Rhé expedition. It was read and approved by Charles and a decision was taken that it should be published. However, at the last moment this was reversed for reasons which, as Tom Cogswell has pointed out, remain obscure. They may have had to do with a concern that publication would hamper Buckingham's efforts to recruit support from other Catholic states. But it appears more likely that the king himself, perhaps encouraged by council hardliners like Dorset or Laud, had second thoughts. Around this time he was expressing alarm over the ways in which the weekly printed 'corantoes', carrying foreign news, 'do abuse the people and oftentimes raise disadvantageous and scandalous reports';[177] and the forced loan provided first-hand evidence of how popular speculation could lead to disobedience and opposition. Rather than attempting to direct the speculation, Charles decided it was safer to shut it down and suspend publication.

---

[174] Cited in W.S. Powell, *John Pory, 1572–1636*, Chapel Hill, N.C., pp. 52–3.

[175] J.P. Vitu, 'Instruments of information in France', in B. Dooley and S.A. Alcorn eds, *The Politics of Information in Early Modern Europe*, 2001, pp. 165–7.

[176] For Buckingham's efforts at public relations, see Cogswell, 'Buckingham and popularity', pp. 211–34.

[177] T.E. Cogswell, 'The politics of propaganda', pp. 187–215; BL, Add. MS 72439, fos. 1–3.

The decision over the 'Manifest' was symptomatic of the king's pre-
ference for a more closed style of government. The trend was not all in
one direction. On occasion the crown demonstrated a capacity for making
well-judged and effective interventions in the public arena. The 1629
Declaration was a case in point, as were several of the better managed Star
Chamber trials of the period.[178] As Anthony Milton has demonstrated, the
crown could also be quite perceptive in counteracting the charge that it was
authoritarian and 'absolutist'. The trial of Cotton and the peers associated
with the tract about bridling 'the impertinency of parliament' was carefully
calculated to distance it from any such sentiments, as was the refusal to
authorise publication of Sir Robert Filmer's *Patriarcha* or Francis Kynaston's
'The true representation of forepast parliaments'.[179] There is no doubt
that Charles and his councillors were capable of presenting positive images
of their actions. The problem was that they did not do this as often or
as tactfully as they needed to. The next big public declaration after 1629
did not come until the *Large Declaration* of 1639; and some of the show
trials of the later 1630s were badly misjudged, most notably Hampden's case.[180]

In contrast to its failure to mount an effective public relations offensive,
the crown did put considerable energy and resources into image-making
at court. The problem was that this had little impact on the perceptions
of the nation as a whole. The idea that images of harmony could instruct
people how to behave in an orderly and civilised fashion may have had
a respectable intellectual pedigree, but it does not seem to have worked in
practice. The court masques are a good example. Most of Charles's subjects
never read a masque or saw one being performed, and those who did showed
little capacity for understanding the philosophical messages it contained.
Reports suggest that audiences were impressed by the lavish costumes,
and some of Jones's special effects, but the deeper meanings washed over

---

[178] Perhaps the most effective of these in terms of putting across the crown's case were
the Leighton case and the first trial of William Prynne: Gardiner, *History of England*,
vol. 7, pp. 143–52, 327–35. The Woodstock meeting of August 1631, accounts of which
circulated in manuscript, was a well-executed, if only partially successful, attempt to put
across the message that the king was applying his preaching ban even-handedly: Como,
'Predestination and political conflict', pp. 265, 291–4.

[179] Milton, 'Wentworth and political thought', pp. 134–5.

[180] On the mishandling of the Hampden case, see below pp. 193–4.

them.[181] Visual images of the king were more accessible and were widely disseminated. Most of Charles's subjects would have known what he looked like from the royal head on a coin or a medal, or from more complex representations in line drawings or public statues. However, as interventions in debates about politics, these images had limited relevance. They could convey very effectively a sense of the majesty and authority of kingship, but, by their nature, could do little to shape attitudes towards specific policies.[182] The crown needed to supplement such images with a steady stream of pamphlets and declarations, justifying its actions in terms that were intelligible to the political nation. The effectiveness of its declarations and propaganda from 1641 onwards demonstrates the opportunity that was missed in the 1630s.

John Morrill has described Charles as a monarch 'unparalleled in his failure to communicate with his subjects'.[183] Enough has been said to show that this is a considerable exaggeration. On occasion he showed that he was quite prepared to communicate and could do so very effectively. The problem was that he did not see this as a political priority and therefore did not do it often enough. There was a mixture of reasons for this. The elitist and inward-looking culture of the court bolstered his sense that it was inappropriate for kings to be always explaining themselves. There was a side of Charles which believed, as Kevin Sharpe has pointed out, that his actions should speak louder than his words.[184] This was not conducive to regular communications about crown policy. Another factor was his abhorrence of 'popularity'. Charles shared with his father a deeply-rooted concern about the dangers of opening up a Pandora's box of popular debate and speculation. His first instinct, therefore, was to try and close down discussion of the *arcana imperii*, rather than open it up. A third factor was

---

[181] Orgel, *Illusion of Power*, pp. 24–5; Smuts, 'Cultural diversity and cultural change', p. 299n; idem, 'Art and material culture', p. 110.

[182] Peacock, 'Visual image', pp. 176–233. For the powerful impact of Van Dyck's portrait of 'Charles I with M. de St. Antoine' on one contemporary observer, see Millar, *Van Dyck in England*, p. 30.

[183] J.S. Morrill, 'Introduction', in J.S. Morrill ed., *Reactions to the English Civil War*, Basingstoke, 1982, p. 4.

[184] K. Sharpe, 'The King's writ: royal authors and royal authority in early modern England', in Sharpe and Lake eds, *Culture and Politics in Early Stuart England*, pp. 132–4.

the absence of any immediate prospect of a parliament. For much of the 1630s the king and his councillors were released from a pressing sense that they needed to account for their actions or engage with the hurly-burly of public controversy. These attitudes were misguided. The constant speculation recorded in diaries of the period, and the plethora of newsletters and manuscript separates, demonstrate that political discussion did not die down because of the absence of parliament.[185] Opinions were being formed that were to have a very harmful impact on perceptions of the crown when the crisis came in 1639–42. Charles's failure to engage more vigorously with this public debate, while he was in a position of relative strength, was one of his most damaging political errors.

Government and politics

'The Personal Rule' was very much what the name implies: government with a high degree of personal direction from the king, in his image, suffused with his values and reflecting his prejudices and priorities. The basic principle on which it operated was explained by Secretary Dorchester in the period after Buckingham's death. 'Everyone walks within the circle of his charge and his Majesty's hand is the chief and, in effect, the sole directory.'[186] Ministers were required to operate in compartments, confining themselves to the matters entrusted to them, leaving the king to pull together the different strands of policy and determine priorities and direction. Charles expected his ministers to discuss their business only with him, which caused Archbishop Laud some awkward moments in the mid-1630s as he sought to monitor the reception of his friend Wentworth's reports from Ireland without revealing prior knowledge of their contents. He was also determined, very much as a matter of personal honour, to be seen to be in charge.[187] The French ambassador noted perceptively that 'nothing would

---

[185] Fielding, 'The diary of Robert Woodford', pp. 777–88; Cust, 'News and politics', pp. 60–90. For a striking account of the extent of private discussions in Kent, see K. Fincham, 'The judges' decision on ship money in February 1637: the reaction in Kent', *BIHR*, vol. 57, 1984, pp. 230–7.

[186] *Court and Times*, vol. 2, p. 2; Clarendon, *History*, vol. 1, p. 64.

[187] Quintrell, *Charles i*, p. 50.

offend the king more than to have it believed' that he was dependent on the wishes of his chief minister, Weston.[188] The upshot of this was that, although Charles had some capable and forceful councillors, none of them was allowed to exercise the amount of influence enjoyed by Buckingham.

Weston came closest to this in the early years of 'the Personal Rule'. He had the enduring trust and confidence of Charles who, according to Clarendon, relied entirely on him in matters relating to royal revenue. He was also the main source of counsel on foreign policy, particularly during the lengthy negotiations with Spain. However, beyond this he never achieved the power he longed for. In 1631 there was a rumour that he was about to take over Buckingham's office of lord admiral; but this did not happen and he always lacked the duke's control over patronage and access to the royal bedchamber. As a result, powerful though he was, he remained essentially as Kevin Sharpe describes him, 'his master's servant and the executor of the king's wishes'.[189]

The most forceful of Charles's ministers and the best equipped, in terms of political skills, was Viscount Wentworth, later earl of Strafford. Given the right circumstances he might have become the English equivalent of Richelieu or Olivares; but he suffered from two debilitating weaknesses. For most of the 1630s he was in Ireland, too far from the centre of power to exert much influence over policy. When he returned to London in late 1639, and effectively became Charles's first minister, his role was mainly confined to damage limitation. The opportunity to shape the direction of 'the Personal Rule' had passed. He also suffered because he found it very difficult to develop an easy personal relationship with Charles. The king was respectful of his abilities, but never seems to have felt comfortable with him, and this robbed Wentworth of much of the confidence to press for what he wanted. In particular, when his big chance came with Weston's death in 1635, he did not have enough self-belief to push himself forward for the vacant lord treasurership.[190]

---

[188] *CSP Ven. 1628–9*, p. 204. Another example of Charles's determination to be seen to be taking personal control was his complaint to the privy council after Pembroke's death that 'he took very ill' the reports that he was about to choose a lord admiral: *CSP Ven. 1629–32*, pp. 263, 270.

[189] Sharpe, *The Personal Rule*, pp. 145–50.

[190] Ibid., pp. 132–40; B. Quintrell, 'The church triumphant? The emergence of a spiritual lord treasurer, 1635–1636', in Merritt ed., *The Political World of Thomas Wentworth*, pp. 86–91.

Of Charles's other ministers, Laud wielded the most influence. He shared to the full his master's anti-puritan/anti-popular instincts and, in spite of his continual anxiety about losing royal favour, remained a close and trusted confidant throughout the 1630s. He was also a shrewd and effective court operator, and an industrious member of the privy council.[191] What limited his power was Charles's compartmentalisation of business, which restricted him mainly to religious matters. For a brief period after Weston's death it looked as if this might change. He began to develop an interest in foreign policy, served on the treasury commission and made a serious bid to become lord treasurer himself. But following Bishop Juxon's appointment to the post in March 1636 he was again confined largely to the affairs of the church.[192] Charles, then, was largely able to maintain the principle that his ministers should stick to their briefs and answer to him personally. There was considerable force in Sir Thomas Roe's observation in 1636 that 'Everything is but discourse until his Majesty gives his consent.'[193]

The king was also much more closely involved in the day-to-day work of his administration than used to be thought. Given the limitations of seventeenth century bureaucracy, no monarch could keep abreast of all aspects of government business; but Charles was more assiduous than most. Sharpe has justifiably depicted him as a princely 'swot'. He would shut himself away for hours at a time to read his state papers, patiently working his way through a mass of reports and petitions, then recording his decisions in longhand in the margins. His annotations on a report from Windebank of 23 January 1636 which, with characteristic thoroughness he turned round within the day, give an indication of his methods.[194] The report covered a range of issues, including the progress of negotiations in Vienna, the Irish customs,

---

[191] Like most of Charles's ministers, Laud had to endure the occasional public put-down, for example at Woodstock in August 1631 (Bod. Lib., Jones MS 17, fo. 303), or in a hearing at Hampton Court in June 1636 (Fincham and Lake, 'Ecclesiastical policies of James and Charles', pp. 46–7). Laud found this extremely uncomfortable and it made him wary of Charles; however, it did not prevent him from manoeuvring with considerable nerve and ruthlessness when the situation at court seemed to require, as Martin Shepherd's account of the coup of September 1634 against the old enemy of the anti-Calvinists, Lord Chief Justice Heath, demonstrates: Shepherd, 'Charles I and political patronage', pp. 284–92.

[192] Sharpe, *The Personal Rule*, pp. 140–5; Quintrell, 'The church triumphant?', pp. 81–108.

[193] *CSP Dom. 1636–7*, p. 250.

[194] Sharpe, *The Personal Rule*, pp. 198–205; NA, SP 16/312/12.

the queen's household and Duchy of Cornwall business, and in each case Charles delivered a clear instruction: 'Do this', 'I like not this', 'Do it if you find that it suit with my service', 'It is reason therefore recommend his business accordingly' and, in response to a plea of innocence from an MP involved in opposition in the recent Irish parliament, 'What he did may easily be seen by his imployment with his fellows, but his intention must be left to God.' As this suggests, Charles would consider carefully and take advice, but once his mind was made up he would act firmly and decisively, often with a strong sense of moral righteousness.

The king was also very much at the centre of the proceedings of the main organ of central government, the privy council. It is difficult to work out how regularly he attended because the sources are not entirely reliable; but he is recorded as present at about forty meetings a year in the late 1630s which was a far higher attendance than his father ever achieved. He sat in on most of the meetings at which important policy initiatives were considered, and would often take the chair and lead the discussion.[195] He was also willing to deal with the small change of government business. He sat on the specialist council committees where many of the executive initiatives were first worked out, and did much to set the agenda and direct discussion. In March 1635, for example, at the committee for trade, he brought forward proposals to tax local maltsters and investigate whether the London poor were receiving their due benefit from the abatement of duties on coal, both of which were later acted on by the council as a whole.[196] Furthermore, Charles was good at making himself available to ministers on a less formal basis. On 24 June 1629, at the height of the crisis over the imprisoned MPs, it was to the king that Attorney-General Heath turned when he needed prompt action. Following a meeting with the lord chief justice, Heath had realised that if Seldon and Valentine were allowed to appear before the King's Bench on the following day they would be granted bail. He urgently required a royal warrant to confine them to the Tower and dispatched an urgent request to Greenwich, with a breathless instruction to the messenger that 'if my lord of Dorchester be not at court intreat one of the bedchamber to show it to the king and desire his majesty to direct

---

[195] Sharpe, *The Personal Rule*, pp. 262–72; Quintrell, *Charles I*, pp. 51–3.

[196] *CSP Dom. 1634–5*, pp. 500, 513, 520, 556, 581, 598; *CSP Dom. 1635*, pp. 11–12, 19, 502, 536.

the answer'. The warrant was duly issued, apparently as a joint effort.[197] This sort of accessibility was important in providing direction and continuity when decisions had to be made quickly.

Charles's command of the direction of government is well documented. Rather less easy to establish is the extent to which he controlled patronage and appointments. The conventional view is that such matters were largely in the hands of Buckingham up until his death and thereafter the dominant influences were a variety of senior court figures, including Laud, Weston and Cottington. However, recent work by Brian Quintrell and others suggests that Charles himself played a much more significant role than had been supposed.

Perhaps the hardest area to assess systematically is Charles's influence over the lesser appointments and minor grants that constituted much of the day-to-day business of government. Analysis of signet office docquet books, showing who procured warrants for the use of the royal signet, suggest that Buckingham's death was an important watershed. Prior to this, most warrants were procured by the favourite or by grooms of the royal bedchamber; however, during the 1630s the king appears to have taken greater control of the process since some 70 per cent of warrants were now being procured by his two secretaries of state.[198] This did not mean that he was exerting a direct personal control in the way Buckingham had done. Pressure of other business, lack of expertise in particular areas and his sense that it was unfitting for a king to reject petitions, largely precluded this. Leading courtiers and other interested parties continued to provide most of the motive force to push grants through the system. Nonetheless Charles was clearly able to get across the message that he expected to be fully involved in patronage and that certain ground rules had to be observed. Evidence from the lord keeper's docquets suggests that this had a considerable impact. After the duke's death, most grants appear to have gone through the proper bureaucratic channels, with the lord keeper regularly referring to the lord treasurer, attorney-general, master of the wards, or whoever else had final responsibility, before approving a grant. This material also shows

---

[197] NA, SP 16/145/40, 41.

[198] R.G. Asch, 'The revival of monopolies: court and patronage during the Personal Rule of Charles I, 1629–1640', in R.G. Asch and A.M. Birke eds, *Princes, Patronage and the Nobility*, Oxford, 1991, pp. 357–92.

the king participating actively, hearing petitions and references in person and giving careful consideration to the terms of grants and charters. This ensured that ministers were conscious of being kept up to the mark and that certain standards were adhered to, for example, in demonstrating that new patents and monopolies were not 'mischievous or inconvenient to the state'. The patronage system remained outdated and in urgent need of reform; but at least by the 1630s it was being operated with reasonable efficiency and without much evidence of the grosser forms of 'corruption' apparent in James's reign.[199]

Charles devoted particular care to matters relating to his own household. We know from Clarendon that he took a keen interest in those who staffed the royal bedchamber, observing men 'long before he received any about his person' and often forming enduring relationships with them.[200] He showed a fatherly solicitude for the welfare of his servants. For example, when Edward Clerk, a groom of the queen's bedchamber, was contemplating marriage he wrote to the prospective bride, urging on her the merits of the young man and predicting that he would prove 'as good a husband as he is subject to me, being descended from a father who besides his laudable behaviour in all private occasions, hath also given sufficient testimony of his loyalty'.[201] This extended to suits involving household officials, where he regularly intervened to promote their interests. In July 1635, for instance, he can be seen holding up the issue of a patent for collecting fines on those convicted of swearing while he amended the terms of the grant to the benefit of Robert Lesley, one of the grooms of his bedchamber.[202]

---

[199] *A Calendar of the Docquets of Lord Keeper Coventry*, 1625–1640, ed. J. Broadway, R.P. Cust and S.K. Roberts, List and Index Soc., Special Series, vol. 34, 2004, introduction; L.L. Peck, *Court Patronage and Corruption in Early Stuart England*, 1990, pp. 44–6.

[200] Clarendon, *History*, vol. 4, p. 490; Sharpe, *The Personal Rule*, p. 205.

[201] BL, Add. MSS 72426–72440 (formerly Trumbull MS, Misc xliii, no. 2–3, Weckherlin draft of letter from Charles to Mrs Oldfield). For a further example of his sensitivity towards the feelings and interests of his servants, see his treatment of the young Sir James Greenfield in May 1645. Prince Charles had appointed him to his bedchamber without his parents' consent. Charles felt he had to reprimand his son, but rather than dismiss Greenfield he kept him on telling the queen that 'the refusal would be a great disgrace to the young gentleman . . . especially considering . . . his own hopefulness': *The King's Cabinet Opened, or Certain Packets of Secret Letters and Papers, written with the King's own hand . . .* , 1645, pp. 10–11.

[202] Birmingham City Archives, Coventry MSS, DV 896, Grants of Offices, 603183/385, inserted letter from Windebank to Coventry.

Given Charles's strong sense of family responsibility, his industry in matters relating to his household is unsurprising. Less predictable is his close involvement in local government and bureaucratic appointments. Myron Noonkester's investigation of the controversial 'pricking' of sheriffs in 1625 suggests that this was not, as had previously been thought, an example of Buckingham disciplining unreliable clients. In fact, it showed Charles himself intervening to punish parliamentary troublemakers and ensure that the right calibre of gentleman was discharging the office.[203] Again in 1635, when it came to his attention that Sir William Manley was failing in his duties as clerk to the court of Star Chamber, he intervened to have him replaced by John Cockshutt who had demonstrated his abilities as clerk to Attorney-General Noy.[204]

Charles's impact was even more apparent in the making of senior appointments. With the exception of posts in the church, where Laud made most of the running, he was undoubtedly the dominant influence after Buckingham's death. Well-informed observers recognised that his decision was crucial in the hard-fought contests for key ministerial posts and that if anyone else pushed too hard for a candidate this was liable to be counter-productive. Henry Percy, an experienced court insider, warned that the queen's personal campaigning for the earl of Leicester to become secretary of state in 1637 was not helping his cause: 'to my knowledge there can nothing destroy the design so much as that; for it will . . . give great distaste to the king to hear how they order those things without his knowledge. . .'[205] The king's dominance is amply demonstrated by Brian Quintrell's meticulous reconstruction of the processes leading to the appointment of Bishop Juxon as lord treasurer in March 1636.[206] Traditionally, the appointment has been seen as a triumph for Laud, since Juxon was the first cleric to hold the post since the fifteenth century and was apparently a trusted adherent who could be relied on to implement the reforms associated with 'Thorough'. Quintrell, however, has shown that the appointment was

---

[203] M.C. Noonkester, 'Charles I and shrieval selection, 1625/6', *BIHR*, vol. 64, 1991, pp. 305–11.

[204] *CSP Dom. 1635–6*, p. 57.

[205] HMC, *Third Report*, 1872, p. 75. The letter should be dated 1637, not 1634. For this episode, also see Shepherd, 'Charles I and political patronage', pp. 153–62.

[206] Quintrell, 'The church triumphant?', pp. 81–108.

very much Charles's own and came as a considerable surprise to leading courtiers, not least Laud who had lobbied hard to secure the post for himself. The king was in charge from the start. On Weston's death, he took the decision to put the treasury into commission, to give himself time to find an appointee who could manage the vital negotiations with the customs farmers and also continue the former lord treasurer's policies. He settled on Juxon because family contacts in the city gave him close links with the customs syndicates, his biddable style could help heal rifts that had developed between Laud and Cottington on the treasury commission, and because he liked and trusted him, having enjoyed his services as domestic chaplain since 1627. After apparently making up his mind at a relatively early stage, however, Charles bided his time and played his cards so close to his chest that few were aware of his choice until just before it was announced. Quintrell's verdict is that the whole episode reveals his 'tight grip on patronage in the years after Buckingham's death and his readiness . . . to use his own judgement in picking men suitable to his purposes wherever he might find them'.[207]

The king's command of court politics was revealed in its most positive light in the absence of the faction feuds that had blighted the second half of his father's reign. During the 1630s no senior English minister was forced out of office by court intrigue and Weston was the first lord treasurer since Robert Cecil to die while still holding the post. This was in spite of the existence of recognisable 'Spanish', 'French' and 'Dutch' factions, and bitter and combustible personal animosities. Laud could not stand Cottington who, on occasion, teased him mercilessly, while the earl of Holland and the queen loathed Weston.[208] The main reason for the stability of the court was Charles's personal success in imposing a relatively restrained pattern of behaviour.

An important element in this was his capacity to compartmentalise the political and the personal. Like any other monarch, Charles was susceptible to the influence of those who got close to him; however, he does appear to have been better than most at setting limits to this. He signalled his intentions at the start of the reign when Sir James Fullerton,

---

[207] Ibid., p. 108.

[208] Sharpe, *The Personal Rule*, pp. 176–8; A.J. Loomie, 'The Spanish faction at the court of Charles I, 1630–1638', *BIHR*, vol. 59, 1986, pp. 37–49; Clarendon, *History*, vol. 1, pp. 132–5.

a political nonentity, was preferred to Buckingham as groom of the stool; and, by and large, he was able to remove the royal bedchamber from the political fray so that it could provide a buffer-zone between himself and his leading politicians. Grooms of the bedchamber, such as William Murray and Endymion Porter, enjoyed considerable trust and played an important role in the scramble for patronage; but they did not become leading players on the political stage.[209]

An instructive example is the role of James, marquis of Hamilton, who came as close as anyone to succeeding Buckingham as the king's personal favourite.[210] Charles felt a genuine warmth and affection for Hamilton. He had accompanied him to Spain in 1623, and enjoyed constant personal access as a gentleman of the bedchamber and successor to Buckingham's crucial office of master of the horse. It also helped that he shared the king's enthusiasm for collecting works of art and was one of the few senior courtiers who was younger than his master. Charles may even have felt that he had saved Hamilton's marriage when he made the somewhat improbable, but nonetheless characteristic, demand that he consummate the relationship before he be allowed to take up the mastership of horse. In matters relating to patronage and appointments the marquis was an influential figure. He and his mother-in-law, the countess of Denbigh (who was Buckingham's sister and first lady of the bedchamber to Henrietta Maria) made a formidable team, using their insider knowledge to time interventions with the king and queen. On one occasion, for example, Hamilton held back from presenting a dispatch that might have jeopardised the diplomatic career of his brother-in-law, Lord Fielding, because, as he explained to Fielding, Charles was 'troubled with a boil on his thigh which makes him unwilling of business but such as will give content rather than breed dislike'.[211] But, in spite of all the advantages that such access gave

---

[209] J. Greenrod, '"Conceived to give dangerous counsel": William Murray, Endymion Porter, the Caroline Bedchamber and the Outbreak of Civil War March 1641–June 1642', University of Sheffield, MPhil. thesis, 2003. This situation changed during the crisis of the 1640s when Charles turned for advice to those he trusted personally, including Murray and Porter.

[210] For Hamilton, see the important and underused study by John Scally, 'The political career of James 3rd Marquis and 1st Duke of Hamilton (1606–1649) to 1643', Cambridge Ph.D. thesis, 1992, chps. 1–4.

[211] Cited in Scally, 'The political career of Hamilton', pp. 128–9.

him, when it came to influencing high policy Hamilton's impact was minimal. As John Scally shows, he was an enthusiastic 'Protestant causer', consistently supporting the interests of Elizabeth of Bohemia and acting as a link with the Swedes. Prior to the Scottish crisis of 1638, however, he found himself largely excluded from the inner circle in foreign affairs, notably while the crucial decisions were being made in 1635–7. The king preferred to take advice from a seasoned professional, like Wentworth, even though his personal relationship with him was much more distant.

Perhaps the most striking testimony to Charles's ability to detach the personal from the political was the limited influence exercised by Henrietta Maria, at least prior to 1641. Charles regarded their relationship as the bedrock of his monarchy; yet he was not prepared to take her advice on matters of high policy. This was not for any want of effort on the queen's part. Malcolm Smuts has shown that she relished the opportunities for scheming and plotting against enemies such as Weston; and during the mid-1630s, urged on by her own courtiers, Holland and Leicester, she worked hard to persuade the king to go to war in alliance with the French. But none of this came to anything. Her efforts to remove Weston were rebuffed or ignored, and the French alliance never materialised. The queen started to emerge as a more significant political force during the Scots crisis, when she and her Catholic courtiers were pressing for all-out aggression; but it was not until 1641 – with Charles feeling vulnerable and isolated – that she became an important adviser on policy. [212]

Charles's strategy for defusing factional conflict also involved being ruthless when it came to any signs of bickering or infighting. He hated the idea that his councillors might be combining among themselves – and Laud had to improvise a hasty response when, on one occasion, he caught sight of a marginal reference to 'Lady Mora' (their nickname for Weston and Cottington) in one of Wentworth's reports and 'would needs know what we meant by it'.[213] He also insisted that councillors deal directly with him and put their trust in him. When Wentworth faced opposition over his policies in Ireland in 1636, the king was at pains to impress on him that

---

[212] Smuts, 'Puritan followers of Henrietta Maria', pp. 26–45; C. Hibbard, 'The role of a queen consort: the household and court of Henrietta Maria, 1625–1642', in Asch and Birke eds, *Princes, Patronage and Nobility*, pp. 393–414; Sharpe, *The Personal Rule*, pp. 168–73.

[213] Laud, *Works*, vol. 7, pp. 102–3.

'the marks of my favour that stop malicious tongues are neither places nor titles, but the little welcome I give to accusers and the willing ear I give to my servants'.[214] The message appears to have got through. Two years later Wentworth was advising his friend the earl of Newcastle, recently promoted to the council, not to put his trust in factions, nor to 'seek to strengthen or value yourself with him [i.e. the king] by any other means than those of his own continual grace'.[215] Where quarrels did break out Charles was quick to defuse them. In 1633, for example, when Holland challenged Weston's son, Jerome, to a duel after he had impugned his honour, he not only stopped the duel, but then made those involved sign submissions that he drafted personally.[216]

Perhaps the most significant factor in avoiding court faction was Charles's loyalty to senior figures who he felt were serving him faithfully.[217] This was the positive side of his tendency to form fixed opinions about those around him. He was capable of displaying considerable tact and sensitivity when it came to assuring servants of his favour. A good example was the boost he gave to Laud, when the archbishop was feeling at his most vulnerable after being passed over for the lord treasurership in 1636. Charles delivered:

a public declaration . . . at the council table that he would have made choice of Canterbury for that place if it had not been out of consideration of over pressing his aged body with affairs, whose fidelity and affection to his service his Majesty did much commend.[218]

The implications of the king's stance became apparent during the 1626 Parliament when Buckingham faced a powerful court conspiracy involving

---

[214] *Strafforde Letters*, vol. 2, p. 32.

[215] Ibid., vol. 2, pp. 174–5.

[216] *CSP Dom. 1633–4*, pp. 14–16; see also, Sharpe, *The Personal Rule*, pp. 178–9 and C. Hibbard, 'The theatre of dynasty', in Smuts ed., *The Stuart Court and Europe*, pp. 163–5.

[217] This did not prevent Charles from acting with considerable ruthlessness where he felt ministers were failing in their duties. Bishop Williams who had got on the wrong side of Charles during 'the Blessed Revolution' was pressurised into resigning the lord keepership in October 1625: Gardiner, *History of England*, vol. 6, p. 31; and Lord Treasurer Marlborough was replaced by Weston in July 1628 after Charles had become frustrated by his inefficiency: Shepherd, 'Charles I and political patronage', p. 208.

[218] Cited in Quintrell, 'The church triumphant?', p. 84.

Pembroke, Arundel and senior members of the queen's household. He made it clear that come what may he would stand by his favourite and Pembroke was faced with either abandoning his campaign or forfeiting his court offices, whereupon he caved in.[219] Much the same thing happened in mid-1634 when the opposition to Weston built up considerable impetus, as accusations of malpractice in the sale of crown woods were backed by Laud, Coventry, Holland and members of Henrietta Maria's household. However, Charles ostentatiously allowed Weston to kiss his hands in the presence of the court and then demonstrated that he was not interested in the charges each side was making against the other.[220] The recognition that the king was able to impose on court politicians, that certain key players were more or less immovable, took much of the venom out of their rivalries. They were forced to accept that they had to muddle along together, which produced some surprising examples of harmony, for instance, when the queen acted as godmother to Jerome Weston's daughter at the height of the quarrel with Holland.[221] The stability achieved at court is one of the success stories of Charles's reign, demonstrating his effectiveness in imposing his desired standards of behaviour on those who came under his immediate supervision. But how far this was entirely a good thing for the political nation is more debatable.

Geoffrey Elton and others have taught us that in early modern monarchies political stability was generally best achieved when the king's court was open to differing opinions of policy and functioned as a 'point of contact' with the political nation.[222] This was not happening for most of the 1630s and, as we shall see, it was to have very damaging consequences towards the end of the decade. The reasons why it was not happening are complex. It had something to do with the culture of a court that emphasised distance and authoritarianism at the expence of openness and accessibility. There was also a strong element of institutional inertia which, as Caroline Hibbard has shown, made it hard for those who did not belong

---

[219] Cust, *The Forced Loan*, pp. 26–7.

[220] *CSP Ven. 1632–6*, pp. 221, 223; Shepherd, 'Charles I and political patronage', pp. 274–9.

[221] Sharpe, *The Personal Rule*, pp. 177–8.

[222] G.R. Elton, 'Tudor government: the Points of Contact. III. The Court', *TRHS*, 5th ser., vol. 26, 1976, pp. 211–28.

to existing courtly families to gain a foothold.[223] And there was the increasing dominance, at the senior levels, of an inner circle of advisers, led by Weston, Cottington, Laud and Arundel, who shared Charles's pro-Spanish/ anti-parliament prejudices. But this was not the whole story. Charles's privy council remained a varied group expressing a wide range of opinions. A quarter of them were to side with parliament in the civil war, and this included experienced operators, like Coke and Manchester, as well as practised courtiers, like Holland and Northumberland, all of whom broadly supported a 'patriot' agenda.[224] In the late 1620s such men had, on occasion, been able to persuade the king to see things their way; but by the late 1630s this was no longer happening. It would appear, then, that an important part of the explanation for the court's 'detachment' from the political nation lay in the changing chemistry of Charles's relationship with his councillors.

One of the strongest impressions one gains from a study of government during the 1630s is of a king displaying much greater assurance in his power of command. A good example is provided by the Woodstock meeting in August 1631. Charles had eight of his senior councillors in attendance on this occasion and yet he took charge of proceedings with considerable skill and confidence. He managed the discussion single-handedly, intervened at opportune moments to pick holes in the argument of those before him and successfully conveyed the impression of being an impartial arbiter.[225] He could never aspire to the subtlety, or intellectual mastery, of his father, but on this, and later occasions, he showed himself a vigorous and effective debater. The contrast with his fumbling encounter with his Scottish advisers in February 1626 is striking.[226] Charles's progress in this respect can probably be attributed to a combination of greater personal maturity, the success of his family life, the partial recovery of English prestige abroad and experience of taking charge. Anxieties and insecurities still betrayed themselves in his fondness for rules and tendency to justify his actions in terms of political maxims. But the indications are that he felt that at last he had mastered the technique of governing and could hold his own with the

---

[223] Hibbard, 'The role of a queen consort', pp. 399–401.

[224] Russell, *Causes of the Civil War*, pp. 189–90.

[225] Bod. Lib., Jones MS 17, fos. 300–9.

[226] See below, pp. 214–16.

veteran politicians around him. His 1636 letter to Wentworth is an illustration of this. Part of the letter was designed to deflect the viscount's plea
for an earldom, and Charles managed this quite adroitly by insisting that
he place his faith in personal favour rather than any external marks of
status. However, he then proceeded to give Wentworth a lecture on how
to deal with his enemies, accompanied by gobbets of sententious wisdom.[227]
The incongruity of advising such a practised operator on how to survive in
the political jungle seems to have been completely lost on Charles. Political
imagination was still not his strong point. But he had evidently developed
considerable confidence in his 'politic wisdom' and 'prudence'. The problem was that, in some respects, this made him rather harder to advise. He
may have paid lip-service to the idea that a good king encouraged honest
counsel, but his somewhat inflexible self-assurance made it difficult for councillors to be totally candid. They were no longer dealing with the callow
politician of the 1620s who could be steered towards particular decisions
by appeals to tradition or practical necessity. Charles now felt that he knew
about such things; and because he was so closely involved in the various
processes of government it was almost impossible to work around him.

The result of all this was that government during the 1630s increasingly
reflected the king's own assumptions and priorities. The scope for presenting alternatives was narrowed and the views of those moderate, 'patriot'
councillors who were most in tune with the opinions of the political
nation were largely sidelined. The consequences for foreign policy, parliament and religion have already been discussed – and the implications for
policy towards Scotland and Ireland will be examined in the next chapter.
But it is also worth exploring how this influenced the crown's domestic
agenda during 'the Personal Rule'.

The ending of the conflict with France and Spain gave the privy
council a breathing space and allowed it to take a longer view of the
problems it faced. Two in particular demanded attention. The first was the
chronic weakness of the royal finances, made worse by the costs of the war
and the short-term expedients used to deal with these; the second was a
general problem of disorder, highlighted by the crisis of 1629–30 in which
the political opposition of merchants and MPs had threatened to become

---

[227] *Strafforde Letters*, vol. 2, p. 32. For a letter to Wentworth similar in tone, see ibid.,
vol. 1, pp. 331–2.

mixed up with agrarian rioting. The council's approach to these problems was heavily conditioned by conventional wisdom. The Book of Orders of 1631, hailed by some historians as an example of Caroline innovative vigour, has been shown to have been based on a scheme worked out by the earl of Manchester in 1620, to ensure the proper enforcement of already existing statutes dealing with vagrants, the poor and dearth. And the methods used for raising extra revenue, such as distraint of knighthood, forest fines and even ship money, were so dependent on precedent that Derek Hirst has described them as 'fiscal antiquarianism'.[228] However, the conservatism of much of what the council was doing should not be allowed to obscure the fact that there were new priorities and initiatives; and a good deal of the drive behind these was supplied by the king.

In three areas, in particular, he was active in imparting a sense of urgency and energy. First, he was successful in highlighting the message that 'private' interests must be subordinated to the 'public' good. As we have seen, Charles grew up with the idea that 'a good king' gave himself over completely to the welfare of his people. From the start of the reign this was one of the most prominent themes of royal rhetoric. Those who opposed him, be they loan refusers, merchants or MPs, were castigated for putting 'private' interests before the 'public', while the signet letters and proclamations that he took a hand in drafting constantly harped on the same issue. It was also an important element in the notion of 'Thorough', which has been seen as a key theme in Laud and Wentworth's approaches to government. In broad terms, 'the rule of Thorough' meant making central government more efficient and more forceful, so that it could push through policies designed to further the 'public interest'. It was all about ensuring, as Laud put it, that 'private ends' should not be allowed to become 'blocks in the public way'.[229] This message was not exactly new. It had been a staple element in government language and thinking ever since such ideas had been popularised by the 'commonwealthmen' in the mid-sixteenth century. But during 'the Personal Rule' it was probably given greater prominence than ever before.

---

[228] B.W. Quintrell, 'The making of Charles I's Book of Orders', *EHR*, vol. 95, 1980, pp. 556–61; D.M. Hirst, *Authority and Conflict. England 1603–1658*, 1986, p. 173.

[229] C.V. Wedgwood, *Thomas Wentworth, First Earl of Strafford 1593–1641. A Revaluation*, 1961, pp. 119–21.

The impact of all this is hard to assess. The 'rule of Thorough', for example, has been shown to have been shot through with contradictions. At times it appears mainly to have been used as a means of attacking political enemies – allowing Laud and Wentworth to accuse arch rivals Weston and Cottington of delay and corruption – or as a cloak for self-interest, disguising Wentworth's own profiteering from projects like the Irish tobacco farm.[230] At the same time, however, it did hold out the ideal of higher standards of public service which Wentworth, for one, took to heart and attempted to imbue into those he worked with.[231] The same ambiguities applied in other areas. The rhetoric of the 'public good' was used to justify projects like the redevelopment of London or the draining of the fens which, while offering the prospect of long-term benefits, also caused a good deal of misery in the short term and allowed massive profits to be made by court projectors. It is important, as Kevin Sharpe has reminded us, not to be too dismissive of such schemes or too cynical about the crown's motivation. Some of them did bring improvements, as well as much needed revenue for the exchequer. On occasion the crown was even prepared to make sacrifices of its own, for example, when Charles allowed saltpetremen to dig up his house at Woodstock as part of an effort to increase production.[232] However, the stress on the 'public' could also have very damaging political implications.

An important part of Charles's understanding of the 'public interest' was that it was something that he himself was best qualified to define. Where other considerations, such as those defined by custom or the common law, appeared to stand in its way, he felt a strong sense of duty to override them in the interests of the 'common weal'. This was, after all, why God had entrusted him with his prerogative in the first place, so that he could take on the ultimate responsibility for his people's welfare, guided by his kingly wisdom and his conscience. When Charles invoked the 'public', then, he was drawing on a strain of moral righteousness that gave his actions added force; and a similar ethos can be detected among crown officials, for

---

[230] Quintrell, *Charles I*, p. 53; Asch, 'The revival of monopolies', pp. 387–9.

[231] Sharpe, *The Personal Rule*, pp. 135–8; T. Ranger, 'Strafford in Ireland: a revaluation', in T. Aston ed., *Crisis in Europe 1560–1660*, 1965, pp. 274–5, 285.

[232] Sharpe, *The Personal Rule*, pp. 121–4, 195; *Proclamations of Charles I*, pp. 116–20.

example in Wentworth's insistence that the law must not be allowed to stand in the way of the king's sovereign responsibility to the 'public'.[233]

Some of the practical implications of this attitude were revealed in the fen drainage project in Lincolnshire. This was managed by a group of unscrupulous court undertakers and an engineer, Sir Anthony Thomas, about whose competence the local commissioners for sewers had severe doubts. In spite of this, Charles was persuaded to give the project more or less unconditional support. In 1629, when a local jury rejected the scheme as unnecessary, instead of referring it to arbitration, the king simply ordered the local commissioners to proceed. This was to ensure, he declared in a signet letter, that 'we be not constrained to interpose our regal power and prerogative . . . to force froward and adverse men to give way to that which is for the public good'.[234] When the commissioners refused he had them dismissed and appointed a new group, packed by the projectors, which authorised the scheme and imposed a tax to pay for it on local inhabitants. In 1634 he accepted Thomas's claims that the project had been successfully completed and granted him 24 000 acres out of the drained lands as a reward. Two years later he discovered that the work was far from satisfactory, but instead of forcing Thomas to finish it, he punished the local inhabitants who protested. This caused enormous resentment. During the 1640 parliamentary election in Lincolnshire fen drainers were depicted as the villains of 'the Personal Rule' and there were numerous complaints to the Long Parliament about the way in which they had 'conjured up prerogative and arbitrary power'.[235]

This project revealed very clearly the dangers of pushing the notion of 'public interest' too far. From Charles's point of view he was supporting a scheme which, like drainage projects in the Low Countries, would eventually yield a rich dividend for the commonwealth. But lacking the means to find out what was happening on the ground, he was prey to corrupt courtiers who were able to portray any opposition as the selfish obstructionism of a few 'private' individuals. In these circumstances the powerful language of the 'public' could become a positive liability, pre-empting any

---

[233] Milton, 'Wentworth and political thought', pp. 137–42.

[234] NA, SO 1/2, fos. 5v–6.

[235] M.E. Kennedy, 'Charles I and local government: the draining of the east and west fens', *Albion*, vol. 15, 1983, pp. 19–31.

further consideration of legitimate grievances and allowing undertakers to ride roughshod over custom and law. Without a parliament to whom the projectors might be answerable, this sort of corruption and abuse was hard to check and it was enormously damaging for good relations with the subject.[236]

A second area in which the king took a particular interest was strengthening the position of the nobility. This was a reflection of his general sense that all would be well in society if each group was pushed back firmly into its place and made to discharge its proper calling. It also encompassed issues relating to honour that were always close to the king's heart. Charles regarded the senior nobles as his natural partners in government, describing them in the Short Parliament as those 'persons in rank and degree nearest to the royal throne' who 'having, received honour from himself and his royal progenitors, he doubted not would . . . be moved in honour and dutiful affection'.[237] At court he afforded them a place of privilege, allowing them access to his privy chamber and dancing with them in the masques. He also took a strong personal interest in their welfare. Philip Warwick, one of the grooms of the bedchamber, recorded how whenever young noblemen came to take their leave before going on a Grand Tour, Charles would give them a mini lecture on moral virtue and tell them that 'if he heard they kept good company abroad, he should reasonably expect they would return qualified to serve him and their country well at home'.[238]

This concern led to a number of important shifts in policy. The sale of honours which had been such a feature of his father's reign, and which continued under Buckingham, came to an abrupt halt. Charles was apparently heeding the advice of social commentators who warned that this was undermining hierarchy by allowing the unworthy to obtain places of honour. Only three baronetcies were sold between 1630 and the crisis of 1641, when Charles was forced into further sales as a means of raising revenue. Peerages

---

[236] For comparable abuses, see the disafforestation schemes that provoked the Western Rising: Sharp, *In Contempt of All Authority*, chps. 4–8; T.G. Barnes, *Somerset 1625–1640*, Oxford, 1961, pp. 156–60; and the soap monopoly: Sharpe, *The Personal Rule*, pp. 259–62.

[237] Rushworth, vol. 1, pp. 1162–5. He also tended to contrast the loyalty of the House of Lords with the 'undutiful and seditious carriage' of the Commons: *LJ*, vol. iv, p. 43.

[238] *Warwick Memoirs*, pp. 73–4.

were also granted very sparingly, with the result that during 'the Personal Rule' the number of peers actually declined.[239] These measures were backed up by a number of significant royal pronouncements. In June 1629 he resolved a dispute between English, Scots and Irish peers by ordering that the English should always take precedence, to preserve their 'ancient lustre';[240] and in April 1636 he issued a proclamation prohibiting the buying and wearing of counterfeit jewellery because this allowed lesser mortals to deck themselves out in the finery properly reserved for noblemen.[241] He also supported the work of Arundel, the earl marshal, in revitalising the High Court of Chivalry. Between 1634 and 1641 it met regularly as a forum in which anyone of 'generous blood' could bring an action for defamation and expect to receive damages and a grovelling apology.[242]

Concern to protect the position of those of 'generous blood' was matched by a determination to ensure that they discharged their social responsibilities. The king sought to achieve this through a series of proclamations ordering nobles and gentlemen to return to their shires so that they could maintain traditional standards of hospitality and carry out their duties as local governors. This was not a new policy. Similar proclamations had been issued as far back as 1596. But, for the first time, Charles made an effort to give it teeth. In November 1632, William Palmer was fined £1 000 in Star Chamber for remaining in town in contravention of the proclamation and the following February some 248 individuals were subpoenaed by the attorney-general to answer for the same offence. As with the forced loan, vigorous enforcement, combined with evidence of the king's personal interest in the matter, appears to have ensured relatively widespread compliance.[243] In this case Charles's initiative showed signs of success. Elsewhere its effects are more difficult to measure, although to judge by the hundreds

---

[239] L. Stone, *The Crisis of the Aristocracy, 1558–1641*, Oxford, 1965, pp. 95, 117–19.

[240] BL, Add 64, 898, fos. 41–2. This is a copy of the council order, corrected and amended by Charles himself.

[241] *Proclamations of Charles i*, pp. 507–8.

[242] G.D. Squibb, *The High Court of Chivalry*, Oxford, 1959, pp. 56–67. Dr Andrew Hopper and I are working on a project to calendar the court's proceedings in this period.

[243] F. Heal, 'The crown, the gentry and London: the enforcement of proclamation 1596–1640, in C. Cross, D. Loades and J.J. Scarisbrick eds, *Law and Government Under the Tudors*, Cambridge, 1988, pp. 211–26.

of suits being brought before the Court of Chivalry in the late 1630s, his initiatives were not unwelcome to the landed classes.

The third area of government that particularly concerned Charles was naval reform and the collection of ship money. The navy had been one of his great enthusiasms ever since his father had encouraged him to take an interest in Buckingham's reform of the fleet in the late 1610s. His eagerness to associate his kingship with the nation's glorious maritime tradition was reflected in his coronation medal, which showed a man-of-war under full sail and the motto 'the love of the people is the king's protection'. With the return of peace, refurbishing the navy became one of his chief priorities. In 1631 he demanded a full report on its current state and undertook a vigorous inspection of the dockyards, clambering aboard every ship and asking searching questions. This led to an extensive programme of shipbuilding, with four new men-of-war completed by 1634 and the launching of the *Sovereign of the Seas* in the autumn of 1637. With 102 guns this was the most heavily armed warship afloat and Charles was so proud of it that he had a model made to show off to visiting dignitaries.[244]

The strengthened fleet played an important role in foreign policy during the 1630s, helping to protect the burgeoning foreign trade against privateers and offering an important bargaining counter in negotiations with the French and the Hapsburgs. It also paved the way for an important new initiative. Charles looked to the navy to restore his personal honour and England's reputation abroad by reviving claims to the sovereignty of the seas surrounding the British Isles. In 1634 Sir John Borough completed a lengthy treatise on the subject and in the same year the admiralty issued new regulations governing the conduct of foreign ships entering British waters.[245] To have any chance of success, however, there needed to be consistent enforcement by the navy; and this was where ship money came in.

Charles originally hoped to launch his strengthened fleet in the summer of 1634, paid for by Spanish subsidies. However, it soon became clear that these would not be forthcoming and that, anyway, he would be in a more powerful bargaining position if he could pay for the fleet himself. Credit for the invention of ship money has often been given to his

---

[244] B.W. Quintrell, 'Charles I and his navy in the 1630s', *The Seventeenth Century*, vol. 3, 1988, pp. 159–79; Autobiography of *Phineas Pett*, ed. W.G. Perrin, Navy Records Soc., vol. 51, 1918, p. 157 (I am grateful to Brian Quintrell for this reference).

[245] Quintrell, *Charles I*, p. 70.

attorney-general at the time, William Noy, but much of the initial impetus undoubtedly came from the king.[246] In June 1634 he instructed the council to consider means for supplying the navy, which led to the initial proposal for the levy. Then over the summer months, as councillors worked out the details, he was kept abreast of proceedings and referred to when decisions needed to be taken.[247] The first ship money writ, of 20 October 1634, very clearly reflected his priorities. The purpose of the levy, it stated, was to protect merchant shipping, get rid of pirates, provide defence against invasion and ensure that, like his predecessors, Charles was acknowledged as 'master' of the seas around Britain, since 'it would be very irksome unto us if that princely honour in our times should be lost or in any thing diminished'.[248]

In financial terms, ship money was a considerable success. The first writ, which applied to maritime towns and counties, raised well over 90 per cent of the £80 000 requested. In subsequent years it was extended to cover the whole country and up to 1640 it became, in effect, an annual tax, worth the equivalent of almost four subsidies. Well over £800 000 of the total assessment of around £1 000 000 was collected and only in 1639–40, when the levy was collapsing under the strains produced by the Scottish war, did non-payment on the final account amount to more than 20 per cent. These figures do conceal a good deal of reluctance and delay as some sheriffs took three years or more to gather their money in; but, even so, by early modern standards, ship money was a remarkably successful tax.[249] On the strength of it Charles was able to dispatch large, well-supplied fleets to sweep the coastal waters in 1635 and, again, in 1636 and 1637. He was less successful than he had hoped in asserting his sovereignty of the seas. The French continued to defy English ships in the Channel and there was only limited success in forcing the Dutch to buy fishing licences. And, embarrassingly, there was nothing the navy could do to prevent a Spanish fleet from being annihilated by the Dutch in English waters at the battle of the Downs in

---

[246] Sharpe, *The Personal Rule*, pp. 548–52.

[247] *CSP Dom. 1634–5*, pp. 68–9, 161–2.

[248] *Constitutional Documents*, pp. 105–8.

[249] Sharpe, *The Personal Rule*, pp. 585–95; A.A.M. Gill, 'Ship money during the Personal rule of Charles I; Politics, Ideology and the Law, 1634–40', Sheffield University, Ph.D. thesis, 1990, pp. 335–41.

1639. But the fleets did enable Charles to re-establish England's reputation as a military power and also provided a basis for the powerful navy of Cromwell's day.[250]

The financial success of ship money owed much to the efforts of privy councillors. They devoted long hours to chivvying local officials and sorting out the ratings disputes triggered by the complicated assessment system. They also showed considerable sensitivity to public relations, for example, inviting the sheriffs responsible for the first writ to view the accounts, so they could see that the money really was being spent on the navy. But, as with the forced loan, Charles was also much in evidence, driving the whole scheme forward. He instituted regular Sunday meetings of the council in 1635 to review the progress of collection. At these he would take the chair, scrutinise accounts and, sometimes, interview officials in person.[251] Sir John Hotham, the sheriff of Yorkshire, described what a boost it was to be told by the king that he was 'well content and satisfied' with his service.[252] Where opposition was encountered he met it with a mixture of firmness and self-assurance. During 1636 the earl of Warwick organised a very effective strike against payment in Essex and then went to the king and told him that he must abandon the levy, because his 'tenants and farmers were all . . . accustomed to the mild rule of Queen Elizabeth and King James and could not bring themselves to consent to such notable prejudices . . .' According to the Venetian ambassador, Charles listened in silence, then simply told Warwick that he 'expected from the example of promptness shown by him that he should be obeyed by the others also'.[253] This unnerving demonstration of royal resolve, together with the threat of legal proceedings in the exchequer, seems to have persuaded the earl and his allies that they would get nowhere and by the autumn of 1637 most of the county's arrears had been cleared.[254] The king and his councillors combined very effectively in managing the process of collection; where they fell down was in handling the politics of the levy.

---

[250] Quintrell, 'Charles I and his navy', pp. 169–74.

[251] Gill, 'Ship money', chps. 2–3.

[252] Ibid., p. 183.

[253] CSP Ven. 1636–1639, pp. 124–5.

[254] V.A. Rowe, 'Robert, second earl of Warwick and the payment of ship money in Essex', Trans. Essex Arch. Soc., 3rd ser., vol. 1, 1965, pp. 160–3.

It might have been possible to contain the opposition caused by ship money had it not been for Hampden's case. As with the forced loan, the levy aroused all sorts of concerns about the legitimacy of unparliamentary taxation, extensions of the royal prerogative and the future of parliaments; however, it appears that these did not become really widespread until after the publicity given to the arguments at Hampden's trial. Charles repeated the mistake he had made in allowing the Five Knights a public hearing, but with even more damaging consequences. To start with councillors were very careful to avoid any test of ship money's legality. They had learnt a lesson from the loan and refrained from inflicting heavy punishments on gentlemen, targeting lesser refusers instead. They were particularly careful to sidestep the various provocations offered by Lord Saye and Sele, and distrained his cattle rather than confronting him directly. When Saye sought to force the issue, by suing the sheriff of Lincolnshire in February 1637, they pre-empted any trial by referring the whole matter to the opinion of the judges. After the usual softening-up process – which involved Lord Chief Justice Finch visiting each judge in turn with a letter from Charles urging compliance with his wishes – the majority declared that the king had the right to collect ship money in a national emergency, and also that he could make his own judgement over what constituted such an emergency. This was rapidly and widely publicised and several commentators concluded that ship money was now a permanent fixture.[255]

The success of the judges' statement, however, made Charles over-confident. Perhaps unaware of the misgivings of three of the judges, in August 1637 he took the decision to call John Hampden before the King's Bench for refusing to pay his 20s. levy. This was supported by a majority of councillors, including experienced legal officers, like Lord Keeper Coventry, who apparently took the view that a decisive judgement now, against someone who was less likely to put up a fight than Lord Saye, would finally destroy the credibility of the opposition. Laud and Wentworth dissented, believing that it was rash in the extreme to expose the levy to any further legal test; but their doubts were brushed aside.[256] This was a serious mistake. The

---

[255] N.P. Bard, 'The ship money case and William Fiennes, Viscount Saye and Sele', *BIHR*, vol. 50, 1977, pp. 177–84; Gill, 'Ship money', pp. 169–73; Quintrell, *Charles I*, pp. 64–5; see the newsletter cited in Sharpe, 'The Personal Rule', pp. 75–6.

[256] Gill, 'Ship money', pp. 173–5; Quintrell, *Charles I*, p. 67; Laud, *Works*, vol. 7, pp. 326–7.

hearings in the Hampden case lasted from November 1637 to June 1638 and aroused enormous public interest. The finding of five of the twelve judges against the crown ensured that, far from closing the issue down, the trial provoked widespread questioning and debate. In the judgement of Clarendon it was the turning point for the levy, since many who had previously been prepared to accept that the law allowed the king a certain amount of leeway in such matters now felt they were being asked to approve a decisive extension of the royal prerogative.[257] This verdict has been endorsed in an exhaustive investigation by Alison Gill who concludes that the case led to a fundamental shift in the pattern of opposition which became both more determined and more violent.[258] Ship money would have been increasingly difficult to collect anyway – because from 1639 other burdens were being imposed on taxpayers as a result of the Scots war – but it was Hampden's case that made it unmanageable. The crown had failed to learn one of the crucial lessons of the late 1620s: that enforcement had to be tempered with a sensitivity to political opinion.

In many ways, this summed up the principal failing of 'the Personal Rule'. There was no lack of energy or drive in the direction of government. By the standards of the day Charles was an active and industrious monarch, and it was important for his sense of self-esteem that he be seen to be in charge. He could not be everywhere and initiatives that have sometimes been credited to him, such as the drawing up of the Book of Orders, have been shown to have been the work of his councillors. But his clear delineation of policy priorities, his readiness to intervene in the day-to-day running of affairs, his determination not to allow his servants to become distracted by faction fighting and his overall grip on government helped to create a climate in which those involved felt they needed to be seen to be working towards meeting his wishes. Of course, this did not always produce the desired results. The ability of king and council to oversee the actions of their servants remained hampered by bureaucratic inadequacies and the difficulties of communicating priorities down the chain of command.[259] There remained many instances where the rhetoric of the

---

[257] Clarendon, *History*, vol. 1, pp. 86–7.

[258] Gill, 'Ship money', pp. 452–72.

[259] Quintrell, *Charles I*, pp. 53–7.

'public' was used to cloak what were essentially selfish, 'private' interests. However, much was achieved. The navy was strengthened, royal finances were improved, local order was by and large maintained and some of the much-criticised 'projects' did produce positive results. In the state, as in the church, 'working towards the king' did much to infuse the system with energy and direction. The problem was that these gains often came at a high political price.

As Charles became more certain of himself during the 1630s, he became less likely to take unwelcome advice. Councillors adjusted to this and it tended to mean that discussion of sensitive issues was closed down before they had been given an adequate airing. The consequence was mistakes over policy, of which the decision to go ahead with Hampden's case was a prime example. At the same time, Charles and the court were increasingly locked into a view of the world in which any dissent from royal policy was seen as emanating from a seditious, selfish, 'popular' opposition. This again tended to make the government's responses cruder and less considered. There was little attempt to understand alternative viewpoints, even when they had a good deal of justification, as, for example, over fen drainage. There was also less energy invested in communicating with people. The requirement of the new style, 'popular' politics, that the crown make a concerted effort to put over its viewpoint and manage the news, was, with a few notable exceptions, disregarded. This might not have mattered so much had Charles possessed the political antennae of his father. But he remained alarmingly insensitive to how his actions appeared to others. His willingness to be drawn into discussions about reunification with Rome at a time of widespread concern about court popery is a prime example. In the event, news of the episode does not appear to have leaked out, but had it done so the effects could have been disastrous.[260]

The combination of policy mistakes, poor communication and what Conrad Russell calls an inability 'to read the political map' prevented Charles from reaping the political dividend that he might have expected from the peace and stability of the 1630s.[261] Instead, there were growing tensions and divisions. However, it should be emphasised that these, in

---

[260] For this episode, see above pp. 146–7.

[261] Russell, *Causes of the Civil War*, p. 208.

themselves, were not enough to bring 'the Personal Rule' to an end. Given a continuation of peace, the king could probably have gone on ruling without parliament more or less indefinitely. It was the Scottish rebellion that transformed the political situation.

Chapter 4

Charles and the British Problem, 1625–1638

Ireland

Any investigation of Charles's role in governing Ireland and Scotland has to be set in the context of what recent scholarship has called the 'British Problem'. Conrad Russell, in particular, has highlighted the difficulties the king faced in ruling a 'composite monarchy' made up of the very different kingdoms of England, Ireland, Scotland and Wales. Each had its own cultural, political and religious traditions and each had a different relationship with the centre of government in London. In the case of Wales there were few problems. The principality had been successfully united with the English political and legal system since the Act of Union of 1536 and its church was part of the Church of England. Ireland and Scotland, however, were much less fully integrated. Scotland remained an independent entity, united with England since 1603 mainly by the fact that both kingdoms had the same sovereign. James had failed to persuade his first parliament to support a full legal and administrative union, so Scotland retained its own parliament, its own legal system and its own privy council. It also had a Presbyterian 'kirk', the independence of which was a source of great national pride. Ireland, on the other hand, was a colonial kingdom, part of the English monarchy by dint of conquest by the Normans that had been consolidated in the sixteenth century. It had its own parliament, lord deputy, council and legal system, but the lord deputy and council were directly answerable to the English privy council and the parliament was hedged around with restrictions, such as Poynings Law, which stipulated that any legislation must be first approved in London. Ireland also had its own Protestant church, but the majority of the population remained Catholic and looked to Rome to serve their spiritual needs.[1]

Charles's problems in ruling these diverse kingdoms were analogous to those faced by other 'composite monarchies', in particular Spain. The commonest cause of instablity in this situation tended to be grievances about the distribution of resources and patronage. The outlying kingdoms felt that because of their distance from the centre they did not get their fair share of offices and grants, and were asked to bear a disproportionate burden of taxation and other demands, especially in wartime. In the British context, however, these problems appear to have been containable. The principal flashpoint, Russell has argued, was religion. Each of Charles's kingdoms contained powerful minorities who preferred the religion of one of the other kingdoms to their own. This created a situation where 'the attractions of an alternative model, tolerated by the same ruler in another dominion, were too great an invitation to instability'.[2] Therefore, from 1633 onwards Charles began to impose the anti-Calvinist measures he was pursuing in England on Ireland and Scotland as well, with disastrous consequences.[3]

The focus on the 'British Problem' has largely been used to explain how each of the three kingdoms came to experience armed rebellion between 1639 and 1642; however, it also raises questions about Caroline government more generally, in particular about how far a British perspective shaped decision-making and the extent to which Charles tried to make a reality of the propaganda about his role as king of a united Great Britain.

If we look first of all at Ireland, there are indications of a broader British perspective, but this was generally supplied by Wentworth and Laud rather than Charles. For most of his reign Charles had little interest in, or awareness of, Irish affairs. He occasionally met Irish politicians at court in London and he was diligent in commenting on the position papers that were presented to him; but he never visited the country and rarely placed its interests at

---

[1] C.S.R. Russell, 'The British Problem and the English Civil War', in *Unrevolutionary England*, pp. 231–51; idem, *Causes of the Civil War*, pp. 39–40; A.L. Hughes, *The Causes of the English Civil War*, 2nd edn, Basingstoke, 1998, pp. 30–5.

[2] Russell, *Fall of the British Monarchies*, p. 28.

[3] Ibid., pp. 37–40.

the top of his agenda. On the two occasions when he was directly involved with its affairs – during negotiations over 'the Graces' in 1626–8, and again in 1641 – his concerns appear to have been entirely Anglocentric: in the first instance securing money and men for the war effort and in the second strengthening his hand in dealing with parliament. This lack of attention left the way open for others to take the initiative in Irish affairs, and Wentworth and Laud became adept at guiding him into the decisions they wanted.

The situation that Charles inherited in Ireland was complicated by the existence of three main political interest groups. Since the start of James's reign, the government had been trying to consolidate royal authority through a policy of 'Anglicisation', which basically meant trying to 'civilise' the Irish by outlawing their cultural and legal traditions, taking over their land and imposing Protestantism. The principal beneficiaries of this were the mainly Protestant 'New English', settlers, officials and members of the military establishment who had colonised Ireland since the Reformation. By the early seventeenth century they held most of the offices in the Irish administration and nearly half the seats in parliament, and they were looking to strengthen their position by extending their landholdings and promoting a Protestant ascendancy. The main losers were the 'native' or 'Gaelic' Irish who still owned much of the land, but whose position was weakened by their continuing resistance to assimilation into the English system of government and their readiness to look to Rome and Spain for support. The English crown treated them alternately as a threat to be subdued and a conquered people to be exploited. The third grouping, the 'Old English', so called because they were descended from the original Anglo-Norman lords of Ireland, were in an ambiguous position. Their main distinguishing feature was their loyalty to the English crown, something that had made them the dominant force in Irish politics for much of the sixteenth century. They continued to hold around a third of the land in Ireland, as well as half the seats in the parliament, and their leaders had good contacts at court in London; however, the majority of them were Catholics, which meant they were gradually being squeezed out of office by the requirement to take the oath of supremacy This in turn was weakening their ability to protect their landholdings and defend themselves from religious persecution. They remained a potent political force, but their privileged position was under threat.[4]

---

[4] Hughes, *Causes of the Civil War*, pp. 38–9.

Crown policy towards Ireland in the late 1610s and early 1620s followed two contradictory approaches that heightened the tension between the main interest groups. Buckingham and his clients in Ireland, who included the two lord deputies of the period, St John and Falkland, joined forces with the 'New English' and sought to enrich themselves under the guise of promoting 'Anglicisation'. They acquired wardships, Irish titles, export licences and the lion's share of the lucrative customs farm, and urged that any shortfall in revenues to the Exchequer in London be met by vigorous enforcement of recusancy fines. At the same time they threatened the property rights of the 'Old English' by extending the policy of plantation, which hitherto had been confined to land confiscated from the 'native' Irish in Ulster. Most of the 'Old English' had Irish titles to their land that were invalid under English law and it now became possible to 'discover' their holdings as 'concealed' crown lands, in which case they were liable to be confiscated and regranted to settlers. The alternative policy, pursued by Lionel Cranfield, during his period as lord treasurer between 1621 and 1624, sought to reverse these measures by allowing landowners with questionable titles to their property to enter into compositions, which gave them security and also brought additional revenues to the crown. Combined with the slackening in the persecution of Catholics that accompanied the Spanish Match, this tilted the balance back in favour of the 'Old English'.[5] Cranfield's policy was brought to an end by his fall from office; but before Falkland and the 'New English' could take advantage of this, the crown became immersed in war with Spain.

Charles and Buckingham's principal concern during the war years was to prevent Ireland becoming a jumping off point for a Spanish invasion of England. Arrangements were quickly made to improve coastal defences and the Irish army was doubled in size; but because of the expenditure elsewhere it was essential to meet the costs out of Irish revenues. This created an ideal opportunity for the 'Old English' to secure confirmation of their status as part of the colonial ruling class by demonstrating their loyalty through financial and military support. Charles's determination to promote the war effort ensured that he took a close interest in the negotiations that followed.

---

[5] T.W. Moody, F.X. Martin and F.J. Byrne eds, *Early Modern Ireland 1534–1691*, The New History of Ireland, vol. 3, Oxford, 1976, pp. 187–229; V. Treadwell, *Buckingham and Ireland 1616–1628*, Dublin, 1998, pp. 301–3.

The first scheme, set up by a gentleman of the bedchamber, Sir John Bath, involved the 'Old English' raising militia units for the defence of Ireland in return for the suspension of recusancy fines and appointments to the commissions of the peace. This was blocked by 'New English' hostility to arming Catholics or allowing them into office. The second scheme emerged in the aftermath of the 1626 Parliament when the crown was desperately casting around for new sources of revenue. A list of 27 concessions was proposed, including suspension of recusancy fines and the replacement of the oath of supremacy with a less stringent oath of allegiance, in return for a promise of supply in a forthcoming Irish parliament. Falkland summoned a 'great assembly' of nobles, clergy and commons to consider this in early 1627, but discussion quickly became bogged down. All the participants were worried by the prospect of heavy taxation and the 'New English', backed by the Protestant bishops, vehemently opposed moves to do away with the oath of supremacy or recusancy fines. The deadlock was not broken until early 1628, when the assembly sent 11 agents, representing a cross-section of Irish opinion, to negotiate directly with the government in London. Out of this, in May, emerged 'the Graces', a list of 51 concessions that the crown was willing to grant in return for subsidies from an Irish parliament worth £120 000. The most important of 'the Graces' were a repeat of the offer to replace the oath of supremacy and a new measure to enact a statute passed by the English parliament in 1624 renouncing royal claims to land held for more than 60 years. This would have had the effect of protecting the property rights of the 'Old English' and putting a stop to the process of confiscation and settlement; however, there was no repetition of the provisions for suspending recusancy fines, or allowing Catholics into office, which confirmed the regime's commitment to maintaining a Protestant ascendancy. The Irish parliament was due to meet in November 1628; but, as part of the agreement over 'the Graces', payment of subsidies began before this, and when there were legal difficulties over the issue of parliamentary writs, the crown simply put off the meeting and continued to collect the money. The 'Old English' were left in the unfortunate position of paying their taxes without formal sanction for any of the concessions they had been granted in return. Things became worse when Falkland was recalled to England and a commission headed by the earl of Cork, one of the most aggressive of the 'New English' planters, took over the running of the government. Measures to harass Catholics were stepped up and the policy of confiscation and settlement was resumed in Connacht.[6] Contrary to the expectations of many, however, Cork did not succeed Falkland as lord deputy. The post went instead to Viscount Wentworth, whose period of office from 1632 to 1640 transformed the pattern of Irish politics and raised the crown's authority to a new level of effectiveness.

The key to Wentworth's immensely powerful position in Ireland was his standing at court. Falkland had been the latest in a line of lord deputies whose power and freedom of manoeuvre had been destroyed by plotting in London. Wentworth recognised this and before he agreed to serve in Dublin secured the king's formal agreement to a series of proposals ensuring that he would have a free hand in running Ireland and would answer only to Charles via his trusted ally Secretary Coke. Charles continued to support his lord deputy even when he appeared to be overreaching himself, as happened when he had Lord Mountnorris convicted of treason in 1635. Wentworth's triumphant reception at court in the summer of 1636 – when the king congratulated him on the 'vigour and force' of his proceedings in front of the privy council – made his position in Ireland virtually unassailable. The other essential prop to his power was his alliance with Laud, which was built initially on a mutual hostility to Weston and then developed through a shared agenda for enhancing royal authority. With Laud to guard his back and inform him of any attempt to undermine his authority, Wentworth was in a far better position to exploit the opportunities that Ireland offered than any previous lord deputy.[7] There was massive potential inherent in the crown's position as a conquering power, and Wentworth set out to make the most of it.

The new lord deputy's principal concern in developing his Irish policy was to impress Charles. As Anthony Milton puts it, 'the whole point of his administration was that it should act as a prolonged advertising campaign displaying the abilities that he would put to use in a similarly elevated position back in England'.[8] Like many another aspiring court politician of the 1630s, he concluded that the best way to achieve this was by representing himself as a staunch opponent of the evils associated with the 'popular' and the 'private'. In his lengthy correspondence with Laud, he

---

[6] *Early Modern Ireland*, pp. 233–8; Treadwell, *Buckingham and Ireland*, pp. 279–83.

[7] *Strafforde Letters*, vol. 1, pp. 65–7; Wedgewood, *Wentworth*, pp. 90–1, 119–23, 135–6, 197–202, 210–12; *Early Modern Ireland*, pp. 259–60.

[8] Milton, 'Wentworth and political thought', p. 145.

developed an image of himself as the public-spirited royal servant, beset by enemies and selfish interests, but determined to battle on. In particular, he made much of the idea of 'Thorough', which basically meant taking a vigorous and forceful line to overcome whatever stood in the way of the 'common weal'. At the same time, he started to use the language of 'anti-puritanism', something he had not done before.[9] Wentworth's rhetoric does not necessarily provide an accurate guide to his motives, but it does reveal much about the assumptions he was making and the challenges that he was seeking to address, which in turn served to structure his actions and define the options open to him.

The concern to impress the king in particular ways – as well as the relative freedom of action that he enjoyed – was demonstrated during the first phase of Wentworth's government in Ireland, when he was dealing with the Parliament of 1634–5. One of his initial moves was to distance himself from the officials and lawyers of the 'New English' interest who had tradi-tionally been regarded as the main prop to the lord deputy's authority. Wentworth took a very jaundiced view of their devotion to the crown and 'public weal', describing them as 'a body of men the most intent on their own ends that ever I met with'.[10] From the outset he sought to use his own patronage to build up a party of loyal servants who could hold the balance of power while he played 'Old' and 'New English' off against each other. In 1632 Cork and his allies in the Dublin government proposed that when the subsidy payments came to an end the shortfall should be met by enforcing recusancy fines. Wentworth, however, favoured negotiation of a continuance of the subsidies and went behind their backs to strike a deal with the 'Old English' based on continued supply in return for a tempor-ary suspension of fines and reconsideration of 'the Graces'.[11] He then began the task of persuading Charles to agree to a parliament that was intended to offer a longer term solution to his financial problems. Here, as we have seen, he prepared the ground carefully, stressing from the outset that he

---

[9] Ranger, 'Strafford in Ireland', pp. 280–2; Wedgewood, *Wentworth*, pp. 120–1; *Early Modern Ireland*, p. 246; H.F. Kearney, *Strafford in Ireland 1633–41*, Manchester, 1959, pp. 115–16. On the novelty of Wentworth adopting an anti-puritan language, see R.P. Cust, 'Wentworth's "change of sides" in the 1620s', in Merritt ed., *The Political World of Thomas Wentworth*, pp. 78–80.

[10] *Strafforde Letters*, vol. 1, p. 96.

[11] *Early Modern Ireland*, pp. 244–5.

would not allow it to challenge royal authority. 'In despite of all popular opinion or opposition', he wrote, 'I assure your Majesty I have courage sufficient to advise the breach of a hundred parliaments rather than my master should suffer in the least circumstance of honour or prerogative.'[12] He also proposed the scheme to divide the meeting into two sessions so that supply would be granted without the appearance of bargaining on the king's part.

When the parliament met events unfolded very much as Wentworth planned. During the first session in July 1634, he achieved his main objective of securing a grant of six subsidies. This was helped by his policy of divide and rule. During this first session he had continued his friendly overtures to the 'Old English', allowing them time to prepare a detailed consideration of 'the Graces', which was then approved by the Commons; however, when he got down to considering 'the Graces' in detail he decided that several of them were unacceptable, including the statute of limitations, confirming estates held for 60 years. He tried to assure the 'Old English' that they would gain greater security from the commission from defective titles, and offered a suspension of measures against Catholics as a gesture of goodwill; but they were not appeased and, when the parliament reconvened in November, began to oppose government legislation. Wentworth retaliated by turning to the 'New English' and invoking the Catholic menace, with a warning that 'friars and Jesuits' were stirring up opposition in the assembly. This was highly effective. The 'New English' MPs rallied behind Wentworth's clients in the Commons and pushed through a whole raft amount of government legislation; then in the final stages of the meeting, Wentworth was able to assert his dominance over the 'Old English' by forcing them to accept two bills that they had earlier refused to proceed with.[13]

Wentworth's triumph in the Parliament of 1634–5 was the high point of his rule in Ireland. His deft manoeuvring had given him money, legislation and freedom of action, and he was able to inform Charles that the 'Ground Plott' had been set for 'the full accomplishment of all your high prerogatives and powers in this kingdom, where undoubtedly your majesty

---

[12] Cited in Milton, 'Wentworth and political thought', p. 143. For Wentworth's attitude to the Irish Parliament, see above pp. 132–3.

[13] *Early Modern Ireland*, pp. 248–51.

may take yourself to be as absolute a monarch as Christendom can set forth'.[14] These predictions were never entirely fulfilled, but the letter does convey Wentworth's complete confidence in his own authority and his sense that it was possible to attempt almost anything he wanted in Ireland since the political constraints operating in England no longer applied. In these circumstances – as Terence Ranger and, more recently, Anthony Milton, have suggested – his rule of Ireland became, in effect, a trial run for introducing a more authoritarian regime in England. His determination to take away parliament's ability to bargain over supply, to accept no enforceable limitations on the king's authority and to disregard established legal and religious traditions amounted to a British version of absolutism.[15] However, his policies gave rise to an increasingly vociferous opposition.

The lord deputy's initiatives were concentrated mainly in two areas: improving the crown's finances and reforming the church. In purely fiscal terms his government was a great success. The income from Irish revenues rose from c.£40 000 to c.£80 000 a year, providing an annual surplus of c.£20 000 that was used to repay debts. Much of this was achieved at a relatively low political cost. A small clique of customs farmers lost out when Wentworth took control of the tobacco import monopoly; but many of the 'Old English' positively welcomed the increased costs on rents and wardships imposed by the commission for defective titles since this gave them greater security in their land tenure.[16] However, the lord deputy's resumption of the plantation policy did cause deep and widespread alienation. No distinction was made between land held by the 'native Irish' and the 'Old English' which, as Aidan Clarke has observed, 'placed at hazard the privileged status upon which the entire "Old English" community depended for the protection of its property'.[17] The main opposition came from the 'Old English' stronghold of Galway, where local jurors refused to find the king's title to local lands and the earl of Clanricard used his considerable influence to lobby against the policy at court; however, Clanricard's premature death in November 1635 enabled Wentworth to gain the upper hand, and he was

---

[14] Cited in Milton, 'Wentworth and political thought', p. 146.

[15] Ranger, 'Strafford in Ireland', pp. 282–93; Milton, 'Wentworth and political thought', pp. 153–6.

[16] Kearney, *Strafford in Ireland*, pp. 74–81, 159–70, 182–3.

[17] *Early Modern Ireland*, p. 253.

able to use the Court of Castle Chamber in Dublin, the Irish equivalent of Star Chamber, to harass the Galway jurors into submission. By the summer of 1637 large tracts of land had been confiscated and the plantation policy was being extended to Clare and Munster. Wentworth had got his way, but at the cost of antagonising a large section of the 'Old English', who started to feel that, perhaps, they had more in common with the oppressed 'native Irish' than the English crown.[18]

If Wentworth's plantation policy alienated the 'Old English', his religious policy upset the 'New English'. The Protestant church in Ireland was staunchly Calvinist. The 'New English' had a strong sense of themselves as a beleaguered minority, and they identified closely with the anti-popery and rigorous adherence to predestinarian doctrine that were embodied in the person of the primate, Archbishop Ussher of Armagh. However, this was precisely the style of divinity that Charles and Laud were trying to eradicate in England and it was predictable that sooner or later they would turn their attentions to Ireland, especially as English Calvinists had looked to the Irish Articles of 1615 to support their predestinarian reading of the Thirty-Nine Articles.[19] Laud's correspondence with Wentworth during the early months of his lord deputyship set out an agenda for reforming the Irish church along ceremonialist and anti-Calvinist lines. He called for the 'reception and establishment' of the Thirty-Nine Articles and the English Canons of 1604, the setting up of an Irish Court of High Commission and the recovery of church property that had fallen into lay hands.[20] Wentworth himself was not particularly interested in religion, but he recognised its importance if he was to make the right impression on Charles and cultivate his friendship with the archbishop.

The first stage in implementing the Laudian programme was to persuade the Irish Convocation, meeting simultaneously with the parliament, to adopt the Thirty-Nine Articles and Canons. This task was largely entrusted to Wentworth's anti-Calvinist chaplain, John Bramhall, recently created

---

[18] Ibid., pp. 253–6, 262–3.

[19] A.L. Capern, 'The Caroline church: James Ussher and the Irish dimension', *HJ*, vol. 39, 1996, pp. 58–64.

[20] Laud, *Works*, vol. 7, pp. 65–71; J.S. Morrill, 'A British patriarchy? Ecclesiastical imperialism under the early Stuarts', in A. Fletcher and P. Roberts eds, *Religion, Culture and Society in Early Modern Britain*, Cambridge, 1994, pp. 226–31.

bishop of Derry. Bramhall's efforts, however, were resisted by Ussher and the Calvinists who tried to disallow those of the Thirty-Nine Articles that they did not consider orthodox and smuggle approval for the Irish Articles into the fifth canon. It was not until the lord deputy discovered their subterfuge and berated them with accusations of 'Brownism' and behaving like 'the fraternities and conventicles of Amsterdam', that they finally gave way. The Thirty-Nine Articles were accepted, while the authority of the Irish Articles was left purposely vague. The bulk of the English canons were also approved, with minor concessions to Ussher's dislike of bowing at the name of Jesus, but also significant new requirements that communion tables be placed at the east end of the chancel and that all communicants kneel.[21]

The lord deputy continued to build on this policy with a blatant disregard of the sensibilities of the 'New English'. The earl of Cork was forced to accept the humiliation of having his wife's monument in St Patrick's Cathedral, Dublin, taken down and boxed up, because it stood in the way of the east end altar. Ussher, worn out by continuous bullying, retired to his episcopal residence in Drogheda, leaving effective control of the church in the hands of Bramhall and another anti-Calvinist bishop, Henry Leslie. And the Irish High Commission caused consternation among Calvinist ministers by its rigorous enforcement of the canons.[22] What made these measures even harder to bear was the *de facto* toleration accorded to Catholics. Wentworth took the view that until the Protestant church in Ireland had been reformed and strengthened it was in no state to undertake the task of evangelising Catholics. It was therefore pointless to antagonise them by enforcing fines or persecution, which meant that they were more or less left alone.[23] The biggest source of grievance, however, was the policy for restoring the church lands and tithes that was implemented far more ruthlessly and effectively than the comparable policy in England. Obstacles to the recovery of church property were removed by legislation

---

[21] J. McCafferty, ' "God bless your free church of Ireland": Wentworth, Laud, Bramhall and the Irish convocation of 1634', in Merritt ed., *The Political World of Thomas Wentworth*, pp. 190–205; Kearney, *Strafford in Ireland*, pp. 115–16; Capern, 'James Ussher and the Irish dimension', pp. 72–8.

[22] Capern, 'James Ussher and the Irish dimension', pp. 70–7; Kearney, *Strafford in Ireland*, pp. 112–19.

[23] *Early Modern Ireland*, pp. 256–7.

in parliament and impropriators were cajoled, bullied and bribed into restoring what they had taken. Proceedings were generally initiated by the commission for defective titles, but appeals were heard by the Court of Castle Chamber which was prepared to ride roughshod over the process of law as it was understood in Ireland. For the first time it seemed that the property rights of the 'New English', who had gained the lion's share of church resources in the past, were being threatened. And to this were added resentments over the lord deputy's personal rapacity – which was particularly hard to stomach given his sanctimonious lectures on the need to put the 'public' before the 'private' – and his coercion of the city of London over the surrender of its Londonderry plantation. The 'New English' were left with a sense that while Wentworth was in charge their privileged position within the colonial system was no longer secure.[24]

Traditionally, lord deputies had built up the support needed to rule Ireland either by cooperating with the 'New English' programme of 'Anglicisation' or offering concessions to the 'Old English'. Wentworth did neither of these things. He was sufficiently confident of Charles's backing to be able to play off the main groupings against each other and rely on a small clique of his own clients to hold the balance. This worked well at the start, but during 1636 and 1637 his increasingly arbitrary policies turned both main interest groups against him at the same time. As Conrad Russell has observed, he was well on the way to being 'the only Englishman ever to break down the religious divide in Irish politics'.[25] The situation became even worse in 1638–9, with the fallout from the Covenanter rebellion in Scotland. 'New English' Calvinists and Scots Presbyterians who had settled in Ulster hoped that this would enable them to reverse the 'Arminianisation' of the Irish church, especially when, in late 1638, Charles offered to revoke the new Scottish service book and canons, and abolish the Scottish High Commission; but they were disappointed. The king eventually opted for war with the Covenanters and Wentworth mounted a campaign to drive out the Ulster Scots who sympathised with them.[26] With his position at court secure, and the considerable Irish army at his back, there was no prospect of the lord

---

[24] Ibid., pp. 258–66; Ranger, 'Strafford in Ireland', pp. 287–91.

[25] C.S.R. Russell, 'The British background to the Irish Rebellion of 1641', in *Unrevolutionary England*, p. 266.

[26] *Early Modern Ireland*, pp. 267–8.

deputy's power being challenged. But he was storing up massive problems for the Irish government should he be removed.

The impact of the Covenanter rebellion is a reminder of the extent to which Irish affairs were connected with those of Charles's other kingdoms. Recognition of this was a feature of Wentworth's government of Ireland. He and Laud had a more developed capacity than most of Charles's ministers to appreciate the British dimension to their policies. Laud's principal aim throughout his dealings with the Irish church was to safeguard his anti-Calvinist vision for the Church of England. He very clearly perceived the danger that his enemies in England would draw encouragement and support if it was allowed to continue as a bastion of predestinarian Calvinism. Hence his determination to impose the Thirty-Nine Articles and the English-style canons. He was also very conscious of operating within a British, rather than just English, frame of reference jesting somewhat ruefully with Wentworth, when called on to send yet more instructions into Scotland as well as Ireland, 'I think you will have a plot to see whether I will be *universalis episcopus* that you and your bretheren may take occasion to call me antichrist.'[27] Wentworth – in part because he was striving to establish his credentials for a job back in England – was equally aware of the connections between the kingdoms. He was, for example, quick to point out to Charles that the success of the Irish parliament, and also the 1633 Parliament in Scotland, 'carries an aspect towards England'.[28] Similarly, comments to Laud on the need to use forceful measures to recover royal authority in Ireland were clearly intended to apply to dealing with 'Common lawyers' and 'Magna Carta men' in England as well.[29] The policies pursued by lord deputy and archbishop in Ireland were an indication of how they would like to have operated in England had they been freed of the existing legal and religious constraints.

But where does this leave Charles? What part did the king play in all this? Most of the time his role in Ireland was relatively limited. He lacked the desire and the opportunities to become involved in day-to-day policy making and he did not possess his ministers' capacity to see things from

---

[27] *Strafforde Letters*, vol. 1, p. 271.

[28] Cited in Milton, 'Wentworth and political thought', pp. 145–6.

[29] Ibid., pp. 138–40.

a British perspective. This was not entirely his fault. Most of the time the information he received on Irish affairs was limited to what the lord deputy and archbishop wanted him to know. Wentworth, for example, was very careful to ensure that he received only positive reports about the parliament lest he take fright and dissolve it prematurely. Similarly, the flow of information about the Convocation was carefully controlled, with great care being taken to prevent Ussher from reporting independently to the king. In these circumstances, Charles's ability to make up his own mind was restricted. The comments he made in the margins of position papers on Ireland suggest he was being nudged and led along in a similar fashion to the bishops' reports.[30] This gave his two ministers maximum freedom of manoeuvre. They were able to secure royal approval for most of what they wanted in Ireland and then use this to browbeat or intimidate opponents.[31] Charles was in the position of authorising policy rather than initiating it. However, this did not prevent him from exercising influence in a broader sense. Both Wentworth and Laud remained acutely aware that they could only continue to function in this way while they retained his confidence, and this depended on continuing to be seen to be addressing his prejudices and priorities. Wentworth, in particular, would have been much more cautious about adopting such a nakedly authoritarian approach had he not received regular assurances that this was how the king wanted him to treat his Irish subjects. Charles was ultimately in charge in Ireland, but operating by remote control rather than directly. It was here, perhaps, that the phenomenon of 'working towards the king' had the greatest impact.

Scotland

Charles played a much more active role in Scotland than he did in Ireland. He felt a greater sense of affinity with the kingdom in which he had been born and which his father had ruled for almost the whole of his life. There was also no one of the stature of Wentworth to cushion him from personal

---

[30] Ibid., p. 148; Capern, 'James Ussher and the Irish dimension', pp. 72, 77–8; *Strafforde Letters*, vol. 1, pp. 183–7.

[31] See, for example, his use of Charles's name in bullying Ussher: Capern, 'James Ussher and the Irish dimension', pp. 64–9.

involvement in its affairs. Charles ruled Scotland directly, issuing regular instructions to his privy council in Edinburgh and responding to their requests on his own initiative. He took advice from a succession of London-based Scottish courtiers, and from Buckingham and, later on, Laud. However, for most of the period up to the rebellion it was he who directed policy. Moreover, because he knew so much less about Scottish politics than English, he felt less inhibited by a sense of the constraints on his power. In consequence, his handling of Scotland offers insights into his attitude to kingship that are not available elsewhere. He often revealed his prejudices and preconceptions with much greater transparency and in the process demonstrated more clearly his shortcomings as a ruler.[32]

The kingdom that Charles inherited from his father was both better governed and more stable than Ireland. James was not a particularly popular king of Scotland, but he was effective and had done much to tame the two most powerful forces in Scottish politics, the nobility and the Presbyterian kirk. His scheme for a full legal and constitutional union with England had collapsed by about 1607, but he was still able to salvage considerable benefits from uniting the two kingdoms. His new prestige as king of Great Britain did a good deal to overawe the Scots nobility and he kept them in line with generous grants and pensions, paid for by the English, as well as the Scottish, Exchequer. Under the capable leadership of the earl of Dunbar, his council was able to quell noble factionalism and bring relative order to the border region between England and Scotland. He also succeeded in outflanking the hardline Presbyterians in the kirk who, in 1596, pressed the claim that the king was subordinate to their General Assembly in matters relating to religion. He was very careful not to be seen to be challenging the autonomy of the Scottish church or its Calvinist doctrine, both of which were sources of great national pride. Nonetheless, he gradually succeeded in reintroducing bishops and re-establishing the principle of the royal supremacy. He even managed to bring a more ceremonial element into its worship, with the Five Articles of Perth, which provided for kneeling at communion, observance of holy days, private baptism, private communion and confirmation by bishops. All this was done with considerable skill and tact, consulting with General Assemblies at every stage and never trying to

---

[32] Russell, *Fall of the British Monarchies*, pp. 30–1.

move too far too fast. By the end of his reign, the church was firmly under royal control, governed by a mixture of episcopacy and Presbyterianism.[33]

James's rule in Scotland was not without its problems. After Dunbar's death in 1611 the government was run by elderly councillors, with little energy or initiative; the crown was never able to remedy its financial deficit, largely because of spending on pensions; and there were protests against the Perth Articles in the 1621 Parliament. However, there was a degree of order and continuity that had rarely been attained during the sixteenth century, and both the nobles and the kirk were broadly supportive of the crown.[34]

Charles began to upset this equilibrium almost as soon as he ascended the throne. Even though he had been born in Scotland, he had little knowledge or understanding of the country. He had not visited it since his infancy and relied for most of his information on a narrow clique of London-based Scots whose main concerns were to promote their own interests. Foremost among these at the start of the reign was a Catholic client of Buckingham's, the earl of Nithsdale, who was so loathed in Scotland that his coach was mobbed when he visited Dalkeith in 1626. The king's own lack of sympathy for the interests of his northern kingdom was revealed in a letter to the Scottish privy council in November 1625 in which he referred to 'your nation', a phrase his father would never have used. None of this, however, deterred him from intervening forcefully in its affairs.[35]

One of his first priorities was to shake up the elderly and rather complacent group of privy councillors who dominated Scottish politics at his accession. Prompted by disparaging reports from Nithsdale, he had taken offence at their failure to persuade the Scottish Convention of 1625 to fund a force of 2 000 men for the war effort. He also resented their sniping and criticism over his principal Scottish initiative in 1625, the Act of Revocation. The means he used to reduce their power was to separate the personnel of the privy council and the senior civil court of Scotland,

---

[33] K.M. Brown, *Kingdom or Province? Scotland and the Regal Union, 1603–1715*, Basingstoke, 1992, pp. 86–94; Russell, *Fall of the British Monarchies*, pp. 31–6.

[34] Brown, *Kingdom or Province?*, pp. 94–9.

[35] A.I. MacInnes, *Charles I and the Making of the Covenanting Movement 1625–1641*, Edinburgh, 1991, pp. 77–8; M. Lee, *The Road to Revolution: Scotland under Charles I, 1625–1637*, Chicago, 1985, p. 9.

the Court of Session. Nobles were to be removed from the former and lawyers from the latter, thus preventing the overlap of functions which had allowed officials to manipulate the land market under James, and which also threatened to obstruct the revocation. Charles's proposals aroused vigorous protest, particularly from the earl of Melrose, secretary of state and president of the Court of Session, who argued that the king had no right to remove members without proper cause. However, Charles stuck to the line that all offices and places of honour were ultimately in his gift and won the day. Melrose resigned, followed by other nobles in the court, allowing him to readmit those he chose. While this was happening, the elderly earl of Mar, the lord treasurer, was being sidelined as the Exchequer was put into commission under the headship of Archbishop Spottiswoode, a strong proponent of the prerogative and an ally of Nithsdale. And the power of the old guard was further reduced when several of the council's functions were transferred to a council of war under Nithsdale's direction. By the summer of 1626 Scottish government was dominated by the earl and his friends among the bishops, and Charles had the sort of administration that he wanted.[36]

The dangers of this were amply demonstrated by the Act of Revocation, which poisoned his early relationship with the Scots landowning classes. The origins of the scheme are obscure. In January 1625, while still Prince of Wales, Charles made discreet enquiries about how he might revoke grants of land made during his minority which were detrimental to the royal interest. This was well-established practice in Scotland where a series of royal minorities had led to the convention that between the ages of 21 and 25 a new monarch could pass an Act of Revocation. James had done so in 1587 with few adverse consequences. Charles's proposed scheme, however, went much further than anything the Scots had experienced before. On the spurious grounds that he had not come to the crown during his minority, and had therefore not damaged the royal patrimony through his own actions, he argued that he was entitled to revoke all grants made by the crown since 1540. His principal aim was to augment the crown's revenues in Scotland, but he also thought that the scheme could be sold on the basis that it would ensure better maintenance for Scots ministers and relieve many gentry of their obligation to acknowledge a feudal

---

[36] Lee, *Road to Revolution*, pp. 7–32.

superiority to those known as 'lords of erection', whose holdings were based on former church lands.[37] However, there was no effort to explain any of this until relatively late in the day.

The scheme was introduced in a great rush to beat the deadline of Charles's 25th birthday and apparently without consultation, except among some of the London-based Scots courtiers. Sir James Skene, one of the leading Scots lawyers of the day and an ally of Nithsdale has been suggested as the likely author, and Nithsdale himself and Sir James Fullerton, the Scottish groom of the stool, were with Charles when the text of the revocation was settled at Salisbury on 12 October 1625. The first his Scottish privy council heard of it officially was in November when it was simply read out to them, without any opportunity for discussion.[38] The haste and lack of consultation were disastrous. Scottish landowners were deeply alarmed because nearly half of all the income-generating land in the country would be affected. Mar warned Charles that no one could feel secure in their holdings since 'they thought it was intended that all their rights given by any of his Majesty's predecessors should be called into question'.[39]

Charles's unwillingness to listen to his senior councillors eventually prompted them to send a delegation to London in early 1626. Mar compiled a record of the resulting discussions that makes fascinating reading, not only for what it tells us about his attitude to Scottish affairs, but also his whole approach to kingship.[40] The Scots councillors were very much on the defensive, begging Charles not to give credence to the 'sinister' reports passed on by Nithsdale and others, and insisting that they were simply fulfilling the terms of their oath 'to give him true counsel according to our knowledge'. Nonetheless, they stood their ground more tenaciously than English councillors generally did and this forced Charles into some revealing responses.

---

[37] Quintrell, *Charles I*, pp. 12–13; D. Stevenson, *The Scottish Revolution 1637–1644*, Newton Abbot, 1973, pp. 35–42; *Register of the Privy Council of Scotland*, ed. P.H. Brown, 2nd Ser., Edinburgh, 1899–1908, pp. 228–9; *A Large Declaration Touching the Late Tumults in Scotland by the King*, 1639, pp. 7–8.

[38] Lee, *Road to Revolution*, p. 35; P. Donald, *An Uncounselled King. Charles I and the Scottish Troubles, 1637–1641*, Cambridge, 1990, pp. 18–20.

[39] HMC, *Supplementary Report on Mar and Kellie*, p. 135.

[40] Ibid., pp. 133–46.

It was evident throughout that he was poorly briefed on Scottish affairs. When justifying the revocation he kept falling back on the argument that he was simply doing what his father and grandmother had done, except for one novel element that he admitted to, but which, Mar records, 'he seemed not to remember'. He was also plainly ill at ease when it came to any sort of debate. He tended to deliver prepared arguments and then simply reiterate them or lapse into silence rather than engaging in any substantive exchange of views. The abiding impression is of a king profoundly lacking in self-belief and who, as a result, was much too quick to invoke royal authority and the power of the prerogative. The meetings themselves were more akin to court audiences than sessions of the privy council. They took place in the withdrawing chamber at Whitehall and when any of the participants wished to speak they had to kneel before Charles. The exchanges over the removal of privy councillors from the Court of Session were particularly instructive. The king's initial line was that he 'thought it strange that we should put in question his power to confer honour on any man he pleased'. Mar responded that, of course, they had no intention of questioning this, but they did feel obliged to point out that the dismissals might discourage others from giving loyal service in future. Rather than accept this, or discuss the point further, Charles demanded to know by what authority councillors continued to sit after his commission had been issued for them to stand down. Mar quickly conceded, again, that 'we had only power from you', but Charles persisted, declaring 'I think I should be obeyed when I send down my directions'; and he added the rather hurt comment that 'you durst not have done so to my father'. It was not easy to advise someone who was both so tactless and so quick to take offence, particularly for those who had no regular access to the king and therefore little opportunity to study his moods and prejudices. Discussion also tended to come up very quickly against the brick wall of Charles's sense of self-righteousness. On another occasion when the Court of Session was being discussed, Mar suggested taking a little more time to consider the dismissals. Charles responded by citing one of the maxims he was so fond of: 'My lord, it is better the subject suffer a little than all lie out of order.' This spoke volumes for his approach to government, summing up an attitude that was as applicable to England as Scotland. The exchange also encapsulated some of his worst faults as a politician: his rigidity and lack of sensitivity, his resort to authoritarianism rather than negotiation or consultation, and his whole conviction that it was more important to abide by abstract principles of virtue and honour than to engage with the concerns and aspirations of his people.

The councillors may have found it hard to debate issues with Charles in a constructive way, but their trip was not entirely fruitless. In February 1626, the king issued a proclamation explaining some of the thinking behind the Act of Revocation and this was followed by another in July which, for the first time, conceded that compensation would be paid to those who surrendered their rights. This was an indication that he accepted the need to moderate his initial demands; however, it was not enough to reassure the 'lords of erection' and in November 1626 they sent their own delega-tion down to London. This led to a crucial change of policy. In February 1627 Charles laid aside the threat to enforce the revocation by legal action and instead set up a Commission of Surrenders and Teinds, consisting of representatives of the nobles, gentry and church, whose brief was to proceed by negotiation and voluntary surrender. This was little more than accepting the inevitable since it had become clear that he lacked the means to enforce legal action; however, it did produce a dramatic change in the political mood. Landowners were reassured by the local controls on the commission and no longer feared, as Spottiswoode was able to report, that the revocation would 'call in question all men's rights since King Fergus'.[41] The commission met on and off until 1637 and devoted most of its energies to sorting out the vexed question of tithes. Its final achievement was relatively limited. There was no obvious benefit to the royal patrimony and few landowners surrendered their feudal superiorities or hereditary offices because the crown lacked the means to compensate them. The one con-crete gain was to put in place arrangements over tithes, which made most Scots ministers a good deal better off than their English counterparts.[42] But this could not justify the political damage the scheme had caused. Charles had failed in one of the first duties of any early modern ruler, to ensure that his subjects felt secure in their property. He had also alienated every section of opinion in Scotland, even the church that had been forced to surrender the cherished principle that they were entitled to all the tithe

---

[41] *Register of the Privy Council of Scotland*, pp. 227–32; MacInnes, *The Making of the Covenanting Movement*, pp. 57–60; Lee, *Road to Revolution*, pp. 44–6.

[42] Lee, *Road to Revolution*, pp. 66–7.

income lost since 1540.[43] Perhaps most damagingly of all he had been seen to back down, thereby demonstrating the limits of royal power when it came to enforcing unpopular policies.[44]

The person largely responsible for persuading Charles to adopt a more conciliatory line over the revocation was another London-based Scot, the earl of Menteith. With Nithsdale out of the way, leading a military expedition to Denmark, Menteith gradually assumed more and more influence. By mid-1628, when he was appointed president of the privy council and justice general, he was the most powerful figure in Scottish politics. Menteith's prominence was based on a combination of personal favour and skill as a political manager. He was not a particularly vigorous or efficient administrator, but he was willing to shuttle between London and Edinburgh to keep channels of communication open. He also got on well with councillors and members of the nobility, he had a shrewd understanding of the realities of Scots politics and, above all, the king liked him and was prepared to listen to him. His greatest success was the Convention of 1630, at which he persuaded the Estates to renew their grant of taxation, worth £100 000 a year in Scots money, for a further four years. This did much to restore crown finances in Scotland after the end of the war. Otherwise he attempted little in the way of policy initiative. A campaign to introduce assize judges in Scotland petered out after just over a year and a scheme to set up an Anglo-Scottish fishing company to challenge Dutch incursions into British coastal waters collapsed through lack of support. In each case Charles had initially been enthusiastic about the project, but he was talked out of it by Menteith when it became clear that it was not popular in Scotland. This was typical of the earl's methods. His emphasis was on restoring the consensual approach to government that had characterised the Jacobean era, and in terms of rebuilding confidence after the shocks of 1625 and 1626 it worked well.[45] It was, therefore, a considerable blow to the king's government of Scotland when he was toppled by a court coup in early 1633.

---

[43] See the advice James gave in the *Basilicon Doron*, that 'the most part of a king's office standeth in deciding that question of *meum* and *tuum* among his subjects': *Basilicon Doron*, p. 24.

[44] Stevenson, *The Scottish Revolution*, pp. 40–2.

[45] Lee, *Road to Revolution*, chps. 2 and 3.

The episode is instructive because, for once, Charles failed to protect a loyal servant against enemies at court. Menteith's problems began in 1631 when he persuaded the king to recognise his family's title to the ancient earldom of Strathearn, which carried with it a claim to the Scottish throne. He seems to have been concerned simply with family prestige and honour, but his enemies at court, led by the ambitious deputy treasurer for Scotland, the earl of Traquair, and the king's Scots favourite, Hamilton, put it about that his real motive was to stake a claim to the succession. At first, Charles was suitably sceptical and, when Menteith confessed that he may have been indiscreet enough to boast about his royal blood while in his cups, he was quite willing to forgive him. However, his enemies kept up the pressure and eventually, in May 1633, Charles gave way and authorised a commission to investigate. Menteith would probably have escaped blame if he had kept his nerve, but he panicked and signed a submission accepting that he may have said the things he was accused of and begging the king's forgiveness. At this point his opponents were able to deny him the access he needed to explain himself, and in October he was stripped of his offices and placed under house arrest.[46] The whole affair demonstrated that there were limits to Charles's constancy. He was as sensitive as the next monarch about issues relating to the royal succession, and, in a crisis, access to his person was crucial to political survival. It also showed just how lacking in understanding he still was when it came to affairs in Scotland.

After the fall of Menteith, Scotland was never managed as smoothly again. This was not for want of capable ministers. The two men most responsible for the coup against him, Traquair and Hamilton, were well equipped to continue his policies of consensus and moderation. Traquair, who became lord treasurer and effective head of the administration in 1636, had a good grasp of what was feasible in Scotland and provided an effective link between London and Edinburgh, while Hamilton, who worked closely with him, enjoyed all the advantages that went with favour and access. The main problem was that their efforts to steer Charles towards the middle ground were undermined by the rising power of the bishops. In 1635 Spottiswoode became the first clerical lord chancellor since the Reformation and the following year James Maxwell, bishop of Ross, the bishops' chief spokesman

---

[46] Ibid., pp. 119–26; J.J. Scally, 'The political career of Hamilton', pp. 168–70.

at court, was only prevented from becoming lord treasurer by a concerted effort from Hamilton. Like Laud and his allies in England, the Scottish bishops found that their best chance of gaining influence with Charles lay in advocating anti-Calvinist reforms in the church and high-prerogative policies in the state; and the lay councillors for Scotland increasingly found themselves drawn into bidding for favour on the same terms.[47] The other problem during this period was that once again the king himself started to intervene directly in Scottish affairs.

This can be dated from the summer of 1633 when he made the long-delayed journey north for his coronation. From the outset, Charles upset his Scottish hosts with a notable lack of tact. In spite of an enthusiastic welcome in Edinburgh, he was distant and standoffish, making it clear that he preferred the company of his London courtiers to the native nobility. He also insisted that the coronation service be performed according to Church of England rites, with the use of an English prayer book, bishops attired in 'Anglican' vestments and a communion table railed off and positioned altarwise. For the Scots, who prided themselves on having purified their church of 'popish' ceremonial, this was highly offensive.[48]

The parliament that met in late June also caused a good deal of discontent. The crown went to considerable lengths to prevent discussion of grievances relating to the revocation and the Perth Articles. The Committee of Articles, which drew up legislation, was packed with royal appointees; bills and petitions critical of royal policy were suppressed by the clerk register; and only a single day was allowed for consideration of the entire legislative package for the parliament – with the king in attendance, reportedly so that he could note the names of any dissenters. The crown's main objectives were achieved. One hundred and sixty-eight pieces of legislation were passed, including retrospective approval for the Act of Revocation. There was also a substantial grant of taxation in the form of a six-year renewal of the land taxes granted in 1630. But the heavy-handed methods caused considerable opposition.[49] Had Charles's councillors been

---

[47] Scally, 'The political career of Hamilton', pp. 180–3.

[48] Lee, *Road to Revolution*, pp. 129–30, 135–6; J.S. Morrill, 'The Scottish National Covenant in its British Context', in idem, *The Nature of the English Revolution*, Harlow, 1993, pp. 92–5.

[49] Lee, *Road to Revolution*, pp. 131–4, 157–8; MacInnes, *Making of the Covenanting Movement*, pp. 86–9, 132–7.

capable of pursuing a united line they might have persuaded him to adopt a lighter touch or, even, make concessions. But both Traquair and the bishops were far more concerned to ingratiate themselves by playing up to the king's prejudices.

Following the parliament, Charles's policies became positively vindictive. First of all he withheld earldoms from Lords Lindsay and Loudoun because they had opposed his proceedings; then he took the disastrous decision to prosecute Lord Balmerino who had been caught in possession of a tract attacking royal policy. Charles was especially outraged because Balmerino's father had previously been pardoned by James for treason. In spite of strong advice to the contrary, he determined to make an example of him. The trial took place in March 1635 and was as damaging to the crown in Scotland as Hampden's case in England. Balmerino spoke eloquently in his own defence, pointing out that he had not actually been the author of the tract and that there had been no reason to regard it as seditious until the judges had declared it to be so in the course of his trial. He was none-theless convicted of 'leasing making' (i.e. slandering the king and council to the people) and was sentenced to death on the casting vote of Traquair. Charles appears to have had no intention of carrying out the sentence, and Balmerino was eventually pardoned. But the damage had been done. There was a storm of protest against the injustice of the proceedings, with the bishops bearing the brunt of the blame. Moreover, by not going through with the sentence, Charles added to the impression that he would back down rather than enforce unpalatable measures. Above all, the trial did more than anything, apart from the revocation, to alienate the Scots nobility. The harsh-ness of Balmerino's treatment suggested that Charles's regime was blind to their interests, dominated by vengeful bishops and self-seeking courtiers.[50] Far from addressing this problem, the king exacerbated it by going ahead with a programme of religious reform.

In trying to make the Scottish church more like the Church of England, Charles was touching on a particularly sensitive nerve. The Scots took enormous pride in the integrity of their church. They were fond of describ-ing it as 'the best reformed kirk in all the world' and were particularly

---

[50] Lee, *Road to Revolution*, pp. 157–63; MacInnes, *Making of the Covenanting Movement*, pp. 137–41; Stevenson, *The Scottish Revolution*, pp. 43–4. For Charles's view of the case against Balmerino, see *Large Declaration*, pp. 13–14.

concerned that its distinctiveness should not be eroded by closer contacts with England. They were also even more fearful than the English of the threat from popery, recognising that their reformation had gone further and deeper than anything achieved in England and that if they were to preserve orthodoxy it was crucial to defend Calvinist doctrine and a purified liturgy. In addition, there was a particularly strong sense in Scotland that religion embodied what was right and lawful. The process of religious change in the sixteenth century had been much more 'popular' and decentralised than in England, carried through without 'tarrying for the magistrate'. Because of this, the traditions of the kirk emphasised local initiative, parity among ministers, a Presbyterian system of self-government and power devolving from below through elected assemblies, all of which had become ingrained features of Scottish political life. The key institution here was the kirk's general assembly, the ultimate governing body, made up of elected representatives in which the prince had no special powers. Anything that threatened its position was liable to be seen as a fundamental challenge, going far beyond just religious issues.[51]

Those features of the church that the majority of Scots found appealing, however, were precisely the ones that Charles found most objectionable. He shared the view expressed by James in the *Basilicon Doron* that the 'democratic' principles inherent in Presbyterianism were an encouragement to 'popularity' and sedition, and were ultimately incompatible with monarchy. This tended to surface in the Scottish context whenever there was a challenge to the bishops. On a number of occasions, in both the late 1630s and 1640s, he gave voice to his conviction that those Presbyterians who wanted to eradicate episcopacy 'aim at nothing but the overthrow of royal authority'.[52] He also shared his father's concern about a lack of set forms in the Scottish service book, encouraging prayers that were often 'plain libels, girding at sovereignty and authority'. The only way to ensure

---

[51] Russell, *Fall of the British Monarchies*, p. 31; idem., *Causes of the Civil War*, pp. 34–5.

[52] NAS, Hamilton MSS, GD 406/1/1031. I am grateful to Sarah Poynting for supplying me with transcripts of Charles's letters in the Hamilton papers. This is part of her project funded by the Leverhulme foundation to produce a definitive edition of *The Writings of Charles I* which will be published by Oxford University Press. Charles also referred to those against episcopacy as being 'in their hearts against monarchy': GD 406/1/1505. See also his statements in 1646 that 'Presbyterian government . . . never came into any country but by rebellion'; and that 'the nature of Presbyterian government is to steal or force the crown from the king's hand': *Charles I in 1646*, pp. 27, 22.

godly order and obedience, he explained in the preface to the new Scottish prayer book , was through a formal liturgy, 'advisedly set and framed, and not according to the sudden and various fancies of men'.[53] In addition, hewas very nervous about the general assembly, apparently regarding it as a challenge to his royal supremacy. James had been careful to call one whenever he sought to introduce religious reforms, confident that he could manage it to his advantage. Charles, however, refused to follow suit, until forced to do so in 1638; and he caused consternation when his new book of canons in 1636 failed to make any reference to its existence.[54] The logic of these various prejudices and concerns was an ecclesiastical policy in Scotland similar to the one he was pursuing in England: more emphasis on set forms and ceremonial at the expense of preaching, increasingly vigorous enforcement of conformity and a greater stress on the role of bishops and the royal supremacy. It was some time, however, before this became obvious.

During the late 1620s Charles was more concerned about the Act of Revocation and the war effort, and his religious policy was deceptively mild. He continued James's approach of non-enforcement of the Perth Articles, requiring that only newly-ordained ministers subscribe to them. He also tended to keep the bishops at arm's length, particularly during the ascendancy of Menteith. Some Scots hoped that he could be persuaded to suspend the Perth Articles altogether and call a general assembly; but for the better informed there were clear indications that his prejudice against Scots Presbyterians was every bit as strong as that against English puritans. In 1625, when told that lay magistrates in Edinburgh held meetings to censure the conduct of ministers, he was horrified, denouncing the practice as an 'Anabaptistical frenzy'. Then in 1628, when two Edinburgh ministers were unwise enough to ask him to authorise the taking of communion sitting in their seats, he immediately wrote to the bishops, and ordered them to enforce the practice set out in the Perth Articles. This was followed by a requirement that all crown officials receive communion kneeling at least once a year in the royal chapel at Holyrood.[55] The first indication of a

---

[53] *Large Declaration*, p. 16; G. Donaldson, *The Making of the Scottish Prayer Book of 1637*, Edinburgh, 1954, pp. 101–2.

[54] Russell, *Causes of the Civil War*, pp. 114–15; Stevenson, *The Scottish Revolution*, pp. 45–6.

[55] Lee, *Road to Revolution*, pp. 10, 12, 62–3.

concern to revise the liturgy came in 1629 when James Maxwell, who was vehemently anti-Presbyterian, drew his attention to a new version of the Scottish service book that he had helped prepare for James. Charles was initially very keen on it; however, Laud persuaded him that it would be better simply to introduce the English prayer book in Scotland.[56] There matters rested until 1633, when Charles's journey north brought him into direct contact with some of the more distasteful aspects of Presbyterian practice.

Between 1633 and 1637 he promoted a systematic campaign to eradicate the unacceptable features of the Scottish church. As in England, ecclesiastical policy was made by king and archbishop working in tandem. Laud gave advice, issued instructions and got the blame for innovations; but Charles set out the priorities and put his prestige behind the policies. In October 1633 a Scottish edition of the English prayerbook was published, with orders that it be used in bishops' chapels and the Chapel Royal. The following year the king and Laud decided to accept the argument of some of the Scottish bishops, that it would be less offensive to their countrymen to have their own version of the English prayer book. This took about two years to complete, and was primarily the work of Maxwell and Bishop Wedderburn, a Scots client of Laud. Charles, however, took a close personal interest in the project, extensively annotating the various drafts to spell out the times when priests and people should sit or kneel, and substituting the term priest for minister, to emphasise their sacramental function. In the final version there were various concessions to Scots sensibilities, including the removal of Charles's references to priests. But it was still much closer to English practice than anything they had experienced before, which allowed a wide spectrum of opinion to brand it as 'popish'. It was also introduced with minimal consultation. The king's lay councillors in Scotland were never given the opportunity to discuss it and even among the bishops only the advice of the more anti-Presbyterian was sought. There was certainly no thought of summoning a general assembly to approve it. Charles simply ordered its use by dint of his royal supremacy.[57]

---

[56] Donald, *An Uncounselled King*, pp. 34–5; Laud, *Works*, vol. 3, pp. 427–8.

[57] Lee, *Road to Revolution*, pp. 137, 201–2; Donaldson, *Making of the Scottish Prayerbook*, pp. 41–59; Fincham and Lake, 'Ecclesiastical policy of James and Charles', p. 42; Russell, *Fall of the British Monarchies*, pp. 45–6.

The prayer book was not the only religious initiative that many Scots found alarming. There was a fresh campaign to restore church property, which caused renewed alarm among noble landowners, and everywhere the bishops appeared to be gaining in strength. There was also considerable disquiet over the new book of canons, introduced in January 1636. Again it made some concessions to Scottish practice, but the whole tenor was to bring this into line with the Church of England. Ministers were no longer permitted to pray *extempore* or preach outside their parishes without licence; communion tables were ordered to be placed at the east end of the chancel; and presbyteries and kirk sessions, as well as general assemblies, were not referred to at all.[58] Offensive as these measures were, however, it was the prayer book that galvanised opposition.

Charles made a major mistake in allowing the prayer book to be introduced over a long period. From late 1636 onwards it was the topic of constant rumour and discussion. Traquair leaked versions of the text as part of his efforts to undermine the bishops; there were meetings of local Presbyterian synods to denounce it as full of 'popish errors'; and there were also discussions among leading nobles about preparing a campaign of protest, in one case involving the advocate general, Sir Thomas Hope. By the time the minister of St Giles, Edinburgh tried to read the prayer book on 23 July 1637, the opposition was fully primed, and the complaints were extensive and well coordinated.[59] They also attracted widespread support, because, as Maurice Lee has pointed out, the new book seemed to sum up everything that was wrong with Charles's government in Scotland. It 'grated on'

every exposed nerve . . . at once . . . fear of popery, of clerical rule, of alien rule, of destruction of the political influence of the landed classes and further encroachments on their property, of the end of Scots law and institutions, of Scotland as an independent entity.[60]

The prayer book rebellion of 1637 was to be the turning point for Charles's government, not only in Scotland, but England and Ireland as well. He had

---

[58] Lee, *Road to Revolution*, pp. 154–5, 166–7, 202–3; Stevenson, *The Scottish Revolution*, pp. 45–6; Morrill, 'A British patriarchy?', p. 234.

[59] Stevenson, *The Scottish Revolution*, pp. 56–64.

[60] Lee, *Road to Revolution*, pp. 200–1.

encountered opposition to a number of his policies in all three kingdoms, but this had been containable. The defiance of the Scots changed everything and set in motion a train of events that led to defeat in the Bishops' Wars and, ultimately, the outbreak of civil war. But how had this disastrous situation been reached?

The main responsibility lay with Charles himself. From the moment of his accession, control of Scottish affairs had ultimately been in his hands. The English privy council had no jurisdiction north of the border and, because of the problems of communication, crucial decisions were often taken without much input from Scots councillors. Insofar as Charles took advice, it was mainly from those at court in London. They ranged from anti-Calvinists and proponents of the prerogative, such as Nithsdale, Laud and Maxwell, to those whose approach was more consensual, like Menteith and Hamilton. In the end, however, it was Charles who took the final decisions, and in doing so he repeatedly revealed not only his ideological preferences, but also many of his weaknesses as a ruler.

Scotland was in many ways a more difficult country for him to govern than England. Leaving aside the problems caused by distance, its political culture was less deferential, more decentralised, more 'democratic', and more accommodating of 'resistance' to the monarch.[61] It also demanded of its rulers a higher degree of craft and flexibility in decision-making and man-management. James's relative success was based on personal contact and face-to-face debate with its political leaders, as well as shrewd judgement over when to compromise and when to stand firm.[62] These were not skills that came easily to Charles. When he needed to engage in personal contact he tended to be stand-offish; he was not good at concealing his distaste when things were not as he would have wished, as was apparent on his coronation visit of 1633; and while his debating skills were certainly improving in the 1630s, he always fell some way short of the relaxed authority of his father. The result was that he never engaged with more than a small cross-section of Scotland's political elite, which prevented him from developing any feel for its politics or building the personal loyalties that mattered so much.

---

[61] Russell, *Fall of the British Monarchies*, p. 203.

[62] Wormald, 'James VI and I', pp. 193–209.

However, to blame Charles's failings in Scotland mainly on lack of contact would be misleading. It is a striking feature of his government there that the less he was involved, the better things worked. It was when he sought to intervene – in the first two years of his reign and again after 1633 – that problems arose. When he allowed Menteith to take over the direction of affairs in the late 1620s and early 1630s, relative stability was achieved. This suggests that the root of the difficulties lay with Charles's own attitudes and policies. His ignorance of Scottish affairs tended to remove some of the inhibitions and constraints he felt in an English context, and ensure that the Scots were exposed to the full force of his authoritarian and anti-Calvinist prejudices. The effects of this were exacerbated by the tendency of Scots advisers seeking his favour to play up to these prejudices. The consequences were apparent in the Act of Revocation, the imposition of the new service book and, above all, in the negotiations that took place during the 16-month period between the initial protests against the prayer-book and the final breach with the Covenanters at the Glasgow Assembly.

The prayer book rebellion

These negotiations can be divided into two phases. The first, which lasted until the signing of the National Covenant on 28 February 1638, re-emphasised Charles's ignorance and lack of judgement in Scottish affairs. While his privy councillors worked for a settlement, the king refused to acknowledge that there was a crisis. The second, which ended at the Glasgow Assembly in December 1638, revealed the more dangerous side of Charles, the authoritarian meddler whose affronted sense of honour led to a disastrous resort to force.

The strength and durability of the opposition to the prayer book was amply demonstrated in the latter half of 1637. During August and September an increasing number of ministers and nobles signed petitions calling for its withdrawal and in October there were further demonstrations in Edinburgh. As these went unpunished, the supplicants became bolder and extended the scope of their complaints to include the book of canons and the bishops, who were denounced for introducing the service book and abusing the king's trust. In November they also established a committee, known as the Tables, to coordinate their actions. In the face of such a widespread and well-organised campaign, the Scottish privy council was

virtually powerless. To start with they tried to quell the disorder by a proclamation forbidding further meetings or discussion about the prayer book.
When this failed they had no option but to talk to the supplicants'
leaders and this produced a scheme for a conference to determine the future
of the prayer book. Traquair travelled south in January 1638 and worked
with Hamilton to sell the plan to Charles, but found him totally unyielding. Instead, the lord treasurer was given instructions to issue a new
proclamation announcing that the prayer book had the king's blessing and
that the supplicants must disperse or else face punishment for treason.[63]

Charles's refusal to face the facts and accept a realistic compromise derived
from a mix of circumstances. His distance from the centre of events, and
the Scottish councillors' reluctance to admit culpability, meant that he did
not receive accurate information about the extent of the opposition in the
early stages. It also did not help that much of the advice he was receiving
in London came from Scottish Catholics, notably George Con and the
earl of Nithsdale, who had resumed his former role in October 1637. Their
line was that the opposition to the prayer book was part of an international
Calvinist conspiracy to subvert Charles's rule, supported by the Dutch,
the Swedes and, even, the French. Any concession would be a threat to
national security, as well as a stain on the king's honour. What was needed
was firm action, not the spineless response of the Scottish privy council,
several of whom were puritans anyway.[64] This sort of analysis bolstered
Charles's existing prejudices and reinforced his instinct against making
concessions. The biggest obstacle to compromise, however, lay in his own
reading of the situation.

From the start he appears to have viewed it as another manifestation of
the 'popular'/puritan conspiracy that caused him such trouble in England.
This was one of the main themes of the *Large Declaration*, issued in early
1639 to explain his reasons for going to war against the Covenanters.[65]

---

[63] Donald, *An Uncounselled King*, pp. 59–62; Scally, 'The political career of Hamilton',
p. 219.

[64] Hibbard, *Charles I and The Popish Plot*, pp. 94–7; Donald, *An Uncounselled King*, pp. 55,
71.

[65] The *Large Declaration* was ghost-written by Walter Balcanquall, but annotated extensively
by the king and 'owned . . . from the beginning as his own': Russell, *Fall of the British
Monarchies*, p. 44n. For Charles's annotations, see *Large Declaration*, pp. 320–4 (comments
on the Acts of the Glasgow Assembly), 337–50 (comments on the Covenanters' response
to Hamilton), 375–401 (comments on the Protestation of the Glasgow Assembly).

The campaign against the prayer book, it argued, followed the pattern of other 'seditions' in that it claimed to be about religion, but was in fact an attempt to overthrow royal government. Allegations that it would lead to 'innovation' or popery were clearly groundless since it was based on a model that had long been acceptable to English Protestants. In fact, the *Large Declaration* insisted, the agitation was part of a plot that had been hatched at the start of Charles's reign by Presbyterian ministers and disgruntled nobles. This had developed through the opposition to the revocation, the difficulties in the 1633 Parliament and the treason of Lord Balmerino until it had burst out in 1637 when 'the base multitude' took to the streets of Edinburgh with encouragement from those above.[66]

These perceptions tended to be strengthened not only by the likes of Con and Nithsdale, but also by the Scottish privy councillors who sought to deflect criticism from their own actions by playing up to Charles's preconceptions. Hence Traquair blamed the troubles on a conspiracy by the 'puritanically affected', while Hamilton complained that power had been seized by 'the multitude', 'combined in a more rebellious manner than I can express to resist and trample under foot . . . royal authority'.[67] This was a dangerous game for the moderates to play since it emphasised the polarities in Scottish politics and made settlement appear less feasible. It also confirmed in Charles a belief that he seems to have clung to throughout the crisis, that the whole thing had been got up by a 'factious' minority of nobles and ministers who, like the 'malignant spirits' in the House of Commons, had 'infected' the loyal majority and temporarily overwhelmed their goodwill and common sense. Experience seemed to show that the worst thing to do in such circumstances was to give ground. If he remained resolute, and offered a clear lead, then there appeared to be every prospect that 'our good, but simple and seduced people' would rally to the crown

---

[66] *Large Declaration*, pp. 2, 6–15, 18–20, 30–1, 34–40. For a similar reading of events in Scotland, see the 'Proclamation and Declaration to inform our loving subjects of the seditious practices of some in Scotland . . .', issued on 27 February 1639 and ordered to be read in every parish church: *Proclamations of Charles I*, pp. 662–7.

[67] Donald, *An Uncounselled King*, p. 47; *The Hamilton Papers . . . 1638–50*, ed. S.R. Gardiner, Camden Soc., New Ser., vol. 27, 1880, pp. 3, 4 and 7. Charles echoed Hamilton's comments on 'the multitude' in his letters back to him: NAS, Hamilton MSS, GD 406/1/10484 and 10493.

and the forces of opposition would retreat.[68] This was the aim of the proclamation that Traquair was ordered to issue in February 1638. It took the form of an unambiguous statement that Charles himself had 'seen and approved' the content of the prayer book, that he was fully satisfied that it would serve 'to maintain the true religion' and that if the supplicants continued in their display of 'preposterous zeal' they would be dealt with as traitors.[69] Unfortunately, it had precisely the opposite of the effect intended.

Hitherto it had suited the supplicants to believe that the prayer book had been foisted on the king by the bishops and that once he was made aware of the problems it caused he would back down. Now, in Traquair's despairing words to Hamilton, 'they conceave by this proclamation and the king taking the same upon himself' that it was 'in effect new ratified'.[70] They also had to face the fact that they were opposing the king directly and could be punished for treason. This transformed their campaign. In the interests of self-preservation, they decided to join together and readopt the 1581 Confession of Faith (the so-called 'Negative Confession') which had been signed by James and the three estates. The National Covenant, as it became known, was designed to attract the widest support possible. The signatories pledged themselves to uphold the 'true religion' as practised in Scotland and accept no changes unless authorised by the general assembly and parliament. They also declared their determination to maintain 'the king's Majesty, his person and estate'. There were no overt references to the role of bishops, or to Charles's ecclesiastical policies, and the only enemies to 'true religion' to be identified were popery and innovation. This was a deliberately moderate appeal to the ingrained loyalties and vitriolic anti-Catholicism of the Scots; but it was also, inescapably, a challenge to royal authority. Whereas the 1581 Confession had taken the form of a covenant between individuals and God, in 1638 the signatories bound themselves to each other as well as God. Such a union could not avoid cutting across their loyalty to their monarch. Moreover, although they

---

[68] *Large Declaration*, pp. 106–7, 124–5, 155–7, 184–6. For Charles's confidence in the residual loyalty of his Scottish subjects, see *Proclamations of Charles I*, p. 663 and his proclamation to the Scots of 25 April 1639: *CSP Dom. 1639*, pp. 77–9.

[69] *Large Declaration*, pp. 48–50.

[70] Scally, 'The political career of Hamilton', p. 221.

affirmed their allegiance to the godly magistrate, as David Stevenson points out, they left open the issue of what to do about 'a magistrate who refused to be godly'.[71] Subscription to the Covenant began in Edinburgh on 28 February 1638 and continued throughout the country during the following weeks. In the end it was signed by most of the adult male population outside the Catholic areas of the Highlands and the royalist strongholds of Aberdeen and St Andrews. This was the culmination of the opposition that had been building up from the start of Charles's reign. The Covenant embraced both opponents of his religious policy and all those aggrieved at heavy taxes, the Act of Revocation and the other challenges to Scotland's legal and political traditions.[72]

The signing of the Covenant opened the second phase of the Scottish crisis, which lasted until the dissolution of the Glasgow Assembly on 20 December 1638. As far as Charles was concerned, it provided ample confirmation for his belief about the real aims of the prayer book rebels. 'So long as this covenant is in force', he told Hamilton, 'I have no more power in Scotland than as a duke of Venice, which I will rather die than suffer.'[73] To this was added a growing realisation that the Covenanters were bent on the permanent destruction of episcopacy in Scotland and a recognition that what happened there had inevitable implications for his other kingdoms.[74] If he yielded before a puritan opposition in Scotland it would have a damaging effect on his whole church, especially in England. Finally, the Covenant struck at the core of Charles's sense of himself as both a monarch and a man. To allow its supporters to succeed in this defiance of his authority would be to accept a massive personal humiliation. As we have seen, Charles, more than most rulers, needed to feel that he was being respected and obeyed. When he started talking about his power being reduced to the level of a duke of Venice what he was envisaging

---

[71] Stevenson, *The Scottish Revolution*, pp. 84–6.

[72] Ibid., pp. 82–7; Russell, *Fall of the British Monarchies*, pp. 52–3.

[73] NAS, GD 406/1/10492. This was a regular refrain of Charles's official statements; for example his proclamation of February 1639 complained that the question raised by the Covenant was not 'whether a service book to be received or not, not whether episcopall government shall be continued or Presbyteriall admitted, but whether we are their king or not': *Proclamations of Charles I*, p. 665.

[74] *Large Declaration*, pp. 115, 131–3, 188–90.

was an act of emasculation. He understood the power of the doge in the terms expressed by his father in *The Trew Law of Free Monarchies*, as a form of government that was 'aristocratic and limited . . . nothing like to Free Monarchies'.[75] For his enemies to seek to unman him in this way was to move beyond the bounds of any legitimate form of political behaviour and invite him to resort to the most drastic remedies. In the case of the Covenanters, this meant treating them as rebels and traitors, and suppressing them by force. But force took time to organise and this gave an opportunity to those around him to explore other means of resolving the crisis.

In the course of 1638, the line-up among Charles's advisers on the Scottish issue became more clearly defined. The most enthusiastic proponents of a war were the Scots Catholics, Con and Nithsdale, now supported by the queen. It appears to have been Nithsdale who in April 1638 came up with a plan for military intervention, based on mobilising the main Catholic families in Scotland, and then supporting them with an invasion from the south by the English and from Ulster by the earl of Antrim and his McDonald clan. The English privy council was divided on the issue. Arundel, Cottington and Sir Francis Windebanke favoured force, while Northumberland, Coke and Sir Henry Vane, treasurer of the household, were urging accommodation. Laud, who seems to have been all too aware of the practical difficulties of mounting a successful invasion, remained uncommitted.[76] However, the English council had no official jurisdiction in Scotland and its involvement was largely confined to supervising the military preparations that got under way in June. The difficult task of putting the case for a settlement was mainly left to Scottish councillors, notably Traquair and Roxburgh, and the man who stepped out of the shadows to play a pivotal role, the marquis of Hamilton.

Hamilton emerges from John Scally's study of him as a much weightier and more substantial politician than has sometimes been supposed. In many respects, he was the classic Caroline moderate councillor. A staunch Calvinist, who favoured a Protestant foreign policy and believed in tradi-

---

[75] 'The Trew Law of Free Monarchies' in *King James VI and I. Political Writings*, J.P. Sommerville ed., Cambridge, 1994, p. 76. Charles talked in these terms on other occasions, and it was generally a signal that he felt he was being pushed too far.

[76] Donald, *An Uncounselled King*, pp. 71, 87–9.

tional methods and solutions in government, he was also an effective administrator (as he showed when he was made collector general for the taxes granted in the 1633 Scottish Parliament) and a shrewd operator at court. His greatest political asset was that he stood high in the king's favour, probably higher than any other leading councillor in the late 1630s. He could talk to Charles and the king was prepared to listen, on one occasion informing the marquis that 'you know my mind and indeed I know none of my subjects that knows it better'.[77] Hamilton would have been the ideal successor to Menteith as first minister in Scotland; but Charles valued his presence at court too much to permit the long absences necessary to oversee Scottish affairs, and Hamilton himself had no wish to give up the influence that went with proximity to the royal person. He therefore settled for acting as court spokesman for Traquair and his other friends on the Scottish council, and counteracting the growing power of the bishops. All this changed, however, in May 1638 when he was appointed king's commissioner in Scotland.

He was perhaps the only politician on the scene with any hope of brokering a compromise, since he was also on relatively good terms with the Covenanter leaders. He spoke their language, understood the strength of their concerns and was not compromised by any role in the formulation of the prayer book. Perhaps most important of all, he appreciated that any resort to force in Scotland would be disastrous in the longer term and that the only durable solution would be a settlement. Failing this, however, he hoped to divide the Covenanter movement and build a party for the king. Charles had little sympathy for the first option; but he did recognise the need to rally support, and Hamilton was able to use this to coax concessions out of him and open up the space to manoeuvre towards a deal. The correspondence between the two men provides some fascinating insights into how Charles worked with his councillors.

The opportunity for Hamilton to divide the Covenanters and make them more amenable to a settlement was created by their very success, which put them in a position where they started to alienate some of their own supporters. During 1638 their movement went from strength to strength and they completely dominated Scottish politics, leaving the privy council

---

[77] NAS, GD 406/1/168/1 and 2. For Hamilton's earlier career, see Scally, 'The political career of Hamilton', partic. chps. 2–5.

helpless and impotent. As they became more confident they steadily increased their terms for a settlement. In April, Archibald Johnston of Wariston and Alexander Henderson, their two chief religious spokesmen, sent Traquair a list of demands in which withdrawing the prayer book and the canons was no longer enough. They now required that the power of the bishops be curtailed and regular meetings held of the general assembly. Episcopacy was not formally condemned at this stage; but antagonism towards it was a growing feature of their rhetoric, and it became obvious that there could be no place for bishops within a Covenanter-dominated church. This produced the first signs of a backlash. Some of the nobles who had supported the Covenant became uneasy about increasing domination of the movement by Presbyterian clerics, while supporters of modified episcopacy began to rally and argue their case. The Covenanters' lay leaders, notably Rothes, displayed a good deal of skill in keeping the movement united, but there was still an opening for Hamilton and the king, if they played their cards right.[78]

Charles sent Hamilton north in June with firm instructions that the signed copies of the National Covenant (the 'bands') should be given up to him, in which case he was to issue a proclamation promising to enforce the prayer book and canons only in 'a fair and legal way' and to 'rectifie' the Court of High Commission. If the Covenanters refused to hand over the 'bands', and, in effect, surrender, Hamilton was ordered to treat them as rebels and prepare for war. When the marquis met the Covenanter leaders he found them unyielding and reported as much to Charles. The king responded with an uncompromising restatement of his priorities. 'When I consider', he declared to Hamilton,

that not only now my crown, but my reputation for ever lies at stake, I must rather suffer the first, that time will help, than the last which is irreparable . . . I will rather die than yield to those impertinent and damnable demands . . . for it is all one to yield to be no king in a very short space of time.

His 'chief end' was now to 'win time, that they may not commit public follies until I be ready to suppress them'. Hamilton was, therefore, to 'flatter them with what hopes you please so you engage me not against my

---

[78] Stevenson, *The Scottish Revolution*, pp. 89, 101–2, 105–6, 115, 124; Russell, *Fall of the British Monarchies*, pp. 53–5, 58.

grounds' – by which he meant the ultimate objectives of his policy. This offered Hamilton an opening – small, but an opening nonetheless – to push forward a dialogue with the Covenanters and begin a game of cat and mouse with his royal master.

As Scally describes it, the dilemma Hamilton faced was 'how to phrase advice that did not overtly suggest concession, but made it the only prudent way forward'.[79] He sought to resolve this by making it clear to Charles that the only way to buy time and divide the Covenanters, while he made his military preparations, was to give the appearance of being willing to accommodate their demands. Charles, who seems to have known very well what was going on, responded with a studied coolness; but he did give his commissioner just enough encouragement to ensure that he did not abandon the mission. Hamilton tried out his new strategy in a letter on 20 June. He had had discussions with the Covenanter leaders, he said, in which, in order to persuade them to disperse their crowds of supporters, he hinted at Charles's willingness to summon a general assembly and parliament. At the same time he cited the opinion of various Scottish councillors, that the Covenant could be neutralised as a threat to Charles's sovereignty if its supporters could be persuaded to enlarge on their assurance of loyalty to Charles. Finally he warned of the danger that a resort to force in Scotland might open the door to rebellion in his other kingdoms.[80] This was an astute and carefully modulated performance. Charles was not yet ready for the U-turn in his thinking on the Covenant that Hamilton's approach implied; however, he did agree to his issuing a different proclamation which reiterated the promises contained in the first version and included a new assurance that in due course he would indeed summon a general assembly and a parliament.[81] Having bought himself some time, the marquis hurried back to London.

Once there, he began lobbying for a scheme devised in conjunction with Traquair and Roxburgh, which enlarged on the hints given in his

---

[79] Scally, 'The political career of Hamilton', p. 235.

[80] Ibid., pp. 241–4; J.J. Scally, 'Counsel in crisis: James, third marquis of Hamilton and the Bishops Wars 1638–1640', in J.R. Young ed., *Celtic Dimensions of the British Civil Wars*, Edinburgh, 1997, pp. 21–3.

[81] *Large Declaration*, pp. 96–8. For Charles's reply to Hamilton's letter, see NAS, GD 406/1/10492.

letter. Far more radical than anything suggested previously, this proposed
that the prayer book, canons and high commission be 'discharged', the Five
Articles of Perth dispensed with until they had been considered by the estates
and the powers of the bishops referred to a general assembly. It also
involved a plan for the king to authorise a fresh subscription to the 1581
Negative Confession that would become, in effect, 'the King's Covenant'.
This last recommendation was an ingenious attempt to break the deadlock
by accommodating the Covenanters' determination to stand by their confession and Charles's insistence that they surrender their 'bands'. Hamilton
worked hard behind the scenes to build support for this, using his access
to Charles to cut out hostile advisers, like Nithsdale, and win over Laud
and the Scottish bishops. The biggest obstacle, predictably, was the king
himself. At first he flatly refused to have anything to do with the scheme,
declaring that 'the remedy was worse than the disease'. But Hamilton
gradually talked him round. In this he was helped by the dawning realisation that the military expedition – which in June Charles had confidently
predicted would take only a matter of weeks to organise – was not going
to be feasible in the current year. He was able to impress on Charles that
his scheme offered the best means of building a royalist party and pre-
empting the Covenanters, who were about to summon their own assembly
anyway.[82]

The proclamation on 22 September announcing the Hamilton concessions
was the high point for the strategy of compromise and negotiation.
Johnston of Wariston and other Covenanter leaders were very nervous about
it, fearing that the marquis had hit on a means of detaching some of their
more moderate supporters and putting pressure on them to back down.
An assessment of the allegiance of the leading Scots nobles made at this
time suggested they were more or less evenly divided between the king and
the Covenanters.[83] However, the Covenanter leadership need not have
worried. From this point onwards the whole scheme began to fall apart.
Hamilton worked hard at organising subscription to 'the King's Covenant';

---

[82] Donald, *An Uncounselled King*, pp. 91–100; Scally, 'The political career of Hamilton',
pp. 248–51. On the slowness of military preparations in 1638, see M.C. Fissell, *The Bishops'
Wars. Charles I's campaigns against Scotland 1638–1640*, Cambridge, 1994, pp. 10–11.

[83] Stevenson, *The Scottish Revolution*, pp. 109–10; Russell, *Fall of the British Monarchies*,
p. 58.

but there was general resistance except in the loyalist north east. Doubts were cast on the advisability of the whole exercise when Lord Advocate Hope, who had thrown in his lot with the Covenanters, declared that signing the Negative Confession implied approval for the abolition of episcopacy.[84] Worse was to follow at the Glasgow Assembly that met on 21 November.

Hamilton and Traquair were prepared to allow the assembly to discuss and determine a whole range of matters – from the prayer book to the Perth Articles – in the hope that this would produce some agreement and keep them off the one issue that was not negotiable, the abolition of episcopacy. At the last moment, however, Charles blocked their efforts by refusing to allow such a broad remit.[85] This killed off any prospect of turning the assembly into a forum for settlement. All that remained was for Hamilton to try to use it as a platform for rallying loyalist support; however, he was not able to achieve even this. As soon as the meeting opened it became apparent that he was powerless to control its proceedings in the face of a well-organised Presbyterian majority. The first few days were taken up with voting Henderson and Johnston into the key offices of moderator and clerk, and arguing about whether the assembly was properly constituted. By 28 November Hamilton had decided that there was nothing to be gained by continuing; so, after issuing his rallying call to moderates – in the form of an attack on the Covenanters for usurping power and seeking to pass judgement on the bishops – he tried to dissolve the assembly in the name of the king. This proved beyond him. The assembly carried on sitting without him and when he tried to secure the privy council's agreement to a proclamation justifying the dissolution, several leading members promptly defected to the Covenanters' side.[86]

Over the next two weeks, the Glasgow Assembly authorised what amounted to a revolution in the Scottish church. Proceedings in the six previous assemblies between 1606 and 1618 were declared invalid because they had been operating under royal and episcopal control; the prayerbook and canons were condemned as 'popish', the high commission denounced as illegal and the Perth Articles revoked; it was voted that the institution

---

[84] Stevenson, *The Scottish Revolution*, pp. 110–12.

[85] Donald, *An Uncounselled King*, pp. 105–7; Scally, 'The political career of Hamilton', pp. 248–51.

[86] Stevenson, *The Scottish Revolution*, pp. 116–23.

of episcopacy had been 'abjured' by the Negative Confession, whereupon the archbishops and bishops in Scotland were deposed; and finally acts were passed affirming the power of the kirk to summon annual assemblies.[87] The Covenanters had effectively overthrown the royal supremacy and established control by the Presbyterian kirk. Hitherto they had been asking the king for concessions, which left open the possibility of a compromise settlement. By acting on their own initiative, in direct defiance of his wishes, they dramatically escalated the whole conflict. In a long, despairing letter to Charles, in which he blamed the bishops for causing the whole sorry mess, Hamilton acknowledged that there now seemed to be no alternative to war.[88]

The main responsibility for the mishandling of the crisis can be laid firmly at the door of the king. It exposed many of the deficiencies in his make-up as a politician. His lack of skills in man-management were once more highlighted. For example, early in 1638 Traquair persuaded him of the importance of cultivating Lord Lorne, head of the powerful Campbell clan. Charles made a big effort, spending an hour and a half listening to Lorne's views on Scotland's problems, but, then, a few weeks later, undid all the good work by supporting a plan for the Catholic earl of Antrim, leader of the Campbells' traditional enemies the McDonalds, to invade Scotland from Ulster. Lorne and the Campbells promptly threw in their lot with the Covenanters.[89] This was not a mistake one could have imagined James making; yet it typified Charles's lack of feel for the practicalities of Scottish politics.

This weakness was compounded by his inability to comprehend any viewpoint that was not close to his own. He never showed the slightest sign of appreciating just how offensive an English-style prayer book was to the Scots. Throughout late 1637 and early 1638 – when it had become unenforceable – he simply went on reiterating that since it amounted to neither 'popery' nor 'innovation', as he understood the terms, they should stop complaining and accept it. The king's lack of political imagination made it very hard to negotiate with him; it also bred distrust in those he was dealing with. When he promised in late 1637 that there would be no

---

[87] Ibid., pp. 123–6.

[88] Scally, 'The political career of Hamilton', pp. 258–61.

[89] Stevenson, *The Scottish Revolution*, pp. 89–90, 99–100.

'innovation' in religion some of the supplicants thought this meant he was about to abandon the prayer book; but this did not happen and it made them much warier in their dealings with him from then on.[90]

The Scottish crisis also revealed other failings. Throughout, Charles displayed a poor sense of timing. There was something to be said for his basic strategy of mixing concession with preparation for the use of force. As he explained to Hamilton, if he conceded too much this would be interpreted as a sign of weakness and risk discouraging 'the little party we have'.[91] However, such an approach required shrewd judgement over when to give ground and when to apply the pressure, and in this the king was singularly lacking. When he made concessions, it always tended to be too late in the day. This was particularly true of his conversion to the proposals that were incorporated into the 22 September 1638 proclamation. As John Scally has observed, had he been prepared to give more of a welcome to the scheme when Hamilton first broached it in June there would have a much better chance of wresting the initiative from the Covenanters.[92] In the event, his sudden volte-face looked like another damaging example of what Conrad Russell calls his 'habit of saying "never" and then retreating'.[93] This lack of judgement – together with the sensitivity about his honour that tended to surface when he felt his authority was being challenged – also led him to stake his personal credit much more conclusively than was wise. A more calculating politician would have held something in reserve. As it was, Charles's repeated declarations that he would rather die than accept a particular demand or restriction, made life very difficult for the councillors who were trying to broker a compromise on his behalf, and left his opponents uncertain how far they could push him, which was a dangerous situation in any attempt to avoid open conflict.[94] When he did make concessions he often insisted on spelling out the fact that he was acting under duress which, again, was hardly conducive to breeding trust in those

---

[90] Russell, *Fall of the British Monarchies*, pp. 50–1.

[91] NAS, GD 406/1/10508.

[92] Scally, 'The political career of Hamilton', pp. 241–4.

[93] Russell, *Fall of the British Monarchies*, p. 67.

[94] Russell, *Causes of the Civil War*, pp. 116–17; idem, 'The British problem', p. 247.

he was dealing with.[95] His all-or-nothing approach also tended to mean that he left himself without a fall-back position. This was the situation during the summer months of 1638 when he pinned all his hopes on being able to crush the Covenanters by force. Once this proved impossible it became clear that he had little choice but to go along with the drastic concession proposed by Hamilton and, moreover, that he had neglected to take some basic measures to prevent the build-up of Covenanter support.[96]

Tied in with these faults, there was also his tendency to take responsibility for unpopular actions onto himself. Charles did this with the best of intentions – to protect those he felt were serving him loyally and in the expectation that it would put an end to opposition – but it was often disastrous. The harm it could do was graphically illustrated by the February 1638 proclamation in which he made it clear that it was he, and not the bishops, who had authorised the prayer book. Far from being reassured, as Charles seems to have expected, the supplicants were now faced with the awful prospect that they were in direct opposition to the king; and it was because of this that they took the fateful step of signing the National Covenant.

However, Charles's failure to achieve a viable settlement of the Scottish crisis was not just about his lack of political skill. It was also bound up with his view of kingship – of what a monarch was for and how he was supposed to behave. Much of the time Charles was not seeking to be judged by modern standards of political success or effectiveness. There was a side of him that understood the need to exercise 'politic wisdom' and engage in tactical manoeuvring, but, in the final analysis, this was not what he believed kings were supposed to aspire to. Their task was to uphold standards of virtue and honour, and fulfil the obligations of conscience and calling. In the context of the Scottish crisis this again reduced the scope for compromise. If he retreated, and failed to uphold his vision of Protestantism and royal authority, then – as he explained in the *Large Declaration* – he would 'betray that trust which the King of Kings hath reposed

---

[95] Russell, 'The British problem', p. 247.

[96] Charles's letters in June 1638 suggest that he was so preoccupied with getting the Covenanters to reveal themselves to the world as rebels that he did not much care whether they issued a protestation against him, or even called a parliament or assembly: NAS, GD 406/1/10490 and 10492.

in us for the maintenance of religion and justice amongst all his people whom he hath committed to our charge'.[97] This high-minded rigidity was reinforced by his perception of the challenge presented by the Covenanters that he assimilated to the 'popular'/puritan threat in England. Any concessions, he believed, would be interpreted as signs of weakness and could only encourage the forces ranged against monarchy. Far better to stand firm and offer a lead to what he generally assumed was the loyal majority.

Having made up his mind about the right course of action, however, Charles was much more flexible about the means he used to pursue this. Where he was required to make concessions he did not regard as legitimate, he felt discharged from any moral responsibility to be overly scrupulous. There is a good deal in S.R. Gardiner's observation that, although he was generally too conscientious to tell a direct lie, he was not above conveying a false impression.[98] He also felt that he was entitled to resort to expedients that might yield temporary advantage in pursuit of his aim of restoring the rightful *status quo*. As he was to explain to the Scottish bishops in August 1639, 'though we may give way for the present to that which will be prejudicial both to the church and our government, yet we shall not leave thinking in time how to remedy both'.[99]

Negotiating with Charles must often have felt like dealing with someone whose fingers were permanently crossed behind his back. It was small wonder that in September 1640, after many months of this sort of thing, Lord Loudoun, one of the Covenanter leaders, was moved to comment – with masterful understatement – that the king's actions 'beget a suspicion that his majesty doth not yet intend a real peace'.[100] Charles's approach also resulted in policies that were sometimes too clever by half. A good example was his handling of the Glasgow Assembly. He admitted that 'I can expect no good by it', and seems to have had no intention of allowing it the latitude implied in the September proclamation; but, in spite of Hamilton's

---

[97] *Large Declaration*, p. 5.

[98] Gardiner, *History of England*, vol. 9, pp. 48–9.

[99] Cited in Russell, *Fall of the British Monarchies*, p. 67. As he indicates, this letter might be read more than one way; my reading follows that suggested by Peter Lake in his 'Review article on C.S.R. Russell *The Causes of the English Civil War, The Fall of the British Monarchies* and *Unrevolutionary England*', *HLQ*, vol. 59, 1994, pp. 178–9.

[100] Russell, 'The British problem', p. 247.

warnings about the dangers it presented to episcopacy, he insisted that it go ahead, apparently on the assumption that it could be used to divide his enemies.[101] In the event, far from weakening the Covenanters, the assembly gave their campaign a renewed sense of purpose and legitimacy.

At the centre of the political events of this period was the relationship between the king and his commissioner. This offers a microcosm of Charles's dealings with his moderate councillors. Hamilton knew the king as well as any of his leading advisers and handled him with considerable dexterity. He was careful to position himself as a cut-out between king and Covenanter leadership, keeping Charles at arm's length from those he was negotiating with. The success of this tactic in the 1628 Parliament had demonstrated that it was as good a way as any of reducing the friction generally caused by the king's personal interventions. Hamilton was also very careful to pay lip-service to Charles's 'grounds', while at the same time trying to nudge him towards a recognition that the only feasible solution to the crisis was to offer realistic concessions. Past experience again showed that this was a sensible way to handle the king. In contrast to the councillors of the late 1620s, however, Hamilton faced a king who was now more confident of his prowess as a ruler. Charles seems to have been well aware of what was going on and played along with him to extract the maximum advantage in terms of buying time and dividing his opponents. But when the moment of decision came, just before the Glasgow Assembly, he pulled the rug from under the marquis's feet. This illustrated another facet of the king's behaviour which has been highlighted by Conrad Russell, that 'he was open to counsel about means, but never open to any counsel about his "grounds" '.[102] It also confirmed the truism that no councillor, however persuasive, could deflect Charles when he was determined to have his way.

Perhaps the most positive aspect of the king's approach was that he recognised that a climbdown in Scotland would have damaging implications elsewhere.[103] This was the main flaw in Hamilton's scheme. He

---

[101] NAS, GD 406/1/10505 and 10514.

[102] Russell, *Causes of the Civil War*, p. 194.

[103] This recognition does not, however, appear to have extended to an understanding of the dangers inherent in the use of force in Scotland. Hamilton highlighted this in his letter of 20 June when he warned that there were 'so many malicious spirits' in England that 'no sooner will your back be turned but they will be ready to do as we have done here': Scally, 'Counsel in crisis', pp. 22–4.

tried to get around it by making it clear to the Covenanters that, while his instructions might allow him to remove the canons and the prayerbook, he could not condemn them in a way 'which might reflect against any public order . . . allowed by my lord of Canterbury and his followers in England or elsewhere'.[104] But, in practice, it was very hard to isolate religious transactions in this way. Charles understood this, which again raises the issue of how far he was thinking in British terms in his policy making.

The absence of any council commission or formal body to deal with all three kingdoms, meant that responsibility for a coordinated British policy rested largely with him. His attention to it was variable and inconsistent. At times he did show some capacity for thinking in terms of what might now be called 'joined-up government'. His religious policy in the three kingdoms, as Russell has stressed, hinged around the aim of implementing his anti-Calvinist vision of the church. The introduction of the Thirty-Nine Articles and canons in Ireland was paralleled by the prayer book and canons in Scotland; and in both countries, as in England, there was a sustained effort to recover the property of the church. The self-consciousness with which these measures were promoted as part of a programme for the whole of Britain was emphasised in the king's preface to the Scots prayer book.

It were to be wished that the whole church of Christ were one, as well in form of public service as in doctrine . . . This would prevent many schisms and divisions, and serve much to the preserving of unity. But since that cannot be hoped for in the whole Catholic Christian church, yet at least in the churches that are under the protection of one sovereign prince the same ought to be endeavoured.[105]

Religious policy was, however, the exception. In most other respects there is little sign of Charles adopting a British perspective. During the late 1620s he was involved with sporadic efforts to integrate support from Ireland and Scotland into the war effort; but after this – outside the religious sphere – probably the only common initiative was over fishing policy.[106] When he was presented with the opportunity to develop a British approach he

---

[104] Russell, 'The British problem', p. 241.

[105] Cited in Russell, *Fall of the British Monarchies*, p. 39.

[106] Ibid., p. 30; Morrill, 'The Scottish National Covenant', p. 97.

generally spurned it. In the summer of 1638, for example, Wentworth pressed the suggestion that in future Scotland, like Ireland, should be governed by an English viceroy, which would make it easier to anticipate problems and gradually lead to the adoption of an English system of law and government. The king rejected this and stuck to Hamilton's line that Scotland should be governed by Scots.[107] There were problems with Wentworth's proposal, but it deserved more consideration than it received and the king's failure to provide this seems to have been, as much as anything, a reflection of his inability to think creatively about policy across the three kingdoms.[108] Most of the positive ideas in this area came from either Wentworth or Laud. Whatever he might proclaim in his court masques and paintings, Charles's perspective was decidedly Anglocentric.

---

[107] Donald, *An Uncounselled King*, pp. 96–7.

[108] On this point, see also N. Canny, 'The attempted Anglicisation of Ireland in the seventeenth century; an exemplar of "British History"', in Merritt ed., *The Political World of Thomas Wentworth*, pp. 184–5.

Chapter 5

Charles and the outbreak of the civil war, 1639–1642

The Bishops' Wars

At Kelso on 4 and 5 June 1639 Charles had his opportunity to resolve the Scottish crisis by force, but he squandered it. Recent work by John Adamson and Mark Fissell has demonstrated that for all its weaknesses the army he assembled in April to May 1639 outnumbered that of the Covenanters, particularly in the all-important cavalry contingents, and was better equipped and funded for a lengthy campaign.[1] Had Charles kept his nerve and worn the Scots down there was every possibility that he would gain the upper hand and achieve the solution he had been seeking ever since the signing of the Covenant in February 1638. He could have crushed the rebellion, vindicated his honour and reimposed his authority over his northern kingdom; in the process he would also have sidestepped most of the problems he later faced as a consequence of defeat in the Bishops' Wars.

Charles's strategy for the Scottish campaign of 1639 was based on the plan for a three-pronged assault devised by Nithsdale in 1638. Antrim, with the assistance of Wentworth, was to invade the western lowlands from Ulster; Hamilton was to lead an amphibious force of 5 000 men to make a

---

[1] J.S.A. Adamson, 'England without Cromwell: What if Charles I had avoided the Civil War', in N. Fergusson ed., *Virtual History. Alternatives and Counterfactuals*, 1997, pp. 95–101; Fissell, *The Bishops' Wars*, pp. 26–33, 38.

Charles I (1600–1649) when Prince of Wales by Hendrik van Steenwyck the Younger, 1619–1621

Charles I by Gerrit van Honthorst, 1628

Charles I and Queen Henrietta Maria with their two eldest children Charles, Prince of Wales and Mary Princess Royal by A. van Dyck c.1632

Charles I on horseback with M. de St Antoine by A. van Dyck c.1633

Equestrian portrait of Charles I by A. van Dyck c.1637

© The National Gallery, London

Charles I à la chasse by A. van Dyck c.1635

A Landscape with St George and the Dragon by Peter Paul Rubens, c.1629

Charles I dictating despatches to Sir Edward Walker, unknown artist, c.1650

landing near Aberdeen and link up with the marquis of Huntly and loyalist forces in north-eastern Scotland; while the king was to lead the main field army of 30 000 men to a rendezvous at York and then march to the border. However, things did not go according to plan. The Antrim/Wentworth invasion force never materialised; Huntly and the loyalists were dispersed when the Covenanters occupied Aberdeen; and Hamilton's revised plan to land near Leith and strike towards Edinburgh came to nothing because his troops were too untrained to be effective. There were also problems with the main English army. Charles's intention was to draw on the support of the nobles whom he regarded as his natural partners in an enterprise of this sort. In January 1639 he sent out a quasi-feudal summons for them to attend him at York with their horse troops; but for the most part this was greeted with little enthusiasm. The force that eventually materialised amounted to not much more than 20 000 men, mostly pressed levies from the Midlands and East Anglia, with little equipment and no training.[2]

On the face of it the Covenanters were in a much stronger position. They assembled an army led by professional soldiers who had served the Swedes in the Thirty Years War and they were united behind their cause. But appearances were deceptive. In spite of dominating the machinery of Scottish government they had difficulties raising men and money, and were suffering from a blockade imposed by Hamilton and the English fleet. They were also conscious that if public opinion in England – which was deeply divided over the wisdom of fighting the war – was to turn decisively against them they would be in an extremely precarious position. For these reasons they made efforts to keep open a dialogue with Hamilton and some of the king's English councillors, and were discussing the possibilities of settlement right up to the outbreak of hostilities.[3]

Charles's position during early 1639 became increasingly uncompromising. In February he issued a proclamation outlining 'the seditious practices of some in Scotland' which, along with the *Large Declaration*, hammered out the theme that the Covenanters were a band of 'captious, busy and traitorously affected men', using religion as a cloak for their aim of shaking off 'all monarchicall government'. They had stirred up the people

---

[2] Stevenson, *The Scottish Revolution*, pp. 138–42; Fissell, *The Bishops' Wars*, pp. 10–26.

[3] Stevenson, *The Scottish Revolution*, pp. 127–40; Russell, *Fall of the British Monarchies*, p. 63.

with 'mutinous libels', spurned his 'princely clemency' and taken up arms with the intention of invading England. The king stuck to his line that this was basically the work of a few 'factious spirits', and in April drafted a proclamation naming the 16 ringleaders and setting a price on their heads. He was talked out of issuing this by Hamilton, but remained convinced that once the leading troublemakers were removed, opposition would fall apart.[4]

Charles initially seems to have believed that simply appearing in the field would be enough to secure him victory, since the Covenanters would never actually have the nerve to fight. As he marched north during April and May, Hamilton's reports of the scale of resistance forced him to revise this view; nonetheless he remained resolute and single-minded. When the marquis offered some belated proposals for 'patching up this business', the king insisted that he would only be satisfied with the Covenanters' complete surrender. His aim, he said, was 'to force them to obedience . . . which rather than not do I shall first sell myself to my shirt'.[5] For Charles, the whole matter had become very personal. Nothing less than the humiliation of his enemies would restore his slighted honour. And as he marched north there were hopeful signs that his offensive was gathering momentum. Reports from York talked of northern gentry flocking into the town to demonstrate their loyalty and beginning to rediscover their traditional antipathy towards the Scots. Initial assessments of the unsuitability of his troops began to change as they turned their attention to some serious training. And by the time his army encamped at Birks near Berwick at the end of May, his mood was one of confident determination.[6]

Within the next few days, however, his whole campaign was undone by an elaborate deception. When he encountered the Scots around Kelso on 4 June he sent forward a force of 3 000 infantry and 1 000 horse under the earl of Holland to probe their strength. As the English approached, Alexander Leslie, the veteran Scottish commander, employed an old Thirty

---

[4] *Proclamations of Charles I*, pp. 662–7; *CSP Dom. 1639*, pp. 77–81; Stevenson, *The Scottish Revolution*, pp. 141–2.

[5] NAS, Hamilton MSS, GD 406/1/10550.

[6] D. Scott, ' "Hannibal at our Gates": loyalists and fifth-columnists during the Bishops' Wars – the case of Yorkshire', *HR*, vol. 70, 1997, pp. 271–3; Adamson, 'England without Cromwell', pp. 98–9.

Years War ruse and drew up his infantry in shallow formation with extra sets of colours. This made it appear that they outnumbered Holland's force several times over. The earl's first impulse had been to charge, but realising that his cavalry might be isolated he decided to withdraw, giving the Scots a psychological victory. The next day Leslie drove home his advantage by arraying his forces on the heights of Duns Law, apparently in readiness to attack. Charles and his commanders surveyed the Scottish host through their telescopes and concluded that they were facing a force in excess of 30 000 men. At this point the king lost his nerve. Seeing the lack of confidence among those around him, and lacking any military experience of his own to fall back on, he decided to withdraw. The following day, when the Covenanters offered to negotiate, he promptly accepted. In fact, Leslie's whole approach was based on bluff. His force was probably smaller than the English army, with no more than 15 000 infantry and a much smaller cavalry contingent (1 500 compared with 4 000). They were also beginning to desert due to lack of pay and victuals. Had Charles delayed treating for a week or two there seems to have been every prospect that the Scottish army would have disintegrated, leaving the way open for him to march on Edinburgh and win the war.[7] As it was, he was forced to negotiate on more or less equal terms.

One of the features of the negotiations at Berwick, which opened on 11 June, was Charles's effectiveness as a debater. He wrongfooted the Scots by arriving suddenly and taking the chair on the first day of discussion, declaring that he was there 'to clear myself of that notorious slander that I shut my ears to the just complaints of the people of Scotland'. He then confronted them with the radicalism of their actions. When they tried to argue that the Glasgow Assembly had done nothing that was not warranted by previous assemblies, he homed in on the unusually large number of lay elders who had been present and insisted that they were sponsoring a brand of lay puritanism which allowed that 'every illiterate person should be able to judge of faith and . . . choose their own religion'. And when they reached the issue of his power to call and dissolve general assemblies, he

---

[7] Fissell, *The Bishops' Wars*, pp. 26–33, 38; Adamson, 'England without Cromwell', pp. 100–1. On the defeatism among his advisers, see Bristol's warning that most of the Lords and councillors in the camp were about to petition the king for a parliament: *CSP Dom. 1639*, p. 294.

forced them to admit that it was not always possible to reconcile their belief that the assembly was ultimately answerable to Christ with loyalty and obedience to their king.[8] Charles had very effectively exposed the revolutionary implications of the Covenanters' position, but this did not prevent the signing of the treaty. Both sides needed an opportunity to regroup.

The terms of the Pacification of Berwick, agreed on 18 June, stipulated that the Covenanters would disband their troops, break up the Tables and restore all property and castles seized from the crown and its supporters. In return, the king undertook to withdraw his forces and summon a general assembly and parliament, the former with power to determine all ecclesiastical matters referred to it and the latter all civil. Charles was not willing to ratify the decisions of the Glasgow Assembly, but he seemed prepared to do the next best thing since the new assembly's remit extended to determining the fate of episcopacy in Scotland. However, these concessions were not quite all they appeared. The dismal performance of his army and the failure of loyalist support to materialise in Scotland had forced him to accept that he could make no further headway as things stood. But he had no intention of surrendering in the longer term, and he entered a vital caveat when he promised to ratify whatever a general assembly and a parliament agreed to, but only on condition that both be 'lawfully constituted'. For Charles, this meant with the inclusion of bishops, which gave him an escape route if he wanted to backtrack later. He also declared his intention to attend the two assemblies in person, apparently confident that his debating skills would win the day.[9]

During the weeks which followed the Treaty of Berwick quickly unravelled. The Covenanters disbanded their army and surrendered the royal castles, but remained highly suspicious of Charles's good faith and sought to pre-empt any effort to withdraw concessions by publishing their version of what he had agreed to verbally.[10] Charles's own position shifted

---

[8] *CSP Dom. 1639*, pp. 310–12; Russell, *Fall of the British Monarchies*, pp. 64–6; Donald, *An Uncounselled King*, pp. 153–7. In these debates Charles was picking up points about the lay dominance of ministers and the general assembly's claim to be answerable to Christ which he had made in the *Large Declaration* (where he described the latter as the 'furious frenzies' of 'Anabaptisticall madness'): *Large Declaration*, pp. 115, 131–3, 416–17.

[9] Gardiner, *History of England*, vol. 9, pp. 39–41; Russell, *Fall of the British Monarchies*, pp. 66–7.

[10] Donald, *An Uncounselled King*, pp. 161, 164.

significantly during the course of July. At the start of the month he told Wentworth that, in spite of the advice of some of his councillors, he fully intended to be present at the general assembly and parliament to prevent the 'irreparable confusion' that would otherwise result.[11] However, he soon lost confidence in this option. This appears to have been partly the result of some gloomy advice from Hamilton, who suggested that the issue of episcopacy had already been determined against him, and also of another, less satisfactory, meeting with the Covenanter leaders at which it became clear that they would block his efforts to argue the case for the bishops. On the 23rd he wrote again to Wentworth, complaining that 'the Scots Covenant begins to spread too far' and ordering him to return to England as soon as possible.[12] This was an indication that the military option was once more uppermost in his mind, something Laud identified in a letter to Sir Thomas Roe. Summarising what was probably the king's thinking at the time, he insisted that any prospect of 'wisdom or moderation' from the Scots had now receded.

Faction and ignorance will govern the assembly, and faction and somewhat else that I list not to name [treason?] the parliament: for they will utterly cast off all episcopal government and introduce a worse regulated parity than anywhere else that I know. How this will stand with monarchy future times will discover; but I am of opinion the king can have neither honour nor safety by it.

Laud was also worried for England: 'considering what a faction we have . . . which leans that way, it is much to be feared this Scottish violence will make some unfitting impressions upon both this church and state'.[13] Charles's earlier misgivings had apparently resurfaced and this put paid to any prospects for a lasting peace.

The meetings of the general assembly and the parliament were, from Charles's point of view, an exercise in damage limitation; but they were mismanaged by his representative Traquair and considerably strengthened the Covenanters' cause. When the assembly met in August 1639, he assented in the king's name to a package of measures that included the 'abjuring' of

---

[11] *Strafforde Letters*, vol. 2, p. 362.

[12] Donald, *An Uncounselled King*, p. 165; *Strafforde Letters*, vol. 2, pp. 372, 374.

[13] Laud, *Works*, vol. 7, p. 584.

episcopacy. News quickly spread through Scotland that the bishops had been 'extinguished by the king's consent' and the Covenanters claimed victory. Traquair tried to retrieve the situation by telling the assembly that the king could only accept the abolition of episcopacy on the grounds that they were against the kirk's constitution, since to do otherwise would cast doubt on its legitimacy elsewhere. However, the damage had been done. Any watering down of concessions now could be made to look as if Charles was reneging on his undertakings. The Scottish parliament met on 31 August and ratified the acts of the general assembly, before going on to approve a tax to cover the costs of the war and a veto on appointments to the keeperships of royal castles. For Charles, this confirmed the Covenanters' determination to dominate the state as well as the church. After initially being prepared to allow Traquair to honour his undertaking to approve the assembly's acts – providing he did not agree to rescind the laws on which re-establishing episcopacy in Scotland had been based – he changed his mind and ordered the prorogation of the parliament.[14]

By the time this took place, in November 1639, preparations for the resumption of war were well under way. Wentworth arrived back in England in September and immediately assumed the position of first minister and royal 'enforcer'. The plan this time was to raise a much larger army of 35 000 men, including 8 000 from Ireland, and to use the garrisons in Scotland and Berwick as the jumping-off points for an attack. Attempts at peacemaking continued into February and March 1640, but with little conviction. Each side was basically seeking an opportunity to blame the other for the final breakdown. Both were also exploring the possibility of foreign aid. Wentworth proposed to the Spanish that they might lend Charles £100 000 in return for future aid against the Dutch and the opportunity to recruit troops in Ireland. Meanwhile, the Covenanter leaders wrote to Louis xiii asking him to intervene with the king to save them from further oppression. This failed to produce any positive results, but the letter fell into Charles's hands and the form of address that it used, 'Au Roi', offered further proof that the Covenanters were committing treason.[15]

---

[14] Stevenson, *The Scottish Revolution*, pp. 162–76; Gardiner, *History of England*, vol. 9, pp. 49–55.

[15] Donald, *An Uncounselled King*, pp. 215, 221; Elliott, 'Year of the three ambassadors', pp. 166–81; Stevenson, *The Scottish Revolution*, pp. 179–87.

The most significant development of this period, however, was the decision to resummon parliament. Charles's original decision to go to war without first meeting his people had caused considerable consternation. Tradition and precedent demanded it, not just as a means of raising money, but also to secure the display of consensus on which a successful war effort depended. Expectation of a summons was growing from late 1638, but Cottington told Wentworth that the king would not hear of it and the council does not appear even to have discussed the matter.[16] The unease this created led to protests by Lords Saye and Brooke when the peers assembled at York in April 1639 and a remarkably frank exchange between the king and Sir Thomas Wilsford, a former MP for Dover, commanding a horse contingent from Kent.[17] Wilsford told Charles that 'if you think to make a war with your own purse you deceive yourself. The only way to prosper is to go back and call a parliament, and so shall you have money enough and do your business handsomely.' Charles, with characteristic self-control, simply smiled and remarked that 'there were fools in the last parliament', to which Wilsford retorted – in an interesting counter to the 1629 *Declaration* – 'True, but there were wise men too, and if you let them alone the wise men would have been too hard for the fools.'[18] Wilsford was bolder than most of his contemporaries, but it seems likely that his views were widely shared and this did much to undermine public confidence in the king's policy.

Charles's councillors were determined not to allow the same thing to happen before the 1640 campaign. They also recognised that there was no other way to raise the necessary funds at short notice. It was estimated that another campaign would cost over £1 000 000 and there was no prospect of a loan from the City of London or other possibilities such as an excise tax. After a brief discussion on 5 December 1639 the summons was agreed to. Rather unexpectedly, Laud was one of the principal spokesmen in favour.[19] Partly this was a measure of the influence now being wielded by his friend the earl of Strafford (Wentworth's new title) who was confident

---

[16] *Strafforde Letters*, vol. 2, p. 246.

[17] Fissell, *The Bishops' Wars*, pp. 18–20.

[18] *CSP Dom. 1639*, pp. 244–5.

[19] Gardiner, *History of England*, vol. 9, pp. 75–6; Russell, *Fall of the British Monarchies*, p. 92; Laud, *Works*, vol. 3, p. 233.

that he could manage an English parliament as he had the one in Ireland. But the grudging mood in which king and council approached the meeting must also have convinced the archbishop that there was little to lose.

A successful parliament could have brought enormous benefits for Charles. Not only would he have had access to considerable funds, but also the advantage of appearing to unite the nation behind the war effort. It was what the Covenanters dreaded most and it was worth the crown's while to offer considerable concessions to achieve it. However, there was a lack of will to make the concessions to the political and religious middle ground needed to secure a settlement. In contrast to 1628, moderate counsels no longer carried the political weight to make a realistic compromise viable. The minimum Charles needed to allow, in order to reach agreement with the Commons, was the abandonment of ship money, but there is no sign that this was even considered until it was too late. The spirit in which the council approached the meeting was summed up in a letter by Windebank presenting it as the Commons' last chance to demonstrate its loyalty and obedience. If it failed then the king would be fully justified in resorting to 'extraordinary means, rather than, by the peevishness of some few factious spirits, to suffer his state and government to be lost'.[20] Parliament was still very much on trial.

Charles set out his agenda for the Short Parliament in the speech by the new lord keeper, Lord Finch, which opened proceedings on 13 April. Finch made it clear that the very fact that it was meeting at all was a gracious concession on the part of the king. He had laid aside 'the memory of all former discouragements in preceding assemblies' and was offering them 'the honour [of] working together with himself' for the good of the common-wealth. He then gave a highly partial account of the Scottish rebellion. Without mentioning the prayerbook or the religious issues, he explained this as a straightforward act of treason contrived by a few disloyal indi-viduals. The king had tried negotiating with them and threatening them with force, but neither had worked. Now they were preparing to invade England and he had no choice except to lead an army against them. However, to do this he needed supply. Finch, therefore, urged the English parliament to emulate its Irish counterpart who in March, under Strafford's supervision, had given four subsidies and a pledge of further support

---

[20] Cited in Gardiner, *History of England*, vol. 9, p. 76.

according to the king's needs. He also announced a promise by the king that he would reassemble parliament later in the year to discuss petitions and grievances, 'according to the ancient way'. His hope was that 'the happy conclusion of this parliament . . . may be a means of many more meetings with you'; however, there must be no delay in granting supply and to this end they must 'for a while lay aside all other debates'. As soon as he had finished, with a theatrical flourish, Charles produced the letter from the Covenanter leaders to Louis XIII which, Finch explained, was cast-iron proof of their treasonable intent.[21]

Finch's address offered a good summary of the king's expectations coming into the parliament, and also demonstrated very clearly the gulf of understanding that separated him from the bulk of the English political nation. As far as he was concerned, the case for unconditional supply was unanswerable. The Covenanters were engaged in an act of treasonous rebellion; it was his duty to suppress them and his subjects' to support him. But he was prepared to be magnanimous, and in return for subsidies forget past wrongs and restore parliament to its traditional role as the 'point of contact' between monarch and people. This was not how most MPs viewed the situation. They believed that parliament was an essential part of a balanced political order, and were disturbed by the king's failure to summon it earlier rather than grateful for his readiness to meet it now. They recognised his needs, but believed that their task was to weigh these against the grievances thrown up by the personal rule. Above all, they expected to proceed through the process of bargaining that had become normal practice in the parliaments of the 1620s. To make a start on supply it was essential for the crown to offer concrete concessions in the early stages, and yet, as one newsletter writer noted with dismay, the lord keeper's speech contained not a single reference to ship money.[22]

In the event, the Short Parliament followed the familiar pattern of repeated attempts by crown spokesmen to obtain agreement over supply while the Commons insisted on giving priority to grievances. The two main differences from the late 1620s were the absence of an effective lobby of moderate councillors and the presence of a group of MPs bent on wrecking

---

[21] *Proceedings of the Short Parliament of 1640*, ed. E.S. Cope and W.H. Coates, Camden Soc., 4th ser., vol. 19, 1977, pp. 115–23.

[22] Sharpe, *The Personal Rule*, p. 863.

the session. These were the pro-Scottish members, several of whom had been involved in active collaboration with the Covenanters. Led by John Pym in the Commons and Brooke, Saye and Warwick in the Lords, they recognised that any settlement could only strengthen the king's hand and make life more difficult for English puritans. They therefore devoted all their energies to preventing it. Well organised and committed as this group was, however, it never comprised more than a minority. The bulk of MPs were keen to settle with the king as long as they could do so on terms that would be acceptable to their constituents. This left the pro-Scots with the tricky task of manoeuvring the majority towards a stalemate, without appearing to do so. Their trump card, as Conrad Russell has observed, was the king: 'they had to hope that Charles would not prove too flexible, and not for the last time [he] did everything that they could have hoped from him'.[23]

The tone of the proceedings was set during the opening two days of debate. Windebank raised the matter of the Covenanters' letter to Louis and Rudyerd gave his customary speech about the dangers for the future of parliament if they failed to settle with the king; but neither received a response. The mood of the house was much more clearly in line with Harbottle Grimstone who insisted that, serious as the danger was from Scotland, there was 'a case of greater danger here at home domestical'. The most influential contribution, however, came from Pym whose speech was built on the premise that there was a 'plot . . . to reduce our land to the pope'. This plot encompassed not only the religious innovations of the 1630s, but promotion of Arminians and Catholics to positions of trust and also the whole gamut of secular grievances, from tonnage and poundage, through knighthood and forest fines, ship money and military exactions, to the absence of parliament. These multiple grievances, he proposed, should be drawn together in a Remonstrance to be presented to the king. This was not, as Russell has observed, the performance of a man seeking a compromise. Suggesting a Remonstrance so early in the parliament was highly provocative, and when the country was on the verge of war questioning the legality of military charges was distinctly unhelpful. The Commons did not follow Pym all the way, but it did resolve that discussion of grievances should precede supply.[24]

---

[23] Russell, *Fall of the British Monarchies*, pp. 98–9.

[24] Russell, *Fall of the British Monarchies*, pp. 104–8; Sharpe, *The Personal Rule*, pp. 863–5.

Over the following days debate focused on the injustices that followed the 1629 dissolution and the grievance of ship money. Then, on 21 April, the Commons was summoned to the Banqueting House where Finch reminded MPs of the urgency of supply and reiterated the king's promise to discuss grievances in due course. This time he did talk about ship money, but only to suggest that if parliament came up with some other means of funding the navy the king was likely to find this acceptable.[25] His speech was discussed in the Commons on 23 April. Rudyerd, Vane and others urged that they should trust the king's assurances and turn to supply, but this was countered by the familiar argument that before they could give anything they had to secure their own freedom of property. Sir Francis Seymour also provided an uncomfortable reminder of the 'false glosses' that had been put on the Petition of Right by 'ill ministers', from which he argued that, although they should normally be prepared to trust the king, in the current circumstances there was a need to be wary.[26] The disillusion caused by Charles reneging on his promises of the late 1620s was rarely articulated so directly, but it was evidently a powerful obstacle in the way of settlement.

On the evening of the 23rd Charles held a meeting with the privy council. It was thought that he was about to dissolve the assembly, but instead he decided to take his case directly to the Lords. This was a risky strategy because the Commons was always liable to interpret it as a breach of its privilege of initiating grants of supply; but it was a measure of the urgency of the situation and Charles's faith in the peers as his natural partners in government.[27] The king's speech to the Lords on 24 April repeated the points made previously by Finch and encouraged the peers to distance themselves from 'the preposterous course of the House of Commons'. What particularly upset him, he explained, was that the Commons did not appear to trust him. The present emergency demanded good faith on both sides. He would eventually have to trust the Commons to behave when he resummoned MPs to discuss grievances later in the year; in the meantime they must

---

[25] *Proceedings of the Short Parliament*, p. 263.

[26] Russell, *Fall of the British Monarchies*, pp. 110–11; Sharpe, *The Personal Rule*, pp. 866–7; *Proceedings of the Short Parliament*, pp. 170, 200.

[27] Russell, *Fall of the British Monarchies*, p. 111; Sharpe, *The Personal Rule*, pp. 867–8.

trust him and if they were not prepared to do so then 'my business this summer will be lost'. He therefore urged the peers to remind the lower house of its responsibilities by taking the initiative over supply.[28] As in the 1620s, Charles's habit of seeing grants of supply as tests of trust and loyalty had unfortunate results. It not only added to the pressures of the situation by injecting a note of personal apprehension, but also cut short discussions with the Commons that had barely begun.

The king achieved what he had hoped for from the Lords. There were some expressions of unease, notably from Bristol who pointed out that goodwill was just as important to the king as money and could only exist if something was offered in return. But, eventually, a majority voted that the king's supply should take precedence. Getting the Commons to agree, however, was another matter. When it met to discuss the Lords' resolution on 27 April the only backing for it came from officeholders. The general reaction was that this was indeed a breach of the Commons' privileges, which must be pursued before anything else could be dealt with. The king's initiative, then, had achieved little beyond pushing another issue onto the Commons' agenda.[29]

Meanwhile, the lower house ploughed on with ship money and religious grievances until, on 2 May, the king played what turned out to be his final card. Secretary Vane was sent down to the house with yet another message urging speedy supply. There was nothing new in this, but the discussion that followed suggested that there had been behind-the-scenes negotiations with some of the more moderate Commons' spokesmen. Seymour, who had previously stood firm on the need for a broad range of concessions, suddenly changed direction and volunteered that 'if he had satisfaction for ship money he should trust the king with the rest'. This was welcomed by Vane who also reminded the house that 'if a rupture should happen . . . the country would not thank us'. Pym and his allies did their best to head off the possibility of compromise by introducing other issues into the bargain; but the ensuing debate suggested that a sizeable contingent of the house wanted to follow up Seymour's proposal. Vane spent the weekend closeted with Charles and on Monday came back with a precise offer. The

---

[28] *Proceedings of the Short Parliament*, pp. 264–5.

[29] Russell, *Fall of the British Monarchies*, pp. 111–14; Sharpe, *The Personal Rule*, pp. 868–9.

king would give up ship money in return for grant of 12 subsidies; in other words, he was prepared to exchange a source of revenue worth about £200 000 a year for a one-off grant that would probably yield about £650 000. From Charles's point of view it was a generous offer, but for MPs and taxpayers it was an alarmingly large sum to pay, at least twice the amount voted by parliament on any previous occasion. Vane's offer was probably intended as an opening for negotiation, since he appears to have had the king's permission to drop the demand to eight subsidies. But he never got the chance to follow it up. Some MPs, including Seymour, took fright at the size of the sum demanded; others tried to introduce new ingredients, like monopolies, into the bargain; and others still, encouraged by the pro-Scots, led discussion off on to the issue of whether a bargain could be struck before the house had finished its investigation of the legality of ship money. One of the diarists present suggests that a considerable number of MPs, recognising that the parliament would be dissolved if the deal was not agreed to, were prepared to go along with Vane's proposal. But the convention that a motion for supply should be supported more or less unanimously prevented it being put to a vote. Having made it clear that any delay at this point would be interpreted as refusal, Charles finally lost patience. The following day he summoned the Commons to the upper house and dissolved the assembly. It had lasted just three weeks.[30]

The closing address given by the king and the *Declaration* of the causes of dissolution that appeared a couple of weeks later, showed that he was still thinking about parliaments in the terms of the 1620s.[31] In spite of his damning comments after 1629, he was still quite capable of acknowledging that these meetings were the customary 'point of contact':

the king for his part graciously hearing and redressing such grievances as his people in humble and dutiful manner should represent unto him, and the subjects on their part . . . supplying his Majesty upon all extraordinary

---

[30] Russell, *Fall of the British Monarchies*, pp. 116–21; Sharpe, *The Personal Rule*, pp. 869–72.

[31] *LJ*, vol. 4, p. 81; Rushworth, vol. 3, pp. 1160–7; E.S. Cope, 'The king's declaration concerning the dissolution of the Short Parliament of 1640: an unsuccessful attempt at public relations', *HLQ*, vol. 40, 1977, pp. 325–31. Charles's closing speech on 5 May was drafted by Hamilton, testimony to the marquis's continued standing with the king: NAS, GD 406/1/1805. I am grateful to Sarah Poynting for this reference.

*occasions for support of his honour and sovereignty and for preserving
the kingdom in glory and safety.*[32]

This passage helps to explain why the option of summoning a parliament
was never entirely excluded as far as Charles was concerned. There remained
a side of him that recognised that he was supposed to follow the 'ancient
way' and left him open to persuasion if it could be shown that the 'turbulent spirits' of 1629 had settled down. But he also continued to expect that
a parliament would be held on his terms and this was what caused problems once a session began. In 1640 he had, he explained, done everything
that could be expected of him. In spite of this, the Commons had 'introduced a way of bargaining and contracting with the king, as if nothing ought
to be given by them but what he should buy and purchase'. This was not
only grossly dishonourable; it also implied that they could not trust him.
However, he did not blame the majority of MPs. As usual, the problem lay
with 'some few seditiously affected men' who had been active in previous
parliaments and were again trying 'to bring ruin and confusion to the state
and render contemptible this glorious monarchy'. He had, he said, been
persuaded that their 'malice' could be overcome by the loyalty of the majority; but this had not happened and he was therefore left with no choice
but to dissolve the assembly.

Given the efforts of Pym and the pro-Scots to wreck the assembly,
there was perhaps more truth in Charles's analysis than on the previous
occasions.[33] But this does not alter the fact that the main responsibility for
parliament's failure rested with him. Past experience should have taught
him that, however much he disliked 'bargaining', it was normal procedure
as far as the Commons was concerned. It was, after all, the way he had
raised supply in 1628. The king was simply not being realistic if he thought
that an English parliament would behave like its Irish counterpart and meekly
yield up supply while allowing grievances to be deferred to a later meeting.
Had he been prepared to offer the abolition of ship money while there was
still time for the negotiating process to operate, there would at least have
been the possibility of reaching agreement since so many MPs were conscious that this was what was expected of them by their constituents. As it

---

[32] Rushworth, vol. 3, p. 1165.

[33] See Hyde's famous story of the pleasure displayed by Pym's lieutenant, Oliver St John,
at the dissolution: Clarendon, *History*, vol. 1, p. 183.

was, Charles stifled any prospect of this with his over-hasty ultimatums and lack of flexibility. His approach is partially explicable in terms of the tight timetable imposed by the military situation – although the later decision to put back the rendezvous of his forces by a month suggests this was less urgent than initially supposed. But more than anything it appears to have been a result of his own perceptions and expectations, and the changing culture of the court. The Personal Rule had bred a narrowness and intolerance of dissent that made decision makers markedly less receptive to the concerns of the political nation than they had been in the 1620s.

The attitude of councillors was displayed very clearly at a meeting that took place on the afternoon of the dissolution. Charles took the chair and sought to pre-empt any debate about whether the war should be continued by directing discussion to the matter of finance. Northumberland, who earlier in the day had voted in council against the dissolution, made an attempt to broaden debate with some cautious queries: 'If no more money then what proposed? How then to make an offensive war, a difficulty? Whether to do nothing and let them alone or go on with a vigorous war?' However, he soon discovered this was 'held by some a disaffection in me', which says a good deal about the difficulty of trying to give Charles unwelcome advice.[34] Cottington and Laud clearly saw that the king's mind was made up. Cottington argued that the likelihood of the Scots making alliances abroad meant that any attack on them was in reality a defensive war, while Laud returned to his favourite theme on such occasions, that the Commons' refusal of a legitimate request for supply meant the king could take it anyway. The person who caught the mood most effectively, however, was Strafford. In a dramatic peroration, summarised in Vane's notes, he urged that now was the moment for the policies he had been pursuing in Ireland to be applied to England.

Go on with a vigorous war as you first designed, loosed and absolved from all rules of government, being reduced to extreme necessities. Everything is to be done that power must admit . . . they refusing you are acquitted towards God and man. You have an army in Ireland you may employ here to reduce this

---

[34] *CSP Dom. 1640*, pp. 112–13; Russell, *Fall of the British Monarchies*, p. 123. Vane may also have tried to argue against an offensive war, as he later claimed; but his notes of the meeting are unclear on this.

kingdom. Confident as anything under heaven Scotland shall not hold out five months. One summer well employed will do it. Venture all I had I would carry it or lose it.[35]

In this drastic scenario one can detect an atmosphere similar to that after the 1626 Parliament, in which the Commons' uncooperativeness was felt to have released the crown from the normal constraints. Also – and not for the last time – one gets a sense that for the king it mattered immensely that he be seen to be doing what was right and honourable, almost without regard to any prospects of success.

The same council meeting also outlined the intended strategy for the war. The king was to raise an army of 30 000 foot and 3 000 cavalry which was to drive into Scotland supported by Strafford's Irish army of 8 000. The garrisons of Berwick and Carlisle were to be reinforced and used as bases, while the Edinburgh garrison was to harry the Covenanters from the rear. The army was to be financed by a loan from the City of London, subsidies from the Spanish and the current round of ship money.[36] Over the following weeks, however, the whole scheme began to unravel. The London aldermen refused point-blank to support the war effort; Strafford's increasingly desperate negotiations with the Spanish collapsed when they found themselves facing their own internal revolt in Catalonia; and ship money proved well-nigh impossible to collect.[37] The king was thrown back on the resources of his near-exhausted Exchequer. Meanwhile the collapse of the parliament and the prospect of a renewal of the war brought out into the open political antagonisms that had hitherto largely been kept beneath the surface. The search for scapegoats became intense and most of the blame fell on the bishops and the papists. Laud was widely blamed for the breaking up of the parliament, and London apprentices gathered to hunt 'William the Fox' and attack Lambeth Palace. Papists were increasingly seen as legitimate targets of popular outrage and troops levied in Devon

---

[35] Cited in Russell, *Fall of the British Monarchies*, p. 126. The phrase about an army in Ireland was later used as evidence of Strafford's intention to subdue an English parliament by force; however, as Russell has argued, it is far more likely that it refers to using the Irish army against the Scots.

[36] Fissell, *The Bishops' Wars*, pp. 39–48.

[37] Gardiner, *History of England*, vol. 9, pp. 130, 140; Elliott, 'Year of the three ambassadors', pp. 165–81.

actually murdered one of their Catholic officers.[38] In the midst of all this, Charles introduced a new source of discontent.

The 1640 Book of Canons was drawn up by Convocation, which represented the different groupings among the clergy; but, perhaps more than any other ecclesiastical measure of the period, it bore the stamp of the king's personal influence. Laud, conscious that he was likely to carry the blame, sought to distance himself from the whole process and it was Charles who ruled that Convocation should go on sitting beyond the end of the parliament, apparently against his archbishop's advice.[39] The king also had a significant input into the canons themselves. The Sixth Canon, containing the controversial 'etcetera oath', was drawn up on his instructions, with a requirement for his final approval before it was administered; while several others, for example, the Seventh Canon, which recommended genuflexion on entering and leaving church, appear to have been drafted with his preferences very much in mind.[40]

Perhaps the most intriguing aspect of the Book of Canons was the lengthy preface, issued in Charles's name.[41] This contains what appear to be the mature reflections of a monarch who had been forced to think through what the Church of England meant for him in the face of the Scottish challenge. Much of the language and argument appeared to have come straight out of the *Large Declaration*. There was the familiar analysis of the sources of trouble that were traced back to the 'ill affected' who under the 'mask of zeal and counterfeit holiness' had spread their 'poisoned conceits', especially among 'the weaker sort who are prone to be misled by crafty seducers'. They had encouraged the king's 'good subjects' to 'take offence' at 'the rites and ceremonies now used in the Church of England', 'upon an unjust supposition' that they were 'introductive unto popish superstitions'. More than this, they also 'aim at our royal person' and would have them

---

[38] Tyacke, *Anti-Calvinists*, p. 237; Russell, *Fall of the British Monarchies*, pp. 129–30, 141–2.

[39] Davies, *The Caroline Captivity*, p. 253. Although this is, perhaps, one of those occasions on which Laud's denial of responsibility needs to be treated with a certain amount of scepticism.

[40] Davies, *The Caroline Captivity*, p. 275; *CSP Dom. 1640*, pp. 175–6; Laud, *Works*, vol. 5, pp. 625–6.

[41] Laud, *Works*, vol. 5, pp. 609–13; Tyacke, *Anti-Calvinists*, pp. 238–9; Russell, *Fall of the British Monarchies*, p. 137.

'imagine that we ourselves are perverted and do worship God in a super-stitious way, and that we intend to bring in some alteration to the religion established'. Against these charges Charles offered the same defence as in the *Large Declaration*. It was absurd to accuse him or his church of popery when they were following the guidelines established by Protestant divines who had suffered martyrdom under Mary. The Church of England rested on the 'pious example of King Edward VI and of Queen Elizabeth' which encapsulated what the Seventh Canon referred to as 'the most ancient custom of the primitive church in the purest times'. What was needed now was 'a return' to this 'true former splendour of uniformity, devotion and holy order', which was what the canons were intended to achieve.

The style of churchmanship they proposed was manifestly anti-Calvinist. The Seventh Canon, for example, dealt with the controversial matter of the place of the communion table and cautiously, but clearly, underwrote its altarwise position and railing off; while the Sixth, with its 'etcetera oath' declaring approval of 'the doctrines and discipline and government estab-lished in the Church of England as containing all things necessary to salvation', implied a wholesale endorsement of the anti-Calvinist *status quo*.[42] The canons aroused a storm of protest when they were published. Groups of puritan ministers in London and Northamptonshire led the way, con-centrating mainly on the shortcomings of the 'etcetera oath'; but they were soon joined by a broad range of more moderate opinion. Robert Sanderson, one of Charles's favourite preachers, warned Laud that the oath was causing such distaste among those 'otherwise every way conformable' that it must be abandoned. At the end of September the king conceded and agreed that it should be suspended until after the next Convocation; however, the damage had been done. A measure intended to unite the English church in the face of the Scots had ended up dividing it more than ever.[43]

The pace and direction of military events in the Second Bishops' War was largely dictated by the Covenanters. The failure of the Short Parliament reassured them about the level of their support in England and

---

[42] Tyacke, *Anti-Calvinists*, pp. 239–40. As Tyacke points out, there was also a highly contentious clause in the First Canon, which declared that 'tribute and custom and aid and subsidy' were all due to the king 'by the law of God, nature and nations'. The lack of any reference to parliamentary approval for taxation made this all too reminiscent of the arguments put forward by Sibthorpe and Mainwaring to justify the forced loan.

[43] Russell, *Fall of the British Monarchies*, pp. 138–9.

they decided there was no longer anything to be gained by the cautious approach of 1639. They therefore took the initiative and crossed the border on 20 August. This gave Charles a political advantage in that there was now no doubt he was fighting a defensive war. He was able to call out the trained bands from Durham, Yorkshire and the Midlands; but in other respects his position was very difficult. Delays and cash shortages meant that his army was divided. The main force of about 15 000 men was encamped at Newcastle under the command of Lord Conway, while Charles himself was still at York gathering the remainder of the pressed levies, many of whom were without arms or provisions. There was also a lack of clarity about his strategy. After the setback of 1639 much of his confidence in military victory appears to have drained away and his instructions to Conway concentrated more on the scorched earth policy to be adopted if Newcastle fell than on how to engage the enemy. Conway decided that his best option was to try to fight the Scots as they crossed the Tyne and he led out a small force of 5 000 infantry and 2 500 cavalry. Leslie made his crossing on 28 August, at Newburn where high ground on the north bank gave his artillery a decided advantage. He also had three times as many men as Conway. The battle followed a predictable course. Heavy fire from the Scots guns forced the English infantry to retire from their earthworks on the south bank and the Scots began to cross. A contingent of English cavalry then bravely charged them, but was forced back by weight of numbers and artillery fire. Once the English defences were breached, Conway's force scattered in disarray. Newcastle was hastily evacuated, leaving the Scots to take the city and then sweep southwards to occupy Durham and the adjacent countryside.[44]

The defeat at Newburn left Charles in a much weakened position, both militarily and politically. He still had a force of around 16 000 men at York, but it was costing £40 000 a month to keep together and at the start of September there was only £1 037 in the Exchequer. The presence of a Scots army on English soil was also threatening to transform English politics. For the first time since the fifteenth century there was an alternative to the crown as a source of power around which critics of the regime could rally. The army's presence was also a stark reminder of the king's failure in battle, which

---

[44] Fissell, *The Bishops' Wars*, pp. 50–61; Russell, *Fall of the British Monarchies*, pp. 142–5.

was still the ultimate test for a monarch. This was particularly damaging for his prestige.[45] Most of the privy council, faced with the unenviable task of trying to raise extra revenue and control London, recognised the hopelessness of the situation. In the two weeks following Newburn they repeatedly advised the king to summon a parliament or a Great Council of Peers (which had last met under Edward III to advise on raising revenue in a wartime emergency), expecting that either course would lead to negotiations for peace.[46] Charles, however, was determined to fight on. He was still at York with his army intact and growing daily as trained band contingents arrived. He also had at his side the forceful figure of Strafford who showed no sign of weakening in his dedication to driving out the hated Scots. When a group of Yorkshire gentry tried to petition the king for a parliament, the earl bullied them into backing down and agreeing instead to a pledge of financial support for the trained bands, which he promptly communicated to Charles. The king showed a similar belligerent spirit. He fired off a series of dispatches to the privy council berating them for their lack of resolve and urging them to set aside any qualms they may have had about overriding custom and tradition. 'Let innovate and spare not', he told them when faced with the need to intervene in the mayoral election in London in order to secure a loan from the City; 'it may be a good example for me to do the like upon occasion hereafter and I see not why you may not use this occasion so as to make them lend the willinger'.[47] Away from York, however, the situation looked very different and, in pursuing what seemed so obviously a lost cause, the king surrendered the political initiative to the Scots and their English allies.

The main objective of both of these groups was to push Charles into summoning another parliament which they could use to put a check on his actions. What became known as the Twelve Peers' Petition, drawn up by Pym and his lieutenant, Oliver St John, under the direction of the earl of Bedford, was subscribed on the day of Newburn and presented to the king in early September. It complained about the spread of popery, the

---

[45] Russell, *Fall of the British Monarchies*, pp. 145–6, 149n.

[46] Ibid., 153–5; Gardiner, *History of England*, vol. 9, pp. 199–200.

[47] Wedgewood, *Thomas Wentworth*, pp. 296–8; Gardiner, *History of England*, vol. 9, pp. 200, 202–6; J.L Malcolm, 'Charles I on innovation: a confidential directive on an explosive issue', *BIHR*, vol. 53, 1980, pp. 252–5.

grievances and disruption accompanying the war and rumours that an Irish army was to be brought to England. It then asked that a parliament be summoned and peace negotiations begun in order to unite the two kingdoms 'against the common enemy of the reformed religion'. Within a few days of their victory the Scots themselves were also petitioning for peace talks and a parliament. Charles eventually decided to follow the course that was being advocated on all sides. He summoned the Great Council of Peers to meet at York on 24 September, then, in his opening address to them, announced that a parliament would meet in November. This did not mean, however, that he had accepted the necessity for peace.[48]

The discussions that followed in the Council of Peers showed that the king was still determined to find some means of driving out the Scots. In the opening speech, he told the peers that he had called them together so that, with their 'advice and assistance', he could undertake the 'chastisement' of the 'army of rebels lodged within this kingdom'. Then, following his usual habit of seeking to limit advice to a specific point, he asked for guidance on how to raise money to keep his army together until a parliament met.

For so long as the Scotch army remains in England I think no man will counsel me to disband mine: for that would be an unspeakable loss to all this part of the kingdom by subjecting them to the greedy appetite of the rebels, besides the unspeakable dishonour that would thereby fall upon the nation.[49]

In his belief that the peers were there to provide him with the means of renewing the war rather than suing for peace, Charles was largely isolated. Strafford continued to support the line and tore into anyone who tried to describe the Scots as anything other than rebels. However, the majority view was represented by Bristol who consistently pointed out that while it might be desirable to bring the Scots to their knees, the practicalities of the situation demanded that 'we must now speak of the business as to men that have gotten these advantages'.[50]

---

[48] Gardiner, *History of England*, vol. 9, pp. 198–202; Russell, *Fall of the British Monarchies*, pp. 149–57.

[49] Gardiner, *History of England*, vol. 9, pp. 207–8.

[50] Russell, *Fall of the British Monarchies*, pp. 157–8; C.S.R. Russell, 'Why did Charles I call the Long Parliament', in *Unrevolutionary England*, p. 260.

The peers did their best to let Charles down gently. They composed a carefully balanced address to him, urging an accommodation to restore 'the perfect union of the two kingdoms', but acknowledging that if the Scots insisted on terms 'dishonourable for his Majesty and the English nation' they would regard themselves as 'obliged . . . in honour and duty to preserve and defend the kingdom'. Charles appears to have seized on the second half of this statement as implying, as Windebank put it, that the peers were 'firm to his Majesty for the repulsion of the Scots'; but this was clearly not what was intended since the council proceeded to nominate a committee largely sympathetic to the Scots to conduct negotiations.[51]

These took place at Ripon during the first half of October. The king seems to have hoped that he could secure a treaty on the same terms as the Pacification of Berwick and then go to the parliament with a request for supply to resume the war. The Scots, however, recognised the importance of not settling too much in advance so that the coming parliament would have to be fully involved in the peace negotiations. In the end, they got their way. Negotiations were confined to the issue of how their army was to be maintained while in England. At first the Scots demanded £40 000 a month, but this was eventually scaled down to £50 000 over two months, or £850 a day. Bristol declared that, while these terms were not as honourable as they might have liked, they were acceptable, and most of the peers agreed with him. Strafford started a row when he took exception to Lord Keeper Finch's description of this as 'a hopeful treaty' and then offered to bring over his Irish army at two days' notice if someone could provide him with ships. However, when Bristol pressed him on whether he could guarantee a military victory he was forced to admit that he 'would not answer for the success'. This seems to have removed any doubts that the peers may have had about accepting the Scottish terms.[52] Only Charles seems to have continued to believe that he could still fight the Scots. In his opening address when the Long Parliament met on 3 November he told MPs that if they had heeded his warnings about invasion in the previous parliament none of the recent mishaps would have occurred. 'But', he added, 'it is no wonder that men are so slow to believe so great sedition could be raysed

---

[51] Russell, 'Why did Charles I call the Long Parliament', pp. 256–7.

[52] Gardiner, *History of England*, vol. 9, pp. 209–14; Russell, *Fall of the British Monarchies*, pp. 161–2.

upon so little ground.' As this last phrase suggests, he continued to view the whole rebellion in the terms presented in the *Large Declaration*, as the conspiracy of a few 'ill affected men'; and this perspective, allied to a burning sense of the humiliation he had suffered at the hands of the Covenanters, persuaded him that he must carry on the fight. He therefore informed the two houses that his agenda for the coming session consisted of just two points: 'first the chasing out of the rebels and secondly the satisfying your just grievances'.[53]

Conrad Russell has described Charles's blinkered belligerence through the period following Newburn as 'a flight from reality'.[54] There is a good deal in this. His readiness to interpret the peers' carefully balanced statement distancing themselves from the war as evidence of support for his line is a striking demonstration of his inability to recognise a viewpoint that was unwelcome to him. In a sense, this had been his problem throughout the Scottish troubles. He was never able to appreciate the strength of feeling against the prayerbook among the Scots and, by the same token, never understood why so many Englishmen were sympathetic to their cause. He was forever banking on a surge of anti-Scottish feeling that never materialised and this led to repeated miscalculations. There is no doubt that Charles's lack of political antennae, and his inability 'to read the political map', frequently prevented him from engaging with the realities of the situation.

But, in seeking to understand Charles, it is important to go further and ask why he found it so hard to comprehend what seemed obvious to the seasoned politicians around him. It is worth stressing that, for anyone who has followed the king through the twists and turns of his Scottish policy, his inflexibility comes as no surprise. It was not a temporary aberration based on an over-optimistic calculation of the odds, or the influence of a particularly assertive first minister; it was entirely in keeping with his mindset throughout, which suggests that it stemmed from an attitude deeply entrenched in his view of himself and his responsibility as a monarch. Here his guiding principle appears to have been to follow the course dictated by his conscience and his sense of honour. Those politicians who came into close contact with the king recognised this and made allowance for it.

---

[53] Russell, 'Why did Charles I call the Long Parliament', p. 258.

[54] Ibid.

Privy councillors and the council of peers were very careful always to pay due regard to the king's sense of honour, and in the latter stages devoted a good deal of energy to trying to persuade him that it was not incompatible with peace. Strafford took a different line and sought to make himself indispensable as the one person who could keep the struggle going in the way that Charles's sense of self-esteem seemed to require. Allied to this was Charles's refusal to abandon the analysis of the Covenanter rebellion set out in the *Large Declaration*. This explains why he so persistently underestimated the strength of support for the Covenanters and other opponents; why he continued to believe that if only he could communicate the dangers effectively the majority of 'loyal subjects' would see the light and rally to his cause; and why he felt he could not be seen to be giving in – because the very survival of monarchy was at stake. At the same time, this was an analysis that allowed him to evade the reality that a majority of the political nation opposed his policies and that if he was to regain the initiative these would have to change. In the event, his inflexibility in the autumn of 1640 created a situation where first of all the Council of Peers and then the Long Parliament were thrust into the role of an alternative government. It was they who had to negotiate with the Scots and pay the army. This was the start, as Russell observes, of 'a habit of carrying on government as if the king was incapacitated' which during the succeeding months transformed the ground rules for English politics.[55]

The Long Parliament

Scottish victory in the Bishops' Wars created immense volatility and uncertainty. The most important thing about it was that a rebellion had taken place against the monarch and had succeeded. This broke the taboo on armed resistance to the monarch which was one of the most significant constraints operating in favour of the *status quo*. The very fact of success destroyed the belief, assiduously cultivated by the Tudors, that rebellion always failed. Moreover, the Scots had rebelled in the name of religion and conscience and had apparently met with divine approval for their actions. All this served to reinstate armed resistance as a legitimate response to dealing

---

[55] Ibid., p. 260.

with a tyrannical ruler, thus opening up a whole range of political possibilities, not just for the English, but the Irish as well.[56]

The other critical consequence of the Scots victory was to provide the king's opponents with a coercive power that they had previously lacked. Since the decline of baronial affinities in the early sixteenth century those who sought to challenge royal policy had lacked the means to take on the monarch in armed conflict. They could put pressure on him by witholding supply and attacking his ministers in parliament, and they could bring influence to bear at court; but, in the last resort, they could not force him to do anything. This situation was changed by the presence of the Scots, in control of what was unquestionably the most potent military force in Britain and willing to use it to promote the interests of their English allies. In the short term this deprived Charles of the power to dissolve parliament at will which, since 1614, had been one of the monarch's greatest political assets. If he did not like the way things were developing in a parliament he could simply call off the game and start again. Often the threat that this might happen was enough severely to curtail a parliament's freedom of action. Now with the Scots occupying Durham and Northumberland, and threatening to march south unless the king kept up payments of £850 a day, dissolution was no longer an option.[57] In the longer term the Scots army guaranteed the security of their English allies and gave them the room to manoeuvre for a lasting settlement. Those who had colluded with the Scots during 1640 left themselves wide open to a charge of treason and there was every likelihood that if Charles could turn the tables he would move against them. The continuing presence of the Scots was their best assurance of personal security, which is one of the main reasons why Pym and his friends were so keen to keep them involved in English politics. Beyond this their insistence that any peace agreement be fully approved by the English parliament allowed their allies to spin out discussion and tie English concessions to those being granted to the Scots.[58]

In these circumstances, the options open to Charles were extremely limited. His one major asset was that he could not be removed. The Scots

---

[56] C.S.R. Russell, 'The Scottish party in English Parliaments, 1640–2 or the myth of the English Revolution', *HR*, vol. 66, 1993, p. 39.

[57] Gardiner, *History of England*, vol. 9, p. 219.

[58] Russell, 'Scottish party', pp. 35–52.

and their English allies would probably have liked to depose him had this been feasible. Medieval precedent suggested that it was the obvious way to deal with a monarch who had become so unpopular that he provoked his people to rebellion. Moreover, they seem to have reached the point where they no longer trusted him to adhere to the terms of any settlement. Loudoun's comment in September 1640, about the Covenanters' distrust of Charles's intention to make peace, summed up a general wariness born out of his track record of reneging on concessions back to the Petition of Right and also his semi-public announcements that he had no intention of standing by any agreement that went against his 'grounds'. The problem was that there was no obvious candidate to replace him. The most viable alternative was Charles Lewis, Elector Palatine and eldest surviving son of Elizabeth of Bohemia, who arrived in England in March 1641. But Charles was careful to cultivate his loyalty by holding out the prospect of renewed intervention in the Palatinate; and there never seems to have been much prospect that the young elector would turn against his uncle. Otherwise none of those with royal blood, such as Hamilton or Lennox, were prepared to put themselves forward.[59] Any final solution to the crisis would have to involve Charles, which gave him the power of veto over its terms. In other respects, however, his position was very weak.

His loss of military power and the power to dissolve parliament left him with only two serious possibilities if he wanted to regain the political initiative. The first of these – to which he was to return again and again during the Long Parliament – was to mount some sort of coup against the parliamentary leadership. This certainly appealed to him. He had few qualms about using force in dealing with those he regarded as traitors and rebels, and his whole analysis of the crisis was posited on the assumption that the 'multitude' had been led astray by a few 'malignant spirits' whose removal would herald a return to normality. In practical terms it was also viable. If he could secure control of the Tower this would give him command of London and he still had the remnants of an army in the north, as well as Strafford's Irish army of some 9 000 men. Moreover, in the lord deputy, he had a minister with the nerve, forcefulness and lack of scruple needed to carry through such an enterprise. When Strafford arrived in London

---

[59] Russell, 'British problem', p. 247; Russell, *Fall of the British Monarchies*, p. 279.

six days after the opening of the Long Parliament, on 9 November, the coup option seems to have been seriously contemplated. According to several accounts, preparations were made for Charles to visit the Tower and take command of the garrison, then round up the Commons' leaders and accuse them of treasonable relations with the Scots. However, everything fell apart on the 11th when the Commons, alert to the danger, pressed charges against the lord deputy as soon as he took his seat in the Lords and had him sequestered and imprisoned.[60] Charles continued to dabble with the possibility of using armed force against his enemies, negotiating through the winter months for a papal loan and a Dutch marriage alliance, either of which might have provided him with the means to recruit foreign mercenaries.[61] But Strafford's removal deprived him of the person who was best equipped to see it through successfully.

The other option was to try to divide his enemies and build his own royal party. This was the approach he had pursued with the Scots in 1638, when, thanks to Hamilton's efforts, it had nearly succeeded. But it required skill, patience and judgement, attributes with which Charles was not over-endowed, and there was always the prospect that he would sink the whole strategy with a reckless intervention. It also took considerable effort to persuade the king that he had little alternative. He appears to have gone into the Long Parliament still believing that he could rally anti-Scots feeling and resume the war. His opening speech on 3 November was a call to his subjects to join him in 'chasing out the rebels' who had inflicted such humiliations and hardships on England. Two days later, however, he was forced to make an apology in which he withdrew the description of the Scots as rebels and accepted that he had to negotiate.[62] This climbdown must have cost him a good deal in personal terms, and, perhaps, helps to explain why, a few days later, he appears to have been willing to back Strafford's proposal for a coup. It also indicates, however, that there was a part of him that recognised the force of the argument being put by his moderate councillors – that he now had no alternative but to acknowledge the *status quo* and make concessions to his enemies. It was to take the rest

---

[60] Gardiner, *History of England*, vol. 9, pp. 231–6.

[61] Hibbard, *Charles I and the Popish Plot*, pp. 168, 171; Gardiner, *History of England*, vol. 9, pp. 257, 262.

[62] *CSP Dom. 1640–1*, pp. 246–7.

of November and much of December before he fully absorbed this. Until he did so, he had little influence on events and it was others who made the running.

These 'others' were chiefly the Covenanters and their friends among the parliamentary leadership, who can be described in this period as the Scots party. They had a clear agenda that involved settling with the king, but on terms that would provide for their own future security. The Scots were aware that England was militarily the stronger nation and that they had been fortunate to face Charles when internal divisions hampered his war effort. They therefore wanted to push through changes that would prevent him starting another war without an English parliament's consent and remove the religious causes that had led to war in the first place. Their English allies were very conscious that the king was not to be trusted, which meant, as Conrad Russell puts it, that they had to 'institutionalise Charles's concessions so thoroughly that he would be unable to reverse them'.[63] Both were agreed on the priorities for achieving these ends. First, they must remove the 'incendiaries' who had led the king astray, especially Strafford, and force him to demonstrate that he had abandoned his earlier policies by giving up those responsible for them. Second, they needed to abolish the bishops to prevent a recurrence of the anti-Calvinist takeover of the church. The latter was more of a priority for the Scots, who, like Charles, believed that there could only be a settled relationship between the British kingdoms when they shared a common religion. But Pym, Saye, Brooke and the others were ready to support it as the price for keeping their alliance together. During the opening weeks of the Long Parliament, the Scots party was the dominant force in the Commons. They had some difficulties over episcopacy, where a clear division of opinion was revealed when the matter was debated in December 1640 and again in February 1641. But their decision to target Charles's ministers was supported right across the political spectum. They were also able to build on the fears of a popish plot outlined by Pym in the Short Parliament, which enabled them to drive forward proposals to dismantle the Laudian apparatus in the church, disband the Irish Army and remove the Catholic advisers around the queen.[64]

---

[63] Russell, 'British problem', p. 247.

[64] Ibid., p. 243; Russell, 'Scottish party', p. 50; idem, *Fall of the British Monarchies*, pp. 167–9.

The Scots party and the king were, however, not the only major players. There was a third force, working for unity and a balanced settlement, which comprised the king's moderate councillors and a substantial element in the House of Lords. Their agenda had been set out immediately after the defeat at Newburn when the council presented Charles with a memorandum insisting that their aim must be 'the uniting of your Majesty and your subjects together, the want whereof . . . is the cause of all the present troubles'.[65] The Council of Peers had followed this line when it met at York and took the responsibility for persuading the king of the need for moderation and compromise. Their programme, as it emerged in the early weeks of the parliament, consisted of upholding the principles enshrined in the Petition of Right, restoring the religious *status quo* of James's reign and getting Charles to signal his acceptance of a change of policy by changing his ministers. It was a programme with something for everyone and it probably represented the best chance of an enduring settlement.[66]

The pivotal figure in pushing it forward was once again the marquis of Hamilton. Restored to Charles's side with the end of campaigning, he continued to enjoy not only the king's confidence, but also that of other leading players. He was a regular attender in the House of Lords; he worked closely with his long-standing client, Secretary Vane, who, via his son, provided a bridge to Pym and the Commons' leadership; he himself had close links with the Scots allies in the Lords, notably the earl of Bedford whose daughter he was rumoured to be about to marry; and he remained on good terms with the Covenanter leaders. He was also no friend of Strafford and was reportedly willing to tell Charles that he had to go.[67] During the winter of 1640–1 court observers repeatedly identified the marquis as the king's most influential adviser. While this remained the case, the prospects for restoring unity were good.

Unfortunately for this period we do not have any equivalent of the revealing correspondence between Hamilton and the king that took place in 1638; however, the indications are that the marquis tried to handle him

---

[65] Cited in Russell, *Fall of the British Monarchies*, p. 236.

[66] Ibid., pp. 210–13.

[67] Scally, 'The political career of Hamilton', pp. 298–304; Russell, *Fall of the British Monarchies*, p. 243.

in much the same way. Like the moderate councillors, he doubtless played on Charles's understanding that a good king sought to unite his people; but, at the same time, he seems to have appealed to his more immediate political concerns by urging that the best way to restore his position was by granting concessions that would divide his enemies. Out of this he hoped to develop enough momentum behind a settlement to make it stick. The first fruits of this approach were apparent in the peace negotiations with the Scots.

The Covenanter commissioners arrived in London in November with a programme of eight demands that went well beyond the previous agreement at Berwick. At the outset Charles was determined to go no further than this and argue his case every inch of the way; but the realities of the situation were soon brought home to him. When he tried to attend the first meeting of the treaty commissioners on 19 November, the Scots refused to treat in his presence and forced him to withdraw. Thereafter the gist of the discussions was relayed to him by the English commissioners who, at the same time, reported everything to parliament. This slowed down negotiations, to the satisfaction of the Scots and their English allies, but it also helped them along in that Charles was kept at arm's length and prevented from making disruptive interventions. The first article, which required the king to authorise the acts passed in the Scottish parliament of June 1640, was a major stumbling block. Charles at first refused, and tried to contest each measure, including the Scottish Triennial Act. However, the English commissioners kept reminding him of the realities of his situation and Hamilton and Traquair talked him round behind the scenes. On 3 December he agreed to let the acts pass. This unblocked the whole process. The second and third articles – covering royal castles and the treatment of those who had taken the Covenant outside Scotland – were rapidly approved and, although Charles predictably held out for some time against the fourth – which required him to allow the authors of the recent troubles to be tried in parliament – this too was passed by the end of December. The fifth and sixth articles – covering the sensitive issue of reparations to the Scots army in the north – were sorted out in January and early February 1641, and by the end of the month only the eighth article – an open-ended proposal for 'securing a settled peace' between the two kingdoms – remained to be determined. Careful management of the king and extensive discussion and manoeuvring behind the scenes had yielded considerable progress; however, at this point, the whole context for the negotiations altered abruptly.[68]

This was due to the collapse of a scheme, carefully nurtured by Hamilton, for bringing leading members of the Scots party into government. It appears to have originated in the meetings between the council and representatives of the Twelve Peers in September 1640. Bedford was the key figure. He carried considerable weight among the Scots party, as chief sponsor of the Twelve Peers Petition and the patron of Pym and St John; and his regular attendance at court also ensured he had a wide range of contacts and personal acquaintances at the heart of government, including Charles himself. Just as important, his Calvinist episcopalianism was broadly compatible with the king's views on church government. From December 1640 onwards there were persistent rumours that he was about to be made lord treasurer. This was doubly significant in that it also indicated that the main incentive he and his friends could offer for engaging their services was a solution to the crown's financial problems. Pym became involved in discussions with Secretary Vane and Sir Robert Pye, auditor of the Exchequer, about augmenting the king's revenues and there were proposals finally to give parliamentary sanction to the collection of tonnage and poundage, to reform subsidy assessment, to revive a version of the Great Contract of 1610 and, even, to introduce a parliament-approved excise tax. These developed slowly, but this suited Bedford and his friends since it meant that progress on a financial settlement could be tied to concessions in other areas.[69] There was also progress on the religious front. On 16 January 1641, at the instigation of the council, the Lords delivered a judgement in the St Saviour's case, which even-handedly condemned puritan separatist refusal to read divine service and anti-Calvinist attempts to introduce 'new ceremonies'. This was accompanied by reports that Archbishop Ussher had been summoned to wait on the king with a programme for restoring episcopacy to 'the ancient

---

[68] Russell, *Fall of the British Monarchies*, pp. 171–9, 183–7; Stevenson, *The Scottish Revolution*, pp. 215–18; Donald, *An Uncounselled King*, pp. 275–9.

[69] Russell, *Fall of the British Monarchies*, pp. 239–43, 252–6; C.S.R. Russell, 'Parliament and the king's finances', in idem ed., *Origins of the English Civil War*, pp. 11–14.

primitive way'.[70] By 21 January Sir John Temple, court informant to the earl of Leicester, was relaying the news that the king 'is brought to a dislike of those counsels that he hath formerly followed and therefore resolves to steer another course'. This, he predicted, would lead to the 'bringing in' of Bedford as lord treasurer, Pym as chancellor of the exchequer and Saye as master of the wards, and 'make up an entire union between the king and his people . . . so to moderate their demands as well as the height of that power which hath been lately used in government'. The credit for this momentous change, he said, was mainly due to Hamilton and the queen's counsellor, Henry Jermyn.[71]

During late January and early February 1641 there was enough progress to suggest that Temple's predictions might not be far wide of the mark. On 23 January Charles delivered a notably conciliatory speech in which he assured the two houses that if they refrained from tampering with the 'present established government of the church', he would 'reduce all matters of religion and government to what they were in the purest times of Queen Elizabeth's days', lay down any parts of his revenue that 'shall be found illegal or grievous to the public' and give his consent to a version of the bill currently being considered for 'frequent parliaments'.[72] This was an astute performance. In taking a stand on bishops he was highlighting the issue most likely to drive a wedge between the Commons and the Scots. But it also contained a massive concession. In promising to assent to the triennial bill – which stipulated that a parliament should meet every three years and that if the king failed to summon it the lord keeper and twelve peers could do so – he was accepting a very significant curtailment of the royal prerogative. The fact that he was prepared to do this indicated the weakness of his position, but also, perhaps, that his moderate advisers were getting through to him. Charles maintained this relaxed approach over the following days when he sought to allay the Commons' fears about popery by giving way to pressure for the execution of a Catholic priest and promising the dismissal of the controversial papal envoy, Rossetti. On

---

[70] Russell, *Fall of the British Monarchies*, pp. 244–5, 249–52; HMC, *De L'Isle and Dudley*, vol. 6, p. 368.

[71] HMC, *De L'Isle and Dudley*, vol. 6, pp. 367–9. Temple was, perhaps, a little too willing to accept Jermyn's own estimation of his influence.

[72] *LJ*, vol. 4, p. 142.

29 January he also made the first of the predicted bridge appointments, naming Oliver St John as solicitor-general.[73]

The high point for settlement came in mid-February. On the 16th he finally assented to the Triennial Act. According to the Venetian ambassador, at the last moment he lost his nerve and responded angrily when a parliamentary delegation tried to hurry him up; but, after thinking long and hard he eventually 'yielded to necessity' and agreed. This produced a great outburst of national rejoicing that promised to carry all before it.[74] Charles delivered his assent in another gracious speech in which he reminded the two houses that he had just given up one of 'the fairest flowers' of the prerogative and asked that they now think of providing for the kingdom's needs and his own. The Commons responded by giving a second reading to a bill for the queen's jointure, 'to express some part of our thankfulness'. Three days later Charles took things a stage further and appointed seven new privy councillors, including Bedford and Saye. Again, however, he had second thoughts and, according to Robert Baillie, the Scots commentator, 'bitterly rejected' the whole scheme until 'the marquis by his wisdom brought him unto it'.[75] Charles's misgivings seem to have reflected his state of mind. These were concessions he bitterly resented having to make, but he was enough of a realist to recognise that he had no choice. Now, at last, it seemed that the momentum Hamilton had been striving so hard to achieve was taking effect. However, within a few days the whole process fell apart.

A series of awkward issues surfaced simultaneously. Questions about whether the queen should be allowed to keep her Catholic servants and what to do about the Irish popish army cropped up again and seemed no nearer to being resolved; and the possibility of a compromise over Strafford, which would involve sequestering him from his offices without actually impeaching him, was apparently sunk when Charles insisted on appearing in the Lords to applaud his defence against the Commons charges.[76] However, these were issues that could be talked through and, in time,

---

[73] Russell, *Fall of the British Monarchies*, pp. 258–61.

[74] *CSP Ven. 1640–2*, pp. 126–7.

[75] Gardiner, *History of England*, vol. 9, pp. 290–1; Russell, *Fall of the British Monarchies*, p. 263. This was confirmed by Temple: HMC, *De L'Isle and Dudley*, vol. 6, p. 387.

[76] Russell, *Fall of the British Monarchies*, pp. 265–7; Gardiner, *History of England*, vol. 9, p. 296.

perhaps, resolved. The real body blow for settlement came on 24 February when the Scots commissioners issued a paper declaring their determination to see episcopacy abolished in England and justice done to Strafford. Their main objective was to force Bedford and his friends to choose sides. The Scots had become alarmed at the ease with which they appeared to be drawing closer to the king and wanted to push them into making some sort of statement of intent. This was the opportunity Charles had been waiting for and he played it for all it was worth. He responded to the Scottish paper with a display of righteous indignation, threatening to withdraw their safe conduct on the grounds that they had violated their role as treaty commissioners. He then summoned a meeting of the English commissioners and vented his anger in an effort to drive a wedge between them and their Scots counterparts. Finally Edward Hyde, presumably acting with royal encouragement, raised the issue of the commissioners' paper in the House of Commons on 27 February. The Scots' friends were divided between those willing to pledge their continuing support openly and those who maintained a diplomatic silence; but it was clear that none was prepared to abandon their alliance. This was not the result Charles had been hoping for, but at least it clarified his position. His principal aim in making the bridge appointments and concessions had been to detach Bedford and his friends from the Scots, at least on the two issues that mattered most to him, Strafford and episcopacy. It was now obvious that this was not going to happen and this led to an immediate change of policy. 'Probably within a few hours', Russell suggests, he decided to abandon the pursuit of settlement and concentrate on building a royalist party.[77]

There was plenty of material with which to do this. During January and February the anti-Scots feeling on which Charles had been banking in 1640 began to develop a critical mass. Hostility to the occupation of the northern shires and the charges of £850 a day to maintain the Scots army was becoming pronounced.[78] At the same time, many MPs were becoming alarmed about Scottish backing for the abolition of episcopacy. This was the most divisive issue of the early stages of the Long Parliament. Differences had been apparent when the Commons first discussed the

---

[77] Russell, *Fall of the British Monarchies*, pp. 268–72; Stevenson, *The Scottish Revolution*, pp. 218–19.

[78] Russell, *Fall of the British Monarchies*, p. 170; Gardiner, *History of England*, vol. 9, p. 294.

London 'root and branch' petition in December 1640, and by the time of the debate on 8–9 February 1641 these were clearly out in the open. The Scots allies made a concerted effort to push the programme forward with more petitions. Several MPs, like Rudyerd, tried to steer a middle course by proposing modified episcopacy. But the most striking feature of the debate was a sustained counter-attack by supporters of the bishops. This was led by George Digby, the earl of Bristol's son, who began by denouncing the original London petition as the product of 'tumultuous assemblies of the people', then warned of the dangers of entertaining appeals against 'the law established', and finally raising the spectre of a bishop in every diocese being replaced by a Presbyterian 'pope' in every parish. He was supported by Hyde, Falkland and Sir John Strangeways, who articulated the worry in the minds of many supporters of episcopacy that 'if we make a parity in the church we must come to a parity in the commonwealth'.[79] Anti-Scots feeling was beginning to merge with long-standing fears of popularity.

This was a constituency that Charles was well qualified to speak to. Even while he was being conciliatory he had continued to warn of the dangers of the multitude. His 23 January speech harked back to some of his favourite themes of the late 1620s, reminding MPs that 'some men . . . will put no difference betwixt reformation and alteration of government: hence it comes that divine service is irreverently interrupted, petitions tumultuously given and much of my revenue detained or disputed'. The Venetian ambassador also reported that behind the scenes he was warning of the dangers of the Triennial Act. If passed it would strike such a blow against royal authority that it might encourage 'the people' to shake off 'the yoke of monarchy' and 'afterwards apply themselves to abase the nobility also and reduce the government of the realm to a complete democracy'.[80] Over the following months this sort of alarmism became a prominent theme of royal rhetoric and propaganda.

---

[79] Russell, *Fall of the British Monarchies*, pp. 181–2, 192–3; Gardiner, *History of England*, vol. 9, 276–89.

[80] *LJ*, vol. 4, p. 142; *CSP Ven. 1640–2*, p. 11. Charles was not the only one experiencing misgivings. Edward Nicholas who, although still only clerk of the council, was working his way into an increasingly important advisory role drafted a response to the proposal to abolish wardship which highlighted the dangers of disinheriting the crown and encouraging puritan 'fanatics'. These were arguments that Charles could readily appreciate: Russell, *Fall of the British Monarchies*, pp. 253–4; see also the comments by Peter Lake, 'Review article on Russell', p. 177.

Meanwhile, the work of building a royal party was proceeding apace. Bristol, promoted to the council with the bridge appointments, emerged as a key royal adviser and recognised that now was the moment to try to seize the initiative in dealings with the Scots. From the beginning of March he was pressing for the Scots to set down all their remaining demands at once since the kingdom could no longer support the charges they imposed. If this motion succeeded it would remove the Scots from the English political scene; if it failed it would still assist the build-up of anti-Scots feeling. At the same time there were the beginnings of a concerted attempt to exploit the issue of episcopacy for the king. Sir Thomas Aston, with royal encouragement, drew up an anti-Presbyterian petition from Cheshire and at the end of February presented it to the Lords.[81] This was the start of an effort to mobilise support for bishops in the localities and also prompted a crown initiative in support of Ussher's scheme for modified episcopacy, which was intended to further marginalise supporters of 'root and branch'. There was also a significant change of mood at court. On 3 March Hamilton, the chief architect of settlement, suddenly found himself facing charges in the Commons. The organisers of this were said to be Arundel and Berkshire, two of the most hardline anti-Scots remaining on the council, and Strafford, who even from the Tower remained capable of striking at his enemies; but none of them would have dared to move without the expectation of backing from the king. This cooling towards the man who less than two weeks earlier had been seen as his most influential adviser was perhaps the most significant political event of the spring of 1641. It is not easy to explain. Hamilton had plenty of enemies at court who were quick to draw attention to his close links with the Scots party. There were also rumours that he and Secretary Vane had been plotting against Strafford. But perhaps the most significant factor was the disjunction between his views and those of the king. As in 1638, he found that once his recommendations no longer fitted the king's perception of the situation, he could be quickly cast aside.[82] This opened the way for the king to listen to more partisan, less consensual sources of advice, with what turned out to be disastrous consequences.

---

[81] Russell, *Fall of the British Monarchies*, p. 199; P.G. Lake, 'Puritans, popularity and petitions: local politics in national context, Cheshire, 1641', in Cogswell, Cust and Lake eds, *Politics, Religion and Popularity*, pp. 277–82.

[82] Donald, *An Uncounselled King*, pp. 289–90; Scally, 'The political career of Hamilton', pp. 298–304.

At this point, however, the king had largely regained the initiative and the situation seemed set fair. 'The likeliest resolution of the crisis', Russell has observed, 'was no longer either settlement or civil war, but the same result parliaments normally produced: a dissolution leaving the king in sole possession of the stage and therefore able to recover from many of the losses he had suffered during the parliament.'[83] That this did not happen was due to a display of political ineptitude which, even by Charles's standards, was spectacular.

Charles's major preoccupation from March to May 1641 was to save Strafford. The lord deputy's impeachment opened on 22 March, with the Commons' managers presenting a series of 28 articles that portrayed him as a classic proponent of arbitrary government. The majority of the charges related to his rule of Ireland, which Pym and his allies saw as a pilot scheme for the government of England. There were also several which rehearsed long-standing causes of friction between crown and subject: for example, the charge that he advised the king to 'break' parliament and raise money 'by ways of force and power', which harked back to issues raised by the forced loan. And, of course, there was the immediate concern about the Irish army which, it was alleged, Strafford intended to bring over to subdue England. If the Commons could make these charges stick, and secure the lord deputy's conviction for treason, this would provide a powerful demonstration that the authoritarian approaches and policies he symbolised were no longer permissible.[84]

Charles could have taken much of the force out of their attack by making concessions, but this was something he deliberately chose not to do. He resisted repeated parliamentary requests to disband the Irish army, even though at the start of May he was forced to do it anyway because of lack of cash. He also refused to accede to suggestions that Strafford be allowed to retire from office. The king's mind was fixed on the idea that the lord deputy should answer his accusers and vindicate himself and his policies.[85] In this he was driven partly by his sense of honour which, as on earlier occasions, persuaded him to stand by a minister he felt had served him

---

[83] Russell, *Fall of the British Monarchies*, p. 272.

[84] Ibid., pp. 281–6; Lake, 'Review article on Russell', pp. 179–80.

[85] Gardiner, *History of England*, vol. 9, p. 323; Russell, *Fall of the British Monarchies*, p. 285.

loyally. When it became clear that Strafford would be forced out of office Charles wrote to him to apologise for 'a very mean reward from a master to so faithful and able a servant' and declared he could not satisfy himself 'in honour or conscience without assuring you . . . that upon the word of a king you shall not suffer in life, honour or fortune'.[86] More than this, owever, the king was determined not to disown the policies that Strafford symbolised. He knew very well that what was taking place was essentially a power struggle in which the coalition ranged against the lord deputy, which included a majority of his own councillors, was seeking to outlaw a style of politics based on authoritarian use of the royal prerogative. The object aimed at was himself as much as his minister. By refusing to give up either Strafford or the Irish army, which he clung to as one of the few remaining instruments of coercion at his disposal, he was signalling his determination to keep open the option of employing these methods when he considered it appropriate and legitimate. This intransigence was what, more than anything, sealed the lord deputy's fate.[87] As Russell has pointed out, it raised the stakes significantly and made it more or less impossible for the Commons to settle for anything less than the death penalty.[88]

The king's inflexible stance need not have been disastrous, however. There were indications that as long as he was prepared to be patient the political advantage might continue to move in his direction. On 10 April, in response to frustration at the slow progress of the case and the effectiveness of Strafford's defence, a bill of attainder was introduced in the Commons which simply enacted that he was guilty as charged and therefore liable to execution for treason. This high-handed procedure did not command universal support. Several MPs were alarmed about the morality of a measure which, as Digby pointed out on 21 April, was tantamount to judicial murder. It also seemed very unlikely that the bill would pass the Lords where peers had already expressed their misgivings over the prosecution case.[89] In addition, there was growing concern about the threat

---

[86] *Letters of Charles I*, p. 115.

[87] Lake, 'Review article on Russell', pp. 179–80.

[88] Russell, *Fall of the British Monarchies*, pp. 208, 221.

[89] Gardiner, *History of England*, vol. 9, pp. 330–41; A. Fletcher, *The Outbreak of the English Civil War*, 1981, pp. 9–13.

from 'the multitude', as crowds of Londoners gathered round the parliament house and intimidated MPs with calls for Strafford's execution. By the end of April there were signs that the nascent royalist party was growing in strength. At the same time the Bedford/Pym group were making new overtures for accommodation based on sparing Strafford's life in return for the king agreeing to his dismissal.[90] There was even a fresh spate of rumours about bridge appointments, although this time with the suggestion that these were aimed at buying off and dividing Charles's enemies rather than promoting settlement. The sudden resignation of Cottington from the mastership of the wards on 27 April appeared to be intended to allow Charles to offer the post to Lord Saye, with the aim of setting him at odds with Bedford and Pym who had plans to abolish wardship as part of their financial reform.[91] Had Charles been prepared to bide his time there seemed every prospect that, although he might lose his minister, he could still gain the political advantage. However, this strategy was suddenly blown apart on 3 May with the revelations about the Army Plot.

Historians have generally been sceptical about the reality of a plot that was supposed to involve the king's northern army marching on London, seizing the Tower, releasing Strafford and dissolving parliament. However, Conrad Russell has demonstrated that this was precisely what was envisaged and, moreover, that Charles was involved from first to last. The Army Plot was originally two plots. The first, born of the sense of frustration at lack of funding for the army still billeted in Yorkshire, involved petitioning parliament to agree to regular pay, removing the threat to disband the Irish army, preserving episcopacy and restoring the king's finances. The manager of this scheme was Henry Percy, master of the prince's horse and an army officer with a seat in the Commons. But Charles was a party to it throughout and later defended the army's right to petition parliament in this way. The second, far more explosive, scheme, devised by the queen's counsellor, Henry Jermyn, and the courtier-poet, Sir John Suckling, was to march the army south and free Strafford. On 29 March Charles arranged a meeting of the two groups of plotters, apparently with the intention

---

[90] Russell, *Fall of the British Monarchies*, pp. 287–90; Gardiner, *History of England*, vol. 9, pp. 340–1.

[91] Russell, *Fall of the British Monarchies*, p. 289.

of bringing the schemes together; but the second plot was dropped after a meeting of officers in Yorkshire on 3 April showed that it had little support within the army. Suckling, however, continued with a plan to recruit mercenaries in London and raised a force of a hundred men under a Captain Billingsley. On 3 May, acting on Charles's orders, Billingsley attempted to occupy the Tower and procure Strafford's escape. The House of Lords was alerted and immediately sent the earl of Newport, master of the ordinance, to defend the Tower. They then dispatched a high-powered deputation to the king which, with some difficulty, persuaded him to back down and discharge Billingsley from his commission. Later statements by those involved implied that the king had drawn a line at getting involved in what was in effect a military coup. But Russell's investigation suggests otherwise. It seems to have been lack of support in the army, rather than any scruples about legality, that caused him to back off. He appears to have recognised that direct military action against his parliament was unconstitutional, and therefore carried a high degree of political risk. But this did not mean he regarded it as illegitimate and, given what he perceived to be the traitorous and rebellious intentions of his enemies, he evidently saw his actions as morally justified.[92]

Two other aspects of the plot are particularly intriguing. The first is the involvement of the queen and her entourage. The principal conspirators were among her closest confidants: Henry Jermyn was her master of horse and principal adviser, while Percy and George Goring, who undertook to fortify Portsmouth as a safe haven for her, were prominent among her courtiers. She herself appears to have been briefed on what was happening throughout and probably did much to reinforce Charles's willingness to pursue the military option.[93] This was consistent with her record of political action at court. She was an inveterate plotter who loathed the House of Commons and had little respect for the constitutional constraints that were recognised by most of the politicians around Charles. During the winter of 1640–1 she had been the intermediary for negotiations with the papacy,

---

[92] C.S.R. Russell, 'The First Army Plot of 1641', in *Unrevolutionary England*, pp. 281–95.

[93] Hibbard, 'Queen consort', pp. 406, 408–9, 412, 413; Russell, 'Army Plot', pp. 285, 287–8. Jermyn's involvement a few weeks after he had been loudly proclaiming his role in trying to promote settlement was a particularly significant indication of the change of mood at court: HMC, *De L'Isle and Dudley*, vol. 6, pp. 367, 382.

which were intended to provide Charles with the money to raise a mercenary force, and in February she sent an envoy to France to request assistance against the parliament.[94] In the past she had had relatively little impact on politics because of her husband's capacity to separate his decision-making from his personal affections. But by early 1641 this was changing, as she herself became an issue because of the attention directed to popish plotting and Catholic courtiers. Charles was seriously concerned that the Commons would not stop at her servants and would attack her. The queen became very adept at exploiting this, employing a form of moral blackmail in which she warned that she would have to flee abroad for her safety if Charles did not display the backbone and resolution needed to protect her.[95] The king now had to take much greater account of her advice, and demonstrate by his actions that he was doing so. As a result, she became a focus for hardline, anti-puritan/anti-parliament elements at court who wished him to solve his difficulties by forceful, direct action. The Army Plot is the first clear example of this, but in the succeeding months there were others.

The other intriguing aspect of the plot was Charles's determination to carry on once it had been discovered. As early as 6 April the Commons signalled their awareness that something was going on by passing a resolution that anyone moving the army without the permission of both king and parliament should be 'taken for enemies to king and state'. If the main objective was to carry out a military coup this makes Charles's persistence hard to understand, since security and surprise were crucial requirements for success. However, the indications are that, for his purposes, discovery did not matter; indeed he seems to have positively welcomed it, encouraging Goring to leak details to the earl of Newport. This has prompted Russell to suggest that the principal aim was to secure compliance with his ends largely through the threat of force rather than force itself.[96] It was part of a repeated pattern, an approach he had used during the Scottish negotiations of 1638, and was to use again with the attempt on the five members and the mobilisation for civil war in the summer of 1642. The problem was that

---

[94] Gardiner, *History of England*, vol. 9, pp. 309–10; Russell, *Fall of the British Monarchies*, pp. 248, 259, 266.

[95] Russell, *Fall of the British Monarchies*, p. 259.

[96] Russell, 'Army Plot', pp. 296–7.

once his bluff was called it became necessary to carry out the threat – and in circumstances that were much more hazardous because his opponents had been forewarned. It was a dangerous tactic that repeatedly backfired.

The effect of the Army Plot was to destroy completely the political advantage that the king had been accruing during March and April. Revelations about Billingsley's attempt to seize the Tower, and other details of the plot, created a frenetic atmosphere in parliament during the early days of May and led to the passage of several measures that severely damaged the king's chances of reimposing his authority. The Commons desperately sought ways of expressing their abhorrence and safeguarding themselves against a coup, and came up with the Protestation. This was an oath of association – based on Elizabethan precedent, and not dissimilar to the National Covenant – which bound those who took it to defend king, parliament, the Protestant religion and laws and liberties 'against all popery and popish innovations'. It was to be a powerful device for rallying support for parliament in later months; however, perhaps its most damaging consequence was to weave together the growing fears of popish plots with a new sense of alarm about the intentions of the king and his advisers. As Russell has observed, 'the code word for "royal plot" became "popish plot"' which was to do much to destroy any residual trust in the king.[97] During the same period the Commons also passed a bill providing that the existing parliament should not be dissolved without its own consent, which was severely to restrict the king's freedom of action. The Lords, recognising that in this crisis Charles could not be relied on to act responsibly, went even further and for a few days effectively took over the reins of government. When he failed to apprehend the plotters they issued a proclamation to arrest them in his name. They also asked him to change various lord lieutenancies and call out the militia to secure Portsmouth. One can see in this the furtherance of a process that began with the actions of the Great Council of Peers in 1640 and culminated in the assumption of military authority in the Militia Ordinance of 1642. Privy councillors and peers were coming to act as if the king was incapacitated.[98]

---

[97] Ibid., pp. 300–1; Russell, *Fall of the British Monarchies*, pp. 293–5; Gardiner, *History of England*, vol. 9, pp. 350–4.

[98] Gardiner, *History of England*, vol. 9, pp. 359–61; Russell, *Fall of the British Monarchies*, p. 298; Russell, *Causes of the Civil War*, p. 209.

The working out of this process lay in the future. In the short-term the most important effect of Charles's plotting was to sweep away his moderate support and seal Strafford's fate. The bill of attainder reached the Lords on 4 May, the day after the revelations about the plot and the passage of the Protestation Oath. This served to frighten off much of the earl's potential support. Attendance dropped from 70 to around 45, with most of the absentees apparently being Catholic peers alarmed at the prospect of having to take the oath or courtiers facing conflicting pressures from the king and public opinion. The bill passed its third reading, leaving Charles to face an uncomfortable decision about whether to give his assent over the weekend on 8–9 May.[99]

He came under immense pressure. The Lords sent a deputation, led by Hamilton and Bristol, urging him to approve the bill promptly. He received similar advice from his privy council. At the same time crowds of Londoners, calling for Strafford's blood, besieged him and his family in the palace at Whitehall. But political pressure was not the only consideration he had to weigh. Charles himself regarded the decision as very much a test of personal good faith and went through agonies wrestling with his conscience. In his final plea to the two houses to spare Strafford, he had made a good deal of this, declaring 'in my conscience I cannot condemn him of high treason' and urging them to 'find a way to satisfy justice and your own fears and not to press upon my conscience'.[100] Strafford attempted to release him from his dilemma by urging him to agree to the passage of the bill as the best means of healing the division between king and people.[101] But Charles was clearly still uneasy on the Sunday when he summoned four of the bishops for advice about how to square his conscience. Eventually he gave his assent at nine in the evening, telling his privy councillors that if it had just been a matter of the safety of his own person 'I would gladly venture it to save my Lord Strafford's life; but seeing my wife, children and all my kingdom are concerned in it I am forced to give way'.[102] It was a decision he never ceased to regret. He ascribed

[99] Russell, *Fall of the British Monarchies*, pp. 296–7.

[100] Rushworth, vol. 4, p. 239; Sharpe, 'Conscience and public duty', p. 657.

[101] Gardiner, *History of England*, vol. 9, pp. 361–2.

[102] Ibid., pp. 366–71.

all his later misfortunes to his sin in agreeing to it and firmly resolved to make amends. The psychological impact of his surrender was apparent in a letter he wrote to Hamilton a few months into the civil war.

I have set up my rest upon the justice of my cause being resolved that no extremity or misfortune shall make me yield; for I will either be a glorious king or a patient martyr . . . the failing to one friend has, indeed, gone very near me, wherefore I am resolved that no consideration whatsoever shall ever make me do the like. Upon this ground I am certain that God has either so totally forgiven me that he will still bless this good cause in my hands, or that all my punishment shall be in this world which, without performing what I have resolved, I cannot flatter myself will end here.[103]

The whole episode had a profound effect on his political stance from this point onwards. Unity and settlement were no longer the priority. He appears to have felt even more strongly than before that any compromise with his enemies could only bring down God's judgements. 'Instead of convincing Charles that he must cooperate with his people', Russell has concluded, 'the execution, by pressing him beyond his conscience, convinced him that he must not do so.'[104]

The party leader

Conrad Russell has described the summer and early autumn of 1641 as 'the slow movement' of the political crisis, a time when the king 'was doing nothing in particular' and some of the earlier tension subsided.[105] This is true up to a point. Charles did adopt a lower profile in English politics and directed much of his attention to Scotland. As a result, Pym and the other political leaders in parliament had less to be anxious about and less to respond to. However, in one important respect it is misleading. Charles may not have been launching dramatic initiatives in England, but behind the scenes he was working hard at building a royalist party that could take on the junto and its Scottish allies. This was to accelerate the development of a style

---

[103] NAS, GD 406/1/167/1 and 2.

[104] Russell, *Fall of the British Monarchies*, p. 301.

[105] Ibid., pp. 303–4, 402–4.

of politics in which the king was no longer raised above the fray, but had entered combat as a party leader. For Charles, of course, this was not a new role. He had performed it with some panache at the time of 'the Blessed Revolution'. The difference now was that he was doing it as king rather than as Prince of Wales, within a political culture in which many of the governing clichés were about the monarch acting as the uniter of his people. This was to have enormously divisive consequences.

The political legacy of Strafford's execution and the Army Plot was uncertain. In some respects, Charles had been considerably weakened. He had conceded the act against dissolution which deprived him of what had long been one of his greatest political assets. He had also been forced to allow parliament to take control of some of his executive functions, thus encouraging the Lords, in particular, to see themselves as an alternative government in waiting. However, in neither case was the damage irreparable. It was possible to envisage a situation in which parliament might agree to dissolve itself. The nascent royalist party in the Commons was becoming increasingly vocal and effective, while MPs were wearying of attendance and anxious to escape the plague that broke out in London in August.[106] It was also probable that if Charles refrained from plotting and confined himself to responsible actions the pressure for further steps to curtail his authority would abate. In addition to this, from spring onwards, two of the most crucial elements in the political equation turned in his favour.

The first of these was the situation in Scotland. There were the first indications of a serious split in the Covenanters' ranks when the earl of Montrose and a group of discontented nobles approached Charles with a promise 'to maintain his honour, power and royal authority against all men' in return for assurances that he would safeguard their religion and liberties. Negotiations began on 3 March 1641 and, as Russell has pointed out, it is no coincidence that it was around this time that Charles abandoned the whole policy of bridging appointments. The division among his enemies opened up, for the first time, the possibility of pressuring the Covenanters from within Scotland and building his own Scottish party.[107]

---

[106] Russell, *Fall of the British Monarchies*, pp. 362–3; Fletcher, *Outbreak of the Civil War*, pp. 68–70.

[107] Russell, *Fall of the British Monarchies*, pp. 308–13; Stevenson, *The Scottish Revolution*, pp. 206–7; Russell, 'British problem', p. 238.

While this was happening, it was also becoming clear that the occupation of the northern counties was unsustainable. The Scots were thoroughly fed up with the cost and inconvenience of maintaining their army there, while their English allies now recognised that as long as Charles's army in the north remained intact it would be a standing temptation to plotting. From late May onwards there was a concerted effort on all sides to pay off the Scots and send the armies home. This released much of the coercive pressure that had hitherto been applied to Charles and allowed him a good deal more freedom in choosing which of the Commons' demands he would accede to and which he would fight.[108] It also widened the split between the Scots and their English allies which had become apparent in late February. The Scots no longer showed much interest in hanging around and trying to effect the decisive changes in the English church that had seemed so necessary earlier in the year. The common interests that had bound them to the junto subsided. With some skill, Charles moved to exploit these opportunities by anouncing in late April that he would journey to Scotland himself in order to oversee the final stages of the Treaty of London.[109] This put added pressure on the Covenanters to settle with him by holding over them the threat that if they did not he would start working with their local enemies. For the moment, the Scots were, in Russell's words, 'a spent force in English politics', which enormously weakened Pym and the junto.[110]

Charles's approach to politics during the summer continued to be based on the mixture of threat and concession. He was still tempted by the idea of resolving all his difficulties by a dramatic coup. This was apparent from the Second Army Plot which came to light in mid-June and involved inviting the army to march on London and petition the Commons to restore his prerogative. At the same time, however, he continued to make conciliatory gestures. He agreed to the bill for tonnage and poundage on 22 June which removed his right to collect duties without parliament's consent and conceded all his earlier claims over impositions. Then, on 5 July, he accepted the abolition of the courts of Star Chamber and High Commission, and at the same time invited parliament to support a new attempt to restore the

---

[108] Fletcher, *Outbreak of the Civil War*, pp. 21–2, 29, 32; Russell, *Fall of the British Monarchies*, pp. 303–5.

[109] Fletcher, *Outbreak of the Civil War*, pp. 42–3.

[110] Russell, *Fall of the British Monarchies*, p. 202.

Elector Palatine.[111] However, unlike the concessions earlier in the year, these measures were not accompanied by overtures to his political opponents. Rumours persisted throughout the summer that Pym and other members of the junto were about to be promoted to the key vacant offices of lord treasurer, chancellor of the exchequer and secretary of state; but when Charles did finally make some appointments, prior to departing for Scotland on 10 August, they were all of loyalists. Bristol, who had emerged as the leader of his party in the House of Lords, was made first gentleman of the bed-chamber, and the earl of Bath, Lord Dunsmore and the former Commons' leader, Lord Seymour, were promoted to the privy council.[112]

The abandonment of bridging appointments in part reflected the shifting balance of the king's inner circle. Hamilton was out of favour and increasingly suspect in the king's eyes because of links with the Covenanter leader Argyll; Sir Henry Vane, who because of his connection with the junto leadership, remained a key figure in any moves to settlement, still held his post as secretary of state, but had forfeited a good deal of credit with Charles since acting as a principal witness against Strafford; while Bedford, the one member of the junto who was on good personal terms with the king, died of smallpox in May.[113] In the absence of moderating influences, the mood at court hardened considerably.

During the summer, the duke of Lennox and Richmond replaced Hamilton as the most influential of Charles's courtiers, mainly because of his personal closeness to the king.[114] His political views are difficult to

---

[111] Gardiner, *History of England*, vol. 9, pp. 398–400, 404–5; *LJ*, vol. 4, p. 283; *CSP Dom. 1641–3*, pp. 44–5.

[112] *CSP Dom. 1641–3*, pp. 62–3; *CSP Ven. 1640–2*, p. 202; Fletcher, *Outbreak of the Civil War*, p. 45.

[113] Scally, 'The political career of Hamilton', pp. 304–7; Russell, *Fall of the British Monarchies*, p. 269.

[114] *CSP Dom. 1641–3*, p. 81; *Evelyn*, p. 789; *Nicholas*, pp. 8, 11. There are parallels with Charles's relationship with Hamilton. Richmond had been brought up in the royal household and, as a gentleman of the bedchamber, spent much of his time in the king's company. He also allowed himself to be guided by Charles in his marriage arrangements, in his case marrying Buckingham's surviving daughter; and he invariably expressed strong personal loyalty to the king, enhanced by the fact that he was his cousin and a fellow Stuart. However, Richmond was much less his own man than Hamilton, partly because he lacked the marquis's Calvinist religious convictions, but also because he was 12 years younger than Charles: D.L. Smith, *Constitutional Royalism and the Search for Settlement, c.1640–1649*, Cambridge, 1994, pp. 39–42; Clarendon, *Life*, vol. 1, pp. 222–3; Clarendon, *History*, vol. 2, p. 528.

ascertain, although it seems evident from the letters of his secretary Thomas Webb that at this stage he was not in favour of the king building bridges with political opponents.[115] There is also evidence, in the correspondence of secretary of state-designate Edward Nicholas, of a siege mentality developing among those close to Charles. Endymion Porter, who remained a central figure in the bedchamber, was very conscious of the threat posed by 'popularity'. He wrote to Nicholas from Scotland in September 1641 complaining of 'the subtle designs of gaining the popular opinion and weak executions for the upholding of monarchy'; and a few days later warned that if concessions to the Covenanters continued Charles's allies would 'repent that ever they showed themselves for the king, for the public applause opposes monarchy and I fear this island before it be long will be a theatre of distractions'.[116] This attitude no doubt fed the comments exchanged between courtiers that the king was not being resolute enough. Webb told Nicholas that it was a common view among royal attendants in Scotland that he 'might carry anything if he did not undo himself by yielding' and Nicholas responded by complaining that many found the king 'faint in his own cause'.[117] Russell has observed that 'party feeling' was reaching the point where it was becoming 'an important limit on Charles's freedom of manoeuvre'.[118] However, it should also be recognised that this was a situation largely of the king's own making. It was his repeatedly expressed concern about the threat from 'popularity' that had helped to create a climate in which such responses were invited and encouraged.

Another important element in the equation was the emergence of the queen as a political force. In the aftermath of the Army Plot she kept a relatively low profile, confining herself to intriguing with fellow Catholics and reminding Charles of the need to protect her against the fate of Strafford. She held a series of meetings with Count Rossetti, the papal nuncio, in which she promised that in return for a subsidy of £150 000 the king would grant more freedom for Catholics in England and Ireland and take steps to 'extirpate' the puritans. Charles was generally willing to follow

---

[115] *Nicholas*, pp. 39, 49, 51.

[116] Ibid., pp. 40, 45–6; Greenrod, 'Conceived to give dangerous counsel', pp. 97–101.

[117] *Nicholas*, pp. 49, 51.

[118] Russell, *Fall of the British Monarchies*, p. 405.

her lead in this area. At her instigation, he reprimanded Secretary Vane for persecuting her chaplain, Father Philip. He also attended a meeting that she arranged with Rossetti, although this yielded no firm committments on either side.[119] Beyond these areas, however, the queen's influence remained limited. This changed in August with the king's departure for Scotland. While he was away he bypassed the privy council – which was increasingly divided and unable to offer a clear lead – and left his wife in charge of making the final decisions on everything from a Declaration about the Commons' attempts to block a General Pardon to his ceremonial entry into London.[120] Henrietta Maria clearly relished the role, and she emerges in this period as a self-confident, even domineering, figure with a clear sense of what she wanted the king to do and how he should do it. The Venetian ambassador, who was receiving much of his information from inside her court at Oatlands, presented a picture similar to that which emerges from her correspondence with Charles in 1642 – of a Lady Macbeth figure constantly prodding forward a husband whom she believed to be irresolute.[121] She was said to be determined that he should act firmly and forcefully, convinced that this would 'encourage those . . . who although at heart supporters of his Majesty's greatness have not had the courage to declare themselves hitherto . . .'[122] She also continued to be drawn to the idea that he could solve all his problems through a military coup, suggesting as much, for example, in her discussions with the French ambassador in October.[123]

Charles's reaction to his wife's aggressive prompting is not easy to discern because most of their letters from this period are not extant. He was certainly more inhibited than she was by a sense of the need to observe constitutional proprieties; but at the same time he seems to have been conscious of the charge that he was not being sufficiently resolute. This may

---

[119] Hibbard, *Charles I and the Popish Plot*, pp. 210–11; *CSP Ven. 1640–2*, pp. 189–92; C. Perceval-Maxwell, *The Outbreak of the Irish Rebellion of 1641*, Dublin, 1994, pp. 196–7.

[120] Fletcher, *Outbreak of the Civil War*, pp. 156–7; *Evelyn*, pp. 752–3, 756–7, 765, 769–70, 781, 783, 785, 789–90.

[121] *CSP Ven. 1640–2*, pp. 210, 229, 232. For a perceptive discussion of the queen's Lady Macbeth role, see Russell, *Causes of the Civil War*, pp. 204–7.

[122] *CSP Ven. 1640–2*, p. 208.

[123] Gardiner, *History of England*, vol. 10, p. 42.

account for the notably 'hawkish' tone of one letter that we do know about, a dispatch sent soon after his arrival in Scotland that strongly hinted at the opportunities offered by the Scots pledge to maintain an army of 5 000 infantry and 1 000 cavalry to be used 'whenever and against whomsoever may best suit his convenience'.[124] It would appear that Charles's readiness to go on contemplating the option of a military coup had at least something to do with his desire to placate his wife. Accepting her as his principal political adviser was not a recipe for a quiet life, which was one of the main reasons why he had delayed doing it for so long. Nonetheless, by the autumn of 1641 she was firmly installed in this role.

As before, however, Charles himself remained the final arbiter of policy. The indications are that in crucial areas his attitudes were hardening, even if they were being voiced less openly. He had made considerable concessions during 1641, accepting the principle that he could not raise taxes without parliamentary consent, and passing the Triennial Act and the act against dissolving parliament. He had even, under enormous pressure, allowed parliament to impeach his principal minister. However, there were two issues on which he was determined not to budge. The first of these was episcopacy. When, in October, he heard from England that it was expected that he would agree to Presbyterianise the church on his return, he immediately instructed Nicholas 'to assure all my servants there that I am constant for the doctrine and discipline of the Church of England as it was established by Queen Elis and my father and resolve (by the grace of God) to live and die in the maintenance of it'.[125] This was a principle to which he was absolutely committed, as a matter of conscience. His other priority was to preserve his right to choose his own ministers and prevent more of them going the way of Strafford. As far as he was concerned, this was one of the main powers that distinguished him from 'a duke of Venice'. It touched deeply on his sense of honour and self-esteem, which meant that it took precedence over everything except his duty to God. Thus, when Nicholas urged him to return to England as quickly as possible and leave his Scottish supporters to fend for themselves, for once he refused to take his advice, insisting that 'I miss somewhat in point of honour if they all

---

[124] *CSP Ven. 1640–2*, p. 208; Gardiner, *History of England*, vol. 10, p. 7.

[125] *Evelyn*, p. 772.

be not relieved before I go hence.' And when Nicholas warned him that the Commons' leaders were planning to force him to allow parliamentary interference in appointments, he immediately urged him 'to advise with some of my best servants there how this may be prevented, for I assure you that I do not mean to grant it'.[126]

Such evidence as there is suggests that Charles continued to interpret the actions of opponents as part of a 'popular' challenge to monarchical authority. One of the most revealing documents from the summer months of 1641 is the petition drawn up for presentation by the army which Charles himself read and approved.[127] This took up the familiar refrain that the king had done everything in his power to remedy the just grievances of his people, but that 'there are certain persons, stirring and practical, who . . . remain as yet unsatisfied and mutinous as ever . . . still attempting new diminutions of your majesties just regalities . . .' 'Those ill-affected persons are backed in their violence by the multitude and the power of raising tumults . . . thousands flock at their call and beset the parliament and Whitehall itself . . .' The petition therefore called on parliament to defeat 'these persons malignity and . . . the licentiousness of those multitudes that follow them . . . by punishing the ringleaders . . .' It was a powerful rhetoric which could be applied equally to puritan schismatics, the crowds thronging the London streets and anyone else who appeared to be threatening order; and, of course, it contained clear indications of a remedy. If the opposition was led by a small clique of ill-affected, anti-monarchical extremists then, as with the Covenanter rebellion, the logical course of action was to mobilise 'the better sort' and destroy the ringleaders. This was to be the principle on which Charles operated during the summer and autumn.

The raw material out of which he was able to build support was largely provided by a backlash against Pym and his allies. They were in a much less advantageous position than earlier in the year. The impending withdrawal of the Scots army had deprived them of the main means of pressuring Charles into accepting further reforms. There was also a growing rift with the Covenanter leadership, summed up in early August when the Commons asked the Scots negotiators in London to help in persuading the king to

---

[126] Ibid., p. 768.

[127] Clarendon, *History*, vol. 1, pp. 323–5. For the evidence of Charles's involvement, see *LJ*, vol. 4, p. 667.

delay his trip north and were refused point-blank. Furthermore, Pym had to contend with the emergence of an increasingly vocal and effective royalist party in the Commons, organised by Sir John Culpepper, Sir Edward Hyde and Viscount Falkland. It was not yet large enough to command a majority, but it restricted his freedom of action and subjected his policies to searching criticism.[128] The junto was therefore in an altogether more exposed and difficult position. They had little choice but to press ahead with reform if they were to make the world safe for themselves and prevent a reversion to the policies of the 1630s; but in doing so they risked alienating the public goodwill they had enjoyed earlier in the year.

Following the Army Plot the junto leaders recognised that a negotiated settlement with the king was no longer a realistic option. They therefore set out, as Russell puts it, 'to Merovingianize Charles, leaving him as a figurehead while real power remained with the council and the great officers'.[129] They were not seeking parliamentary sovereignty, but the more traditional solution of taking power out of the king's hands and entrusting it to his leading nobles. The first move in this direction came in mid-June in response to the Second Army Plot and the alarming prospect of the king passing through the two armies on his journey to Scotland. It took the form of the Ten Propositions, a set of proposals for discussion with Charles, framed by the Commons and agreed to by the Lords. The most important aimed at persuading the king to remove 'evil counsellors' and appoint only such 'as his people and parliament may have just cause to confide in'. It was accompanied by measures to disband the armies before Charles headed north, purge the queen's court of Catholics and put the defence of the kingdom in the hands of 'good lord lieutenants and deputy lieutenants'.[130] This last proposal anticipated the Militia Ordinance of 1642 and showed that Pym and his allies were already thinking of how to remove control of military force from Charles's hands.

Measures to limit the king's executive authority were generally acceptable in the aftermath of the Army Plot; but in other respects the actions

---

[128] Russell, *Fall of the British Monarchies*, pp. 344–5, 368–9; Gardiner, *History of England*, vol. 9, pp. 415–16.

[129] Russell, *Fall of the British Monarchies*, p. 333.

[130] *Constitutional Documents*, pp. 163–6.

of Pym and the junto were beginning to provoke a backlash. The new poll tax levied by the Commons to pay for the disbanding of the two armies was not popular. Neither was the junto's religious policy which combined measures to abolish the 'superstition' of the Laudian church with continuing efforts to eradicate episcopacy. The Commons' order of 8 September, which sanctioned the pulling down of altar rails and the destruction of images, was particularly controversial, since it appeared to offer a licence to sectaries to dismantle divine service and smash up church interiors.[131] With the Scots out of the way, Pym and his colleagues were increasingly targeted for blame. Stories of their personal ambition and arrogance were circulating in newsletters and the epithet 'King Pym' was in general use by October.[132] 'For the first time', Conrad Russell concludes, the actions taken by a junto-led House of Commons 'were making it possible to turn the rule of law into an effective royalist slogan'.[133]

The reaction against the junto was initially most evident in the House of Lords. There was a significant minority of godly peers, led by Pym's allies, Brooke and Saye, who tended to vote with the Commons; however, the majority were veering towards Charles, as increasingly he came to appear the defender of the *status quo*. The revelations surrounding the Army Plot

---

[131] Russell, *Fall of the British Monarchies*, p. 402; Gardiner, *History of England*, vol. 10, p. 9; Fletcher, *Outbreak of the Civil War*, pp. 115–20.

[132] Fletcher, *Outbreak of the Civil War*, pp. 88–9; Russell, *Fall of the British Monarchies*, p. 404.

[133] Russell, *Fall of the British Monarchies*, p. 371. These various sources of hostility were brought together in a facetious list of 'Queries to be decided by a committee of the House of Commons', thought to be the work of the anti-Calvinist master of St John's, Cambridge, Dr Beale. Was it right, the author asked, that the church should be treated 'like a watch, that may be taken to pieces and set together again'; and were ministers still to be allowed to preach obedience and respect for the Scriptures? Were there 'any laws, divine or human [which] allow subjects to keep an army of strangers to master their king' and would 'statutes enforced upon the king with the awe of an army . . . be of any force hereafter?' Referring to the Protestation Oath, which was circulating round the country, he asked if subjects had the right to 'impose an oath upon their fellow subjects without the king' and was it 'not to be expected that the Protestation will raise a sedition in pure zeal?' Finally, was it the case that 'subjects must rule the king or the king the subjects?' This was, of course, a travesty of the junto's policies, but it was circulating widely in August and the Commons took it sufficiently seriously to order that it be publicly burned: *CSP Dom. 1641–3*, p. 113; Fletcher, *Outbreak of the Civil War*, pp. 88–9; *The Journal of Sir Simonds D'Ewes from the First Recess of the Long Parliament to the Withdrawal of Charles I from London*, ed. W.H. Coates, New Haven, 1942, pp. 326–7.

had persuaded them to support the Ten Propositions; but they were not prepared to give their assent to further actions which threatened to undermine order or divide the political nation. When, in May, the Commons tried to push through a bill excluding bishops from sitting in the Lords, they vigorously resisted and sought to shift the focus on to popular disorder by requesting a conference about tumultuous petitioning. And when, in July, the lower house tried to make the Protestation Oath compulsory, they again resisted, on the grounds that it would exclude those who had qualms about taking it – like Catholic peers – from holding office or sitting in parliament. The biggest rift came over the Commons' Order of 8 September, which the Lords interpreted as a calculated snub, as well as an invitation to further disorder. They responded immediately by publishing their own order of 16 January 1641, which demanded that divine service be performed according to law and enjoined punishment on 'all such as shall disturb that wholesome order'.[134]

The peers' determination to stand as the self-appointed guardians of the political middle ground held out the possibility during the summer months of building a new coalition that might rally moderate opinion and act as the catalyst for settlement. Achieving this probably depended on Charles reaching an agreement with the Covenanters and also adopting some of the more conciliatory policies on offer, such as promoting Archbishop Ussher's programme for 'modified' episcopacy, or stepping up efforts to restore the Elector Palatine. But, given the hints that the king was dropping, there seemed no reason why such things should not happen and in some quarters there was considerable optimism. Secretary Vane, for example, was predicting in late August that the king's enthusiastic reception in Scotland heralded an end to their 'troublesome storms and tempests' and the onset of a 'peaceable calm' and 'happy union'.[135] Charles, however, had little commitment to such a vision. He wanted accommodation with the Scots and moderate support in England, but more out of a partisan desire to gain the upper hand on his enemies than any concern for reconciliation.

---

[134] Russell, *Fall of the British Monarchies*, pp. 330–1, 342, 370; Gardiner, *History of England*, vol. 9, pp. 413–14; vol. 10, pp. 14–17.

[135] Cited in C.S.R. Russell, 'The British background to the Irish Rebellion of 1641', in *Unrevolutionary England*, p. 263. See also letters from Bristol and Culpepper: *CSP Dom. 1641–3*, pp. 105–6; Russell, *Fall of the British Monarchies*, pp. 348–9.

From May onwards his energies were devoted almost wholly to building a royalist party, in both parliament and the country. The process was at its most visible in the House of Lords. As John Adamson has demonstrated, he worked closely with Nicholas to identify 11 lay peers, led by Bristol, who could be relied on to carry out royal instructions. In early October each was sent a letter declaring the king's recognition of their loyal service and ordering them to attend the opening of the new session on the 20th. Thereafter they received regular directives, with guidance on which issues to respond to and how to vote. There is also evidence that Nicholas approached William Juxon, bishop of London, and former lord treasurer, to organise between ten and fifteen of the bishops to act in a similar way.[136] Over the opening weeks of the autumn 1641 session this group of loyalists provided the nucleus of a royalist party that held the upper hand in the Lords.

Nicholas's correspondence over the autumn makes it clear that much of the guidance on political strategy was coming from himself and the queen; but Charles's own input was still considerable. Edward Hyde, later earl of Clarendon, has left an intriguing account of an interview with him which probably took place in late April or early May 1641.[137] Charles began by telling Hyde how he had 'heard from all hands how much he was beholden to him', then asked him what he thought of the prospects for the Commons passing a 'root and branch' bill. Hyde replied that he thought it could be prevented, whereupon Charles urged him that 'if you'll

---

[136] J.S.A. Adamson, 'Parliamentary management, men-of-business and the house of lords, 1640–1649', in C. Jones ed., *A Pillar of the Constitution: The House of Lords in British Politics, 1640–1784*, 1989, pp. 21–9; *Evelyn*, pp. 775, 778, 787.

[137] Clarendon, *Life*, vol. 1, pp. 92–4. There is some debate over when this happened. Russell opts for the late April/early May date, while Gardiner prefers June: Russell, *Fall of the British Monarchies* p. 289; Gardiner, *History of England*, vol. 9, pp. 387–8. I prefer Russell's dating because of Hyde's clear reference to being introduced to the king by Henry Percy who fled abroad on 5 May. I have made considerable use of Clarendon's *Life* in both this chapter and the next, conscious of the problems it presents as a source. As C.H. Firth pointed out, it was written in the late 1660s, without the assistance of the notes and contemporary accounts that Clarendon used for his *History*. It contains mistakes over detail and uncertainties over dating, and it was intended to vindicate Hyde's own conduct and demonstrate his perspicacity as a royal councillor. In spite of these shortcomings, however, I would argue that in its recollection of what was said in meetings with the king – which would have been inherently memorable occasions for Hyde – it is likely to be as reliable as most contemporary politicians describing such encounters: C.H. Firth, 'Clarendon's "History of the Rebellion". Part II – The "Life" of Himself', *EHR*, vol. xix, 1904, pp. 246–62.

look to it that they do not carry it before I go for Scotland . . . I will undertake for the church after that time'.[138] This was the first occasion on which Hyde had met the king face to face, and it showed Charles making very effective use of an ability to inspire loyalty through personal contact. It also demonstrated his capacity to think ahead and plan a political campaign.

Both qualities were on display on other occasions. The king was very adept at encouraging subordinates with expressions of personal interest, like the assurances relayed to the Cheshire loyalist, Sir Thomas Aston, in March 1641 to boost him in his campaign on behalf of the bishops.[139] He also showed himself to be a supple and responsive tactician. When Nicholas warned in September that the junto were planning moves for parliament to appoint officers and councillors, he reacted with a prompt order to ensure that 'some of my servants met likewise to countermand their plots, to which end speak with my wife'.[140] In October he was planning to use the plague as an excuse for adjourning the parliament to Cambridge, which would have done much to counteract the advantages Pym enjoyed through his support on the London streets. When this was blocked he fell back on another scheme to build Commons' support by issuing a proclamation for all parliament men to attend the new session.[141]

Charles backed up these moves with a public relations offensive reminiscent of the 'Blessed Revolution'. With Nicholas offering a stream of perceptive advice, he looked for every opportunity to win over public opinion. In August, when the disbanding of the armies was held up by parliament's lack of cash, he embraced Nicholas's suggestion that he write to the speakers of the two houses urging them to hurry things up. 'Such a letter', Nicholas urged, 'would let your people here see your care and affection to them and make appear clearly to the world that there is no intention to make use of the army here.'[142] Later in the same month he seized on the possibilities offered by the Commons' reluctance to accept his General Pardon by ordering the lord keeper to issue a declaration 'to

---

[138] Clarendon, *Life*, vol. 1, pp. 92–4.

[139] Lake, 'Puritans, popularity and petitions', pp. 282–3.

[140] *Evelyn*, p. 765.

[141] Ibid., pp. 771–2, 778.

[142] Ibid., p. 754.

make my favourable intention known to all my English subjects'.[143] Public opinion was also uppermost in the king's mind when he appointed various Calvinists to bishoprics in October. Nicholas urged that there was no better way to refute the charge being made by Pym and his allies that 'popery is too much favoured by your clergy here and in your own court'; and the king was prepared to go ahead with the scheme even though it meant, as he put it, that 'I have altered somewhat from my former thoughts to satisfy the times'.[144] The promotions – which included unexceptionable moderates like Hall, Prideaux and Ussher – signalled that the church was safe in Charles's hands and did much to undermine the case for 'root and branch' reform.[145]

The public relations offensive came to a climax with the campaign to woo the citizens of London. Again Charles was quick to identify an opportunity in parliament's failure to allow for the abatement of duties on re-exports in the tonnage and poundage bill. This could have been very damaging for the interests of the City trading companies; so in early September he ordered the lord keeper 'to tell the city in my name that though their own burgesses forgot them in parliament yet I mean to supply that defect out of my affection to them'. The political dividend was apparent almost immediately and Nicholas was able to report that 'your gracious letter . . . hath wrought much upon the affections not only of the merchants but of divers others of this city'.[146] Nicholas also suggested that the king press home his advantage by arranging a ceremonial entry into London when he returned from Scotland. This would enable him not only to woo the City elite, who, he believed, were 'weary of the insolent carriage of the schismatics', but also appeal more widely and 'gain the affections (especially of the vulgar)'.[147] In the past the king had often gone out of his way to shun anything that suggested demagoguery. But this time he quickly agreed, and ordered Nicholas to make the necessary arrangements with the queen.

---

[143] Ibid., p. 756.

[144] Ibid., pp. 763–4, 769.

[145] Fletcher, *Outbreak of the Civil War*, pp. 121–2.

[146] *Evelyn*, pp. 759, 767.

[147] Ibid., pp. 768, 791.

Charles's transformation from a monarch struggling to come to terms with defeat in war to a purposeful party leader was remarkable. It is a reminder not to underestimate his abilities as a politician. Where he was following a line he believed in, rather than trying to reconcile conflicting interests, he could be energetic, decisive and persuasive. The prospect of destroying the junto had become his principal goal, and it gave him a new sense of drive and determination. There was always the danger that his rather blinkered perspective on politics, and his inability to comprehend the views of others, would lead to some disastrous miscalculation. But, as long he kept in mind the strength of Englishmen's attachment to the rule of law, his sense of conviction, allied with a flexibility which, in these circumstances, allowed him to bend his otherwise rather inelastic conscience, were sources of considerable strength.

Before the king could concentrate on England, however, he had to sort out his Scottish affairs. His prospects here had been transformed by the split among the Covenanters. The first sign of this had emerged in August 1640 when the earl of Montrose and 17 other nobles subscribed to a document known as 'the Cumbernauld Band', which declared their loyalty to king, country and religion and denounced 'the particular and indirect prackticing of a few'. It was aimed mainly at the marquis of Argyll, who Montrose resented on a personal level, but who was also rumoured to be working for the king's deposition. The 'Band' proved largely ineffective, so from Christmas 1640 onwards Montrose began negotiating with a more select group of nobles who became known as 'the Plotters'. Their main preoccupation, highlighted in a 'Letter on Sovereign Power' composed by Montrose's brother-in-law and former tutor, Lord Napier, was the danger of a 'tyranny of the subjects'. This was another version of the populist threat described in the *Large Declaration* in which it was feared that ambitious demagogues and seditious preachers would encourage the people to rise up, overthrow authority and destroy the nobility.[148] News of the existence of 'the Plotters' reached Charles in February 1641 and, together with evidence of the Scots army's desire to disband, it encouraged him to take a much more assertive line in dealings with the Covenanters. During March he was

---

[148] Russell, *Fall of the British Monarchies*, pp. 308–11; Stevenson, *The Scottish Revolution*, pp. 225–7. For a fuller discussion of the 'Letter', see Cust, 'Charles I and popularity', p. 256.

able to secure an important concession with the abandonment of the scheme for appointing 'conservators of the peace' to sit between parliaments and perpetuate the links between the Scots and the junto. Then in April he put them on the defensive by announcing his journey to Edinburgh and also proposing that the Act of Oblivion be applied to the so-called 'incendiaries' in Scotland, ministers like Traquair whom the Covenanters regarded as responsible for the recent troubles. During June, Charles lost the initiative temporarily when the Covenanters uncovered evidence of a coup against Argyll, and Montrose, Napier and some of the other 'Plotters' were imprisoned at Edinburgh. However, he managed to recover the situation by assuring Argyll of his good intentions towards him and then offering Lord Rothes a place in the royal bedchamber, which caused considerable jealousy among the Covenanter leadership. For most of the summer he held the upper hand, and, by hinting at ways in which he could offer a final solution to their problems, was able gradually to draw them away from their English allies. Treaty negotiations were finally concluded in London on 9 August and the king set out for Scotland with high hopes.[149]

His main concern throughout his northern journey appears to have been his political position south of the border. Nicholas fed him a constant stream of advice on how his actions were playing in London, and by and large he followed it. As Gardiner suggests, he may have entertained hopes of using the nucleus of Leslie's Scottish army to pressurise parliament; but, if so, they were relatively short lived since by mid-September these troops were being disbanded.[150] His main aim, as Russell argues, was to reach a settlement which would finally break the link between the Covenanters and the junto, and thus remove the Scots from English politics. In pursuit of this he was prepared to be remarkably conciliatory. Having been reprimanded by Alexander Henderson for missing the afternoon sermon on his first day in Edinburgh, he swallowed his very considerable reservations and diligently attended Presbyterian services. The contrast with his behaviour in 1633 was not lost on his hosts, and again it demonstrated Charles's willingness to restrain his conscience when there was an important objective in sight.

---

[149] Russell, *Fall of the British Monarchies*, pp. 198–202, 307–8, 313–15; Stevenson, *The Scottish Revolution*, pp. 227–8.

[150] Gardiner, *History of England*, vol. 10, pp. 6–7, 19–20.

He displayed the same flexibility in dealing with parliament. He allowed all the acts passed by the June 1640 assembly to be published in his name without having touched them with his sceptre, thereby implicitly accepting that acts could be legal without his consent. He also allowed Lord Balmerino to act as president of the assembly and agreed that the royalist peers attending on him should subscribe to the Covenant before taking up their seats. The goodwill generated by these actions enabled progress to be made on the two most contentious issues that remained: proceedings against the 'Incendiaries', who had finally been excluded from the Act of Oblivion, and the question of who should appoint royal officers in Scotland.[151]

Charles's determination that no more of his servants should suffer the fate of Strafford was directly at odds with the Covenanters' resolve that Traquair, Montrose and others must stand trial to expose the enormity of their crimes. However, a compromise was gradually worked out whereby the 'Incendiaries' and 'Plotters' were to be tried, but the king would be allowed to determine their sentence, on the understanding that he would not employ them in future. The appointment of royal officials was more complicated because Charles was acutely aware that any concession could set an unfortunate precedent for England. However, he eventually accepted a scheme by which parliament would be allowed to advise on appointments on the grounds that his residence in England meant he did not always know who was best qualified. This was agreed on 16 September, at which point there was a good deal of optimism about the prospects for settlement.[152]

Over the following three weeks, however, the various schemes unravelled. First, there were problems over who should actually fill the major offices. Lord Loudoun was accepted as lord chancellor by both Charles and the Covenanter leadership, but the king was adamantly opposed to allowing Argyll into high office, and Argyll objected to the various candidates he put forward. At the same time, it began to seem much harder than had at first appeared to break the link between the Covenanters and the junto. Pym had arranged for a parliamentary delegation to travel north to oversee the conclusion of the treaty and disbandment of the army precisely in order

[151] Russell, *Fall of the British Monarchies*, pp. 316–18; Stevenson, *The Scottish Revolution*, pp. 228–34.

[152] Russell, *Fall of the British Monarchies*, pp. 318–20; Stevenson, *The Scottish Revolution*, pp. 235–6.

to avoid this eventuality; and once in Edinburgh, they renewed their contacts with the Scots leaders and put forward a scheme to bind the English and Scots parliaments together by requiring the consent of both for any decision to go to war. To add to Charles's discomfort, there was also growing evidence, much of it provided by the malicious Montrose, that his former favourite Hamilton had defected to the Covenanters and was working hand in glove with Argyll. His growing sense of frustration and personal resentment provided the context for the attempted coup on 11 October known as 'the Incident'.[153]

As with the earlier plots, it cannot be proved beyond doubt that Charles was involved; but the fact that the scheme was organised by 'little' Will Murray, one of the most trusted servants in his bedchamber, makes it highly probable.[154] 'The Incident' was a plot to seize Argyll and Hamilton, and either put them on trial for treason or simply have them murdered. Russell has pointed out that unlike Charles's other plots it was not deliberately leaked, which suggests that 'it was meant not to terrify but to succeed'.[155] Had it done so it would have removed the lynchpins of the Covenanter/junto connection, opened the way for a takeover by Montrose and his allies in Scotland and struck terror into the king's opponents in England. The most surprising aspect of the plot was Charles's readiness to turn against the man who a few months earlier had been regarded as his closest friend. But this was, perhaps, yet another indication of the bitterness and turmoil he was experiencing in 1641, particularly in the wake of Strafford's execution. The plot failed after Argyll and Hamilton received a warning and fled for safety to the country. Charles wanted to insist that they be tried anyway since their flight cast a slur on his honesty; but he was forced by the Scottish parliament to back down, and a compromise was patched up at the start of November that left both sides with their honour intact.[156]

---

[153] Russell, *Fall of the British Monarchies*, pp. 321–2; Stevenson, *The Scottish Revolution*, p. 237.

[154] Murray was also the main go-between for the king and queen at this time: *Evelyn*, pp. 754, 759, 764, 781, 783, 786; Greenrod, 'Conceived to give dangerous counsel', p. 104.

[155] Russell, *Fall of the British Monarchies*, pp. 325–7.

[156] Donald, *An Uncounselled King*, pp. 314–15; Russell, *Fall of the British Monarchies*, pp. 327–8.

By this stage both the Covenanters and the king were anxious to reach agreement. News of the Catholic rebellion in Ireland had reached the Scots and they were eager to organise a relief force which needed the cooperation of the king and parliament in London. Charles himself was weary of Scotland and impatient to get back and sort out his problems south of the border. During early November both parties made concessions, although the most significant ones came from the king. He allowed the earlier compromise on the trial of 'the Incendiaries' and 'the Plotters' to stand and agreed to accept Argyll as one of the heads of his treasury commission in Scotland. He was also forced to accept the creation of the 'conservators of the peace', a commission of senior Scots politicians appointed to confer regularly with the English parliament on the performance of the articles of the treaty and other issues, like trade and relief to Ireland. This threatened to perpetuate precisely the sort of links that he had been fighting so hard to avoid; but it was the price he had to pay to extricate himself. Much more damaging than any of these concessions, however, was the outbreak of the Catholic rebellion in Ireland on 23 October 1641.[157]

Charles himself played an important role in the genesis of the rebellion. Royal authority in Ireland had remained intact as long as Strafford was around to command the army and bully the various competing interests. His mastery had been shown very clearly during the parliament convened in March 1640, which approved a grant of four subsidies to the crown and also provided a fulsome declaration of willingness to give more as the king's 'great occasions . . . shall require'.[158] However, when Strafford was imprisoned in November 1640, and his deputy Wandesford died soon after, the whole situation changed. There was a power vacuum that was only partially filled when two of the 'New English' lord justices were appointed to lead the administration. For a time the 'New' and 'Old English' were able to bury their differences and join together in denouncing the lord deputy and his administration; but once it was clear that both were finished – by about March 1641 – old rivalries resurfaced.[159] The committee that had been sent

---

[157] Stevenson, *The Scottish Revolution*, pp. 239–41; Donald, *An Uncounselled King*, pp. 316–17; Russell, *Fall of the British Monarchies*, pp. 328–9.

[158] *Early Modern Ireland*, pp. 272–4.

[159] Ibid., pp. 280–2; Russell, 'The British background to the Irish Rebellion of 1641', pp. 266–8.

over to London by the Irish parliament to assist in preparing the charges against Strafford began to divide into competing factions. The 'New English' members developed close links with Pym and the Scots and began to explore an agenda that involved resuming the policy of plantation, bringing the Irish parliament under the control of Westminster and stepping up repression of Catholics. The 'Old English', meanwhile, were looking to the king for their salvation. In early March it was reported that two of their leading spokesmen, Thomas Burke and Nicholas Plunkett, had gained access to him, via Lord Cottington, and were engaged in renewed negotiations for 'the Graces'. Charles's main priority in Ireland at this time was raising enough money to maintain Strafford's Irish army and thus keep control of one of his few remaining instruments of coercion. The Irish council and the Irish parliament made it clear that they could not provide for this, but 'the gentlemen of Connacht' came forward with an offer to fund the army in return for stopping the policy of plantation. Charles set up a council committee to consider this and, on 3 April, formally agreed to legislation in the Irish parliament to confirm 'the Graces'. This would have had the effect of making Ireland safe for Catholic landowners and blocking Anglo/Scots interference in the country. The timing, as Russell has noted, followed closely on the abandonment of bridging appointments and the beginnings of a more aggressive search for 'a king's party'. The 'Old English' were being lined up alongside Montrose and his allies to outflank the junto in both Ireland and Scotland.[160]

During the weeks that followed, however, Charles's scheme fell apart. The Irish council ran out of money to pay the Irish army and, for reasons that are unclear, the 'gentlemen of Connacht' withdrew their offer of funding. Charles had little choice but to accept disbandment, which removed his main incentive for approving 'the Graces'. At the same time the 'New English' fought a very successful defensive action, forcing the council in London to consider the financial turmoil likely to ensue if plantation was abandoned and 'the Graces' were allowed. Discussion about the legislation continued until early August 1641 at which point the House of Lords intervened and requested that Charles stay 'the Graces' in pursuit of claims that they were making for jurisdiction over the Irish parliament. Charles

---

[160] Russell, 'The British background to the Irish Rebellion of 1641', pp. 268–70; idem, *Fall of the British Monarchies*, pp. 384–6, 388–9.

agreed, which allowed him to escape any blame for the breakdown of negotiations; but this left the 'Old English' bitterly disillusioned.[161]

This was the context in which some of the 'Old English' nobles were prepared to countenance rebellion. Planning for an uprising had been under way among native Irish leaders since at least February 1641. They were encouraged by the Scottish example of a successful rebellion in the name of religious liberty, and also by the collapse of Strafford's regime. However, to have any prospect of success they needed 'Old English' support. This was where the abandonment of 'the Graces' was so significant. It appeared to leave the 'Old English' exposed to the three things they feared most: more plantations, increasing persecution of Catholics and subjection of the Irish parliament to parliament at Westminster. They continued to believe that Charles was their best hope of salvation, but it was no longer clear that he could deliver. In these circumstances, 'Old English' nobles became involved in discussions with the rebel leaders and, although they remained aloof when the rising began in Ulster in October, many joined in by the end of the year.[162]

Charles's prevarication over 'the Graces' certainly alienated the 'Old English' to the point where some were prepared to countenance rebellion. But did he also contribute to the uprising by keeping together Strafford's Catholic army and plotting to use it against the English parliament? The formal order for disbandment was proclaimed on 21 May 1641, but the troops did not disperse immediately and during the summer there were negotiations to recruit them for the service of the king of Spain in Flanders. These collapsed in late August leaving the bulk of the partially disbanded force still in Ireland where it eventually provided armed support to the rebels. The suggestion that Charles contributed to this state of affairs rests on claims made in 1650 by the earl of Antrim, the Anglo-Irish courtier who had been in charge of the abortive scheme to use an Irish army against the Scots in 1638–9. Antrim stated that during 1641 he received two messages from Charles urging him to keep together the Irish army and persuade it to declare for him against the English parliament, 'if occasion should be for so doing'. He also claimed that, after receiving the second message, he had met with Irish nobles loyal to Charles and was preparing to place his request before

---

[161] Russell, 'The British background to the Irish Rebellion of 1641', pp. 270–4.

[162] Ibid., pp. 276–8; Gardiner, *History of England*, vol. 10, pp. 48–9.

the lord justices and the Irish parliament when the rebellion broke out. There has been considerable debate among historians about the veracity of Antrim's claims; but, if true, they provide evidence of another way in which Charles was implicated in the uprising.[163]

Much depends on the dating of the messages to Antrim. Most historians have assumed that these came quite close together in the period July–August 1641 in which case it is difficult to reconcile them with Charles's other actions at the time. However, if, as Jane Ohlmeyer has argued, the first message was sent in late April–early May then the initial scheme makes much more sense.[164] The messenger was Thomas Burke, the 'Old English' committeeman, who had been meeting with Charles to discuss 'the Graces'; and a proposal to mobilise the Irish army at this time can be seen as an extension of the First Army Plot, designed to bring additional pressure to bear on the English parliament. After the failure of the Army Plot Charles appears to have lost interest in keeping the Irish army together and was committed to supporting the scheme for employing the troops abroad. It was not he who prevented this happening, but the English and Irish parliaments. Having initially welcomed foreign service as a solution to the problem of the army, they became worried about supporting Spain at a time of renewed efforts to recover the Palatinate, and during July and August did their best to obstruct the plan. Charles showed considerable annoyance at this, telling the English delegation in Edinburgh that it 'would tend highly to his dishonour with other princes'.[165] But by the end of August he seems

---

[163] The debate can be followed in Russell, 'The British background to the Irish Rebellion of 1641', pp. 274–6; J.H. Ohlmeyer, 'The "Antrim Plot" of 1641 – a myth?', *HJ*, vol. 35, 1992, pp. 905–19; M. Perceval-Maxwell, 'The "Antrim Plot" of 1641 – a myth? A response' and J.H. Ohlmeyer, 'The "Antrim Plot" of 1641: a rejoinder', *HJ*, vol. 37, 1994, pp. 421–30, 431–7.

[164] Ohlmeyer, 'The "Antrim Plot" of 1641: a rejoinder', pp. 432–3. In addition to the arguments adduced by Ohlmeyer for an early date, it is worth noting that Burke would have been much more likely to gain access to Charles at this time, rather than later on when negotiations over 'the Graces' had fizzled out. A later statement made by Count Rossetti, the papal nuncio, in close touch with queen, recalled that Charles had planned a seizure of power by his allies in Ireland at the time of the First Army plot: Hibbard, *Charles I and the Popish Plot*, p. 301 n.70. The case for a later dating is put in Perceval-Maxwell, 'The "Antrim Plot" of 1641 – a myth? A response', pp. 424–5; A. Clarke, *The Old English in Ireland 1625–42*, 1966, p. 159.

[165] Clarke, *The Old English in Ireland*, pp. 153–61; Perceval-Maxwell, *Outbreak of the Irish Rebellion*, pp. 179–91; Russell, *Fall of the British Monarchies*, p. 315n.

to have started to think again about the possibilities that the army offered. The prospect of the Scots putting a military force at his disposal may have encouraged him in this; and the queen also appears to have been pushing him in this direction.[166] If the second message to Antrim was indeed delivered, this would have happened at about this time. A plausible case, then, can be made for accepting the earl's story as essentially true.

In the final analysis, the existence of a plot to use the Irish army against the parliament in England cannot be proved one way or the other. But it does fit with the picture we have of Charles's policy in 1641. This was essentially opportunistic. He was prepared to use whatever means came to hand in order to destroy his enemies, and this probably included exploiting the possibilities offered by the Irish army. To argue, as Russell does, that the 'Antrim plot' was inherently unlikely because during the summer Charles seemed likely to achieve his ends by legal means, is to underestimate his capacity to keep two apparently contradictory lines of policy going at once.[167] His hints to Henrietta Maria in late August about the possible use of a Scottish force showed that he was still mindful of the possibility of a military coup, and she was apparently keen to encourage such thoughts. All this undoubtedly contributed to the genesis of the Irish rising. Although Charles can be absolved from blame for preventing the dispersal of the Catholic army, his plotting and meddling helped to create a context in which its use against the English parliament could appear legitimate.

Back in England, during the days leading up to news of the rebellion, Charles's political prospects were improving. The Long Parliament reconvened on 20 October and it was immediately apparent that the royalist party was becoming more coordinated and more effective. On the 21st, when the long anticipated proposal for parliamentary choice of great officers was introduced, it was resisted by Edward Hyde and a battery of royalist spokesmen who argued for leaving things as they were. The proposal was referred to a committee which was widely interpreted as a victory for the king.[168] Two days later the bill for Bishops' Exclusion was revived and once more the king's supporters mounted a robust defensive action, ensuring that it passed only

---

[166] Gardiner, *History of England*, vol. 10, p. 42.

[167] Russell, 'The British background to the Irish Rebellion of 1641', pp. 274–6.

[168] Russell, *Fall of the British Monarchies*, pp. 412–13; Evelyn, pp. 778–9.

by the relatively narrow majority of 70 to 59.[169] They were learning to play Pym at his own game and even ventured into the difficult territory of news management. When reports of 'the Incident' reached England in mid-October the junto predictably seized on it to revive fears of popish plots which, as Nicholas observed, 'amuse and fright the people here more than anything'. Instead of simply accepting this, however, the king's allies held a series of meetings and came up with their own version of events, which appears to have involved laying the blame on an embittered Hamilton.[170] They were unable to make this stick much beyond the court; but at least they were showing a recognition of the need to get their story into the public domain. During the final week of October, then, Charles was making considerable headway towards recovering the political initiative. He could still rely on a majority in the Lords to block the junto's more radical agenda; his supporters were beginning to take on Pym on his own ground; and he had an increasingly persuasive narrative to put before the country in which he was cast as prime defender of law and order and the *status quo*. When news of the Irish Rebellion reached Westminster on 1 November, this progress was disrupted, but not halted altogether.

Charles's initial response, when he received the news in Scotland, constituted one of his most serious political misjudgements of the period. He told Nicholas that he hoped 'this . . . may hinder some of these follies in England' and then sat back as if nothing had happened.[171] This was not what was expected. Initial reports suggested that it might yet be possible to contain the rising and the Commons immediately voted to send £50 000 and 8 000 men to assist the Protestants. Charles's failure to respond force-fully allowed a dangerously distorted reading of his intentions to emerge which gave credence to claims later made by the rebels that they had royal warrant for their actions. It also gave Pym the opportunity to spin a version of events which suggested that the king was willing to tolerate popery in return for 'Old English' support in placating the rebels.[172] The extent to which

[169] Fletcher, *Outbreak of the Civil War*, pp. 133–4.

[170] *Evelyn*, pp. 773, 776, 777, 780.

[171] Ibid., p. 776.

[172] Gardiner, *History of England*, vol. 10, pp. 53–4; Russell, *Fall of the British Monarchies*, pp. 396–7.

Charles was directly blamed by contemporaries is difficult to ascertain because most stopped short of openly criticising their monarch. But there was certainly a renewed concern about Henrietta Maria and other 'evil counsellors' – with the rising being described in some quarters as 'the queen's rebellion' – coupled with widespread alarm about 'popish plotting' which was often taken as code for 'royal plotting'.[173]

This situation gave the junto an immediate political advantage. Pym was able to make a clear connection between evil counsel and Catholic conspiracy, and then use it to push forward his domestic agenda. The queen's Catholic attendants were targeted for dismissal, unless they took the oaths of supremacy and allegiance, and there were calls for the disarming and arrest of prominent recusants, including peers. It was a measure of the sense of emergency that both measures were supported by the Lords. In the 'Additional Instructions' to be sent to the parliamentary committee in Scotland, Pym tried to go further, proposing that unless the king remove 'evil counsellors' and 'take such as might be approved by parliament' the Commons would not hold itself bound to assist him over Ireland. On this occasion, however, he overreached himself and Hyde and other royalist spokesmen forced him to back down.[174]

The most significant parliamentary response to the rebellion was the Grand Remonstrance. This had originally been drafted in August 1641 to justify the Commons' actions in the face of mounting public criticism. When it was revived in November it also became part of the attempt to persuade the king to change his counsels. It set out at much greater length than had been attempted before what had gone wrong since 1625, tracing the nation's misfortunes to 'a malignant and pernicious design' to subvert fundamental laws and the Protestant religion. It also outlined what the Commons' leaders still wished to happen: the removal of bishops and Catholic peers, the reform of the church and the employment of parliament-approved counsellors. Pym and the junto took a decision to go ahead without any pretence of seeking the approval of king or Lords, and appealed directly to the country.[175]

---

[173] Hibbard, *Charles I and the Popish Plot*, pp. 213–14.

[174] Russell, *Fall of the British Monarchies*, pp. 420–1; Gardiner, *History of England*, vol. 10, pp. 5–6.

[175] Gardiner, *History of England*, vol. 10, p. 60; Fletcher, *Outbreak of the Civil War*, pp. 145–6; Russell, *Fall of the British Monarchies*, pp. 424–6.

It was this aspect that caused most dismay when the Remonstrance was debated on 22 November. A battery of royalist spokesmen attacked it as naked populism, their case summed up in Sir Edward Dering's memorable lament that 'I did not dream that we should remonstrate downward, tell stories to the people and talk of the king as a third person.' The Remonstrance was eventually passed, by only 11 votes, after dramatic scenes in which MPs came close to drawing their swords on each other.[176] The junto had set its case before the country, but at the cost of appearing to countenance 'popularity' and disorder.

As the king progressed south, then, there was still much to play for. He had lost ground over the Irish Rebellion; but he looked more and more like the chief bastion of order and hierarchy. He could still draw on majority support in the Lords; and his party in the Commons was challenging the junto with increasing success. One of his main problems at this point was over supply. Well over half of his income derived from tonnage and poundage, but in spite of repeated assurances, and lengthy discussions over the summer, he was unable to secure a bill that would enable him to collect it on a permanent basis. This was mainly because Pym and his allies engaged in a subtle process of obstructionism, recognising that withholding supply was still one of their most potent weapons.[177] The difficulty of securing a financial settlement was one of the most frustrating aspects of the situation, as far as the king was concerned; but if he was able to overcome it there lay ahead the possibility of an adjournment and getting back to ruling without parliament.

The king's most urgent task on his return, however, was to shore up his position among 'the better sort' in London. Pym's ability to draw large crowds on to the streets had been an important advantage at critical moments like the signing of Strafford's death warrant; but this could be counteracted if Charles was able to rally his own support. Hence the long-planned ceremonial entry that took place on 25 November. The king was at his most gracious and outgoing, working the crowds and parading himself before them in a manner reminiscent of Elizabeth. As he entered the City, with the queen and Prince of Wales,

---

[176] Russell, *Fall of the British Monarchies*, pp. 427–9; Gardiner, *History of England*, vol. 10, pp. 76–9.

[177] Russell, *Fall of the British Monarchies*, pp. 346–50, 357–9.

the people [responded] with loud and joyful acclamations, crying God Bless and
long live King Charles and Queen Mary, and their majesties reciprocally and
heartily bless[ed] and thank[ed] the people with as great expressions of joy.[178]

Outside Moorgate, the recorder of London gave an elaborate speech of
welcome to which Charles replied on the basis of a careful briefing from
Nicholas. He expressed his pleasure at the reception he had been given and
his confidence that 'all these tumults and disorders' he had heard about
had 'only risen from the meaner sort of people', with 'the affections of
the better and main part of the City . . . ever . . . loyal'. He then assured his
audience of his intention to protect the Protestant religion and govern
according to the laws. Finally, he promised to restore the City's charter for
Londonderry, which had been confiscated in 1635.[179] The whole event was
a public relations triumph, making full use of the drama of his return after
a long absence, as in 1623, and demonstrating what might have been achieved
with a more open approach earlier in the reign. The outpouring of popular
loyalty that accompanied it shifted the political mood to such an extent
that some commentators concluded that London had now 'deserted the
parliament' and aligned itself with the king. Things had not gone as far as
this; but anti-puritan demonstrations over the following weeks suggested
that at least part of the local populace shared Charles's concerns. He was
also able to consolidate his support among 'the better sort' by entertaining
the City fathers at Hampton Court and promising to spend Christmas at
Whitehall.[180] This put him in a powerful position. As long as he had the
confidence of the aldermanic elite he could command the City's trained
bands, which meant that, in the last resort, he could police the streets.

During early December Charles sought to make the most of his advantage with a calculated appeal to moderate opinion. He was advised in this,
primarily, by the earl of Bristol, who managed his following in the Lords,
and his son, Lord Digby, who was in close touch with Hyde, Culpepper

---

[178] Cited in Smuts, 'Public ceremony and royal charisma', pp. 91–2.

[179] *Constitutional Documents*, pp. 201–2; Fletcher, *Outbreak of the Civil War*, p. 161; *CSP Dom. 1641–3*, pp. 177–8.

[180] V. Pearl, *London and the Outbreak of the Puritan Revolution*, Oxford, 1961, pp. 128–30; Fletcher, *Outbreak of the Civil War*, pp. 161–3.

and Falkland in the Commons.[181] Their strategy was basically to exploit the issue on which he had the strongest case, the church, and neutralise two of the weaker ones, 'evil counsellors' and Ireland. It began with a concerted effort to show that Charles was now the best person to safeguard the Church of England. The appointment of Calvinist bishops was followed up by a proclamation on 10 December in which he ordered that 'laws and statutes' relating to the church be enforced 'against all wilful condemners and disturbers of divine service'.[182] This was in effect a repetition of the Lords' order of 16 January 1641 and firmly aligned the king with their policy of defending a Jacobean-style church against radicals and sectaries. Charles himself hammered home the message in his replies to the Grand Remonstrance at the end of December, reminding his audience that the church was threatened by 'schismatics and separatists' as well as papists, and promising that if parliament advised him to call a 'national synod' to undertake reform of 'unnecessary ceremonies' he would seriously consider it.[183] This case had a powerful resonance. The Lords received a large number of county petitions in defence of the established church during December, and when his proclamation was read out in Dover, it was reported to have 'caused much rejoicing, the people crying out God bless his Majesty, we shall have our old religion settled again'.[184] 'The church in danger' was an extremely effective rallying cry.

The second plank of Charles's strategy was to counter the suggestion that he was dominated by 'evil counsellors'. This was a principal theme of his responses to the Grand Remonstrance. He picked up the charge that there was 'a wicked and malignant party' at the heart of government and interpreted it as applying to his privy council, which made it relatively easy

---

[181] Gardiner, *History of England*, vol. 10, pp. 94, 100–1; HMC, *Buccleuch and Queensberry*, pp. 286, 288.

[182] *Proclamations of Charles I*, pp. 752–4.

[183] *An Exact Collection of all Remonstrances, Declarations, Votes, Ordinances, Proclamations . . . from . . . December 1641 . . . untill March the 21 1643*, 1643, pp. 26–7; see also his response to the petition accompanying the Grand Remonstrance: *Constitutional Documents*, pp. 233–6. The Declaration was based on a draft by Hyde, which was brought to the king's attention by Digby: Clarendon, *Life*, vol. 1, pp. 97–100.

[184] *CSP Dom. 1641–3*, p. 207; Fletcher, *Outbreak of the English Civil War*, p. 437. The petitions included one from Cheshire in which Sir Thomas Aston was able to rally a wide range of moderate opinion behind the king's stance: *The Papers of Sir Richard Grosvenor, 1st Bart. (1585–1645)*, ed. R.P. Cust, Record Soc. of Lancs. & Cheshire, vol. 134, 1996, pp. xx–xxii.

to refute. He then underlined his willingness to allow errant ministers to be brought to justice, as had been demonstrated in the trial of Strafford; and robustly defended 'that natural liberty all freemen have' to choose their own advisers.[185] This was backed by practical measures. During December and early January there was a revival in the activity of the privy council, with the king himself chairing a number of well-attended meetings. Then, on 1 January 1642, after weeks of speculation, he made two key appointments. Sir John Culpepper became chancellor of the exchequer – after Pym had reportedly been offered and refused the post – and Viscount Falkland secretary of state. Both men were loyalists, but the sort of loyalists against whom it was difficult to take exception since they had been involved in so many of the Commons' reforms of 1641.[186] Charles doubtless had some way to go in convincing the public of the soundness of his choice of advisers, but he was moving in the right direction.

The same could be said for Ireland, which became a much more problematic issue for the junto during December. The public expected Pym and his allies to act vigorously in suppressing the rebellion, but this was bound to be difficult without putting an army into the hands of the king. They attempted to resolve the issue with an impressment bill that legalised conscription, but only for this particular service, and with limits on the king's freedom to employ soldiers beyond their counties. This immediately ran into objections in the Lords where it was seen as a serious curtailment of the royal prerogative. When the junto tried another approach by proposing to send 10 000 Scottish volunteers to Ireland, the Lords again blocked this by insisting on a force of 10 000 Englishmen as well.[187] Charles bided his time and made the most of his opponents' discomfort by offering to pass any impressment bill that did not infringe on his prerogative and to lead the relief force in person.[188] This served to bind him more closely than ever to the Lords and further the impression that the Commons was

---

[185] *Constitutional Documents*, pp. 234–5; *An Exact Collection*, p. 28; B.H.G. Wormald, *Clarendon. Politics, History and Religion 1640–60*, Cambridge, 1951, pp. 30–6.

[186] Fletcher, *Outbreak of the Civil War*, pp. 163, 180; Gardiner, *History of England*, vol. 10, p. 127.

[187] Russell, *Fall of the British Monarchies*, pp. 416–17, 434–5; Gardiner, *History of England*, vol. 10, pp. 94–6, 101–3.

[188] *An Exact Collection*, pp. 3–4, 29; *Constitutional Documents*, pp. 235–6.

evading its responsibility. An issue that should have worked to the junto's advantage was steadily being turned around.

The one issue on which the king was still not able to make headway was supply. On 2 December he accepted another temporary bill on tonnage and poundage, but this brought him no nearer a lasting settlement and seems to have added to his sense of frustration. A few days later, he asked the privy council to consider whether he could live off his ordinary revenues since he found it 'dishonourable' to accept any more through temporary grants or to be 'starved or bought out of any more flowers of his crown'.[189] The answer came back on 28 December that he was running a deficit of £285 000 a year on his ordinary account and that he could not subsist without a permanent grant of tonnage and poundage.[190] Whether this news influenced his decision-making in the days that followed is uncertain; but it must have reinforced his sense of grievance over the whole issue which became a prominent theme of statements during 1642.

Up to 23 December Charles was more than holding his own in the battle against the junto. He was outmanoeuvring them in the Lords and mounting an increasingly effective opposition in the Commons. He was also managing to keep control of the streets of London where the support of the lord mayor meant that the trained bands could still be relied upon to disperse demonstrations. For many in 'the country' it had come to seem that, whatever his faults, at least he stood for the maintenance of the *status quo*. At this point, however, just when it seemed that his efforts were coming to fruition, he threw away his advantage with a series of grotesque misjudgements.

The first of these was the decision to replace Sir William Balfour, the lieutenant of the Tower who had held out against Billingsley during the First Army Plot, with a notoriously unscrupulous 'swordsman', Thomas Lunsford. Charles was probably hoping to reinforce his control of the streets by appointing someone willing to clear away the 'tumultuous petitioners' round Westminster. But this was taken in some quarters as signalling the start of another attempted coup. There was near panic in the City as merchants removed their cash from the Royal Mint in the Tower.

---

[189] Russell, *Fall of the British Monarchies*, pp. 436–7; NA, SP 16/138/63.

[190] C.S.R. Russell, 'Charles I's financial estimates for 1642', in *Unrevolutionary England*, pp. 165–76.

Pym protested that this was all part of yet another popish design against the kingdom's security and on 24 December, after the Lords had refused to join in a request for Lunsford's removal, the Commons appealed directly to Newport, the constable of the Tower, whom Charles promptly sacked. Two days later the king did dismiss Lunsford after representations from the lord mayor, but he then gave him responsibility for guarding parliament. Between 27 and 29 December Westminster was in uproar as crowds swarmed round parliament demonstrating against bishops and papists. Lunsford's men fought a series of running battles in which stone-throwing citizens confronted soldiers with drawn swords. Several Londoners died as a result and Charles added fuel to the fire by hosting a dinner for the 'cavaliers' in apparent celebration.[191] The king had not created the demonstrations which were an extension of the 'tumultuous petitioning' of previous weeks; but he did provide them with legitimate targets and helped to produce an atmosphere in which the normal rules of political engagement went out of the window. The Commons became positively vengeful, and on 27 December named Bristol and Digby as 'evil counsellors' and began treason proceedings. On the streets there was open talk of civil war, and the labels 'cavalier' and 'roundhead' were applied for the first time.[192]

Charles's second mistake was to encourage a protest by the bishops. During the post-Christmas demonstrations, Archbishop Williams had been jostled by a crowd of apprentices and this had frightened most of the other bishops into absenting themselves from the Lords. The peers responded by asking the Commons to join them in a declaration against riotous assemblies; however, this was rejected, with Pym stating in remarkably frank terms the lower house's sense of its dependence on popular support: 'God forbid that the House of Commons should proceed in any way to dishearten people to obtain their just desires in such a way.'[193] The Lords then reacted by debating a motion brought forward by Digby, that because of the pressure from the mob the parliament was no longer free. At last there seemed a

---

[191] Fletcher, *Outbreak of the Civil War*, pp. 171–3, 176; Russell, *Fall of the British Monarchies*, pp. 439–4; Gardiner, *History of England*, vol. 10, pp. 110–12.

[192] Gardiner, *History of England*, vol. 10, pp. 116–17, 121; Fletcher, *Outbreak of the Civil War*, pp. 177–8.

[193] Gardiner, *History of England*, vol. 10, pp. 117–20; Russell, *Fall of the British Monarchies*, pp. 442–3.

possibility of the adjournment that Charles had long been hoping for. A resolution that parliament was acting under duress could be held to override the statute against dissolving without its own consent. On 28 December, however, the upper house voted by a bare majority that parliament was free and could continue sitting. At this point the king seriously overplayed his hand. Hoping to capitalise on the Lords' alarm over the mob, he approved a protest drawn up by Williams in the name of 12 of the bishops declaring that, since they could find neither 'redress or protection' from parliament, all proceedings in their absence should be declared null and void. This would have invalidated the vote that parliament was free and reopened the possibility of adjournment. But when the Lords discussed it on the 30th they showed considerable irritation over the contradicting of their earlier vote; and the godly minority were able to push through a resolution that the protest entrenched on parliament's fundamental privileges. As soon as this was communicated to the Commons, Pym seized the initiative, ordered the doors of the house to be locked and, with great drama, explained that this was the precursor to a forcible dissolution. He then urged MPs to send to the City to provide a guard from the trained bands. The majority refused to follow him in this, but they did agree that the bishops involved should be charged with treason. Later in the day this was also accepted by the Lords and 10 of the 12 were immediately incarcerated in the Tower.[194] The whole episode was enormously damaging to the king. The line that a majority of the Lords had held in defence of the bishops had at last been breached and the number of his natural supporters in the house significantly reduced. Something Pym and the junto had been struggling to achieve for months was handed to them on a plate.

The mistakes over Lunsford and the bishops, however, were as nothing compared with the folly of the attempted coup against the junto leadership. This was a policy Charles had been considering on and off ever since Strafford had first suggested it in November 1640; however, the final decision to go ahead appears to have been taken suddenly on 1–2 January 1642.[195] Throughout New Year's Day, the king was ostensibly sticking with

---

[194] Gardiner, *History of England*, vol. 10, pp. 122–5; Russell, *Fall of the British Monarchies*, pp. 443–4.

[195] See the rumours picked up by the Venetian ambassador: *CSP Ven. 1640–2*, pp. 261–2, 269.

the gradualist policy of party building, although there are hints that he was also accustoming himself to the idea of a general purge of his enemies. A fascinating vignette of the behind-the-scenes politicking at this particular moment is provided by Hyde. He describes how Digby, on whose advice Charles was particularly reliant, summoned him to a secret interview with the king and queen in the evening. There he was offered the post of solicitor-general which was held by Pym's ally Oliver St John. Hyde was dismayed and urged Charles to reconsider on the grounds that, although St John would 'never do much service', he would be in a position 'to do much more mischief if he be removed'.[196] His assessment presumed that the king was still committed to the long game implied by the appointment of Culpepper and Falkland earlier in the day. However, Charles's action suggested that his thoughts were turning towards a more vengeful approach, perhaps prompted by Pym's rejection of the chancellorship a few hours before which he may well have felt absolved him from having to appease his enemies. And the presence of the queen seemed to point in the same direction.

The following day Charles moved quickly and instructed the attorney-general, Sir Edward Herbert, to bring treason charges in the Lords against Pym, Hampden, Hazelrig, Holles, Strode and, as a late addition, Lord Mandeville. He also told Herbert to ask for a secret committee to take evidence. At the same time, according to Hyde, Digby undertook to speak up and offer to prove that Mandeville had encouraged the mob to march on Whitehall. Herbert presented the charges on 3 January; but, in spite of the presence of a majority of the king's allies, the house showed itself in no mood to countenance such naked political aggression. Digby lost his nerve – perhaps, as Gardiner suggests, when he saw the reaction on the peers' faces as the charges were read out – whispered to Mandeville that 'the king was mischievously advised' and promptly left the house. Instead of moving to examine witnesses, as Charles had anticipated, the Lords appointed a committee to decide whether the charges were 'a regular proceeding according to the law' and voted to join the Commons in requesting an armed guard. Later in the day, when the sergeant at arms arrived with an order for arrest of the MPs, the Commons defied him and announced that it would

---

[196] Clarendon, *Life*, vol. 1, pp. 100–1.

appoint a committee to determine whether this was breach of privilege.[197] That evening Charles took the fateful decision to go in person to arrest the Five Members.

This time he made preparations for the use of force. The garrison at the Tower was reinforced, and the lord mayor was instructed to ignore any requests from the Commons and prepare his men to open fire if there was rioting. After several hesitations, at about 3 o'clock on the afternoon of 4 January, he set out from Whitehall Palace, marching through the streets with the Elector Palatine and three or four hundred armed men. The Five Members were forewarned and escaped by river. Charles was left in the hugely embarrassing position of arriving at the Commons to demand their surrender only to find they had already departed; however, his sense of decorum did not desert him. He took the speaker's chair and, after explaining that privilege was no defence against a treason charge, declared that, 'by the word of a king, I never did intend any force, but shall proceed against them in a legal and fair way, for I never meant any other'.[198] This was not entirely disingenuous. A more ruthless monarch than Charles would probably have tried to seize the MPs in their beds, as Digby later urged him to do.[199] But this was not Charles's style. He needed to feel that his actions accorded with his understanding of legality and tradition. Political murder was self-evidently the act of a tyrant and therefore something he would find difficult to square with his conscience or his worries about divine retribution. He kept to the legalist line the following day when he visited the Guildhall to request extradition of the MPs. In the face of cries of 'Privilege of parliament!', he again stated his case, but found that the City's committee of safety had already decided that the charges against the Five Members were illegal. On 6 January he made a final attempt to secure the MPs, issuing a proclamation for their surrender. But, by this stage, the bankruptcy of his policy was so evident that the lord keeper refused to seal it and the lord mayor refused to read it out.[200]

---

[197] Gardiner, *History of England*, vol. 10, pp. 129–32; Russell, *Fall of the British Monarchies*, pp. 448–9; Clarendon, *History*, vol. 1, p. 484.

[198] Gardiner, *History of England*, vol. 10, pp. 133–40.

[199] Clarendon, *History*, vol. 1, p. 485.

[200] Gardiner, *History of England*, vol. 10, pp. 142, 147; Russell, *Fall of the British Monarchies*, pp. 450–1; *Proclamations of Charles I*, pp. 757–8.

The events of these six days in January 1642 were arguably the most critical of Charles's reign. He had openly committed himself to armed aggression and failed to achieve his ends, which meant that he must either accept a massive humiliation or else raise the stakes and fight a civil war. On the other hand the counter-coup that his actions provoked ensured that in any such war he would start with the huge disadvantage of having lost his capital. It is important to analyse his thinking over this period and try to identify the main considerations that influenced him.

The first of these appears to have been fear of losing control of the London streets. For most of December, Charles had been able to command the support of a majority of the City's aldermanic elite and keep control through use of the trained bands. But on 21 December there were new elections to the Common Council which tilted the balance in favour of Pym's supporters. From this moment onwards he became increasingly nervous about his authority over the bands, particularly during the post-Christmas riots, which seemed to show that London was about to turn against him.[201] The turning point came on 1 January when a Commons committee followed up Pym's motion of 30 December with a proposal that it appeal to the Common Council to call out the bands on its behalf. In attempting to put military force on to the streets without royal authorisation they were, in Russell's words, crossing 'a line which Charles was watching very carefully indeed . . . the line between politics and rebellion'.[202] The king's agitation was plain in the message to the lord mayor on the evening of the 3rd in which he claimed the Commons had 'sent to have a guard of the trained bands' and insisted that this could only be allowed by his 'special warrant'. He seems to have assumed that their actions signalled the start of their own attempted coup and decided that the most effective response was a pre-emptive strike.[203]

Another fear that weighed heavily with Charles was that of losing control in the Lords. Deprived of the votes of most of the bishops, and with continuing intimidation of his supporters, there was every prospect that unless he did something his advantage would be steadily eroded. The person who

---

[201] Russell, *Fall of the British Monarchies*, p. 432; Pearl, *London and the Puritan Revolution*, pp. 132–40.

[202] Russell, *Fall of the British Monarchies*, pp. 444–5.

[203] Ibid., pp. 445–6.

spelt out how he should act was probably Digby who had seen his strategy for securing an adjournment backfire on 30 December. He seems to have persuaded Charles, on 1 or 2 January, that the rejection of the bishops' protest had been a temporary aberration and that, given a clear lead, the majority of the Lords would still be firmly behind him.[204] Only this can explain the huge gamble of preferring treason charges. Had it come off Charles would have gained a considerable advantage. All that was needed was for the house to move to take evidence which would have led to the immediate imprisonment of several of the junto leaders and aligned the majority with the king in the eyes of the public. However, anyone able to take a detached view of the Lords' proceedings since the Army Plot would have recognised that this was unlikely to happen. Most peers remained deeply suspicious of Charles's intentions and unwilling to countenance anything that looked like a coup. It is significant that the earl of Bristol, who would surely have advised against the move, is not mentioned in any of the sources about royal counsel in this period. As it was, his son displayed an impetuosity and degree of wishful thinking that bore out the verdict of his erstwhile friend Hyde, that 'his fatal infirmity' was to think 'difficult things easy and . . . not consider possible consequences'.[205]

It is unlikely, however, that Charles would have acted on Digby's advice alone. Another critical consideration was the role of the queen. Following accusations about her role in the Irish Rebellion, she had adopted a lower profile in domestic politics; however, behind the scenes the indications are that she was exerting far more influence than had been the case prior to August 1641. Several commentators believed her to be responsible for the abrupt dismissal of Vane from the secretaryship in early December; and she was also rumoured to be seeking the removal of Northumberland from the lord admiralty.[206] As far as it is possible to tell, Henrietta Maria had been a consistent advocate of the coup option throughout 1641 and Charles's acceptance of her as his principal adviser can only have increased the likelihood of his moving in this direction. There was also another reason why Charles was especially willing to listen to her at this time. On 30 December it was

[204] Gardiner, *History of England*, vol. 10, pp. 122–3, 129–30.

[205] Clarendon, *History*, vol. 1, p. 462.

[206] *CSP Dom. 1641–3*, pp. 194, 214.

rumoured that the Commons intended to impeach the queen over her role in the Irish Rebellion.[207] For a monarch as concerned for the welfare of his family as Charles this was not something that could be brushed aside. It gave Henrietta Maria a very powerful argument for urging him to decisive action. Whether, as one story suggests, on the morning of 4 January she said to him 'Go you coward and pull these rogues out by the ears, or never see my face more', it was certainly in character to use her predicament to stiffen his resolve.[208] The queen's closeness to the centre of the political action, then, was another important influence on Charles's thinking. There is some truth in Gardiner's view that his policy in this period was the result of a contest between the counsels of Bristol and Henrietta Maria.[209]

However, such a verdict is not entirely satisfactory since it does not allow sufficiently for Charles's determination to make up his own mind. He believed that a good king worked things out for himself, through the application of his God-given wisdom and reason. This meant that it was essential for him to be convinced that his actions were both legitimate and sensible. There were two elements to achieving this. In the first place, as Russell has explained, he was able to persuade himself that the treason charges against the Five Members were justified in law. The first charge, that they had 'traitorously endeavoured to subvert the fundamental laws and government', could be sustained by reference to parliamentary efforts to legislate by ordinance and by the Commons' Order of 8 September; and the charges of endeavouring 'to alienate the affections of his people' and having 'raised and countenanced tumults' could be linked to the printing of the Grand Remonstrance and the encouragement given to the crowds. Moreover, Charles could point out that the first move to introduce treason charges had been made by his opponents, with the accusations against Bristol and Digby on 28 December.[210] In strictly legal terms his case against the Five

---

[207] Gardiner, *History of England*, vol. 10, pp. 128–9; Fletcher, *Outbreak of the Civil War*, p. 179.

[208] Gardiner, *History of England*, vol. 10, p. 136. The language cited here was rather less deferential than that which she was normally reported as using towards her husband, but otherwise, as Gardiner suggests, the story is not implausible. She reminded him late in 1642, 'You see what you have got by not following your first resolution when you declared those of parliament traitors': *Letters of Henrietta Maria*, p. 70.

[209] Gardiner, *History of England*, vol. 10, pp. 94, 100–1, 129.

[210] Russell, *Fall of the British Monarchies*, p. 448.

Members was rather stronger than the Commons' case against Strafford; but what seems to have persuaded him that his actions were also politically prudent was his belief in 'popular' conspiracy.

This was the thread running through many of the key decisions of his reign. His speeches and declarations, and, even more, his off-the-cuff comments, are peppered with allusions to 'that hydra', 'the many headed monster of the multitude', which dragged all who came into contact with it into a vortex of chaos and disorder. The agents of this monster were the politicians he was confronting in early 1642. This belief is clearly set out in a declaration he issued from York on 12 August 1642.[211] Allowing for a certain amount of retrospective insight, and the need to present his own actions in the most favourable light, this offers valuable evidence about the concerns that structured Charles's thinking. It was similar in approach and content to the declarations issued after the dissolution of parliaments and the *Large Declaration* of 1639. The story was taken back to the start of the Long Parliament. Charles had set out with every intention of winning 'the hearts and affections' of his subjects, but had found himself opposed by 'a faction of a few ambitious, discontented and seditious persons'. They had refused to acknowledge gestures of goodwill, such as the Triennial Act or the abolition of ship money, and, instead, had entered into 'combination . . . for an alteration in the government of the church . . . to ruin the government of the kingdom and to destroy us and our posterity'. An integral part of the plot was to 'startle the people' with 'false reports' of plots and stir them up to 'rage and fury' through 'seditious preachers and agents'. This had been frighteningly effective, producing 'great multitudes' who had 'trained down to Westminster . . . with swords and clubs', intimidating peers, bishops and any other supporters of the king. The whole set-up was reminiscent of the collapse of royal authority outlined by James in the *Basilicon Doron* or, indeed, the genesis of the Covenanter rebellion that Charles himself described in the *Large Declaration*. At first, he explained, he had held back from direct action, hopeful that the malicious aims of 'the faction' would become obvious and there would be revulsion among 'the better sort'. However, by the time of his return from Scotland it was becoming evident that this was not happening. 'Tumults' had increased, attacks on the fabric of the church had become more sustained

---

[211] *An Exact Collection*, pp. 514–62.

and appeals to 'the people' – in the Grand Remonstrance in particular – more open and more dangerous. All this had finally prompted him to bring treason charges against the leaders, so that 'all the world might see what ambitious malice and sedition had been hid under the vizard of conscience and religion'.[212] Viewed in these terms, his response was a logical attempt to expose and cut off the head of 'the malignant party' before it could do any more damage. It was a policy that had been used – with some apparent success – against the MPs in 1629 and which he had belatedly tried to implement in dealing with the Covenanters. If it worked it seemed reasonable to assume that the opposition would fall apart.

Charles's decision-making in early January 1642 may have been rational, but this did not make it any less disastrous. It provoked a reaction that lost him his capital. On 5 January the Commons voted that the king had breached its privileges and it could no longer safely sit at Westminster. The Commons therefore adjourned to the Guildhall where it continued to meet as a committee and worked closely with its allies on the Common Council. This led to series of resolutions that effectively gave military control of London to the parliament. The Lords agreed to request a guard from the City; the sheriff was empowered to raise a *posse comitatus* for parliament's safety; and the City's forces were put under the command of Sergeant Major Skippon, an ally of the junto. There was also a widespread popular reaction against Charles as news of his actions spread. On 6 January huge crowds came out on to the streets when it was rumoured that he was about to seize the Five Members by force; and when the Commons made its return to Westminster on the 11th, the Five Members in its midst, there were again massive demonstrations of support, with the city bandsmen carrying copies of the Protestation stuck into their pikes. By this stage the king had had enough. On the 10th he took his family and fled to Hampton Court, arriving so unexpectedly that the beds had not even been made up, and he and the queen had to sleep with the royal children.[213] He told the Dutch ambassador that he was anxious above all for the safety of his wife which, given the proximity of a military force no longer under his command, was

---

[212] Ibid., pp. 514–35. On the importance to Charles of exposing his enemies as men of 'no conscience', see Sharpe, 'Conscience and public duty', pp. 652–3.

[213] Russell, *Fall of the British Monarchies*, pp. 450–1; Gardiner, *History of England*, vol. 10, pp. 147–51; Fletcher, *Outbreak of the Civil War*, pp. 182–4.

understandable; however, in the process, he had surrendered control of London to his enemies. What he had begun as an attempted coup ended as a counter-coup against him.

The events of early January ensured that civil war was now not just possible, but highly probable. Both sides had taken up positions from which it was very difficult to retreat, and by withdrawing from London Charles had physically separated them into two camps. The confrontations of the period had also introduced a crucial element of violence that made the final resort to armed force less unthinkable. If this had happened anywhere else, the French ambassador observed, 'la ville serait à feu et sang dans 24 heures' (the town would have been alight and awash with blood within 24 hours). In England there was still the restraining influence of deeply rooted traditions of unity and legality; however, the leadership on both sides was approaching the point of no return. As Russell has explained, Charles had effectively been deprived of his capital by a rebel insurrection and if he now 'wanted civil war . . . he was only doing the obvious thing for a king in his position to do'.[214] Meanwhile the junto, having been publicly accused of treason, were unlikely to feel secure in any undertaking given by the person who had brought the charges. What held back the final confrontation at this stage was largely Charles's sense that he was not yet strong enough to win a civil war. The story of the following months was, in many respects, the story of how he was able to gather enough support to fight.

The outbreak of war

The counsel available to Charles in early 1642 was as sharply divided as at any stage in his reign. On one side were the hardliners, advocating a policy of no concessions and forceful action. Most prominent among them were the queen and Lord Digby (who fled to Holland late in January), but they probably also included Secretary Nicholas who was in close attendance on Charles throughout. Henrietta Maria's role was paramount. It was her strategy, worked out in discussions during January and February, which provided the basic structure for much of Charles's activity during 1642; and even after she had gone into exile at The Hague in March he continued

---

[214] Russell, *Fall of the British Monarchies*, p. 454.

to take her advice. Her recommendations appear to have been guided by a mixture of fear and resentment. She later explained to her old governess, Madame St George, that parliament had been intent on blaming her for the rebellion in Ireland and determined to separate her from her husband. Moreover, they had terrorised her and her family, 'coming to my house whilst I was at chapel, bursting open my doors and threatening to kill everybody'.[215] Much of this was exaggerated or simply untrue, but it reveals the extent to which she felt personally threatened. She was also very hurt by the 'dishonourable conditions' to which she felt Charles was being subjected, reiterating his own claim that these left him with less power than a Doge of Venice.[216]

An intriguing insight into the dynamics of the relationship between king and queen is provided by the survival of her half of their correspondence while she was in exile. She cast herself as the Lady Macbeth figure occasionally glimpsed in earlier letters. She appeared far more willing than her husband to countenance aggressive, and even violent, action; and she was constantly browbeating him for a lack of resolve and readiness to make self-defeating concessions. 'That want of perseverance in your designs has ruined you', she insisted in March, when it was reported that he was about to abandon the plan they had drawn up together. In May she was reminding him of 'your own maxims that it is better to follow out a bad resolution than to change it so often'. And she rarely missed an opportunity to point out that it was his flexibility which kept encouraging parliament to demand more: 'if they saw you in action . . . perhaps they would speak after another fashion'.[217] Charles, for his part, emerges as meek and indecisive, anxious to please, but incapable of following through the logic of his decisions.[218] This was evidently how he appeared to his wife; but, as we shall see, the appearance was deceptive.

---

[215] *Letters of Henrietta Maria*, pp. 71–2. Her letters to Charles also reveal the extent to which she felt she had been betrayed by those around her: ibid., p. 116.

[216] Gardiner, *History of England*, vol. 10, p. 158; *Letters of Henrietta Maria*, p. 119.

[217] *Letters of Henrietta Maria*, pp. 55, 65, 60; in September she reminded Charles 'of what you promised me at Dover, and have since often written to me, that you would never consent to an accommodation without my knowledge and through me': ibid., 118–19.

[218] For Charles's anxiety to create a favourable impression, see her reference to an exaggerated account he had given of his reception at York in March 1642: ibid., p. 59.

On the other side there was an array of counsellors urging moderation, including Bristol, Chief Justice Bankes, Sir John Culpepper, Viscount Falkland and Sir Edward Hyde. We have much less direct evidence about the advice they were giving, but Hyde's autobiography, although written in the late 1660s, offers some interesting, and apparently reliable, insights.[219] Conrad Russell has suggested that Hyde took on the Hamilton role in this period.[220] This is a little misleading since he never enjoyed the close friendship and personal access that made Hamilton so effective; but it does point to the similarities in the ways in which both tried to persuade Charles to pull back from the brink. Like the marquis in 1638, Hyde warned Charles that a resort to force would be counter-productive and would simply strengthen the already powerful hand of his enemies. He told him in early March, as he was progressing towards York, that there could not be 'so cunning a way found out to assist those who wish not well to your Majesty (if any such there be) as by giving the least hint to your people that you rely upon any thing but the strength of your laws and their obedience'. His 'greatest strength' lay in 'the hearts and affections of those persons who have been the severest asserters of the public liberties'. He must strive to quell rumours about his 'designs of immediate force' and demonstrate that 'however your affairs and conveniences have invited you to York, you intend to sit as quietly there as if you were at Whitehall'.[221] The key to royal policy, as far as Hyde was concerned, was for the king to present an image of moderation and constitutional propriety. He appears to have sold this line to Charles as his best chance of building up political support; and, like Hamilton before him, he hoped that it would open up a space to discuss accommodation and allow the leading players on both sides time to come to their senses. He was clinging to the hope that no one in their right mind could want a civil war.

A major problem for both sets of counsellors was that Charles himself remained extremely hard to read. Neither seems to have had a great deal of confidence that he would actually follow their advice. Hyde's dark hints about hardliners giving assistance to those 'who wish not well to your

---

[219] On the role of Culpepper, Falkland and Hyde, see Clarendon, *Life*, vol. 1, pp. 102, 122–3. For the reliability of Clarendon's, *Life*, see above, p. 299n.

[220] Russell, *Fall of the British Monarchies*, pp. 480–1.

[221] *Clarendon State Papers*, vol. 2, pp. 138–9.

majesty' were mirrored by Henrietta Maria's regular warnings about the danger in listening to the voices for accommodation. To those advising him, Charles's inscrutability often looked like a lack of resolve or a failure of judgement. But since the king eventually achieved much of what he appears to have been striving for we should, perhaps, be wary about endorsing their verdict.

For much of the first half of the year a civil war seemed beyond him because he was simply too weak to confront parliament effectively. This frailty was demonstrated by the events of mid-January 1642 when, with the queen's encouragement, he attempted a resort to armed force. The earl of Newcastle was appointed governor of Hull and Captain Legge was ordered to take control of the town, in order to secure its munitions and provide a base for reinforcements from the Netherlands or Denmark. At the same time, Digby and Lunsford tried to seize the magazine at Kingston. However, Sir John Hotham, acting on orders from parliament, reached Hull first and Digby and Lunsford were turned away by the Surrey trained bands. On top of this, various foreign envoys made it clear that he could expect no military aid for a struggle against his parliament.[222] Friendless and lacking any obvious leverage, Charles bowed to the inevitable and on 20 January embarked on a more conciliatory approach.

In a message to the two houses, which was probably drafted by Bristol, he expressed concern at the 'manifold distractions' and undertook to 'exceed the greatest examples of the most indulgent princes in their acts of grace and favour to their people'. He then urged them to consider measures for safeguarding their privileges, securing the religion of the Church of England and settling the royal finances. He was in effect falling back on Bristol's strategy for dealing with the Scots the previous March and, in Russell's words, calling 'on the houses to state their uttermost demands'.[223] The main purpose of this policy appears to have been to drive a wedge between Lords and Commons. After the attempt on the Five Members the royalist party in the lower house largely collapsed. The most effective opposition to Pym in the following months came not from Hyde and his allies, but from 'peace-party' parliamentarians. In the upper house, however, there was still a

---

[222] Gardiner, *History of England*, vol. 10, pp. 152–4, 158–9; Russell, *Fall of the British Monarchies*, pp. 457–8.

[223] *An Exact Collection*, pp. 54–5; Russell, *Fall of the British Monarchies*, p. 465.

potential majority for the king. This was apparent on 24 January when the Lords rejected a proposal for parliamentary control of the militia. The king's message, which the Lords promised to take into speedy consideration, was designed to consolidate this support. However, Charles's advisers reacted with urdue haste and gambled everything on another attempt to secure an adjournment. On 28 January Richmond – acting in concert with his old ally Bristol – proposed that the house adjourn for six months. Why the two peers should make such a move when it had backfired so disastrously a month earlier is unclear. Perhaps they felt that royalist support was already ebbing away and it was the last chance to push it through. At any rate, it was rejected and Richmond was fortunate to escape being branded an enemy of the state. The following day he and Bristol withdrew to join the king at Windsor.[224]

This was the beginning of the end for the king's allies in the Lords. The new balance of power was evident by 1 February when the upper house agreed to join the Commons in petitioning Charles to put the militia in the hands of those whom parliament could trust. Four days later they passed the Bishops' Exclusion bill, having steadfastly resisted it since the previous autumn. Thereafter there was a gradual exodus of royalist peers.[225] However, this did not mean that the junto had things all their own way. There was still a strong feeling in the Lords that they bore responsibility for preventing moves by the Commons that might start a civil war. The majority, including privy councillors who stayed in London, like Manchester, Holland, Northumberland and Pembroke, remained wedded to what Russell describes as 'a sort of aristocratic conciliarism which would enable the peers and the great officers to continue government in the king's name unless or until he came to his senses . . .'[226] Over the following months most of the serious efforts at accommodation on parliament's side emanated from this group.

The collapse of Charles's support in the upper house destroyed much of the rationale for the policy initiated on 20 January; but he stuck with it for want of any feasible alternative. Meanwhile, behind the scenes, he was

---

[224] Gardiner, *History of England*, vol. 10, pp. 159–60; Russell, *Fall of the British Monarchies*, pp. 467–70.

[225] Gardiner, *History of England*, vol. 10, pp. 162–3; Russell, *Fall of the British Monarchies*, pp. 470–1.

[226] Russell, *Fall of the British Monarchies*, p. 472.

working on a much more aggressive strategy. The outlines of this – and also the attitude that prompted it – were revealed in an interview with the Dutch ambassador at Windsor on 7 February. Charles told Heenvliet that he particularly resented the way in which, whenever he made concessions, parliament asked for more. They seemed determined to humiliate him.

How am I to take away the bishops, having sworn at my coronation to
maintain them in their privileges and pre-eminences? At the beginning
I was told that all would go well if I would allow the execution of the
Lord-Lieutenant of Ireland; then it was if I would grant a triennial parliament;
then it was if I would allow the present parliament to remain sitting as long as
it wished; now it is if I will place the ports, the Tower and the militia in their
hands; and scarcely has that request been presented when they ask me to
remove the bishops. You see how far their intentions go.[227]

He then explained his future plans. To content parliament and his people, he said he was willing to give way over the militia and name the persons they approved of to take command. He would then dispatch the queen abroad for her safety and head for Yorkshire, not with any intent of taking up arms, he assured the ambassador, but simply to see how parliament would react. If they became more compliant then all well and good. But if they responded with hostility then he hoped the Prince of Orange and the Dutch States would not suffer him to perish.

This was essentially the scheme which Henrietta Maria later referred to as 'the resolutions which you and I had taken' and which Charles tried to implement over the following weeks.[228] The queen was deeply involved throughout. It was she who first mooted the idea of a journey into the north and who engineered a later change of direction on the militia. But on her account the whole intent was much more aggressive. The king was to set up camp in a part of the country that was presumed to be much friendlier to him than London; Hull was to be seized as a base for recruiting a royalist army; she was to be dispatched to the Netherlands, partly for her own safety, but also to purchase weapons by pawning the crown jewels; and finally parliament was to be coerced into backing down and

---

[227] Gardiner, *History of England*, vol. 10, pp. 164–5.

[228] *Letters of Henrietta Maria*, p. 68.

acknowledging obedience to their monarch.[229] Charles now had a viable strategy for a military offensive; however, while Henrietta Maria remained in England, vulnerable to parliamentary sanction, he had to maintain his conciliatory front.

The same day as he was explaining his position to the Dutch ambassador he dispatched a soothing message to the Lords, offering to abandon the prosecution of the Five Members and appoint those whom parliament recommended to take control of the militia. He followed this up on 11 February by moving from Windsor to Greenwich – so as to be more accessible – and also agreeing to parliament's call for Sir John Conyers to be made lieutenant of the Tower. On 14 February, at Canterbury, he considered their request to approve the Bishops' Exclusion bill.[230] Hyde's account of what followed provides a fascinating glimpse into his decision-making at this juncture.

Initially Charles refused to countenance the bill, for the reasons he had given the Dutch ambassador. If he had to make a substantial concession he was resolved that it should be over the militia. However, according to Hyde, Sir John Culpepper and the queen were then able to persuade him to change his mind. Culpepper argued that the king had to make a big concession, in order to relieve the pressure from parliament and avoid the risk that they would block the queen's passage abroad. If he gave way on the bishops this would 'gratify the major part' and 'the church would be free from further apprehension', whereas if he sacrificed his control over the militia 'it would be the next day in their power to depose him'. Charles listened, but remained unconvinced. Culpepper then went to the queen, warned her of the danger that she might be prevented from going abroad and urged her to 'so use her credit with the king that he might pass the act concerning the bishops'. This did the trick. As far as Henrietta Maria was concerned the bishops were dispensable, whereas she was seriously worried about her own safety and believed that control of the militia was essential to realising Charles's bigger plan. On Hyde's account, 'she gave

---

[229] Gardiner, *History of England*, vol. 10, p. 164. Henrietta Maria recapitulated the whole scheme in a letter of 9 September 1642: *Letters of Henrietta Maria*, p. 118.

[230] Gardiner, *History of England*, vol. 10, pp. 164–6; Russell, *Fall of the British Monarchies*, p. 475.

not over her importunity with the king till she had prevailed with him'.[231] What this episode shows is that Charles was prepared to listen to argument and advice, but remained determined to make up his own mind on the basis of what he saw as certain essential principles. In the circumstances of early 1642, the one person who could circumvent these principles was Henrietta Maria; and she was able to do so because she could trump all his other arguments with reminders of the threat to his family's security. Once the queen was safely stowed abroad, however, her capacity to carry out this sort of emotional blackmail was severely diminished.

The king's assent to the bishops' exclusion helped to buy the time that he sought and on 23 February Henrietta Maria boarded ship for the Netherlands. Charles was said to have galloped along the cliffs at Dover keeping his eyes fixed on her ship until it was out of sight. His thoughts then turned to his eldest son who was still at Whitehall in the custody of his governor, the earl of Hertford. Young Charles was summoned to Greenwich, where he eventually arrived in spite of the Commons' efforts to bar him from going. The king's sense of relief was palpable. He told Hyde, who accompanied a parliamentary delegation asking for a decision on the militia, that he was now 'without any fear to displease them' and that having 'gotten Charles I care not what answer I send to them'.[232] This brought to an abrupt end the conciliatory phase of his policy. A few days later he set out on his journey north, turning a deaf ear to parliament's pleas that he carry on negotiating in London.

Charles's progress to York was extremely leisurely, allowing plenty of opportunities for representations from parliament. The junto leadership was keen to pursue these since its strategy at this time was basically to prepare for war while giving every appearance of wishing to preserve the peace. Having been accused of treason, Pym and the other leaders recognised that their only security lay in emasculating Charles to a degree that he could not possibly find acceptable. This made any resolution of the conflict short of civil war highly improbable. However, if they did have to fight, the junto needed to carry with them the bulk of the Commons and a substantial part of the political nation which, given the deeply-ingrained traditions of

---

[231] Clarendon, *Life*, vol. 1, pp. 112–15. Hyde's account is partially corroborated by William Montagu's newsletter: HMC, *Buccleuch and Queensberry*, vol. 1, p. 290.

[232] Gardiner, *History of England*, vol. 10, pp. 168–9; Clarendon, *Life*, vol. 1, pp. 122–3.

non-resistance, was never going to be easy. This was why Pym had to go on giving the appearance of seeking accommodation, while, as Russell puts it, trying to 'needle the king into beginning a civil war himself'.[233] It was a difficult balancing act, but he largely carried it off, with, as we shall see, Charles's willing cooperation.

Pym's first task was to defeat the hopes of conciliation raised by the king's message of 20 January. He was able to do this partly by taking every opportunity to remind the lower house of the military preparations Charles had been making in January, and partly by pulling various rabbits out of his hat, such as an intercepted letter from Digby to the queen which appeared to show that the king was again readying himself to fight. Out of these discussions came the militia bill which proposed that local defence forces be put into the hands of lords lieutenant nominated by parliament. The Commons completed its debate on the bill on 31 January, and this was the measure Charles refused in mid-February. The king's decision to then head north played into Pym's hands and the junto leader immediately pushed through the Commons a 'declaration of fears and jealousies', providing the strongest statement yet of how 'evil counsellors' had schemed for years to undermine religion and the constitution. It also contained a menacing reference to 'advertisements' from foreign parts 'that your majesty has some great designs in hand for the altering of religion and breaking the neck of your parliament'.[234] Pym was raising the stakes and getting nearer and nearer to laying the blame on Charles himself.

This declaration was delivered to the king at Newmarket on 9 March by a high-powered parliamentary delegation. His response, which for once appears to have been largely unscripted, was highly revealing of the strain he had been under in recent weeks. He lost his customary composure and, as the declaration was being read out, interjected 'That's false!', 'Tis a lye' and – after a passage referring to Henry Jermyn's removal abroad following the Army Plot – that it was 'a high thing to tax a king with breach of promise'. His anger had barely subsided the following day when he made his answer to the delegation. If anyone had cause for 'fears and jealousies', he insisted, it was he, since parliament had done nothing about the

---

[233] Russell, *Fall of the British Monarchies*, pp. 459–62.

[234] Wormald, *Clarendon*, p. 59; Gardiner, *History of England*, vol. 10, pp. 171–2; Russell, *Fall of the British Monarchies*, pp. 479–80.

'tumults' at Westminster in December or 'seditious pamphlets and sermons'. He also referred again to the familiar theme of the grotesquely one-sided bargaining process by which he had conceded everything to parliament and they had given nothing in return.

What would you have? Have I violated your laws? Have I denied to pass any bill for the ease and security of my subjects? I do not ask what you have done for me.

When Pembroke, who was representing the Lords, gently suggested that Charles might give his assent to the militia bill, he exploded and 'swore by God, not for an hour; you have asked that of me in this was never asked of any king and that with which I will not trust my wife and children'.[235]

This was a king at the end of his tether. During recent weeks he had been subjected to the most intense conflicting pressures. On the one hand there were his wife's urgings to do something aggressive and decisive, and his own embittered sense that parliament was steadily stripping him of his power and authority; on the other there was his concern to do what was right and act the part of a good king. His claim to the delegation that 'my fears . . . are greater for the True Protestant Profession, my people and laws, than for my own rights or safety' was sincerely meant, and it simply increased the stress he felt he was being subjected to.[236] In spite of all this, Charles showed that he was still capable of functioning politically and making calculations about the options open to him; and what is, perhaps, most interesting is the indication that in his own mind he had passed a point of no return. In an aside to the parliamentary delegation, he remarked that 'God, in his good time, will, I hope, discover the secrets and bottoms of all plots and treasons and then I shall stand right in the eyes of my people.'[237] When Charles invoked God and his conscience in this way it usually meant that he was preparing to wash his hands of the consequences of his actions. He was aware he was about to do something that went beyond the bounds of what was normally permissible, but he felt that those he was dealing with had left him no alternative. He was responding as much in sorrow as in anger, as he had done over the forced loan or the war against

---

[235] Rushworth, vol. 3, pt. 1, pp. 532–3.

[236] Ibid., p. 532.

[237] Ibid.

the Scots. The emergence of such an attitude at this juncture suggests he had come to accept that war was now the likely consequence of his actions. This was the last time in 1642 that Charles was close enough to Westminster to engage in significant face-to-face negotiations. His dismissive response indicated the gulf now separating the two sides.

If Charles had accepted the probability of war, however, he was still far from possessing the means to wage it. This was forcibly demonstrated when he reached York on 19 March. He 'appeared almost abandoned by all his subjects', according to Henry Wilmot, one of the former army plotters. His attendance at court was severely diminished and the rallying to him by the northern gentry that the queen had envisaged failed to materialise. At the end of March he was reported to have no more than 39 gentlemen and 17 guards waiting on him. He was also cut off from much of the machinery of royal government, which he had been forced to leave behind in London. The functions of the privy council were, for the most part, being performed by the councillors still sitting in the House of Lords; he was largely denied access to the exchequer and the ordnance office, two of the most important departments if he was to mount a military campaign; and he did not even have possession of his Great Seal until Lord Keeper Littleton journeyed north with it in late May.[238] In these circumstances, it became clear that he was losing much of his capacity to command. On 23 March he summoned Essex and Holland, his lord chamberlain and groom of the stool, to join him at York, along with Lord Savile, his household treasurer, and the earl of Salisbury, captain of his gentlemen pensioners. None of them complied, and Essex and Holland promptly resigned their posts, with the full approval of the Lords and Commons.[239]

Hurt and abandoned, Charles's initial declarations from York, on 21 and 26 March, reflected the resentment he had expressed at the Newmarket meeting. He emphatically rejected the charges of 'harbouring evil counsellors' and encouraging the Army Plot; reiterated his sense of grievance at the way in which, despite all his concessions, parliament never got around to addressing his needs; and demanded again why nothing had been done about

---

[238] Fletcher, *Outbreak of the Civil War*, p. 231; Russell, *Fall of the British Monarchies*, pp. 495–6, 502–3. He also had only £600 in ready money when he set off to the North: Gardiner, *History of England*, vol. 10, p. 207.

[239] Russell, *Fall of the British Monarchies*, pp. 502–3.

the tumults and seditious pamphlets.[240] But amidst his bitterness Charles was also beginning to put together the platform for an appeal to the country.

The main architect of this was Edward Hyde. He had been secretly commissioned to prepare answers to parliamentary declarations when he attended Charles at Greenwich in late February. According to his memoirs, over the next three months he supplied the king with a variety of texts which Charles diligently transcribed, even though it 'sometimes took him up to two or three days and a good part of the night', then presented to councillors as his own handiwork.[241] The tone of Hyde's efforts was apparent from the first of his drafts, an open letter to the parliament dispatched from Huntingdon on 15 March.[242] This picked up on the approach of the 20 January message and sought to put parliament on the spot by asking what they had done in response to his request for constructive measures. Hyde also, ingeniously, turned the king's refusal to give ground over the militia into a positive statement of his intention to abide by the rule of law. He pointed out that the king's subjects could not be obliged to obey any order or injunction to which 'his Majesty hath not given his assent' and that in seeking to enforce the Militia Ordinance parliament was passing beyond the bounds of constitutional propriety. Then he concluded with a ringing affirmation of the king's resolve 'to observe the laws himself and to require obedience to them from all his subjects'. This depiction of Charles as the champion of the legal, as well as the religious, *status quo* was to provide an extremely effective pitch over the following months. Sometimes the king would drift 'off message' as his sense of resentment got the better of him;[243] but, for the most part, Hyde and others were able to persuade him to keep the focus on the moderate face of royalism.

It is in the light of this propaganda campaign that we should view Charles's attempt on Hull in late April 1642. The aim of this has been misunderstood because it appeared to be bound up with the announcement on 8 April that he intended to go to Ireland with a force equipped from the Hull magazine.[244] Charles's intentions in this are unclear. The official

---

[240] *LJ*, vol. 4, pp. 667–9, 686–7.

[241] Clarendon, *Life*, vol. 1, pp. 123–4, 139.

[242] *CJ*, vol. 2, p. 481. For Hyde's authorship, see *Clarendon State Papers*, vol. 2, pp. 138–9.

[243] Russell, *Fall of the British Monarchies*, pp. 483–4, 487.

[244] See Fletcher, *Outbreak of the Civil War*, pp. 231–2.

aim, as he told the Lords, was 'to chastise those wicked and detestable rebels
... thereby to settle the peace of that kingdom and the reuniting of this'.[245]
However, it also appears that, as in 1641, he was tempted by the idea of
using an Irish army to sort out his problems in England. This may have
been part of the plan worked out with the queen in January, although on
balance this seems unlikely.[246] It is more probable that the scheme was worked
out by Charles himself and was linked with a proposal mooted by the
'Old English' envoy, Lord Dillon of Costello, in Scotland the previous
September. This involved Charles granting a toleration for Irish Catholics
in return for the 'Old English' withdrawing their support from the rebellion, and thus freeing the Irish army to help him in other ways.[247] The
king was quick to assure the Lords that he had no such intention, but this
did nothing to allay the suspicions of Pym and the junto. In the end,
however, the whole scheme came to nothing. When the Lords resolved on
20 April that the operation of the militia bill be extended to two years, Charles
used this as an excuse to quietly drop his plan. He had probably been talked
out of it by his advisers who realised that in his absence royal supporters
would be cruelly exposed to the power of the junto.[248]

Charles had probably made up his mind to abandon the Irish venture
before his attempt on Hull on 23 April. Otherwise it is hard to explain why
he should be so hesitant about actually seizing control of the town. If this
had been his primary objective he could have achieved it simply by riding
in unannounced before Hotham could take a decision to shut the gates.
The main aim, as Russell has pointed out, was probably somewhat different
– to flush out his opponents and demonstrate to the world that they were
engaged in an act of rebellion against him.[249] For much of early April, to
the queen's intense frustration, Charles bided his time and appeared to

---

[245] *LJ*, vol. 4, p. 709; Russell, *Fall of the British Monarchies*, p. 488.

[246] The only mention we have of such a scheme in their correspondence is a veiled reference by Henrietta Maria in a letter of late April in which she refers to Charles's intention
to 'join the army of the Catholics' and advises against this because it will be so difficult
for him to get to Ireland safely: *Letters of Henrietta Maria*, p. 66.

[247] Russell, *Fall of the British Monarchies*, pp. 396–8, 488.

[248] Gardiner, *History of England*, vol. 10, pp. 187, 191; Russell, *Fall of the British Monarchies*,
pp. 488–9.

[249] Russell, *Fall of the British Monarchies*, pp. 503–4.

follow the advice of Culpepper and others not to try 'taking [the town] by force unless the parliament begins'.[250] His first move came on the 14th when, in response to a parliamentary request that Hull's munitions be removed to London, he sent a message that has all the hallmarks of Hyde. It abandoned the recriminations of late March and struck out for the legal and moral high ground. Parliament was asked why it had placed a garrison in Hull and billeted soldiers there in contravention of the Petition of Right; how it could justify usurping the king's rights in appointing its own governor; and why it was still failing to take the measures required to meet the needs of 'the public'. Then, with a brilliantly ironical flourish, it quoted Pym's own words from his speech against Strafford: 'the law is that which puts a difference betwixt good and evil, betwixt just and unjust. If you take away the law all things will fall into a confusion.'[251] Parliament's response was a peremptory order that the munitions should be removed from Hull anyway.

Having satisfied himself that he was in the right, and that parliament had indeed struck the first blow, Charles decided to raise the stakes by going to Hull in person. The elaborately theatrical negotiations that followed suggest that his actions were still aimed as much at provoking his enemies as actually capturing the town. He approached on 22 April, with a party of 300 cavalry. The Elector Palatine, the duke of York and the earl of Newport, master of the ordnance, were sent on ahead to warn Hotham that the king was coming and that he expected to be admitted. In the interim, Hotham took his decision to shut the gates, giving as his reason the danger posed by a large party of cavalry when there were rumours of popish activity in the area. The next day Charles arrived and there ensued the farcical scene of Hotham up on the town walls conducting a shouted negotiation with his monarch down below. When Charles demanded that the gates be opened, Hotham replied that he could not do this without breach of the trust placed in him by parliament. Charles then tried to persuade the men alongside Hotham to let him in. When they refused he had them all proclaimed traitors and retired to a house outside the walls. An hour later he returned with an offer to enter the town with no more than 20 cavalry,

---

[250] *Letters of Henrietta Maria*, p. 60.

[251] *LJ*, vol. 4, pp. 722–3.

but this failed to reassure Hotham and the gates remained shut.[252] The king then retreated to Beverley and immediately wrote to the two houses giving his version of Hotham's treasonable behaviour and offering them a chance to disown it. When the two houses proceeded to endorse the governor's actions, and declare that pronouncing him a traitor without due process of law was a breach of the subject's liberties, he had the admission he had apparently been looking for.[253] The town was still in his opponents' hands, but he could now represent both Hotham and parliament as in rebellion against him. This was important not just in terms of the developing propaganda war, but also to assuage his own conscience. It confirmed the belief, implicit in his Newmarket pronouncement, that he had done everything possible to discharge his duty to his people and that the responsibility for any breakdown lay with his opponents. Increasingly Charles could feel that he was being released from the moral constraints against waging civil war.

During May the paper war intensified and Hotham's defiance at Hull appeared to give the king a considerable advantage. The declarations of the period focused principally on the Hull episode and parliament's order to execute the Militia Ordinance on 5 May. On both issues Charles had a powerful case. He could justifiably argue that Hotham's action amounted to 'no less than plain high treason' and that parliament's countenancing of it amounted to 'actual war levied against us', while the Militia Ordinance could be seen as a challenge to the traditional view that the king was a part of parliament and that without his consent legislation was not binding.[254] These arguments reinforced his basic claim that defiance of his authority was tantamount to a rejection of the principles of property and the rule of law.

We would fain be answered what title any subject of our kingdom hath to his house or land that we have not to our town of Hull? Or what right hath he to his money, plate or jewels that we have not to our magazine or munition there?[255]

---

[252] Gardiner, *History of England*, vol. 10, pp. 192–3; *LJ*, vol. 5, pp. 28–9.

[253] *LJ*, vol. 5, pp. 16–17.

[254] *An Exact Collection*, pp. 163–7; Rushworth, vol. 3, pt. 1, pp. 571–4, 588–99; Russell, *Fall of the British Monarchies*, pp. 510–11.

[255] *An Exact Collection*, p. 163.

They also enabled him to resurrect the potent theme of the popular threat to order. His quarrel, he insisted, was not with parliament as a whole, but with 'a faction of malignant, schismatical and ambitious persons whose design is and always hath been to alter the whole frame of government, both of church and state, and to subject both king and people to their own lawless arbitrary power and government'.[256]

Countering the king's case was by no means straightforward. The staple of the rhetoric deployed by Pym and the junto leaders remained the threat posed by evil counsellors and a 'popish design of altering religion'; but they could not escape the fact that in many respects parliament was passing beyond the bounds of constitutional precedent and that some new justification was needed for its actions. This was provided by two lines of argument which, while not exactly novel, were given far more prominence than hitherto. The first of these was the notion that parliament was both 'the representative of the people' and the highest court in the land, and there-fore uniquely qualified to interpret what was in the 'public interest'.[257] This was coupled with the idea that it was possible to distinguish loyalty to the body of public authority that the king stood for from loyalty to his own private person. It was this doctrine of the king's two bodies that was used to justify the Militia Ordinance.

Acts of justice and protection are not exercised in his [the king's] own person, nor depend upon his pleasure, but by his courts and ministers who must do their duty therein though the king in his own person should forbid them; and therefore if judgements should be given by them against the king's will and personal command, yet are they the king's judgements.[258]

Once this was linked with the increasingly frequent argument that, following medieval precedent, the king should be treated as if he were a minor, a cap-tive or insane, parliament had a powerful claim to act on his behalf. The great value of this doctrine, as Russell has pointed out, was that it did not require the two houses to offer any justification for rebellion, or argue the case for parliamentary sovereignty: 'if the authority of the king could once

---

[256] Rushworth, vol. 3, pt. 1, p. 588; see also *An Exact Collection*, pp. 175, 240.

[257] Russell, *Fall of the British Monarchies*, pp. 481–3.

[258] Cited ibid., pp. 506–7.

be separated from the angry man at York their members could claim to be truly loyal to it'.[259]

The problem with this line of argument was that while it might reassure those already committed to parliament's cause, it did not present a particularly convincing case to win over waverers. For the generations who had grown up with the oath of allegiance and divine right of kings, the notion of separating the king's two bodies was by no means easy to grasp. There seemed no obvious evidence that he was either 'idiot', 'infant', or 'incapable of understanding to command', which, as Charles himself pointed out, were the grounds on which such a separation had been made in the past.[260] Moreover, the fear of evil counsel and popish conspiracy which provided the alternative rationale for taking this line seemed to carry less force now that the queen was safely abroad. The king was, therefore, able to respond with a robust restatement of what was probably the view of the majority. Against those who have 'gone about subtly to distinguish betwixt our person and our authority', he insisted that the 'allegiance' of 'all our good subjects . . . is due unto the natural person of their prince, and not to his crown or kingdom distinct from his natural capacity'.[261] In many respects, he appeared to be getting the better of the battle for hearts and minds.

Anthony Fletcher's survey of the growth of royalist support in the spring and summer of 1642 tends to confirm this. The criticisms of the junto leadership and puritan religious policy, which had surfaced intermittently during 1641, were coming together to provide a coherent platform for a royalist party. Petitions of support for episcopal government and the prayerbook were widespread, especially in the western counties. Several contained passages suggesting that Charles's message about the dangers presented by popular puritan sectaries was getting through.[262] There was also growing recognition for the king's portrayal of himself as the guardian of constitutional tradition. An open letter drawn up by a group of Herefordshire justices in April described the constitution as bound together by 'a triple cord', comprising king, Lords and Commons: 'Every one of the

---

[259] Ibid., p. 507.

[260] Ibid., pp. 507–8.

[261] *Proclamations of Charles i*, pp. 773–4.

[262] Fletcher, *Outbreak of the Civil War*, pp. 283–9.

three has a negative voice and if any should have the power of binding it should rather be thought the king than the Commons.' This was supported by a request that the king's revenues be settled with a grant of tonnage and poundage and that there be an accommodation on the basis of Charles's resolution to govern 'by law for the future'.[263] These were relatively sophisticated arguments which anticipated some of the themes of the king's *Answer to the XIX Propositions*. They suggested that Charles was beginning to attract the sort of provincial support that he needed if he was to fight a civil war.[264]

Charles's success in rallying local opinion was accompanied by a gradual strengthening of his position at York. From mid-May onwards, when he gave his supporters leave of absence from parliament, there was a steady flow of nobles and gentry to join him. Savile, who had refused his invitation in March, now travelled north, as did Bristol and Lord Chief Justice Bankes. When the king sent an emissary to demand the Great Seal from Littleton, the lord keeper surprised him by accompanying it to York. Perhaps the most impressive recruit was Lord Paget who had formerly supported the junto in the House of Lords.[265] Just as significantly, Charles also had offers of money. During June the leading loyalists among the peerage pledged themselves to maintain a force of 2 000 cavalry and Lord Herbert arrived with a staggering donation of £100 000.[266]

In other respects, however, the king's prospects appeared less promising. He was still failing to mobilise support in the north, which had been one of the main aims in heading there in the first place; and his repeated pleas for assistance to deal with Hotham's defiance at Hull largely fell on deaf ears. The great open air meeting on Heworth Moor, outside York, on 3 June, which was intended to be the rallying point for loyalist support,

---

[263] J. Eales, *Puritans and Roundheads. The Harleys of Brampton Bryan and the Outbreak of the English Civil War*, Cambridge, 1990, pp. 132–5; Fletcher, *Outbreak of the Civil War*, pp. 302–5.

[264] On the effectiveness of the propaganda, see T. Harris, 'Propaganda and public opinion in seventeeth century England', in J. Popkin ed., *Media and Revolution: Comparative Perspectives*, Lexington, Ky., 1995, pp. 56–60. For the constant flow of publications and declarations from the royal court which Falkland ordered to be delivered to the county sheriffs so that they could circulate locally, see Flintshire Record Office, D/DM/271, letter book of the sheriff of Flintshire, David Pennant Esq.

[265] Russell, *Fall of the British Monarchies*, pp. 511–12; Clarendon, *Life*, vol. 1, pp. 142–9; HMC, *Cowper*, vol. 2, pp. 316–17.

[266] Gardiner, *History of England*, vol. 10, pp. 206–7.

produced what one eye-witness described as 'nothing else but a confused murmur and noise as at an election for knights of the parliaments (some crying "the king", some "parliament")'.[267] Just as disappointingly, it became clear that the king could expect little help from Scotland. Part of the plan devised with the queen had involved him journeying to his northern kingdom to rally loyalist support; but while Argyll was still there, at the head of the army intended for the relief of Ireland, this was both difficult and dangerous. He therefore turned his attention to persuading the Scottish privy council to declare for him. In late May, with the advice of Montrose and other 'Banders' who were with him at York, he instructed the council to issue a condemnation of parliament's proceedings. He then sent his friends back to Edinburgh to apply further pressure. However, the junto leadership was alive to the danger and moved to exert counter pressure via its Covenanter allies. When the Scottish council finally made its decision on 2 June it did its best to remain neutral. Charles was promised that it would do everything in its power to bring about a settlement of the crisis in England; but there was to be no pledge of support for his cause.[268]

During May and June both sides passed beyond the stage where they were still trying to give the appearance of seeking an accommodation. Their principal aim became to blame the other camp for opening hostilities. One of the puzzles of this period – and indeed the whole stay at York – is who Charles was looking to for advice. With the queen and Lord Digby in exile at The Hague, the two most conspicuous royal counsellors of earlier in the year had been removed from the scene. The fragmentary nature of the evidence for what was going on at York makes it very hard to tell who, if anyone, replaced them. Secretary Nicholas was with the king throughout this period, and it is likely that he was continuing to offer the sort of shrewd advice on party building that he had given the previous autumn. But Nicholas was never thought of by his contemporaries as a political heavyweight.[269]

---

[267] Ibid., pp. 199–200; *The Diary of Sir Henry Slingsby of Scriven*, ed. D. Parsons, 1836, p. 77.

[268] Russell, *Fall of the British Monarchies*, pp. 490–4; Stevenson, *The Scottish Revolution*, pp. 248–9. For the important role played by Will Murray as Charles's emissary in these negotiations, see Greenrod, 'Conceived to give dangerous counsel', pp. 145–56.

[269] *CSP Dom. 1641–3*, pp. 300–1, 307, 316, 318, 325–6, 336, 340. On Nicholas's own lack of confidence in his ability to influence the king, see the way in which he passed on to Hyde the responsibility for pressing Charles to resume bridging appointments with Northumberland in March 1643: Clarendon, *Life*, vol. 1, p. 181.

Another councillor who was with the king for most of this time, and who continued to enjoy his favour, was the duke of Richmond and Lennox; but again the contemporary evidence suggests that he was doing little to influence the king's thinking.[270] The person whose name cropped up most often in this respect was Sir John Culpepper. As Charles's chancellor of the exchequer – at a time when he did not have a lord treasurer – his advice inevitably carried considerable weight. Hyde believed that he was responsible for encouraging the king to carry out the plan to head north when others were advising Charles to stay near London; and coded entries in Henrietta Maria's correspondence suggest that she thought he was the person to whom Charles looked for advice on the timing of the operation against Hull.[271] However, until early June Culpepper remained in London, still rallying royalist resistance in the Commons.[272]

In the absence of an influential adviser on the spot, the king appears to have taken control himself. When a parliamentary delegation arrived in early May to remonstrate over Hull, it was he who dealt with them and threatened to 'clap' them up if they tried to 'make any party or hinder his service in the country'.[273] Throughout the period he continued to receive regular letters from the queen, and on some issues – such as summoning Essex and Holland in March – he appears to have followed her advice closely. But there was a limit to the amount of influence she could exert at long distance. It is significant that he did not respond to her appeals that he

---

[270] Smith, *Constitutional Royalism*, pp. 93–4. Hyde described him as 'so diffident of himself' that he tended to be led by others rather than taking the lead: Clarendon, *History*, vol. 2, p. 528.

[271] Firth, 'Clarendon's, "History of the Rebellion"', p. 250; *Letters of Henrietta Maria*, pp. 68, 75.

[272] Smith, *Constitutional Royalism*, pp. 89–90. For evidence of a visit by him to York in April, see *CSP Dom. 1641–3*, p. 310. Culpepper's political stance at this point is difficult to pin down. His efforts to align himself with the queen, and his willingness to support the queen's journey north suggests that he was parting company with his former allies Hyde and Falkland, and favouring more forceful solutions to the king's difficulties; however, he was still capable of collaborating with Falkland over the *Answer to the XIX Propositions*: *Letters of Henrietta Maria*, pp. 56, 75; Wormald, *Clarendon*, pp. 60–2; David Scott, 'Rethinking royalist politics: faction and ideology, 1642–1649' (forthcoming). This important paper provides the best account we have of the royalist politicians around the king during the civil war. I am grateful to David Scott for allowing me to read it prior to publication, and for some very helpful discussion about Culpepper and other matters.

[273] *CSP Dom. 1641–3*, p. 317.

make another attempt on Hull, and the queen admitted in her letter of 10 September that this part of their plan had been 'changed and retarded upon some ground that I have never known'.[274]

Charles, then, appears to have been in charge, and, from what we can glean, he was also displaying quite a shrewd appreciation of political realities. This is certainly the impression received from Hyde's description of a long interview which took place when he reached York in late May. One of Charles's first acts was to thank him profusely for his work in drafting declarations, acknowledging the 'great benefit he had received from it, even to the turning of the hearts of the whole nation towards him again'. He evidently recognised the value of propaganda and public relations. He also responded favourably when Hyde pleaded for Lord Keeper Littleton to be readmitted to his favour, apparently taking Hyde's point that if he punished Littleton for his earlier vacillations 'he would discourage many good men' who desired to 'serve him faithfully'.[275] This was the sympathetic face of Charles, a leader who, in spite of his stiffness, was capable of inspiring considerable personal loyalty. But, perhaps, his greatest achievement during this period was in keeping on board those moderate royalists whose ends appear to have differed from his own.

He did this by sending out mixed signals. If the present reading of Charles is correct then he had probably made up his mind after the defiance at Hull that the use of armed force against his enemies was both legitimate and necessary. The main consideration holding him back was the need to assemble adequate support. However, this was not how it appeared to those around him. In late May, Thomas Ellyot, the royal page who had been sent to take the seal back from the lord keeper, offered the hawkish perspective to his patron, Lord Digby. 'Our affairs . . . are now in so good a condition', he judged, that 'if we are not undone by hearkening to an accommodation, there is nothing else can hurt us.' The main difficulty he feared was that 'the king is too much inclined' to the latter and he hoped that a missive from the queen 'will make him so resolved that nothing but a satisfaction equal to the injuries he hath received will make him quit the advantage he now hath'.[276] If Charles still appeared open to compromise

---

[274] *Letters of Henrietta Maria*, pp. 53, 112.

[275] Clarendon, *Life*, vol. 1, pp. 146–8.

[276] *An Exact Collection*, pp. 486–7.

to an unyielding character like Ellyot, it was even more the case with those hoping for a belated settlement. The earl of Dorset who was with the king from late May onwards was one such. He wrote to his old friend the earl of Salisbury in June urging on him

the tractable and counsellable disposition of the king, who though apt to take extempore resolutions upon the first impression, yet upon pause and second thoughts changes to the better.[277]

As an example he cited the way in which Charles had been persuaded to retreat from using force against the earl of Stamford in Leicestershire. There was an element of special pleading here. Salisbury was back at Westminster and Dorset was plainly hoping to persuade him to use his best efforts to further the peace process. However, the fact that he could still persuade himself that the king was 'counsellable' and 'tractable' says much for Charles's effectiveness in reaching out to moderates. How far he deliberately set out to do this is unclear. It was, perhaps, more the case that his inscrutability was proving an asset, since it allowed different groups of his supporters to project their own aspirations on to him while continuing to work for the common cause. Those, like Dorset, who continued to hope for accommodation, would have been less effective in presenting the moderate aspect of royalism had it been obvious that the king had set his face against it.

One of those who responded to the mixed signals was Lord Chief Justice Bankes. In late May he approached his friends in the House of Lords, Essex, Saye and Northumberland, expressing the belief that their differences might still be reconciled if the king could be given satisfaction over Hull and assured that there would be no alteration in church or state. This led to a motion by Northumberland in the Lords which, on 28 May, resulted in the first draft of parliament's Nineteen Propositions. The effect of this document, however, was simply to emphasise the gulf that now existed between the two sides. Its impact would have been to exclude Charles almost entirely from the process of government. Russell has suggested that the only parallels to such a drastic curb on the king's authority were the captivity of Richard I and the insanity of Henry VI.[278] Operating on the assumption

---

[277] Cited in D.L. Smith, ' "The more posed and wise advice": the fourth earl of Dorset and the English Civil Wars', *HJ*, vol. 34, 1991, pp. 809–11.

[278] Russell, *Fall of the British Monarchies*, pp. 513–6.

that the main cause of the present 'distractions' remained 'evil counsels', it proposed that parliament have the right to choose both privy councillors and the great officers of state, that all councillors and judges take an oath to uphold the Petition of Right and that the king pass a militia bill devised by the two houses. It also insisted that he reform the church along lines determined by parliament and an assembly of divines, and that safeguards be put in place to prevent his children being brought up as Catholics or marrying without parliament's consent. The effect, as Charles's *Answer* put it, would have been to turn him into 'but the outside, but the picture, but the sign of a king'.[279]

In spite of the exasperation he must have felt, the king gave the responsibility for drafting the *Answer to the xix Propositions* to Culpepper and Falkland. They produced a masterful statement of moderate royalism.[280] This included the usual stress on Charles's willingness to meet as many of parliament's demands as was feasible and his determination to retain his power of vetoing legislation. There was also an extended condemnation of the restrictions on his choice of councillors and his right to educate his own children and arrange their marriages which, as the *Answer* pointed out, was a liberty enjoyed by the lowliest of his subjects. But the centrepiece of the whole response was a ringing affirmation of the monarch's role within a balanced polity. Using the language of civic humanism, it depicted the English constitution as the ideal amalgam of 'absolute monarchy, aristocracy and democracy' in which it was the mixing together of the three elements that counteracted the shortcomings inherent in each. Within such a system the monarch must preserve his authority in order to enforce laws, protect the subject's liberties and curb the 'tumults, violence and licentiousness' of the people. The effect of the limitations now being proposed by parliament would be to destroy the balance, open the way to faction and dissention, bring about the end of aristocracy and eventually usher in a popular anarchy as terrifying as anything envisaged in Charles's earlier declarations.

At last the common people . . . grow weary of journey-work and set up for themselves, call parity and independence liberty; devour that estate [the house

---

[279] *Constitutional Documents*, pp. 249–54; *An Exact Collection*, p. 316.

[280] M.J. Mendle, *Dangerous Positions. The King's Answer to the Nineteen Propositions*, Alabama, 1985, pp. 5–21; *An Exact Collection*, pp. 311–27.

of commons] which had devoured the rest, destroy all rights and properties,
all distinctions of families and merit; and by this means this splendid and
excellently distinguished form of government end in a dark, equal chaos of
confusion, and the long line of our many noble ancestors in a Jack Cade or
a Wat Tyler.[281]

This was the crux of the royalist case in the summer of 1642. The king was
speaking directly to the worst nightmares of the propertied classes. If parliament offered the best safeguard against popery, then the king was the
main bulwark against popularity. It was a powerful source of appeal.

The king's *Answer* was debated in the Commons on 23 June and there
was considerable support from an emerging 'peace party' for toning down
some of the original propositions. But such moves were soon overtaken by
the escalating military preparations. On 9 June parliament had stepped
up the execution of the Militia Ordinance by calling on everyone willing
to assist their country to bring in money, plate and horses. On the 12th
Charles began issuing commissions of array, which were a reversion to
the medieval means of raising local defence forces, intended to circumvent
parliament's hijacking of the militia. The first clashes over this occurred on
22 June in Leicestershire when Henry Hastings was resisted in his attempt
to seize the county magazine for the king. On 9 July the Commons voted
to raise an army of 10 000 volunteers under the command of Essex and on
the 11th the two houses adopted a declaration that the king had already
begun the war.[282] The outbreak of actual fighting was still delayed, however, and in the meantime both sides sought to mobilise armed force.

Charles's efforts to recruit support in the summer months of 1642 have
met with considerable criticism. Joyce Malcolm, in particular, has castigated
him for failing to persuade large enough numbers of ordinary citizens
to join his infantry regiments, with the result that he had to rely on Catholics,
Welshmen and Irishmen, and jeopardised his longer-term support in
England.[283] Such criticism, however, fails to take account of the difficulties

---

[281] *An Exact Collection*, pp. 320–2.

[282] Russell, *Fall of the British Monarchies*, pp. 516–17; Gardiner, *History of England*, vol. 10,
pp. 200–2, 205–6, 208, 211.

[283] J.L. Malcolm, 'A king in search of soldiers: Charles I in 1642', *HJ*, vol. 21, 1978,
pp. 251–73; M.D.G. Wanklyn and P. Young, 'A king in search of soldiers: Charles I in
1642. A rejoinder', *HJ*, vol. 24, 1981, pp. 147–54.

he still faced. His first priority remained winning the battle for hearts and minds without which there would be no royalist army. This meant that most of his efforts still had to be directed towards appealing to the gentry and securing their support. Moreover, during the summer of 1642 the provinces remained in a state of high anxiety about a Catholic invasion, which made it particularly difficult to persuade the local citizenry to join a marching army. Given the weakness of his position as recently as April, the fact that he got an army into the field at all was a remarkable achievement.

It was based largely on a continuation of the policy of taking every opportunity to claim the middle ground and present himself as the upholder of the *status quo*. A good example of this was his open letter to the assize judges on 4 July, which reaffirmed his commitment to defending law and order and the Church of England. This led to grand juries in several parts of the country signing up to petitions condemning the Militia Ordinance and the puritans.[284] The effects of this propaganda were bolstered by a series of excursions from York in which Charles rallied support in person. Perhaps the most successful of these was the visit to Lincoln on 13 July. Charles received a rapturous welcome from the crowds who lined his route and responded with a gracious address, thanking them for their loyalty and stressing the usual theme of his defence of the traditional order. He then got down to what Hyde described as the process of 'caressing the principal gentlemen, severally, familiarly and very obligingly'. This produced immediate results. Seventy-five of the gentry and clergy agreed to subscribe to a body of 400 cavalry to serve him over the next three months. They also drew up a petition calling on parliament to withdraw the Militia Ordinance, surrender Hull, stop the attacks on the government of the church and reconvene to where they could meet the king peacefully. Charles did not achieve everything he wanted. In spite of broad hints, the gentry failed to execute the commission of array.[285] Nonetheless the whole occasion was a powerful demonstration of his continuing ability to command his subjects' loyalty; and during the summer this was above all what he needed.

---

[284] *An Exact Collection*, pp. 442–3; Fletcher, *Outbreak of the Civil War*, pp. 300–2.

[285] C. Holmes, *Seventeenth Century Lincolnshire*, History of Lincolnshire, 1980, pp. 147–50; Clarendon, *History*, vol. 2, pp. 343–4.

Charles's success in winning the political battle during this period was demonstrated by the splits that were emerging within the ranks of the governing classes. By this stage many MPs and a majority of the peers were in the process of abandoning Westminster, and eventually some two-fifths of the Commons and three-quarters of the Lords were to do so. Not all of them, by any means, took up arms for the king, but, at least, they were distancing themselves from parliament. The king also had more success than he had any right to expect in getting local gentry to execute the commission of array. Given the lack of familiarity with its procedures, the fact that some 24 counties made an attempt to execute it during the summer months was a considerable demonstration of support. Even in the most unpromising circumstances local gentry were prepared to stand up and be counted on his behalf. Moreover, outside East Anglia and the home counties, active royalist gentry generally outnumbered parliamentarians in a ratio of at least two to one.[286] From a very unpromising start, then, Charles had achieved the critical mass needed to fight a civil war.

Of course, the situation was by no means an easy one. The raising of the royal standard at Nottingham on 22 August, which should have been the cue for a symbolic rallying to the cause, turned into something of a damp squib. The reading of the royal proclamation was botched, after Charles insisted on last-minute amendments; the standard itself blew down; and only 30 volunteers actually materialised.[287] The king also started to make mistakes, largely because he appears to have been panicked by news that Essex's army was on the march across the Midlands. He began taking away weapons from the local trained bands to equip his army and also relaxed his earlier ban on Catholics joining his ranks. For a leader who had trumpeted his commitment to defending property rights and the Protestant religion neither was a sensible move, and the parliamentary press was quick to depict him as the tyrannical head of a popish army.[288] But these

---

[286] Young, *Charles I*, pp. 208–9, n.122; Fletcher, *Outbreak of the Civil War*, pp. 356–68; Hughes, *Causes of the English Civil War*, p. 169. The near suicidal effort made by Lord Montagu in the strongly puritan county of Northamptonshire was a case in point: E.S. Cope, *The Life of a Public Man. Edward, First Baron Montagu of Boughton, 1562–1644*, American Philosophical Soc., vol. 142, 1982, pp. 193–4.

[287] *Proclamations of Charles I*, pp. 777–9; Malcolm, 'A king in search of soldiers', pp. 264–5.

[288] Fletcher, *Outbreak of the Civil War*, pp. 327–9; Malcolm, 'A king in search of soldiers', pp. 259, 267–8, 270–1.

mistakes could not detract from the magnitude of his achievement. As recently as mid-May Pym had predicted that lack of support for the king would 'so over-awe' his party 'as to keep them quiet'.[289] By September Charles had turned the situation around to the extent that he had the backing of the majority of the non-neutral nobles and senior gentry, and he could confront parliament in the field with a reasonable prospect of success. He had demonstrated beyond doubt his capacity to assemble and lead a royalist party.

The descent into civil war in England took place by a series of discernible stages during 1641–2. The first of these was the king's abandonment of bridging appointments in late February 1641, which marked the end of his serious pursuit of settlement. This was followed by the First Army Plot of March–May, which transformed a crisis that was still negotiable into a power struggle that neither side could afford to lose. Another stage was reached with the events of December 1641–January 1642 when an element of violence was injected into the struggle which made the final resort to force less unthinkable. The king's departure for York in March 1642 marked a further turning point, since it cut him off from the possibility of face-to-face negotiation with parliament and reinforced the division into two camps. Finally the revival in the king's political fortunes from May onwards gave him the means to fight a civil war. Throughout this process it was Charles who made the political weather. His actions and his decisions did much to set the agenda; and it was his determination to defeat and punish his enemies which, more than anything else, overwhelmed the efforts of those who continued to work for settlement.

The process began moving with the decision to abandon bridging appointments. The reasons behind this are still somewhat mysterious. Russell has provided a brilliant dissection of the whole event, highlighting the importance of Scots pressure to abolish episcopacy, the emergence of the first rifts among the Covenanters and the collapse of Hamilton's position with the king.[290] However, he still leaves unanswered questions about why Hamilton was so vulnerable and why the process of settlement was so fragile. Perhaps the explanation, at least in part, is provided by the ideological tone of the court. In spite of the high profile of Hamilton, and all the talk of admitting opposition leaders into office, this had apparently

---

[289] Russell, *Fall of the British Monarchies*, p. 497.

[290] Ibid., chp. 6.

changed little since the 1630s. If the king's comments on the Triennial Act and the important memorandum on wardship by Edward Nicholas are anything to go by, it remained predominantly anti-popular and anti-puritan. This meant that advocates of settlement faced a constant uphill struggle, having to work against the assumptions and prejudices of those who dealt with the king on a day-to-day basis. Moreover, from February onwards, they had to contend with the fact that these were the themes on which Charles based his appeal to the country. The turning point here was the Commons' debates on episcopacy of 8–9 February in which Digby and Strangeways pointed out the dangers of puritan reform. For the first time in months Charles had an issue on which he could regain the political initiative and he pushed it for all it was worth. The message was dressed up in moderate language by royal apologists like Hyde and Falkland, but essentially it remained the same – that the king alone could offer a safeguard against the excesses of the puritans and the popular multitude. Once adopted, this platform also helped to entrench a mindset in which plotting against the factious demagogues who threatened the crown appeared legitimate, and any attempt at compromise a dangerous encouragement to the enemy. The letters of court insiders, such as Endymion Porter, suggest that this line was being presented to the king on a regular basis. It appears not only to have confirmed his existing ideological prejudices, but also to have had a profound impact on the overall direction of royal policy.

Once Charles abandoned the serious pursuit of settlement there were two obvious courses of action open to him. One was to follow the advice of his wife and seek to destroy his enemies by a *coup de main*; the other was to adhere to the counsel being given by Hyde and others, that he must hold back, negotiate, offer moderate MPs terms on which they could settle, and thus divide his enemies and accomplish his ends by political means. However, neither entirely accorded with Charles's own perceptions and needs. While the queen's proposals might be appropriate to the courts of Renaissance France – where coup and counter-coup were a way of life – he recognised that in England the game was played by very different rules. The instinctive constitutionalism of the governing classes made any resort to open violence potentially counter-productive. Moreover, there was his nagging sense that this was not how a good king should behave and also his recognition that he never quite had enough military force to carry it through successfully. But Hyde's proposals did not entirely fit the bill either. He could see the rational arguments for building a party and following a script that presented him as the model constitutional monarch; but this did nothing to assuage his deep sense of anxiety and grievance. Not only did he feel that he was being dishonoured and humiliated by the one-way traffic in concessions to parliament, he also experienced something approaching panic whenever he contemplated the designs of 'malignant popular spirits' against his family and his monarchy. In consequence, Charles tried to pursue both courses at once, without fully committing himself to either. He dabbled with plots throughout the period, but lacked the nerve and ruthlessness to see any of them through to their logical conclusion. And he continued to make concessions and act the part of a constitutional monarch, but without real conviction that this could deliver the results he wanted.

Charles was much criticised by contemporaries, not least the queen, for his apparent lack of resolve and direction during 1641–2. This criticism has been echoed by later historians, such as Brian Wormald who argued that his vacillation gave him 'the worst of both worlds'.[291] However, in view of the fact that he did eventually achieve much of what he was striving for, this verdict would appear to be in need of revision. Charles certainly made mistakes. His failure to provide a more vigorous response to the Irish Rebellion and his decision to impeach the Five Members were both disastrous misjudgements; and his handling of the various coup attempts brought him all the stigma of plotting with none of the potential benefits. However, in his central objective – which was to form a strong enough party to challenge the political dominance of the junto – he did finally succeed. As Russell has reminded us, he demonstrated 'a skill in nursing and strengthening "my partie" which he never showed in the task of leading the whole country'.[292] It is worth looking more closely at what this skill consisted of because it helps to correct the widely-accepted image of Charles as a political incompetent.

The king's success as a party leader was based on much the same abilities as he had displayed in leading the patriot coalition in 1623–4, the sort of skills associated with most successful leaders of a political cause in late Tudor and early Stuart England. At the core of these was a strong enough display of conviction to reassure his followers that he was sound on the

---

[291] Wormald, *Clarendon*, p. 105.

[292] Russell, *Causes of the Civil War*, p. 187.

basics of what they believed in. In Charles's case these core beliefs were an unswerving commitment to defending the Church of England against puritan excesses and a determination to uphold the principles of constitutional monarchy in the face of popular assault. Charles's record in both areas was, in fact, less consistent than he liked to believe; but with the help of Bristol, Hyde, Nicholas and others he did a very good job of convincing potential supporters that this was where he stood. This positive image was combined with a much greater degree of tactical awareness than Charles has generally been given credit for. Kevin Sharpe has argued that almost any element of political calculation – what Charles himself called 'design' or 'policy' – was anathema to a king who was seeking to put conscience and service to God before everything else.[293] But, like most politicians, Charles was more flexible than he claimed.[294] There are several occasions during this period when he deliberately set aside his conscientious scruples in pursuit of immediate advantage. The most striking was his approval of the bill for bishops' exclusion in February 1642 after he had repeatedly proclaimed that this was an issue on which his duty to God would allow no concession. He sometimes appears to have been quite self-conscious about what he was doing, for example when he wryly remarked 'I have somewhat altered from my former thoughts to satisfy the times' on approving the appointment of Calvinist bishops.[295] Perhaps his greatest tactical achievement was to steer a middle course between the advice of Hyde and the queen in the spring and summer of 1642. In terms of a party-building strategy he seems to have got this just about right and for once enjoyed the best of both worlds.

Shrewdness and flexibility were also allied with a somewhat unexpected capacity for playing 'the popular game'. As Hyde recognised, this had to be done with considerable skill and judgement. He who sought 'popularity . . . too immoderately or importunately' courted disaster, as the earl of Essex had discovered under Elizabeth. On the other hand it could be equally disastrous if one 'too affectedly despises or neglects' what the people thought,

---

[293] Sharpe, 'Conscience and public duty', pp. 648–9.

[294] The encounters described in Clarendon's *Life* repeatedly illustrate this. Indeed one could argue that they show that one of the main reasons why Charles was drawn to Hyde, as both a confidant and adviser, was because he saw in him a fellow practitioner of the 'prudential' approach to politics: see, for example, Clarendon, *Life*, vol. 1, p. 193.

[295] *Evelyn*, p. 769.

or 'too stoically condemns the affections of men, even of the vulgar'.[296] The successful politician had to strike just the right balance. Charles's first instinct was, of course, to spurn the 'popular' and play the 'stoic'. But he was enough of a politician to recognise that there were times when he needed to communicate with his people and put himself on display. Moreover, as he had demonstrated at the time of the 'Blessed Revolution', he had a certain talent for it. His entry into London on 25 November 1641 was a public relations triumph and some of his encounters with the local gentry in the summer of 1642 were similarly productive. He was also good at face-to-face meetings, sending followers like Hyde away with a sense of having been touched by the royal charisma. These qualities, combined with a resilience that enabled him to recover from a whole series of political disasters, made him an effective leader of a cause.

Unfortunately, it was this very effectiveness that brought about civil war. As Russell has argued, if Charles had simply been incompetent he would never have been able to gather sufficient support and could have simply been deposed or turned into 'the picture' of a king envisaged in the Nineteen Propositions. It was his skill as a party leader that enabled him to fight back.[297] What was so disastrous was the imbalance between this skill and the skills of a uniter and reconciler that were so much more evident in his father. During both the Scottish and English crises, Charles appears to have given up believing that he could achieve his ends by negotiation and compromise far too early in the process. In Scotland this point was reached when he absorbed the news of the signing of the National Covenant; in England it is harder to date, but Strafford's execution, and the mixed feelings of guilt and shame that it engendered, was probably the critical watershed. The thought processes behind this rejection of compromise are not easy to pin down. Partly they seem to have had to do with his doubts about his own capacity. One needed to be self-confident when it came to negotiating with the seasoned politicians Charles was having to deal with and, in spite of the enormous strides he had made in this respect during the 1630s, he still seems to have been prey to nagging doubts. This led to a rigidity in sticking by his 'grounds' which allowed little room for the constructive flexibility needed to bridge the differences between

---

[296] Clarendon, *History*, vol. 3, p. 224.

[297] Russell, *Causes of the Civil War*, p. 209.

the two sides. Linked to this was his extreme sensitivity about matters which touched on his conscience or his honour. He was terrified of divine disapproval and personal humiliation, and the demands being made by his opponents seemed likely to lead to both. Finally, there is little doubt that he harboured exaggerated fears about the threat offered by his opponents. The tendency to view them as engaged in a popular conspiracy to bring down monarchy and the church made any concessions feel like weakness and betrayal. The only acceptable response was to destroy them.

The unfortunate result of the king's approach was to cut away the ground from under those seeking a realistic settlement and assist those most determined to strip him of his power. It set in train the spiral of events that led to rebellion in Scotland and civil war in England. Charles was by no means the only cause of these conflicts, but there is no escaping his central role in their genesis. It would be hard to disagree with Conrad Russell's verdict that 'civil war without him [is] almost impossible to imagine'.[298]

---

[298] Ibid., p. 211.

Chapter 6

Charles and civil war, 1642–1649

The warrior

During the opening weeks of civil war Charles lurched from one emotional extreme to the other. A few days after raising the standard 'he broke out into tears' at the prospect of having to treat with parliament. The earl of Southampton, who had watched by his bedside, reported that he had never seen him in 'so great an agony': 'he had not slept two hours the whole night'.[1] Six weeks later, however, the young Lord Spencer was able to declare that 'I never saw the king better'; he was so cheerful that judging by 'the bawdy discourse' circulating in the royal presence Spencer thought 'I had been in the drawing room'.[2]

These early weeks of the war were some of the most traumatic of Charles's life. He had just committed himself to the momentous step of waging civil war and however much he might rationalise this as necessary to counter the actions of a few 'malignant' rebels, he was keenly aware that it would lead to the shedding of innocent blood. He was also very frightened. Until his main army came together at Wellington on 19 September 1642 there was nothing to prevent Essex's army from simply marching

---

[1] Clarendon, *History*, vol. 2, p. 301.

[2] *Letters and Memorials of State*, ed. A. Collins, 2 vols., 1746, vol. 2, p. 668.

on Nottingham and seizing him. That it did not do so seemed little short of miraculous. To add to his misery he had been separated from his wife and children for six months, and the queen was hinting that she might be safer moving to France.[3] After the emotional turmoil that he had experienced it must have been a positive relief finally to be able to fight the enemy at Edgehill on 23 October. But getting there was by no means straightforward.

Charles's immediate prospects after raising the standard were distinctly gloomy. He may have been winning the propaganda war, but this had not yet translated into supplies of men and weapons. At a council meeting on 23 or 24 August he was told that any one of the three parliamentarian armies at Northampton, Sherborne and Portsmouth was strong enough to destroy him. His only alternatives were to sue for peace or allow himself to be taken prisoner. Charles argued that the least parliament would demand would be the terms set out in the Nineteen Propositions which were plainly unacceptable. For the sake of his honour, it was better to remain steadfast and 'oppose that torrent'. However, after a sleepless night, he agreed to negotiate, mainly, it would seem, on the grounds that parliament was in such a strong position that it was bound to reject his overtures, which would make it 'odious to the people'. Southampton, Dorset and Culpepper, who appear to have persuaded him, headed a delegation to parliament with a notably soothing message in which the king offered to talk whenever and wherever parliament wanted, without preconditions. However, as expected, parliament refused to deal and negotiations quickly petered out.[4] Nonetheless, the more conciliatory members of Charles's council kept lines of communication open and this was to be the first of many attempts to arrange an accommodation.

This first round of negotiation temporarily crystallised the political groupings around the king. As David Scott has demonstrated, throughout the war these were to be in a permanent state of flux, continually breaking up and reforming around different issues and circumstances. The labels that historians have customarily applied to them – 'war party'/'peace party', 'constitutional royalist'/'ultra' and so on – suggest a degree of consistency that

---

[3] Clarendon, *History*, vol. 2, pp. 299, 305, 313; *Letters of Henrietta Maria*, pp. 124–7.

[4] Clarendon, *History*, vol. 2, pp. 300–5; S.R. Gardiner, *History of the Great Civil War 1642–1649*, 4 vols., 1893–1905, vol. 1, pp. 13–14.

simply does not accord with individual responses and patterns of behaviour. Leading courtiers and counsellors were constantly shifting their alliances and reformulating their advice.[5] Nonetheless, in these opening months it is possible to draw a broad distinction between those who wanted the king to settle his differences by force and those in favour of negotiation.

These groupings were similar to the ones that had emerged in the summer of 1642, but with the added ingredient that Charles now had to take account of the soldiers. Foremost among these was his 22-year-old nephew, Prince Rupert of the Rhine, who arrived at York in August and was immediately commissioned as general of the horse. At the head of those seeking a military solution was the queen who, even in exile, was firmly established as Charles's principal counsellor. Her return was thought to be imminent, but until it actually happened those who opposed a negotiated settlement lacked leadership at court. Rupert and Lord Digby – who had attached himself to the prince's entourage since his own return in June – were its most influential spokesmen; however, their impact was diluted by their regular absences on campaign and by a certain coldness that Charles displayed towards Digby, perhaps because he felt he had abandoned him earlier in the year.[6] Nonetheless, they had a powerful case, based on appealing to his sense of slighted honour. Henrietta Maria continued to push this theme in her letters. She urged him to remember that 'the factious men in the parliament' had responded with 'so much insolence after you sent with such gentleness'; and to recognise, that while those advising him to embrace accommodation may have meant well, their advice was unlikely to secure him 'the glory which you may have'. 'As to believing that they would wish to see you absolute', she insisted, 'their counsels visibly show the contrary.'[7] Charles's susceptibility to such arguments – as well as her customary jibe that lack of resolution would discourage his natural

---

[5] David Scott, 'Rethinking royalist politics'. As Scott demonstrates, the common description of Prince Rupert as a 'swordsman' or 'ultra' can be misleading since he showed himself in favour of a negotiated settlement at several points, even before the king's military situation became hopeless. Similarly, Hyde, the supposed 'arch-constitutional royalist', on occasion set his face against peace negotiations because they offered insufficient safeguards for episcopacy and the preservation of the royal prerogative.

[6] R. Hutton, 'The structure of the royalist party 1642–6', *HJ*, vol. 24, 1981, pp. 555–7; Smith *Constitutional Royalism*, pp. 110–11; *Letters of Henrietta Maria*, pp. 90–1.

[7] *Letters of Henrietta Maria*, pp. 131, 134, 143.

allies – helped ensure that his first inclination was to press for military victory. However, this did not preclude continuing efforts to reach a settlement.

In the early months the privy council and senior ministerial posts were dominated by those seeking a political solution. Hyde and Falkland, together with the more erratic Culpepper, continued to make much of the running; but they were now reinforced by the earl of Southampton – who Hyde identified as a particularly forceful presence in council[8] – and less influential figures, such as Lord Keeper Littleton, Lord Chief Justice Bankes and the earl of Dorset. Their most productive lines of argument were to appeal to Charles's sense of duty and to his tactical awareness. There was a side of the king that recoiled at the prospect of spilling his people's blood and genuinely believed (as even the queen acknowledged) that it was 'the part of a good and just king' to pursue 'the paths of mildness'.[9] At the same time he recognised that considerable political advantage would accrue to whichever side was seen to be working hardest for peace. The 'honest men', as Lord Spencer termed them, kept working away steadily on these two issues, relying on what they saw as the king's 'counsellable disposition'.[10] However, their task was not made easier by the dramatic improvement in the king's military prospects during the first two weeks in September.

His recruiting efforts at last began to bear fruit. Charles's method of raising an army was to issue commissions to local supporters to recruit regiments on his behalf. The commissions went out in late July and early August, and by the time he left Nottingham on 13 September they had produced seven or eight regiments of infantry. On his march across the Midlands he was joined by several cavalry regiments that had been shadowing Essex's army and, once he reached Shrewsbury on 21 September, by companies from Wales, the Marches and the north-west. This made up an army of around 14 000 men, which was the equal of Essex's in size and was better equipped in terms of the quality of its cavalry and its officers, many of whom had seen professional service. There remained problems over the supply of arms, but it was now a relatively well-paid force, since large

---

[8] Clarendon, *History*, vol. 2, p. 530.

[9] *Letters of Henrietta Maria*, p. 132. Attendance at the only council meeting of this period recorded in the register reflects the dominance of the moderates: NA, PC 2/53, fo. 102.

[10] *Letters and Memorials of State*, vol. 2, pp. 667–8.

numbers of voluntary donations were coming in from noble and gentry supporters.[11] Above all, morale was extremely high, especially after Rupert's victory at Powick Bridge on 23 September. It was being confidently predicted that the war would be settled by the first clash of arms and that Essex's 'puritan rabble' would be swept aside.[12]

Two of Lord Spencer's letters from this period provide a fascinating glimpse of the mood at court. For the time being, he reported, all talk of negotiation had ceased: 'the king is of late very much averse to peace by the persuasions of 102 and 111 [probably Rupert and Digby]. It is likewise conceived that the king has taken a resolution not to do anything in that way before the queen comes.' The 'honest men' were still talking up the prospects of an accomodation, but most men's thoughts were already turning to the nature of a post-war settlement. Here Spencer was worried that a swift victory for the king would open the way for a takeover by what he called 'the papists' – presumably the allies of the queen. They were becoming 'insupportable' and had 'so awed' Charles that 'he dares not propose peace or accept'.[13] Henrietta Maria's references to making the king 'absolute', and securing 'the glory which you may have', perhaps pointed to the sort of attitudes that so alarmed him. For moderate royalists outright military victory was coming to look almost as unpalatable as defeat by parliament.

In this context, the manifesto that Charles issued to his army at Wellington on 19 September became a highly significant political event. In a short speech, he reminded his listeners of the worthiness of their cause and the lack of credibility of their enemies – 'most of them Brownists, Anabaptists and atheists'. He then delivered a Protestation in the form of a royal oath to defend 'the true reformed Protestant religion established in the Church of England', 'to govern by the known laws of the land', 'to maintain the just privileges and freedom of parliament' and 'to observe inviolably the laws consented to by me this parliament'.[14] There was

---

[11] Wanklyn and Young, 'A king in search of soldiers – a rejoinder', pp. 150–1; R. Hutton, *The Royalist War Effort 1642–1646*, Harlow, 1982, pp. 22–3, 28–31; Gardiner, *History of the Civil War*, vol. 1, pp. 36–7.

[12] Clarendon, *History*, vol. 2, pp. 325, 341.

[13] *Letters and Memorials of State*, vol. 2, pp. 667–8.

[14] Clarendon, *History*, vol. 2, p. 312.

nothing new in the Protestation. It kept to the line articulated by Hyde on the king's behalf throughout the spring and summer – and indeed Hyde probably wrote it.[15] But the fact that the king was taking a solemn oath, and that the Protestation was immediately published and widely distributed, made it something like a definitive statement of the principles on which he was going to war.[16] This was a considerable coup for those who sought a political solution to the conflict and lived in dread of the 'papists' and 'swordsmen'. It gave coherence to their efforts in pursuit of an accommodation and provided a point of reference to which they could return in later debates about policy. It also signalled that in constitutional matters Charles would listen to his civilian councillors. The queen immediately recognised the significance of what had happened and administered a sharp reprimand. 'Had I been with you', she declared, 'I should not have suffered it'; 'I beg you to be a little more careful in the oaths you take'.[17] At a distance, however, there was not much more she could do.

Early in October, the decision was taken to march on London and engage Essex's army in the field.[18] Charles set out from Shrewsbury on the 12th and the campaign that followed provides an opportunity to assess his performance as commander-in-chief. In contrast to later campaigns, he was in charge of a single, unified force and had a relatively simple strategic objective; but this did not mean his task was straightforward. The facilities available to a seventeenth-century commander were still extremely primitive. As Martin Van Creveld has pointed out, he had to operate without adequate intelligence of enemy movement and with few reliable means of communicating with his own side. Once on the battlefield, his ability to make decisions was severely hampered by the lack of visibility – caused by the black powder muskets – and also by the knightly convention that still required him to lead by example, fighting at the head of his men.[19] In

---

[15] Ibid., vol. 2, p. 390.

[16] This message was underlined in the royal coins being produced within a few days at the newly established mint at Shrewsbury. These replaced the royal arms with the motto 'RELIGI. PROT. LEG. ANGI. LIBER PAR.': Peacock, 'The visual image of Charles I', pp. 186–7; *CSP Ven. 1642–3*, pp. 186–7.

[17] *Letters of Henrietta Maria*, pp. 142–4.

[18] Clarendon, *History*, vol. 2, p. 349.

[19] M. Van Creveld, *Command in War*, Cambridge, Mass., 1985, chp. 2.

Charles's case there was the added difficulty that he was almost completely lacking in military experience. He had been trained for war since boyhood, and he was the inheritor of a long chivalric tradition that command of his armies in battle was the supreme expression of his sovereign power. Van Dyck's great equestrian portraits, showing him in full battle armour, were the visual expression of this role. But he had never been involved in actual combat. The closest he had come was the deadlock at Kelso in June 1639, when he spied the Scottish army through a telescope. In these circumstances, it would have been surprising if he had not felt daunted by the task facing him, and he clearly did. However, he had the sense to recognise his limitations and allow the professionals to guide him.

Before he even left York he had appointed a council of war. This was made up of senior soldiers and civilian politicians who had the responsibility of advising him on strategy and supervising the war effort. During the Edgehill campaign Charles consulted the council every time an important decision had to be made. However, he also drew heavily on the guidance of his charismatic young nephew, and the order to deploy at Edgehill on 23 October seems to have been given mainly on his advice.[20] Van Creveld has suggested that the most successful commanders avoided councils of war because their advice was usually a recipe for indecision.[21] But, in Charles's case, consulting them was surely the most sensible thing to do.

During the battle at Edgehill the king's role was severely restricted. He entrusted the important task of ordering his army to Patrick Ruthven, Lord Forth, a Scottish commander with long experience of serving under Gustavus Adolphus. He then rode up and down the ranks urging on his troops, reportedly 'with great courage and cheerfulness which caused hurras through the whole army'. And, at the critical moment when it looked as if his foot might break under the weight of the parliamentarian assault, he rode forward and helped to rally them. However, his control over events was very limited, and he could do nothing to prevent the royalist cavalry reserve charging off the field at an early stage in the battle, thus surrendering the advantage gained by Rupert's initial attack.[22] Overall,

---

[20] P. Young, *Edgehill 1642*, Kineton, 1967, pp. 62, 77–8.

[21] Van Creveld, *Command in War*, p. 38. Rupert largely ignored them, although this caused some dissatisfaction among his officers: *Rupert & the Cavaliers*, vol. 3, p. 8.

[22] Young, *Edgehill*, pp. 108–9, 113, 118, 124–5, 267–9.

Charles performed creditably enough and had certainly displayed considerable courage and willingness to lead by example. But it was evident that he still lacked the confidence to assert himself convincingly as a military leader; and this was to deny him, perhaps, his best opportunity of winning the war.

Edgehill ended in a draw, but it was the king who enjoyed the advantage because Essex retired to Warwick and left open the road to London. Early reports that the earl had been defeated plunged the capital into panic and parliament rushed to reopen negotiations.[23] The initiative lay with Charles more clearly than at any time since November 1641. He faced a critical decision. Either he could either press forward and attack London before Essex's force was able to recover; or he could hold back and negotiate, but this time from a position of great strength. In the event he did neither. The crucial discussion appears to have taken place at a council of war meeting soon after the battle. According to later accounts giving Rupert's side of the story, the prince requested that he be allowed to march on Westminster immediately, with 3 000 horse and musketeers. This was, reportedly, opposed 'by the advice of many in the council who were afraid lest his Majesty should return by conquest'. The clinching argument was apparently put by the earl of Bristol who warned that Rupert, 'being a young man, and naturally passionate, might be urged in the heat of blood to fire the town'. Charles, it was said, 'did not disapprove' of the prince's proposal but was 'so overpressed by other importunities that he could not do it'.[24] In spite of its partisan origins, this account looks broadly plausible. It suggests that the 'honest men' continued to worry about the consequences of winning

---

[23] Ibid., pp. 129–30; Clarendon, *History*, vol. 2, p. 377; Gardiner, *History of the Civil War*, vol. 1, pp. 53–4.

[24] Young, *Edgehill*, pp. 279–80, 286. The two accounts that describe this meeting, one known as Rupert's diary and the other as the duke of York's account, are retrospective and appear to have drawn on a common source; however, they are unclear over precisely when the meeting took place. The duke of York's account dates it to 24 October, the day after the battle, although, as Malcolm Wanklyn has pointed out, this is unlikely since Rupert spent the day harrying Essex's army. Rupert's diary dates it to 27 October after he had taken Banbury, which is more plausible. A royal proclamation issued on that day included a promise by Charles that his army would not offer violence to the inhabitants of London: *Proclamations of Charles I*, pp. 806–8. I am grateful to Malcolm Wanklyn for advice on the military aspects of the war and for allowing me to read parts of his book on the subject in advance of publication: M. Wanklyn and F. Jones, *A Military History of the English Civil War 1642–1646*, 2005.

the war by 'conquest' and were sufficiently influential, even on the council of war, to talk the king out of an immediate attack, while Charles was still too unsure of himself as a commander to go against the advice of the majority, even when the counter argument was being put by Rupert.

The king's decision to turn aside, and take first Banbury and then Oxford, lost him the opportunity to reach London before Essex; but he still had the upper hand. When his army captured Reading virtually unopposed on 4 November, and then advanced to Colnbrook, he had the option of either pressing forward to attack London or settling for negotiation. This, according to Hyde, was the great missed opportunity to secure a favourable settlement. In his *History* he presents a scenario in which Charles could have withdrawn to Reading until parliament had acceded to his request to restore Windsor Castle, which would then have opened the way for a cessation of arms and a treaty.[25] This probably reflected the hopes – and possibly the advice – of the peace lobby at the time. But they were to be disappointed. On 11 November Rupert's patrols encountered Essex's army at Brentford and he insisted that the king bring up the royal army in support. Brentford was taken on the 12th; but the king's apparent treachery in breaching the proposed cessation, together with the threat of being pillaged by Rupert, turned the mood in London against negotiation. The following day the city bands rallied in huge numbers at Turnham Green and the king was forced to back away. Hyde's *History* blamed Rupert for persuading the king into an advance on London and thus wrecking the prospects for peace; but Gardiner has argued that Charles never seriously intended to negotiate, and points to his later admission that it was he who gave the order to advance on Brentford.[26] Perhaps the most credible interpretation lies somewhere in between. Rupert could have deliberately engineered a confrontation with Essex by sending ahead his cavalry patrols, leaving Charles with no alternative but to advance. But the king may also, typically, have been trying to keep his options open, pushing the peace negotiations to see what they would produce, while retaining the military threat as an alternative and an added source of pressure. The problem was that, in the circumstances, what was required was a commitment to one course or the other. Charles's

---

[25] Clarendon, *History*, vol. 2, pp. 391–4.

[26] Ibid., vol. 2, pp. 394–5; Gardiner, *History of the Civil War*, vol. 1, pp. 56–61.

attempt to have it all ways looked like dithering and sent out the wrong message. The result was to invite pressure from both 'hawks' and 'doves' within the royal entourage, which pushed him first one way then the other and, eventually, lost him the opportunities which had beckoned after Edgehill.

Following the withdrawal from Turnham Green, Charles set up head-quarters at Oxford and proceeded to turn it into a seat of government. He took over the dean's lodgings at Christchurch and equipped it as a royal palace, with the usual separation between public and private rooms. The law courts relocated from Westminster to the Oxford Schools and reopened for business in the spring of 1643; the exchequer operated out of All Souls; and the ordnance office established workshops at Christchurch and the Schools.[27] The formal centre of this system of government remained the privy council, but it now shared much of its authority with the council of war.

During early 1643 the council of war seemed set to become the dominant institution of the new royalist government. It was responsible for oversee-ing every aspect of the war effort, from raising taxes and supplying the army to planning campaigns and directing troop movements. Charles sat in on nearly every meeting and during the campaigning season it convened almost daily. However, as Ian Roy has demonstrated, its potential was never fully realised. The council's reach tended to be limited to the vicinity of Oxford, or wherever the king happened to be at a particular time, and it rarely exercised much control over the regional armies. It could also be bypassed in decisions on strategy, as Charles took advice from favoured courtiers or generals in the field, especially Rupert. There were times – usually when the king himself was on campaign – when the council functioned to its full capacity. Perhaps the best example of this was the Lostwithiel campaign of July–August 1644. But overall its influence was intermittent.[28]

The privy council, on the other hand, remained a powerful presence at the heart of government. The fragmentary nature of its registers for the civil war period, together with its relative lack of involvement in foreign policy and military affairs, has persuaded some historians to downplay its

---

[27] I. Roy and D. Reinhardt, 'Oxford and the civil wars', in N.R.N. Tyacke ed., *The History of the University of Oxford, vol. 4. Seventeenth-Century Oxford*, 1997, pp. 703–5; I. Roy, *The Royalist Ordnance Papers*, Oxfordshire Rec. Soc., vol. 43, 1964, pp. 25–8.

[28] I. Roy, 'The Royalist Council of War 1642–6', *BIHR*, vol. 35, 1962, pp. 105–68.

significance.[29] But this is misleading. It met much more regularly than the council registers imply and continued to discuss and give advice on a wide range of matters (including peace negotiations, the Oxford Parliament and overall political strategy).[30] Charles himself remained highly respectful of the obligation to consult his civilian councillors on matters of high policy. And, perhaps most significantly, it provided a power base for those who sought a political solution to the conflict. They recognised that such a solution – whether it was to be achieved by persuading the king to moderate his demands to the point where settlement might be reached or by reaching out to moderate elements on the parliamentarian side and engineering a coup against the 'war party' at Westminster – depended on persuading the king to keep to the 'constitutionalist' line set out at Wellington. This was what the majority of the privy council generally tried to do, and, as we shall see, they were often more successful in achieving it than they had been prior to 1642.[31]

It is important, however, not to exaggerate the privy council's influence. Policy continued to be made first and foremost by the king, generally acting in consultation with his favoured adviser of the moment. For much of the early part of the war this position was held by the queen. Her return to court had been anticipated since September 1642, although she did not actually reach Oxford until July 1643, having sheltered for several months with the earl of Newcastle at York.[32] Once she was reunited

---

[29] I. Roy, 'The Royalist Army in the First Civil War', Oxford University, D. Phil thesis, 1963, p. 76; J. De Groot, 'Space, patronage and procedure: the court at Oxford 1642–6', *EHR*, vol. 117, 2002, p. 1222.

[30] See, for example, Clarendon's account of its role during the peace negotiation of 1643: Clarendon, *History*, vol. 2, p. 521.

[31] A good example of the council's ability to influence Charles is provided by a debate about bishops described by Hyde, which took place in February or March 1643: Clarendon, *Life*, vol. 1, pp. 188–93. The king came to the meeting determined to issue a statement of the *iure divino* case for episcopacy in response to a Scottish Presbyterian paper on the subject. However, the majority of councillors opposed this and Charles became annoyed. There was a good deal of heated discussion until Hyde himself stepped in and calmed things down by persuading the king that now was not the time to issue such a statement since it would simply give the Scots an opportunity to engage him in public dispute. This was a relatively minor incident, but it demonstrated that the privy council was a long way from being emasculated during the civil war.

[32] Gardiner, *History of the Civil War*, vol. 1, pp. 94–5, 165–6.

with her husband, Henrietta Maria's power was as great as it had ever been. Charles still doted on her and Hyde later commented of this period that he 'saw with her eyes and determined by her judgement'.[33] Her greatest influence was in high-level diplomacy and negotiations for aid from overseas, which she and Charles appear to have managed almost entirely between themselves, often using special ciphers that not even the secretaries of state were privy to.[34] She was also a powerful voice against any sort of negotiated settlement with parliament. Charles received a stream of reproachful missives from York while he was discussing the Treaty of Oxford in early 1643. 'If you make a peace and disband your army before there is an end of this perpetual parliament', she warned, 'I am absolutely resolved to go into France, not being willing again to fall into the hands of these people.'[35] Her hapless husband could only assure her that he had no intention of making peace and that the main purpose of the negotiation was to 'undeceive the people by showing it is not I but those who have caused and fostered this rebellion that desire the continuance of this war'.[36]

Once Henrietta Maria was back in England her entourage also began to re-establish itself and this added to the weight of her influence. Henry Percy was made general of the ordnance at her insistence in May 1643 and immediately began to upset all and sundry with his usual lack of tact. Henry Jermyn, her chief counsellor, was made a peer, Henry Wilmot became lieutenant general of the horse, Jack Ashburnham became treasurer to the army and a member of the council of war and, most significantly, in October 1643, Digby became secretary of state. The post, made vacant by Falkland's death at Newbury, had originally been promised to Hyde, but seeing which way the wind was blowing he was quick to withdraw his suit. By late summer the queen's followers were the dominant faction at court. The earlier balance had been overturned, the careful demarcation between the

---

[33] Clarendon, *Life*, vol. 1, p. 185.

[34] I. Roy, 'George Digby, Royalist intrigue and the collapse of the cause', in I. Gentles, J.S. Morrill and B. Worden eds, *Soldiers, Writers and Statesmen of the English Revolution*, Cambridge, 1998, pp. 79–81, 89.

[35] *Letters of Henrietta Maria*, p. 177.

[36] Ibid., p. 174.

different institutions of government was being abandoned and everyone, from Rupert downwards, had to defer to her influence.[37]

Charles's withdrawal to Oxford did, however, provide a fresh opportunity for peace negotiations, with the impetus this time coming from parliament. The Londoners' alarm at the prospect of another attack, combined with the heavy taxation introduced to support the war, led to a series of demonstrations during December 1642 and January 1643 which strengthened the hand of the parliamentarian 'peace party'. By mid-January Lords and Commons had agreed on a package of measures that would require Charles to abide by the bills approved by parliament, allow the trial of certain named delinquents and agree to the disbandment of the two armies.[38] These represented a considerable lowering of their demands since the Nineteen Propositions, but Charles was unenthusiastic. When parliament's commissioners arrived in Oxford on 1 February, he countered with his own proposals that his revenues, ships and forts be restored immediately and that there be a truce rather than disbandment. The commissioners at Oxford and the MPs at Westminster debated these at length and eventually came back with an offer of a 20-day cessation while the return of the ships and forts was discussed; however, Charles then raised his demands by pressing for an end to 'illegal' imprisonments by parliament and for the navy to be placed under the command of his nominees. Discussions continued throughout March and early April, but eventually the two houses decided that he was asking too much and terminated the process on 14 April.[39]

With hindsight it is apparent that these negotiations had little chance of success. The royalists appeared to enjoy a military advantage at the time and, even among the civilian privy councillors, there was little enthusiasm for the sort of concessions needed to break the deadlock. Most of the effort of Hyde and his allies was directed towards trying to bring about a split in the parliamentarian ranks by winning over some of the more moderate

---

[37] *Royalist Ordnance Papers*, pp. 20–1; Gardiner, *History of the Civil War*, vol. 1, p. 164; Hutton, 'Royalist party', p. 558; Roy, 'George Digby', p. 74; Clarendon, *Life*, vol. 1, p. 204. As David Scott points out in 'Rethinking royalist politics', several of the queen's inner circle, notably Jermyn, Percy and Wilmot, had been involved in the Army Plot and had a charge of treason hanging over them at Westminster. Just as for Pym and the leaders of the junto, almost any settlement would have been personally hazardous.

[38] Gardiner, *History of the Civil War*, vol. 1, pp. 78–82.

[39] Ibid., pp. 90–3, 99–101, 108–9.

delegates sent to Oxford.[40] Each time parliament came forward with proposals the king raised his demands. Most historians have concluded that
there was no serious intent to settle, and Gardiner cited a letter to the
marquis of Ormond on 2 February in which Charles himself declared that
'no less power than his who made the world of nothing can draw peace
out of these articles'.[41] However, it is important to recognise that this
was not necessarily how it appeared to the participants. Both Hyde and
Bulstrode Whitelocke, one of the Commons' commissioners at Oxford,
were impressed by the statesmanlike demeanour of the king and the
seriousness with which he pursued the treaty. They believed that the
source of opposition lay elsewhere. Whitelocke referred guardedly to 'some
in the bedchamber and some higher than they', while Hyde pointed the
finger firmly at the queen, observing that the king had promised that he
would 'never make any peace, but by her interposition and mediation'.[42]
Hyde was probably correct. Charles was anxious that the queen should
be seen to be involved in any settlement so as to restore her credit with
parliament.[43] He had also made various undertakings in his correspondence
with her which meant it was almost impossible for him to conclude a peace
on any terms that would be acceptable to his opponents. But, if this is
the case, it is worth asking why he appeared to take the negotiations so
seriously. The likely answers help to explain why supporters of a settlement
remained hopeful during the succeeding months, in spite of the apparent
difficulty of their task.

One of the main considerations appears to have been that, by continuing to talk the king gained a significant military advantage. Essex had
a large army at Windsor which was threatening both Reading and Oxford,
and the only thing holding it back was the truce that accompanied the
negotiations. A second concern was to retain the political advantage. As
Charles told the queen, he wanted the blame for breakdown to fall squarely
on the parliament. This was apparent throughout the negotiations in his

---

[40] Clarendon, *History*, vol. 3, pp. 9–12; Clarendon, *Life*, vol. 1, pp. 179–84.

[41] Gardiner, *History of the Civil War*, vol. 1, p. 89.

[42] *The Diary of Bulstrode Whitelocke 1605–1675*, ed. R. Spalding, British Academy Records
of Social and Economic History, new ser. XIII, 1990, pp. 143, 145–6; Clarendon, *Life*, vol. 1,
p. 187.

[43] *Letters of Henrietta Maria*, pp. 118–19.

constant reiteration of his desire for peace and his attachment to the rule of law. One can, perhaps, again detect the influence of Hyde, who was made chancellor of the exchequer in February 1643. The king's demands for measures to defend the prayerbook against sectaries and an end to the imprisonment of those refusing to pay parliament's illegal taxes were nicely judged to reinforce his stance of moderate constitutionalism and reach out to those on the parliamentarian side who wanted peace. However, perhaps, the most significant consideration was Charles's own strong sense of duty, and need to feel that he was occupying the moral high ground. He told the parliamentarian commissioners, 'I was always for peace and I am more concerned in it than any, being the Father of my country next under God.'[44] There is no doubt that he believed this; not, perhaps, sufficiently to make the sort of concessions that would allow a settlement, but certainly enough to go on talking and listening until his conscience was satisfied.

As usual, however, Charles had more than one set of irons in the fire. While he was negotiating at Oxford he was also working hard to secure armed support from overseas. Initially he directed his efforts towards the Danes who, in November 1642, supplied him with a large cache of arms. But they insisted on the secession of the Orkneys and Shetland before they would offer more substantial assistance, and this was something Charles was reluctant to do, for fear of offending the Scots. France offered possibilities after the deaths of Richelieu (November 1642) and Louis XIII (May 1643) removed the main obstacles to an alliance. But Mazarin was determined to proceed cautiously and his envoy did not reach Oxford until November 1643.[45] The best hope of aid appeared to lie in Ireland where Charles still had an army under the command of his lord lieutenant, the marquis of Ormond. However, before this could be made available a truce had to be arranged with the Catholics of the Irish Confederacy. This was finally agreed on 15 September 1643, after lengthy deliberations between Ormond and the Confederacy assembly at Kilkenny. By November the first contingents of the Irish army were being shipped over to England to join

---

[44] *Rupert & the Cavaliers*, vol. 2, pp. 159–60; Clarendon, *History*, vol. 3, pp. 8–9; *LJ*, vol. 5, p. 590.

[45] Gardiner, *History of the Civil War*, vol. 1, pp. 39, 64, 140–1, 270–3.

him; however, as usual, developments in Ireland set off a reaction in his other kingdoms.[46]

In England, news of negotiations with the Irish Catholics was relentlessly exploited by parliament's propagandists and undermined support for Charles among Londoners at a crucial juncture in June 1643. The greatest damage, however, was probably in Scotland. Here Charles had adopted delaying tactics. He recognised that he could probably hope for little in the way of positive support; but he wanted to hold off an alliance between parliament and the Covenanters, at least until he had had the opportunity to deliver a decisive blow in the 1643 campaigning season. Initially he was able to make use of the Scots' desire to broker a peace in the southern kingdom. When their emissaries arrived at Oxford in early 1643 he was able to keep them waiting with procedural queries until the middle of April. He then faced a choice of policies. He could either go along with a group of ultra-royalists, led by Montrose, who for months had been begging him to authorise an uprising in Scotland; or he could opt for the more cautious policy being advocated by Hamilton, who was now back in favour. This involved the building of bridges with the moderates who formed a majority of the senior Scottish nobility. Charles supported Hamilton and launched a northern propaganda offensive in which he circulated declarations announcing his hatred of popery and his determination to stand by the laws passed in Scotland in 1641. However, the marquis, characteristically, overestimated his ability to control the situation. The Covenanters were allowed to summon a convention of the Scottish parliament in June 1643, which authorised negotiations with the English parliament and eventually produced the Solemn League and Covenant. Their case was helped by revelations of a planned uprising in Scotland organised by the earl of Antrim and, even more, by news of Charles's negotiations with the Irish Catholics.[47] Nonetheless, Hamilton had at least ensured that the military intervention promised under the Solemn League would not materialise until 1644.

---

[46] *Early Modern Ireland*, pp. 302–9; Gardiner, *History of the Civil War*, vol. 1, pp. 120–5, 220–5, 248–9.

[47] Stevenson, *The Scottish Revolution*, pp. 248–93; Gardiner, *History of the Civil War*, vol. 1, pp. 176–8, 232–6.

At the start of 1643 the balance of military advantage lay with the king. He had a relatively unified and professional high command; morale was buoyant after early victories; and Rupert's cavalry were acknowledged to be the most effective fighting force on either side. He was hampered by a shortage of arms and ammunition, and during the spring he had to contend with the threat from Essex's army at Windsor; but, overall, he retained the initiative. The nature of his strategy at this juncture has aroused considerable debate. The traditional view, based on a hypothesis put forward by Gardiner, is that he planned a triple advance on London. This would involve Newcastle's northern army pushing down into East Anglia and Essex, Sir Ralph Hopton's Cornish contingents advancing from the West Country into Kent and Charles's main army confronting Essex near Oxford. The three armies would then surround London and starve it into submission.[48] However, various objections have been raised to this account. Malcolm Wanklyn has pointed out that there in no positive evidence for such a scheme in any of the king's correspondence or council of war minutes; and that the report by the Venetian ambassador in January 1643 which Gardiner cited as evidence was in reality no more than optimistic speculation on the part of the king's London agent.[49] Ian Roy, the leading authority on the royalist army, has also argued that until the king's shortage of ammunition was remedied in May it was almost impossible for him to contemplate offensive action with the Oxford army.[50] However, the most compelling objection to the whole hypothesis – again emphasised by Roy – is that it assumes a degree of centralised command and strategic control over the king's armies that simply did not exist.

The direction exercised by Charles and the council of war was for the most part confined to the Oxford army. Partly this was because of the shortcomings in intelligence and communications; but it was also a consequence of the king's lack of assertiveness as a commander-in-chief.[51] This was most apparent in his dealings with Rupert who was given enormous

---

[48] Gardiner, *History of the Civil War*, vol. 1, p. 67.

[49] M.D.G. Wanklyn, 'Royalist strategy in the south of England 1642–1644', *Southern History*, vol. 3, 1981, pp. 64–6; *CSP Ven. 1642–3*, p. 231.

[50] Roy, 'The Royalist Army', pp. 72–5.

[51] Ibid., p. 71; Roy, 'Council of war', p. 162.

latitude in deciding what action to take on his campaigns. Typical of the deferential tone that Charles adopted towards him was a letter of March 1643 in which he recommended 'to your consideration the assisting of the west', before adding 'I write not this to put the thought of Gloucester out of your mind, but only to lay all before you that you may choose the best . . . '[52] This was hardly calculated to inspire either confidence or obedience, and it allowed commanders like Rupert, and his brother Maurice, to assume that much of the time they could make their own decisions. It was a similar story with the earl of Newcastle and the northern army, although here the king seems to have felt constrained more by feelings of obligation and respect for his social position. He was keenly aware that in military terms his position was more like that of the leader of an aristocratic host than a national army. Newcastle and other peers had made monumental sacrifices to provide him with the men and money needed to fight and, in such circumstances, the king tended to be very hesitant about giving direct orders. 'I may propose many things to you', he told the earl in December 1642, 'but I will never impose anything on you.'[53] There is little doubt that he wanted Newcastle's army to advance south to assist him in 1643, but instead of commanding him to do so, he made various recommendations and suggestions that tended to get lost amid the complex processes of local lobbying that dictated the northern army's movements.[54] Evidence of communication with Hopton's western army is sparse; but here, again, there seems to have been a lack of any firm, central direction. All this has prompted Roy to conclude that 'it was hardly possible for the king seriously to put forward . . . a nation wide plan which could unite all these disparate forces'. His decision-making, at least up to the queen's arrival at Oxford in July, bore 'the stamp of improvisation rather than lengthy deliberation'.[55] However, this did not mean that he lacked a strategy for winning the war.

---

[52] *Rupert & the Cavaliers*, vol. 2, p. 140.

[53] Cited in Roy, 'The Royalist Army', p. 72. Charles had a similar relationship with the marquis of Worcester: ibid., p. 71. For the often difficult relationship between senior member of the nobility and the crown in military matters in this period, see D. Parrott, *Richelieu's Army: War, Government and Society in France 1624–1643*, Cambridge, 2001, pp. 463–504.

[54] These processes are illustrated in Henrietta Maria's letters from York in this period: *Letters of Henrietta Maria*, pp. 190, 195, 200, 203, 204–5, 208–9.

[55] Roy, 'The Royalist Army', pp. 72, 75.

Charles's main offensive in the early part of 1643 was political rather than military, and it was directed towards the City of London. In spite of having been expelled in January 1642 he had never given up hope of winning the sort of support he had enjoyed in November 1641. He was encouraged in this by constant reports of Londoners' dissatisfaction with parliamentarian rule and by the presence in Oxford of an influential lobby of exiled aldermen and merchants.[56] Charles prepared the ground with a series of proclamations and declarations aimed at reassuring Londoners that he would protect their interests and pardon those who refrained from bearing arms against him. When a delegation from the City came to Oxford in January 1643, he was careful to reiterate his desire for peace and his faith in their loyalty, while calling for the arrest of Mayor Pennington and the parliamentarian leaders. The constant refrain of these statements was that opposition in the capital was the work of a small group of 'stirrers of sedition' – including 'schismatical, illiterate and scandalous preachers' and 'desperate persons of the suburbs' – who had hoodwinked the majority of 'good subjects' and engineered a popular takeover.[57] This familiar analysis structured his whole policy. He acted on the assumption that if he could open the eyes of Londoners to the reality of their situation he would then be able to mobilise support for a coup against the rebel leadership.

Preparations for a coup began in January 1643 when he sent a young courtier, Henry Heron, to sound out support and probably also drop hints that it would soon be in the king's power to cut off trade to the capital. Then in March, while the Oxford negotiations were in full flow, Charles drew up a secret commission for Sir Nicholas Crispe and other London exiles to organise an armed uprising. This was sent to Edmund Waller, a royalist supporter still sitting in the Commons, with instructions to approach senior parliamentarians thought to be sympathetic to the king. Waller's Plot was a scheme to involve loyalist members of the London trained bands in seizing the City magazine, arresting the parliamentarian leaders in their beds and then opening the gates to a royalist army. However, it was thwarted by the discovery of the king's commission, and Waller escaped with his life

---

[56] I. Roy, ' "This proud, unthankfull City": a Cavalier view of London in the Civil War', in S. Porter ed., *London and the Civil War*, 1996, pp. 152–6.

[57] Clarendon, *History*, vol. 2, pp. 424–9, 433–5; *Proclamations of Charles I*, pp. 806–8, 825–6.

only by implicating Viscount Conway and Lord Portland.[58] As usual, the revelation of one of Charles's plots was enormously damaging. Coming at the same time as news of the talks with Catholics at Kilkenny, it suggested the king's stance in the Oxford negotiations had been a sham. It also did much to discredit the links that had been forged between the 'peace party' at Westminster and some of the civilian councillors at Oxford, because Pym was able to weave into the story evidence that Waller had been in close communication with Falkland. By mid-June the 'war party' had regained the political initiative in parliament and were able to push through measures such as a new loyalty oath. Charles responded with a much tougher line towards London. 'Our good people', he now claimed, had been overwhelmed, and the City had become 'the head of that traiterous faction and the receptacle of all such as are disaffected to our government'.[59] The attempt to divide his enemies was abandoned and, for the time being, he settled for a policy of trying to starve the capital into submission; however, the rapidly fluctuating military situation soon changed his approach again.

During July 1643 there was a dramatic upturn in the king's prospects. The gradual disintegration of Essex's army in Berkshire, followed by victories at Adwalton Moor (30 June) and Roundway Down (13 July) , the queen's arrival in Oxford at the head of a sizeable army (14 July) and finally Rupert's capture of Bristol (26 July) gave him a significant military advantage. When his main Oxford army joined up with Hopton's troops in Bristol at the beginning of August he appeared, at last, to have a force capable of delivering a decisive blow. Meanwhile, pressure for peace was pulling the parliamentarian leadership apart. The 'peace party' in the Lords, led by Bedford and Holland, came forward with a new set of proposals which represented a considerable climbdown from those on offer at Oxford. On 4 August the Commons voted in favour of considering these, only to reverse its decision three days later, prompting angry demonstrations in London and causing Bedford and Holland to defect to the royalist garrison at Wallingford.[60] Charles

---

[58] *CSP Ven. 1642–3*, pp. 230–1; Roy, 'London in the Civil War', pp. 159–62; Gardiner, *History of the Civil War*, vol. 1, pp. 111, 144–9, 156–8.

[59] Gardiner, *History of the Civil War*, vol. 1, pp. 148–9; Roy, 'London in the Civil War', pp. 162, 164; *Proclamations of Charles I*, pp. 932–4.

[60] Gardiner, *History of the Civil War*, vol. 1, pp. 183–4; Clarendon, *History*, vol. 3, pp. 142–3.

had already moved to make the most of these divisions with a carefully judged declaration on 30 July, again probably written by Hyde. This exploited the impact of the king's victories by arguing, in providential terms, that these demonstrated the justness of his cause. It then reaffirmed his commitment to the Protestation made at Wellington and invited all 'good subjects' to show their loyalty by turning against the 'state imposters' who claimed to act in the name of parliament.[61] It was a powerful plea which, in Hyde's words, presented the king as 'an indulgent father' rather than an avenging warrior, and it repaired some of the damage done by the Waller Plot. Charles's prestige and self-confidence were at their height, and it made good sense to be generous. If he could sustain his efforts to win over waverers and keep up the military pressure it seemed possible that the parliamentarian movement might split apart. At this point, however, he lost his way with a series of mistakes, both military and political.

Whether the king did the right thing in besieging Gloucester in August has long caused considerable debate. J.P. Kenyon and others have argued that this was the moment when he might have succeeded in executing a combined advance on London and achieving a decisive victory.[62] However, Malcolm Wanklyn has suggested that this was simply not feasible. The royalist army was too weak in infantry to defeat Essex in prepared positions around London, and anyway they needed to wait to see whether Newcastle responded to the king's calls to advance into East Anglia. Capturing Gloucester, on the other hand, could give the royalists control of the Severn Valley and unlock forces in South Wales to join their main army.[63] Even with hindsight, it is difficult to be certain what Charles should have done; however, it is clear that the guidance he received from his council of war was virtually unanimous in favouring the attack on Gloucester. There was a strong expectation that Edward Massey, the parliamentarian governor, would defect as soon as the king's army approached; and when this proved unfounded royalist commanders still confidently predicted that the town would fall within ten days. Even Rupert does not appear to have

---

[61] Clarendon, *History*, vol. 3, pp. 118–20.

[62] J.P. Kenyon, *The Civil Wars of England*, pbk. edn. 1989, p. 80; Roy, 'The Royalist Army', p. 77.

[63] Wanklyn, 'Royalist strategy in the south', pp. 64, 68–9.

dissented from this view.[64] It would have taken a much more confident commander than Charles to go against such clear professional advice.

The king was forced to raise the siege of Gloucester when Essex's relief force arrived at the outskirts of the city on 5 September. But he now had an opportunity to defeat the last main parliamentarian army in the field. After a chase across the Midlands, the two forces clashed in the First Battle of Newbury on 20 September. This was a confused encounter, fought among enclosed fields and ditches. The terrain denied Rupert's cavalry their usual opportunities for rapid manoeuvre and the parliamentarian infantry, stiffened by the London trained bands, were able to hold off repeated assaults. By nightfall the armies had fought each other to a standstill; however, the king still blocked Essex's line of retreat to London and one last push might have defeated his exhausted force. It was here that Charles made what was arguably the biggest blunder of the campaign. At a council of war that evening he received advice from Lord Percy, general of the ordnance, that his troops were so low on powder and shot that they must withdraw. This was opposed by several cavalry commanders, including Rupert, but Charles opted in favour of caution and ordered the retreat. Essex was free to make his way back to base and entered London in triumph on 25 September. The fortunes of the 'war party' at Westminster were restored and calls for peace were silenced.[65]

At the same time the king missed a considerable political opportunity. It had been apparent since early 1643 that several senior parliamentarian peers were on the verge of declaring for him and Hyde was keen to further this process by reviving the policy of bridging appointments. During the Oxford treaty negotiations he was involved in discussions about restoring Northumberland to the position of lord admiral in the expectation that this would further negotiations or, at least, deepen divisions within parliament's ranks. Charles, however, refused to agree to it on the grounds that Northumberland's recent record of disloyalty made it an unacceptable risk.[66] The defection of Bedford and Holland offered another opening, but

---

[64] Clarendon, *History*, vol. 3, pp. 129–34, 149.

[65] P. Young and R. Holmes, *The English Civil War. A Military History of the Three Civil Wars 1642–1651*, 1974, pp. 144–9; Gardiner, *History of the Civil War*, vol. 1, p. 237.

[66] Clarendon, *Life*, vol. 1, pp. 179–85.

this time the king faced an even trickier decision. Among his councillors there was a good deal of the jealousy felt towards any new converts to a cause and the queen was said to be implacably hostile. Hyde was quick to point out the potential for bringing about other defections; but he was virtually alone in recommending a generous reception, and Charles was reluctant to swim against the tide. In the end the whole issue resolved itself into a question of whether he would restore Holland to his position as groom of the stool. The earl felt that this was the least he deserved for the risks he had taken; but the king had already promised the post to the earl of Hertford, and was disinclined to go back on this unless Holland made an explicit apology for being involved in rebellion. There followed a deadlock in which pride and honour prevented either from giving way. Hyde coached Holland on how to make his apology, but he refused to act until the king made a clear gesture of goodwill. Charles, for his part, showed the earl every politeness, but was insistent that he must make the first move. Finally, in November 1643, he confirmed Hertford's appointment, where-upon Holland sneaked back to Westminster.[67] The king could hardly be blamed for acting the way he did. By all the standards of political protocol he was entitled to his apology. But a more calculating and ruthless politician would surely have taken the initiative, recognising that whatever the risks of offending against propriety and upsetting his own supporters this was a golden opportunity to divide the enemy leadership. As it was, Hyde reckoned that the treatment of the peers made Charles look 'implacable' and undid most of the good achieved by the 30 July declaration.[68]

Charles's main political initiative during the winter of 1643–4 was the Oxford Parliament. Hyde later claimed that it was he who first mooted the idea in the autumn of 1643. To start with Charles was uneasy, on the grounds that such an assembly would press him to make peace and disrupt pre-parations for the next campaigning season; but he agreed to refer it to the privy council. There followed an internal debate reminiscent of the late 1620s. The hardliners on this occasion appear to have urged that any concession to the constitutionalist position would weaken the king's cause. The majority, however, were able to trump this by demonstrating the

---

[67] Clarendon, *History*, vol. 3, pp. 146–52, 155–6, 193–200.

[68] Ibid., pp. 199–200.

tactical advantages of the parliament. It would rally royalist support against the impending invasion by the Scots, highlight the rebelliousness of the assembly at Westminster and deprive the 'ill affected' there of a means of hoodwinking 'the people'. Charles showed – as he tended to when the arguments were finely balanced and the case was put in language he understood – that his instinct was to follow the constitutional line. He would later profess to regret the summons of this 'mongrel' parliament; but at the end of 1643 it appeared to him as a shrewd, and entirely acceptable, means of building political support.[69]

The king's agreement to a summons was not, however, the end of the matter. The queen's party then intervened and urged Charles to take this opportunity to declare the Westminster Parliament dissolved. The king floated this with Hyde, putting a view which had surfaced repeatedly in his correspondence with the queen, that 'there was too much honour done to those rebels at Westminster in all his declarations by his mentioning them as part of his parliament'. Hyde was appalled. If the king took this step it would destroy one of the chief planks of his platform as a constitutional monarch. He replied with some carefully chosen comments about how suspicion of Charles's readiness to stand by the 1641 legislation had been 'the first powerful reproach they had corrupted the people with towards his Majesty'. He also observed that a breach of the act against dissolution 'would confirm all the fears and jealousies which had been infused into them and would trouble many of his own true subjects'. These were arguments that Charles could understand and he quickly backed down. Hyde was commissioned to draft the proclamation for the summons to Oxford which, while urging members of both houses to join the new assembly, carefully avoided any claim that it was the only true parliament.[70]

The assembly that convened in Christchurch Hall on 22 January 1644 was, in many respects, Charles's most successful parliament. In spite of initial worries, there was a healthy turnout, which made it a credible alternative to the assembly at Westminster, and it proceeded to deliver much

---

[69] By the end of December 1643 even the queen's ally Digby was putting a positive gloss on it: *CSP Dom. 1641–3*, p. 510.

[70] Clarendon, *Life*, vol. 1, pp. 206–13; *Proclamations of Charles I*, pp. 987–9. The case appears to have been put initially by Attorney-General Herbert who had formerly been the queen's attorney-general.

of what the king hoped for. Peace overtures were made to the earl of Essex during January and February, but these were rebuffed, which led to a declaration by the two houses at Oxford blaming those at Westminster for starting the war and destroying hopes of peace.[71] The parliament also delivered a wholehearted condemnation of the Scottish invasion, voting that members at Westminster, and anyone else who assisted the Scots, were guilty of high treason. Furthermore, MPs broadly accepted the king's case for supply for the coming campaign, authorising him to issue privy seal letters (which Hyde claimed brought in £100 000) and also to levy the controversial excise. Much of the credit for this success lay with Hyde and Culpepper who were given responsibility for managing the lower house. They consulted extensively with MPs before opting for privy seal letters as the least onerous way of raising money, and allowed them considerable leeway in criticising the army and wartime profiteering. They also made use of their pivotal position to push the constutionalist agenda before king and council. According to one report, Culpepper came forward at the start of the parliament with a proposal that as pledges of his goodwill the king pass 'an act against papists' and offer to deliver up those proclaimed as delinquents before the war and still serving in his army. This got short shrift from Digby, Jermyn and Percy, and Henrietta Maria herself was said to be 'much offended at it'.[72] But the fact that it could be proposed at all indicated the way in which the existence of the parliament had given the initiative to the constitutional royalists. This was also apparent from the tone of the king's speeches which showed him at his most gracious and emollient. He told MPs that he welcomed the opportunity to take advice from 'such counsellors', commended their overtures for peace, encouraged them to pursue any grievances against his army and promised that he would abandon

---

[71] Gardiner, *History of the Civil War*, vol. 1, pp. 300–1; Clarendon, *History*, vol. 3, pp. 294n, 296–7. Contemporary estimates suggest that as many as 137 members of the Commons and 44 members of the Lords (which was a considerable majority of able-bodied peers) were in attendance in late January 1644: Huntington Library, California, Hastings MSS, HA 8060; Smith, *Constitutional Royalism*, p. 118.

[72] Clarendon, *History*, vol. 3, pp. 293n, 305–6; *The Kingdom's Weekly Intelligencer*, no. 41, 23–30 January 1643/4, E30 (19). As David Scott points out, Culpepper's motion may have had more to do with a desire to embarrass some of his rivals in the circle around the queen than any concern for peace; however, it still illustrates the force of the constitutionalist agenda in this particular forum: 'Rethinking royalist politics'.

'extraordinary' measures, like the excise, as soon as circumstances allowed. Hyde probably had a hand in writing these speeches, but the king himself was plainly aware of the need to appease the assembly's members.[73]

This was made easier, of course, because it was basically a meeting of loyalists. Once their peace overtures had been rejected at Westminster, MPs recognised that they had to give Charles the means to go on fighting or else everything they had struggled for would be lost. They also appear to have been conscious of the need to draw a distinction between their own behaviour and that of the squabbling rebel assembly. Observers commented on how well behaved MPs at Oxford were, with a high degree of consensus and unanimity.[74] At last, Charles had a lower house of the type he had been seeking throughout the late 1620s and early 1640s. It was probably the nearest he ever came to the assembly of those 'wise and well tempered men' that he was forever appealing to in his declarations and speeches.

The first session at Oxford, which ended on 16 April 1644, was also a high point in the king's efforts to present himself as a constitutional monarch. He sent members back to their shires on 16 April 1644 with a plea to 'inform all my subjects . . . how solicitous I have been for peace . . . assuring them that my armies are raised and kept only for the defence of their religion, laws and liberties which once being secured and vindicated I shall most cheerfully lay them down'.[75] Peace had not actually been achieved, but the king had been able to take the moral high ground by reiterating his 'unwearied desire' for a settlement and his determination to uphold tradition and legality. As John Morrill and Ronald Hutton have shown, this was a principal theme of the royalists' management of their war effort. Throughout the war they lagged several months behind parliament in taking emergency powers over matters such as compulsory impressment or the introduction of the excise, and when they did so they were careful to emphasise that these were temporary expedients, born of 'extraordinary necessity'. They also made every effort to administer the war through the traditional machinery of quarter sessions and assizes. Local assemblies were

---

[73] Rushworth, vol. 5, pp. 560–1, 565, 599–600, 601–2.

[74] A.L. Hughes, 'King, parliament and the localities during the English Civil War', *JBS*, vol. 24, 1985, pp. 256–7; *Rupert & the Cavaliers*, vol. 2, pp. 377–8.

[75] Rushworth, vol. 5, pp. 601–2.

required to sanction decisions about monthly contributions or sequestration and provided courts of appeal for those aggrieved at military decisions.[76] Hutton, in particular, has criticised this approach and argued that Charles would have been more successful if he had more readily entrusted power to 'the swordsmen'; however, such a verdict places too heavy an emphasis on the purely military aspects of winning the war. If Charles was to be successful, he had to win the political battle. The 1643 campaign demonstrated that even if he was victorious in the field he would still find it very hard to mobilise the resources needed to take London. His best chance lay in negotiation from a position of strength, with a divided and demoralised enemy. To succeed in this he needed to take every opportunity to assure the 'peace party' at Westminster that he was sincere in his attachment to the principles set out in the Wellington manifesto. This was basically the course advocated by Hyde and the supporters of a constitutional agenda in his privy council. Just as in 1642 their approach had enabled him to fight a civil war, now it probably offered his best chance of winning it.

Charles had enough of a grasp of political realities to recognise this – especially when it was explained to him by the reassuring figure of Sir Edward Hyde. However, he was always susceptible to other influences, notably that of the queen. Up to the moment of her departure for Exeter in April 1644, Henrietta Maria remained the most powerful figure at court, after Charles himself. The loose coalition between her own entourage and the 'swordsmen', led by Prince Rupert, held firm and continued to control the distribution of patronage and the running of the war.[77] However, as at other times during the reign, court observers tended to overestimate the queen's influence on policy making. It is harder to assess the extent of this than in 1642–3 because we no longer have her revealing correspondence with her husband; but it would appear that Charles remained stubbornly insistent that there were certain key areas – to do with peace overtures and the Oxford Parliament – which were his preserve and that of his civilian councillors. The queen seems to have acquiesced in this, recognising that it was important not to overplay her hand. Her approach was summed up in a

---

[76] J.S. Morrill, *Revolt in the Provinces*, 2nd edn, Harlow, 1999, pp. 111–18; R. Hutton, 'The Royalist war effort', in Morrill ed., *Reactions to the English Civil War*, pp. 55–7.

[77] Roy, 'George Digby', pp. 74–5; *Rupert & the Cavaliers*, vol. 2, pp. 400, 405–6; Hutton, 'Royalist party', pp. 561–2.

letter to Newcastle in February 1644 in which she acknowledged that it was right and proper that the king should 'listen to a peace provided that it was honourable for him'; but at the same time she drew encouragement from the fact that 'they are so haughty in London that they will make no propositions', in which case the French were likely to come in on the royalist side.[78] She could also console herself with the knowledge that she was pushing forward her agenda on other fronts.

The most hopeful of these appeared to be the negotiations with the French. In October 1643 the Comte de Harcourt arrived in England, with the declared aim of making peace. After a brief, and unproductive, stay in London, he arrived in Oxford amid high expectations that France was about to declare for the king. A special council committee was established which drew up a 'wish-list' for French aid, while the queen lobbied hard and mobilised her contacts in Paris. At the end of the day, however, Harcourt remained unmoved. He left Oxford in February 1644 without making any commitments, and it later transpired that his instructions from Mazarin were not to back either side in the war, but to keep the conflict simmering.[79]

Another area where the queen was hopeful of progress was Ireland. She had long urged Charles to use 'all means possible' to make peace with the Confederacy so that he could deploy extra troops in England.[80] When the earl of Antrim, husband to her close friend the former duchess of Buckingham, arrived at court in December 1643 there seemed to be an opportunity to achieve this. Antrim offered to use his influence with the Irish Catholics to raise an army of 10 000 men for use in England – in addition to around 20 000 who were already in transit as a result of Ormond's treaty of September 1643 – and a further force of 2–3 000, to join up with Montrose in Scotland. In return, the Confederacy wanted a peace based on repeal of the penal laws, an end to plantation and security of tenure for the 'Old English', and the establishment of a free Irish parliament which could deal with the crown on the same terms as that in England. Their negotiators arrived in Oxford in March 1644, but from the start were treated with a good deal of suspicion. The Oxford Parliament was still in

---

[78] *Letters of Henrietta Maria*, p. 235.

[79] Gardiner, *History of the Civil War*, vol. 1, pp. 271–3; Roy, 'George Digby', p. 80.

[80] *Letters of Henrietta Maria*, p. 156.

session and was adamantly opposed to concessions to Catholics in Ireland or anywhere else. This was a view shared by Hyde, Nicholas and the majority of the privy council who appreciated how damaging such concessions could be to the king's image as defender of the church. Charles himself prevaricated. He badly wanted the troops, but he recognised that the political price was too high. It was left to the queen and Digby – neither of whom felt much compunction about offending Protestant opinion – to keep the negotiations moving forward. By the time the Confederacy's agents left Oxford in May they had achieved some modest success, with the 'Old English' contingent on the brink of an agreement.[81]

The other area where the queen made her presence felt was in the continuation of plotting. Charles continued to be attracted to the idea of simply cutting through the tangled web of calculation and compromise with a sudden *coup de main*. Over the winter of 1643–4 he became involved in two separate conspiracies. There was the Ogle Plot, arranged by Digby and his father, Bristol, which involved concessions to disgruntled Independents in return for the surrender of the parliamentary garrison at Aylesbury; and the Brooke Plot, promoted by the queen and the duchess of Buckingham, which was another attempt to divide the mayor and City of London from the parliament. All too predictably, both plots miscarried. The Ogle conspiracy was betrayed by the garrison commander at Aylesbury, and when Rupert turned up to seize the town he walked into an ambush. Charles's letter to the Catholic Sir Basil Brooke fell into parliament's hands in January 1644 and, by exploiting the involvement of Digby and the queen, parliamentarian propagandists were able to make this look like another instance of 'popish plotting'. The fall out once again made the king look devious and insincere, and damaged the prospects of the peace lobbies on both sides.[82] As long as the king continued to dabble in plots and engage in negotiations with the Irish, those seeking a political resolution faced an uphill struggle. However, on 17 April, their prospects improved

---

[81] J.H. Ohlmeyer, *Civil War and Restoration in the Three Stuart Kingdoms. The Career of Randal MacDonnel, Marquis of Antrim 1609–1683*, Cambridge, 1993, pp. 49–50, 129–30; J. Lowe, 'Charles I and the Confederation of Kilkenny, 1643–9', *Irish Historical Studies*, vol. 14, 1964, pp. 1–6; *Early Modern Ireland*, pp. 306, 311–12; Roy, 'George Digby', pp. 78–9.

[82] Gardiner, *History of the Civil War*, vol. 1, pp. 264–70, 273–5; A. Sumner, 'The Political Career of Lord George Digby until the end of the First Civil War', University of Cambridge, Ph.D. thesis, 1985, pp. 211–17.

considerably when the heavily pregnant queen left Oxford to seek refuge in the south-west.[83] The resulting shift in the balance of power at court opened the way for the Uxbridge negotiations of the following winter.

Meanwhile the king's attention turned once more to the war. Devising a positive strategy for the 1644 campaigning season was largely impossible. From the start the royalists were thrown onto the defensive. Early defeats at Nantwich (25 January 1644) and Cheriton (29 March) largely prevented them from enjoying the benefit of their Irish reinforcements; and they now had to deal with the formidable Scots army that crossed the Tweed on 19 January and rapidly advanced into Yorkshire. The royalist high command also continued to be plagued by poor communication and lack of central direction. The council of war met regularly, under Charles's supervision, but it could still do little to control the movements of provincial armies. It also suffered increasingly from internal divisions between the soldiers and the civilians. There was a general sense that the Scots were the main threat, but little consistency or agreement over how to deal with them. In late March, following Rupert's dramatic relief of Newark, there was an opportunity to act decisively; but the prince was first told that the council would not interfere in his decision about what to do next, then, a few days later, ordered to march back to Oxford immediately to provide protection for the queen.[84] Perhaps the clearest indication of the lack of grip at the heart of royalist planning was the famous letter from Charles to Rupert before Marston Moor, which the prince interpreted as a command to fight the Scots.

This was written on 14 June when the king was near Bewdley, short of supplies and being chased around the Midlands by the combined forces of Essex and Waller. It was one of a series of increasingly despondent missives in which Charles conveyed the impression that unless Rupert could do something dramatic in the north, the game would be up.[85] 'If York be lost,' the king lamented,

---

[83] Gardiner, *History of the Civil War*, vol. 1, pp. 330–2.

[84] Young and Holmes, *English Civil War*, pp. 173–6; Roy, 'Council of war', pp. 162–6; *Rupert & the Cavaliers*, vol. 2, pp. 397–405.

[85] 'The happy progress and success of the arms of the ever blessed memory from the 30th of March to the 23rd of November 1644', in Sir Edward Walker, *Historical Discourses on Severall Occasions*, 1705, pp. 23–4; *Rupert & the Cavaliers*, vol. 2, pp. 415–16.

I shall esteem my crown little less, unless supported by your sudden march to me and a miraculous conquest in the south before the effects of their northern power can be found here. But if York be relieved and you beat the rebels' army of both kingdoms which are before it, then (but otherwise not) I may possibly make a shift (upon the defensive) to spin out time until you come to assist me.[86]

What is most striking about this is its lack of clarity. It is not hard to see why Rupert interpreted it as an order to fight no matter what. By the standards of Charles's previous communications it was unusually emphatic.[87] But the tortured and qualified phraseology suggests a king who lacked the confidence to issue clear instructions. This impression is compounded by the reports that Digby and Wilmot had a hand in writing the letter, and that the crucial words '(but otherwise not)' were inserted at Wilmot's insistence.[88]

The defeat at Marston Moor destroyed the king's hold on the north; but he was saved from disaster by some equally inept decision-making on the part of his opponents. During May, Essex and Waller had encircled Oxford and driven the king to seek refuge in Worcester. However, on 6 June they took a misguided decision to divide their forces, leaving Waller to continue the pursuit of the king while Essex marched into the West Country to relieve Lyme Regis. Charles was able to rejoin his main army at Oxford and get the better of Waller's force at Cropredy Bridge on 29 June. He then pursued Essex, trapped his army of 10 000 men at Lostwithiel in Cornwall and finally forced it to surrender at the end of August.[89] It has been argued that this campaign was his finest hour as a commander. He became, according to Peter Young and Richard Holmes, 'generalissimo in practice as well as in name', displaying 'a firm grip' throughout and handling operations with

---

[86] *Rupert & the Cavaliers*, vol. 2, pp. 438–9. A few days later, with the news that Essex and Waller's armies had divided, Charles's situation had improved dramatically and had he been able to get another letter through to Rupert it would probably have been couched in very different terms; but this was the last instruction from the king that Rupert received before the battle.

[87] Roy, 'The Royalist Army', pp. 89–90.

[88] *Rupert & the Cavaliers*, vol. 2, pp. 436–8.

[89] Young and Holmes, *The English Civil War*, chps. 13–15.

'a cool confidence in himself'. His personal success amounted to the 'most striking' royalist military achievement of the war.[90] This is somewhat over-stating the case;[91] nonetheless, it does point to a significant improvement in the king's performance as a soldier.

The first point to address here is the extent to which Charles was, in fact, in command of his army. This was the one campaign in which he took charge for long periods without the guidance of Rupert; but this does not necessarily mean that he was taking the crucial decisions. Gardiner has argued that he leaned heavily on the professional skills of his senior general, the earl of Forth; and Ian Roy suggests that much of the credit was due to the council of war which was particularly effective in coordinating tactics and logistics.[92] However, both these verdicts would appear to underplay the king's role. Much of the time he was having to make the choice between conflict-ing conciliar advice, as is evident from the contemporary account by the secretary to the council, Sir Edward Walker.[93] Sometimes he got it wrong: for example, in late June when he wasted several days considering a fruitless proposal to attack London; or after Cropredy when he had to be talked out of marching to the aid of the marquis of Winchester at Basing House. (As usual, Charles regarded it as a matter of honour to be seen to be respond-ing to pleas for help from those who were serving his cause loyally.[94]) But he also showed that he could act promptly and decisively, notably in early June when the council dithered and it was he who took the bold decision to cut himself free from Oxford and thereby gain a crucial advantage.[95] Hyde's view was that Charles should have backed himself more in his dealings with the council of war.[96] He 'always suspected, at least trusted less to his own judgement than he ought to have done which rarely deceived him so much as that of other men'. The 1644 campaign suggests that Hyde had a point.

---

[90] Ibid., p. 212.

[91] For a more judicious assessment see Jones and Wanklyn's account of the campaign in *A Military History*, chp. 17.

[92] Gardiner, *History of the Civil War*, vol. 1, p. 351; vol. 2, p. 13; Roy, 'Council of war', pp. 163–4.

[93] Walker, 'The happy progress . . . 1644', pp. 5–81.

[94] Ibid., pp. 28–9, 38.

[95] Ibid., pp. 18–19.

[96] Clarendon, *History*, vol. 3, p. 344.

The king also showed himself to be a competent tactician. At Cropredy he had been quick to recognise the danger of allowing his army to become divided and gave instructions for the crucial cavalry charge which saved the day.[97] In the operations around Lostwithiel he relied heavily on the expertise of his nephew, Prince Maurice, but also made important contributions of his own. After tightening the noose around Essex's force, he personally directed the attack on 21 August which closed off its retreat; and at the final engagement on 31 August he joined his men in the field and inspired the decisive charge by his own lifeguards. In the event, much of the strategic value of Charles's victory was lost, because of the length of time it took to defeat Essex and the terms granted to his army which allowed the bulk of it to march away to Portsmouth.[98] Nonetheless, it was a considerable fillip to royalist morale which owed much to his own performance as commander-in-chief.

The boost this gave to the king's self-confidence was reflected during the final phase of campaigning in 1644, culminating in the Second Battle of Newbury. At a meeting in early October, Charles and Rupert came up with a bold plan to join forces for an attack on the Eastern Association. This had to be abandoned because of the slowness of the king's advance out of the West Country, and calls for relief of the royalist garrisons at Banbury, Basing and Donnington. But with the assistance of Goring, who was now in charge of his cavalry, Charles made a series of forays to disrupt parliamentarian rendezvous in the south.[99] He continued to consult the council of war at every stage, but was now providing a much clearer sense of direction. He also showed that he was not afraid to give clear advice to Rupert. Letters to the prince were still prefaced with assurances that he would be allowed to do 'what in your judgement you shall think fit', but 'his Majesty's wishes' were now much more straightforwardly explained.[100] If anything, the king became a bit too confident on this campaign. Having detached Rupert's force, and another under Northampton, he left himself

---

[97] M.R. Toynbee and P. Young, *Cropredy Bridge, 1644*, Kineton, 1970, pp. 92–4.

[98] Young and Holmes, *The English Civil War*, pp. 207–10; Walker, 'The happy progress . . . 1644', pp. 63–6, 74–5; Jones and Wanklyn, *A Military History*, chp. 17.

[99] Jones and Wanklyn, *A Military History*, chp. 17; Young and Holmes, *The English Civil War*, pp. 214–15.

[100] *Rupert & the Cavaliers*, vol. 3, pp. 12–13.

with only 9 000 men when he faced the much larger parliamentarian army at Newbury. Undismayed, he took the decision to dig in and try to exhaust the enemy. The battle that took place on 27 October allowed little scope for him to display his generalship because he was mainly fighting on the defensive. But he does appear to have been responsible for the decision to retreat through a gap in the parliamentarian army and recover the safety of Oxford. He returned in November, reinforced by Rupert, and successfully accomplished the relief of the three garrisons before settling back at Oxford on the 23rd.[101]

Because of the loss of the north Charles ended 1644 in a much weaker position militarily than he had begun. But he was still in the fight, largely due to his own success in the West Country. All the indications are that on this campaign the king grew up as a military commander. The nervous and deferential novice of 1643 and early 1644 had been replaced by a leader who was not frightened to act decisively and take the fight to the enemy. He was still better at the tactics than the strategy; but his leadership was becoming an asset to the royalist cause rather than a handicap.

On his return to Oxford Charles was greeted by parliamentarian commissioners with fresh proposals for accommodation. These had been drawn up at the behest of the 'peace party' at Westminster and the Scots who were increasingly desperate to head off the possibility of a radical/Independent takeover.[102] They opened the way for the negotiations at Uxbridge in February 1645, which represented the last big push by those royalist councillors seeking a negotiated settlement. It was recognised, even by the normally upbeat Digby, that the king's prospects for the 1645 campaigning season were not good and that this overture offered a final chance of securing a realistic peace.[103] Parliament's initial 'Propositions' called for Charles to take the Solemn League and Covenant and agree to the introduction of Presbyterianism. They also required him to authorise control of the militia passing into the hands of their commissioners, to allow various named

---

[101] Young and Holmes, *The English Civil War*, pp. 215–23; Walker, 'The happy progress . . . 1644', pp. 110–21.

[102] Gardiner, *History of the Civil War*, vol. 2, pp. 76–8, 99.

[103] For a pessimistic assessment from the normally upbeat Digby, see Hyde, *Life*, vol. 1, p. 216.

royalists to be proceeded against as delinquents and to rescind the treaty with the Irish Confederacy.[104] These were considerably tougher than the demands made at Oxford in early 1643 – reflecting the deterioration in the king's military position – but they still appeared to privy councillors to offer the basis for a negotiation. There seemed to be scope for compromise over articles on the militia and delinquents, and few of them had any sympathy for the Irish. The main sticking point was likely to be Presbyterianism; but, with the exception of Hyde, most councillors did not share Charles's devotion to episcopacy and probably believed there was room for movement even on this.[105]

From the start, it was civilian councillors, such as Richmond and Southampton, who drove the process forward. They appear to have secured the king's cooperation mainly by appealing to his sense of duty and his recognition of tactical advantage. Charles clearly remained open to the notion that a good king should do everything in his power to bring an end to bloodshed and civil war.[106] Alongside this he understood that there was considerable advantage to be gained by reopening discussions at this juncture. As he told the queen, the divisions within parliament's ranks offered 'a very good hope' that 'the ring-leading rebels could not hinder me from a good peace'.[107] Even if 'a good peace' was out of reach, there was still an excellent opportunity to sow dissension in their ranks with the sort of personal approaches that Hyde had managed in 1643.[108]

The 'peace' lobby also benefited from the changed climate at court. With the queen in Paris and her party in disarray, one of the main obstacles to accommodation was removed. Moreover, Rupert, who had previously

---

[104] Gardiner, *History of the Civil War*, vol. 2, p. 124.

[105] David Smith's view that most 'constitutional royalists' felt as strongly as Charles did about preserving episcopacy does not appear to hold water. Hyde probably did, but, as Charles himself acknowledged on several occasions, he was very much in a minority. His views were certainly not shared by the likes of Culpepper: Hyde, *Life*, vol. 1, p. 213: *Charles I in 1646*, p. 30. In 1646 Culpepper and Jermyn were to claim that at Uxbridge even the royalist divines present were not willing to make the case for *iure divino* episcopacy; *Clarendon State Papers*, vol. 2, p. 263. On this point, see also, Scott, 'Rethinking royalist politics'.

[106] See, for example, *A Forme of Common Prayer to be used upon the solemne fast appoynted by his Majestie's proclamation of 5 February for a blessing on the treaty now beginning . . . 3 Feb., Thomason 1644*, E27 (4), pp. 10–12.

[107] *King's Cabinet Opened*, p. 11.

[108] Whitelocke, *Diary*, p. 158; *Evelyn*, p. 797; Clarendon, *History*, vol. 3, pp. 494–5.

opposed peace negotiations, could now see the tactical advantages, and gave the process his blessing.[109] This allowed the supporters of settlement a clear run at court, and they were able to build up such momentum that Charles was forced to admit that had he not gone along 'the breach of treaty had been laid upon me, even by my own party'.[110] Richmond, Lindsey, Southampton and others warmly welcomed the parliamentarian commissioners at Oxford and then persuaded the king to take seriously a suggestion by Holles and Whitelocke that he go to London to negotiate in person. When this was blocked at Westminster, they were able to persuade him to adopt the alternative of negotiations at a neutral venue. These were to take place without his being present, which the councillors believed, according to Hyde, would allow more 'freedom of their communications' with their parliamentarian counterparts.[111] Perhaps their greatest coup was talking Charles into acknowledging 'the two houses sitting at Westminster to be a parliament'. This happened at a packed council meeting on 5 December, with Rupert in attendance. Charles later claimed to the queen that 'if there had been but two (besides myself) of my opinion I had not done it'.[112] He was allowed to save face by means of an entry in the council register declaring that 'the calling did no ways acknowledge them to be a parliament'; but there was no disguising the fact that he had made a major concession which confirmed the success of the constitutionalists in binding him to the legislation of 1641. The queen was predictably furious. She reminded him that in allowing 'the title of parliament of England' he had just gone back on the first of the 'grounds' that he had promised he would 'never relax'.[113]

The discussions that preceded Uxbridge demonstrated that, given the right circumstances, Charles's moderate councillors were still capable of managing him; but they also showed that this could only be done up to a point. The king continued to hold firm opinions of his own, and also to

---

[109] *Rupert & the Cavaliers*, vol. 3, p. 47.

[110] *Letters of Henrietta Maria*, p. 278.

[111] Clarendon, *History*, vol. 3, p. 464.

[112] NA, PC 2/53, p. 231; *King's Cabinet Opened*, pp. 4–5. The only support Charles had was from Nicholas: *Rupert & the Cavaliers*, vol. 3, p. 42.

[113] *Letters of Henrietta Maria*, pp. 276–7.

be influenced by the queen.[114] For her part, Henrietta Maria was determined to curb what she saw as his dangerous instinct for compromise. She bombarded him with a stream of letters reminding him of the 'grounds' which, he had assured her – apparently in a written memorandum – he would never abandon. As well as doing everything possible to put an end 'to the perpetual parliament', these consisted of standing by the bishops and 'poor Catholics', remaining faithful to 'those who have served you' and preserving 'the sword that God has placed in your hands . . . not to quit it till you are a KING'.[115] With slight differences of emphasis, Charles shared these objectives and much of his correspondence over the winter was aimed at reassuring her that he would never be 'threatened or disputed' from them. However, as Conrad Russell has observed, he does seem to have harboured nagging doubts about his capacity to achieve this.[116] Therefore, to secure himself, he resorted to a negotiating technique that he was to follow in the post-war period.

This involved beginning the discussion by fixing his 'negatives'. He explained in October 1646 that by resolving 'what is not to be done . . . the degrees of inconveniencies (in my judgement) are easilyest discerned, and men are not so readily stolen into errors'.[117] In the context of Uxbridge, this meant drawing up a series of 'Directions' for the royalist commissioners in which he reiterated his determination to stand by the bishops, keep control of the militia and avoid being dictated to over Ireland.[118] Russell has pointed out that such an approach allowed little scope for the 'constructive embracing of opportunities', which was what was needed if compromise was to be achieved.[119] But, then, this was not what Charles wanted. He wanted peace, but it had to be 'a safe and honourable peace', which meant preserving episcopacy and maintaining control of the militia. Anything less was, in his view, not worth having. So deciding

---

[114] Charles's scepticism about the likely outcome of negotiations was apparent in his letters to the queen: *King's Cabinet Opened*, pp. 7, 38.

[115] *Letters of Henrietta Maria*, pp. 276–7, 279, 283, 286, 288.

[116] Russell, *Causes of the Civil War*, p. 205.

[117] *Clarendon State Papers*, vol. 2, p. 273.

[118] *Evelyn*, p. 797; *King's Cabinet Opened*, pp. 6–7, 15, 26–7.

[119] Russell, *Causes of the Civil War*, p. 206.

first on what was non-negotiable made a good deal of sense, not least as a means of controlling his councillors.

In spite of these constraints the councillors ploughed on, making several brave attempts to give impetus to the talks. During the first round of discussion on the church the marquis of Hertford proposed that they resolve that neither Presbyterianism nor episcopacy were *iure divino*. This was certainly something that Charles did not agree with, but it might have laid the basis for a compromise. Then, in the second round of talks on the militia, Southampton attempted to move discussion forward with a contro-versial scheme for the joint nomination of a body of commissioners.[120] In the final analysis, however, what wrecked negotiations was not so much Charles's meddling as the mutual suspicions on the parliamentarian side, which prevented the commissioners going much beyond the initial pro-positions. On 20 February 1645 the royalists made a final effort to keep the process alive by again proposing that Charles go to London to treat in person; but once more this was blocked at Westminster.[121]

Uxbridge was the high water mark for those seeking a settlement to end the war. Almost as soon as the negotiation was over, their power at court was effectively dismantled. First of all, on 10 March, Charles prorogued the Oxford Parliament. He had become increasingly irritated with its persistent lobbying for peace and told the queen how glad he was to be rid of this 'place of base and mutinous motions (that is to say our Mongrel Parliament here)'.[122] By removing it he signalled that he was turning his back on the constitutionalist agenda which was essential for reaching out to moderate parliamentarians. This was surely a mistake. As James Daly has pointed out, the king's strongest political card in 1645 was probably to offer to reunite the Westminster and Oxford assemblies. This was rumoured to be a condition of his going up to London in February 1645.[123] Had it happened – or even been suggested – it would have further divided his enemies and might, even, have created a majority in favour of peace on reasonable terms.

---

[120] Whitelocke, *Diary*, pp. 163–4.

[121] Gardiner, *History of the Civil War*, vol. 2, pp. 129–30.

[122] *King's Cabinet Opened*, pp. 12–13.

[123] J. Daly, 'The implications of royalist politics, 1642–6', *HJ*, vol. 27, 1984, p. 754; Gardiner, *History of the Civil War*, vol. 2, p. 130.

The other development that damaged the cause of accommodation was the revival of a scheme for setting up a council for the Prince of Wales at Bristol. This was sold to the king as a means of ensuring that he and the prince should not be captured together – the likely outcome of which would be 'murdering him and crowning his son' – and of putting some backbone into the newly constituted Western Association.[124] But for its chief proponent, Digby, it also offered a means of strengthening his position at court and clearing away some of the opposition to the plan for bringing over another Irish army. Among those dispatched to Bristol was Hyde, who had long been one of the scheme's main opponents.[125]

The aftermath of Uxbridge also brought out into the open a bitter rivalry between Digby and Rupert. Following the departure of the queen, Rupert was in prime position to take over as the king's favourite. As a member of the royal family he enjoyed a special relationship, which Charles was in the habit of describing as similar to that with his own son.[126] He was also the pre-eminent soldier on the royalist side, something the king recognised by making him captain general in November 1644. And he was well positioned at court, succeeding Hamilton in the crucial post of master of the horse in May 1645.[127] However, in political matters Rupert was often his own worst enemy. Like the earl of Essex in the 1590s, he tended to interpret every appointment to office as a test of favour and every setback as a slight on his honour. Charles never got the measure of him and veered between over-indulgence and loss of patience. He tried to calm things down by arranging a reconciliation with Digby in August 1644; but this was no more than temporary and by November Rupert was threatening to resign when he did not get his way over the command of the royal lifeguards.[128] The urbane Digby was able to run rings round his foe. Since

---

[124] Gardiner, *History of the Civil War*, vol. 2, pp. 180–2; Clarendon, *History*, vol. 3, p. 502; Clarendon, *Life*, vol. 1, pp. 216–17, 219.

[125] Scott, 'Rethinking royalist politics'.

[126] *Rupert & the Cavaliers*, vol. 3, pp. 152, 212.

[127] Hutton, 'The royalist party', pp. 562–5; *King's Cabinet Opened*, p. 4.

[128] *Rupert & the Cavaliers*, vol. 3, pp. 23; HMC, *Fourth Report*, 1874, p. 297. As in the 1630s, Charles placed a high premium on ensuring that his councillors got on with each other. For his efforts to reconcile quarrels between Richmond and Ashburham, and Hyde and Culpepper, see Clarendon, *Life*, vol. 1, pp. 223, 227, 229–30.

his appointment as secretary of state he had steadily been making himself indispensable, demonstrating his effectiveness as a man of business and taking on tasks that other councillors shied away from, like managing the Irish negotiations. His polished, courtly manners and almost feline instinct for intrigue were a complete contrast to his blundering rival. He was always careful to avoid confronting Rupert directly, especially when it came to the delicate business of passing on royal instructions. But he rarely neglected an opportunity to undermine him by reminding the king and fellow courtiers of his touchiness and unreliability.[129] By March 1645 he was on the way to becoming established as Charles's most influential adviser. The ill feeling between the two would-be favourites was to be a feature of the summer campaigns, and eventually caused considerable damage to the royal cause.

After a bout of pessimism following the fall of Shrewsbury on 22 February, Charles became increasingly upbeat about his military prospects for 1645. By late March he was declaring to the queen that 'I am confident to be in a better condition this year than I have been since this rebellion began'.[130] This optimism had two principal sources. First of all the king had come to believe that, at last, divine providence was starting to work in his favour. Charles always attached great weight to God's providential judgements and had been convinced that his misfortunes in the early stages of the civil war were a punishment for his weakness in signing Strafford's death warrant. What persuaded him that this was about to change – apparently at the suggestion of Digby – was parliament's execution of Archbishop Laud on 10 January 1645. 'This last crying blood being totally theirs', he informed the queen, 'I believe it is no presumption hereafter to hope that his hand of justice must be heavier upon them and lighter on us . . . having passed by our faults.'[131] Confidence in divine deliverance was to be an increasingly prominent theme in the letters of both Charles and Digby and was to play an important role in military decision-making.

---

[129] Sumner, 'The political career of Digby', pp. 188–217, 220–3, 238–40; Roy, 'George Digby', pp. 75–82; *Rupert & the Cavaliers*, vol. 3, pp. 135–6, 160–1.

[130] Clarendon, *Life*, vol. 1, p. 216; *King's Cabinet Opened*, p. 3.

[131] *King's Cabinet Opened*, p. 24. For further evidence of Charles's belief in providence, see *A Forme of Common Prayer*, pp. 11–15.

The other event that fuelled Charles's sense of optimism was the earl of Montrose's success in Scotland. Following the discrediting of Hamilton at the end of 1643, Charles had agreed to support the earl's plan for an uprising in the Highlands. In February 1644 Montrose was given a commission as lieutenant general and headed north to raise an army. By July he had united several of the highland clans with Antrim's 2 000 Irishmen and set off on a devastating campaign of conquest. In September he defeated Lord Elcho at Tippermuir and captured and sacked the Covenanter town of Aberdeen. Then, during the winter, he marched across Scotland to the Campbell strongholds of the Western Highlands and on 2 February 1645 destroyed Argyll's clan army at Inverlochy. With Scotland at his mercy, he wrote to Charles urging him to abandon the Uxbridge negotiation and march north to join him.[132] It was this letter which, more than anything, raised the king's hopes. He could now envisage recapturing northern England with Montrose's assistance, and then returning south to deliver the decisive blow.

As the campaigning season opened, Charles appeared to have three options. He could concentrate his army at Oxford and continue the strategy of the previous autumn, using Rupert's cavalry to make rapid strikes against weak points in the parliamentarian defences. The problem with this was that Oxford remained too exposed and vulnerable to provide a secure base for a large army.[133] The second possibility was to concentrate on the west, where Goring had achieved some success over the winter and the prince's council was beginning to get to grips with recruiting. The key to the situation here was the parliamentarian stronghold at Taunton. If this could be captured it would give the royalists complete dominance of the area. A siege might also draw Fairfax's New Model Army into the field before it was ready to fight.[134] The third option was a northern campaign that would relieve pressure on Chester – thus clearing the way for the expected landing of the 10 000 troops from Ireland – and also open up the possibility of defeating the Covenanter army in England. This was the strategy that both

---

[132] Gardiner, *History of the Civil War*, vol. 1, pp. 297–9, 336; vol. 2, pp. 135–55.

[133] Ibid., vol. 2, pp. 180, 201; Kenyon, *The Civil Wars*, pp. 124–5.

[134] Kenyon, *The Civil Wars*, p. 134; Gardiner, *History of the Civil War*, vol. 2, pp. 181–3, 205–6.

Charles and Rupert appear to have favoured from March onwards.[135] However, the final decision was not taken until a critical council of war meeting at Stow-on-the-Wold on 8 May.

The previous day, Charles had marched out of Oxford at the head of an army of over 11 000 men, including both Rupert and Goring's cavalry. Present at the meeting was an array of senior commanders and councillors, and, according to the two principal sources, Walker and Hyde, it resolved itself into a faction battle between Rupert and Digby. The secretary, supported by Goring, Ashburnham and most of the others present favoured the western campaign; but Rupert, backed by Sir Marmaduke Langdale, commander of the Northern Horse, held out for the march into the north. Rupert basically prevailed. It was decided that the bulk of the army should head north-west, but that Goring and his 3 000 cavalry should reinforce the Prince of Wales and undertake the siege of Taunton.[136] This division of the king's main army has been seen by historians as a colossal blunder – having more to do with Rupert's desire to separate his enemies Digby and Goring than any military priority – and Charles has been allotted much of the blame for allowing it to happen.[137]

It is difficult to be certain what happened at Stow; however, it is possible to read the evidence in a way that presents Charles's actions much more favourably. It is important to recognise that both Walker and Hyde were writing at some distance from the events and both wished to portray royalist defeat in 1645 as a consequence of factional squabbling.[138] They, therefore, tended to play down the role of the king almost to the point of excluding him from the decision-making process. This seems implausible,

---

[135] Gardiner, *History of the Civil War*, vol. 2, pp. 185, 203, *King's Cabinet Opened*, p. 3; Walker, 'Brief memorials of the unfortunate success of his Majesty's army and affairs in the year 1645', in *Historical Discourses*, p. 125; Clarendon, *History*, vol. 4, p. 34.

[136] Walker, 'Brief memorials . . . 1645', pp. 125–6; Clarendon, *History*, vol. 4, pp. 35–6.

[137] Gardiner, *History of the Civil War*, vol. 2, pp. 209–10; Kenyon, *The Civil Wars*, p. 141; A. Woolrych, *Battles of the English Civil War*, pbk. edn., 1966, p. 107.

[138] Walker's account of 1645 is much less well informed and authoritative than that for 1644 and it is far from clear that he actually attended many of the important council of war meetings. He was writing it in exile in 1647, and from the opening page (p. 125) it is clear that he wished to place most of the blame on Rupert, and his quarrels with Digby. Hyde was not present at the meetings and was drawing on Walker as his principal source: Firth, 'Clarendon's "History of the Rebellion"', pp. 52–3.

given his prominent role in previous council of war meetings and his enhanced confidence in his abilities as a general. It is also not the impression given in a letter written by Charles to Henrietta Maria a few days after the meeting. Here the strategy decided on at Stow is presented very much as his own. In supporting the northward march he was remaining consistent to the plan he had been contemplating since March, and also to the general principle of endorsing the judgement of his captain general. Moreover, as he explained to the queen, it was a plan that gave him several positive options. He would be able to keep the gateway open for Irish reinforcements and then choose either to continue northwards to deal with the Scots army, or head south to meet Fairfax, or even break into the counties of the Eastern Association. Based on the information he had at the time, the Scots appeared to be the main danger, but with Montrose in their rear he now had the opportunity to defeat them decisively. Fairfax's New Model seemed to offer the lesser threat, and by reinforcing the Prince of Wales with Goring's cavalry he was confident of containing him until he was able to march his main army southwards.[139] As so often in the summer of 1645, Charles was acting on faulty intelligence but, given the information at his disposal, the decision to divide off part of his army at Stow did make military sense.

For most of the campaign that followed, Charles and Rupert were in the position of reacting to events rather than controlling them. But they played their hand quite skilfully and avoided serious mistakes until the eve of the battle at Naseby. Charles's army headed initially for Chester, then turned back when they received news that the siege of the town had been lifted and Fairfax was advancing into the Midlands. Goring was summoned to rejoin the main army in Leicestershire, reinforcements were ordered from Sir Charles Gerrard in Wales and preparations were made for a decisive battle. Then on 26 May news reached the king that the New Model Army had laid siege to Oxford, which was short of provisions and in danger of being captured. Charles and Rupert kept their nerve and recognised that this was also an opportunity. If Oxford could hold out for a few weeks and pin down Fairfax's force then they would be able to run free in the Midlands and the North. The benefits of this were demonstrated at

---

[139] *Letters of Henrietta Maria*, pp. 303–4. See also his letter of 14 May: *King's Cabinet Opened*, p. 10.

Leicester on 31 May when, after a sharp assault, the town fell to Rupert.[140] Throughout May and early June strategic decisions continued to be referred to the council of war which, according to Walker and Hyde, remained riven by faction. Rupert himself saw things very much the same way, complaining bitterly to his client William Legge that Digby and Ashburnham's advice at the council was guided by a fear that 'the soldiers should take from them the influence which now they possess with the king'.[141] These differences certainly caused a good deal of disharmony; however, it is not obvious, as historians have tended to assume, that, at this stage, they seriously hampered military decision-making. For the most part, Charles continued to back the judgement of his captain general and when he did not it was to pursue the sensibly cautious approach of shadowing Fairfax and waiting for him to make the next move.

More damaging problems were caused by a lack of accurate information and the king's own overconfidence. Poor intelligence was one of the hazards of early modern warfare, but even by the standards of the day Charles was particularly badly informed on the Naseby campaign. The reports he receeived consistently underestimated the strength and cohesion of the New Model Army, and he had little knowledge of its whereabouts, due apparently to Rupert's failure to organise adequate patrols.[142] He was also in the dark about the reinforcements he had ordered from Goring and Gerrard. Goring had in fact decided to stay put and besiege Taunton, while Gerrard was stuck in South Wales. But this information did not get through and the royalist high command went on assuming that reinforcements would arrive any day. These problems were compounded by Charles's overestimation of his own strength and prospects. Buoyed by news of more successes for Montrose and reports that the New Model Army was falling apart after failing to capture Oxford – as well as by his continuing faith in a providential deliverance – he told the queen

---

[140] Young and Holmes, *The English Civil War*, pp. 236–7; Gardiner, *History of the Civil War*, vol. 2, pp. 231–3.

[141] Walker, 'Brief memorials . . . 1645', pp. 125–8; Clarendon, *History*, vol. 4, pp. 34–7; *Rupert & the Cavaliers*, vol. 3, p. 100.

[142] Van Creveld, *Command in War*, pp. 19–23, 33–4; R.N. Dore, 'Sir William Brereton's siege of Chester and the campaign of Naseby', *Trans. Lancs & Cheshire Arch. Soc.*, vol. 67, 1957, pp. 36–7; Kenyon, *The Civil Wars*, p. 143; Young and Holmes, *The English Civil War*, p. 249; Gardiner, *History of the Civil War*, vol. 2, p. 240.

on 8 June that 'since this rebellion my affairs were never in so fair and hopeful a way'.[143] In fact, he was dangerously exposed. His army was now reduced to around 9 000 men and faced a force totalling around 14 000.[144] In these circumstances, the decision to give battle at Naseby on 14 June was an appalling error.

Historians have tended to follow Walker's version of events and attribute this decision to the factional divisions within the council of war.[145] 'A council being presently called,' Walker records, 'resolutions were taken to fight . . . contrary (as 'tis said) to Prince Rupert's opinion, it being our unhappiness that the faction of the court, whereof the most powerful were the Lord Digby and Mr Ashburnham, and that of the army ever opposed and were jealous of others.'[146] There are, however, several circumstances which, again, cast doubt on Walker's veracity. First the rather vague and distanced terms in which he recorded the episode suggest he was reporting a story he had heard rather than an event he had witnessed; and there were other stories circulating at the time which suggested that Rupert actually favoured giving battle but was opposed by some of the 'old commanders', notably Lord Astley.[147] Second, it seems highly unlikely that Charles would have contradicted his captain general over such as critical decision. And third – and most tellingly – Lord Digby emphatically denied that any council of war meeting actually took place, telling William Legge a few weeks later 'I am sure no council was called'.[148]

A more probable scenario is that the crucial decision was taken by Rupert and Charles at the last minute. When news reached the royal army that the New Model Army's cavalry were only eight miles away, the initial orders were to withdraw. On 13 June the army moved back from Daventry to Market Harborough with the intention, as Charles explained to Nicholas that

---

[143] *King's Cabinet Opened*, p. 14.

[144] Charles claimed in a letter to Nicholas in early June that he had only 7 000 men, but he may have been economical with the truth in order to convince him that he could not go to Oxford's rescue: *Evelyn*, p. 800. I am grateful to Malcolm Wanklyn for guidance on the size of Charles's army.

[145] Woolrych, *Battles of the English Civil War*, p. 120; Hutton, The royalist party', p. 566.

[146] Walker, 'Brief memorials . . . 1645', p. 129.

[147] Bulstrode Whitelocke, *Memorials of the English Affairs*, 4 vols., 1853, vol. 1, p. 447.

[148] *Rupert & the Cavaliers*, vol. 3, p. 127.

evening, of marching the next day to Melton Mowbray and then on to Newark, where they could join up with reinforcements before confronting Fairfax.[149] This entirely sensible strategy appears to have been overturned at 2 a.m. on the night of the 13th–14th, when news was brought to Charles's quarters that Fairfax and the New Model Army were close at hand.[150] What followed is unclear, but it appears that after a hurried consultation with Rupert, Charles gave the order to draw up his army for battle. No council of war meeting was held because at that time of night it was impractical. But why Charles should change his resolution of the previous evening is still a puzzle. He could have retreated if he had wanted to, even with the New Model Army breathing down his neck. His army was preparing to do this anyway and, as Walker observed, in seventeenth-century warfare it was very difficult to bring the other side to battle unless they wanted to fight.[151] The assumption must be that Charles and Rupert made a positive calculation that they had more to gain by fighting than retreating. And, although unprovable, it appears likely that this calculation was based on ignorance of the strength of the New Model Army and the feeling that Charles had had since the spring, that providence was now working in his favour.[152] The decision to give battle at Naseby was arguably the most important military decision of the entire war. It was the supreme test of Charles's judgement as a commander and he failed it.

During the battle itself Charles played only a limited role. Rupert took charge of the deployment of the royalist army and then led the charge on the right wing, which scattered Ireton's cavalry. If he had been able to draw rein and turn against the parliamentarian infantry, the royalists might have had a chance of victory. As it was, by the time his cavalry returned to the field the weight of numbers in the centre and the attack by Cromwell's cavalry on the left had forced the rest of the royalist army to give ground. Charles was positioned to the centre and the rear with the royalist reserve consisting of his own life-guards. As resistance crumbled in front of him

---

[149] *Evelyn*, p. 802.

[150] 'Iter Carolinum', in *Somers Tracts*, vol. 5, p. 271; *Richard Symonds' Diary of the Marches of the Royal Army*, ed. C.E. Long, Cambridge, 1997, p. 193.

[151] Walker, 'The happy progress . . . 1644', p. 12; Van Creveld, *Command in War*, p. 26.

[152] Digby's letter to Legge at the end of June confirms that the royalists had no clear idea of the strength of the New Model Army: *Rupert & the Cavaliers*, vol. 3, p. 127.

he prepared to charge the parliamentarian cavalry, but just as he was about to do so the earl of Carnwarth pulled him away and 'swearing two or three full blooded Scottish oaths said "Will you go upon your death in an instant" '. Seeing the king in apparent retreat the life-guards moved back and by the time they had sorted themselves out the bulk of the royalist infantry were surrendering.[153]

Naseby shattered the king's main field army and greatly damaged his political prospects. Less than a thousand royalists were killed, but 4 500 were taken prisoner, many of them veteran infantry. The king's coach was also captured and with it much of his recent correspondence with the queen. This was immediately published as *The King's Cabinet Opened*, which dealt a considerable blow to supporters of a settlement on both sides since it suggested that Charles's stance at Uxbridge had largely been a sham. Whatever he might say in public, his letters showed that he was far from willing to accept the legitimacy of the Westminster Parliament. Even more damagingly, they revealed that he was continuing to negotiate to bring over a Catholic Irish army, with concessions which included abolition of the penal laws not only in Ireland, but England as well.[154]

During the weeks following Naseby, Charles's strategy was to con-solidate his position in the West and await the arrival of Scots and Irish aid. Rupert was sent to Bristol to organise its defence and the king set up base at Raglan Castle in South Wales where he attempted to recruit fresh levies.[155] A royalist revival was still not out of the question; but Charles did much to forestall it by his inept handling of the quarrel between Rupert and Digby.

After his second defeat in a major battle, Rupert needed reassurance that the king still valued his military judgement and would defend him against his critics. But this Charles signally failed to provide. His confidence in the prince's military prowess had been shaken and at Raglan he was surrounded by advisers like Digby who steadily undermined Rupert's reputation with snide comments about lack of loyalty and judgement. Nonetheless, he should have recognised that any revival of his military fortunes depended

[153] Young and Holmes, *The English Civil War*, pp. 246–8; Kenyon, *The Civil Wars*, pp. 143–6.

[154] Kenyon, *The Civil Wars*, p. 146; Gardiner, *History of the Civil War*, vol. 2, pp. 257–8.

[155] Kenyon, *The Civil Wars*, p. 14; Gardiner, *History of the Civil War*, vol. 2, p. 275.

on cooperating closely with his captain general. Rupert tried to rescue the situation at a full council of war meeting at Blackrock, near Cardiff, on 21 July. There Charles agreed to join him at Bristol and concentrate on repairing the damage caused by Goring's recent defeat at Langport. Had he made this move it would probably have done much to restore their relationship. But three days later he wrote to inform the prince that he had changed his mind and that Digby would explain the reasons in a covering letter, 'I not having time myself to do it'.[156] Even by Charles's standards, the letter was a particularly crass misjudgement. In his state of anxiety about the malign influence of Digby, the last thing Rupert needed was a rebuff by his king. To make matters worse, the letter was accompanied by rumours that Charles was about to head north to join the Scots without him.[157] He reacted by writing to Richmond, his closest friend at Raglan, explaining that it was his considered view that 'his Majesty hath now no way left to preserve his posterity, kingdom and nobility, but by a treaty'. Richmond passed this on – which may not have been an entirely friendly act – and the king was predictably incensed.[158] Such defeatism confirmed the doubts he had about his nephew and appeared calculated to undermine his prospects for recovery. He responded with a long and pained justification for his actions, followed by a firm injunction 'not in any wise to hearken after treaties' since 'the very imagination . . . will lose me so much the sooner'.[159] Rupert must have realised that he had made a grave tactical error; but once the king departed for the North, on 5 August, there was little he could do about it.

The breach between king and captain general was a disaster for the royalist cause. Not only was Rupert the royalists' most capable soldier, but he also enjoyed the confidence and loyalty of other key military figures, notably his brother Maurice and Sir Charles Gerrard. By alienating his nephew, Charles disrupted his high command and contributed to the loss of Bristol a few weeks later. The premature surrender of the town appears to have had a good deal to do with the prince's sense of rejection. For the king it

---

[156] Gardiner, *History of the Civil War*, vol. 2, p. 276; *Rupert & the Cavaliers*, vol. 3, p. 148.

[157] *Rupert & the Cavaliers*, vol. 3, p. 156. For Rupert's suspicion of Digby, see ibid., pp. 121, 145.

[158] Ibid., pp. 149–50.

[159] Clarendon, *History*, vol. 4, pp. 74–5.

was the last straw. He wrote bitterly to Rupert of his sense of betrayal and promptly dismissed him from all his commands.[160]

It can be argued, of course, that the prince brought his fate upon himself, through his naivety and petulance. He was in many ways the most difficult and unstable senior politician that Charles ever had to handle. But the king must bear the brunt of the blame, for failing to protect him against his enemies and displaying obtuse insensitivity when he needed reassurance. During the early part of the civil war he had managed the court relatively effectively and kept a grip on faction; but by 1645 the politicians around him were out of control and had become, in Ian Roy's memorable phrase, 'like a basket of crabs where each member struggled for survival against the rest'.[161] Partly this had to do with the circumstances. It was harder for Charles to command amid the stresses and strains of a war going badly and he greatly missed the controlling influence of the queen. But it was also a reflection of his own shortcomings as a political leader. One of the things he was not good at was cracking the whip and imposing his will. This weakness was graphically illustrated when Rupert visited the king at Newark in October 1645, in an attempt to vindicate himself. The visit ended with a shouting match in which the prince, accompanied by Maurice, Gerrard and Sir Richard Willys, the recently dismissed commander of the garrison, burst in on Charles and told him to his face that 'the cause of all this is Digby'. The king at first tried to stand firm, demanding to know 'Why do not you obey me, but come to expostulate with me?'; but Gerrard responded by telling him plainly that it was 'because your Majesty is ill informed'. Charles then resorted to a characteristically plaintive sarcasm: 'Pardon me, I am but a child. Digby can lead me where he list. What can the most desperate rebel say more?' When this failed, he finally silenced his antagonists by telling them that they were 'all rogues and rascals that say so, and in effect traitors that seek to dishonour my best subjects'.[162] This remarkable cameo – assuming that it was accurately reported – says much about the dynamics of Charles's relationship with senior court politicians.

---

[160] Kenyon, *The Civil Wars*, pp. 150–1; *Rupert & the Cavaliers*, vol. 3, p. 185.

[161] Roy, 'The Royalist Army', p. 79.

[162] *The Bloodie Treatie, or Proceedings Between the King and Prince Rupert*, 1645, Thomason E 311 (27), pp. 4–6. On the veracity of this account, see Roy, 'George Digby', p. 68.

Most of the time he dealt with them at a distance, shielded by a carapace of formality and deference. In a situation like this, where he was divested of much of his royal authority and faced by men with little to lose, he lacked the force of personality needed to command respect. He was not good at the shouting matches and bullying that any political leader needs to be able to resort to on occasions. Instead, he tended to fall back on a hurt sarcasm, or else foreclose discussion by invoking his royal authority. This made him look weak and ineffectual, and left those he was dealing with with an intense sense of frustration. What was required, above all, as the royalist cause disintegrated, was strong leadership. It was something Charles was unable to provide.

During the late summer and early autumn of 1645 Charles's military prospects went from bad to worse. Goring's defeat at Langport on 10 July, followed by the fall of Bristol on 11 September allowed Fairfax and the New Model Army to range freely across the South West, mopping up royalist garrisons. The effort to recruit fresh levies in Wales came to nothing and by the end of July, with the peace negotiations stalled, it was clear there would be no new troops from Ireland either. In retrospect it is apparent that Charles's best hope of a breakthrough on this front had been the previous summer, when the 'Old English' were close to an agreement. But his misgivings about making concessions over Catholicism and the difficulties of negotiating at long distance had prevented a settlement. By mid-1645 the native Irish and clerical groupings within the Confederacy were asserting themselves much more effectively and the concessions being demanded had risen accordingly.[163] Charles's main hope remained Scotland where Montrose appeared to be on the brink of forcing the Covenanters to settle and then use their army against the parliamentarians. However, on 27 September he received news that the earl's army had been destroyed at Philiphaugh.[164] This put an end to any hopes of a military revival in 1645 and by the beginning of November he was back in Oxford attempting to shore up his position.

During this period Charles's mood oscillated between optimism and near despair. The confidence of the spring and early summer had not entirely evaporated and Digby, who was now firmly established as his

[163] *Early Modern Ireland*, pp. 314–16; Lowe, 'Charles I and the Confederacy', pp. 6–19.

[164] Gardiner, *History of the Civil War*, vol. 2, pp. 215–28, 277–86, 291–300, 347–57.

chief councillor, was always ready to feed his hopes of a providential deliverance. Even after the disaster of Philiphaugh he clung to the hope that Montrose would be able to raise another army and regain the initiative.[165] However, the steady stream of disasters undermined his generally fragile sense of self-assurance. The fall of Bristol was a particularly severe blow, which he described to Prince Maurice as causing him 'more grief than any misfortune since this damnable rebellion'. He also wrote to Prince Charles ordering him to get ready to leave for France, and impressing on him that should he be captured he must, on no account, 'yield to any conditions that are dishonourable, unsafe for your person or derogatory to royal authority'.[166] In his own mind, then, Charles was preparing for the worst.

The main effect of this was to make him more determined than ever not to 'quit his grounds'. In a letter to Nicholas during August, he reaffirmed his intention

never to yield up this church to the government of papists, Presbyterians, or Independents, nor to injure my successors by lessening the crown of that ecclesiastical & military power which my predecessors left me, nor forsake my friends, much less to let them suffer, when I do not, for their faithfulness to me.[167]

These were in essence the same 'negatives' as he had set out at Uxbridge; but this time he added a warning for Nicholas to pass on to his fellow councillors. Any who advised him 'to recede in the least title, I shall esteem him either a fool or a knave'.

This inflexibility was closely connected with Charles's thinking about providence and conscience. He remained convinced that God would ensure ultimate victory for the royalist cause, but he was coming to accept that he might not necessarily be the instrument for achieving it. His role, therefore, must be to remain 'constant' and trust to God's purposes. To do otherwise would be to invite further judgements against him. These ideas

---

[165] *Evelyn*, pp. 806, 809. For Digby's optimism, see *CSP Dom. 1645–7*, pp. 118, 122.

[166] *Rupert & the Cavaliers*, vol. 3, p. 189; Clarendon, *History*, vol. 4, pp. 168–9.

[167] *Evelyn*, p. 806. See also his letter to Ormond on 31 July 1645: T. Carte ed., *The Life of James Butler, Duke of Ormond*, 6 vols., Oxford, 1851, vol. 6, pp. 305–6.

were spelt out in the letter to Rupert rejecting the suggestion of a treaty. 'Speaking either as a soldier or as a mere statesman', he confessed, 'I must say there is no probability but of my ruin.'

But as a christian I must tell you that God will not suffer rebels to prosper, or this cause to be overthrown; and whatever personal punishment it shall please him to inflict upon me, must not make me repine, much less to give over this quarrel; and there is as little question that a composition with them at this time is nothing else but a submission which by the grace of God I am resolved against, whatever it cost me.[168]

There was a side of the king, then, that was very consciously turning away from what at other times he referred to as 'policy'. His priority was to make his peace with God by remaining firm to his principles.

The stoical strain that was a feature of Charles's thinking became much more pronounced in this period, to the point where he began, openly, to contemplate the possibility of his own martyrdom. It was something he had alluded to as early as December 1642 when he told Hamilton that he was 'resolved that no extremity or misfortune shall make me yield, for I will either be a glorious king or a patient martyr'.[169] This resolution now became a regular point of reference in his letters. Writing to his son in June 1645, he emphasised that 'the saving of my life by complying with them [measures to diminish royal authority] would make me end my days with torture and disquiet of mind . . . But your constancy will make me die cheerfully.' To Digby the following March he insisted 'that if I cannot live as a king, I shall die like a gentleman'.[170] This determination set the tone for his approach to the final stages of the civil war and severely restricted his scope for political manoeuvre.

During this period Charles became isolated from the majority of his own councillors. In October 1645 Digby departed the court in a final, fruitless attempt to link up with Montrose. This left him with only two senior courtiers whom he regarded as reliable: the ever-loyal Nicholas and Jack Ashburnham who now took over as his principal adviser. The rest he dismissed as

---

[168] Clarendon, *History*, vol. 4, p. 74.

[169] NAS, GD 406/1/167/1 and 2.

[170] Clarendon, *History*, vol. 4, pp. 168–9; *Letters of Charles I*, p. 176.

'inclinable to the most flexible counsels', and he made no effort to conceal his disgust at their defeatism and disloyalty.[171] His privy councillors, for their part, made one last bid to get him to see sense. Soon after his return to Oxford, Dorset, Hertford, Lindsey and Southampton – first of all one by one and then in full council – pleaded with him to negotiate for peace. Charles's reported response was that he 'would place his crown on his head and preserve it with his sword if the swords of his friends failed him'. This appears to have been the final straw. If the French envoy is to be believed, they then approached the two houses at Westminster with an offer to surrender Charles's person in return for guarantees of his safety and their own inclusion in a general pardon. The scheme came to nothing because the king heard rumours about it and made his own offer to travel to London.[172] But the readiness of four such senior and long-standing royal servants to contemplate what was, in effect, a coup against their king, was a measure of the desperation induced by Charles's determination to reject the negotiating process.

During the winter of 1645–6 the various military alternatives collapsed. Hopes of bringing over the 10 000 troops from Ireland evaporated as the papal envoy Cardinal Rinuccini mobilised the Catholic clergy to block the Confederacy's efforts at settlement. Another scheme for the queen to provide troops from France had to be abandoned when Charles ran out of places for them to land safely. And his last field army capitulated at Stow-on-the-Wold on 21 March.[173] Seemingly all that was left to him was to try to divide his enemies by playing them off against each other. This was the policy to which he now applied himself.

The political circumstances of early 1646 offered Charles plenty of opportunity. The divisions at Westminster between Presbyterians and Independents had deepened, and the Scots Covenanters had become seriously disenchanted with their English allies. There was continual

---

[171] Gardiner, *History of the Civil War*, vol. 2, p. 371; *Charles I in 1646*, pp. 11–12. See, for example, his reply to Dorset's speech welcoming him back to Oxford in November 1645, that 'his voice was the voice of Jacob; but his hands were the hands of Esau': Smith, 'Dorset and the Civil Wars', p. 824.

[172] Smith, *Constitutional Royalism*, pp. 126–7; Gardiner, *History of the Civil War*, vol. 3, pp. 16–17.

[173] *Early Modern Ireland*, pp. 318–21; Gardiner, *History of the Civil War*, vol. 3, pp. 58–68; Kenyon, *The Civil Wars*, pp. 155–6.

bickering over the payment and deployment of the Scots army and it was becoming clear that the Westminster Parliament would not accept a Presbyterian church along Scottish lines. Charles recognised there was an opening and was prepared to offer all sorts of vague assurances to deepen the splits between his enemies. His proposal to come to London in December–January, for example, was accompanied by hints that he would allow toleration for Independents.[174] What he was not prepared to do, however, was shift from his 'grounds', and this undermined his best chance of success.

Since the late summer of 1645 Mazarin's envoy, Montereuil, had been working to broker a deal with the Scots. The basis of this was that if Charles accepted a Presbyterian church settlement in England, the Scots would press the English parliament to reinstate him and, if they refused, would take his side against them. In this eventuality, Mazarin also agreed to provide military aid. Henrietta Maria in Paris accepted the conditions on Charles's behalf in November, then set about persuading him to agree.[175] However, she found herself running up against the immovable obstacle of her husband's conscience.

The sticking point in the whole negotiation was Charles's unwillingness to give up the bishops and accept Presbyterianism. Digby had warned in August 1645, when the matter was first raised, that no one could get the king even to pretend to go along with it.[176] Charles spelt out his reasons in a lengthy correspondence with the queen during January and February 1646. Partly these had to do with overconfidence. He consistently overestimated the strength of his own position, believing that if he held out, the Scots would have to soften their demands, to avoid the risk that he would do a deal with the Independents. But the main consideration was his conscience. Abandoning the bishops and the Church of England, he insisted, was contrary to his coronation oath, which would be 'a sin of the highest nature'. It would be a denial of his very faith, comparable to asking the queen 'to leave the communion of the Roman church'. It would also 'ruin'

---

[174] D. Stevenson, *Revolution and Counter Revolution in Scotland 1644–1651*, 1977, pp. 54–64; Gardiner, *History of the Civil War*, vol. 3, pp. 16, 22, 27; *Clarendon State Papers*, vol. 2, pp. 196–7; *Letters of Charles I*, p. 176.

[175] Stevenson, *Revolution and Counter Revolution*, pp. 58–9.

[176] Gardiner, *History of the Civil War*, vol. 2, p. 286.

his crown since the 'chief maxim' of the Presbyterians was 'that all kings must submit to Christ's kingdom, of which they are the sole governors'.[177] Seen in the light of his past failings and future prospects, to concede on these points now would be to reject the destiny that he believed God had mapped out for him.

I must confess (to my shame and grief) that heretofore I have for public respects . . . yielded unto those things which were no less against my conscience than this, for which I have been so deservedly punished that a relapse now would be insufferable; and I am most confident that God hath so favoured my hearty (though weak) repentance that he will be glorified either by relieving me out of these distresses . . . or in my gallant sufferings for so good a cause, which to eschew by any mean submission cannot but draw God's further justice upon me, both in this and the next world.[178]

These arguments went to the heart of Charles's psychological make-up and sense of self. In the last resort, he clung to the belief that as long as he remained a true defender of the Church of England God would deliver him, in this world or the next. Faced by such conviction there was little that even the queen could do.

Charles's obduracy wrecked any chance of an alliance with the Scots while he was still in a position to benefit militarily. Discussion continued through early 1646, with neither side willing to give way. He did not give up hoping and calculating, telling Digby in March 1646 that he was 'endeavouring to get to London' where he aimed 'to draw either the Presbyterians or Independents to side with me, for extirpating the one or the other', and that he was confident 'I shall really be king again'.[179] Eventually, however, his hand was forced by the advance of Fairfax's army on Oxford. After several hesitations and false starts, he decided that continuing to work with the Scots offered his best chance of salvation and on 2 May 1646 surrendered to their army at Newark.[180] Nothing had been settled, and the discussions with the Scots would continue to the end of the year; but the king's had, at least, brought the first civil war to an end.

---

[177] *Charles I in 1646*, pp. 7, 19, 22–3.

[178] Ibid., p. 19.

[179] *Letters of Charles I*, p. 176.

[180] Stevenson, *Revolution and Counter Revolution*, pp. 64–6.

Historians have generally been quick to saddle Charles with the blame for the royalists' defeat. S.R. Gardiner condemned him for duplicity and defects of character which alienated the bulk of the political nation from his cause; C.V. Wedgewood criticised a lack of realism and flexibility which made him determined to pursue his basic objectives regardless of the prospects of success; and Ian Roy has accused him of failing to get a grip on the royalist high command and allowing his military advantage in the early part of the war to be wasted amid factional squabbling.[181] The verdict against him appears damning, and yet contemporaries were much less quick to pass judgement. Sir Edward Walker, in his account of the royalists' military collapse in 1645, laid most of the blame on the self-interest of various individuals in the royalist high command; while Hyde, in recognising that the king needed to be more assertive in his dealings with both politicians and generals, acknowledged that when he did use his discretion it was generally to good effect.[182] Both these commentators were, of course, writing while Charles was still alive, and blaming him was not an option. Nonetheless, their carefully argued judgements do suggest the need for a reassessment of the king's wartime performance.

The most straightforward aspect of this is his military role. The task of a commander-in-chief was particularly difficult during the civil war. He was expected to be personally brave, tactically aware and capable of dealing with the myriad problems over communications, intelligence and logistics that beset early modern armies. But, in addition, compared with continental conflicts of the period, the English Civil War placed a high premium on flexibility and quick decision-making. It was a war of rapid marches, fought with relatively small armies operating along short supply lines, in which the cavalry were masters of the battlefield. Commanders needed to be able to think on their feet, execute speedy manoeuvres to surprise the enemy and then weigh the odds when it came to the all-important judgement on whether to give battle. This was a form of warfare at which, for the most part, Rupert excelled. By comparison Charles was inflexible and cumbersome. His habit of consulting the council of war before making almost every

---

[181] Gardiner, *History of the Civil War*, vol. 3, pp. 80–1; vol. 4, pp. 326–8; C.V. Wedgewood, *The King's War 1641–1647*, pbk. edn, 1966, pp. 408–9; Roy, 'The Royalist Army', pp. 71–98; idem., 'Council of War' pp. 167–8.

[182] Walker, 'Brief memorials . . . 1645', p. 125; Clarendon, *History*, vol. 3, p. 344.

important military decision – which was a safeguard against his inexperience in the early stages of the war – became a severe handicap. At critical meetings he lacked the confidence to make a clear choice and was very hesitant about asserting himself over his regional commanders. The royalist successes of 1643 happened largely in spite of his contribution rather than because of it. The culmination of this indecisiveness was the disastrous letter to Rupert before Marston Moor. However, during the summer of 1644 Charles's performance as a commander improved considerably.

He was probably helped by the fact that Rupert was out of the way and he had to make up his mind for himself. He was also the sort of person who needed things to go right before he became convinced that he could carry off a particular role. Whatever the psychological mechanisms at work, he suddenly emerged as a more confident and capable leader, building on the success at Cropredy to defeat Essex's army and then carry the fight to the parliamentarians in the autumn. He maintained this self-belief during the Naseby campaign of 1645, when he and Rupert combined to put themselves in a relatively advantageous position. However, this was all thrown away when, for once, he failed to consult the council of war and made his greatest military mistake. Faulty intelligence played a large part in this, but so too, it seems, did a certain amount of royal overconfidence. After Naseby Charles lost his way. If there was to be any chance of a military revival he had to work as closely as possible with Rupert; but, for reasons which had more to do with politics than strategy, he alienated the prince and precipitated the collapse of his cause. Charles was no Henry v or Gustavus Adolphus, but he was a brave soldier, with a reasonable grasp of tactics and, once he had developed some self-belief, a capacity for making sound, and sometimes bold, decisions. He failed the greatest test of his judgement by giving battle at Naseby, but prior to this he had done much to retrieve the damage inflicted at Marston Moor. He was a better soldier than many monarchs and his efforts kept the royalists in the war longer than might otherwise have been the case.

Charles's effectiveness as a wartime political leader also appears to have been seriously underestimated. Roy, Hutton and others depict him as being pushed first one way then the other by squabbling court factions, unable to exert control or direction.[183] However, their accounts overstate both the

---

[183] Roy, 'The Royalist Army', pp. 79–96; Hutton, 'The royalist party', pp. 562–8.

extent of this factionalism and the amount of damage that it caused. Up until 1645 Charles had considerably more success than the parliamentarians in keeping together the senior politicians who supported his cause.[184] He was also able to limit the extent to which court rivalries were allowed to interfere with the deliberations of the council of war. And he managed this is spite of having to deal with a much more assertive group of councillors than had been the case prior to 1640.

The causes of this assertiveness are not easy to pin down. They seem to have had something to do with the fact that Charles was now having to function as a party leader as much as a monarch. This gave his councillors scope to argue about the meaning of the cause they were fighting for and ensured that diversity of opinion was much more readily expressed in fora such as the privy council. The *iure divino* case for episcopacy, for example, which would never even have been discussed by councillors before the civil war, now became a legitimate topic for debate. The greater forcefulness of councillors also seems to have had to do with the revival of aristocratic constitutionalism associated with the Nineteen Propositions. Conrad Russell and John Adamson have focused on the effects of this for the parliamentarian peerage; but it also had an impact on royalists.[185] Councillors like Bristol, Hertford and Saville had developed the habit of taking the political lead when the king appeared incapable before the civil war, and they were not about to abandon it. The debates prior to the Oxford Parliament and the preliminaries to Uxbridge showed that they were quite willing to seize the initiative and drag Charles along with them. The king, then, had a difficult hand to play. For the most part, however, he managed it quite effectively, continuing to command the respect and loyalty of the majority of senior court politicians.

He was helped in this by the fact that the royal cause was closely identified with his person. It was one of the defining features of royalism that it rejected the notion of the 'king's two bodies'. 'Our natural allegiance and the oaths of allegiance and supremacy', according to a statement issued by the Oxford Parliament, 'do bind us and all his other subjects to loyalty and

---

[184] With the exception of Lord Savile's defection in 1645 there were no royalist defections to compare with those of Holland and Bedford in 1643.

[185] Russell, 'Army Plot', pp. 301–2; J.S.A. Adamson, 'The baronial context of the English Civil War', in R.P. Cust and A.L. Hughes eds, *The English Civil War*, 1997, pp. 83–99.

allegiance to his natural person.'[186] This meant that in the final analysis the king's word remained absolute. The effects were not always advantageous. Ann Hughes has demonstrated that those who got on the wrong side of Charles often felt rejected, and deprived of means of redress for their grievances, with the result that they abandoned the struggle and damaged the cause.[187] However, when it came to commanding the allegiance of court politicians it proved a considerable asset. It also helped greatly that Charles continued to give the impression of being 'counsellable'. Hyde found that when he was able to gain access the king was willing to listen and broadly sympathetic to his point of view. Others, such as Richmond, had a similar experience. This feeling that they could get through to Charles was critical in securing personal loyalty; and the loss of it led directly to the remarkable attempted coup of November 1645.

Until 1645 Charles also kept a grip on court faction. Much of the credit for this must go the queen. While she was at Oxford between July 1643 and April 1644 she finally came into her own as a court politician and played what was, effectively, the role of royal favourite. Her presence and that of her urbane chief adviser, Henry Jermyn, did much to defuse the rivalries at court, especially between Rupert and his opponents. It was clear that her position could not be challenged and that, ultimately, she had to be deferred to in matters of both patronage and policy. However, she was careful not to overplay her hand. She accepted that privy councillors had a legitimate role when it came to advising the king on peace negotiations or the Oxford Parliament, and did not try to over-interfere. It was an accomplished performance that allowed Charles to stand above the fray and perform the role of ultimate arbiter.

Following her departure this all changed. The king was dragged into face-to-face confrontations, which were never his forte, and now had to deal with Rupert on his own. The prince's spikiness, sense of insecurity and lack of judgement repeatedly upset those he had to deal with and at the same time exposed his own position to challenge, notably by Digby. Charles could have managed this if he had been prepared to bang heads together, but this was not his style, and the quarrels, with Digby in particular, rapidly

---

[186] Hughes, 'King, parliament and the localities', p. 243.

[187] Ibid., pp. 254–60.

got out of hand. In the aftermath of Naseby it was the lack of firm leadership, as much as anything, which caused the rapid disintegration of his party. Up to this point, however, Charles had continued to function as a relatively effective coordinator of the royal cause.

Where he was much less successful was in identifying and bringing to fruition a strategy for winning the war. Following the failure to capture London in November 1642, outright military victory was unlikely. His best chance appeared to lie in a negotiated settlement reached from a position of armed strength. This required him to strike a difficult balance. On the one hand, he needed to be flexible and alert to military opportunities so that he could take advantage when these arose. On the other, he had to present himself as a firm adherent to religious and constitutional tradition, so that the door to negotiation with moderate elements on the parliamentarian side would remain open and potential defectors would not be put off. The problem was, perhaps, highlighted most clearly in his dealings with the Irish rebels, where the prospect of considerable military assistance depended on religious compromises which could destroy his political credibility. In the event, Charles never quite managed to pick his way through this particular minefield. Much of the time, however, he does seem to have understood what was required, especially when it was being explained to him by Hyde. His constitutionalist instincts and his appreciation of the need for tactical manoeuvre – even, on occasion, to be 'popular' – created several openings for pressuring parliament towards an acceptable settlement, notably during the spring and summer of 1643 when his military successes went hand in hand with Hyde's charm offensive. In the end, however, he lacked the balance of opportunism and integrity required to carry the strategy off. He was not ruthless enough to take advantage of openings like the defection of Holland; and he was not trusted enough for those he was dealing with to have confidence in his assurances.

One of the main problems here was his deep sense of injury at the way in which he had been treated by the parliamentarians. They had stripped away his royal authority and spurned their obligations of loyalty and obedience, and he felt degraded and dishonoured. His basic instinct was that they must be made to pay the price, and any concessions on his part would simply encourage them. In a telling aside at the start of the Uxbridge negotiations, he instructed Nicholas that if the parliamentarian commissioners hesitated over accepting his offers he was to remind them 'that they were arrant rebels and that their end must be damnation, ruin and infamy, except they repented'.[188] The queen and other opponents of negotiation were able to tap into this with reminders of the need to restore his honour and humiliate his opponents as they had humiliated him. In consequence, Charles was repeatedly drawn to the 'quick fix' of plotting. The effect was similar to the failed plots of 1641–2. Each time his actions were exposed to public view it made him look devious and untrustworthy, and squandered the political capital built up through Hyde's patient efforts to present him as a constitutional monarch.

The other main stumbling block was Charles's unwillingness to shift from his 'grounds'. The reasons for this were complex. They had something to do with his determination to answer the queen's jibes about inconstancy and something to do with his understanding of the fundamentals of royal authority. But more than anything they appear to have rested on a conviction that God was punishing him for a lack of resolve in standing by Strafford. This can be traced back at least as far as December 1642 when he told Hamilton that 'God has either so totally forgiven me that he will bless this good cause in my hands, or that all my punishment shall be in this world, which without performing what I have resolved, I cannot flatter my self will end here.'[189] The belief that unless he mended his ways there would be no deliverance, either on earth or in heaven, made peace negotiations a much less open-ended process than they would have been if he had simply been concerned about preserving his royal authority. His determination to fix his 'negatives' and not be shifted from them did much to prevent the possibility of finding common ground during the negotiations at Oxford in 1643 or Uxbridge in 1645. It also blocked the possibility of alliance with Scots late in 1645. With a monarch who was so firm in his convictions that he was prepared to face death rather than compromise the scope for implementing the strategy of negotiation from strength was severely limited. In the final analysis, then, the beliefs that made civil war possible – and gave the king much of his strength as a party leader – also deprived him of his best chance of winning it.

---

[188] *Evelyn*, p. 796. This point has been stressed in a later context by John Adamson: J.S.A. Adamson, 'The Frighted Junto: Perceptions of Ireland and the Last Attempts at Settlement with Charles I', in J. Peacey ed., *The Regicides and the Execution of Charles I*, Basingstoke, 2001, p. 56.

[189] NAS, GD 406/1/167/1 and 2.

The negotiator

On 4 May 1646 William Sancroft, the future archbishop of Canterbury, dispatched one of his regular newsletters to his father in Suffolk. The talk of the town was that the king was about to leave Oxford, give himself up to Fairfax and then insist on proceeding to London.

The faction that hath the vogue at Westminster fear nothing more than that; they know not what to do with him if he comes . . . his presence will attract hearts and animate many of the members to appear for him with open face who now mask under a visor, and sigh to see a party they like not carry all before them.[190]

The London newsmongers were mistaken in their main assumption. Charles surrendered to the Scots and was whisked away to Newcastle before he could go anywhere near his capital. But in other respects their gossip was highly perceptive. There was strong support for the king's restoration among Presbyterians and the London citizenry, as the attempted counter-revolution of 1647 was to demonstrate. There was also a state of near panic within the Independent leadership at Westminster ('the faction that hath the vogue') at the prospect of Charles coming up to negotiate face to face. Above all, Sancroft's report underlined the fact that, although he had lost the war, the king appeared to have every chance of winning the peace.

This was partly because of the squabbling among his opponents. The Independents and Presbyterians in parliament were even more divided than they had been at the start of the year. New quarrels had arisen over the disbanding of the army and the terms for getting rid of the Scots. The Scots themselves were increasingly alienated from the Westminster leadership, but they too were starting to experience internal divisions as a moderate royalist party led by Hamilton emerged to challenge the dominance of Argyll and the kirk.[191] Amid these competing factions Charles appeared to be the one stable element in the political situation. His deliberate decision to stay and negotiate, rather then fleeing into exile, made

---

[190] H. Cary ed., *Memorials of the Great Civil War in England from 1646 to 1652*, 2 vols., 1842, vol. 1, p. 17. I am grateful to Ann Hughes for this reference.

[191] Stevenson, *Revolution and Counter Revolution*, pp. 66–72.

it very difficult to get rid of him. There was some scattered talk of deposition, but his precaution of sending Prince Charles overseas made this largely impractical.[192] Anyway, it had little support. The majority view, at Westminster and in the country, was that the sooner the king was reinstated the better. Since it appeared that only he could provide the basis for a return to normality.

Charles was also in a strong bargaining position. There were now lots of opportunities to play off his enemies against each other. He could continue to dangle the prospect of toleration before the Independents, while receiving instruction in Presbyterianism and encouraging the Scots to believe that he was about to embrace their system. In addition to this, he was prepared to put his own life on the line. 'I have already cast up what I am like to suffer which I shall meet (by the grace of God) with that constancy that befits me', he told Jermyn, Culpepper and Ashburnham in July 1646;[193] and throughout the negotiations that followed he rarely missed an opportunity to remind those involved of his willingness to face martyrdom rather than give way on the key issues relating to his sovereignty or his conscience. How far this was a negotiating ploy, and how far a fixed resolution, it is impossible to say. Probably Charles himself did not know for certain. However, he was undoubtedly very aware of the way in which it strengthened his position. It meant, in effect, that his opponents would have to give ground or eliminate him.

Charles had a strong hand in the aftermath of the civil war, but the consensus among historians is that he played it badly. S.R. Gardiner argues that there were several moments during the negotiations of 1647 and 1648 when he had the opportunity to settle on relatively advantageous terms; but his deviousness and duplicity drove those he was dealing with to conclude that he was simply not to be trusted. In the end he left them little choice but to get rid of him. Robert Ashton and Austin Woolrych highlight his aimlessness in pursuing the Micawberite strategy of simply playing off

---

[192] Conrad Russell has made the point that one of the most significant features of this period – in contrast to previous civil wars or the crisis of 1688 – was the lack of a suitable pretender to the crown. None of Charles's sons was prepared to cooperate with the victors, which forced them to deal with him, and him alone: C.S.R. Russell, *The Crisis of Parliaments. English History 1509–1660*, Oxford, 1971, p. 381n.

[193] *Clarendon State Papers*, vol. 2, p. 243.

opponents against each other in the hope that something would turn up. Specifically, they castigate him for failing to recognise that in the Heads of Proposals he was being offered the best terms he was ever likely to achieve. Conrad Russell, on the other hand, points to his rigid determination to assert whatever he thought his conscience required, which ultimately amounted to a rejection of the whole political process.[194]

Each of these criticisms is valid. Charles certainly was guilty of deviousness, lack of judgement and inflexibility. But this was not the whole story. From his point of view the primary objective for most of this period was not a settlement, but a resumption of the war. He continued to believe that rebels should be coerced not conciliated. He would no doubt have accepted peace on his own conditions, but he recognised these were unlikely to be satisfactory for those he was dealing with. A more attainable objective was to restart the war on more advantageous terms. In this context, the fact that the Second Civil War took place at all must be seen as some sort of achievement for Charles. Of course, he lost again, but this was by no means a foregone conclusion. He had succeeded in giving himself a second chance, which again suggests that he cannot simply be dismissed as a political incompetent.

Charles did not, however, make a good start. During the opening months of negotiation – in the summer of 1646 – he overestimated the strength of his own position and underestimated the distrust that his opponents felt towards him.[195] He also failed to recognise that those he was dealing with were just as attached to their principles as he was.[196] The result was that he united his opponents rather than driving them apart. His aim was to play off the various parties against each other by making offers first to the English Independents and then to his Scots hosts. This strategy was undermined when he failed to come up with any concrete concessions. The two things

---

[194] Gardiner, *History of the Civil War*, vol. 4, pp. 326–8; R. Ashton, *Counter Revolution. The Second Civil War and its Origins 1646–8*, 1994, pp. 24–5, 27, 30, 35; A. Woolrych, *Soldiers and Statesmen: The General Council of the Army and its Debates 1647–1648*, Oxford, 1987, pp. 166–7, 174–9; Russell, *Causes of the Civil War*, pp. 198–9.

[195] For evidence of this distrust, see Thomas Juxon's comment that 'no prince ever used such dissimulation', cited in Ashton, *Second Civil War*, p. 13.

[196] Russell cites Charles telling the queen at the time he surrendered that the Scots had no sincere attachment to Presbyterianism and only wanted a share of bishops' lands: *Crisis of Parliaments*, p. 379.

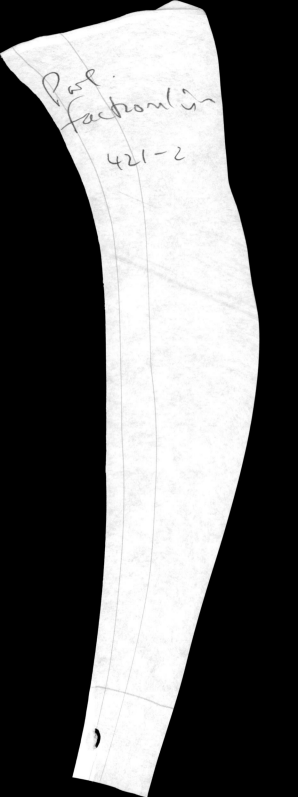

Prof.
Factomlin

421-2

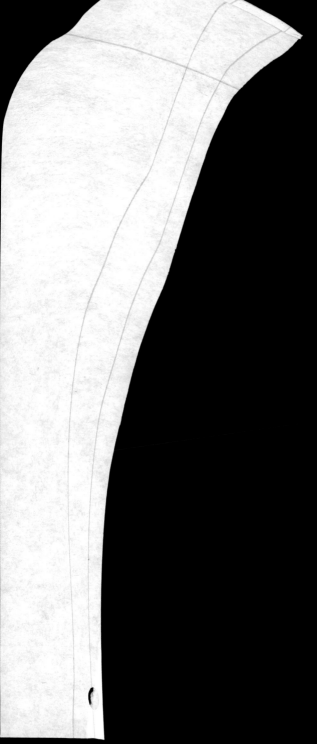

that really mattered to the Scots were that he should take the Solemn League and Covenant and agree to establish Presbyterianism in England. His refusal to give ground on either, in spite of long exchanges with the Presbyterian divine, Alexander Henderson, frustrated them sufficiently to push them back into the arms of the English parliament. By June, Argyll and the Covenanter leadership had buried some of their differences with the Independents and agreed to back the peace proposals they had drawn up the previous winter.[197]

The Newcastle Propositions were a disaster for Charles. The terms on offer were considerably tougher than those he had rejected at Uxbridge in 1644–5. It was again demanded that he take the Covenant and agree to the abolition of episcopacy; but he was now required to surrender the militia to parliamentary control for at least 20 years and also exempt a total of 58 of his supporters from any general pardon.[198] Charles felt he could not even begin to discuss these terms, telling the queen that 'all my endeavours must be delaying my answer (till there be considerable parties visibly formed)'.[199] Meanwhile he replied to parliament by declaring his inability to decide anything without further advice and requesting that he be allowed to come to London. The problem with this approach was that it antagonised the Scots even more. By August they were talking openly of giving him up to the English parliament and retiring north of the border.[200]

This put the king in a very difficult position. For a brief period during the mid summer it looked as if he might be able to rely on assistance from either Ireland or France. But hopes of an Irish peace evaporated when Cardinal Rinuccini and the Catholic clergy vetoed the proposals agreed between Ormond and the Confederates, and then engineered a coup against the moderate Confederacy leadership. The French, meanwhile, proved as evasive as ever when it came to turning promises into concrete assistance. By September Charles was ready to admit that his most realistic hope of salvation lay with the Scots.[201] Yet the two things they insisted on were the very things he was most averse to agreeing to. The whole issue became

---

[197] Stevenson, *Revolution and Counter Revolution*, pp. 66–70, 111–12.

[198] *Constitutional Documents*, pp. 290–307.

[199] *Charles I in 1646*, p. 50.

[200] Stevenson, *Revolution and Counter Revolution*, pp. 73–4.

[201] *Early Modern Ireland*, pp. 317–21; *Clarendon State Papers*, vol. 2, pp. 249, 261, 264, 274.

the subject of a lengthy correspondence with Henrietta Maria and her leading advisers, Jermyn, Culpepper and Ashburnham. It is worth looking at this more closely because it tells us a good deal about the thinking which underpinned the king's approach to negotiations.

The queen's line throughout the correspondence remained as it had been since late 1645. She wanted Charles to give up episcopacy, at least for the time being, since this was the only way to get the Scots on his side and put himself 'at the head of an army' again. Otherwise she was determined that he should concede nothing. He must not take the Covenant, not agree to anything that would prolong the life of the parliament and, above all, not surrender control of the militia.[202] Jermyn, Culpepper and Ashburnham supported the queen with a carefully reasoned case for making concessions on episcopacy. Their basic argument was that Charles had no alternative. His 'piety, courage and constancy' in standing by the bishops were to be applauded, but he had now reached the point where he could only save them by saving himself. 'Presbytery or something worse will be forced upon you whether you will or no', they argued. He was not obliged 'to perish in company with bishops merely out of pity'; rather it was his duty to rescue his own authority and then use it to relieve the church. 'A disease is to be preferred before dissolution: the one may in time admit of a remedy, the other is past cure.'[203] This was a powerful case, cogently argued, but Charles appeared unmoved.

The arguments he countered with were twofold. First of all, abandoning episcopacy was against his conscience; and second, it would lead inevitably to the 'destruction of monarchy'. For Charles, as for most of his contemporaries, conscience took the form of a series of moral and spiritual imperatives, which his duty to God bound him to obey. These were defined partly by his understanding of his religious obligations and partly by specific oaths that he had taken, the most important of which was his coronation oath. He always had a very strong sense of the binding nature of oaths, which helps to explain his persistent refusal to take the Covenant; however, it seems likely that this was reinforced during 1646 by his close reading of Robert Sanderson's great work on promissory oaths, *De*

---

[202] *Letters of Henrietta Maria*, pp. 326, 327, 329, 330, 335.

[203] *Clarendon State Papers*, vol. 2, p. 263.

Juramento.[204] To abjure an oath would be to invite eternal damnation, as he explained to Henderson.[205] But it would also, he believed, undermine his credibility as a monarch since no ruler could be trusted by his people unless he remained true to God. At the time there were three issues that Charles saw predominantly as matters of conscience: abjuring episcopacy, taking or establishing the Covenant, and consenting 'to that undoubted sacrilege of alienating the church lands'. So when Jermyn, Culpepper and Ashburnham argued that it would be political wisdom to give way on episcopacy, he retorted furiously that 'conscience and policy' were inseparable: 'the prudential part of any consideration will never be found opposite to the conscientious; nay here they go hand in hand'.[206]

The proof he offered for this maxim constituted the second main plank of his case – that if he were to allow Presbyterianism to be established he would be opening the way to the destruction of his kingship. This was a view that he appears to have held for at least as long as he had been on the throne, but he was given the opportunity to refine his thinking in the exchanges with Henderson. The basis for his case was that, whereas bishops were part of the primitive church and dated from apostolic times, Presbyterianism was a recent innovation, the product of 'a popular reformation' and therefore inherently threatening to royal power. He reiterated his father's maxim 'No bishop, no king', glossing it as a statement of the fact that 'Presbyterian doctrine' was 'incompatible with monarchy'. Removing episcopacy would 'take away all the ecclesiastical power of government from the crown' and place it in the hands of parliament and the people. This was a recipe for disaster. 'Orthodox divines' would be 'expelled or silenced'; there would no longer be anyone to instil obedience; and the Presbyterians would have licence 'to introduce that doctrine which teaches rebellion to be lawful and that . . . kings . . . ought to give account and be corrected when they do amiss'. The result would be 'anarchy' and

---

[204] According to the preface this was 'revised and approved under his Majesty's own hand': Sharpe, 'Conscience and public duty', pp. 653, 659. Charles's attitude here was in marked contrast to his son who yielded very quickly to Scots' demands that he take the Covenant during the Second Civil War: Gardiner, *History of the Civil War*, vol. 4, pp. 170–1, 195.

[205] *The Papers which passed at Newcastle*, pp. 3–4.

[206] *Clarendon State Papers*, vol. 2, pp. 260, 274.

'perpetual rebellion'.[207] Presbyterianism, in short, embodied the whole 'popular' threat which loomed so large in the king's thinking.

The inflexible attitude that Charles displayed in these letters was, however, deceptive. While announcing his resolute determination not to give ground, he was in fact preparing to make some very significant concessions. The extent of these has largely passed historians by because their image of Charles has been shaped by the rhetoric he deployed in his lengthy correspondence with the queen. But, as with any piece of justificatory writing, it is important to understand the ground rules. In this case, the two main parties were following a routine which, over the years, had become familiar. The queen continued to castigate her husband for his lack of resolution. 'I tell you again, for the last time', she warned on 1 December, 'that if you will grant more you are lost, and I shall never return to England, but shall go and pray to God for you.' Charles, for his part, responded with his usual mixture of patient argument and weary rebuttal. He persisted in pointing out that he had never yielded on his basic 'grounds' and that for the queen to think otherwise was the result of misunderstanding or misinformation.[208] Within the conventions being observed in the correspondence he could not afford to appear flexible. Nonetheless he was preparing for a significant climbdown.

This process began in early September 1646 with the arrival at Newcastle of his old companion, Will Murray. Up to this point Charles had felt isolated and largely friendless. He was confined to the mayor's lodgings with limited freedom of movement, and was subjected to regular harangues by Presbyterian ministers. His main source of contact with the outside world was Bellièvre, the French envoy, who tended simply to amplify the views of the queen. It was an indication of the king's beleaguered state that at first he did not trust Murray, suspecting him of being yet another emissary from the marquis of Argyll. However, when it became clear that he was not going to press him to agree to the Newcastle Propositions, Charles relaxed. At last he had a counsellor on the spot whom he felt he could trust. By mid-September, he could inform the queen that 'he and I are consulting for the best means how to accommodate [the religious differences] without

---

[207] *Clarendon State Papers*, vol. 2, pp. 243, 247, 254, 274; *Charles I in 1646*, p. 71.

[208] *Letters of Henrietta Maria*, pp. 334–6; *Charles I in 1646*, pp. 83, 85–6.

going directly against my conscience'.[209] The scheme they came up with involved accepting the *status quo* in England – with Presbyterian church government and use of the Directory – for a period of three years, while an assembly of 60 divines (20 Presbyterians, 20 Independents and 20 chosen by Charles) came up with recommendations about the future structure of the church which could then be put to both king and parliament. In the meantime Charles and his household were to be allowed to worship in the way they chose. To make absolutely sure that he could propose this 'with a safe conscience' he communicated the whole scheme to Bishops Juxon and Duppa. Without waiting for their reply, however, he dispatched Murray to London to discuss the proposal with the Scots commissioners.[210]

Murray spent much of October and November in negotiation with the Scots. When their initial response proved unenthusiastic, Charles authorised him to agree to the *status quo* remaining in place for five years rather than three. He also prepared a second answer to the Newcastle Propositions, which was much more accommodating than the first. The key concession here was agreement to hand over control of the militia for ten years – or even the duration of his own lifetime – provided that at the end of the period control reverted to his son on the same terms as had been enjoyed by his predecessors. This provoked an angry response from the queen who declared that such a concession would 'cut your own throat; for having given them this power you can no longer refuse them anything, not even my life'.[211] Charles, however, pressed on; and to put extra pressure on the Scots, he again hinted at the possibility of religious toleration for the Independents. In the end, the Scots commissioners refused to accept anything less than full compliance with their religious demands and the negotiation collapsed. Charles was reduced to near despair. For the first time he seems to have seriously contemplated abdication, asking Bellièvre to sound out opinion on the possibility of Prince Charles acting in his name to give the Scots what they wanted. He also made the first of his many attempts to

---

[209] Wedgewood, *The King's War*, pp. 521, 567; Gardiner, *History of the Civil War*, vol. 3, pp. 133, 141; *Charles I in 1646*, pp. 45–6, 63, 65.

[210] *Clarendon State Papers*, vol. 2, pp. 265–7; Gardiner, *History of the Civil War*, vol. 3, pp. 165–8.

[211] Gardiner, *History of the Civil War*, vol. 3, p. 168; *Clarendon State Papers*, vol. 2, pp. 275–6; *Letters of Henrietta Maria*, p. 335.

escape. But, in spite of all this, he refused to give in. Right up to the moment of handing him over to the English in January 1647, the Scots made it clear that if he would take the Covenant and agree to introduce Presbyterianism they would do all in their power to reinstate him. But he remained adamant.[212]

Charles's stubbornness has puzzled later historians, just as it puzzled his wife. If he could 'dispense with a thing which went against [his] conscience for three years', why, she reasoned, could he not 'go further' to save his kingdom?[213] The explanation lies in Charles's struggles with his conscience. Duppa and Juxon confirmed his view that it would not be a breach of his coronation oath to allow 'a temporary compliance' with the *status quo* in order 'to recover and maintain that doctrine and discipline wherein [he had] been bred'. An 'absolute' allowance of Presbyterianism on the other hand, even if he had no intention of abiding by it, would constitute 'a sin against . . . conscience' and would bring down God's judgements.[214] Charles's explanation of this to the queen revealed the extent to which his thinking was still dominated by a fear of divine retribution.

I made that base sinful concession concerning the earl of Strafford for which – and also that great injustice to the church in taking away the bishops' votes in parliament – though I have been most justly punished, yet I hope that God will so accept of my hearty (however weak) repentance and my constant adhering to my conscience that at last his mercy will take place of his justice. But a new relapse, as my abjuration of episcopacy, or my promise without reserve for the establishing of presbyterian government, will both procure God's further wrath upon me, as also make me inconstant in all my other grounds.[215]

If the dictates of Charles's conscience ultimately prevented him from reaching an accommodation with the Scots in 1646, this did not mean, however, that he was totally inflexible. He was prepared to negotiate up to

---

[212] Ashton, *The Second Civil War*, pp. 13–14; Gardiner, *History of the Civil War*, vol. 3, pp. 172–4, 186–7; *Charles I in 1646*, p. 81; Stevenson, *Revolution and Counter Revolution*, pp. 79–80.

[213] *Letters of Henrietta Maria*, pp. 328–9.

[214] *Clarendon State Papers*, vol. 2, pp. 265–8.

[215] *Charles I in 1646*, pp. 80–1; See also the remarks by Bellièvre, cited in Stevenson, *Revolution and Counter Revolution*, p. 78.

the limits of what he felt his conscience would permit and, as he put it, try 'to find such a present compliance as may stand with conscience *and* policy'.[216] The result was the scheme worked out with Will Murray in September and October. In the circumstances this could not be made to stick; but it did provide the basis for his third answer to the Newcastle Propositions in May 1647 and, eventually, for the Engagement under which the Scots entered the Second Civil War.

Although it was not immediately obvious, Charles gained considerably by the withdrawal of the Scots. In personal terms, he was able to feel that he was acting as a king again. On the journey south from Newcastle he was greeted by huge crowds and was able to touch for 'the king's evil'. Once installed at Holdenby House in Northamptonshire he was given a household staff appropriate to his dignity and was able to socialise with the local gentry. He was still not allowed to take part in Church of England services, and his communications with the queen were cut off until April 1647; but he felt much better off.[217]

At the same time support for him was growing. The irritant of the Scots army's presence in northern England had been a major source of support for the Independents at Westminster. Now that they had returned to Scotland the balance of advantage shifted towards the Presbyterians, who favoured Charles's speedy restoration. Their main power base was in London, where militant Presbyterianism among the ministers and leading citizens was combined with a yearning for peace and a return to stability; but they were also gaining ground in the provinces as a result of growing hostility to high taxation and the presence of the New Model Army. In Scotland too there were signs of a royalist resurgence. Those who had agreed to hand Charles over to the English began to regret their action and fear that they had opened the way to dethroning their king. This benefited Hamilton and his allies who were able to gain a majority on the committee of estates in March 1647 and secure the appointment of the pro-Royalist Lauderdale to head the Scottish commission negotiating in London. The first result of these changes was an approach by a group of English Presbyterian peers to Bellièvre. They proposed that if the king agreed to the

---

[216] *Charles I in 1646*, p. 65; my italic.

[217] Gardiner, *History of the Civil War*, vol. 3, pp. 212–13; Carlton, *Charles I*, pp. 313–14.

concessions he had offered in October 1646, they would support his return to London to negotiate.[218]

This was a major opportunity and Charles responded skilfully and positively. Apparently on his own initiative, he drew up a third answer to the Newcastle Propositions, which was published on 12 May 1647.[219] In it he set out to be as conciliatory as possible. He repeated the concessions of the previous October over religion and the militia and made a point of accepting those propositions that he felt he could, including steps to curb popery and confirm acts passed under parliament's Great Seal. On other matters, such as the Covenant, he was considerably vaguer, but he was careful not to shut the door on discussion. Throughout he pressed to be allowed to come to London to negotiate directly. It was a cleverly pitched appeal that had the desired result. On 18 May his answer was read out at Westminster and accepted by the English Presbyterians and the Scots commissioners as the basis for an accommodation; then on the 20th the Lords voted that he be invited to come up to his palace at Oatlands, near London. It seemed that at last he was about achieve the return to his capital that he had sought for so long. However, the opportunity was plucked away from him when, on 4 June 1647, he was seized from Holdenby by Cornet Joyce and his New Model troopers.[220]

In retrospect this can be seen as a disaster for Charles. By denying him this opportunity to get to London, the army deprived him of his best chance of an immediate restoration; and by entering the political arena themselves they introduced a volatile new element into the negotiations over his fate. At the time, however, the change of custody offered benefits. Charles was pleasantly surprised by the treatment he received. He and his counsellors had always assumed that the army and its Independent allies were much more anti-monarchical than the Presbyterians. But during the summer of 1647 there was considerable goodwill towards the king, among ordinary

---

[218] V. Pearl, 'London's counter revolution', in G.E. Aylmer ed., *The Interregnum*, 1972, pp. 42–4; D. Underdown, *Pride's Purge*, Oxford, 1971, pp. 76–9; Stevenson, *Revolution and Counter Revolution*, pp. 85–8; Gardiner, *History of the Civil War*, vol. 3, pp. 213–14.

[219] *Constitutional Documents*, pp. 311–16. Charles was isolated from the queen and his former servants during this period: Gardiner, *History of the Civil War*, vol. 3, pp. 237–8.

[220] Gardiner, *History of the Civil War*, vol. 3, pp. 253–4, 259–60; Ashton, *The Second Civil War*, pp. 17–18.

soldiers as much as the officers.[221] At his own request he was conveyed to Newmarket, where he stayed a fortnight, before setting out towards Hampton Court. He was allowed to communicate freely with the queen and receive visits from former servants, such as Richmond and Lindsey, as well as his children, James and Elizabeth. Just as importantly he was given access to two of his chaplains and at the end of June was able to attend a prayerbook service for the first time in over a year. Charles appreciated the treatment, but he interpreted it mainly as a sign of how badly the army needed his cooperation.[222] Once again he overestimated the strength of his position and failed to make the most of what was on offer.

During early July the General Council of the Army, in conjunction with the Independent leadership in parliament, worked out the scheme known as the Heads of Proposals. As the name implied, this was a provisional statement of where negotiations might lead rather than the draft of a final agreement. Even so, it was far more generous to Charles than anything he had been offered hitherto. On the militia, it proposed that control be transferred to parliament for 10 years, rather than 20, with the same condition to apply to the appointment of the great officers of state. The number of royalist delinquents excluded from any pardon was to be reduced from 58 to 5. And on the vexed issue of religion it proposed building on the offers of liberty of conscience that Charles had made in his earlier approaches to the Independents. Bishops and magistrates were to lose their coercive power in religious matters, and acts enforcing the prayerbook and church attendance were to be abolished. But no one was to be forced to take the Covenant, and bishops and the prayerbook were to be allowed to continue where so desired. The most original provisions, however, related to the existing parliament's own power which, in response to army and Leveller pressure, was to be considerably reduced. It was to be dissolved within a year and thereafter parliaments were to be elected biennially.[223]

These terms appeared to offer Charles the opportunity to achieve much of what he was aiming for by peaceful means. Sir John Berkeley, who was sent by the queen to act as an emissary between Charles and the army,

---

[221] Woolrych, *Soldiers and Statesmen*, pp. 141–3.

[222] Gardiner, *History of the Civil War*, vol. 3, pp. 306, 317; Carlton, *Charles I*, pp. 316–17; *Memoirs of Sir John Berkeley*, 1702, p. 28.

[223] *Constitutional Documents*, pp. 316–26; Gardiner, *History of the Civil War*, vol. 3, pp. 329–33.

believed that these were the best terms he could reasonably hope for. 'Never was a crown so near lost so cheaply recovered', he insisted, 'as his Majesty's would be if they agreed on such terms.'[224] In the hands of a shrewd tactician – like his father or his eldest son – they could have provided the basis for a substantial restoration of royal authority. Biennial parliaments, and the prospect of eventually recovering control over appointments and the militia, offered plenty of scope for party building and manoeuvre. But Charles was not interested. Assenting to even these relatively generous terms still appeared to be conceding more than his concept of sovereignty, or his conscience, would permit. Moreover he had his sights fixed elsewhere.

During July 1647 the long-threatened counter-revolution finally took place in London. It was prompted by the Independents' efforts to impeach 11 of the Presbyterian leaders in the Commons and gain control of the London militia. On 21 July huge crowds turned out in the City to support the signing of a Solemn Engagement which pledged to uphold the Covenant and secure the king's restoration on the terms set out in his letter of 12 May. Four days later there was widespread rioting, which led to the return of the 11 members and the flight of the Independent leadership. Meanwhile, on 22 July, Lauderdale had approached Charles with an assurance that the Scots were willing to invade England to secure his authority.[225] Charles's self-confidence soared as it seemed that he was about to be carried back to power through a combination of Scots arms and popular reaction. As a result, he missed the opportunity to push for a settlement at the moment when the army needed him most. A more astute tactician would have taken out insurance by at least appearing to welcome the army's proposals when they were presented to him on 28 July.[226] But the king was at his most brutally dismissive. Berkeley recalled that he subjected the army delegates to 'very tart and bitter discourses saying sometimes that he would have no man suffer for his sake . . . and that he would have the church established according to law by the proposals'. He also started telling them, 'You cannot be without me. You will fall to ruin if I do not sustain you.' Berkeley had to take Charles on one side and warn him that if he 'had some

---

[224] *Memoirs of . . . Berkeley*, p. 30.

[225] Pearl, 'London's counter revolution', pp. 49–51; Underdown, *Pride's Purge*, pp. 81–3; Gardiner, *History of the Civil War*, vol. 3, p. 334.

[226] Woolrych, *Soldiers and Statesmen*, pp. 178–9, 183–4.

secret strength and power that I do not know of' he should conceal the fact. The king duly 'recollected himself' and adopted a more conciliatory tone.[227] But the damage had been done. Lauderdale was barred from further access on the assumption that he was plotting a Scottish invasion and Colonel Rainsborough went back to the army Agitators and told them that there was no longer any point in trying to do a deal. A few days later Charles's hopes collapsed when Fairfax marched into London at the head of 16 000 troops, restored the seceded members and snuffed out the counter-revolution.[228]

The king, however, adjusted quickly to the changed circumstances. With the Presbyterians crushed and the Scots on the defensive, he was left little choice but to work with the army. He made his peace with a rather grudging letter to Fairfax on 3 August in which he disowned the Presbyterian demonstrations and praised the Heads of Proposals.[229] He then sat down with the army negotiators and his own advisers, Berkeley and John Ashburnham (who had been sent by the queen as another emissary), and went through the proposals clause by clause. Unfortunately our knowledge of these negotiations is very fragmentary. It appears, however, that over a period of two weeks, in mid-August, Charles fought the proposals every inch of the way. He resisted the removal of his control over the militia and contested the loss of his power to make war and peace. He also tried to secure an amnesty for all his supporters, and ensure that the revenues of the bishops and clergy were safeguarded.[230] These were probably the most prolonged and detailed discussions Charles entered into in either 1646 or 1647. He had his back against the wall, forced to confront the fact that he had to settle with the army because he had nowhere else to go. But even in such circumstances his conviction that he must put his duty to God and his crown before all else remained undiminished. He would negotiate to buy time, but not with any serious intent to settle. By the end of August it seemed that this might pay off as the situation changed yet again.

---

[227] Memoirs of . . . Berkeley, pp. 34–5.

[228] Gardiner, History of the Civil War, vol. 3, p. 342; Memoirs of . . . Berkeley, pp. 35–6; Pearl, 'London's counter revolution', pp. 52–6.

[229] Woolrych, Soldiers and Statesmen, p. 180; Clarendon State Papers, vol. 2, pp. 373–4.

[230] Gardiner, History of the Civil War, vol. 3, pp. 353–4.

To appease the Scots and head off the threat of an invasion, the Independent leadership in parliament agreed to reintroduce the Newcastle Propositions (which now became known as the Hampton Court Propositions). They calculated that if the king was confronted with these again he would see the advantages of the Heads of Proposals. Charles, however, with strong encouragement from Ashburnham, drew the conclusion that once more there were divisions and differences which he could exploit. Meanwhile a messenger arrived from Hamilton informing him that the Scots were extremely hostile to the army's actions in England and were still ready to send an army to his rescue.[231] The king now set his sights on binding the Scots to deliver on their promise of military assistance.

This was not easy. The kirk and majority opinion in Scotland still demanded that he take the Covenant and abolish episcopacy, while he remained just as determined to abide by his conscience. Moreover, Hamilton, although broadly supportive of intervention in England, was reluctant to undertake an invasion while the Scottish army remained under the control of Argyll's ally David Leslie.[232] Charles had to manoeuvre the Scots into a position where they would commit themselves without demanding too much in return. This he was able to accomplish with no little skill, although at the cost of adding to his reputation for duplicity and alienating the army sufficiently to lead to calls for his deposition.

Charles's trump card with the Scots was their fear that he might still come to an agreement with the Independents and the army. During September and October he exploited this by continuing to make encouraging noises about the Heads of Proposals. He rejected the Hampton Court Propositions and compared them disparagingly with the Heads, which prompted the army to reopen discussions via Berkeley and Ashburnham.[233] Charles was invited to a meeting in early October, along with Hertford, Richmond, Southampton and other former councillors who were in favour of him settling with the Independents rather than the Scots. This broke up after two days with nothing to show for its efforts. The king's prevarication over the army's terms frustrated the grandees and their Independent allies

---

[231] On Charles's relationship with Ashburnham, see *Memoirs of . . . Berkeley*, pp. 32–3.

[232] Stevenson, *Revolution and Counter Revolution*, pp. 89–90.

[233] Gardiner, *History of the Civil War*, vol. 3, p. 361; Ashton, *The Second Civil War*, pp. 36–7; *Memoirs of . . . Berkeley*, p. 43.

to the point where they began to run out of patience.[234] However, it did have a positive impact on the Scots. In late September the committee of estates in Edinburgh dispatched Lanark and Loudoun to join Lauderdale, with instructions to negotiate on the basis of his 12 May letter and do all in their power to prevent an agreement with their enemies. The three commissioners met Charles at Hampton Court on 22 October and delivered a paper declaring that if he would 'give satisfaction in the point of religion' then the Scots would 'engage themselves for your restoration and civil interest'.[235] The following day they reappeared with 50 horsemen and urged him to escape to Scotland. Charles refused on the grounds that he had given his word of honour not to do so; but he was also holding out for better terms.[236] They had not yet made any binding commitment, and 'satisfaction in the point of religion' still appears to have included taking the Covenant.

In early November majority opinion in the army turned decisively against Charles. His delays and prevarications, combined with rumours of a Scots invasion, led to open talk of bringing him to justice and altering the constitution. Crucially the officers on the Army Council changed direction and on 5 November passed a resolution supporting a policy of 'no further addresses'. Lord Saye and the grandees made a final effort to isolate the king from the Scots and pressurise him into accepting the Heads of Proposals, but their initiative was rapidly overtaken by events.[237] Charles became alarmed at the rumours that the army intended his deposition and instructed Ashburnham to draw up plans for his escape. Various options were considered. Berkeley favoured fleeing to France; Ashburham wanted him to stay in southern England where he could continue playing off the various parties against each other, while the king himself came up with a scheme to take refuge at Berwick where he could be protected by the Scots, but still retain his independence of action. In the end, he was panicked into

---

[234] Gardiner, *History of the Civil War*, vol. 3, pp. 370–1; Smith, *Constitutional Royalism*, pp. 134–5.

[235] Stevenson, *Revolution and Counter Revolution*, pp. 93–4; G. Burnet, *The Memoirs of the Lives and Actions of James and William, Dukes of Hamilton and Castleherald*, 1677, Oxford, p. 332.

[236] Gardiner, *History of the Civil War*, vol. 3, p. 411.

[237] J.S. Adamson, 'The English nobility and the projected settlement of 1647', *HJ*, vol. 30, 1987, pp. 598–600; Gardiner, *History of the Civil War*, vol. 4, pp. 2–3, 9.

acting prematurely and escaped from Hampton Court on 11 November with no clear idea of where he was going. He headed south rather than north because, as he confided to Berkeley, he still did not trust the Scots to deliver on their assurances. But he found there were no boats available to transport him overseas and for want of anything better eventually entrusted himself to the custody of Robert Hammond, governor of the Isle of Wight.[238]

Charles reached Carisbrooke Castle on 14 November and carried on acting as if he could keep the army and Independents interested in negotiation simply by increasing his offer. He wrote to the speaker of the Lords promising to accept the ecclesiastical *status quo* for three years, and hand over control of the militia and the appointment of great officers for the remainder of his lifetime, in return for a 'personal treaty'.[239] But his flight had confirmed the army's suspicions about a deal with the Scots and destroyed what little credibility he had retained as a negotiator. The overture was ignored and, instead, Saye and the Independent leadership in the Lords came up with an ultimatum. Charles was to be presented with Four Bills based on the Hampton Court Propositions. If he assented to them he would be allowed to come to London to treat in person; if he refused, parliament would proceed on the basis of a vote taken earlier in November and remove his power to veto a settlement.[240]

The prospect of the king accepting the Four Bills was always remote. The bill on the militia gave parliament control of the armed forces for 20 years, but with no provision for it to revert to the crown thereafter; and there were 'additional propositions' tacked on covering such matters as the abolition of episcopacy and the sale of church lands. Accepting the package, as Charles pointed out, would prejudge any further negotiation and divest him of 'all authority . . . without possibility of recovering it'.[241] However, he was able to use it finally to tie in the Scots. During early December his tussle over the terms of an agreement continued. The Scots commissioners

---

[238] Gardiner, *History of the Civil War*, vol. 4, pp. 9–10, 12–15; *Memoirs of . . . Berkeley*, pp. 50–2; Carlton, *Charles I*, pp. 322–3.

[239] *Constitutional Documents*, pp. 328–32.

[240] Gardiner, *History of the Civil War*, vol. 4, pp. 31–2; Adamson, 'The projected settlement', pp. 598–600.

[241] Ashton, *The Second Civil War*, pp. 37–8; *Constitutional Documents*, pp. 354–6.

persisted in the demand that he take the Covenant, and also tried to frighten him into escaping to Berwick with warnings that the army was about to arrest him. But the king kept his nerve and continued to hint that he might come to an agreement with parliament. The breakthrough came when the parliamentary delegation arrived at Carisbrooke on 24 December to present the Four Bills. The Scots commissioners were two days behind and Charles was able to use the interval to create the impression that he was seriously considering the bills. The Scots commissioners finally caved and, on 26 December, signed the Engagement. They pledged support for his request for a 'personal treaty' in London and, if this was denied, undertook to invade England to restore his authority. In return, Charles agreed to establish Presbyterianism in England for three years, approve various acts of the Scottish parliament and appoint Scots to the English privy council. On the issue of the Covenant he won decisively. It was to be ratified by act of parliament, but neither he nor any of his subjects was to be compelled to take it.[242]

Rumours that Charles was about to come to an understanding with the Scots prompted parliament to pass the 'Vote of No Addresses' in early January 1648. This should have put an end to negotiations; however, the Independent leaders and the army grandees continued to work behind the scenes to try to head off a Scottish invasion. Cromwell mooted the possibility of persuading the king to abdicate in favour of either Charles or James, while Lord Saye consulted Southampton and travelled to the Isle of Wight in the hope of restarting discussions.[243] The problem was that Charles was no longer interested even in keeping up the appearance of negotiation. He had secured the Engagement and prepared the ground for a resumption of war, and now his priority was to escape. The first attempt on 28 December was prevented by adverse winds in the Solent, but he went on trying in spite of Hammond placing him under increasingly close confinement.[244] The Scots, meanwhile, were gearing up for war. When a new Scottish parliament met on 2 March 1648 there was a strong majority in

---

[242] Stevenson, *Revolution and Counter Revolution*, pp. 95–7; Gardiner, *History of the Civil War*, vol. 4, pp. 35, 37–41; Burnet, *Memoirs of . . . the Dukes of Hamilton*, pp. 326–33; *Constitutional Documents*, pp. 347–52.

[243] Gardiner, *History of the Civil War*, vol. 4, pp. 51, 56, 59, 85, 96–7, 99–101; Underdown, *Pride's Purge*, pp. 88, 95–6.

[244] Carlton, *Charles I*, pp. 326–8.

favour of the Engagement and Hamilton was able to use this to overcome opposition from Argyll's allies in the army and the kirk. On 11 April the Scottish parliament approved an ultimatum requiring their English counterparts to establish Presbyterianism, disband the army and allow the king to go to London. A week later they ordered the mobilisation of their own army of 30 000 men. By the end of the month the Second Civil War had effectively begun.[245]

From Charles's point of view this was a vindication of his tortuous negotiating strategy. Resumption of the war with Scottish help had been his primary objective since the autumn of 1645 and this should be borne in mind when it comes to assessing his capabilities as a politician. Historians have generally been very disparaging about his role in these negotiations, criticising him for deviousness, inflexibility and lack of judgement. Such verdicts, however, tend to assume that Charles was aiming for a settlement when, in fact, most of the evidence points in another direction. His basic instinct – evident throughout his surviving correspondence – was that his enemies should be punished and humiliated. As in Scotland in 1638, he regarded peace talks largely as a means of buying time and dividing his opponents while he assembled sufficient force to destroy them. He recognised that he would have to negotiate in the end – and he was no doubt sincere in his professions of a desire to bring to peace to his people – but he seems to have envisaged it as happening only after another period of bloodletting. Understanding this makes his approach look less misguided than has often appeared.

One of the main criticisms made of him, by Gardiner in particular, was that he engaged in a degree of deception that was both morally reprehensible and counter-productive.[246] Charles, of course, did not see things in these terms. As far as he was concerned there was an important distinction to be drawn between those occasions when he had specifically pledged his word – such as giving his parole not to escape in November 1647 – and those where he had made undertakings which might be interpreted in different ways. In the former case he felt that his word was his bond and he refused to break it until he had found a way of satisfying himself that he was not acting dishonestly. The latter circumstance, however, was very different, and

---

[245] Stevenson, *Revolution and Counter Revolution*, pp. 98–9, 105.

[246] Gardiner, *History of England*, vol. 4, pp. 327–8.

he appears to have had no compunction about equivocating with those who were rebels and traitors. Thus he could cheerfully admit to the Scots commissioners in November 1647 that 'many things may be fitly offered to obtain a treaty that may be altered when one comes to treat'. In other words, there was a world of difference between what he was prepared to say to keep negotiations going and what he would be finally willing to agree to.[247] This approach made Charles exasperating to deal with and it undermined goodwill and trust in him as a negotiator; but the extent to which it damaged his cause can be overestimated. It probably put paid to any prospect of parliament agreeing to invite him to London for 'a personal treaty', although given the nervousness of the army and Independents over this even when they were well disposed towards him in June 1647 the possibility was always remote. On the other hand, his changes of position and his willingness to tell those he was dealing with what they wanted to hear did much to keep the different groupings in play and open up what little room for manoeuvre he actually enjoyed. There was always a constituency on the parliamentarian side that was desperate to believe the king's assurances because the alternatives were so unpalatable. As long as he was able to give them some hope that he might be won round he could keep them talking and exploit their differences.

A more serious criticism can be made of his tactical misjudgements. A number of blunders occurred because he overestimated the strength of his position. Had he been less dismissive of the motives of the Scots and more aware of the distrust his actions had provoked, for example, he could probably have avoided his antagonists uniting over the Newcastle Propositions. He was also at fault over the planning of the escape from Hampton Court in November 1647, which considerably reduced his scope for exploiting the divisions among his enemies. Perhaps most damagingly of all, he failed to recognise the opportunity offered by the Heads of Proposals. Had he welcomed these, instead of dismissing them at the height of London's counter-revolution in July 1647, he could probably have achieved much of what he sought by peaceful means. The army was desperate for his support and apparently in the mood to give him back enough of his power to be

---

[247] NAS, GD 406/1/2177. On another occasion he boasted to the queen that he was deliberately misleading the parliamentarian commissioners when he promised to 'give full satisfaction' over Ireland: *Charles I in 1646*, p. 84.

able to restore his position without fighting. His brutal rebuff to the army delegates on 28 July – probably born of an understandable desire to see his enemies humiliated as he had been – was surely his biggest single mistake of the period.

These faults, however, need to be balanced against the political acumen and resilience displayed by Charles. On several occasions he proved flexible enough to adjust his tactics and recover his position. Following the failure of the counter-revolution he was quick to recognise the need to make his peace with the army, while after September 1646 he was able to work his way out of the impasse with the Scots with the proposal to accept the ecclesiastical *status quo* for three years. In addition he displayed consider- able nerve as a negotiator. He recognised that the Scots' fear of an army takeover was greater than any reservations over his failure to take the Covenant, and used this to clinch their agreement to the Engagement. Above all he continued to display a good grasp of how to pitch his appeals to the various constituencies he was dealing with. His letter of 12 May 1647 was a particularly accomplished performance; but so too were other declarations that probably came from his own pen, such as his response to the Vote of No Addresses on 18 January 1648 in which the reader was confronted with the full horror of England without a king.[248] There were moments, particularly during the summer of 1647, when it looked as if he would be able to accomplish most of what he wanted without the need for another civil war. Had he been able to make his return to London, the momentum behind the campaign for his restoration might well have become unstop- pable. In the end, it was not just his own failings and miscalculations, but also a large measure of bad luck that proved his undoing.

How far Charles was acting of his own volition, and how far he was relying on others during this period, is sometimes difficult to ascertain. He continued to receive a more or less constant stream of advice from the queen. But by this stage he was inured to many of her arguments and appears to have been quite willing to ignore them when it suited him, notably in making concessions over the militia. He always tended to pay more atten- tion to counsellors on the spot and in this respect the arrival of his old

---

[248] *The King's Declaration to all his Loving Subjects, 18 January 1647/8*, Thomason E 426 (5), pp. 1–6. For Charles's isolation at the time this was written, see Gardiner, *History of the Civil War*, vol. 4, p. 49. On the impact of responses to the Vote of No Addresses, see Ashton, *The Second Civil War*, pp. 40, 212–13.

friend Will Murray was probably crucial in helping him devise a workable compromise on religion. The presence of another trusted courtier, John Ashburnham, also appears to have been important in boosting his self-confidence in the final stages of his dealings with the Scots. In one respect, however, there is no doubt that the king was drawing on his own resources. This was in the sheer willpower and determination that he displayed in keeping going. He was on his own for long periods and frequently felt depressed and abandoned; yet he refused to take the easy way out by escaping to France. Instead he stood his ground, convinced that if he fought on, and remained true to his principles, God would ensure ultimate victory. This display of resolution and conviction exerted a powerful influence on his supporters and ensured that (as in 1641–2) his cause was kept alive in very difficult circumstances. Charles may have lacked the qualities that the country needed to heal its divisions in the aftermath of civil war, but he remained an effective party leader.

During the Second Civil War (May–August 1648) the king was effectively consigned to the sidelines. After his failure to escape in March he was placed under increasingly close confinement at Carisbrooke. He was able to keep in touch with the Scots up to the end of April, but thereafter most of his contact with the outside world had to be via coded letters smuggled out in the heels of his servants' boots.[249] For the time being, command of the royalist cause passed to the queen and Prince of Wales.

At the start of the war the royalists had the political upper hand. The southern counties were seething with discontent over taxation, high prices and rule by the army. There was a longing for the order and stability which, it was believed, would accompany the king's restoration. Petitions to parliament and widespread demonstrations culminated in rioting in London on Charles's Accession day (26 March), which piled the pressure on MPs at Westminster. At the end of April the Presbyterian majority were able to secure a suspension of the Vote of No Addresses. This led to the resumption of their control in the City and moves to invite the king to London for a personal treaty. The problem was that this political strength was not matched by effective military action. The royalists completely failed to coordinate the risings by their sympathisers in the South with Hamilton's invasion from

---

[249] Carlton, *Charles I*, pp. 328–33; Burnet, *Memoirs of . . . the Dukes of Hamilton*, pp. 337–8, 344–5.

the North. The marquis was not ready until early July, by which time the rebellion in Kent had been put down and the royalist attempt to enter London had been repulsed. Cromwell was able to march north in early August and block Hamilton's advance at Preston, leaving the king's forces in disarray.[250] Charles appeared to have little choice but to negotiate.

Meanwhile the coalition ranged against him had hardened its stance. At the Windsor prayer meeting in late April 1648, the army had passed its momentous resolution 'to call Charles Stuart, that man of blood, to an account for the blood he had shed'. From this point onwards there was substantial support within its ranks for putting him on trial. This was the threat that hung over the proceedings of the following months, inducing occasional panic in Charles, but also concentrating the minds of those he was dealing with. Within parliament the majority remained committed to a negotiated peace, but on much tougher terms than those on offer in 1647. The Independent grandees continued to take the lead, and they had learnt by bitter experience that they could not afford to trust Charles's assurances. They believed that the only way to deal with him was to tie his hands by ensuring that control of the militia and the appointment of ministers remained with parliament, preferably for 20 years. They were also willing to appease the Presbyterian majority at Westminster by pressing for the com-plete abolition of episcopacy and the sale of bishops' lands. The result was that the terms with which the king was presented at Newport in September 1648 closely resembled the Hampton Court Propositions that he had roundly rejected a year earlier.[251]

At first it seemed to Charles that there was little point in further negotiation; however, once it became clear that he would be restored to much of his royal dignity for the duration of the treaty he warmed to the prospect. Discussions began on 18 September at Newport Grammar School on the Isle of Wight. The king took the lead, sitting under his canopy of state flanked by his former councillors, Richmond, Hertford, Lindsey and Southampton. Once again he impressed observers with his statesmanship

---

[250] Underdown, *Pride's Purge*, pp. 90–105; Kenyon, *The Civil Wars*, pp. 179–93; Stevenson, *Revolution and Counter Revolution*, pp. 105–14.

[251] Gardiner, *History of the Civil War*, vol. 4, pp. 118–20, 212–15; Underdown, *Pride's Purge*, pp. 101–9.

and mastery of the arguments.[252] The negotiation quickly settled into the pattern of the wartime treaties at Oxford and Uxbridge. The councillors pressed the king to be accommodating, but he remained determined not to be pushed too far. He was conscious as before of his kingly duty to abide by 'the rule of charity which looks to the good and peace of many . . . before the public maintaining the right of any one single cause'. On this basis, as he told his son, he was willing to make various concessions to keep the negotiations going. However, he was also adamant that he would not be drawn into giving away too much and, therefore, insisted that nothing be regarded as binding until a complete package had been agreed.[253] This was Charles returning to a policy of fixing his 'negatives'.

The negotiating process at Newport was scheduled to last 40 days, but in the end went on for considerably longer. The parliamentarian commissioners were under instructions to present the Hampton Court Propositions in order. Charles jibbed at the first of these – that all declarations against parliament be withdrawn – on the grounds that it contained a statement that the two houses 'had been necessitated to undertake a war in their just and lawful defence'; however, he eventually let it go, not wishing to appear 'irreconcilable' as he told his son. The critical point was reached on 25 September when the commissioners presented their ecclesiastical demands, which included the abolition of episcopacy, the sale of bishops' lands and the compulsory taking of the Covenant. The king responded three days later with his old offer to allow Presbyterianism to be established for three years and a proposal for a 99-year lease on bishops' lands. He also declared that he was ready to allow control of the militia and appointment of ministers to pass to parliament for ten years (although not twenty) and permit the two houses to take control of affairs in Ireland.[254] This last was in many ways the most interesting concession because it suggested that Charles had abandoned hope of military assistance from that quarter. His attitude was to change a few weeks later when Ormond returned to Dublin and made a promising start in rebuilding a pro-royalist

[252] Carlton, *Charles I*, pp. 336–7; *Warwick Memoirs*, pp. 358, 360.

[253] *Clarendon State Papers*, vol. 2, p. 431; Gardiner, *History of the Civil War*, vol. 4, p. 214.

[254] Gardiner, *History of the Civil War*, vol. 4, pp. 214–18; Underdown, *Pride's Purge*, pp. 110–11, 4–15, 17–18.

alliance. But, for the time being, Charles appeared to accept that he had no choice but to negotiate. Whether he would have gone through with any agreement based on these terms, however, appears doubtful. He still tended to view negotiation as a means of buying time until something turned up and he was clinging to the hope that the undoubted justness of his cause would lead to some sort of providential deliverance. Had parliament responded positively to his offers it is likely that he would have discovered some new reason for spinning out the process. In the event, he was spared this because on 2 October the Commons rejected his proposals.[255]

Charles could now feel that he had done all that could reasonably be expected of him and was therefore released from any moral ties in dealing with the commissioners. Once again he prepared to make his escape. On 9 October he told his chief accomplice William Hopkins, master of Newport Grammar School, that henceforth his negotiating strategy would be to 'deny them nothing' to put his captors off their guard. The same day he offered assurances that the type of episcopacy that would be restored after the three years of Presbyterianism would be the modified version proposed in 1641, and that he would give up control of the militia and ministerial appointments for 20 years. Over the following weeks he conceded, in all, 38 of parliament's demands.[256] However, there were still certain areas on which he would not yield.

On 'the businesses of the church', he told Hopkins, he would go no further than his 9 October concessions since this was 'a point of conscience' on which 'I durst not dissemble'. He also took the same line over 'my friends'. Having bitterly regretted allowing Strafford to go to the block, he refused to agree to his leading supporters being exempted from a post-war pardon.[257] The other area where he now held out was over Ireland. News reached him in late October that Ormond had come to an agreement with Lord Inchiquin, who had defected from the parliamentarians earlier in the year and now commanded a considerable force in Munster. The marquis was also hopeful once more of forming an alliance with the Confederacy at

---

[255] Gardiner, *History of the Civil War*, vol. 4, p. 219.

[256] C.W. Firebrace, *Honest Harry. Sir Henry Firebrace 1619–1691*, 1932, p. 344; Gardiner, *History of the Civil War*, vol. 4, pp. 220–1.

[257] Firebrace, *Honest Harry*, pp. 343, 345.

Kilkenny. It was being rumoured in London that he would soon have an army of 16 000 men, and was simply waiting for the final breakdown at Newport before launching an invasion. On 28 October the parliamentarian commissioners demanded that the king disavow Ormond's negotiations; but this he refused to do, pointing out that he had already agreed to allow parliament to take control of all Irish business and it was therefore unnecessary. At the same time he wrote to Ormond, urging him to go on with his discussions with all speed and ignore any reports that he was about to settle at Newport. 'Do not startle at my great concessions concerning Ireland', he insisted, 'for . . . they will come to nothing.'[258] Very deliberately, Charles was opening the door to a third civil war.

At the same time, however, he began seriously to face up to the possibility of his trial and martyrdom. His letters and asides were now strewn with references to his impending fate. He told his servant Philip Warwick that he felt like the commander in a besieged town who in spite of being given permission by his superiors to surrender believed that he must 'hold it out till I make some stone of this building my tombstone'.[259] When the parliamentarian commissioners took their leave of him on 27 November he warned them, rather melodramatically, that 'we shall surely never see each other again', adding that he took comfort from having made his peace with God and come to terms with 'whatsoever he shall be pleased to suffer men to do unto me'.[260] There was a strong element of calculation in this, of course, because Charles was determined to confront moderate MPs with the awful consequences of allowing him to be put on trial. But it is also clear that he was increasingly preoccupied with his possible fate and that, at times, the strain became too much. Warwick tells of how one day he came upon the king standing by a window as the commissioners talked at the other end of the room. He suddenly noticed that he was crying, 'the biggest drops that ever I saw fall from an eye'.[261]

---

[258] Adamson, 'The Frighted Junto', pp. 47–8; *Early Modern Ireland*, pp. 331–2; Gardiner, *History of the Civil War*, vol. 4, pp. 224–6; Carte, *The Life of Ormond*, vol. 5, p. 24.

[259] *Warwick Memoirs*, p. 363.

[260] *A Royalist's Notebook*, p. 126. See also his letters to Prince Charles at this time: *Clarendon State Papers*, vol. 2, p. 449; *Letters of Charles I*, pp. 239–41.

[261] *Warwick Memoirs*, p. 362.

During his time at Newport Charles also began a concerted effort to fashion an image of himself for posterity. The most plausible reconstruction of the authorship of *Eikon Basilike* suggests that it was during this period that the marquis of Hertford presented him with John Gauden's manuscript, based on a vindication of his actions that he himself had been working on since 1642. Having corrected and revised it Charles then apparently authorised publication in his name, although the manuscript did not reach his printer until late December 1648.[262] At the same time he was working on a series of lengthy letters to the Prince of Wales which served both as a justification of his approach to the treaty negotiations and a guide to kingship. A number of familiar themes resurfaced – the importance of preserving episcopacy, following one's conscience, promoting peace and so on – but the one that stood out most clearly was Charles's determination to present himself as a constitutional monarch. At one point he explained how he conceived of his role as that of 'a politic parent', by which he meant someone whose duty it was 'to seek [his people's] peace in the orthodox profession of the christian religion' and ensure that 'the ancient laws, with the interpretation according to the known practice, may once again be a hedge about them'. There was again an element of political calculation in this. Charles presumed that once the importance of this role was acknowledged it would also be recognised 'how useful a king's power is to a people's liberty'. However, he was also prepared to concede that his stance placed a heavy responsibility on the prince. He must be willing to make concessions in a 'parliamentary way, to agree the bounds for prince and people'. He must also be sure 'never to affect more greatness or prerogative than that which is really and intrinsically for the good of subjects, not satisfaction of favourites'.[263] It is, perhaps, tempting to see this as belated recognition on the king's part of the policies which would have avoided civil war. But this would surely be to read too much into it. What it does demonstrate, however, is his grasp of the constitutionalist language that Hyde

---

[262] *Eikon Basilike*, pp. xxx–xxxii; S. Kelsey, 'The King's Book. *Eikon Basilike* and the English Revolution of 1649', in Tyacke ed., *The English Revolution and its Legacies* (forthcoming).

[263] *Clarendon State Papers*, vol. 2, pp. 425–54; *Letters of Charles I*, pp. 239–41. According to Warwick, Charles dictated several of these letters in the evenings as he reviewed the day's proceedings in the treaty: *Warwick Memoirs*, p. 361.

had deployed so successfully in royalist declarations. During the last weeks of his life Charles was to go back over this ground again and again. In the process, he not only found an effective means of dividing his enemies, but also provided his supporters and apologists with a powerful legacy.

By late October, the negotiations at Newport were collapsing. Charles came up with a final offer on the church, which was rejected by the Commons on 21 October. The parliamentarian commissioners were able to secure an extension to the original 40-day negotiating period, but with the king unwilling to budge on episcopacy there was little prospect of agreement. In these circumstances the initiative passed to the army, where Ireton was orchestrating pressure from the regiments to bring Charles to justice. In early November he produced the Remonstrance of the Army, which called for a purge of parliament and the trial of the king and leading royalists. Fairfax and the more conservative of the officers were still hoping to persuade their fellow soldiers to abide by the outcome of the Newport negotiations; but, as pressure built from the regiments and Charles showed no sign of disowning Ormond, they shifted towards a more radical position. On 18 November the General Council of the Army endorsed the Remonstrance and the way was open to bringing Charles to justice. Three days prior to this, however, the Presbyterian majority persuaded the Commons to agree to the king's repeated request to be allowed to come to London to negotiate in person.[264] Once again it must have appeared to Charles that his enemies were dividing.

It is probably this which explains his curious refusal to escape from Newport when the opportunity presented itself on 30 November. There are two versions of this episode. One has it that Charles refused to flee because he would not violate his parole. In reply to grim warnings from Richmond, Lindsey and Southampton of the dangers he faced, he was said to have declared 'never let that trouble you. I would not break my word to prevent it.'[265] This is certainly in keeping with the attitude of stoical indifference that Charles was seeking to present as he prepared himself for the possibility of martyrdom. However, he had found ways of getting round his parole in the past and, presumably, could have done so

---

[264] Underdown, *Pride's Purge*, pp. 115–22; Gardiner, *History of the Civil War*, vol. 4, pp. 233–45.

[265] Gardiner, *History of the Civil War*, pp. 254–9.

again. The more likely explanation appears to be that given by Colonel Edward Cooke who was party to the escape plan. He claimed that Charles had worked out that 'if the army should seize him, they must preserve him for their own sakes, he being convinced that no party could secure their own interests without joining his to it, his son being out of their reach'.[266] He therefore decided at the last moment to stick it out. This sort of reasoning would have been typical of Charles. It accorded with the image he had of himself as a shrewd political tactician, well able to out-manoeuvre his enemies. As so often, however, there was an element of being too clever by half and, with hindsight, his action looks like an outrageously optimistic gamble.

The final collapse of the negotiations at Newport in late November, together with the Commons' refusal to accept the Remonstrance when it was presented to it on the 20th, eventually persuaded the General Council to sanction a march on London. The Presbyterian majority in the Commons mounted a final act of defiance on 5 December by voting that the terms discussed at Newport constituted a basis for further negotiation. But the following day Colonel Pride moved in with his troopers and purged the house.[267] The traditional view has been that these events led inexorably to the king's trial and execution. With the Presbyterian majority in the Commons neutralised, and the Lords seemingly set for extinction, the way was now open for the army and its radical allies to push through the programme outlined in the Remonstrance and bring Charles to justice, as 'the capital and grand author of our troubles'.[268] However, recent work by John Adamson and Sean Kelsey has put a very different complexion on these events.[269] They demonstrate that the leaders of the army/radical junto were deeply fearful of the consequences of removing the king and continued to make every effort to reach a settlement. This makes a crucial difference

---

[266] Cited in S. Kelsey, 'The death of Charles I', *HJ*, vol. 45, 2002, p. 732.

[267] Underdown, *Pride's Purge*, pp. 130–50; Gardiner, *History of the Civil War*, vol. 4, pp. 263–70.

[268] C.V. Wedgewood, *The Trial of Charles I*, 1964; Gardiner, *History of the Civil War*, vol. 4, chps. lxvii–lxx; Underdown, *Pride's Purge*, chps. 5–7.

[269] Adamson, 'The Frighted Junto', pp. 36–70; Kelsey, 'Death of Charles I', pp. 727–54; idem., 'The trial of Charles I', *EHR*, vol. 118, 2003, pp. 583–616; idem, 'Staging the trial of Charles I', in Peacey ed., *The Regicides and the Execution of Charles I*, pp. 71–93; idem., 'Politics and procedure in the trial of Charles I', *Law & History Review*, vol. 22, 2004, pp. 1–25.

to our understanding of Charles's actions during the final weeks of his life. If he was effectively doomed from early December onwards then, as Conrad Russell puts it, he had little option but to try to end his days 'with honour and a good conscience'.[270] If, however, there was everything still to play for then his decision-making and tactical judgements become much more significant.

Even after Pride's Purge, the king continued to enjoy considerable room for manoeuvre. The leaders of the army/radical junto were anxious to build a lasting post-war settlement and recognised that working with him was much the most desirable means to achieve this. The alternatives of deposition or execution both appeared fraught with danger. The possibility of replacing Charles with the only one of his sons who was still in parliamentarian custody, the nine-year-old duke of Gloucester, was being mooted in some quarters. But contemporaries were very conscious of the precedent of Richard II who had been a focus for intrigue as long as he remained alive. Regicide appeared even more hazardous. It was recognised that it would prompt a Europe-wide outcry against whoever was responsible and cede the initiative to the king over the water. Charles II would be in a position to mount a powerful military challenge. He already had the nucleus of a royalist fleet – made up of those ships which had deserted the parliamentarian navy in May 1648 – and he could rely on support from his Dutch brother-in-law William II of Orange. He also had every opportunity to recruit a mercenary army from among the forces recently released by the Treaty of Westphalia. In the civil war which, it seemed, would inevitably follow, there could be no certainty that the new regime would survive. It was a much better option to work with the existing king, keep him alive as a bargaining counter if things went wrong, and persuade him to defuse the biggest immediate threat by calling off Ormond's negotiations with the Confederacy.[271]

Charles's approach was to go on buying time in the hope that the marquis would come to his rescue. He therefore refused to disown Ormond's negotiations and tried to take the political initiative himself. He spent the early part of December closely confined at Hurst Castle in Hampshire; but

---

[270] Russell, *Crisis of Parliaments*, p. 383.

[271] Adamson, 'The Frighted Junto', pp. 38–50; Kelsey, 'Trial of Charles I', pp. 586–8, 593–4; idem, 'Politics and procedure', pp. 6–8; idem, 'Death of Charles I', p. 732.

he still seems to have been able to keep in touch with news of what was going on, and smuggle out the occasional letter to Ormond or the Prince of Wales.[272] His *Declaration Concerning the Treaty*, which was published at this time, set out to exploit the Commons' vote on 5 December by reminding the public of how earnestly he had sought peace and how close Newport had come to succeeding. It also repeated earlier warnings of the danger to his person and the hazards of an army takeover. Reverting to the language of popularity, he insisted that 'there is nothing can more obstruct the long hoped for peace of this nation than the illegal proceedings of them that presume from servants to become masters and labour to bring in democracy and abolish monarchy'.[273] This was a calculated appeal to the Presbyterian constituency which had rallied to Charles in the past and which he still seems to have expected to head off the threat of a trial. The problem was that the Presbyterians had lost much of their power as a result of Pride's Purge. Those who mattered now were the members of the army/radical junto, and the critical fault line within their ranks was that between the leadership (consisting of the army grandees led by Fairfax and Cromwell and the Independent peers of the Derby House Committee, such as Denbigh and Pembroke) who wanted to negotiate and the more radical MPs, with their allies among the junior officers and regiments, who were determined to press ahead with a trial.[274] For much of December the leadership was in control, but they were very conscious that their grip on power remained insecure. If it came to having to choose between keeping the talks with the king going and surrendering to army pressure to preserve the unity of their coalition, there was every likelihood that they would give ground. It does not seem that Charles understood this until quite late in the day and it led him to squander his best opportunity of averting a trial.

Events came to a head on 18–19 December when the Derby House Committee and the grandees were informed that a naval treaty had been concluded between the Irish Confederacy and the Dutch Republic. This not only offered Ormond the means of convoying an army to England, it

---

[272] Francis Peck ed., *Desiderata Curiosa*, 2 vols., 1732–5, liber x, p. 30.

[273] *His Majestie's Declaration Concerning the Treaty*, Thomason, 1648, E 476 (13), pp. 4–7.

[274] Underdown, *Pride's Purge*, pp. 163–7; Adamson, 'The Frighted Junto', pp. 38–9; Kelsey, 'Trial of Charles I', pp. 588–94.

also introduced the threat of a full-scale naval war with the Dutch. The decision was taken to make a new approach to the king once he had been moved from Hurst Castle to Windsor, and Denbigh was chosen to lead the mission. It was reported that he would propose that Charles surrender his 'negative voice', agree to the alienation of bishops' lands and 'abjure the Scots'. In addition, he was almost certainly to be required to call off Ormond. At the same time Cromwell was to explore the possibility of readmitting some of the secluded members to the Commons and appeasing the radicals by bringing other leading royalists to justice. By Christmas Day, when Denbigh was due to meet Charles, it was widely expected that the king's trial could be avoided, or at least stage-managed to ensure his acquittal.[275]

Charles, however, refused to cooperate. It is unclear what happened but it seems that he either refused to meet with Denbigh or else rejected his proposals outright. In some respects, this was hardly surprising. One of Edward Nicholas's correspondents remarked that losing his 'negative voice' would have left him with no more power than 'a duke of Venice' and the king had never been prepared to accept such a surrender in the past.[276] However, the unpalatable nature of the junto's demands does not explain why he did not at least talk to Denbigh and, perhaps, string him along with counter proposals. The reason would appear to be that he was subject to one of his bouts of overconfidence. There were reports from Windsor that he had been 'very pleasant and merry since his coming thither' and was taking delight in picking holes in the army's case. He was also said to be optimistic that 'though he suffers under restraint . . . yet his Irish subjects will come in this time and rescue him'. So, instead of negotiating, Charles decided to go on to the offensive and draft his own ultimatum. According to *His Majesties Last Proposals to the Officers of the Armie*, this consisted of a request that he be allowed to come to London to confer about the grievances afflicting the kingdom, and a warning that if the army went ahead with his trial they would be opposed by the City of London, the Irish and his own son.[277] As John Adamson has observed, 'these gestures were vintage Charles I:

[275] Adamson, 'The Frighted Junto', pp. 43–7, 51, 54; Underdown, *Pride's Purge*, pp. 167–70.

[276] Gardiner, *History of the Civil War*, vol. 4, pp. 284–6.

[277] *His Majestie's Last Proposals to the Officers of the Armie*, 1648, Thomason, E 536 (13), p. 6.

concessions with menaces'.[278] But they were not well judged. The king was placing a huge reliance on Ormond delivering a treaty with the Confederacy, something he had repeatedly failed to do in the past. He was also continuing to target his appeal to the Presbyterians who, for the time being, had little power to assist. This approach might have worked before Pride's Purge, but now it simply served to push the various elements in the army/radical coalition together.

The failure of Denbigh's mission meant that Cromwell and the other junto leaders could no longer hold back the pressure for a trial. On 27 December the Council of Officers decided to allow it to go ahead and the following day the Commons began the process of setting up a high court of justice. When this was opposed by the Lords they went ahead anyway, and on 4 January 1649 voted that since the Commons House was 'the original of all just power' and 'the supreme power of this nation', they could legislate without the consent of the king or the upper house. This was affirmed two days later when they passed the 'Act for a High Court of Justice' naming 135 commissioners, drawn from MPs and supporters of the new regime, who were to act as the king's judges.[279]

The Commons' revolutionary action was driven by a group of reforming MPs and their allies in the army who were now committed to sweeping away the key features of the ancient constitution. This radical coalition was apparently bent on pushing through a Leveller/Republican agenda which would lead to the abolition of the monarchy and the Lords, and government by 'the people'. However, a sizeable contingent of MPs, as well as the junto leadership, did not support such innovation and wished to preserve as much of the existing constitution as possible. Over the following days they sought to limit the implications of the 4 January vote. When the Lords met again on the 9th they attempted to get back into the process by offering to recognise the High Court of Justice on condition that the king only be tried if he attempted to start another civil war. This came to nothing. But two days later the Independent peers were reported to be holding discussions with Richmond, Hertford, Lindsey and Southampton about the possibility of a new settlement on the terms agreed at Newport. There was also speculation that Charles himself was in contact with the army grandees via

---

[278] Adamson, 'The Frighted Junto', pp. 50, 56–7.

[279] Gardiner, *History of the Civil War*, vol. 4, pp. 286–92.

the Independent minister Hugh Peter, whom he had invited to Windsor to confer on matters of conscience.[280]

The main effort by those who were anxious to preserve the ancient constitution focused on arrangements for the trial. There was an initial proposal to hold it at Windsor, rather than Westminster, where proceedings could take place behind closed doors under the supervision of the castle's constable, the earl of Pembroke. This was rejected by the trial judges in favour of a more public hearing in the Great Hall at Westminster; however, even here, respect for the existing order was emphasised by the presence of the royal coat of arms, emblazoned on a shield hanging behind the trial judges. The principal struggle took place over the charges that the king was to face. The radicals among the commissioners and hardline army officers backed a lengthy indictment of Charles's conduct going back to the start of his reign. This was intended to demonstrate his full culpability in tyranny, treason and bloodshed with the object of blackening his name sufficiently to make the case for doing away with kingship altogether. However, after a debate between the trial judges lasting well over a week, it was rejected in favour of a more limited accusation which centred on the charge of levying war against his people since 1642. This was a victory for the more conservative of the commissioners. It would make it harder to sustain a capital judgement and offer the king the opportunity to plead a defence of evil counsel. The way would thus be open for a settlement at some stage in the future. However, everything depended on Charles being willing to plead. If he did so this could be taken as an acceptance of the court's authority which, in turn, would imply a surrender of his 'negative voice'. If he did not then the options open to the defenders of the ancient constitution would be severely limited.[281]

The king was fully aware of the implications of pleading to the charges and was determined to avoid doing so. But in other respects he was now quite willing to let it appear that he might come to an accommodation. He continued to pin his hopes on Ormond and an Irish army, and was doubtless encouraged by a joint letter from the marquis and Inchiquin in

---

[280] Kelsey, 'Trial of Charles I', pp. 588–94; Adamson, 'The Frighted Junto', pp. 58–9; Gardiner, *History of the Civil War*, vol. 4, pp. 593–4; Kelsey, 'Death of Charles I', pp. 741–3.

[281] Kelsey, 'Trial of Charles I', pp. 594–8; idem, 'Staging the trial of Charles I', pp. 82–3; idem, 'Politics and procedure', pp. 12–20; idem, 'Death of Charles I', pp. 734, 753.

late December, which warned Fairfax that if any harm came to the king they would exact speedy revenge.[282] His strategy, therefore, was to go on buying time and trying to exploit the divisions between his opponents. By early January he appears to have recognised that the critical fault line lay between the radical and conservative wings of the junto. He therefore set out to build bridges to the leadership. His invitation to Peter, who was held in high regard by Cromwell, looks like an attempt to put out feelers to the grandees. It could also be interpreted as a signal that Charles might be willing to soften his stance on episcopacy. Whether he went further and made 'certain offers' to 'an eminent officer' when he was moved to St James's Palace on 19 January seems doubtful; but the fact that this was being rumoured indicates an expectation that he was ready to talk. He may also have been in contact with the Independent peers, via his principal manservant at the time, Thomas Herbert, who was a kinsman and client of Pembroke. The discussions involving Richmond and his other former councillors were probably begun without his knowledge, and had they threatened to reach any sort of agreement he would presumably have disowned them.[283] For the time being, however, it suited his purposes to allow these to continue. While the preparations for the trial were going ahead, then, Charles was carefully positioning himself as someone with whom the junto leadership might still do business.

The trial itself opened on 20 January 1649 with the solicitor to the Commonwealth, John Cooke, reading the charge. Charles was accused of being 'a tyrant, traitor, murderer, and a public and implacable enemy to the commonwealth of England'. The president of the court, John Bradshawe, then asked the king how he would plead, whereupon Charles demanded to know 'by what lawful authority I am seated here'. Bradshawe replied that it was 'by the authority of the Commons of England, assembled in Parliament, in the behalf of the People of England, by which People you are elected king'. This blunt assertion of Commons' sovereignty gave Charles the cue to launch into a sustained defence of mixed monarchy and the rule of law.[284] For the remainder of the hearing on this first day – and

---

[282] Adamson, 'The Frighted Junto', p. 58.

[283] Kelsey, 'Death of Charles I', pp. 741–3; idem, 'Trial of Charles I', pp. 602–3.

[284] *Trial of Charles I*, ed. J. Muddiman, 1928, pp. 78–83.

again when he returned to the court on the 22nd and 23rd – he hammered away at this fundamental theme.

He began by pointing out that England was 'never an elective kingdom'; then mounted a robust attack on the court's authority to bring him to trial. 'It is not my case alone', he insisted,

it is the freedom and liberty of the people of England . . . For if power (without law) may make law, may alter the fundamental laws of the kingdom – I do not know what subject he is in England can be assured of his life or anything he can call his own.[285]

He presented himself as the surest safeguard of legal rights and liberties, bound 'by the duty I owe to God and my country' to resist any attempt to undermine constitutional propriety or subvert the fundamental laws. If he could be removed by this arbitrary and 'pretended power' then nothing could be secure.[286] This was his basic argument throughout. At one point he reverted to the language of divine right and insisted that, in the final analysis, he was answerable for his actions only to God.[287] But for the most part he stuck closely to the line that he was the servant of 'the people of England', a hereditary monarch whose actions were bounded and limited by law.

He supported this by repeating that there was a need for the trial to be authorised by a properly constituted parliament. There was a marked difference, he insisted, between the present proceedings and those at Newport where 'I entered into a treaty with the two houses of parliament with as much public faith as is possibly to be had with any people in the world'. Now he could see 'no House of Lords that may constitute a parliament' and was having to deal with a Commons in which 'it is too well known that the major part of them are detained or deterred from sitting'.[288] In a remarkable passage which he prepared for the hearing on 22 January – but probably never delivered – he went further and confronted the Commons' claim to be uniquely representative of 'the people of England'.

---

[285] Ibid., pp. 82, 90.

[286] Ibid., pp. 83, 99–100; Kelsey, 'Trial of Charles I', pp. 604–5.

[287] *Trial of Charles I*, p. 82.

[288] Ibid., pp. 81–3.

Certainly you never asked the question of the tenth man in the kingdom, and in this way you manifestly wrong even the poorest ploughman if you demand not his free consent; nor can you pretend any colour for this your pretended commission without the consent of the major part of every man in England of whatsoever quality or condition.[289]

This implied a vision of a participatory political order that was some way removed from anything the king had been willing to sanction before. Had he survived he might have had cause to regret such remarks, even in draft form. However, their appearance here does emphasise how thoroughly he had embraced the language of the balanced constitution and how determined he was to present himself as its principal defender.

There was also a good deal of shrewd political calculation behind Charles's approach. His repeated references to his role as guarantor of the subject's liberties were designed to strike a chord with the more conservative of the trial commissioners; while his comments on the House of Lords chimed in with their efforts to take control of the whole process.[290] Even more significantly, he continued to tantalise the judges with the possibility that he might actually plead to the charges. He repeated on several occasions that if he could be shown 'by what legal authority I am seated here . . . I will answer it'; and on 22 January he tried to enter a demurrer which, although intended as another way to avoid pleading, at least implied a recognition that the court constituted some sort of legal tribunal.[291] The arguments Charles deployed, then, were targeted very effectively on the fault line dividing those who wished to see him condemned and those still hoping for a settlement. He was able to dictate the terms of the hearing in such a way as to open this up even further.

Gilbert Mabbott's *A Perfect Narrative*, which is the fullest account we have of the court's proceedings, suggests that over these first three days it was Charles who made most of the running. Legend has it that for the first time in his life he was able to overcome his stammer, and he delivered a fluent and impressive performance.[292] In spite of repeated demands that

---

[289] *Letters of Charles I*, p. 260.

[290] Kelsey, 'Trial of Charles I', pp. 606–8.

[291] *Trial of Charles I*, pp. 83, 91, 93; Kelsey, 'Trial of Charles I', pp. 603–4.

[292] Kelsey, 'Trial of Charles I', p. 613.

he enter a plea, he succeeded in keeping the discussion focused on the question of the court's legitimacy and, in doing so, highlighting the reluctance of the bulk of the commissioners to condemn him. At the start of proceedings on 22 January, Cooke urged that the court should take his refusal to plead two days earlier as an admission of guilt and move immediately to sentence. But, in spite of Bradshawe's best efforts, Charles was able to keep the hearing going over this day and the next while he rehearsed his arguments about the rule of law and the monarch's role within a balanced constitution. By the end of the third day he had been given the opportunity to plead on at least six separate occasions and the court had still not reached the point of condemning him.[293] As Sean Kelsey has pointed out, this not only exposed the divisions among the commissioners, it also encouraged Charles to believe that he had them on the run.[294]

The king's refusal to plead left the trial commissioners with a difficult decision on where to go next. They bought themselves some time by hearing the various witnesses against the king. At the conclusion of this, on 26 January, they finally proceeded to sentence and condemned Charles to death as 'tyrant, traitor, murderer and public enemy to the people of England'. However, at the same time, they reversed an earlier decision that he should not be allowed to plead again and agreed to bring him back to Westminster to hear the sentence in person.[295] There were those who were still willing to give him another chance.

Meanwhile the junto leadership was at work behind the scenes. In a series of sermons on 21 January, preached by Peter among others, the trial commissioners were urged to look for ways of dealing with the king which stopped short of execution. The arrival of the Dutch ambassador in London, and the receipt of a mysterious letter from the Prince of Wales to the Council of Officers, prompted talk of fresh negotiation. There also appears to have been a clandestine approach to Charles himself, possibly via Peter. Certainly it was understood by the king that when he came before the court again on 27 January he would be allowed to speak before sentence was passed. The expectation – encouraged by reports in Henry Walker's *Perfect*

---

[293] *Trial of Charles I*, pp. 89–94, 96–100.

[294] Kelsey, 'Death of Charles I', p. 744.

[295] Kelsey, 'Trial of Charles I', pp. 609–10; Gardiner, *History of the Civil War*, vol. 4, pp. 305–8; Kelsey, 'Death of Charles I', p. 747.

Occurrences, which was the mouthpiece of the leadership – was that he would make some fresh offer of terms, either in the form of an undertaking to abdicate or else an agreement to plead.[296] The stage was set for what appeared to be the king's last opportunity to save his life.

Charles was well aware that the death sentence was hanging over him, but he calculated that he could keep his opponents talking. News came through on 24 January that Ormond had finally signed a treaty with the Confederacy. If the king could spin out negotiations for a few weeks longer it seemed that he might once more have an army at his disposal.[297] In these circumstances, as Kelsey has demonstrated, he was tempted to overplay his hand. When Bradshawe gave him his opportunity to speak on the 27th, instead of coming forward with a concrete proposal, he requested that he be heard in the Painted Chamber before the Lords and Commons, since he had 'something to say which concerns both the peace of the kingdom and the liberty of the subject'.[298] On the face of it this was quite a clever move. If allowed it would bring the Lords back into the process and strengthen the hand of all those concerned about preserving the ancient constitution. But it was also a massive gamble because if the commissioners rejected his request he would be left with nowhere to go.

When the judges withdrew to consider it became clear that Charles had misjudged those he was dealing with. What he was asking them to do in effect was collapse the trial proceeding and abandon the whole claim to Commons' sovereignty advanced since 4 January. There appear to have been commissioners who were willing to do this – and they were able to keep the discussion going for the best part of an hour – but they were evidently in a minority. The majority view was that they could simply not afford to take the risk. Partly this was because they did not believe Charles could be trusted, but more importantly because it would have prompted an outcry among the new regime's supporters. As Kelsey has observed, the collapse of the trial would have 'sent shock waves of potentially catastrophic proportions through the army, the city and the "honest" radical

---

[296] Kelsey, 'Death of Charles I', pp. 745–8.

[297] Adamson, 'The Frighted Junto', p. 61.

[298] Kelsey, 'Trial of Charles I', pp. 613–14; idem, 'Death of Charles I', p. 748; *Trial of Charles I*, pp. 105–10.

constituencies in the country at large'.[299] This would probably have destroyed the fragile coalition that had come to power since Pride's Purge.

When the court reconvened Charles still seems to have believed that he held the upper hand. Bradshawe gave him two further opportunities to plead, but he simply repeated his request that he be heard before the Lords and Commons. The president then delivered a long speech about the punishment of tyrants, citing the precedents of Edward II, Richard II and Mary Queen of Scots.[300] This seems to have shaken the king and he tried to interrupt, only to be told that he had been given 'too much liberty already'. Bradshawe then read the sentence, which finally convinced Charles that the game was up. For a moment he lost his composure and began to bluster; but when Bradshawe finally ordered the guards to take him away he collected himself and delivered a final, stinging, retort: 'I am not suffered for to speak. Expect what justice other people will have.'[301]

Sean Kelsey has presented Charles's trial as an extended negotiation which eventually collapsed because each side misjudged the other. The junto leadership calculated that faced with the threat of execution Charles would finally back down and plead, while the king remained convinced that his enemies would go on talking rather than face the consequences of putting him to death.[302] There is a good deal in this assessment. It explains the delays and the hesitations, and the repeated invitations to Charles to plead even after it became clear he was not going to do so. It also highlights the extent of the king's tactical error which, not for the first time, was based on overconfidence about the strength of his position. However, to explain the outcome of the trial solely in these terms would be to underplay the importance of Charles's own convictions.

At the final hearing on 27 January he insisted that he had refused to plead because he was determined to preserve that which 'is much dearer to me than my life which is my conscience and my honour'.[303] This goes to the heart of Charles's inner motivation. He was always acutely sensitive

---

[299] *Trial of Charles I*, pp. 110–11; Kelsey, 'Trial of Charles I', pp. 610–11.

[300] *Trial of Charles I*, pp. 113–14; Gardiner, *History of the Civil War*, vol. 4, p. 312.

[301] *Trial of Charles I*, pp. 125–9.

[302] Kelsey, 'Trial of Charles I', pp. 615–16; idem, 'Death of Charles I', pp. 743–5.

[303] *Trial of Charles I*, pp. 107–8.

on matters of honour and he seems to have regarded giving in at this point as one humiliation too far. But, even more importantly in the circumstances, he saw not pleading as a matter of conscience and therefore closely linked to his providential interpretation of events. He remained firm in the belief that, given the justness of his cause, God was bound to ensure final victory – and the unexpected turn of events in Ireland looked like a precursor to just the sort of semi-miraculous deliverance that might be anticipated in this situation. However, if it turned out that he was not to be the instrument of this victory, he was determined to avoid God's further wrath by standing firm on matters of conscience. To surrender his 'negative voice', which all along he regarded as an essential, God-given, component of his sovereignty, would be to undo all the benefits of his perseverance elsewhere.[304] Charles, then, refused to give the junto leadership what it wanted because, in the final analysis, he was more afraid of God's judgement than he was of death.

Even the passing of sentence, however, did not finally extinguish the junto's efforts to secure a settlement. The trial commissioners set up a committee to decide on the time and place of execution, but then adjourned proceedings until Monday the 29th. In the meantime there was extensive lobbying by the Dutch ambassador and the Westminster Assembly, and Fairfax was reported to be trying to persuade the Council of Officers to spare Charles's life. There was also – if Clement Walker's *History of Independency* is to be believed – a final approach to the king in which 'some of the grandees of the army and parliament tendered . . . a paper booke, with promise of life and some shadow of regality if he subscribed to it'. If such an approach was made, however, it was unavailing. Charles appears to have decided during the hearing on the 27th that he could not keep the talking going any longer and he must now simply stand firm. Cromwell and Ireton seem to have recognised this and on the 29th they finally took the step of formally disavowing the Treaty of Newport and thereby effectively bringing negotiation to an end.[305] What eventually appears to have persuaded them was the strength of feeling in the army – which could only be appeased by the

---

[304] One account of the proceedings on 20 January has Charles remarking that on this point it would be sinful for him 'to lay down that power wherewith he was entrusted': Kelsey, 'Trial of Charles I', p. 613.

[305] Kelsey, 'Death of Charles I', pp. 749, 752; Wedgewood, *Trial of Charles I*, p. 171.

sort of concrete concessions that Charles was evidently not prepared to make – and the continuing threat from Ireland. The king remained unshaken in his refusal to order Ormond to back down and, as John Adamson has observed, it must now have seemed that the only way to overcome the danger was to remove the lynchpin of the anti-Independent coalition, Charles himself.[306] Executing the king was a step into the unknown, but it finally came to appear less risky than keeping him alive.

Having made the decision not to concede any more, Charles faced the prospect of death with extraordinary serenity. Throughout his final days he displayed none of the anguish and uncertainty that tended to surface when he was confronting difficult choices. He was clear in his own mind what he must do and buoyed up by a sense that he had persevered to the end and was about to receive his final reward. He woke on the morning of his execution and cheerfully announced to Herbert that 'this is my second marriage day . . . for before night I hope to be espoused to my blessed Jesus'.[307] This was not mere bravado. He really did believe that he was about to attain salvation. He was able to draw on this, and on all the reserves of stoical self-control that he had built up over the years, to deliver a remarkably assured final performance.

Charles had two priorities at the end of his life. The first was to discharge his conscience and make his peace with God; the second to construct a political legacy that would benefit his son. He spent much of his final morning in prayer with Bishop Juxon and drew considerable solace from the lesson for the day, Matthew 27, on the passion of Christ. On the scaffold he emphasised his willingness to die in charity, going out of his way to forgive his enemies and once again underlining his commitment to peace. Finally he affirmed that he was dying 'in the profession of the Church of England as I find it left me by my father'.[308] On his last day, then, the king provided Anglican apologists with the raw materials to fashion an image of Charles the martyr, the Church of England saint. This was to be an inspiration to royalists in the 1650s and to later generations of Anglicans. Even more significant, however, was his final political testimony.

---

[306] Adamson, 'The Frighted Junto', pp. 60–2.

[307] *Trial of Charles I*, p. 144.

[308] Ibid., pp. 145, 262–3.

He had the tricky task of answering the charge that he was a tyrant and warmonger, and also deflecting the claim that his execution was a providential judgement which confirmed his guilt. In his scaffold speech he managed to accomplish both these things with considerable skill. The noise and hubbub of the occasion diminished the immediate impact of his words; but there were scribes standing by, and his speech was rapidly and widely circulated. He began by acknowledging that, like everyone else he was irredeemably tainted by sin and fully deserving of God's judgements. However, he insisted that he was being judged not for his actions in the civil war but for the earlier 'crime' of allowing Strafford to go to the block.

God forbid that I should be so ill a Christian as not to say God's judgements are just upon me. Many times he does pay justice by an unjust sentence, that is ordinary. I will only say that an unjust sentence that I suffered for to take effect is punished now by an unjust sentence on me.[309]

These words appear to have been a genuine expression of Charles's inner convictions; but they also provided a very effective way of answering claims about his divinely-sanctioned guilt.

He then focused specifically on the origins of civil war, insisting that the blame here lay not with himself, or parliament, but with 'ill instruments between them and me'.[310] Again this was a skilfully constructed response. By 'ill instruments' he presumably meant the 'seditious spirits' whom he had repeatedly identified as the prime movers of rebellion against him. But equally it could be taken to refer to 'evil counsellors' within his own court, which would probably have given his words greater purchase with moderate parliamentarians dismayed at the removal of their king. It was to this constituency that he directed much of the remainder of his speech. The current regime, he insisted, had come to power 'by way of conquest' which, unless sanctioned by the justness of their cause, was little better than 'robbery'. The surest safeguard of the people's liberties lay in 'government'; but this did not mean the sort of government outlined in the claim to Commons' sovereignty – for if 'you put the people in that liberty . . . they will never enjoy themselves' – it meant government by a constitutional

---

[309] Ibid., p. 261.

[310] Ibid.

monarch, limited by 'the laws of the land'. It was this that Charles had set himself up to preserve and for this that he was prepared to die.

If I would have given way to an arbitrary way, for to have all laws changed according to the power of the sword, I needed not to have come here. And, therefore, I tell you, and I pray God it be not laid to your charge, that I am the martyr to the people.[311]

Some may have felt that this last claim was a bit rich. But, again, it emphasised how determined he was to wrap his actions in the rhetoric of constitutional monarchy; and if there was one overriding political lesson he could draw from the civil war period it was that he was most effective in gathering political support when he did precisely this. The king's last speech, then – given enormous potency by the courage and dignity of his bearing on the scaffold – consolidated the message of his final months and helped to establish an enduring image of the benefits of constitutional monarchy.

One of the features of the last months of Charles's life was that for long periods he had to rely on his own counsel. For a variety of reasons, those who had advised him in the past were no longer doing so. The most notable casualty of this was the queen whose forthright opinions had forced the king to spend so much time thinking through and justifying his policies in 1646. By 1648 their correspondence appears to have dwindled to no more than the occasional hurried letter. Partly this was a result of the general difficulties Charles had in communicating with the outside world, and partly also the queen's decision to spend much of the latter half of 1648 in a Carmelite monastery.[312] However, there are indications that even when the king had opportunities to seek her advice – while he was at Newport, for example – he did not take them. The main reason for this appears to have been the emergence of the Prince of Wales as a significant political player in his own right. During the Second Civil War he had taken the initiative in negotiations with the Scots and proved himself an effective naval commander. Now that the young Charles had come of age both the king and queen seem to have felt that he was the one who should be consulted

---

[311] Ibid., p. 262.

[312] Firebrace, *Honest Harry*, pp. 185–6, 188; C. Oman, *Henrietta Maria*, 1930, pp. 190–2.

over political decisions. This meant, however, that Charles was deprived of some very challenging, and often perceptive, counsel. His relationship with the prince, who was still only 18, was not one between political partners, with shared perspectives and experiences; it was that of father and son, in which the father's principal concern was to pass on advice for the future. During his final months, then, the king was largely alone when it came to making his decisions. This provides an opportunity to look again at Hyde's judgement that he was at his most effective when he was following his own instincts and determining things for himself.

From late October 1648, when news came through of Ormond's successes, his main political objective was to buy time until he could once again put an army into the field. It could be argued that, given his previous experience of being let down by the Irish, the king was being unduly optimistic – although it is worth remembering that Ormond did reach agreement with the Confederacy in January 1649.[313] However, it is clear that, as far as he was concerned, there was no alternative. It would have gone against all his political instincts to agree to a lasting settlement with those he regarded as rebels; and, as John Adamson has observed, ever since the Army Plot of 1641 – or indeed the prayerbook rebellion of 1637 – 'when cornered he had always placed his trust in force'.[314] If he could not achieve deliverance through a third civil war then the only other course he could see open to him was to stand firm and trust that his martyrdom would prepare the ground for his son's victory. Charles's pursuit of these two objectives met with mixed results.

He did succeed in buying time and dividing his enemies, but not enough to create the conditions for a military victory. This was partly a consequence of his own mistakes. Not taking the opportunity to escape in late November 1648 and not offering a more positive response to Denbigh's mission in December were both serious errors of judgement, once again apparently born of overconfidence. His reading of the tactical situation was also at fault. He was slow to appreciate the loss of power for the Presbyterians after Pride's Purge and he seems to have completely misjudged the pressures on the trial commissioners at the fateful hearing on 27 January. However, having just lost a second civil war Charles was facing

---

[313] *Early Modern Ireland*, pp. 331–4.

[314] Adamson, 'The Frighted Junto', p. 56.

a situation that would probably have defeated a far more skilful politician. As it was, his flexibility and resilience did at least create opportunities for a revival. His concessions at Newport, which (as the letters to Hopkins indicated) were never meant to be anything more than a means of deceiving his enemies, opened up serious splits between the Presbyterians and the army. In different circumstances he might have been able to exploit these more effectively. Similarly his careful cultivation of the Lords and the army grandees in January 1649 came close to providing him with a significant opening. More importantly for the long term, he kept his nerve and stood firm under enormous pressure. His refusal to give way on what he saw as the fundamentals of royalism ensured that many of his followers remained determined to fight on. So, in spite of failing to deliver a third civil war, Charles continued to display many of the qualities of a good party leader.

Where he was most successful was in achieving the second of his objectives and bequeathing a powerful legacy to his son. Here his courage and conviction came into their own. He drew on all his reserves of stoical self-control, and even more on the sense that he was now in God's hands, to deliver an inspiring display of bravery and defiance. He also exploited to the full his instinctive understanding of the rule of law and the ancient constitution. More than at any time previously in his reign he embraced the language of constitutional kingship. He talked of following the 'parliamentary way', ensuring that the prerogative was bounded by law, refusing to submit to the tyranny of an arbitrary power and governing for the people. This helped to create a powerful image of the benefits of limited monarchy which significantly assisted his son at the Restoration.[315] The Declaration of Breda, which did much to win round moderate opinion in 1660, picked up on precisely these themes. Charles II's return to the crown was the victory that his father had long anticipated, and it owed much to his final performance as a kingly martyr.

---

[315] Smith, *Constitutional Royalism*, pp. 290–2; S.R. Gardiner, 'Draft by Sir Edward Hyde of a Declaration to be issued by Charles II in 1649', *EHR*, vol. 8, 1893, pp. 300–7.

Conclusion

There are no simple judgements to be made of Charles I. He was a complex man whose career intersected with some of the most dramatic events in English history; and the tragedy and nobility of his end have often appeared hard to relate to the ordinariness of his day-to-day dealing with servants and politicians. Historians have struggled to get him into perspective. The tendency has been to veer between the outright condemnation of S.R. Gardiner and the measured sympathy of Kevin Sharpe. The present study is no exception. It exaggerates some facets of Charles and underplays others. However, it does represent an attempt to take stock of him in the light of current historiography; and it is worth elaborating on some of the conclusions that have emerged from this process.

One of the main themes has been that there were a number of constants in Charles's political make-up that repeatedly influenced his actions. Two that stand out were his loathing for puritanism and his fear of popularity. From his first entry into the political arena in the 1621 Parliament to his final scaffold speech, these encompassed the things he dreaded and detested most in politics. Another constant was his very strong sense of personal honour. This was based on a mixture of neo-Stoic ideas about virtue and 'honesty', and deep-seated anxieties about masculinity and personal authority. It meant that he could aspire to the highest standards of nobility and self-control in his personal conduct, while at the same time harbouring anxieties and grudges that made him vengeful, prickly and hypersensitive. His negotiations with the Covenanters in the late 1630s, and various parliamentarian opponents during the 1640s, continually ran up against his sense that he had been humiliated in a way that demanded retribution. In such circumstances, settlement became very hard to achieve.

A further, perhaps more surprising, continuity was his reverence for a mixed and balanced constitution. Charles consistently presented himself as a 'constitutionalist' who favoured the rule of law and partnership with parliament. In this respect he was both temperamentally and ideologically some way removed from the queen, who was probably the nearest thing to a continental-style 'absolutist' among his principal advisers.[1] This did not preclude his policies from appearing 'absolutist' to others, or producing outcomes which were 'absolutist' in their practical application. As Anthony Milton has demonstrated, a good deal depended on where one struck the balance between the rights of the subject and the prerogatives of the crown.[2] Charles's approach tended to be based on the assumption made in his *Answer to the xix Propositions*, that the greatest danger to the *status quo* lay in the emergence of a 'tyranny of the people'. Over issues like unparliamentary taxation this led him to interpret what was customary and legitimate in ways that were plainly at odds with the majority of his subjects. However, there were also plenty of occasions – particularly when he was seeking to work with parliament or build up for support for royalism – when Charles could present himself as a model of constitutional propriety. He was only able to do this because the tone of so much of his rhetoric was 'constitutionalist', and because he himself genuinely believed that a 'good king' worked to uphold a balanced constitution.

If one turns to looking at which of Charles's attitudes changed over time, again, there are a number of significant findings. One of the most interesting of these is the increasing importance he attached to providence. A belief in God's providential judgements has normally been associated with puritans and Calvinists.[3] But G.C. Browell has demonstrated in a recent doctoral thesis that there was a 'royalist' providentialism which drew its force

---

[1] For an example of the ideas circulating in Catholic circles around the queen, see L.L. Peck, 'Beyond the Pale: John Cusack and the language of absolutism in early Stuart Britain', *HJ*, vol. 41, 1998, pp. 121–49.

[2] Milton, 'Wentworth and political thought', pp. 133–56.

[3] B. Worden, 'Providence and politics in Cromwellian England', *P & P*, vol. 109, 1985, pp. 55–99; Walsham, *Providence in Early Modern England*, partic. chp. 1.

from the shared belief in an interventionist deity.[4] Charles's early Calvinist upbringing and strong sense of the demands of conscience predisposed him to a belief that God's judgements were visited on those who sinned; however, it was not until the 1640s that this had an obvious impact on his political conduct. The change was, perhaps, partly due to the onset of middle age, and the anxieties that accompanied it; but, more obviously, it was a response to the trauma and agonies he went through over Strafford's execution. He convinced himself that in going against his conscience and signing the death warrant he had committed a grievous sin, for which both he and the nation were being punished. This had a powerful effect on his decision-making thereafter. It persuaded him not to give ground to those he perceived to be his, and God's, enemies; and, on occasions, it encouraged a dangerous overconfidence in judging his political and military prospects. During the latter part of his life the belief in providence was, perhaps, as profound an influence for Charles as it was for Oliver Cromwell.[5]

Perhaps the most striking transformation in Charles's political make-up, however, was the growth in his self-confidence as both a monarch and a ruler. The hesitant, rather taciturn figure glimpsed in discussions with councillors during the late 1620s was replaced by a far more assertive and self-assured individual who could take charge of proceedings and impress onlookers with his grasp of argument. He never aspired to the subtlety or intellectual mastery of his father, and his lack of political imagination continued to find him out; but during the 1630s he took charge of the direction of government in the way monarchs were supposed to. This was a transition, perhaps, best summed up, as Kevin Sharpe points out, in the contrast between the somewhat faltering and anxious prince painted by Daniel Mytens, and the mature and substantial sovereign of Van Dyck.[6]

An overview of Charles's career should be sufficient to dispel some of the judgements made by modern historians about his unfitness to rule

---

[4] G.C. Browell, 'The Politics of Providentialism in England, c. 1640–1660', University of Kent, Ph.D. thesis, 2000, partic. chps. 2 and 3.

[5] For Cromwell, providence and decision-making see B. Worden, 'Oliver Cromwell and the sin of Achan', in D. Beales and G. Best eds, *History, Society and the Churches*, Cambridge, 1985, pp. 125–45.

[6] Sharpe, *The Personal Rule*, p. 183.

or his 'apolitical personality'.[7] He discharged the first responsibility of a monarch, which was to provide for his succession; he controlled his court and avoided the factional infighting that was one of the classic signs of a weak or incapable monarch; and he did not cave in or give up in the face of political setbacks. In terms of personal ability and aptitude for the task, he was at least as impressive as his contemporaries Louis XIII of France and Philip IV of Spain. However, one cannot escape the fact that he presided over a disastrous civil war and a temporary end to monarchical government in England. Part of this can be attributed to the peculiarly difficult conditions that the English monarchy faced during the early Stuart period – with the 'British problem', the divided religious legacy of the Reformation and an insecure financial base. But this cannot be the whole story because his father had managed to cope with many of the same problems. A large measure of responsibility must be laid on Charles himself. This brings us back to the king's specific shortcomings, and the ways in which, as a ruler and as a politician, he contributed to the conflicts of the late 1630s and 1640s.

One approach, addressed in Peter Donald's study of the Scottish Rebellion, has been to look at the extent to which Charles was 'an uncounselled king'. Was he a monarch who failed to listen to and take moderate advice? As Donald has indicated, the answer to this question is complex and ambiguous.[8] Charles was certainly very respectful of the notion that a 'good king' listened to his counsellors, while those who served him generally believed that he was 'counsellable'. On the other hand, everyone recognised that it was for the monarch to make the final decision, drawing on his God-given wisdom and reason. What often happened, as Conrad Russell has pointed out, was that Charles took advice on 'means', but was not open to being persuaded about his 'ends', or what he called his 'grounds'. He was prepared to talk about compromise and make limited concessions to opponents – as in Scotland in 1638 or England in 1641 – but he would not follow through to the point at which reconciliation became achievable. For reasons which often seem to have had to do with a particular sense of personal injury and a near paranoia about the ultimate objectives of his opponents, he was much keener to punish than to settle. He was not insincere in his desire to promote peace and unity; but it had to be on his

---

[7] See, for example, Reeve, *Road to Personal Rule*, p. 200.

[8] Donald, *An Uncounselled King*, partic. pp. 320–7.

own terms, which generally went so far beyond anything his opponents were likely to agree to that they had little choice except but to struggle on until one side emerged as the victor. As a consequence, moderate councillors found that while they might persuade Charles to compromise on tactical grounds, or because he was too weak to do anything else, when it came to the point of decision he would dig his heels in and they would find that their approach was no longer viable.

Another way of summing up Charles's weaknesses has been to argue that he was insufficiently 'popular'. This was a charge made by contemporaries such as Peter Heylyn and Sir Philip Warwick, and it has been echoed by later historians who have argued that in an era when politics was increasingly about the manipulation of public opinion, Charles paid too little attention to politics 'out of doors'.[9] This charge touches on one of the classic dilemmas of the period: how far politicians should go in sacrificing their moral integrity to appeal for popular support.[10] It was a dilemma Charles himself was very conscious of. He had a particularly strong sense of his kingly duty to set an example of virtuous conduct and discharge his duties to God; but, at the same time, he did understand that 'policy' often required a ruler to woo the people. His first instinct was to try to follow the dictates of conscience and morality; however, when he had to he could play the popular game effectively, as he demonstrated at the time of the 'Blessed Revolution', or his entry into London in 1641. It can certainly be argued that for long periods of his reign he failed to make the most of the assets available to the crown. In terms of news management and selling his case to the public, the 1630s was a decade of missed opportunities. But to characterise him as a monarch with a 'fatal' propensity to 'shut down public debate rather than engage with it', or who was 'unparalleled in his failure to communicate with his subjects', is to overstate the case.[11]

---

[9] For Heylyn and Warwick, see Smuts, 'Public ceremony and royal charisma', pp. 90–1; *Warwick Memoirs*, p. 365. Among modern historians this view has been stated most bluntly in T. Harris, 'Understanding popular politics in Restoration Britain', in A. Houston and S. Pincus eds, *A Nation Transformed*, Cambridge, 2001, pp. 145–6 and Morrill, 'Introduction' to *Reactions to the English Civil War*, p. 4; but it is also implicit in Cust, 'News and politics', p. 81n and Smuts, 'Public ceremony and royal charisma', pp. 89–93.

[10] This was highlighted in Clarendon, *History*, vol. 3, p. 224.

[11] The quotations are from Harris, 'Understanding popular politics', p. 145 and Morrill, 'Introduction', p. 4.

Perhaps the most interesting judgement made in recent work on Charles is Conrad Russell's verdict that he was much more effective as a party leader than as a king. Russell's assumption is that a king should be essentially a uniter and reconciler, somebody sufficiently flexible and open to compromise to be able to overcome differences and bring his people together. The party leader, on the other hand, is a more partisan figure with the convictions to pursue a particular line, and the resilience to keep going and rally 'the faithful'. Charles, Russell argues, was a disaster in the former role, but possessed many of the qualities required for the latter.[12] One of the themes of this study has been that in many respects he is right. Charles patently lacked the consensus-building and negotiating skills of his father and felt much more at home following his convictions. Such aptitude as he had for politics tended to emerge when he was drawing together those who supported his line, or developing a strategy for outmanoeuvring his opponents. However, to characterise this as a contrast between the roles of 'king' and 'party leader' is not entirely satisfactory. Being an effective ruler was generally an amalgam of the two. One had to project the image of the 'good king', aspiring to harmonise and conciliate, while at the same time engaging in the day-to-day practice of political management and manoeuvre. James, who is generally depicted as a far more irenic figure than his son, nonetheless displayed a highly partisan approach to his politics. He fully recognised that he was operating in a polarised political world in which he had to angle for support and appeal to particular constituencies in order to maintain the authority of the crown. It was James who identified the magnitude of the 'popular' threat from the House of Commons and took steps to neutralise it, and James who laid the basis for the anti-Calvinist takeover of the church in the 1620s. It is certainly true that after 1640 Charles was operating in a context in which the authority of the crown had been fundamentally challenged, and party building had come to be regarded as a more open and legitimate part of the political process. But the shift was one of degree rather than substance.[13] Successful kings needed to be

---

[12] Russell, *Causes of the Civil War*, pp. 187, 198, 209–10.

[13] Much has been written about the extent to which the politics of the period was dominated by notions of consensus or division. For a summary of some of the main arguments in favour of viewing the political world in terms of polarities, see Cust and Hughes, 'Introduction: after Revisionism', in *Conflict in Early Stuart England'*, pp. 1–46 and more recently Cust, '"Patriots" and "popular spirits"': narratives of conflict in early Stuart politics'.

effective party leaders in this and, indeed, most other eras. Charles was not as effective a ruler as either his father or his eldest son. But to place too much weight on his failure to display 'kingly' qualities is to misconstrue what was required of him.

This brings us, finally, to the verdict of S.R. Gardiner, which has stood the test of time better than most.[14] Gardiner depicts Charles as a fatal combination of the obstinate, the unrealistic and the untruthful. He describes him as a politician who had 'no power of stepping out of himself to see how his actions looked to others', who was unable 'to subordinate that which was only desirable to that which was possible', and who 'lacked an elemental quality of veracity'.[15]

On the evidence presented in this study the first charge stands up well. Charles was generally not good at reading how his actions would play with the various constituencies he was dealing with. This was not invariably the case. Ian Atherton has remarked perceptively that he was much better when it came to dealing with other kings than with his own subjects.[16] This could be extended to cover his negotiations with the Presbyterian and Independent leaderships after the civil war. In such circumstances he could be quite astute about calculating the options and playing on the weaknesses of opponents. However, for reasons which seem to have had to do with a lack of political imagination and an unwillingness to engage with views which were out of line with his own, he could be very bad at reading the likely reactions to his policies among the politically-informed public. On occasions such as the signing of the National Covenant in 1638, the Army Plot of 1641 and the Attempt on the Five Members in 1642 this had disastrous consequences.

The second charge – that Charles was reluctant to accept that politics was the art of the possible – also carries considerable weight. His refusal to internalise what seemed obvious to his advisers was sometimes remarkable. The most striking example was his inability to come to terms with the fact that he had to give up trying to defeat the Scots by force after Newburn;

---

[14] See M. Young's discussion of Gardiner in *Charles I*, pp. 2–3, 173–4.

[15] Gardiner, *History of England*, vol. 5, p. 434, vol. 6, p. 328; idem, *History of the Civil War*, vol. 4, p. 328.

[16] I. Atherton, *Ambition and Failure in Stuart England*, Manchester, 1999, p. 178.

but one could also cite his failure to recognise the need for serious concessions if he was to obtain supply from the Short Parliament, or his assumption that he could go on dividing his enemies indefinitely during the final
negotiations of 1648–9.[17] He was sometimes still flexible enough to back
down and retrieve a situation; but his lack of judgement about what was
feasible and realistic did much to precipitate the various crises of the reign.

Gardiner's third charge – that the king engaged in a degree of deception that was both reprehensible and counter-productive – needs to be
treated more cautiously. There is a strong element of moral disapproval in
Gardiner's verdict which makes insufficient allowance for political realities.
There were situations in which Charles needed to be economical with the
truth in order to give himself some room for manoeuvre, particularly in
the post-war negotiations. However, it did not help his cause that early on
he acquired a reputation for duplicity. He appeared slippery and devious in
ways that put those he was dealing with on their guard, and made them
reluctant to accept his assurances without the sort of guarantees that he
felt no king should have to give. The Commons in 1629 might have
been more amenable to the carefully crafted programme on offer from the
'patriots' had it not been for the king's apparent double-dealing over the
Petition of Right; and the army might have been more willing to allow him
to come up to London during the negotiations of 1647–8 had he not been
so obviously angling to play off his opponents against each other. Charles's
reputation did not help his own cause, and it certainly did not help the
cause of settlement.

If one adds to these shortcomings, Charles's fears and prejudices, his
oversensitivity to anything that might be construed as a slight to his
honour and his tendency to panic and take the wrong option when under
pressure – at its most damaging in the crisis of late December and early January
1641–2 – then one probably comes close to understanding his weaknesses
as a politician. He was an exasperating man to deal with and he had an
immense capacity to make a bad situation worse. However, as Russell has
emphasised, in the end it was his strengths as much as his weaknesses that
brought disaster. Had he simply been incompetent he could have been
deposed or reduced to a figurehead. It was his capacity to recover, and

---

[17] Russell gives further examples: *Causes of the Civil War*, p. 200.

form a party, after first alienating the bulk of the political nation, which produced a civil war.

The complexity and many-sidedness of Charles's political make-up is perhaps best illustrated by revisiting the disappointments of the period following Buckingham's assassination.[18] With the favourite out of the way and a realignment at court, there seemed every possibility of implementing a 'new deal' with the subject based on a return to the politics of the Elizabethan era. To court insiders the king appeared to be favourable to a *rapprochment* with parliament, a return to the Calvinist *status quo* in the church and, perhaps, even the resumption of a 'patriot' foreign policy. Yet within a few weeks, faced by a House of Commons that appeared to be out of control, the crown had reverted to 'new counsels' and anti-Calvinism. It was a shift that summed up many of the wrong turnings and missed opportunities of the early Stuart period, and at the heart of it was Charles. It was his 'constitutionalist' instincts and willingness to listen to moderate counsels which had opened up the opportunity in the first place. But in the end – as had always been most likely – it was his sensitivity to slights and challenges to his authority, his wariness of the 'popular' and his loathing for the puritans which closed it down.

---

[18] For this, see Cust, 'Was there an alternative to the Personal Rule?', pp. 350–2.

Index